The Mammoth Book of

BATTLES

The Mammoth Book of
BATTLES

Edited by
Jon E. Lewis

Carroll & Graf Publishers, Inc.
NEW YORK

Carroll & Graf Publishers, Inc.
19 West 21st Street
New York
NY 10010–6805

First published in the UK by Robinson Publishing 1995

First Carroll & Graf edition 1995
This edition 1999
Reprinted 2000, 2001

Maps by András Bereznay

Front cover picture:
Indochina wars/Vietnam War 1964–75, AKG London/AP.
Back cover picture: "The German offensive in the West. Cavalry
advancing", World War I/Western Front, AKG London.

ISBN 0–7867–0689–9

Printed and bound in the UK

Contents

List of Maps

Acknowledgements

The editor has made every effort to locate all persons having any rights in the selections appearing in this anthology and to secure permission from the holders of such rights. Any queries regarding the use of material should be addressed to the editor c/o the publishers.

Parts of this work previously appeared in the partwork *War Monthly*, unless otherwise stated all material is copyright © Marshall Cavendish Partworks Ltd.

'The Relief of Ladysmith' is an extract from *Great Military Battles* by Howard Green. Copyright © 1971 Leo Cooper Ltd. Reprinted by permission of the publishers.

'Tsushima' is an extract from *Great Battles of the 20th Century*, edited by Barrie Pitt. Copyright © 1977 Phoebus Publishing and BPC Publishing Ltd.

'The Somme' is an extract from *A Sergeant-Major's War* by Ernest Shephard. Copyright © The Crowood Press. Reprinted by permission of the publishers.

'Battle of Britain 1940' by Christopher Dowling was first published in *Decisive Battles of the Twentieth Century*, edited by Noble Frankland and Christopher Dowling, Sidgwick & Jackson, 1976. Copyright © 1976 Dr Christopher Dowling. Reprinted by kind permission of the author.

'Stalingrad' and 'Ardennes' are extracts from *World War 1939–45: A Short History* by Peter Young. Copyright © 1966 Brigadier Peter Young. Reprinted by kind permission of Mrs Mary Delion and London Management and Representation Ltd.

'El Alamein' is an extract from *Decisive Battles of the Western World* by J. F. C. Fuller, Vol III. Copyright © 1974 J. F. C. Fuller. Reprinted by permission of David Higham Associates.

'Imjin River' by A. H. Farrar Hockley and E. L. Capel is an extract from *Cap of Honour* by David Scott Daniell. Copyright © 1951 David Scott Daniell and 1975 The Gloucestershire Regiment.

'Ia Drang' by Ian Westwell was first published in *The Elite: Special Forces of the World*, Marshall Cavendish 1987. Copyright © 1987 Marshall Cavendish Ltd. Reprinted by permission of Marshall Cavendish Ltd.

'Jerusalem' by Ashley Brown was first published in *The Elite: Special Forces of the World*, Marshall Cavendish 1987. Copyright © 1987 Marshall Cavendish Ltd. Reprinted by permission of Marshall Cavendish Ltd.

'Hamburger Hill' is an extract from *Vietnam: The Decisive Battles* by John Pimlott, Marshall Editions, 1990. Copyright © Marshall Editions Developments Ltd 1990. Reprinted by permission of Marshall Editions Developments Ltd.

'Wireless Ridge' is an extract from *2 Para Falklands* by Maj-Gen John Frost, Buchan & Enright Publishers Ltd. Copyright © 1983 by Maj-Gen John Frost.

'Desert Storm' is copyright © 1995 Jon E. Lewis.

Introduction copyright © 1995 Jon E. Lewis.

Introduction

If war is not an inevitable part of human nature, it is an enduring one. The profession of arms is man's oldest, and the moments in the last three millennia when peace has existed across the globe have been few. The twentieth century, the timespan covered by this book, differs from its predecessors only in that it has been even more war torn; it has also been the age in which warfare has, thanks to technological advance, reached new destructive depths.

Modern warfare is not quite synonymous with the 1900s; the 'industrialization' of slaughter began with the American Civil War of the 1860s, when entire ranks of close-pressed troops were felled by the Gatling gun. This was but a portent, however, and the mechanics and methods of mass slaughter would only truly proliferate as the new century turned. The replacement of cavalry by artillery, the invention of the aircraft, the tank, missile technology and the atomic bomb are peculiar to this age of violence and have transformed the killing power of armies into realms unimaginable by those who took the field at Agincourt, or even Gettysburg and Bull Run. Technology has not just given humankind more powerful arms, it has changed the ways – the strategy and tactics – in which war is waged. This is perhaps most clearly seen in the addition of airpower to land warfare, leading to the theory and practice of the Wehrmacht's *Blitzkrieg* (lightning war), and its several descendants, including the AirLand Battle Doctrine of the US armed forces, used so devastatingly in Operation Desert Storm (1991). And, as the war in the Persian Gulf proved – if proof were needed – with its skies traversed by Scud and Cruise missiles, war is becoming increasingly automated, due to breakthroughs in robotics, electronics and computer technology. War by remote control is no longer science fiction. A book of battles of the twenty-first century will have a very different content.

In this century, however, no war has yet been won without the small but necessary business of the mud soldier. And I would argue that the strain on that soldier over the last hundred years has become greater and greater. War is increasingly unendurable, because it is increasingly lethal and increasingly far removed from anything the soldier undergoes in ordinary civilian life. Most of the post-1950s generations have no experience of war beyond images on the television screen, leaving the soldier isolated from his (and sometimes her) peers. War, as the general said, is hell. It always has been, and it is only getting worse.

I have never been in a battle, never heard, in Churchill's phrase, 'a bullet whistle'. I find myself in awe of those who have, but also find that sometimes, through their eyes, I can get a glimpse of the intensity and uniqueness of combat, and what it means to have taken part in history. To read the testimonies of 'those who were there' seems the very least that the rest of us can do. Accordingly, a number of the 42 battles described on the following pages are eye-witness accounts. The rest are by a distinguished company of military historians, or soldiers who have taken up the pen in place of the sword. As for the battles selected, most are important twentieth-century clashes of arms which have changed the course of wars and thus our times. Some of these are directly decisive – like the naval battle of Tsushima (1905) which saw the spectacular sinking of the Russian fleet, like El Alamein, like Stalingrad – while others are indirectly so. The battle of Dien Bien Phu (1953) was a relatively small engagement, but the shock of losing it broke the morale of the French army and people, and ended France's reign as a colonial power in the Far East. But I have also selected a few remarkable, if obscure, 'non-decisive' battles which deserve to be better known (the epic Kokoda Trail, 1942, being a case in point), and others which seem typical and illustrative of the war in which they were fought (Hamburger Hill, Vietnam 1969). Taken together they make a history of war, its nature and its art, in our century. It is perhaps the last in which the human factor, the courage of soldiers and the tactics of battlefield commanders, will be of supreme importance. This book is dedicated to those who fought and fell in the battles it describes.

Jon E. Lewis
October 1994

1
The Boer War

The Relief of Ladysmith (1900)

Howard Green

Occasioned by the discovery of vast reserves of gold and diamonds in an area of South Africa outside British jurisdiction, the Anglo-Boer War (1899–1902) began as an exercise in imperial humiliation, with the volunteer Boer army scoring impressive successes over Queen Victoria's regulars. Not the least of these was at Ladysmith where Sir George White and 12,000 troops were shut in on 2 November 1899. In an effort to relieve the situation in South Africa – where imperial forces were also under siege at Mafeking and Kimberley – the British government dispatched two divisions and appointed General Sir Redvers Buller, Adjutant-General in the War Office, as Supreme Commander. A vastly experienced soldier (Buller had won a VC in the Zulu War), he decided to take personal command of the campaign to relieve Ladysmith, making his forward base at Frere, south of Colenso, where the Boers had blown the bridges and entrenched themselves on the north bank of the Tugela River.

By mid-December 1899 Buller was ready to relieve Ladysmith. His first plan was to send a brigade up to Colenso, ten miles to the north to 'demonstrate' his intention of forcing the Tugela there while he

marched the whole of the rest of his army off to the west, intending
to cross the river at Potgeiters Drift, 11 miles from Frere and so come
round the Boers' right flank in the Tugela Heights – a goodish plan,
but it overlooked the Boer mobility and the positions of observation
they could have used along the line of the hills.

However, on 13 December, he heard of the defeats at Magers-
fontein and Stormburg, the beginning of the 'Black Week', and
then realized that he was Commander-in-Chief in the whole of South
Africa, and not only in Natal. Clearly he was indirectly responsible
for these defeats and he felt that something must be done quickly to
counteract them. A quick success was imperative and its news must
arrive in London very soon.

Accordingly he abandoned the Potgeiters Drift plan entirely and
decided to attack Colenso with his whole strength. He rode up
from Frere to Chieveley on the 14th and that afternoon he told
his brigadiers that he would attack Colenso in the morning and,
having crossed the Tugela, bivouac on the far bank. It was to be
his first great attempt, and he led out next morning the finest and
largest force which any British general had handled since the Alma.
Four brigades of four battalions each, two regular cavalry regiments
with six regular and five other batteries of field artillery with 16 naval
guns under command made up a force of 21,000.

The plan was simple. A line of three brigades was to advance to
the river and across it where possible. Objectives allotted to each
brigade were very vague and almost unspecified.

The left brigade consisting of three Irish regiments and the Border
Regiment moved out to their left-front, trying to find a ford which a
local civilian thought he knew well. He was wrong, and disappeared,
and the brigade blundered on into the 'Loop', an area surrounded on
three sides by a great curve of the unfordable Tugela, a mile long and
half a mile wide. The Boers around two sides of the 'Loop' waited
until the brigade had halted well inside the trap, and had sent one of
the scouts out to find a ford. Then fire opened, heavy casualties were
caused and in spite of gallant attempts by companies and individual
men to rush forward down to the water's edge, not one man reached
it, and not one man of the enemy was seen. The brigade withdrew,
badly shaken.

The centre brigade, of four typical English country regiments,
Queen's, Devons, West Yorks and East Surreys, fared scarcely
better. Under the cover of the village of Colenso itself they advanced

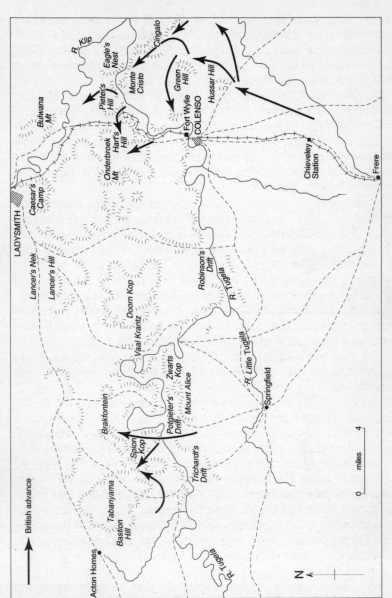

1.1 *The Relief of Ladysmith*

well for a while, making for the two bridges, rail and road, that crossed the river 500 yards beyond the last houses. The fact that no battalion in this brigade had been given a specific bridge as an objective was of little matter, as all were held up soon after leaving the cover of the houses and gardens, by rifle fire from across the river. The two leading battalions, Queen's and Devons, infiltrated up the water's edge and the two bridges but could not cross, while the reinforcing West Yorks only added to the targets along the river bank. Not a man crossed the river.

On the right the Fusilier Brigade, of Royal, Scots, Welsh and Irish Fusiliers, advancing sometime after the other two brigades were in action, had orders to probe for the river and act as a right flank guard. Its latter task was unnecessary and like the other brigades it too was held up by accurate rifle fire from across the river and pinned to its ground. A flanking movement by one battalion out to the right petered out.

Three brigades were now halted short of, or only just up to, the river bank, not a man was over the water and the enemy was still concealed in the superb cover in the foothills over the river.

But the biggest disaster of all occurred in the centre, between the English and the Fusilier Brigades. Here Colonel Long, commanding the artillery, had been ordered to support with two batteries the advance of the centre and right brigades. He was a zealous and dashing officer with very distinct ideas of his own on the tactical employment of guns. His previous battle experience, always against natives whose rifles were usually obsolete and their marksmanship rudimentary, had taught him to fear little from defensive small-arms fire.

His principle, always successful previously, of getting his guns up into action quickly, close to the enemy, was put into practice yet again. Getting his two batteries forward at the trot he quickly got in front of the brigades he was supposed to support and advanced across the open plain in line, eventually outdistancing the Fusilier and the English Brigades by nearly a mile.

Seven hundred yards from the line of the tree-covered river bank and well short of the cover provided by the houses, gardens and railway station, in full view, with no infantry near him and the nearest cavalry far out on his right flank he halted, and his 12 guns, neatly drawn up as though on Queen's Parade at Aldershot, meticulously carried out all points of drill. The teams were led away to a donga 300 yards in the rear and Colonel Long was about to open fire at the clear, low, scrub-covered hills only a few hundred yards away, and where he thought the enemy might be.

The Boers anticipated his order to fire by a few seconds, and several hundred of the finest marksmen in the world, firing from behind cover, opened up. Heavy casualties occurred at once, among the first being Colonel Long, who was mortally wounded. He and those that could be moved were carried back to the donga where the horses were sheltering, and where he died that evening.

The gun detachments, as might be expected, fought their guns to the end despite devastating casualties. Their target was the low hills beyond the river, 800 yards away – wherein the enemy casualties were negligible – and they fired until their ammunition was exhausted. Then, withdrawing to the shelter of the donga, they waited, the guns silent. Captain Reed, one of the battery captains, galloped up some scratch teams to pull out the guns, but was driven back losing seven men out of 13, and 13 horses out of 22. Buller then called for volunteers from his staff to bring the guns in, and miraculously two were saved. Their casualties, though, were heavy, among them Lieutenant Roberts, son of the field-marshal, who died in hospital two days later. The VC was awarded to him after his death, as it also was to three other officers and a driver. Among the Indian bearers who carried back the wounded was a young man called Gandhi, who learned here the hatred of violence that made him so successful in his campaign of non-violence in India, 26 years later. The remaining ten guns were left out on the plain, and after dark were removed by the Boers who used them against the British at Ladysmith a month later. At dusk the centre and right brigades withdrew as best they could, and next morning the force marched back to Chieveley.

Nine hundred men were killed or wounded with 250 missing. The latter were mostly wounded who could not be moved from the donga or the 'Loop' and who were taken prisoner.

The disaster at Colenso, when none of the 16 battalions reached their objective and ten of the 12 field-guns were lost was General Buller's greatest defeat. As a result of the 'Black Week' Lord Roberts was ordered out to South Africa as Commander-in-Chief. On his arrival it was thought that he did not remove Buller from his command because Lieutenant Roberts had been killed whilst on Buller's staff, and he feared that a removal might be taken personally.

Buller was much depressed by this defeat. It was the third in a week – the 'Black Week' – and he was deeply disappointed that a resounding success had not been achieved, to show alongside the two defeats elsewhere. His never-optimistic nature now became defeatist and he informed London and his goal, Ladysmith, that he could not succeed, advised the latter to destroy all documents, fire away all ammunition and to surrender. He sat back, not knowing what to do next. Severely reprimanded by Downing Street for his defeatist attitude he awaited supercession, but none came. Instead yet another division was ordered out in reinforcement.

Its Commander was Major-General Sir Charles Warren. He was a difficult man to get on with, with a distinct tinge of acerbity in his temper and tongue. Buller was brusque, with an overbearing manner and the frequent clashes between them must have been most unedifying to those of their staff who overheard them.

Roberts had telegraphed Buller to remain on the defensive and attempt no further advance until he, Roberts, and the new division had arrived. But Buller, however, being somewhat affronted by his coming supercession in the Chief Command by Roberts, whom he knew and disliked, suddenly changed drastically his recent defeatist policy for the relief of Ladysmith. He determined to have another try while still his own master. Telling his army that he had found the key to Ladysmith, he left Chieveley on 10 January for the west, marching along the line of the river barrier. Reinforced by Warren's division he had now 30,000 men, 20,000 of whom he took with him.

It was a slow and tedious march. Usually the leading unit had reached its night's destination before the last wagons had marched out of the previous camp, and it took five days to cover the 16 miles to Springfield, where Buller set up his advanced HQ.

Not only was the vast column frequently in sight from the Tugela Heights on its right, but the incessant dust cloud indicated its whereabouts. The Boers marching through the hills on the far side of the river kept up with the British, having no difficulty whatever in assessing their enemy's moves and intentions. When the British halted, they halted too, and the two marches were parallel – the only difference being that every British move was seen in full view whereas the movements of the Boers were not only invisible but their presence largely unsuspected.

Pushing on from Springfield the army reached the village and ridge of Spearman's, opposite two drifts over the river and beyond which were a high and imposing series of hills. Several days were spent here while preparations were made to cross the Tugela. The two drifts available had to have their approaches widened and metalled, water points set up on the far bank, roads improved, bakeries built, the Boers having as perfect a view from the hills of the preparations and obvious intentions of their enemy as they could possibly wish. During these five days of waiting (when the infantry and artillery were much employed in finding work parties for the sappers building or expanding the crossing and other works) the cavalry crossed to the north bank and probed for the enemy.

Buller now took an extraordinary step. He handed over the command of the whole force at Spearman's to Warren, leaving him only with his normal divisional staff to command a large force, and convoy it across a difficult river into rugged unreconnoitred country in which a dangerous enemy might or might not be lurking. He withdrew from the growing camp to his new headquarters at Springfield, some four miles away.

Meanwhile the cavalry found no sign of the enemy on one of the great mountains, Tabanyama, the most westerly of the group. The cavalry Brigade Commander, Lord Dundonald, reported this to Warren, asked for reinforcements and permission to push on and round the north side of the range of hills. It was a sensible and feasible tactical move. But this was too enterprising for Warren and he not only refused both reinforcements and permission but severely reprimanded Dundonald for presumption. However, he did send one brigade on a rather half-hearted attack on Tabanyama, which was recalled for no apparent reason when within sight of success.

During these days while the crossings were being enlarged, and the Tabanyama operations were carried out, General Buller frequently rode over from Springfield to see Warren, bombarding him with advice, suggestions, and criticisms – but no orders. Warren seemed quite unable to make up his mind as to the best tactical course to take, and Buller became more and more impatient. Finally Warren selected the next hill to Tabanyama, Spion Kop, for attack, although he admitted he did not like the look of it. Buller acquiesced, thankful to have some plan made at last.

On the late evening of 23 January, the Lancashire Brigade of Royal Lancasters, Lancashire Fusiliers, South Lancashires and Thorneycroft's Mounted Infantry left camp, and started to climb the hill, the most formidable, and the highest in the whole range,

1,500 ft above the river. The night was dark, a fine drizzle was falling and the going very difficult. Moreover, the Brigade Commander, Major-General Woodgate, an ex-Royal Lancasters CO, was 55 years of age and in poor health. The operation bore many similarities to the disaster of Majuba, 19 years earlier.

Spion Kop has three very steep sides, with one convenient and less acute shoulder up which the brigade climbed. Towards the end of the climb the hill flattens out considerably, the top being a shallow inverted saucer. At the farther (northern) end the high ground runs away into a long narrow saddle, terminating in a pronounced knoll. To the east and 200 ft below the main hill, and quite separate from it, rises another small feature, Aloe Knoll.

Advancing on a two-battalion front, the Royal Lancasters on the left and the Lancashire Fusiliers on the right followed by Thorneycroft's Mounted Infantry and led by the Brigade Commander in person, the brigade reached the first 'flattening out' without incident after climbing for most of the night. Owing to their weight and the noise inseparable from carrying them, many of the picks and shovels were dumped, but the men were still encumbered with greatcoats and ammunition, though not with rations or water. At about 6 a.m. the thick dawn mist gave the impression that the summit had been reached, the only Boer encountered had been bayoneted and the men ordered to give three cheers to indicate success to Warren below.

An hour or so later the mist suddenly lifted to disclose the summit 200 yards further on up the hill. The ensuing movement on to the hilltop in the now broad sunlight warned the main enemy force on the far side of the hill and on the plain below of the occupation, and they immediately started to climb the Aloe Knoll and the north-western end of the main feature at the end of the saddle. From the former they were soon able to accurately enfilade the shallow trench being built on the summit by the Lancashire Fusiliers on the right, while the Royal Lancasters, prolonging the line to the left, came under accurate though frontal fire from the knoll at the far end of the saddle. From Tabanyama Hill, 3,000 yards to their left front across the intervening valley, an enemy battery enfiladed both battalions.

The extreme rockiness of the hill precluded any serious trench digging although both battalions scraped together some skeleton forms of breastwork two feet high. The picks left behind would now have come in useful, although the Lancashire Fusiliers could

only have protected themselves from the accurate enfilade fire from
Aloe Knoll by changing direction through 90 degrees. Even then it
is doubtful whether much entrenching could have been done under
this fire.

Thorneycroft's Mounted Infantry passed through the two battalions and tried to reach the far end of the inverted saucer, but were
prevented from doing so by the fire from the north-west knoll. A
few men from the two left-hand companies of the Royal Lancasters
managed to crawl forward individually, around the left (outer) flank
of the MI, meeting some success but also meeting enemy scouts who
had crept up along the saddle on to the far segment of the saucer.
Attempting to relieve this complete hold-up, the South Lancashires
were ordered forward to support. They too were quickly pinned
down before reaching the three forward battalions. About an hour
after the two forward battalions had commenced their trench digging,
General Woodgate was mortally wounded, standing at the right of the
Lancashire Fusiliers trench – the nearest man to Aloe Knoll. He was
carried down the hill and died in hospital some days later.

Woodgate left chaos behind him in the command on the hill and
Colonel Crofton, CO of the Royal Lancasters, as the senior officer
present, assumed command. Losing his head he sent a panic signal
to Warren below: 'Reinforce at once or all is lost. General dead.'
Buller intercepted this message before it reached Warren and he rode
over with his usual advice, suggesting that an officer more vigorous
than Crofton should be appointed. Warren chose Thorneycroft, and
as he was junior to Crofton heliographed to him his promotion to
Brigadier-General. The news of his promotion reached Thorneycroft
later but he neglected to tell Crofton.

Later in the day Warren sent up the Middlesex to the summit, and
the Scottish Rifles to work round the right flank, in order to relieve
the pressure on the Lancashire Fusiliers. They were unsuccessful,
however, and not only added to the general confusion on the hill,
but also further confused the problem of command. Colonel Hill of
the Middlesex was senior to both Crofton and Thorneycroft.

When Hill arrived he assumed command at the eastern end of the
summit, while Thorneycroft was commanding with vigour at the
other end. They did not meet for several hours. The commander
of the brigade to which the Middlesex and Scottish Rifles belonged,
Major-General Talbot-Coke, felt that he too should ascend the hill
to see his two battalions and was then, of course, the senior officer

present. However, he did not attempt to take command and the delicate point as to who was in fact the commander on the hilltop was never settled.

During the afternoon the CO of the 60th Rifles (from yet another brigade), acting on his own initiative and without orders from any superior officer, moved his regiment far out to its right and, climbing a long low ridge, came up behind the Boers on Aloe Knoll, causing them considerable casualties from long-range fire. The Boers, seeing the British were in front of and now apparently behind them, were about to leave the Knoll, when General Buller rode up to Warren and demanded to know who had ordered the 60th on its lone though effective mission. On hearing that the CO had done so without orders Buller immediately and peremptorily ordered the battallion to withdraw, on the grounds that he would not tolerate such independence, almost amounting to impertinence.

At dusk the problem of who in fact was in command on the hilltop became acute. General Talbot-Coke advised Colonel Hill, whom both believed to be in charge, to retire to the plain during the night. Thorneycroft at the other end of the hill had now run into Crofton. Both felt that they should stay for some time yet and therefore sent a heliograph message to Warren for orders. Warren had by now heard from Hill, advising retirement, yet Thorneycroft was, as far as Warren knew, in command. However, Warren took Hill's advice and ordered withdrawal. As the left-hand units were on their way down they met Hill, who, having by now changed his mind, ordered them back. Thorneycroft came along and met Hill and, after a considerable wrangle, the latter had to admit that Thorneycroft as a Brigadier-General was the senior. The withdrawal continued.

And so the British left their objective leaving 300 dead behind them. Probably at about the same time, the Boers, quite certain that the British troops were immovable, withdrew too, and for several hours Spion Kop remained unoccupied. At dawn next day a Boer scout, finding the hill empty, signalled to his commander below and the hill was re-occupied.

It must be remembered that Woodgate's brigade did not capture Spion Kop. It took possession of it on finding it untenanted after the climb – and there remained unmolested for some hours. Had the Lancashire Fusiliers only advanced another 300 yards over the top to the far rim, they would have reached the edge of the plateau and so seen the Boers leave their laager on the plain below when commencing their climb. To assault such a slope against the fire of the defending British infantry was an impossible task for the enemy, no matter how mediocre the British shooting. But Woodgate did not see the obvious advantage he held.

Amongst the might-have-beens that are found in every account of every defeat must appear Warren's failure during the day to visit the hilltop where seven of his battalions, parts of his three brigades, were closely in action. A firm grip of the situation taken there must have shown a general with dominance how the battle could be controlled. The *junta* of five or six colonels on the site was quite incapable of doing so.

By 4 a.m. the next morning the last battalion had left Spion Kop, and rejoined the camp at Spearman's. When it was all over Buller moved Warren's command away to the east again, and out of range of Boer guns.

After Spion Kop a curious psychological change came over the Boers along the Tugela. They knew they had successfully invaded Natal, had surrounded and were now successfully besieging behind them a garrison of 8,000 British soldiers, had won resounding victories at Colenso and Spion Kop, all in less than three months. Their morale should indeed have been high. But it wasn't.

Many of them felt they had done enough and that their farms and families were now again top priority. Many applied for, and got, leave for 'private affairs' and went back to Transvaal. Others, more fearful, wondered whether they had not taken on too much. They felt that their invasion of friendly territory and then the defeats of their enemy would sooner or later bring retribution on them from the ever-growing and professional British Army. These Boers did not apply for leave. They quietly left their comrades in the hours of darkness and also rode back to Transvaal. By the time the next British advance took place there were only 4,000 Boers to face Buller's 20,000 British soldiers.

Unlike his behaviour after Colenso, Buller did not have a fit of deep depression following his defeat at Spion Kop. Instead he decided to have another go at a small hill, Vaal Krantz, six miles farther to the east.

Vaal Krantz was much lower than Spion Kop and had it been captured the cavalry could comfortably have passed round both its east and west extremities. They would then have found themselves in a plain with little or no obstacles in front of them and from where they could have taken the Boers in the rear and from both flanks.

After a week's rest and excellent rations of vegetables and fresh meat, the British soldiers were full of high spirits and very ready to go again. But the attack on Vaal Krantz was miserably slow.

It began at 6 a.m. when Wynne's Brigade (which had been Woodgate's and had led the assault on Spion Kop) advanced up to the Tugela, making a feint attack. It advanced well towards a smaller hill to the right of the Vaal Krantz but failed to draw the Boer fire.

A pontoon bridge was then built in front of the main hill and Buller led the remainder of his forces across it. It took time for the several thousands of men, in double file only, to cross the swaying bridge and the horse-drawn guns had to go very slowly. The Boers were left in no doubt as to where the attack would come.

The day passed into afternoon, the sun got hotter and hotter, the crossing of the bridge took longer and longer and Buller's natural pessimism returned. He decided to give up any idea of an attack in force that day, and told General Lyttelton, the commander of the leading brigade: 'You'll never carry the hill before dark, we had better put it off.' Lyttelton replied: 'Let me go now, and I'll guarantee I'll be on the top of Vaal Krantz by 4 o'clock.' Buller let him go.

The Durham Light Infantry led the attack and, after stiff resistance from the naturally very thinly spread Boers, reached the top of the ridge – soon followed by the Rifle Brigade – at precisely 4 o'clock.

But the position now became like Spion Kop. The top of the hill was taken but no reinforcements arrived and the Boers on the next hill were able to enfilade the Rifle Brigade. Buller, with his customary pessimism, ordered Lyttelton to withdraw – but Lyttelton ignored the order, and advised an additional attack on Green Hill whence the fire enfilading the Rifle Brigade was coming. But Buller would have nothing to do with such a common-sense suggestion, and decided to leave Lyttelton, exposed and unsupported, with no attempt to help him, on the hill all night. Buller then went to bed.

It was a very similar situation to that at Sulva Bay in the Gallipoli campaign in 1915, when 900 Turks on a low but clearly defined ridge several hundred yards inland from the beach held up two British divisions for three days before Turkish reinforcements arrived.

During the night the enemy concentrated his force, and all his guns, to defend Vaal Krantz. But for Lyttelton's tactical skill, another Spion Kop would have developed. Next day Buller vacillated all the morning between telling Lyttelton to withdraw and 'asking' him to hang on, and then reached the nadir of his professional incapacity. He telegraphed Roberts, who had just arrived in Cape Town 700 miles away, asking him what he should do and could he have tactical advice on a situation Roberts did not know, on ground he had never seen. Roberts replied that Buller must do what he could to relieve Ladysmith, his prime task, and that he was the best judge of the situation.

Buller's next step was at least positive. He relieved Lyttelton's brigade on Vaal Krantz with Hildyard's, which spent that night improving their positions on the ridge. On relief Lyttelton and Major Wilson (later to be CIGS in 1918) went to see Buller, who was dining. He asked them to share his champagne and enquired how they had got on. Lyttelton was very angry that Buller had failed to support him and so avoided victory, but the champagne worked wonders and Lyttelton and Wilson returned to their lines.

The next day Warren was sent out personally on reconnaissance, and returned with some sketches he had made of enemy-held territory. Buller saw them, and making only a sarcastic comment, called a Council of War of his brigadiers and Warren. Some advised going on, though most advised withdrawal. Buller, glad to have his mind made up for him by a democratic vote, ordered withdrawal. The troops got back across the Tugela without disturbance, the pontoon bridges were dismantled, and Buller's army marched back to Chieveley again.

Vaal Krantz, the third major defeat for Buller in trying to relieve Ladysmith, was much less costly than either Colenso or Spion Kop. Thirty men only were killed with some 300 wounded. The loss of prestige was negligible, it was already very low. Ladysmith was getting used to disappointments and Roberts had his hands full.

The new Boer position holding the Tugela around Colenso was extended two miles further to the east than they had done when Colenso was attacked in December. Buller, now in an optimistic period of thought decided to out-flank this long extension to the east.

A cavalry reconnaissance secured a hill five miles from Chieveley, and Buller arrived with his telescope. The result of his observations was that he ordered everyone back to Chieveley, intending to advance again with his whole army, eastward, along the south bank of the river, as he had done to Spearman's before Spion Kop, hoping to find a crossing.

But the next day when he intended to start was very hot, and the start was postponed for 24 hours. Then for three days the army crawled eastward parallel to the river, but well to the south. The Boers had, unwisely, left their excellent positions on the north bank and, crossing over, occupied lines not nearly so good in the open country to the south of the river.

On the 18th the British Army turned left and attacked the new Boer lines with two brigades. The Boers nervously conscious that they had their backs to the river turned and fled. For two days they were not followed and were allowed to get clear away over the river.

By the 20th Buller was not only in possession of the south bank of the river for several miles, but there was no sign of the enemy on the north bank. He could have crossed anywhere he liked by building pontoon bridges at the most suitable sites, suitable both from an engineering point of view and for tactical reasons. But he moved back almost to Colenso where he built one bridge only, leading directly into a hollow surround, enclosed by hills. Despite the expressed opinions of his staff on the unsuitability of this site, he took no notice and 15 battalions and 40 guns got across without opposition. But if anything more than a rearguard were to oppose them they would indeed be in trouble. But Buller was over the Tugela, his army now very experienced, the weather was gradually cooling, the Boers were obviously failing, and Ladysmith was only seven miles away. The end was in sight.

For three months since the Boers invaded Natal and its withdrawal from Talana Hill at Dundee the British Army had, with the single exception, at Caesar's Camp and Wagon Hill, suffered nothing but setbacks. The retreat to Ladysmith, Elandslaagte, Lombard's Kop, Nicholson's Nek, Pepworth, the armoured train, Colenso, Spion Kop and Vaal Krantz had all seen the superiority of the Boer fighting.

But now, over the Tugela at last, everything was to change. The advance through the hills and the actual relief of Ladysmith was pursued with energy, speed, concentration and success. In contrast to the previous 80 days of marching, bivouacking, marching, attacking, marching, withdrawing, covering a tragic 30 miles, littered with defeats, repulses, casualties, depression, the new phase was to be indeed different. The seven miles to Ladysmith was to take seven days only, four successful brigade attacks were to be carried out, the Boers were constantly kept on the run, less than 1,800 total casualties were suffered, of which the vast majority were wounds, frequently not serious. Press correspondents, painfully accustomed to witness assaults that failed, could hardly believe their eyes.

The brigades attacked in succession four sizeable hills, Wynne's Hill, named after the brigade commander, with Green Hill, were the first to be assaulted and it gave the most trouble. It is in fact two abutments of the same feature. Between them is a small re-entrant which peters out before it reaches the summit. The Royal Lancasters led the attack on the twin hills, the left two companies reaching the crest without great difficulty. The right companies were held up by Boer trenches and the rather steeper slope, with much more difficult going. The CO, who had only taken over the command that morning (Colonel Crofton having gone to Brigade in place of General Wynne, wounded earlier in the day), went up to the left companies to assess the situation and make a plan for a flank movement to release the right companies. While there and holding a brief 'O-Group' conference he was shot and mortally wounded. The bullet came almost from the rear, and undoubtedly one of the Boers holding up the right companies whose position was not so far forward, saw the O-Group with all its paraphernalia of officers with swords and maps and took the wonderful opportunity. Shortly after the CO's death the right companies were able to move again and the hill was captured.

Next day the Irish Brigade came through and the Royal Inniskilling Fusiliers took Inniskilling Hill a mile further on. This regiment too had considerable resistance to overcome and suffered many casualties. The hill is much more bare than Wynne Hill, with no trees, bushes or grass, and the Boers must have had great difficulty in finding positions. There is no top soil whatever on the rock, no digging was possible, and the graves are like those on Spion Kop, the bodies being covered with stones and rocks. However, Inniskilling Hill and Wynne being held and forming a strong flank protection, the next hill, Railway Hill, another mile on, was the objective for three days later.

But the plan was changed and the fourth hill, Pieters Hill, of which

Railway Hill was an off-shoot, was the next objective. Its capture must 'pinch out' Railway Hill and clearly Buller was beginning to show some tactical knowledge and to use his experience. Indeed his staff could hardly recognize the man they had served for the past two months. His previous pessimism, vacillation and indecision seemed to have disappeared and he had a firm grasp of the operations. He dictated his orders at speed and omitted nothing.

The Fusilier Brigade advanced up to, and captured, Pieters, the Irish Fusiliers losing many men. The Scots Fusiliers and the Dublin Fusiliers supported them, and the Dublin Fusiliers were able to open fire on the Boers still on Railway Hill from the rear. The West Yorks had assaulted this hill as a feint attack, and while containing the Boers thereon, had allowed Buller's 'pinch out' tactics to be successful. Buller then followed up his success with the kind of pressure that no one in his army had ever seen or suspected before. Gunfire continued through the night, and next morning, the 28th, the Boers disintegrated, fleeing across the plain past Ladysmith.

That afternoon Lord Dundonald's cavalry brigade entered Ladysmith. The 92 days of operations were over, and success had at last reached Buller. He had relieved Ladysmith.

The sudden change in Buller's attitude was quite extraordinary. His normal pessimistic, introvert, rude nature could not stand a rebuff or failure or opposition. Hence his colossal defeat at Colenso, his first engagement in the South African War, affected him deeply, greatly shaking his self-confidence and inducing indecision. He remained the same man for two months, setback following setback, his doubts always remaining.

Then the first success, when after returning to Chieveley from Vaal Krantz he got his army across the Tugela without opposition. His sudden elation, optimism, vitality, showed him to be a man whom success encouraged, a man who did not like, perhaps couldn't take, hard knocks, but who thrived on good news. Never was there a clearer case of nothing succeeding like success.

2
The Russo-Japanese War

Tsushima (1905)

C. P. Campbell

The great sea battle that was fought on 27 May 1905 in the straits dividing Tsushima island from Japan ended with the complete destruction of a first-class European battle squadron by the navy of a country with only 50 years of modern industrial and organizational experience. In those 50 years warship design had progressed from wooden sailing-ships firing cannon broadsides to steel steam-powered battleships, equipped with wireless, fire-control systems and mounting guns capable of engagement at ranges over five miles. When the battle came it was a clash of design ideas and tactical doctrines, but above all of two different social systems' will to win. As the Japanese commander, Admiral Togo, wrote after the battle, 'The *Mikasa* [Togo's flagship] and the 11 others of the main force had taken years of work to design and build, and yet they were used for only half an hour of decisive battle. We studied the art of war and trained ourselves in it, but it was put to use for only that short period. Though the decisive battle took such a short time, it required 10 years of preparation.'

On 30 January 1902 Japan announced the conclusion of an alliance with Great Britain. The Royal Navy's tactical doctrines and British shipbuilding practice had already permeated the thinking of those directing Japan's emergence as a world naval power. Japan's transformation from a medieval to a modern state had proceeded at breakneck speed. They had imported 200 years of Europe's industrial revolution wholesale, but in choosing their military mentors – Germany for the army, and Britain for the navy – they had chosen well. There had even been a modern naval action for Japan to test and show her efficiency at sea.

In 1894 the Chinese Empire seemed on the verge of breaking up. Korea and the vast Manchurian hinterland were tempting targets for Japanese military ambition. The Japanese successfully convoyed a large army to Korea in August, 1894, until the Chinese Admiral Ting sought battle off the mouth of the Yalu River.

When the time came, however, the contest was not so clear; Admiral Ting adopted outdated tactics, throwing away his advantage in gunpower, and the Japanese Admiral Ito decided the action by out-manoeuvring and encircling the Chinese line of battle. Four Chinese ships were sunk by gunfire and one by collision, but their battleships proved the value of armour against hits from smaller guns. Ito's flagship, the *Matsushima*, was hit three times by 12-in and once by 10-in shells, causing great damage and over a hundred casualties. Both fleets retired, but Japan was left in command of the Yellow Sea and free to continue her military adventure in Korea.

The prize of the Liaoutang Peninsula, with the ice-free port, Port Arthur, at its base, was snatched away when the European powers put on diplomatic pressure to 'protect' China. The wound to Japanese pride was deepened when, as soon as Port Arthur had been returned to China, Russia bullied the ailing Empire into allowing the Trans-Siberian Railway to be completed to Vladivostok across Manchuria. By March 1898 the Russians were in Port Arthur itself and developing an ice-free naval base to complement Vladivostok, 300 miles to the north. The Japanese, however, had already started a programme of naval expansion which would bring their fleet up to six new battleships, six armoured cruisers, and eight light cruisers by 1903.

Russia watched with alarm, and commenced production in Baltic yards of eight battleships. In contrast to the Anglophile Japanese, these ships were strongly influenced by French practice, with pronounced tumblehome and high freeboards (high hulls bellying out at the waterline), long waterline armour belts, and massive masts and built-up superstructures.

The Russo-Japanese War began on the evening of 8 February 1904. Japanese destroyers in two waves made a precision night attack against the Russian First Pacific Squadron lying in the roadstead of

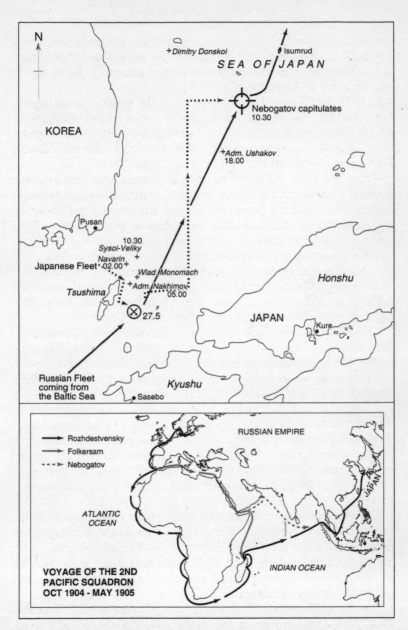

N

Dimitry Donskoi +   • Isumrud

SEA OF JAPAN

Nebogatov capitulates
10.30

KOREA

Adm. Ushakov +
18.00

Pusan •

10.30
Sysoi-Veliky
Navarin +
Japanese Fleet + 02.00
Wlad. Monomach
Tsushima   + *Adm. Nakhimov*
05.00

⊗ 27.5

Honshu

JAPAN   Kure •

Kyushu

Russian Fleet
coming from
the Baltic Sea

• Sasebo

→ Rozhdestvensky
→ Folkersam
- -▸ Nebogatov

RUSSIAN EMPIRE

*ATLANTIC
OCEAN*

JAPAN

INDIAN OCEAN

**VOYAGE OF THE 2ND
PACIFIC SQUADRON
OCT 1904 - MAY 1905**

2.1   The Battle of Tsushima, 28 May 1905

Port Arthur. Seven battleships, six cruisers, and 25 destroyers lay anchored in the harbour, their lights blazing and their defences woefully ill-prepared. Only three torpedoes found their mark, but they crippled three battleships. The *Tsarevitch*, *Retzivan* and *Pallada* settled on the shallow bottom, stranded without dry-dock facilities, and for a vital month the Japanese controlled the Yellow Sea and began the transfer of their armies to the mainland.

When the dynamic Admiral Makarov arrived in March to take command of the dispirited Russian fleet, the squadron was roused from its somnolence and the damaged battleships were raised in coffer-dams. As the new spirit and the renewed threat to their lines of troop transports became evident to the Japanese, they redoubled their efforts to block the harbour. Admiral Togo was forced to use his ships in close blockade, with its wear and tear on his vessels (although keeping the crews combat trained), and face the increasing hazards of Russian minefields. However, on their few sorties out of harbour, the lack of skill of the Russian commanders was painfully obvious. Coming out in the battleship *Petropavlovsk* to cover the return of a disastrous destroyer sortie, Makarov led his whole squadron over a freshly laid minefield. There was a muffled explosion under the flagship, then suddenly two vast explosions threw a great chunk of the battleship's superstructure into the air. The big ship heeled over and slid to the bottom, her propellers still turning, taking Makarov with her.

His ability had been the Pacific Squadron's hope, and with his death the offensive power of the fleet, even to stop a landing on the peninsula behind the port, collapsed. 'The squadron went back to slumber in the basins of the inner harbour,' wrote an observer.

The Japanese, however, had their problems. Togo's repeated attempts to block the harbour with suicide assault blockships had failed. The battleships *Habuse* and *Yashima* were claimed by mines. The Vladivostok cruisers were harrying troop transports. It was clear that the Russians were gathering a fleet in the Baltic to come to the aid of embattled Port Arthur, and Togo was still forced to keep his fleet concentrated should the new if reluctant Russian commander, Admiral Vitgeft, attempt a breakout.

It was not Togo, however, who had to make the first move. Vitgeft received direct orders from the Tsar to take the squadron to Vladivostok and, led by minesweepers, the fleet left harbour on 10 August 1904. There was little hope aboard the Russian ships and already Japanese scouts were signalling the news of the attempted break-out to Togo's battle-squadron, now steaming north to engage. Togo had hoped the Russian fleet could be kept inside harbour where it would be destroyed or captured by the besieging army. Now his Combined Fleet, the entire battleship strength of Japan, would have to accept battle, with the threat of the Baltic Fleet still to come. He could afford to lose no more ships.

The Japanese purpose would be served by barring the way out, if not destroying the Pacific Squadron in battle. Suitably the opposing heavy squadrons opened fire at extreme range, with the Russian gunnery surprisingly accurate. As the long daylight action continued and the opposing fleets manoeuvred for the best position, the Japanese were taking serious punishment. Mutual destruction would bring Togo a tactical victory but would lose him the strategic object.

Then suddenly, with darkness beginning to fall, two 12-in shells struck the Russian flagship *Tsarevitch*, killing every man on the bridge. Of Vitgeft only a bloody piece of one leg remained, and the battleship lurched out of control, turning the battle-line into a milling throng. After minutes of utter disorder, Admiral Prince Uhtomski, flying signals from the bridge-rails of *Pereviet* (the signalling masts had been shot away), led the squadron back to Port Arthur as *Retzivan* and *Pobieda* put up a gallant rearguard. Japanese destroyers closed in for the kill, but in the darkness the Russian stragglers managed to regain the harbour they had so recently left. The crippled *Tsarevitch*, hit by over 15 12-in shells, was interned in German Kiau-Chow, and two cruisers suffered similar fates. The sortie had been a fiasco, but until the hit on *Tsarevitch* the Russians had held their station. With their leadership gone, their fighting ability collapsed. The Vladivostok squadron was brought to action on 14 August, but again this resulted in a Russian defeat. The cruiser *Rurik* was sunk and the cruiser *Gromoboi* ran aground. All that was left was the cruiser *Rossiya* and three Russian admirals, unable to reach Port Arthur, where the leaderless Russian battleships had retired to lick their wounds.

The humiliations in the East made the dispatch of reinforcements inevitable. The Russian confidence of 1904 that the 'yellow monkeys' would be crushed had been shattered by Admiral Togo Heiacho and his British-built battleships. In the Baltic a force of new first-class battleships were under construction, while older cruisers and battleships were undergoing refits. If Port Arthur held out, and a powerful new fleet could come to the rescue, Japan might still be denied her mainland ambitions.

The man appointed to command this 'Second Pacific Squadron', Rear-Admiral Zinovei Petrovitch Rozhdestvenski, faced immense problems in even getting his ships ready for sea. Food and clothing had to be procured for the fleet's 12,000 seamen, and machinery prepared for an ordeal beyond any design endurance. In the brief periods of manoeuvres nothing had gone right, with ships colliding and wildly inaccurate gunnery. The overriding problem, however, was coal. Great Britain, with her virtual monopoly of high-grade smokeless Welsh coal, had declared it contraband, but not before the Japanese had built up large stockpiles. The Royal Navy's dominance in the world's oceans was maintained by a strategic chain of coaling stations. Russia had none and only a fitful access to 'neutral' French and German colonial ports. The Baltic Fleet would have to cover 19,000 miles of sea, round the Cape and across the Indian Ocean, consuming 17,000 tons of coal per 1,000 miles. The bunkering capacity of the most modern Russian battleship was 1,063 tons. The solution was a fleet of 60 German colliers dispatched in succession to meet the slow-moving fleet at prearranged rendezvous between Libau in the Baltic and Port Arthur on the other side of the globe.

On 15 October 1904 Rozhdestvenski raised his flag on *Kniaz Suvorov* and, with flags waving and bands playing, the fleet steamed out of Libau to avenge the humiliations in the East. It comprised seven battleships – the recently completed *Suvorov, Aleksandr III, Borodino, Orel* and *Oslyaba*, and the *Sissoi Veliki* and *Navarin*, with two armoured cruisers, *Admiral Nakimoff* and *Dmitri Donskoi*, four light cruisers, *Aurora, Svietlana, Zhemtchug* and *Almaz*, plus seven destroyers and nine transports. The modern battleships mounted four 12-in and seven 6-in guns in paired turrets and had complete waterline armour belts 10 inches thick. The pronounced tumblehome and built-up superstructures, following French design practice, made them bad seakeepers. The overloading of coal and stores added to the miseries of the voyage.

Once at sea, the morale and incompetence of the fleet was revealed to the world when fantastic rumours of a Japanese torpedo attack were taken seriously. To the men on the bridges who remembered the surprise night attack on Port Arthur, however, an attack from British bases did not seem that fantastic. In the North Sea the repair ship *Kamchatka* lost contact with the main fleet, and her frantic signals of sighting torpedo-boats (in fact a Swedish steamer) reached the line of battleships just as they ran into British trawlers working off the Dogger Bank. Wild alarm seized the Russians and equally wild gunnery tore into the trawlers. The voyage had opened in fiasco, and meanwhile Britain seemed on the brink of war.

At Tangier the fleet divided. Admiral Velkerzam was ordered to take the older shallow-draught ships through the Suez Canal and rendezvous at Nossi Bé on the northern tip of Madagascar. At a halting pace the main squadron crawled around the coast of Africa. Ships got lost. Engines broke down. Sailors went made in the heat, cursing the back-breaking ritual of coaling from the faithful German colliers. Inside the ships coal was piled everywhere, 'not up to the neck but over the ears', as an officer wrote, blinding and choking, but, worst of all, making any combat training impossible.

At Nossi Bé the divided squadron rejoined and learned the news that Port Arthur had fallen. Worse still, the coaling arrangements had broken down and the fleet was stuck. All the Russian Admiralty could do was dispatch a 'Third Pacific Squadron' under the command of Rear-Admiral Nebogatov. The fleet did manage an epic crossing of the Indian Ocean, coaling at sea from lighters, until on 9 May, off the coast of French Indo-China, Nebogatov's 'tubs' caught up to further embarrass Rozhdestvenski.

On 23 May the Russians coaled off the China coast for what was going to be the last time. The force heading into the battle-zone was organized in four divisions. The first, led by Rozhdestvenski's flag-ship *Suvorov*, comprised the battleships *Aleksandr II*, *Borodino*, and *Orel*. The Second Division was commanded by Admiral Velkerzam aboard the *Oslyaba*. The unfortunate admiral had succumbed to a tropical disease on the day of the last coaling, but Rozhdestvenski kept this information from the fleet. The *Sissoi Veliki*, *Navarin*, and *Admiral Nakhimoff* followed the dead admiral's flagship. In *Nicolai I* Nebogatov led the Third Division, *Apraxin*, *Seniavin* and *Ushakoff*, while Admiral Enquist, in the *Oleg*, commanded the eight cruisers.

On board the *Mikasa*, flagship of the Combined Fleet lying in the anchorage of Masan on the Korean mainland, Togo directed the operations to meet Rozhdestvenski's ships, now heading for Vladivostok. The most likely route, the Tsushima Strait separating the island of that name from Japan, was divided into boxes, each patrolled by Japanese cruisers. The Tsugau Strait and the northern route around the top of Japan itself was left thinly protected, but it was a gamble that would pay off. The Russian crews prayed for fog to conceal the seven miles of the ships under their black smoke haze until they reached the safety of Vladivostok, which now seemed like the promised land. But for Rozhdestvenski merely to evade Togo and take refuge in another Port Arthur might merely repeat the fate of the First Pacific Squadron. The Russian admiral had at least to inflict some damage on the enemy, so the squadron's speed was adjusted so that it would enter the zone of maximum danger at daylight on 27 May 1905.

A Japanese armed merchant cruiser, the *Shinano Maru*, made the first contact at 0330. The wireless message reached Togo in the *Mikasa* – 'The enemy sighted in section 203, he seems to be heading for the eastern channel.' Ninety minutes later Togo led the battleships of the First Division out of Masan, the *Mikasa*, *Shikishima*, *Fuji*, and *Asahi*, the armoured cruisers *Kasuga* and *Nisshin*. Vice-Admiral Kanimura led the Second Division, the armoured cruisers *Izumo*, *Azuma*, *Tokira*, *Yagumo*, and *Iwate*. The cruisers *Naniwa*, *Takachino*, *Tsushima* and *Akashi* made up the Third Division. Every ship was fuelled and armed for maximum combat efficiency and able to make 18 knots, in contrast to the worn-out Russian ships' nine or ten. Togo's fleet could bring to action 16 12-in guns, and 112 8-in and 6-in guns. The Russians had 26 12-in, 10-in and 121 8-in and 6-in. Any disparity in gunpower mattered little, however; it was how the rivals used their gunpower that would decide the battle.

Togo's operations officer, Commander Akiyama, had set a seven-stage trap for the Russians to sail into. The battle would open with torpedo and destroyer attacks and the third phase would be the direct fleet engagement. The remaining stages envisaged the piecemeal destruction of any survivors who might break through towards Vladivostok. The Russian fleet was detected too late for torpedo attacks, but shadowing cruisers forced Rozhdestvenski into weakening his formation. Fearing an attack, he ordered a manoeuvre designed to give him the advantage of crossing the 'T' of the main Japanese force that must be waiting somewhere ahead. When the shadowing cruisers disappeared, the Russian admiral ordered the First and Second Battleship Divisions to make an eight-point turn to starboard to bring the ships in line abreast. As *Suvorov* began the turn, the Japanese cruisers reappeared and the order to the Second Division was contradicted. The Russian captains could not execute the change with any kind of precision and, as Nebogatov wrote, 'The enemy continued to turn to port and lay parallel to our mob, since this is the only word to describe our formation.' Thus the Russians were suddenly steaming towards Togo's battlefleet at a closing speed of 24 knots in a ragged battle formation exposed on the port side.

It was not Togo's intention to make a north–south broadside pass which, although it might damage the weaker Russian ships, would leave them travelling in the direction of Vladivostok. At 1355 the Japanese line swung to port, following the *Mikasa* in line ahead. Rozhdestvenski meanwhile had ordered the First Division to increase speed and come out from behind the weaker line to his left and take up battle formation in one line ahead. Then, as Togo reached the chosen position, the battle ensigns were unfurled, and in a breathtaking manœuvre the whole Japanese line swung round 180 degrees, turning in succession, with the *Mikasa* leading. At the moment of the turn they were helpless targets, but only the lighter Russian shells were making hits. Coming out of their turn, one after the other, the Japanese ships opened a slow deliberate fire at a range from 5,000 to 6,000 yards. Then they put on speed, sprinting north-east at 15 knots across the head of the labouring Russian column. The classic manœuvre that the pirates of the Inland Sea had known for centuries, crossing the 'T', had been achieved.

As the Japanese gunners found the range, the leading Russian ships were subjected to a fearful battering. *Suvorov* and *Oslyaba* were soon set ablaze, while, on board, stunned Russian seamen struggled with primitive damage-control procedures. At 1455 *Suvorov* fell out of line on fire. At 1505 *Oslyaba* sank, throwing the following ships into chaos. *Aleksandr III* turned to port to escape under the smoke haze and slip behind the stern of the Japanese line, all steaming in perfect formation at 15 knots, all guns in action. As they looped back to intercept them, only the *Suvorov* was left in sight, still fighting back with one remaining 12-in gun and a few remaining 12-pounders. From the shattered bridge the severely wounded Rozhdestvenski was carried to a gun turret.

An hour later the missing Russian main body was resighted and forced to turn away south-east as Togo's ships poured fire into them at a range of 1,000 yards. *Aleksandr III* was forced out of formation until, at 1800, it capsized and sank. The *Orel* was raked with fire and the *Borodino* burned until her exploding magazines ripped the ship apart. At the same time the gallant *Suvorov* was being finished off with torpedoes. The agony of the battleships could not relieve the cruisers *Oleg* and *Zhemtchug*, set ablaze, and the sinking of several auxiliary ships.

At darkness, with Vladivostok still 300 miles away, Admiral Nebogatov, in the old *Nicolai I*, attempted to achieve some sort of order from the decimated survivors of the First and Second Divisions and his still largely intact Third Division. The gathering darkness, however, brought the torpedo-boats. Pressing home vicious attacks at ranges under 300 yards, the Japanese sank *Navarin* and *Sissoi Veliki*. Admiral Enquist, in the *Oleg*, led *Zhemtchug* and *Aurora* away from the slaughter out by the southern exit of the Tsushima Strait, but the cruisers *Admiral Nakhimoff* and *Monomakh* were scuttled on the island of Tsushima itself.

At dawn the next day Nebogatov's shattered fleet was found again by the Japanese battlefleet. The tragic Rozhdestvenski lay critically wounded in the destroyer *Bedovi*. By 1115 the Japanese had formed a great circle around the Russian ships. There was no other choice. A white tablecloth was run up on *Nicolai I*, but Togo did not cease fire until the Russians had stopped their engines. Victory was complete when the unconscious Admiral Rozhdestvenski was carried into captivity. Of the 12 Russian ships that had made up the battle-line, eight had been sunk and four captured. Four cruisers had been sunk, three scuttled and Enquist's three escaped to the Philippines and were interned in Manilla. One cruiser, the *Almaz*, and two destroyers reached Vladivostok. The Russians lost 4,830 men killed, 7,000 prisoners and more interned. The Japanese lost three torpedo-boats, 117 killed and 585 wounded.

What had happened? How had two battlefleets – on paper, at least, evenly matched – met and fought with such an uneven outcome? The reports of the British naval attachés who had gone into action with the Japanese fleet were eagerly studied, and they indicated several things: that Russian gunnery had been surprisingly accurate at long range but had rapidly deteriorated as soon as the Russian ships themselves took damage; high-explosive shells had caused the most damage, and a high proportion of Russian shells found their target but failed to explode; that shells, not torpedoes, were the deciders; that both sides had fought bravely, but that the Japanese were vastly more competent than their opponents. All this was true, and the reports strongly influenced naval thinking up to the start of the First World War and beyond, however, the Second Pacific Squadron had been disadvantaged from the very start.

The ships were worn out by the voyage from across the world. Of the men themselves, many were sick. Ironically, after the repeated stops and the backbreaking task of coaling, the Russians had gone into action with too much, some of it stacked on the decks in bags. The Japanese, taking the advice of a Royal Navy report by Admiral Fisher, had actually dumped coal, losing weight to fighting trim and giving them the crucial speed advantage which allowed Togo's in succession turn and the foiling of Russian evasive manoeuvres. The Japanese had concentrated fire on the Russian flagships, and as soon as they had been battered out of line, their squadrons' formation and fighting qualities fell to pieces.

Finally, the initiative and competence of the Japanese commanders and seamen was something that could not be quantified in the reports drafted by naval attachés. As they had closed for action, Admiral Togo had been urged to take cover as he stood on the exposed bridge. He shook his head. 'I am getting on for sixty, and this old body of mine is no longer worth caring for. But you are all young men with futures before you, so take care of yourselves and continue living in order to serve your country.' The Imperial Japanese Navy was a curious mixture of Royal Navy traditions of understatement and Oriental determination to triumph. Togo had signalled to the fleet: 'The rise and fall of the Empire depends upon the result of this engagement. Do your utmost, every one of you.'

3
The First World War

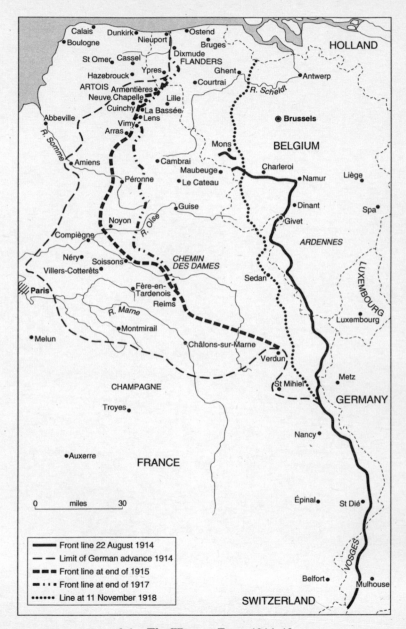

Calais •   Dunkirk •   Ostend
Boulogne •   Nieuport •   Bruges
St Omer •   Cassel •   Dixmude   FLANDERS   HOLLAND
Hazebrouck •   Ypres •   Ghent •   Antwerp
ARTOIS •   Armentières •   Courtrai   R. Scheldt
Neuve Chapelle •   Lille
Cuinchy •   La Bassée •   Brussels
Abbeville •   Vimy •   Lens
Arras •   Mons   BELGIUM
R. Somme
Amiens •   Cambrai •   Charleroi
Péronne •   Maubeuge •   Namur   Liège
Le Cateau
Guise •   Dinant   Spa
Noyon •   R. Oise •   Givet
Compiègne •   ARDENNES   LUXEMBOURG
Néry •   Soissons •   CHEMIN DES DAMES
Villers-Cotterêts •   Sedan
Paris •   Fère-en-Tardenois   Luxembourg
Reims
R. Marne
Melun •   Montmirail •   Châlons-sur-Marne •   Verdun •   Metz
CHAMPAGNE •   St Mihiel   GERMANY
Troyes •   Nancy
Auxerre •   FRANCE
Épinal •   St Dié

0   miles   30

Belfort •   Mulhouse   VOSGES

SWITZERLAND

——— Front line 22 August 1914
– – – Limit of German advance 1914
▬ ▬ ▬ Front line at end of 1915
▪▪▪▪ Front line at end of 1917
•••••• Line at 11 November 1918

3.1   The Western Front 1914–18

Nun's Wood (1914)

Peter Banyard

It is not often in the history of warfare that elite corps clash head on. The occasions when they do such as at Waterloo when the British Guards faced Napoleon's Imperial Guard are usually well-recorded and dramatic struggles. Yet 11 November 1914, when Prussian Guards broke the line held by 1st British (Guards) Brigade, during the First Battle of Ypres, is not the date of a well-remembered contest. This may be because neither side had much to celebrate at the end of the day or because the British brigade contained so few actual guardsmen that they could plead that it was hardly a fair contest. But, although the battle lacked the drama of an equal stand-up fight between the Guards of two Royal Houses, it was nevertheless a moment in the First World War during which the Germans were within an ace of seizing a decisive advantage.

It had long been a basic tenet of German military thinking that France and her Allies in the West must be crushed swiftly in any general conflict, so that the German Army would be free to turn on Russia. When this strategy was frustrated in September 1914 by the Anglo-French victory on the Marne, General Helmuth von Moltke, the younger, was replaced as Chief of the German General Staff by General Erich von Falkenhayn. Although von Falkenhayn realized that he had little chance of driving the Western Allies from the field during 1914, he knew that the capture of the Channel ports would prevent any easy reinforcement of the French from Britain and might provide Germany with an advantage which could, eventually, be decisive.

The Allies, whose command was co-ordinated in Belgium and Northern France by the irrepressible French General Ferdinand Foch, were concerned not only to parry the threat to the ports but also to liberate and hold as much of Belgium and France as they could – however high the cost. The result of these decisions in high places was a series of bloody engagements in Flanders beginning on 19 October and collectively known as the First Battle of Ypres. Throughout the battle the Germans enjoyed a numerical and material advantage over the Allies and, despite Foch's repeated attempts to counter-attack, began to exert a near intolerable pressure on the Allied line. Through October and into early November fresh German troops pressed attack after attack on the severely strained Anglo-French forces holding the infamous Ypres Salient. By 11 November the Allies and particularly the British had no reserves left worth the name. They were logically a beaten army.

During the night of 9/10 November the Germans inserted a fresh, elite Army Corps into the line opposite Gheluvelt. The move was carried out in secret and the troops were Pomeranians and West Prussians of 4th Division and the men of Lieutenant General von Winckler's Guard Division. They were commanded by General Baron von Plettenberg of the Guard Corps and their role was to be spearhead of a great, final assault to break the Allied line. Other German units to the north launched an attack on 10 November to keep the French busy and prevent them from reinforcing the weak British formations in the path of the Prussian steamroller. Early on the morning of 11 November the long lines of guardsmen formed up well to the rear of their front line as a powerful preliminary barrage plastered the British trenches. Although German forces to the south were meant to join in the attack, they made only a half-hearted attack and the real blow was delivered by the Guard and 4th Divisions. Together they made up 25 battalions – at least 17,500 infantry – as they advanced astride the Menin road, east of Ypres.

The entire available British forces in the path of the attack (from 1st and 3rd Divisions) including reserves, cavalry and cooks totalled no more than 7,850 men and only a proportion of these were in the fire trenches. Besides this all British units were now very reduced after three weeks constant fighting. Although new armies were being formed in England there were no reinforcements left for the old

Regular Army which was withering away under continuous attrition. Most British battalions could muster only 200–300 men from their original wartime establishment of more than 900 and they had already used up all their trained reinforcements. Besides this all British units were exhausted by long exposure to battle without relief and their clothing and health had suffered in the rain and sleet. It had proved impossible to feed front-line units promptly and adequately during First Ypres and there was a very marked German superiority in the available quantity of shells and guns. All in all it was remarkable that any British troops kept on fighting.

But the professionals of the British Regular Army were very accomplished soldiers. They were not all heroes but constant indoctrination with regimental and unit loyalty made them, in general, as loyal and enduring as soldiers can be. They were also experts with their weapons as seen in the famous 'rapid fire'. In the 'mad minute' of rapid fire on the rifle range the best of them could hit a target with 30 shots; it must have been a spectacular feat, using a bolt-actioned rifle and three magazine changes. They had also been given practice with the bayonet and were prepared to use it. But fond hopes for a war of maneuver had led British military theorists to rely too heavily on shrapnel rather than high explosives (HE) – which was more effective on earthworks. In fact, the Royal Artillery was hampered by a dire shortage of shells of any sort, but the more readily available shrapnel was effective enough against massed formations, even if not much good for softening up prepared defenses.

The German Army should have been able to match the British in military virtue. The Prussians were picked troops of unusual size and courage. They were to display an enthusiasm for the bayonet at least equal to the British, and they were backed by far greater resources in artillery. But their counter-battery work was defective and the British guns were seldom shelled during the day. There was also, at least among the Prussian Guard, a certain narrowness of military outlook which is best illustrated by the fact that, in spite of new regulations, it prided itself on sticking to the methods of the 1870–1 Franco-Prussian War. It was ironic that in 1906 a German military theorist had described 'clockwork guards from Potsdam' as being soldiers of the past. Throughout 11 November the Prussian Guard, relying chiefly on courage and discipline, seems to have been confused and dismayed when called upon to show initiative and flexibility.

The British had also made primitive beginnings at defense in depth. Their front line was pitifully inadequate by later standards and consisted of a single, shallow and roughly continuous trench. This was not revetted by timber or sandbags and so was a death-trap under bombardment as near misses collapsed it, burying defenders. There were no proper communications trenches and no buried telephone cables for safe contact with supporting batteries. Then the GOC 1st Corps, Lieutenant-General Sir Douglas Haig, had one of his rare flashes of imagination. He ordered engineers to construct vestigial strongpoints in a chain immediately behind the lines. These five strongpoints were revetted and surrounded by a single fence of barbed wire; this was not much by later standards but it made them almost impervious to infantry assault in 1914, unless they had been softened up by artillery.

So there were a few shocks in store for both sides when the German bombardment began at dawn (a little after 0630) on the 11th. As the barrage built up, the British, who had been taken by surprise, soon felt the lack of buried cables as their telephone links to the rear were swiftly destroyed. Many of their infantry were forced out of the dangerous front-line trenches to shelter in nearby woods. It was the heaviest bombardment which the Germans had mounted at Ypres. Lieutenant William Congreve of the Rifle Brigade wrote: 'I never have seen the like before . . . the shrapnel played up and down our lines exactly as one waters a line of flowers, backwards and forwards. Also there were heaps and heaps of crumpets, crumps and super-crumps – all over the place they were.'

At 0900 the barrage began to lift towards the rear areas and the British infantry ran forwards from sheltered positions to firing positions in the trenches. In most places they were in time to see the Germans advancing out of the morning mist. For most of the attackers this spelled disaster. The braver and more determined they were the greater their losses would be. The magnificent 4th Division of Pomeranians and West Prussians was to suffer most. Their 12 battalions (about 8,500 men) received the staggering blow of a full minute's 'rapid fire' from eight and a half British battalions (about 4,600 men). After that, they tried to advance in 'a sort of dazed way as if they were drugged' until a last attempt at 1600, but they never came near the British trenches, although some of their companies took 75 per cent casualties.

Winckler's Guard Division had considerably better fortune; 4th

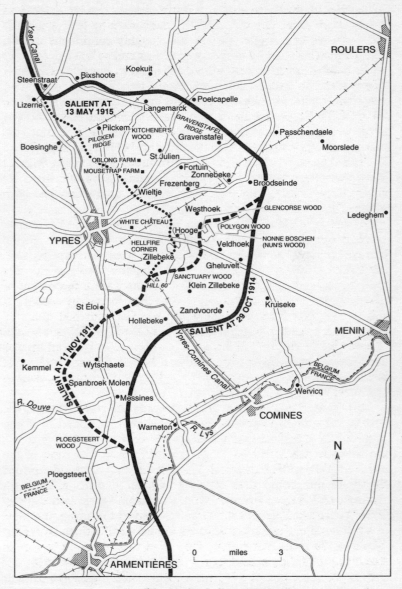

3.2 The Ypres Salient, 1914–15

Prussian Guard Grenadier Regiment was the only part of the division to attack south of the Menin road, and it soon received its first unnerving experience of rapid fire. The regiment's official account records that it 'at once suffered such heavy losses that the first two attacks made no headway.' But, the success of the rest of the Prussian Guard north of the Menin road forced the British to retire. At the end of the day, and after much bitter fighting with 4th Royal Fusiliers, 1st Royal Scots Fusiliers and 1st Northumberland Fusiliers, 4th Prussian Guard Grenadier Regiment managed to take and hold a small section of the British front line south of the Menin road.

North of the Menin road the full weight of 2nd Prussian Guard Grenadier Regiment's three battalions fell on 2nd Battalion, The Duke of Wellington's Regiment. Some 2,100 Prussians reached the British trenches before the 846 defenders could come forward from their shelter in the woods to man them. The leading (Fusilier) battalion of 2nd Guard Grenadiers pressed on over the British front line into Weldhoek Wood. As it went on into the wood this battalion became more and more heavily engaged by its British opponents and its losses became heavier by the minute amid the dense undergrowth. All might still have gone well for the Prussians if their following 1st Battalion had come up in support. Amazingly these picked troops declined to come forward because of shrapnel fire from the British 1st Division's artillery. It is hard to believe that unsighted guns suffering from shell shortage could have put up a deadly and continuous barrage, but it was evidently quite enough for 1st Battalion which did no more than occupy the already captured British front line. A few of the Fusilier battalion's survivors escaped back to join it before evening.

It was the rest of Winckler's Guard Division that was to punch a big hole in the British line. Opposed to them was the British 1st (Guards) Brigade with 1st Battalion, The King's (Liverpool) Regiment, at right angles to their northern flank. This was where the epic clash of Guard against Guard should have taken place but, in the event, it was hardly a real test. For there were only about 200 guardsmen on the British side and they were the survivors of 1st Battalion, The Scots Guards. The rest of the so-called Guards Brigade was made up of the men from two badly mauled Scots line regiments – 1st Cameron Highlanders and 1st Black Watch – the whole brigade amounted to no more than 800 men. The Prussians moved against them with two full-strength regiments, each of three battalions. Some of the Prussian force was used for an attack on the 456-strong 1/King's which quickly shot down its assailants and maintained its position throughout the day.

The mass of the Prussian 1st and 3rd Foot Guard Regiments had very little opposition to face before reaching the British lines. The three 18-pounder gun batteries of 41st Brigade, Royal Field Artillery (2nd Division) were out of touch with the infantry but, realizing that something was up, were firing shrapnel on their 'night lines' (preset traverse and elevation to be used in emergency, these 'night lines' brought down fire in likely places in No Man's Land). This did not stop the lines of Prussians, as Major H. C. Rochfort-Boyd of 41st Brigade, RFA, noticed: 'The German Infantry moved forward at a shuffling run through the mist – then, without firing but using the bayonet with a sort of grunting cheer, they closed with and passed over our front line.' Rochfort-Boyd was able to escape on this occasion and doubled back to his battery with the news that the line was broken.

The fight between Scot and Prussian for the front line was short but very bitter. *Domprediger* Baumann, chaplain of the 4th Prussian Guard Division, was impressed by it: 'Our Brothers [the British] are cold-blooded and tough and defend themselves even when their trenches are taken, quite different to the French.' Only five Scots Guardsmen came back from the fire-trench alive. The survivors of the Scottish regiments quickly fell back upon the garrisons of the newly built strongpoints and fortified battalion HQs. This new British concept of defense in depth was to save the day for them. The German breakthrough was bottlenecked between the Black Watch strongpoint held by a lieutenant and 40 men of that regiment in the north, and a combined battalion HQ at Verbeck Farm in the south which was stoutly defended by battalion COs Lieutenant-Colonels C. E. Steward and D. L. McEwan and their staffs of the Black Watch and Cameron Highlanders.

To all intents and purposes, the Prussian Guard were through the British line and it seemed that they might go on to Calais. At this point the difference in training and experience began to tell. Most British units and individuals seemed to know exactly what they should do but the Prussians, who had been effective in storming the carefully defined objective of the British line, seemed to become confused when they stumbled upon the unexpected. They had not known about the existence of the Black Watch strongpoint and they suffered heavy casualties passing it – they were unable to take it. As they pressed on they were enfiladed by the survivors of the Scottish regiments from the edges of Glencorse Wood and the majority of them stumbled thankfully into the sanctuary of the undefended Nonne Bosschen (Nuns' Wood). From the edges of the Nonne Bosschen the Prussians could actually see the last obstacle between themselves and complete breakthrough – the three 18-pounder batteries defended only by their gunners. But at this critical moment the British kept their nerve while the Germans failed to realize their opportunity.

The British gunners made no attempt to limber up and run for it. In the front line, 1/King's made no move to fall back and cover their exposed flank; indeed the battalion diary merely noted that it was 'supported on the right by the Prussian Guard.' For the gunners, Lieutenant P. H. Murray (orderly officer to the 39th Brigade, RFA) did a lightning horseback reconnaissance of the German position. Once they knew that the enemy was in the Nonne Bosschen the British batteries concentrated their fire on it and sent out dismounted parties of gunners, cooks, stragglers and veterinaries to use their rifles against any attack.

Between 0930 and 1000, between 700 and 900 Prussians of 1st Foot Guard Regiment were assembling in the Nonne Bosschen. There were other parties of Prussians both to east and west. Ahead were the British batteries protected by small groups of riflemen amounting to about 30 bayonets all told. But the Foot Guards knew nothing of this and milled about the wood in confusion lashed by shrapnel and convinced that they were faced by numerous enemies. After 1000 the British commanders calmly built up the forces around the wood until a threatening German spearhead became a beleagured and beaten mob.

The strongpoints still holding out behind the Germans made their communications difficult and added to the uncertainty of their position. On their right flank they might have gone into Polygon Wood and taken 1/King's in the rear but this option was soon closed to them by Lieutenant-Colonel C. B. Westmacott, commanding 5th Brigade (2nd Division). He immediately sent 5th Field Company, Royal Engineers, and 2nd Connaught Rangers to line Polygon Wood and protect the flank of 1/King's. Westmacott's divisional commander, Major-General Charles C. Monro, ordered three companies of Highland Light Infantry, the divisional cyclists and 1st Coldstream

Guards to be placed at his disposal for counter-attack. General Monro also moved 2nd Oxfordshire and Buckinghamshire Light Infantry right across the battlefield to the western edge of the Nonne Bosschen.

Meanwhile Brigadier-General Charles FitzClarence, commander of the ill-fated 1st (Guards) Brigade, found the Prussians almost in his HQ and appealed to his divisional commander, Major-General H. J. S. Landon (1st Division), for help. General Landon sent the 1st Northamptonshire Regiment. These units sound more impressive than they were, for all had been heavily engaged very recently (the Coldstream battalion was only about 100 strong), but the balance of strength was tilting against the Germans.

Meanwhile, casualties were mounting in the Nonne Bosschen. Small parties of Prussian infantry which tried to work their way forward out of the wood had been met by accurate shrapnel from 41st Brigade and rifle fire from its dismounted groups. This was enough to convince the Prussians that they faced serious opposition and they began, methodically, to dig fire positions on the edge of the wood to prepare for a full-dress assault. Time was running out for this as British reinforcements hurried to the spot and the Allied artillery began singling out the Nonne Bosschen for heavy bombardment. As many guns of 41st Brigade as could register sent shrapnel into the wood (one of the batteries had been given 24 rounds of 'experimental' 18-pounder HE and much of this was used in and around the Nonne Bosschen). Farther away, 35th Heavy Battery (four 60-pounders) NW of Westhoek joined in the shelling. Elsewhere, 51st Battery (39th Brigade) and 22nd Battery (34th Brigade) found time to send contributions crashing into the German positions and French 75 mm field guns added their quick-firing help. The German shelling was heavy at times but their counter-battery work and target indication left much to be desired, so that Allied casualties were light, but many German shells rained in on the luckless Prussians in the Nonne Bosschen.

While the Prussian strength was being sapped, their counter-attackers were forming up. The 2/Oxfordshire Light Infantry (Lieutenant-Colonel H. R. Davies), 306 strong, arrived behind the guns of 41st Brigade at about 1300. When Col. Davies learned of the situation he eagerly formed his men up for an assault to clear the Nonne Bosschen. By one of the strange coincidences of war, 2/Oxfordshire were the direct descendants of the 52nd Light

Infantry which had dealt the mortal blow to Napoleon's Imperial
Guard at Waterloo by leading a charge into their flank. Traditions
are long remembered in British regiments and 2/Oxfordshire were
eager to add the scalp of the Prussian Guard to that of Napoleon's
veterans. Just before 1500 the battalion moved off and charged the
western edge of the Nonne Bosschen.

The Foot Guards may have been adversely affected by the shelling
and have lost most of their officers but they put up very little
resistance to the disciplined assault. The Light Infantrymen moved
steadily through the wood, killing or capturing all who stayed to meet
them and sustaining very few casualties (they had only five killed and
22 wounded from all causes, including shellfire, on the 11th). Once
through the wood 2/Oxfordshire found 1/Northamptonshire on their
right and the doughty 5th Field Company, RE, on their left. These
troops pressed on together and cleared Prussian resistance up to the
old British support lines and relieved the Black Watch strongpoint,
which was still holding out. Just as they prepared to retake the
old front line they were caught by shrapnel from the guns of the
French 9th Corps near Frezenberg. It took time to send word to
the French guns that they were shelling their friends and the final
attack was stillborn. Early next morning Brig.-Gen. FitzClarence
was killed while trying to organize a new attack and the project
was abandoned.

So the great German attack of 11 November gained them less than
a mile of front to a depth of less than 300 yards. Their casualties had
been fairly heavy and some of them provided the British with grisly
proof of the splendid physique of the Prussians. Second Lieutenant
Titherington of 2/Oxfordshire complained that three of the Prussians
he had had to bury were over 7 ft tall while many of their wounded
proved too long for the British stretchers and ambulances.

The battle of Nonne Bosschen was one of strange and sometimes
meaningless coincidences. Its very date, 11 November, seems oddly
prophetic of Armistice Day 1918 and it resulted in a clash between
two so-called Guard formations on very unequal terms. But these
strange coincidences mean nothing when one recalls how close
11 November 1914 came to being the date when the Prussian
Guard broke the British line and won a decisive victory. It was
only because the Prussians did not realize how close they were to
success that they did not grasp it. For one of them realization was
blinding and bitter.

Feldwebel-Leutnant Schwarz was wounded and captured. As he was led past the guns of 16th Battery, 41st Brigade, he saluted and spoke to Major W. E. Clark. He asked where the British reserves were. Major Clark pointed silently to the guns. Unbelieving, Schwarz asked what troops stood behind. The curt answer was 'Divisional HQ!' Amazement and disappointment made the German exclaim, 'Heilige Gott!'

Gallipoli (1915)

Nigel Bagnall

The order to 'fall in' came ringing down to the men of the 10th Australian Battalion resting on the lower decks of HM battleship *Prince of Wales*. They were approaching the Gallipoli peninsula. There was only a dim glow from the stars as the men calmly assembled and formed into dark, shapeless groups. Between these were the smaller Naval beach parties, whose duty it was to put the men ashore. After the final breathless orders, the Australian and New Zealand Army Corps (ANZACs) clambered down the improvised ladders and ship's gangways into the waiting barges.

The expedition was made for a number of reasons. The Russians were asking Britain for aid against the invading Turks. At this time the British War Cabinet were alarmed at the seemingly endless war of bloody attrition in France. Alternative strategies were needed. And an attack on the Turks would help the Russians, make new British Allies in the Balkans and raise home morale. The War Cabinet were unsure about the attack but it was First Lord of the Admiralty Winston S. Churchill's enthusiasm that convinced them. But although the concept was bold, it was marred by indecision, delay and bad planning. Time was lost and with it the chance of surprise and success.

By March 1915 the Turks were alerted to possible British intentions after a failure by the Fleet to force past the Turkish forts and minefields defending the Dardanelles. This unmistakable warning had been realized by the Turks, who, under their energetic German commander, Marshal Liman von Sanders, began improving their defenses.

The Turkish Fifth Army were to defend the Dardanelles, a 50-mile peninsula with mountainous cliffs falling down into the sea. The ground was rugged and scrub-covered, with little cultivation. All landing sites were dominated by Turkish defenses. Three of their six divisions were on the peninsula, two on the Asiatic mainland and one astride the narrow isthmus of Bulair.

Reports of the preparations for the expedition reached the Turks from their agents. They secretly watched the gathering concentrations of shipping, troops and stores at Alexandria and the island of Lemnos. Exactly where the enemy planned to land remained a mystery. Fearing the effects of the supporting naval bombardment, von Sanders had ordered each division to remain concentrated – maintaining only the minimum forces necessary near the coastline. His defences were to be mobile. With this in mind, he exercised his 60,000 troops with forced marches, developed the paths and bridle tracks on the peninsula into roads, and assembled barges at specially chosen harbors. At the same time, the field fortifications were strengthened by all means possible – mainly by night. Stores were not plentiful, so considerable improvisation was necessary. Torpedo heads were used as mines. Wire and posts were taken from fences enclosing the cultivated areas, and pressed into service as assorted obstacles – both above and below the water line.

General Sir Ian Hamilton, Commander of the 78,000-strong BEF, planned to make two converging attacks at the southern end of the peninsula. The first would be by the British 29th Division. They were to make five separate but simultaneous landings on small beaches near Cape Helles. The ANZACs were to mount the second attack near Gaba Tebe. It was hoped that these separate actions would link up to roll the Turks back along the whole length of the peninsula. Two diversionary operations were also planned. The French contingent would land near the ruins of Troy on the Asiatic mainland, while the Royal Naval Division in transports accompanied by warships, feinted at Bulair.

Late on the afternoon of 24 April the armada, assembled in Mudros Bay, set sail. At 1000 on the 25th the three battleships and seven destroyers carrying the 3rd Australian Brigade, which formed the assault wave, stopped short of the peninsula. The final preparations

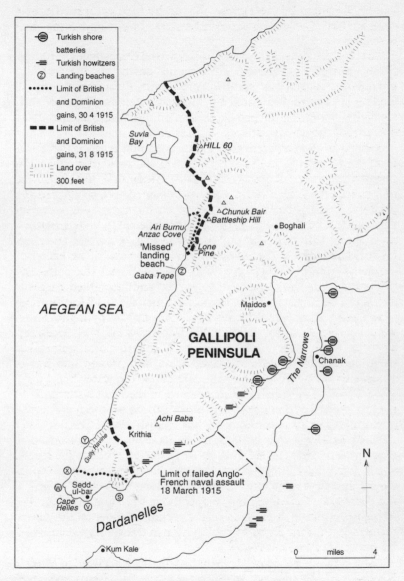

Key:

- ⊖ Turkish shore batteries
- ≡ Turkish howitzers
- ⓩ Landing beaches
- •••••• Limit of British and Dominion gains, 30 4 1915
- ▬ ▬ Limit of British and Dominion gains, 31 8 1915
- ⌇⌇⌇ Land over 300 feet

Suvla Bay

△ *HILL 60*

△ *Chunuk Bair*
△ *Battleship Hill*

● *Boghali*

Ari Burnu
Anzac Cove

'Missed' landing beach

Lone Pine

Gaba Tepe ⓩ

AEGEAN SEA

Maidos ●

GALLIPOLI PENINSULA

The Narrows

● *Chanak*

△ *Achi Baba*

Krithia ●

Gully Ravine

Ⓨ
Ⓧ
Ⓦ *Sedd-ul-bar*
Cape Helles Ⓥ
Ⓢ

Limit of failed Anglo-French naval assault 18 March 1915

Dardanelles

● *Kum Kale*

N

0   miles   4

3.3   *Gallipoli*

for disembarkation were completed. Each of the battleships had towed astern three steam pinnaces – in addition to her own. These now took in tow the ships' boats which had already been lowered. Once alongside, they waited to receive the assembled troops.

Thanks to the rigorous rehearsals there was no confusion. As the midshipman in the stern reported each boat full, the officer in charge ordered 'Cast off and drift astern.' The boats fell behind until arrested by the hawsers connecting them. Once in position the battleships moved slowly towards the shore, each ship trailing four tows. At about 0430, the ships came into line. They were about 3,000 yards from the coast. The signal was given for the tows to cast off and make for the beach. Like so many snakes, they slowly forged their way ahead packed with men – gunwales almost flush with the water. Behind them, until the water became too shallow, the warships followed to cover the final approach. Thirty minutes after the tows had left the battleships, the seven destroyers moved forward right behind them ready to disembark their troops 20 minutes later in a second wave.

General Sir William Birdwood, commander of the ANZACs, planned to land 4,000 men of the 1st Australian Division in three successive waves, on a front of about 2,000 yards. The essence of his plan was speed and surprise. There would be no preliminary naval bombardment. Once ashore, the troops were to strike rapidly inland for some 2,000 yards and secure three prominent hill features. Having captured these, the main body would be passed through and the advance extended over comparatively easy ground for a further 3,000 to 4,000 yards. This was to be the limit of the first day's objectives.

Exactly what happened next remains in dispute. Some blame a northerly current, others a last-minute and largely unknown change of plan, while a Turkish source attributes it to deception on their part. They claim that they found and moved a previously positioned British marker buoy – causing the battleships to anchor too far north. Whatever the cause, instead of approaching the shore over a 2,000-yard front just south of the Ari Burnu promontory, the boats crowded together in the direction of the promontory itself.

This error became apparent to some of the troops and naval officers in the landing boats. But it was too late for the majority to do more than hope to reach the beach before the Turks saw them. Fifty yards from the water line the pinnaces cast off and the boats were rowed in by the sailors until grounding on the shelving beach. During this final approach they were seen. The Turks opened fire from the high ground. Scrambling out of the boats – often into several feet of water – the Australians struggled to the shore and rushed across the beach to take cover where they could. After quickly reorganizing and discarding their heavy packs, they charged the Turkish trenches on the foreshore and bayoneted the enemy. Then, heaving themselves up the steep, broken slope by the roots and branches of trees or shrubs, they doggedly pressed inland as ordered.

Not all the men were so lucky. Some of the packed boats were hit by Turkish machine-gun fire and their occupants suffered severely. Other boats ran aground at the foot of sheer cliffs. The troops were forced to move along the beach until they could find an exit. One effect of this was that the sheer cliffs protected them from Turkish guns. It caused confusion and delay, however, sub-units became hopelessly mixed, and objectives impossible to identify.

But by 0600 the Australians had secured the first ridge and began to infiltrate the second. On the left flank the greatly outnumbered Turkish survivors were falling back in disorder. Waves of Australians were landing unhindered. Some 4,000 men were already ashore and the advance inland gathered strength. By 0700 small groups of Australians had reached the third ridge. Looking down, they could see the Dardanelles only three miles away. Success appeared within reach. But the situation was to change.

The Australians' progress was delayed and then halted by the growing confusion on the beach. As a result of landing on a beach only a few hundred yards long instead of one of 2,000, the confusion and delay in bringing ashore the two follow-up brigades was immense. The control organization ashore had all but collapsed. Wounded were beginning to flow back in an ever-increasing stream and choked the beach from where many of them could not be moved. Others were loaded into boats which were meant to land further reinforcements. The one hospital ship was soon full. Successive waves of troops were landing in an increasingly chaotic manner and – on coming ashore – could be given no precise orders in the absence of any clear knowledge as to what the situation was inland.

The beach itself soon became a scene of confusion. Heaps of hastily dumped ammunition and stores lay around. Among these lay the dead. Overhead the sky was rent with the flash of shrapnel, and the air hummed with bullets. Fortunately, most of the Turkish fire was wild and casualties were not heavy. The same sanctuary was not available farther out to sea where fountains of water were thrown up around the tows operating to and from the ships.

. The New Zealand Brigade was part of the reinforcements. They were given the job of lengthening the line to the left of the Australian 1st Division. The transports with their field guns on board were delayed in the face of the Turkish guns, and the New Zealanders were to feel the full bitterness of being subjected to enemy shellfire with no means of retaliation. Eventually some support was given by an Indian Mountain Battery which skilfully maneuvered themselves into seemingly inaccessible vantage points. Unloading, they would fire a dozen or so shots and be down the gully and up to a new position before the Turks could find them.

Of greater impact than even the chaos on the beach was perhaps the arrival of 34-year-old Mustafa Kemal Pasha, Commander of the Turkish 19th Division. Like all able commanders, he contrived to arrive at the critical part of the front when most needed. Alerted by the sound of gunfire from Gaba Tepe where the Australians had first landed, he at once alerted the 19th Division and at 0630 received orders to send one battalion to the heights of Ari Burnu, where the leading Australians were reported to have arrived. Kemal instinctively sensed that a major threat had developed. Far more than one battalion would be needed.

Disregarding orders, he gave instructions for the whole division to move to the coast and he himself led the first regiment which was ready towards the threatened key ridge. On arrival, he ordered the men to rest after their forced march over broken ground while he continued on his way, accompanied only by his ADC, a second officer and an orderly. Then he saw some Turkish troops fleeing towards him. Confronting them he demanded to know why they were running away. The reason was clear enough. Their ammunition was exhausted and the Australians were close behind. This explanation did not satisfy Kemal. He ordered them to fix bayonets and lie down and take up firing positions as the leading Australians came into view. The Australians did the same and unwittingly lost the initiative to the Turks.

Then Kemal ordered an officer to bring up his resting regiment at the double. They soon arrived at the position. The small band of Australians – isolated and unable to resist the ever-increasing weight of Turkish fire – withdrew to the next ridge. It was held by their countrymen. But they were widely dispersed and largely uncoordinated.

From about 1000 the Turks started to push against the Australians' left flank and filter round the seaward slopes of Baby 700 – the main hill feature held by their leading troops. A little later the second Turkish regiment started to arrive. The Turks mounted a series of savage counter-attacks. Baby 700 was lost but retaken again by two companies newly arrived from the beaches.

By now the Turks were arriving in increasing numbers and Baby 700 changed hands no fewer than five times before the Australians were finally driven off. The Australians and the New Zealanders, who had joined them during the afternoon, were suffering heavy casualties. No more than scattered and mixed up elements of seven battalions were trying to stem the advance of most of the Turkish 19th Division which were attacking in massed waves. Silhouetted against the sinking sun, they screamed 'Allah' as they advanced. They were cut down *en masse* but successive waves continued the frenzied attacks over the corpses of their fellows.

Neither side were taking prisoners. Groups of ANZACs were cut off and could not repel the Turkish charges any longer. They died where they fought. The firing line was indeterminable. Isolated groups of Australians and New Zealanders clung grimly to a number of key features as night fell and a steady drizzle set in. In the tangled gullies, when not actually fighting, men dug for their lives until, trumpets blowing and still calling on 'Allah!' the Turks again surged forward. One New Zealander remembers how they would counter these attacks by running forward themselves 'cursing in loud round English and very bad Arabic.' Many strange duels were fought that night. One Turkish rush was stemmed by a small band commanded by a corporal armed with nothing more effective than a pick-handle.

Not only the fighting men showed such tenaciousness. From the firing line it took two and a half hours to get a wounded man back onto the beach. Ignoring both bullets and shells, carefully threading their way down the twisting tracks made ever more treacherous by the endless rain, the stretcher bearers and doctors worked unstintingly. Only the most severe cases could be dealt with on the crowded beaches. Many a man, when asked whether he was badly hurt, replied quietly that 'he was all right,' then died uncomplaining.

Shortly after 2200 General Birdwood came ashore at the request of his two Australian and New Zealand divisional commanders. He found a demoralized force, tired and shaken by the day's events and disorganized by the confusion on the beach. But he was taken aback when it was proposed that there should be an immediate evacuation. Tired themselves, neither the divisional commanders nor their brigadiers believed their men could resist the renewed Turkish counter-attack. They all believed this would be mounted in overwhelming strength by fresh troops at daybreak. With no reinforcements to replace their own exhausted and fragmented units, there seemed no alternative but to evacuate and save what they could. Reluctantly Birdwood agreed. He dictated a message to Hamilton recommending that re-embarkation should start immediately.

In response to this totally unexpected proposal, Hamilton held a conference with his principal advisors. Among them was Rear-Admiral C. F. Thursby, his naval commander. The Admiral was emphatically opposed to evacuation. He did not regard it as being administratively feasible. The men were tired and disorganized and it was a dark and stormy night. Control on the crowded beaches would be virtually impossible. Under such conditions the losses could be dreadful. Hamilton needed no further persuasion. His instructions were explicit and ended with the exhortation: 'You have got through the difficult business, now you have only to dig, dig, dig, until you are safe.'

Admiral Thursby was given the job of delivering the message. He landed on the right of the ANZAC position. Here he saw for himself the chaos and suffering which had provoked such despair among the commanders. They felt too much was being demanded of their men. However, he found Birdwood cheerful, though not exactly hopeful, and the two divisional commanders more inclined to stay and fight it out.

What had not been allowed for was the courage and resolution of the troops. Had the order to evacuate been given it is probable that it would have been received with incredulity – possibly even contempt. In the succeeding days' fighting the few orders to withdraw which were given were usually queried and as frequently countermanded.

Although it was known that their own landing and that of the British at Helles should converge, it was as well that neither Birdwood nor his men counted on getting any early help as a result of this plan. The initial British landing had resulted in appalling casualties. The survivors were fighting as grimly as the ANZACs themselves to maintain their positions ashore.

Preceded by a naval bombardment, the British 29th Division had begun to land at five beaches in the vicinity of Cape Helles shortly after the Australians had got ashore at Ari Burnu. The landings at 'V' beach by the 88th Brigade were intended to be the most important. An old ruined fort dominated the beach but it was hoped that the Turkish defenders – dug in along the cliff edges as well as concealed in the fort itself – would be largely accounted for by the Navy's guns. The plan was to run the *River Clyde* – an old collier turned 'Trojan Horse' specially adapted for landing troops – as close to the beach as possible and bridge the intervening water gap with two lighters. At the same time, other troops would be landed by boat.

Because of a strong current which had delayed their arrival, there was a long interval between the lifting of the naval bombardment and the landings. This allowed the Turkish defenders to recover and take up their positions. When the *River Clyde* gently grounded, the 2,000 men of the Dublin and Munster Fusiliers and the Hampshire Regiment began to cross the improvised causeway. But as they did so, whole platoons were shot down as they raced into the withering Turkish fire. Those in the boats fared no better. The Turks had laid wire below the water and along the beach. Holding their fire until the packed boats became entangled and crowded together on the obstacles, they devastated the leading wave. There were few survivors. A handful of men managed to cross the beach and shelter under the cliffs. Others, who had been ordered to stay below and cease the senseless slaughter, remained aboard the *River Clyde*. With the brigade commander dead, any further attempt to land at 'V' beach was suspended until nightfall.

Farther north on 'W' beach the Lancashire Fusiliers suffered similar carnage. The naval bombardment had little impact on either the defenders or their defenses. Holding their fire until the last possible moment the Turks reduced the Fusiliers to a handful as they struggled through the water and wire entanglements and tried to cross the open beaches. One officer, who died later, described the scene he saw as he looked behind.

There was one soldier between me and the wire, and a whole line in a row on the edge of the sands. The sea behind was absolutely crimson, and you could hear the groans through the rattle of musketry. A few were firing. I signalled to them to advance. I shouted to the soldier behind me to signal, but he shouted back that he was shot through the chest. I then perceived they were all hit.

In spite of their appalling losses and suffering, the Fusiliers re-formed into a thin line and began to assault the cliffs. Six VCs were won on that desperate morning, but it is unlikely that the survivors would have had the strength to dislodge the Turks had not one of the companies been landed unopposed under a promontory slightly farther to the north. From here the Fusiliers scrambled up onto the high ground and, after being reinforced, extended this foothold to relieve the survivors on the beach. On the other three subsidiary beaches – 'X', 'Y' and 'S' – only light opposition had been encountered and the few troops assigned established themselves ashore without great difficulty.

The Turks had fought resolutely. Of the 9,000 men who had been disembarked onto the five beaches, 3,000 had been killed or wounded and the survivors had secured little more than precarious toeholds. Only 'W' and 'V' beaches were linked together after dark. The troops who had been kept on board the *River Clyde* were landed and helped extend the bridgehead to make contact with those advancing south from 'W' beach.

The landing of the French regiment on the Asiatic mainland near the site of Troy occurred after a preliminary bombardment from French warships at about 1000. There appears to have been some delay and confusion. But by the afternoon the whole force was ashore after encountering only light opposition. The Turkish units in this area initially showed little of the tenacious determination which had been displayed on the peninsula. Progress was easier for the French. Later, however, they were unable to advance farther. After withstanding a series of Turkish counter-attacks during the night, they were withdrawn the following day to reinforce the right flank of the British line on the European side of the straits. 'V' beach was handed over to them as their base.

None of these details was known to the ANZACs. Most of them only had time to concern themselves with their own immediate difficulties. After the close-quarters fighting during the earlier part of the night, exhaustion and confusion forced a lull. There was still continuous firing. Here and there the front would flare into angry violence. Generally, however, both sides had reached the limit of exertion. They concentrated on holding on to what they had. Some reinforcements came ashore during the night. The Wellington Regiment were disembarked and sent straight up Plugge's Plateau – a prominent feature behind the firing line. Here the sappers were already hard at work preparing a second and last line of defense. Behind this position no organized resistance would be possible.

Most of the 4th Australian Brigade was also landed but arrived in a very irregular order. Some elements came from one ship and some from another. As each platoon or company came ashore it was immediately sent under the senior officer present to the right flank where the 1st Australian Division was particularly hard pressed. In this manner units became further mixed up.

Elsewhere, the gunners labored through the night to prepare positions and improve access routes for the guns which it was hoped would be disembarked urgently. Stores and supplies poured ashore onto the congested beach. Movement was further hampered by the darkness and the running sea. It was therefore not until daylight on the 26th that the first howitzer was landed. It went into action shortly afterwards. The gun's arrival did not significantly affect the situation, but its steady, reverberating fire acted as a tonic to the hard-pressed infantrymen.

After a night of feverish activity, bitter fighting and at one time near despair, the expected Turkish dawn attack never materialized. Instead, a series of piecemeal assaults took place. These were fiercely mounted but containable because they were neither overwhelming nor sustained. The Turks had themselves suffered heavily. Further reinforcements were slow in arriving, co-ordination was difficult and the situation no clearer to them than to their enemy. The front started to stabilize. Shell scrapes became trenches, outposts became firm strongpoints, the firing was incessant. But it became possible for the troops to snatch a few moments of sleep, eat and adjust to their condition.

However immediately welcome this stabilization of the front may have been to Birdwood and his senior commanders after their earlier anxieties, it represented the first small step towards reproducing the stalemate of Western Front trench warfare which the Dardanelles expedition had been intended to break. As the days turned into weeks and then months, the deadlock became firm. The ANZACs could not materially extend their positions beyond where they had been established during the first night's fighting. The Turks had suffered the most dreadful losses as a result of repeatedly attempting to dislodge them.

In the five weeks since the expedition had begun the British and Dominion troops had suffered almost 40,000 casualties, and the French a further 20,000. Hospitals throughout the Middle East were crammed with the wounded and sick. Large numbers had been shipped back to England. The toll of sickness had arisen alarmingly. All that had been gained was a 6,000-yard-deep front across the peninsula. In the wearing heat of a Mediterranean summer swarms of flies and vultures feasted on the unburied dead that littered the battlefield and invaded every sanctuary of the living. Disease became rife, especially in the crowded conditions at ANZAC, from where an ever-increasing number of sick were having to be evacuated daily. Many of those who remained were gaunt and weak – they were barely recognizable as the same robust, exhuberant men who had so recently terrorized Cairo.

After heavy deliberations, it was decided by the War Cabinet that a great endeavor would be made to break the deadlock with large reinforcements. Three separate attacks would be mounted at the same time. First, a new landing would be made due north of the ANZAC position by two British divisions at Suvla Bay. Secondly, the ANZACs would break out and link up with the Sulva Bay landings. Finally, at Helles a holding attack would be mounted to stop the Turks switching reinforcements to the north. Including reserves available either at sea or on the adjacent Aegean islands, the Allies had some 120,000 men. Against this the Turks had an approximately equal number. About 100,000 of these were on the peninsula.

Despite great courage and impressive fighting skill by British, Dominion and Indian troops, by the end of August it was clear that the operation had failed. With certain notable exceptions the inertia of the senior commanders and the rawness of many of the troops at Suvla resulted in an over-cautious advance inland. This allowed the Turks to move their reserves to the threatened area and stem all further progress. About 1,000 men had been lost on the day of the landings. Nearly 8,000 were killed or wounded during the two days following. Another bridgehead had been established but it only served to strain the expedition's administrative resources even more and increase the need for reinforcements to maintain units at fighting strength. A break-out seemed as unrealizable at Suvla as it had proved to be at ANZAC and Helles. The weeks and months dragged on. With the approach of winter, storms added to the supply difficulties. Piers and barges were pounded and smashed on the beaches. Inland, the trenches were flooded and tracks washed away or blocked – preventing ration parties from getting forward. No sooner had the storms abated than a November blizzard swept the peninsula. The battlefields were blanketed in snow and ice. Blankets were frozen solid, weapons jammed and a lull in the fighting was enforced while men struggled to survive in the savage cold. Frostbite increased the sick-rate and deaths occurred amongst the already physically exhausted troops on both sides. One morning at stand-to, 30 men of a British battalion were found frozen to death on the fire-steps of their trenches.

Inevitably – but after much conflicting advice and painful debate – the decision to evacuate the entire peninsula was taken. Planning for such a possibility had already been put in hand. Clear, carefully considered instuctions were issued to selected officers. Unless anything unforeseen happened, the evacuation would be conducted in three stages. All surplus men, equipment and animals would begin to be withdrawn immediately. Then the force would be progressively reduced by formed units between 13 and 18 December. Finally, on the nights of 19 and 20 December the last rearguard would be withdrawn.

If the evacuation was to be undertaken successfully the highest degree of security and deception was essential. Losses of up to 40 per cent were already being expected in some quarters. Every night the outgoing barges were jammed full. But as it grew light a show of landing troops would be made. By day stores and ammunition which could not be evacuated were prepared for destruction, barricades were erected in all the principal communication trenches and a final covering position to be manned by machine-gunners was prepared.

Smoothly and methodically the evacuation continued. Only 3,000 volunteer 'Diehards' were left in each of the three divisions to hold the bridgeheads for the last 24 hours on 19 December. About 1,500 of them manned the forward trenches moving from position to position to keep up the usual pattern of fire. Others marched uphill where they could be heard and even seen to impersonate reinforcements, kept the cooking fires burning and maintained the atmosphere of general activity. To accustom the Turks to complete inactivity, periods of total silence had been imposed at irregular intervals during the preceding weeks.

Soon after dusk on the last night the rearguard started to thin out. The guns opened fire for the last time before they too were withdrawn or destroyed when this was not possible. Midnight came and the firing died down on both sides – as was usual. At 0145 the silence was broken on the New Zealand sector when the duty machine-gunner fired three rapid bursts. This was the signal for the brigade's machine-guns to withdraw. At 0200 the already sparsely populated trenches were further depleted as the infantry started to thin out. Individuals slipped away from their positions to form a shadowy stream as they flowed into the main communication trenches from the web of forward posts and trenches.

Those left behind stared into the darkness. They watched fearfully for any signs of Turkish suspicions being aroused, before it was time for they themselves to withdraw. Not all the positions could be abandoned at the same time. Those farthest from the beaches were vacated at 0130. Others, covering the more direct and short approaches, were held until 0315.

As the last of the men were being checked through the control posts manned by staff officers, a huge mine which had been tunnelled under the forward Turkish trenches was detonated. Its deafening roar abruptly shattered the silence and tension of the last few hours. The Turks took this as a signal for an all-out attack and opened fire along the entire front. They kept this up with unrelenting vigor until long after the last of 83,000 soldiers had been safely embarked from both Suvla and ANZAC. As dawn broke the Turks realized at last that their enemy had vanished. With a mixture of disbelief and awesome relief, they left their trenches to work their way down to the abandoned piles of stores and equipment lying burning and broken along the beaches.

Against all expectation of being able to surprise the Turks again, the evacuation of 35,000 men from Helles was equally successfully carried out on the night of 8 January. This was in spite of a Turkish attack taking place when the front line had already been withdrawn.

Few military expeditions create such controversy – even today – as does Gallipoli. But whether or not it was ill-conceived, hesitant in its implementation, a sad saga of 'might-have-beens', it remains an epic of heroism. Its tragedy was that it was all for nothing, but, as one New Zealander wrote, 'It was not our wasted energy and sweat that really grieved us. In our hearts it was to know that we were leaving our dead comrades behind. That is what every man had in his mind.'

Suez (1915)

Anthony Burton

In the 1973 Yom Kippur War both the Egyptians and the Israelis crossed the Suez Canal. They were not the first to do so – some 50 years before them a Turkish army had marched across the forbidding wastes of Sinai and put men on the western bank of the Canal.

In the middle of January 1915 a Turkish Expeditionary Force of 25,000 men left its base at Beersheba and prepared to cross the Sinai peninsula. Its goal was the Suez Canal – a vital link in Britain's Imperial chain. Djemal Pasha, Commander-in-Chief of the Turkish force, despite his arrogant proclamation as he left Constantinople for the front – 'I shall not return until I have conquered Egypt' – should have been under no illusions as to the magnitude of his task.

On the far bank of the Canal there was a British force much stronger than the Turks. Its base was only a few miles to the rear. The Turkish troops would find it difficult to carry sufficient stores across Sinai to maintain an offensive for more than a few days. Yet Djemal considered that the political situation was promising. Agents of the German Baron Oppenheim were busy stirring up a rebellion in Cairo which was timed to break out at the approach of the army of another Islamic Power. In the west of Egypt the Senussi tribes were revolting against the British. Djemal Pasha hoped that the infidels would soon find themselves faced with a holy war, a *jihad*, in their very midst. He had, he believed, already scored a propaganda triumph by the insulting messages he had sent to the British generals, inviting them to come out and fight in the open. Understandably, the British had ignored these suggestions and remained behind their Canal defenses.

They did not commit the error of underestimating their enemy. The contemporary issue of *War Illustrated* (13 March 1915) said: 'Whatever may be thought of his intelligence and skill, the ordinary Turkish soldier is at least no coward. He can usually die as bravely and stubbornly as men of any race.'

If German agents and the promise of a Turkish invasion could succeed in inciting rebellion in Cairo then Djemal could hope to repeat the exploits of Sultan Selim, the first Turkish conqueror of Egypt in 1517. Even if the hoped-for risings did not materialize, the Turks still reckoned on being able to seize a portion of the Canal and hold it long enough to destroy or block it. At the very least they would be able to sink some of the ships which would be trapped *en route* by the advance. Their hulks would take weeks, perhaps months, to shift. So Djemal took with him nine batteries of field artillery and one 150 mm (5.9 in) howitzer battery – supplemented by a quantity of mines – to attack the British shipping.

The Turks possessed one other advantage. They had with them as adviser the true architect of the advance to the Canal, the Bavarian Colonel Kress von Kressenstein – 'a most excellent and efficient Officer', wrote the German General Liman von Sanders. Von Kressenstein's forte was desert warfare.

The German Major Fischer saw to it that the problem of watering man and beast on the trek were overcome. Nature also helped the passage. The winter of 1914 had been exceptionally wet and the force was to find a number of springs and pools of water as it marched towards the Canal and the waiting British. Fischer had charge of 5,000 water-carrying camels. A similar number were loaded with stores and ammunition.

British Intelligence knew of the impending assault but the short range of their available aircraft made early discovery of the direction of the attack difficult. The defenders only had three Maurice Farmans, two Henri Farmans, one BE2a and seven French seaplanes at their disposal. Therefore, Djemal and Kress believed that an element of surprise might be achieved by avoiding the traditional coastal route, which would be under the guns of the British and French navies. Instead they decided to strike across the center of Sinai at the section of the Canal between Lake Timsah and the Great

Bitter Lake. This approach would provide the possibility of access to Ismailia. He who controlled that town controlled the Canal. Here were the sluices which would enable the water supply to be cut off from its whole length.

Of the three possible routes – the central, the coastal strip and the Akaba–Nekhl–Suez line – that chosen was the worst watered. Also, none of the routes was at that time more than a camel track. However, the central approach via Jifjaffa had the advantages of reasonably firm going and immunity from British naval attack.

To confuse his enemy, Djemal sent out two diversionary columns, one in the north against Kantara, the other to his south towards Kubri. Guided by local Bedouin tribesmen, the main Turkish force crossed central Sinai in two contingents, patiently laying brushwood tracks when the surface deteriorated into areas of sand dunes – sometimes several square miles in extent. It is a tribute to German organization and Turkish doggedness that the force crossed Sinai in ten days without losing a single man or animal. By the end of January the Turks were poised before their objective. Djemal then issued a flowery exhortation:

'Warriors! Behind you lie the vast deserts; before you is the craven enemy; behind him the rich land of Egypt, which is waiting impatiently for you. If you falter, death will overtake. Before you Paradise lies.'

After this rhetorical flourish Djemal gave his orders and the Turks moved forward.

On the right flank, in the north, a weak force of irregulars and Bedouin was sent with some Turkish infantry detachments to mount a feint attack on Kantara. In the south, a pack battery accompanied the 69th Regiment, 23rd Division, as it moved towards Kubri while in the center 20,000 of the best Turkish troops prepared for the attack. Kress von Kressenstein was with the first group of the central force while his fellow German, Colonel von Frankenberg und Proschlitz, accompanied Djemal Pasha and the crack 10th Division in the second contingent.

By now the British were ready for them. Small raids against Kubri (27 January) and Kantara (29th) did not disguise the Turkish intention to thrust at the center. Spies as well as aerial reconnaissance confirmed that the attack would concentrate on that sector. Accordingly, Major General A. Wilson, GOC Canal Defenses, reinforced Serapeum with the 2nd Rajputs.

Thirty thousand troops, mainly Indian, now awaited the attack along the line of the Canal. The 10th and 11th Indian Divisions were supported by the Imperial Service Cavalry Brigade and the Bikanir Camel Corps. Behind them the 42nd (East Lancashire) Division, Australian and New Zealand contingents and some Yeomanry units lay in reserve. The total overall strength was 70,000 men, but not all were fully trained. The defenders were short of artillery. There were only three batteries of Indian mountain artillery and a battery of Egyptian artillery available in the threatened sector. This deficiency was made up for by stationing British and French warships in the Canal. Eight were eventually used in this role. The most powerful of these were HMS *Ocean*, a *Canopus*-class pre-Dreadnought battleship of 12,950 tons (four 12-in, 12 6-in and 12 12-pounder guns) and HMS *Swiftsure* (formerly the Chilean Navy battleship *Constitution*, bought by the Royal Navy in 1909), 11,800 tons, armed with four 10-in, 14 7.5-in and 14 14-pounders. Other vessels involved included the *Eclipse*-class second-class cruiser HMS *Minerva* (5,600 tons), the sloop HMS *Clio*, the armed merchantman *Himalaya* and the Royal Indian Marine armed troopship *Hardinge*. *D'Entrecasteaux*, the French cruiser, and the coastguard ship *Requin* were also to be involved. The latter, together with the *Hardinge*, was destined to play an important part in the action on the central sector.

The attack began on the night of 3 February. It was cloudy and the waiting British strained their eyes into a darkness made more impenetrable by the blown sand which stung their faces and against which they had to wrap their rifles for protection. Three posts on the east bank, Tussum, Serapeum and Deversoir – two companies in each – watched for a sign of the Turkish advance. Behind them on the west bank 11 smaller posts, each manned by two platoons, covered the opposite shore – and waited. Among the 62nd Punjabis was a 30-year-old subaltern who was to achieve fame in the Second World War. The defense of the Canal was his first experience of action ('I remember the first bullet that went over my head, which made me duck damn quickly'). His name was Claude John Eyre Auchinleck.

At 0325 Arab irregulars – calling themselves the 'Champions of Islam' – disobeyed orders and gave away their positions south of Tussum by calling loudly upon Allah and cursing the infidel. After sporadic firing on both sides there was once again silence. A little after 0400, the clouds cleared and the moonlight illuminated hundreds of the attackers struggling down to the water's edge, carrying rafts and pontoons. At 0420 this party was engaged by an Egyptian artillery battery and by rifle fire and driven back. Immediately after this, larger groups appeared to the north, near Tussum. These troops tried manfully to launch their cumbersome craft – galvanized iron pontoons and rafts of kerosene tins in a simple wooden frame. Over their heads fierce fire raged between defenders and their own supporting infantry. Three boatloads succeeded in crossing the Canal but were attacked by a bayonet charge from the 62nd Punjabis and the 128th Pioneers. As Auchinleck laconically remarked, 'We were on the west bank and they came over and our men charged down the bank and put a bayonet into them – that was all.' In these engagements every Turkish soldier on the west bank was either killed or captured. At the same time as the Tussum incident the Turks launched a half-hearted attack on the Ismailia ferry post.

In the weary dawn the cost of the attack became clear. Turkish dead lay among their abandoned rafts and pontoons on the east bank. The defenders of the east bank outposts sallied forth from their perimeters. More troops crossed the Canal to support them and put paid to any surviving Turk from the eastern margins of the waterway. A torpedo boat was sent north from Deversoir to destroy any pontoons still intact.

But these British counter-attacks were halted by the appearance of a superior Turkish force. Artillery duels between the ships anchored in the Canal and the Turkish batteries continued throughout the rest of the day.

Here the Turkish artillery was efficient. Two batteries of field artillery and the 150 mm howitzer battery succeeded in hitting the outgunned 6,520-ton *Hardinge*, armed only with six 4.7-in guns. She was forced to break off action at 0845. A duel now began between the *Requin* and the Turkish battery. At first the Turks had the better of it, but at 0900 their position was betrayed by a puff of smoke. Their range was estimated and their howitzers silenced. *Requin* and the cruiser *D'Entrecasteaux* – ordered up to replace the *Hardinge* – now concentrated their fire on the assumed position of the main Turkish force. Artillery engagements were fought elsewhere on the front, particularly between HMS *Clio*'s six 4-in and two Turkish field guns which had scored some direct hits on El Ferdan railway station. At 1030 these too were silenced.

Next day, to the surprise of the watching British and Indian troops, the Turks began to retreat. Djemal had in fact ordered it on the evening of the 3rd. The speed of the withdrawal, which both Kress and Djemal believed to be necessary, left some of the Turkish troops behind. These were duly attacked and captured before they could escape from their trenches facing the Canal. The remainder of the Turkish army escaped without incident since the British were neither physically nor psychologically prepared for pursuit. Djemal fell back to Beersheba, leaving Kress in the desert with three infantry battalions and a squadron of cavalry with two mountain batteries to support. Kress's orders were to exploit his mobility to keep the enemy occupied, to hamper shipping movements and slow down preparations for any British advance across Sinai.

British casualties numbered only 32 killed and 130 wounded. Enemy losses were heavier. Kress gives figures of 192 killed, 371 wounded and 727 missing, a total of 1,290 – but the true numbers were higher, since the Turks did not record the casualties of their irregulars. British archives show that they buried 238 of the enemy dead and captured 716 prisoners. One of the dead was the German Staff Officer who had been in charge of the crossing, Captain von dem Hagen.

While Turkish expectations of a rising in their favor were certainly over-optimistic, their less ambitious plan of seizing a section of the Canal for a few days was more realizable. Therefore, their failure to come anywhere near to achieving this objective is puzzling.

Kress claimed that the sandstorm delayed his preparations, that the force lacked the training necessary for a night crossing of the Canal under enemy guns and, finally, that the use of an Arab, rather than a Turkish division was an error – the former's loyalty being suspect. While the first two of these reasons may have some plausibility the third does not bear examination. It would indeed have been more sensible to have used the 10th Division in the first place, instead of holding it in reserve to pass through the Arab 23rd (Homs) and the 25th (Damascus) Divisions after they had made an initial breach in the British defenses. The assertion, made by General Liman von Sanders among others, that Arab units went over to the British is certainly untrue. On the contrary, the crossing was bravely attempted against an entrenched enemy who had prepared the ground – even to the extent of putting range markers out in the desert – and had excellent fields of fire.

The warships were the eventual victors of their clash with the Turkish artillery. The reluctance of the Turkish troops to press their attacks later on the morning of the 3rd must be attributed to the warships' shelling accuracy, not least with their 12-pounders and smaller quick-firing guns.

Djemal Pasha and Kress von Kressenstein argued later that the raid had in any case been worth the effort. It had demonstrated the vulnerability of the Canal and had floored British assumptions as to the numbers of men who could cross the Sinai peninsula. In 1906 the British War Office had estimated that, in view of the water situation, the largest force that could cross would be 5,000 men and 2,000 camels. Technically, the expedition had been impressive and this demonstration of German/Turkish expertise made necessary the continuation of a huge British presence – first to defend and then to move out from the area of the Canal. One British commentator, Major-General Sir M. G. E. Bowman-Manifold, is generous in his praise for the Turkish achievement.

> The Turkish effort deserves admiration. To bring thousands
> of men, artillery and pontoon train across 140 miles of desert
> was creditable; to assault a front defended potentially by 70,000
> men and the heavy metal of ships' armament, was audacious:
> to depart again with artillery and baggage intact, and a loss of
> not 10 per cent of infantry was clear gain and left the defenders
> with little to boast of.

Troops occupied in Egypt – and the next time the Canal was threatened, early in 1916, 400,000 troops were massed to oppose any expedition – were at least kept out of the European theater. This, to von Kressenstein, was reason enough for the original attack. Djemal had escaped without serious loss, while the British were to pay dearly for letting Kress von Kressenstein escape them. It is difficult to avoid the impression that the British were much too cautious in their counter-attack, even allowing for the fact that their reconnaissance capabilities were reduced by damage to the French seaplanes.

Djemal and Kress had twisted the lion's tail – and got away with it. There was little glory in the affair. But what there was must, on the Turkish side, go to those who crossed the Canal.

Nearly 60 years before the SAMs and the Phantoms, the T62s and the Centurions, a few infantrymen struggled over the one hundred yards of the Canal, paddling rafts made of kerosene tins.

Verdun (1916)

Brenda Ralph Lewis

In choosing Verdun as the main German objective for 1916, General Erich von Faikenhayn, Chief of the German General Staff and Minister for War, pre-dated the jibe that the British would fight to the last man in the armies of their allies. Falkenhayn reasoned that, for the British, the European fronts in the First World War represented nothing more than a sideshow, with the Russian, Italian and French armies as their whipping boys. The Italians and Russians, Falkenhayn believed, were already foundering on their own ineptitude. Only France remained.

'France has almost arrived at the end of her military effort.' Falkenhayn wrote to the German Kaiser Wilhelm II in December 1915.

If we succeeded in opening the eyes of her people to the fact that in a military sense they have nothing more to hope for . . . breaking point would be reached, and England's best sword knocked out of her hand . . . Behind the French sector on the Western Front, there are objectives for the retention of which the French General Staff would be compelled to throw in every man they have. If they do so, the forces of France will bleed to death, as there can be no question of a voluntary withdrawal.

The objective Falkenhayn chose to put France in this moral and military dilemma was the massively fortified town of Verdun, on the canalized river Meuse. Verdun fitted Falkenhayn's bill admirably. It had immense historic and emotional significance for the French and formed the northern linchpin of the double defense line of fortifications built to protect France's eastern frontier after the Franco-Prussian War of 1870–1. Mount an assault here, with enough threatening potential, Falkenhayn reckoned, and the French Army would be inextricably lured to Verdun and mangled to extinction by the Germans. The mangle would be provided by a series of limited, but attritionist advances, intensively supported by artillery and spiced with surprise.

Falkenhayn's proposals appealed to the Kaiser and to his son, Crown Prince Wilhelm, whose Fifth Army had been pounding away at Verdun with little success since 1914. But the prince and his Chief of Staff, General Schmidt von Knobelsdorf, seemed to see the Verdun campaign more in terms of shattering the French with a bombardment than of bleeding them dry by attrition. Wilhelm, who wanted to attack on both sides of the Meuse, not on the right bank only, as Falkenhayn proposed, stated the campaign's purpose as 'capturing the fortress of Verdun by precipitate methods'. Compared with this fierce phraseology, Falkenhayn's notion of 'an offensive in the Meuse area in the direction of Verdun' seemed enigmatic. Despite the suitably malevolent codename of Operation *Gericht* (Judgement) given to his offensive, Falkenhayn's essentially half-hearted approach to it planted the seeds of ultimate German failure at Verdun. Basically, that failure was rooted in Falkenhayn's timid choice of too narrow a front for the initial attack and also in his extreme parsimony in doling out reserves.

Although Crown Prince Wilhelm and others seemed to suspect this outcome, preparations for the campaign went ahead as Falkenhayn had originally planned. It did so at a pace remarkable for those leisurely times. Weeks, rather than the usual months, divided Falkenhayn's preliminary consultations with the Kaiser at Potsdam on or about 20 December 1915 from the issue of final orders on 27 January 1916 and the projected attack date of 12 February.

During this period, the Germans amassed in the forests that surrounded Verdun a massive force of 140,000 men and over 1,200 guns – 850 of them in the front line – together with 2.5 million shells brought by 1,300 munitions trains, and an air arm of 168 aircraft as well as observation balloons. A superlative standard of secrecy

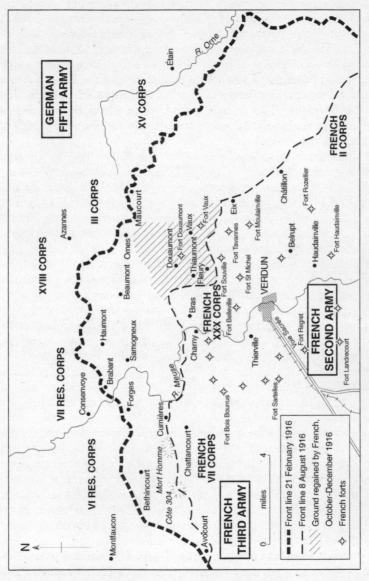

3.4 Verdun, 1916

was achieved by deft camouflage of the guns, by the building of underground galleries to house the troops instead of the more usual, give-away 'jump-off' trenches, and by dawn-to-dusk air patrols to prevent French pilots from casting spying eyes over the area.

These gargantuan preparations were, however, being directed against a military mammoth whose teeth had been drawn. By early 1916, Verdun's much-vaunted impregnability had been seriously weakened. It had been 'declassed' as a fortress the previous summer and all but a few of its guns and garrison had been removed. This was primarily the work of General Joseph J. C. Joffre, C-in-C of the French Army, who, with others, had presumed from the relatively easy fall in 1914 of the Belgian fortresses at Liège and Namur that this form of defense was redundant so far as modern warfare was concerned. Between August and October 1915, therefore, Verdun was denuded of over 50 complete batteries of guns and 128,000 rounds of ammunition. These were parcelled out to other Allied sectors where artillery was short. The stripping process was still going on at the end of January 1916, by which time the 60-odd Verdun forts possessed fewer than 300 guns with insufficient ammunition.

The result was that on the eve of the German offensive, the French defenses at Verdun were perilously weak, from the trench-works, dugouts and machine-gun posts to the communications network and barbed-wire fences. Far-sighted men who protested at the headlong disarmament of Verdun did so in vain. One of them, General Coutanceau, was sacked as Governor of Verdun and replaced in the autumn of 1915 by the ageing and apparently more tractable General Herr. Another, Colonel Emile Driant, commander of 56th and 59th *Chasseur* Battalions of 72nd Division, 30th Corps, warned as early as 22 August 1915: 'The sledge-hammer blow will be delivered on the line Verdun–Nancy.' After his opinion reached the ears of Joffre, Driant was sharply reprimanded in December for arousing baseless fears. Gen. Herr quickly realized that Coutanceau's alarm had been perfectly justified, and that he was in dire need of reinforcements to prepare the defense line Joffre had ordered at Verdun. But Herr's pleadings did little to penetrate the cloud of smugness that swirled about the question of defending Verdun. This mood remained impervious for some weeks, despite information from German deserters about troop movements and cancelled leave and other glimpses at the dire truth.

The very last moment had almost arrived before a glimmer of sense started to seep through. On 24 January General Nöel de Castelnau, Joffre's Chief of Staff, ordered a rush completion of the first and second trench lines on the right bank of the Meuse, and a new line in between.

On 12 February, two new divisions arrived at Verdun – much to Herr's heartfelt relief – to bring French strength up to 34 battalions against 72 German. Had the German attack begun on 12 February as planned, it would doubtless have smashed through the weak French defenses to score a stunning steamroller victory.

As it was, 12 February was not a day of savage battle, but of snow-blizzards and dense mist which afforded less than 1,100 yards visibility. The Verdun area was said to 'enjoy' some of France's filthiest weather. For a week it lived up to its reputation with snow, more snow, rain-squalls and gales.

Not until 21 February – just before 0715 – did a massive shell, almost as high as a man, burst from one of the two German 15-in (380 mm) naval guns and roar over the 20 miles that separated its camouflaged position from Verdun. There, it exploded in the courtyard of the Bishop's Palace. At this signal, a murderous artillery bombardment erupted from the German lines and a tornado of fire – including poison gas shells – began to flay the French positions along a six-mile front. The earth convulsed and the air filled with flames, fumes and a holocaust of shrapnel and steel which, the Germans clearly hoped, would destroy every living thing within range. The bombardment hammered on and on until about 1200, when it paused so that German observers could see where – if anywhere – pockets of French defenders survived. Then the artillery began afresh, smashing trenches, shelters, barbed wire, trees and men until the whole area from Malancourt to Eparges had become a corpse-littered desert.

Between 1500 and 1600, the barrage intensified as a prelude to the first German infantry advance along a 4.5-mile front from Bois d'Haumont to Herbebois. The advance began at 1645 when small patrol groups came out over the 656 to 1,203 yards of No Man's Land in waves 87.5 yards apart. Their purpose was to discover where French resistance might still exist and to pinpoint it to the artillery – which would then finish off the surviving defenders. This tentative approach, the result of Falkenhayn's excessive caution, was not to the taste of the belligerent General von Zwehl, commander of 7 Reserve Corps of Westphalians. Von Zwehl, whose position lay opposite Bois d'Haumont, paid brief lip-service to Falkenhayn's orders by sending out probing patrols first, but only a short while elapsed before he ordered his fighting stormtroopers to follow them. The Westphalians surged into the Bois d'Haumont, overran the first line of French trenches and within five hours had seized the whole wood.

To the right of the Bois d'Haumont lay the equally devastated Bois des Caures. Here, 80,000 shells had fallen within one 500,000-square-yard area. In this shattered wasteland, the advance patrols of the German 18 Corps expected to find nothing but mounds of shattered bodies in the mud. Instead, they were faced with a fierce challenge from Colonel Driant's *Chasseurs*. Of the original 1,200 men under Driant's command, fewer than half had survived the artillery bombardment. Now, these survivors poured machine-gun and rifle fire at the infiltrating Germans from the concrete redoubts and small strongholds which Driant had cunningly scattered through the trees.

Similarly ferocious isolated resistance was occurring all along the front, causing the Germans more delay and more casualties – 600 by midnight – than they had reckoned possible. By nightfall on 21 February, the only hole decisively punched in the French line was in the Bois d'Haumont, where Gen. Zwehl's Westphalians were now solidly entrenched. Elsewhere, the Germans had captured most of the French forward trenches, but were held up when darkness put an end to the first day's fighting which had yielded only 3,000 prisoners.

On the next two days, the Germans attacked with far greater force and much more initiative. On 22 February they blasted the village of Haumont, on the edge of the wood, with shellfire and flushed out the remaining French defenders with bombs and flamethrowers. That same day, the Bois de Ville was overwhelmed and in the Bois des Caures, which the Germans enveloped on both sides, Col. Driant ordered his *Chasseurs* to withdraw to Beaumont, about half a mile behind the wood. Only 118 *Chasseurs* managed to escape. Driant was not among them. On 23 February, the Germans saturated Samogneux with a hail of gunfire, captured Wavrille and Herbebois, and outflanked the village of Brabant, which the French evacuated. Next day – 24 February – despite their inch-by-inch resistance, the pace of disaster accelerated for the French with 10,000 taken prisoner, the final fall of their first defense line and the collapse of their second position in a matter of hours.

The Germans were now in possession of Beaumont, the Bois de

Fosses, the Bois des Caurieres and part of the way along La Vauche ravine which led to Douaumont.

Incredibly enough, at first the magnitude of the disaster did not sink in at Joffre's HQ at Chantilly, where the Staff had persuaded themselves that the German attack was a mere diversion. 'Papa' Joffre, who had long believed a serious German offensive was more likely in the Oise valley, Rheims or Champagne, maintained his customary imperturbability to such an extent that at 2300 on 24 February, he was fast asleep when General de Castelnau came hammering on his bedroom door bearing bad news from the front. Armed with 'full powers' from Joffre, who then went calmly back to bed, de Castelnau raced overnight to Verdun.

At about the time he arrived there, early on 25 February, a 10-man patrol of 24th Brandenburg Regiment of 3 Corps walked into Fort Douaumont and took possession of it and its three guns while the French garrison of 56 reserve artillerymen slept. This farcical episode, which German propaganda exaggerated into a hard-fought victory, shocked the French into melancholic despair and realization of the true state of affairs. At Chantilly, many officers openly advocated abandoning Verdun.

There, de Castelnau drew the conclusion that the French right flank should be drawn back and that the line of forts must be held at all costs. Above all, the French must retain the right bank of the Meuse, where de Castelnau felt that a decisive defense could, and must, be anchored on the ridges. The hapless Gen. Herr was replaced forthwith by 60-year-old General Henri Philippe Pétain. De Castelnau cannibalized Pétain's Second Army with the Third Army to form for him a new Second Army.

Pétain took over responsibility for the defense of Verdun at 2400 on 25 February, after arriving that afternoon to find Herr's HQ at Dugny, south of Verdun, in a chaos of panic and recrimination. Pétain, however, judged the situation to be far less hopeless than it seemed, even though the loss of Fort Douaumont and its unparalleled observation point was a serious blow. He decided that the surviving Verdun forts should be strongly re-garrisoned to form the principal bulwarks of a new defense. Pétain mapped out new lines of resistance on both banks of the Meuse and gave orders for a barrage position to be established through Avocourt, Fort de Marre, Verdun's NE outskirts and Fort du Rozellier. The line Bras–Douaumont was divided into four sectors – the Woevre, Woevre–Douaumont, astride the Meuse, and the left bank of the Meuse. Each sector was entrusted to fresh troops of the 20th ('Iron') Corps. Their main job was to delay the German advance with constant counter-attacks.

Pétain saw to it that the four commands were supplied with fresh artillery as it arrived along the Bar-le-Duc road – which was soon rechristened 'Sacred Way'. Three thousand Territorials labored unceasingly to keep its unmetalled surface in constant repair so that it could stand up to punishingly heavy use by convoys of lorries – 6,000 of them in a single day. Along *La Voie Sacrée* came badly needed reinforcements to replace the 25,000 men the French had lost by 26 February – five fresh Corps of them by 29 February. Already, Pétain was topping up his stock of artillery from the 388 field guns and 244 heavy guns that were at Verdun on 21 February towards the peak it reached a few weeks later of 1,100 field guns, 225 80–105 mm guns and 590 heavy guns. He also set the 59th Division to work building new defensive positions.

His injection of new strategy, new blood, new supplies and new hope into the Verdun defense soon began to disconcert the Germans. In any case, their impetus was gradually grinding down. On 29 February, their advance came to an exhausted halt after the last of their initial energy had been expended in three days of violent attacks against Douaumont, Hardaumont and Bois de la Caillette.

At that juncture, apart from their own mood of 'grievous pessimism', the most damaging factor for the Germans was the French artillery sited on the left bank of the Meuse. Here, more and more Germans came under fire the farther along the right bank they advanced. The solution was obvious, as Pétain had long feared and Crown Prince Wilhelm and Gen. von Knobelsdorf had long urged. On 6 March, after a blistering two-day artillery barrage, the German 6 Reserve and 10 Reserve Corps, partly pushed across the flooded Meuse and in a swirling snowstorm, attacked along the left bank. A parallel prong of this new onslaught was planned to strike along the right bank towards Fort Vaux, whose gunners had been savaging the German left flank.

Despite a plastering from French artillery in the Bois Bourrus, the Germans sped along the left bank and swept through the villages of Forges and Regneville – ending by nightfall in possession of Height 265 on the Côte de l'Oie. This ridge was of crucial importance, since it led through the adjacent Bois des Corbeaux towards the long mound known as Mort Homme. Mort Homme possessed double peaks and offered two advantages to the Germans. First it sheltered a particularly active battery of French field guns, and secondly, from its heights there stretched a magnificent all-round vista of the surrounding countryside. This gave whoever possessed it a prize observation point.

But Mort Homme soon lived up to its grisly name. After storming the Bois des Corbeaux on 7 March and losing it to a determined French counter-attack next day, the Germans prepared another attempt on Mort Homme on 9 March – this time from the direction of Béthincourt in the NW. They seized the Bois des Corbeaux a second time, but at such a crippling cost that they could not continue.

Results were depressingly similar on the right bank of the Meuse, where the German effort faded out beneath the walls of Fort Vaux. Difficulties of ammunition supply had made the attack there limp two days behind the left bank assault. With that, the parallel effect of the German offensive was ruined.

Inexorably, perhaps inevitably, the fighting around Verdun was acquiring that quality of slog and slaughter, and of lives thrown away for petty, short-lived gains that was so familiar a characteristic of fighting in the First World War.

Both Pétain and, in his own way, von Falkenhayn, were devotees of attrition by gunpower rather than manpower, but between March and May, the struggle at Verdun, like some Frankenstein's monster renouncing its master, assumed a will of its own and reversed this preference. German casualties mounted from 81,607 at the end of March to 120,000 by the end of April, and the French from 89,000 to 133,000, as the two sides battered each other for possession of Mort Homme. By the end of May, when the Germans had at last taken this vital position, their losses had overtaken their enemy's. On the right bank of the Meuse, in the same three months, the fighting swung to and fro over the 'Deadly Quadrilateral' – an area south of Fort Douaumont – to the tune of maniacal, endless artillery barrages, never resolving itself decisively in favor of one side or the other.

The process greatly weakened both contestants. Mutinous behavior and defeatist gossip became more common in the French ranks and French officers tacitly condoned this mood. More and more Germans, many of them terrified, clumsy 18-year-old boys were becoming sickly from exhaustion, the din of the guns and the filth in which they were forced to live.

Ennervation and dismay affected the heads as well as the bodies of the two opposing war efforts. By 21 April, Crown Prince Wilhelm had made up his mind that the whole Verdun campaign was a bloody failure and ought to be terminated. 'A decisive success at Verdun could only be assured at the price of heavy sacrifices, out of all proportion to the desired gains,' he wrote. These sentiments were echoed by Gen. Pétain, who was being nagged by Joffre to mount an aggressive counter-offensive. Pétain baulked at the increase in human sacrifice which that implied and clung to the principle of patient, stolid defense. Pétain was in a difficult position. Verdun had already become a national symbol of implacable resistance to the Germans, and Pétain himself a national idol. On the other hand, Verdun was threatening to gobble up the whole French Army and it certainly presented a serious drain on the manpower being reserved by Joffre for the coming Anglo-French offensive on the Somme.

For both sides at Verdun, these falterings at the top opened the way for men more ruthlessly determined to escalate the fighting onto even more brutal levels. On 19 April, Pétain was made Commander of Army Group Center, a position which placed him in remote rather than direct control of operations. His place as commander of Second Army was taken by General Robert Georges Nivelle, whose freebooter style of warfare had caught Joffre's attention during his series of audacious, if expensive, attacks along the right bank of the Meuse. Nivelle took over on 1 May, and arrived at headquarters at Souilly with the brash announcement: 'We have the formula!' He was also responsible for a quotation attributed sometimes to Pétain: 'Ils ne passeront pas!'

Nivelle's formula displayed itself in all its gory wastefulness on 22/23 May, when General Charles Mangin staged a flamboyant attack on Fort Douaumont. After a five-day bombardment, which barely chipped the fort's defenses, Mangin's troops streamed out of their jump-off trenches straight into a hurricane of deadly German gunfire. Within minutes, the French 129th Regiment had only 45 men left. One battalion had vanished. The remnants of the 129th charged the fort and set up a machine-gun post in one casemate against which the defending Germans flung themselves in a matching mood of suicidal madness. Out of 160 *Jägers*, *Leibgrenadiers* and men of the German 20th Regiment who attempted to overcome the French nest, only 50 returned to the fort alive. By the evening of 22 May, Fort Douaumont was in French hands, but the Germans staged violent counter-attacks, capping their onslaught with eight massive doses of explosive lobbed from a mine-thrower 80 yards distant. One thousand French were taken prisoner, and only a pathetic scattering of their comrades managed to stagger away from the fort.

This bloody fiasco ripped a 500-yard gap in the French lines and greatly weakened their strength on the right bank of the Meuse. Together with the fact that German possession of Mort Homme largely nullified French firepower on the Bois Borrus ridge, the self-destructive strife at Fort Douaumont gave great encouragement to the so-called 'May Cup' offensive which the Germans planned for early June.

The inspiration behind 'May Cup' was Gen. von Knobelsdorf, who had temporarily eclipsed Crown Prince Wilhelm. As Nivelle's new opposite number, von Knobelsdorf soon displayed an equally implacable resolve to overcome the enemy by brute force. 'May Cup' comprised a powerful thrust on the right bank of the Meuse by five divisions on under half the 21 February attack frontage. Its purpose was to lift Verdun's last veil – Fort Vaux, Thiaumont, the Fleury ridge and Fort Souville.

On 1 June, the Germans crossed the Vaux ravine and after a frenzied contest forced Major Sylvain Raynal – commander of Fort Vaux – to surrender on 7 June. By 8 June, Gen. Nivelle had mounted six unsuccessful relief attempts, at appalling cost. He was stopped from making a seventh attempt only when Pétain expressly forbade it. Elsewhere – notably round the Ouvrage de Thiaumont – the fighting brought both sides terrible losses. The French alone were losing 4,000 men per division in a single action. By 12 June, Nivelle's fresh reserves amounted to only one brigade – not more than 2,000 men.

With the Germans now poised to take Fort Souville – the very last major fortress protecting Verdun – ultimate disaster seemed imminent for the French. Eleventh-hour salvation came in the form of two Allied offensives in other theaters of war. On 4 June, on the Eastern Front, the Russian General Alexei A. Brusilov threw 40 divisions at the Austrian line in Galicia, in a surprise attack that flattened its defenders. The Russians took 400,000 prisoners. To shore up his war effort, now threatened with total collapse, Field Marshal Conrad von Hötzendorf, the Austrian C-in-C, begged Falkenhayn to send in German reinforcements. Grudgingly, Falkenhayn detached three divisions from the Western Front. Meanwhile, the French had been doing some pleading on their own account. In May and June, Joffre, de Castelnau, Pétain and French Prime Minister Aristide Briant had all begged General Sir Douglas Haig, the British C-in-C, to advance the Somme offensive from its projected starting date of mid-August. Haig at last complied on 24 June, and that day the week-long preliminary bombardment began.

At this juncture, a German 30,000-man assault on Fort Souville, which had begun with phosgene – 'Green Cross' – gas attacks on 22 June had already crumpled. Despite its horrifying effects on everything that lived and breathed, the novel phosgene barrage was neither intense nor prolonged enough to sufficiently paralyze the power of the French artillery. This shortfall, together with German failure to attack on a wide enough front, their recent loss of air superiority to the French, their shrinking store of manpower and the ravages thirst was wreaking in their lines, combined to scuttle the German push against Fort Souville on 22 June. July and August saw increasingly puny attempts by the Germans to snatch the prize that had come so tantilizingly close, but all ended in failure and exhaustion. German morale was at its lowest. On 3 September, the German offensive finally faded in a weak paroxysm of effort. Verdun proper came to an end.

For the Germans, this miserable curtain-fall on the drama of Verdun was assisted by the fact that after 24 June, the exigencies of the fighting elsewhere denied them new supplies of ammunition and, after 1 July, men.

All that remained was for the French to rearm, reinforce their troops and counter-attack to regain what they had lost. By 24 August 1917, after a brilliant series of campaigns masterminded by Pétain, Nivelle and Mangin, the only mark on the map to show the Germans had ever occupied anything in the area of Verdun denoted the village of Beaumont.

During this counter-offensive, the formerly maligned forts reinstated themselves as powerful weapons of defense. As the French recaptured them, they found how relatively little they had suffered from the massive artillery pounding they had received. This discovery made forts fashionable among French military strategists once more. It did so most notably, and later mortally for France, in the mind of André Maginot, Minister for War from November 1929 to January 1931 and in that time sponsor of the Maginot Line of fortifications.

Of course, fortress-like durability was given neither to the 66

French and 43.5 German divisions which fought at Verdun between February and June 1916, nor to the terrain they so bitterly disputed for so long. Both suffered permanent scars. The land around Verdun, raked over again and again by saturation shelling – over 12 million rounds from the French artillery alone – became a ravaged, infertile lunar-like wasteland. By 1917, the soil of Verdun was thickly sown with dead flesh and irrigated by spilled blood, having claimed more than 1.25 million casualties. Between February and December 1916, the French had lost 377,231 men and the Germans about 337,000 in a scything down of their ranks. In these circumstances, the Western Front ceased to be a sideshow for the British – if it had ever been so. They were forced to assume the star role in the Allied war effort which the French had formerly played. A repetition of Verdun was simply inconceivable.

The Somme (1916)

Sergeant-Major Ernest Shephard

In the memorable phrase of Basil Liddell Hart, the Somme was the 'glory and the graveyard' of Kitchener's army. After a week's heavy shelling British troops 'went over the top' on 1 July 1916 along a 15-mile sector of the Western Front, expecting little opposition. They met instead a hurricane of German fire, and 60,000 officers and men were lost on this day alone. Their deaths secured 1,000 yards of ground. It soon became clear to the Allies that a breakthrough on the Somme, despite some French successes, was impossible and they settled down for a campaign of attrition. The battle ended on 18 November, with an Allied advance of only seven miles, won at a cost of 418,000 British and 195,000 French casualties. The Germans lost 650,000 killed or wounded. Sergeant-Major Ernest Shephard, whose diary covering the first days of the Somme offensive is extracted here, served with the Dorset Regiment. He was killed in action in January 1917 in the Beaumont Hamel sector.

Saturday 1st July 1916

Place already nearly crammed, only four dug-outs for Company, two-thirds of us slept outside, enemy sending heavy shell and shrapnel all round us. A heavy shell caught a store containing flares, etc., a big fire caught some petrol and Bangalore Torpedoes. Some troops of the KOYLI were there, ten were killed by shell, two burnt to death. Fire continued until dawn. I got no sleep, it was bitterly cold. Had a limited walk round at 4 a.m., roused troops as all breakfast to be finished by 6.30. Wind change from favourable to dead against us at 5 a.m. At 6.30 a.m. our artillery were bombarding intensely, a most awful din. At 7.30 a.m. we moved to 'the attack' by companies at 200 yards intervals in the order C, D, A, B. We took the track in rear of the batteries by Brookers Pass, turned left on and over the road, into the Authuille Wood (which we call Blighty Wood) and followed the Dumbarton Track. A battery of artillery was in action half way in wood, enemy sending heavy shrapnel all over the place searching for us. (Naturally we got the thickest time, as the 97th Bde had already debouched from the front of wood, and the enemy guessed more to follow.) We had a number of casualties there, and passed by a number of killed and wounded from our leading companies. We had a terrible dose of machine-gun fire sweeping us through wood, could not understand why. If front and second line had been carried, enemy machine-guns would be out of action. We found reason quick enough. Had to wait nearly two hours on the track waiting for the brigade ahead of us to get forward, most infernal noise all the time, had a rough time from enemy artillery. Finally we got to Wood Post. This lies on the forward edge of the wood, a lot of killed and wounded there. Here we had to wait again, I went forward to see what was happening. Across the opening I saw the last platoon of A Coy going over the open ground in front of wood to our original front-line trench, a distance of about 120 yards. Half of this platoon were killed and almost all of remainder wounded in the crossing and I at once realized that some part of the attack had gone radically wrong, as we were being enfiladed by batteries of enemy machine-guns from the ridge on our right front held by the enemy.

I saw the Adjutant at this moment, and sent signal to our leading platoon to advance. We were told to cross as quick as possible. I went on ahead, Gray the Company Orderly behind, and No. 5 platoon behind him. How I got over I cannot imagine, the bullets were cracking and whizzing all round me. I got bullet holes through my clothing and equipment in several places and was hit in left side. The ground was covered with our dead and wounded men. When nearly over I dropped into a shell hole for breath and to see how the platoon was getting on. Gray was shot dead alongside me, and very few of No. 5 platoon left. I pulled two wounded men of

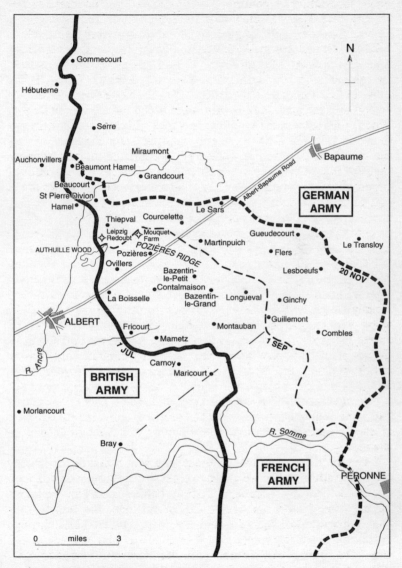

N

Gommecourt

Hébuterne

Serre

Miraumont

Auchonvillers

Beaumont Hamel

Beaucourt

Grandcourt

St Pierre Divion

Hamel

Thiepval

Le Sars

Albert-Bapaume Road

Bapaume

GERMAN ARMY

Courcelette

Leipzig Redoubt

Mouquet Farm

Gueudecourt

Le Transloy

AUTHUILLE WOOD

Pozières

POZIÈRES RIDGE

Martinpuich

Flers

Lesboeufs

20 NOV

Ovillers

Bazentin-le-Petit

Contalmaison

Bazentin-le-Grand

Longueval

Ginchy

La Boisselle

ALBERT

Fricourt

Montauban

Guillemont

Combles

1 JUL

Mametz

1 SEP

R. Ancre

Carnoy

Maricourt

BRITISH ARMY

Morlancourt

R. Somme

Bray

PÉRONNE

FRENCH ARMY

0   miles   3

3.5   The Battle of the Somme, July–November 1916

A Coy into the shell hole for cover, and then went on again, and got to a communicating trench. This I could not get into as it was simply crammed with troops of all units in utter confusion, some badly wounded and a number of dead. I pushed on again half left and got into our fire trench which was almost level from shell fire in places. From here I directed my Company behind to cross further to the left where the fire was not so hot, nevertheless they grew very thin in the crossing. I joined my Company Officer (2/Lt Webb) and we tried to find out from men of other units what was the situation. These were chiefly men of the Bns of 96th Bde, who should have passed through the 97th Bde (in enemy front and second line) to enemy 3rd line and Ferme du Mouquet. Of these most could only say they were the sole survivors of their Bn, but we got news that at any rate some of our own Bn had gone on to the enemy trenches, but no one knew exactly what portion of enemy trench or trenches were in our possession. There were a number of NCOs and men of C, D, and A Coy in with us. We gave orders for these to get ready to push on to enemy line, meanwhile 2/Lt Mainhood came up, and I got No. 6 and 7 platoons together, and he led them on to enemy trench. Meanwhile Captain Lancaster took command of the remnants of C, D and A Coys and they went over. By this time my No. 8 platoon had come up and I got them together with No.5 platoon and was just going to push over with them when orders arrived from Major Shute that we were to wait until he could get information from our troops in enemy line and report same to our Brigadier. A portion of the 19th Lancs now arrived (2 Companies). Some of these pushed straight through, others were stopped in time. Of the 11th Borders only one officer was left. The Colonel, 2nd in Command, and several other officers were killed. The Adjutant (we got him in) and remainder of officers were wounded. RSM also killed. We had lost most of our officers also. At this moment our Commanding Officer (Major Shute) was wounded (he had arrived in trench five minutes before with our Adjutant). Our Adjutant now took command of us, also he took command of the 11th Borders. Message from Brigade in reply to our report on situation, that we were to hold on and consolidate where we were, as owing to the Division on our right having failed in their attack our advance was impossible, as every inch of the ground in front of us was commanded by enemy.

The remainder of our Brigade, i.e. 19th Lancs, 2nd Manchesters and 15th HLI, had of course remained behind on getting orders not

to push on. The 19th Lancs who had come up were now withdrawn
to Blighty Wood to reorganize. Manchesters and HLI also in wood.
This left remnants of us and 11th Borders to hold the line. I took
charge of trench from Chequerbent St to the left of 'The Nab'. CSM
Stehr took from my left to Chowbent St CSM Pedder of C Coy had
been killed and CSM Mills slightly wounded in leg. My wound was
not very deep. I stuck a bandage on and managed to keep going. Our
troops in front are carrying on a bombing attack, bombs are being
sent to them via a big underground sap called the Russian Sap.

A lovely day, intensely hot. Lot of casualties in my trench. The
enemy are enfilading us with heavy shell, dropping straight on us. A
complete trench mortar battery of men killed by one shell, scores of
dead and badly wounded in trench, now 1 p.m. Every move we make
brings intense fire, as trenches so badly battered the enemy can see
all our movements. Lot of wounded in front we got in, several were
hit again and killed in trench. We put as many wounded as possible
in best spots in trench and I sent a lot down, but I had so many of
my own men killed and wounded that after a time I could not do
this. Sent urgent messages to Brigade asking for RAMC bearers to
be sent to evacuate wounded, but none came, although Brigade said
they had been despatched. Meanwhile the enemy deliberately shelled
the wounded between the trenches with shrapnel, thus killing, or
wounding again most of them. Our own Regtl stretcher bearers
worked hard to take cases away. Counted all Dorsets at 1 p.m.
Total 53 all ranks. At 3 p.m. the Manchesters went through the
Russian Sap and made an attack, captured a portion of the Leipzig
Redoubt. Brigade sent message to say we would be relieved by 15th
HLI as soon as possible. Meanwhile we were to hold tight.

We needed to; literally we were blown from place to place. Men
very badly shaken. As far as possible we cleared trenches of debris
and dead. These we piled in heaps, enemy shells pitching on them
made matters worse.

Wounded suffering agonies. I got them water from bottles of
dead, a few managed to crawl away to the Aid Post in wood.
At dusk we got more wounded in from the front. 8 p.m. we
got shelled intensely, and continued at intervals. I had miracu-
lous escapes. The HLI arrived at midnight. I handed care of
wounded to them, and took remnants of B and C Coys, only
ten NCOs and men, back via Mounteagle and Rock St, through
Wood Post and over same track (Dumbarton) through Blighty

Wood, down the valley to Crucifix Corner. Arrived there at 1 a.m. on

Sunday 2nd July

Had a halt there, then on as ordered to the Authuille defences in Kintyre St. Got to top of hills, met messenger, orders to go to Blackhorse dug-outs for night, arrived there absolutely dead beat at 2 a.m. No dug-outs available, place crammed with troops of another division, camped out in the open. Very cold, had some sleep for an hour. Terrible bombardment going on all the time. The 17th HLI and 11th Borders say their Bns nearly wiped out, also the Ulster Div. who attacked Thiepval on left.

A number of our men came in at 4 a.m., some had been mixed up with other units, others had to lie in shell holes unable to budge owing to machine-gun fire, some from various jobs detailed for before the attack, and a number from the enemy trenches on relief by 15th HLI. This party had been commanded by Capt. Lancaster. He got wounded but held on and our men did very good work there. They bombed and captured a large portion of the enemy second line, and completed the capture of enemy 1st and 2nd line up to the Hindenburg Fort on right and Leipzig Redoubt on left. Very strong position held them up. We lost a lot of men there, but we have satisfaction over them as they killed a large number of the enemy. The enemy troops against us were the Prussian Guards, whom we have fought against at Ypres and previously at La Bassée. A prisoner said they only came there two days ago, and had lost heavily. Our men say they fought very bravely, and were of splendid physique, all over 6 feet in height. Also, they say enemy trenches very substantial and wanting nothing. Good dug-outs fitted luxuriously with electric lights, boarded and even wallpapered, plenty of good food, cigars, wines, in fact everything required. Plenty of German helmets as souvenirs. Enemy trenches choked with their own dead. Three Companies of 15th HLI are holding enemy trenches now, with two companies of Manchesters. At 6.30 a.m. came orders we were to be at Kintyre Trench by 7.30 a.m. On arrival there we had a roll call of the Bn. After all were in I mustered 90 all ranks, out of 201 who went into action. I lost 111 all ranks. Total casualties in Battalion reckoned as 490 NCOs and men, and 20 officers. I lost all my Platoon Sgts and three Platoon Officers.

A fine day. I reorganized my remnants, made new Platoon Sgts, etc., sent in my list of casualties and had a little sleep. Major Thwaytes now arrived and took over command of Bn. Needless to say, we are all bitterly cut up at practically losing our fine Battalion in getting to our own fire trenches. Had we lost so many in actual grip with the enemy we should have felt more satisfaction. This is a repetition of Hill 60, where we lost nearly the Battalion with hardly a fighting chance. That happened on 1st of month as well.

Of course the 8th Division caused it through not being able to capture the ridge with machine-guns on our right. Really our Division ought never to have attacked until that ridge had been gained, but either the 97th and 96th Brigade Commanders did not inform our Divisional Commander of the situation (possibly the orderly was killed or wires destroyed) or else, if our General did know and yet decided that we should carry on, he is not fit for his job.

At 2.30 p.m. an intense bombardment of our artillery started on Beaumont Hamel. At 4.30 p.m. smoke bombs were used, so I presume our troops attacked. We could see quite plainly, but no troops. The enemy retaliated on us, and we had a hot time from 'Jack Johnsons'. Great aerial activity going on. Rumour at 6 p.m. that the cavalry are in action on left. Got rations up later and just going to settle down for a decent sleep at 8.30 p.m. when we were sent for and told to be ready to move in one hour for trenches to relieve 17th HLI. All day we have been expecting to go right back out of it for the Division to reorganize. I sent a Sgt to take over our portion of trench. Our Bn is to hold our own original front line from Chequerbent St to Tyndrum St as support to 2nd Manchesters in enemy trench in front between the Leipzig and Hindenburg Forts. The 15th HLI are relieving Manchesters at 3 a.m. and are to make an attack to capture the forts. We act as supports to them with 19th Lancs and Manchesters in reserve. Stood by for orders which came at 1.30 a.m. on

Monday 3rd

We moved up via Campbell Av. and got blocked there by a company of Cheshires with 'wind up'. Hell's own bombardment going on by our artillery preparatory to the attack, and enemy retaliating heavily all round us. Got clear of Cheshires and cut across the New MG Trench. Here we found half of our men had got cut off by Cheshires and lost touch. Waited half an hour trying to connect up, nothing doing so I sent on what we had and went back to find the others. I found nine of them and they said the remainder were sure of the way on, so I decided to get the nine up. Got to Oban Av. and up to the front trench expecting to find the others there. Most terrible fire from enemy on the trench from howitzer shells dropping dead in trench, also the enemy were using gas shells, which almost stifled us. Evidently by the intense shelling from enemy, they have news of our attack and shelling this trench to prevent troops getting up. Shells dropping all round us, hairbreadth escapes. L/Cpl Lillington and Jenkins killed by one shell. The trench almost level with ground. Finally got to Chowbent St, still no sign of our men so came to conclusion they had all been killed and buried by debris in trench. I turned into Chowbent, worked way to junction of Bury Av. – Hough St, and through Hough St to Oban Av., met no one, so I put the men in a shelter for a rest, while the HLI passed up to relieve Manchesters. Now almost break of dawn. At 4 a.m. the remainder of lost party came up, so I decided to hold Hough St (instead of the fire trench), and I put two groups on duty there. Later I found my OC Coy at the Aid Post and found that he had, on arrival with first party, decided not to hold fire trench owing to intense fire, and he had put his party on duty in Chequerbent St on the right of Hough St. Time now 6 a.m., devilish row going on ahead.

The attack started at 6.30 a.m. I went along the fire trench and put out another post in the new communicating trench across the salient from Chowbent to Iona St. From there I had fine view of the attack. Apparently the HLI are getting on alright, as they have not asked for our help yet. We are getting a lot of heavy shell and machine-gun fire. I returned to Coy HQ at 11 a.m. to find the OC in a great stew over my absence. They thought I had been killed and reported me as 'Missing' to Bn HQ. Had breakfast. Enemy brought one of our aeroplanes down at noon. I have only one officer in the Company, i.e. the OC, Lt Webb. In afternoon had little sleep. Heavy shelling continues all day. At 7 p.m. message to say we are being relieved by 1st Wilts tonight, so sent guides down and made all preparations. They arrived at 9.30 p.m. and we got out fairly easily as enemy eased down a little at that time. The Wilts have a lot of raw reinforcements of officers and men. We led out via Oban Av. through Authuille, over Blackhorse Bridge and Road to Pioneer Road, Northumberland Av., skirted Martinsart and arrived Bouzincourt at midnight. Here we collected the Company, a few enemy shells dropped close by. We pushed on and got in by singing, quite exhausted, at 1 a.m. on [billets in Senlis].

Tuesday 4th

Issued rum and tea, saw men settled and slept until 10 a.m. Nasty day, very hard storms of rain and wind continued all day. Road outside my billet flooded 2 feet deep. Adjutant told me General Joffre came round here yesterday, and says it will cost us 20,000 men to take Thiepval and trenches close to it, by frontal attack. The 15th Lancs Fus. reported to have attacked there and completely swallowed up. Joffre says it is the best situated and most strongly fortified enemy position on the Western front. I see in today's paper same thing mentioned, also a paragraph mentioning the 'Dorsets' hard fight'. By what I read and hear our offensive has been quite successful generally, certain strong points are holding against us. I hear we are not going to attack Thiepval now. We are going to wedge them out from round Pozières. I felt very queer all day, have a bad attack of bleeding piles, also the relaxation is telling.

Wednesday 5th

During morning held kit inspection. Company bathed in afternoon from 2 to 4 p.m. At 5 p.m. the Bn paraded and marched via Hédauville to Forceville where we occupied huts, arrived 7 p.m. All the Brigade are here close by. Quiet night.

Thursday 6th

Fine day. During morning sorted out kits of casualties. Company parade for arms drill 10–11 a.m.

Rained hard in afternoon. Just settling for night when urgent orders arrived to be ready to move for Senlis or Bouzincourt at an hour's notice. We were ready at 9 p.m. Raining hard, fierce bombardment going on.

Friday 7th

Operation orders arrived at 3 a.m. The 19th Lancs Fus. and we go to Bouzincourt, Manchesters and 15th HLI to Senlis. Our Brigade

is in Corps Reserve. Packed up, paraded and moved off at 4.45 a.m.
in order B, A, D, C; marched via Hédauville direct to Bouzincourt.
There we handed in packs, drew bombs and extra SAA, all ready to
go. We are reserve to 49th Division, who are attacking at 8 a.m. to
capture completely the Leipzig and Hindenburg redoubts. Intense
bombardment going on now. I went to a high point to watch the
attack. At 8 a.m. the smoke screen was flying in front of enemy
trenches and the troops moved to attack. Could see nothing more.
While waiting news I went to the cemetery to see what men of ours
had been buried there. Only L/Cpl Woolfries from my Company.
After I went over to see Lizzie, the heavy gun fire – shells so large
can be seen quite plainly on leaving muzzle. After I went to billet and
had little sleep. Heavy rain from 1 p.m. and all the afternoon. Lot
of Colonial (Australian) artillery just come round here. We expected
to move in evening, as our Brigade is now lent to the 12th Division,
who are continuing the attack on Ovillers. No orders yet.

Saturday 8th

We were heavily shelled all night, some just cleared roof of billet
and exploded on yard. Fritz is after Lizzie, but is a long way out.
No moving orders yet. Sent for by Adjt at 10 a.m. All Bns in the
Brigade are now forming two Coys out of the remnants of the four
Coys to simplify work. Also all officers, warrant officers and NCOs
over the complement of the two Coys are to be left behind when we
go into action again, thus forming a reserve of ranks to keep the Bn
going. The Adjt had already listed CSM Miller and myself as the two
CSMs to stay behind, as we both have been on active service longest,
Miller since start of war, and I since January 1915. I selected Sgts
Stroud, Charles and Gilchrist to stay as well from my Coy. A and B
Coys will be joined together and called the 'Right Company', C and D
same and called the 'Left Coy'. CSM Cobb to be CSM of Right Coy,
CSM Stehr to be CSM of Left Coy. We have to go back to Hédauville
and be under orders of 97 Bde while the Bn is in action. I do not like
the idea at all, but orders must be carried out. I turned my No. 5
and 6 Platoon into No. 3 Platoon, and 7 and 8 into No. 4 Platoon
of Right Coy. Handed over all documents to Cobb. I decided to stay
with Coy until they moved to go into action. Fine day. Went up to
high ground to watch the fighting. Lot of observation balloons up.
At 5 p.m. orders came for Bn to move tonight. I collected the party

staying behind, 13 officers, 20 WOs, Cpls and Sgts, and moved off for Hédauville. Half way orderly came, orders to go to transport lines; went there, and later in night orders to move to Senlis where 97 Bde are now. Decided to go there in morning. Very heavy bombardment all night. Rather interesting to be back from trenches with transport and peep behind the scenes. Continued passage of troops and supplies all night. Had a good bivouac, slept well.

Vimy Ridge (1917)

Brenda Ralph Lewis

Four divisions of the Canadian Corps, with the 5th British Division in support, began their assault on Vimy Ridge on 9 April 1917. This six-mile hogsbacked pleat in the plains near Arras in NE France possessed an almost legendary reputation for impregnability. French forces had battered incessantly against it in 1914 and 1915, only to gain the Lorette Spur next to the Ridge and part of the slopes. They gained it in the typically wasteful and bloody style of the First World War with the loss of 150,000 men. In 1916, when the British took over from them, they, too, employed the same dismally ineffective tactics of repeated shelling, mining, raiding and skirmishing by night. The British, like the French, lost men by the thousand – 2,500 in the three days 23–26 May alone.

The slaughter of all these men, like that of millions of others on the Western Front, achieved absolutely nothing from a strategic point of view. For while the Germans remained firmly entrenched in their warren of tunnels and deep dugouts, and while they stayed strongly in possession of the crest of Vimy Ridge, which dominated the Lens–Douai Plain, they were able to keep their opponents' position in Arras, six miles away, in a constantly precarious condition.

The apparent unshakeable hold of the Germans on Vimy Ridge also maintained the Allied High Command in a mood of fuming frustration. These were men to whom territory gained equalled success, no matter what the cost, and territory lost (or like Vimy

Ridge, not captured), spelled failure. It was this rigid mentality – divorced from the realities of modern, mechanized warfare and untempered by humanitarian considerations – that helped account for the quality of attrition that so quickly characterized hostilities on the Western Front. Among the firmest exponents of attrition and the mass assault by thousands of human lemmings, was Marshal Joseph Joffre, C-in-C of the French Armies on the Front between 1914 and 1916. Joffre's methods were so successful in killing off his own troops that in 1916 he stated they could stand just one more great battle, after which France's pool of men of military age would virtually dry up.

But by the end of 1916 the French were no longer able to countenance the wholesale slaughter of their men for the sake of a few patches of gain, or, more commonly, for none at all. In 1916 alone, a year of almost unmitigated failure on the Western Front, the inconclusive battles of the Somme (1 July to 15 November) and Verdun (21 February to 24 August) had taken more than 500,000 French lives and left thousands of survivors gassed, crippled, blinded and otherwise ruined.

French patience and trust in Joffre finally ran out and he was relieved of his command. He was replaced on 12 December 1916, by General Robert Georges Nivelle. He had won instant popularity in the public imagination by master-minding two successful French counter-attacks at Verdun. Nivelle appeared to have a more mobile and more promising concept of warfare. The enemy was to be violently and repeatedly hammered by masses of artillery and assaulted by vast numbers of infantry. Nivelle's ideas seemed to herald the decisive victory for which the French now thirsted. As 1917 began, the impression mushroomed that the hour had found the man and the man could produce with one stunning strike the longed-for miracle of a complete and permanent rupture of the German lines.

In this atmosphere, the plan Nivelle conceived – that the French should mount an offensive along a 50-mile front between Soissons and Champagne – was as much of a public relations venture as a battle campaign. To draw the German reserves away from the French sector, the British were to attack along the Hindenburg Line, which was held by the German Sixth Army under General Freiherr von Falkenhausen. The Hindenburg Line skirted Queant and Bullecourt in the south, crossed Telegraph Hill, part of Vimy Ridge, and ended

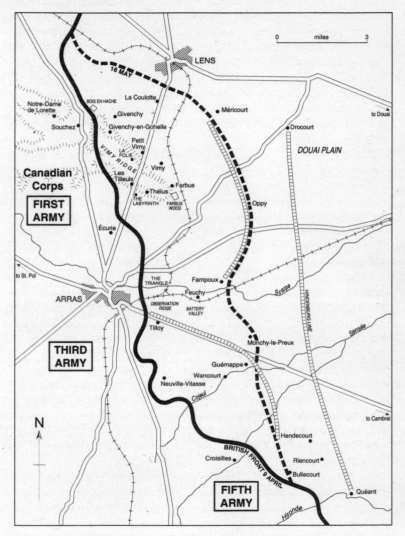

3.6 *Vimy Ridge and the Battles of Arras, April–May 1917*

at the Railway Triangle about two miles east of Arras. It was intended that the British Third Army, under General Sir Edmund H. Allenby, would break through the line and advance south-eastwards towards Cambrai. At the same time, the British First Army, of which the Canadian Corps formed part, would advance towards Douai to the north-east. During these offensives – the battles of Arras which began on 9 April and cost 150,000 casualties – the Third Army succeeded in puncturing the Hindenburg Line with a dent 11 miles long and 3.7 miles deep. But, although Monchy-le-Preux and Hill 102 were also gained, the British effort round Arras fell short of most of its other objectives.

The onslaught on Vimy Ridge, on the other hand, was a brilliant success. The Ridge, which ran NW to SE from south of Givenchy to the edge of Farbus Wood, was the northernmost part of the British front. It was a depressing wasteland. The continuous struggle staged there since 1914 had pulverized it into a quagmire of mud and waterlogged pot-holes and trenches, scattered with the rotting flesh and stripped bones of thousands of unburied dead, numerous rats, lice, bugs and nits, the jagged debris of countless shells, bombs and bullets, torn-up fragments of barbed wire and corrugated iron and the empty cans and litter that were the junk of everyday living.

Early in 1917, the Canadian Corps began to replace the British on this derelict compost heap. It was assumed on both sides that they would repeat the melancholy mixture as before, and do no more than wage fruitless running warfare resulting in heavy losses. The five regiments of the German Sixth Army, who were occupying the Ridge, together with their commanders, were confident that this was the case. The German reading of the situation was well founded. The mediocre performance Allied troops had so far made in the war convinced them that incompetence was inherent in the Allied war effort. Any attack – on Vimy Ridge or anywhere else – was bound to fail.

Therefore, it was in complacent mood and without undue alarm that the Germans fended off occasional Canadian raiding of their lines and observed the quickening pace of the British build-up around the Ridge in late 1916 and early 1917. During that winter, the British dug thousands of feet of new tunnels in the chalk of Vimy Ridge, together with caves capable of housing men by the hundreds. In March, 1917, piles of ammunition and supplies were stockpiled in the area, the roads leading to it and from it bustled with activity, fresh wire barricades were erected and strongpoints reinforced. Early in April, the Allied artillery bombardment, which had been more or less continuous in the months before, suddenly intensified. The Germans' former superior firepower began to be overwhelmed. The number of rounds fired rose sharply – doubling the Allied expenditure in March and rising to a peak of 90,000 rounds on 5 April: this was three times the number pumped out by the Germans in reply. The bombardment flattened several German trenches and smashed huge gaps in the wire. Each hammering was followed up with British and Canadian forays, made in greater strength than before, to discover the damage caused.

Despite all this, the Germans concluded only that some time soon, some strenuous effort – bigger than a raid, but not so powerful and much more limited than a 'Big Push' – was about to be made. But they believed that they could deal with anything their enemies would throw at them. In this complacent mood, General von Falkenhausen not only failed to move up the best part of his reserves, but kept them so far back that they had little chance to intervene should the coming battle put the front line under impossible pressure. The men of von Falkenhausen's First Guards Reserve Division and 18th Infantry Division were in fact, still 12.5 miles behind the lines on 9 April. What was more, von Falkenhausen did not order his artillery to the rear, where they might have mounted a defence in depth, until the Canadian attack was imminent. To make the Germans' plight worse their sluggish supply system failed to deliver rations and reinforcements. They also suffered from an ammunition shortage.

The magnitude of the threat to the Germans on Vimy Ridge was considerably greater than they imagined. For one thing, their Canadian opponents possessed qualities unusual in ordinary soldiers of the First World War. The nature of Canadian society encouraged tenacity and toughness to a far higher degree than did the rigid class societies of Europe. Similarly, the plan of battle for Vimy Ridge was not the sort the Germans' experience so far had led them to expect. Though it was a set-piece offensive, it contained the uncommon element of surprise. The preliminary artillery barrage was to be much briefer than the usual days or even weeks. It would last only three minutes before the Canadians went 'over the top' and would creep forward at the rate of about 33 yards per minute. The infantry would march behind at a careful synchronized pace.

At the same time, 150 Vickers machine-guns would thicken up the barrage and spray the ground 40 yards ahead of the advance, while HE and gas shells saturated the German positions and mortars spread a smokescreen in selected sectors. The overall effect would be to provide the infantry with a devastating artillery umbrella to get them to the German front line long before they were expected.

On the night of 8/9 April, the first attack wave of Canadian troops – 15.000 men – stood packed shoulder to shoulder in the jump-off trenches in freezing and unseasonable weather. They were weighted down with full battle kit, extra ammunition and rations and – as was all too familiar – were standing knee-deep in freezing, muddy water. At 0530, a large gun coughed out a throaty signal from nearby Mont St Eloi. Immediately, 1,000 Allied guns, the heaviest of them 15-in howitzers, responded with a huge concerted roar. The air was rent with shells that whooshed over the heads of the men hunched in the jump-off trenches. The barrage speared out over No Man's Land ripping apart the semi-darkness blanketing the German front line with a flickering, flashing curtain of light. At the same time, counter-battery fire thundered down upon the German gun emplacements, and to add to the cacophony, two large mines were detonated in the German lines, tearing massive holes in the wire.

After three minutes, the guns of the 'creeping barrage' lengthened their range and the bombardment leapt 100 yards ahead. The deluge of shells pounded its way foward as the Canadians scrambled out of the trenches and moved over the mud-wastes that led up the slopes of Vimy Ridge. Their rate of advance – drummed into them by intensive training – was the same as that of the barrage. Some of the most heavily laden troops had trouble keeping up even with this crawling pace. It was snowing fairly heavily and the sticky mud beneath their feet made the Canadians slither and slide. The eight MK 1 'Female' tanks, armed with machine-guns, which were moving forward with 2nd Division, soon lumbered to a complete halt – their tracks quite unable to grip the near-liquid sludge beneath them. Three of the tanks were wrecked by German gunfire.

Overhead and in front of them, the advancing Canadians could see amber-coloured flares leaping up into the gradually lightening sky as the Germans fired desperate signals for immediate artillery support. They signalled largely in vain. The best part of the German heavy artillery – accurately plotted earlier by Allied sound ranging or aerial photography – had been neutralized or destroyed. Those guns further back which were still intact were not in communication with their beleaguered front line, and could not lay down fire where it was needed. All that the German guns were able to do was to fire at the known position of the Canadian front line, which the initial attack wave had already left.

Only the German machine-guns, which were strongly emplaced almost flush with the ground, were able to retaliate to any advantage. Their answering fire streamed out among the Canadians. Many fell dead in the mud. Even if they were not mown down in neat rows – as had happened during infantry advances on the Somme and elsewhere – the Canadians suffered considerable losses. For example, the 7th Battalion of the 1st Division, which lost half its men during the battle of Vimy Ridge, lost most of them to machine-gun fire in the first half-mile of their advance.

The deadly machine-gun nests could only be silenced by close personal onslaught. This tactic was extremely dangerous and likely to be fatal to the attacker. Two Victoria Crosses won at Vimy Ridge – both awarded posthumously – went to a 1st Division private who crawled up to the gun-slit of a machine-gun and slammed a hand grenade inside, and to a 2nd Division lance-sergeant who charged another nest single-handed and bayoneted the crew.

If the machine-gunners on the Ridge were able to defend themselves adequately, the German infantry were the exact opposite. The preliminary barrage, which had been directed with punishing accuracy from Forward Observation Posts, observer balloons and aircraft of the Royal Flying Corps, had smashed the German trenches to near-oblivion along with many of their deep dugouts – most of them unwisely placed in the first 700 yards of the front line. This bombardment had buried hundreds of Germans alive in the dugouts and those who managed to survive were taken completely by surprise. They had not expected an attack to arrive for hours, perhaps days. Several were taken prisoner while sitting down to breakfast. Others were captured in their beds or skulking sockless, shirtless and otherwise half-dressed in tunnels, shafts and dugouts. The shock of surprise was quickly followed by terror, as the Germans realized that the roarings and shudderings they could hear and feel close by were caused by Canadians tossing Mills bombs into neighbouring dugouts.

Germans who had been surprised underground, but who managed to avoid capture, rushed down their tunnels to the rear in a frantic effort to escape, carrying the dire news of disaster to gun-crews in the German artillery area of Farbus Wood. There was immediate panic and those crews able to began to pull out across the Douai Plain. The demoralization the Canadians achieved by swiftness and surprise proved a valuable, even economic, weapon in their armoury. One German machine-gun crew which opened fire a few hundred yards ahead of troops of the 31st Battalion of 3rd Division gave themselves up as soon as a Canadian fired a Mills bomb at them from his .303 rifle. Another lone Canadian, a member of the 29th (British Columbia) Battalion of the same division, achieved even easier success while reconnoitring in Farbus Wood. A short burst of bullets from his rifle, fired in the general direction of a German howitzer crew, resulted in the instant evacuation of their position.

By 1100 – after five and a half hours of battle – the German defences were in almost total disarray. Some scattered spots on the front, in the areas covered by the 2nd and 3rd Canadian Divisions, were still held by the Bavarian 79th Reserve Infantry Division, but the Germans' centre had been pushed well over the crest of Vimy Ridge. The German left wing had fallen back as far as Intermediate Position No. 11, which coincided roughly with the Canadians' 'Brown Line'. The overall picture now was that the most important parts of Vimy Ridge, including Telegraph Hill and its south-eastern contour, were in Canadian hands. Also, men of the 1st Division were swarming through Farbus Wood. There, they were performing an unprecedented function for Allied troops in the First World War – capturing German guns, several of them the much-dreaded 5.9-in howitzers.

The dictum that 'artillary conquers, infantry occupies' had for once come true – and much faster than anyone had forseen.

However, the rapid and spectacular success of the 1st, 2nd and 3rd Divisions and most of the 4th Division was not being matched on Hill 145, a vital part of the 4th Division's area. Hill 145 (475 ft), the highest point of Vimy Ridge, lay in the centre of the 4th Division's operation and was the objective of its 11th Brigade, under Brigadier V. W. Odlum. Opposing the 11th Brigade was the Reserve Infantry Regiment No. 261, a unit of the Bavarian 79th Division. The Germans were dug into strong defences – the normal three forward trenches, with a strong tunnel, the *Munchener-Lager*, between trenches two and three. On the crest and reverse slope of Hill 145 lay a twin-trench system which included the deep defences of the *Obere*

Hangstellung, the *Untere Hangstellung*, a reserves' double tunnel, and a large encampment, the *Hanseaten-Lager*. This defence system was basically no different from those faced by the other three Canadian divisions, and the method of attack used by them was the same as on Hill 145. There was, nevertheless, one crucial difference, and a difference ironically created by a Canadian commanding officer.

Before the battle began, the CO of the 87th (Montreal) Battalion of the 4th Division had requested that the artillery barrage should leave intact and undamaged a German trench of the second line, which he wished to capture and exploit. The CO seemed confident of seizing the trench – only 150 yards from the Canadian jump-off trenches – before its defenders had time to emerge from their deep tunnels and fight back. In these circumstances, the CO's request was granted. Unfortunately, in keeping this trench sacrosanct, the CO had also preserved unharmed several machine-gun nests and infantry sections of the German 5th Company of 261st Regiment. This factor, combined with German reserve machine-guns farther back on Hill 145, and the peculiarly stubborn fighting qualities of the 5th Company, brought the Canadians near to disaster.

Machine-gun fire, rifle fire and hand grenades were unleashed from the undamaged trench, slaughtering half the advancing Canadians in minutes, and producing piles of khaki corpses in front of the German position. All around them, shell-holes full of water were stained a deep red.

Despite their appalling losses, the Canadians managed to overwhelm the left wing of Regiment No. 261 and the opposition they faced narrowed down to the centre. Here, the Germans scrambled from their tunnels and viciously counter-attacked. Soon, the fighting degenerated into confusion and discernible lines of Canadians and Germans disappeared. The battle dissolved into small close-quarter skirmishes, fought by groups of isolated men. Battered battalions of the ill-fated 11th Brigade, together with neighbouring units of the 12th Brigade, on their left, broke up into scattered remnants. Of the 11th Brigade battalions, the 54th on the left flank was rapidly reduced to about 90 men, the 102nd to not many more and the manpower of the 87th was scythed in half. As for the 12th Brigade, 'A' Company of its 78th Battalion lost all its officers, either killed or badly wounded, and out of the 700 men the battalion sent into the battle, only 199 reported at the first roll call afterwards.

The 11th Brigade Commander, Brigadier V. W. Odlum, was

distraught. Reports reaching him were non-existent or scanty. As far as he could tell, the 54th, 102nd and 87th Battalions had gone up Hill 145 and disappeared. Of the 30 scouts Odlum had sent out to reconnoitre and report, only one had returned. And he brought dismal news that the Germans were still holding their Second Line on the left of the 11th Brigade's front. The major part of Hill 145 was still in German hands long after the battle plan had specified that it should have been wrested from them.

At 1450 Brigadier Odlum summoned officers of the 85th Battalion, Lieutenant-Colonel J. Warden commanding, to urgent consultations at Tottenham Tunnel, the communications trench that served as 11th Brigade HQ. The result of this anxious get-together was orders for the 85th, which consisted mainly of untried men, to prepare to take Hill 145. A covering artillery bombardment was promised but, in the event, failed to materialize.

At 1745 the 85th Battalion began to advance without the comfort and reassurance of covering fire. They ran straight into a barrage of German machine-guns. Bullets whipped through the Canadian ranks. Many men fell to the ground but the advance was not halted. Several men of the 85th had been trained in the tricky job of firing Mills bombs from rifles. This daunting marriage of two weapons had a terrifying effect on the Germans. Corporal H. M. Curll, of the 85th's 'C' Company, fired a Mills bomb to within five yards of one machine-gun crew, producing instant surrender. Curll's initiative was followed by other rifle-bombers and by the time 'C' Company got within 50 yards of the Germans' Second Line five crews had leapt from their gun positions and fled.

At nightfall on 9 April, troops of the 85th Battalion were passing over the crest of Hill 145. Isolated Germans in scattered positions on the Hill were still resisting, but their main defence effort had been effectively quelled. At 1600 on 10 April, under cover of an artillery barrage, the 44th and 50th Battalions of the 10th Brigade (4th Division) crossed over the north of Hill 145 and down the reverse slope to the *Untere Hangstellung*. A few hours later, as night closed in, Hill 145 was in Canadian hands and the 'Southern Operation', the main part of the Vimy Ridge offensive, was over. The cost had been 3,000 Canadians killed, over 4,000 wounded, and the reward, 4,000 German prisoners taken and unknown numbers killed.

The hiatus on Hill 145 had, however, put the timetable out by about 48 hours. The 44th and 50th Battalions had originally been detailed to spend 10 April carrying out the 'Northern Operation' to take the wooded knoll – known as the 'Pimple' – commanding the Souchez Valley. Because of the rescue operation on Hill 145, the attack on the 'Pimple' which was made with very heavy artillery support, did not start until 0530 on 12 April.

The weather, which had alternated between squalls of snow, hail, sleet and rain, leaden skies and brief glimpses of bright sunshine since 9 April, was now decisively in favour of the Canadians. It was snowing as the 44th and 50th Battalions, together with the 46th Battalion, struggled towards the German positions on the 'Pimple', sunk up to their knees in gluey sludge. Fortunately for them, the freezing wind was blowing the snow straight at the Germans, and their machine-gunners were so blinded and bemused by it that the Canadians were upon them before they had a chance to mount an effective defence. The ensuing fight was vicious and the result never in serious doubt. By 0900, after three and a half hours, the Canadians had taken the 'Pimple' and had completed the capture of Vimy Ridge. Their toll of casualties was now climbing towards the final figure of 10,000 which was officially acknowledged on 14 April. The Canadians had lost one tenth of the men they put into the battle. In human terms, this is a chilling toll, but in cold statistics, in terms of the ratio between sacrifice and success, nowhere near as costly as other battles in the First World War.

Already, during the night of 12/13 April, the Germans had withdrawn to their well-fortified defence line between Avion, Mericourt and Arleux, near the Scarpe River. Here, their strength was reinforced by 14 April with reserve divisions, and with one man to every 6 ft of ground, their resistance markedly stiffened. The reaction of the British High Command was to attack quickly and prise the Germans out. Three attacks were made to this end, one at Arleux (28–9 April) and two on the Scarpe (23–4 April and 3 May). They failed to dislodge the enemy. Twelve days later, on 15 May, the battles of Arras, of which these were almost the final flickers, petered to an inconclusive close, leaving the Canadian capture of Vimy Ridge very poorly exploited.

However, Arras and Vimy did have uncomfortable consequences for General von Falkenhausen. He was fired for his gross unpreparedness. The French General Nivelle of whom so much, perhaps too much, had been expected was also removed from his post after his Champagne offensive – launched on 16 April in the vilest possible weather – failed to break through the German defence-in-depth. The French lost 100,000 men and on 3 May, the French armies mutinied. On 15 May, Nivelle was replaced as French C-in-C by General Henri Philippe Pétain.

In these circumstances, with the British effort round Arras something of a damp squib and the French campaign an embarrassment and disaster, it was not surprising that so much lustre had attached itself to the Canadians' exploit on Vimy Ridge. This was, in the first place, the first Allied effort in the First World War that could even vaguely be called a success, and the gains made there proved in time to be permanent.

Vimy gave a striking demonstration of just how much could be achieved and just how quickly when warfare was conducted along intelligent, well-coordinated and efficient lines. Marshal Joffre and the other apostles of attrition had shown that sending thousands of men to certain death in the hope of swamping the enemy by force of numbers was neither necessary nor efficacious if battles were to be won.

But in practice the lessons of Vimy Ridge were forgotten as soon as they had been learned. For in the history of the First World War, the Vimy battle makes a fresh filling in a stale and melancholy military sandwich. Six months before it was fought, the battles of the Somme ended. Here, British and French troops were thrown at the enemy in droves – 350,000 of them were mown down like corn. Six months after Vimy Ridge came the battle which cost the British 250,000 men and which serves, even today, as a synonym for nauseating waste and mindless butchery – Passchendaele.

Passchendaele (1917)

Hubert Essame

Much has been written about Passchendaele, or the Third Battle of Ypres, 1917 – a lot of it by writers who were not there. In the process, they have created many myths ranging from the belief that the troops were 'lions led by donkeys', and that the generals lived in luxury chateaux whilst the soldiers died in the mud, to the claim that Field Marshal Sir Douglas Haig was a 'great master of the field' and justified in his decision not only to stage an offensive on the grand scale east of Ypres on 31 July 1917 but also to continue attacking there for a further 14 weeks. I belong to neither of these schools of thought but prefer to tell what happened to me and what I saw just north of the Menin Road in late July and August.

There was something sinister about the ruins of Ypres in 1917. The painters Hieronimus Bosch, Gustave Doré and Sidney Nolan, had they been living at the time, could, perhaps, have conveyed the eerie horror of the place. A stink of decay from the moat mixed with that of HE defiled the air. In June and July 1917 it was under day and night bombardment. Everybody going to the front had to pass either through the Menin Gate and take the road to Hellfire Corner or the Lille Gate whence a plank road called the Warrington Track ran just north of Zillebeke Lake. Men anxiously waited for the next shell as they marched over the cobble stones of the *Grande Place*. In the ramparts there was some cover from the shellfire. By night the Very lights of the front line cast a loop round the city.

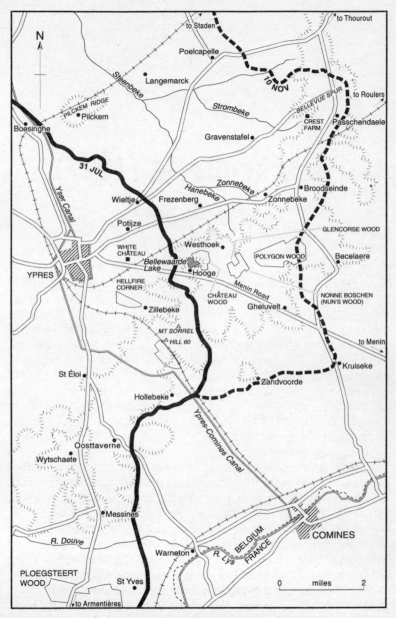

3.7 Passchendaele, July–November 1917

Never can the point of attack have been more blatantly advertised. On 7 June we, 2nd Battalion, The Northamptonshire Regiment were in reserve for the Messines battle but not used. A few days later, we, with the rest of our division, the 8th Infantry, were moved into the line to hold the sector about Hooge and to familiarize outselves with the ground over which we were destined to attack. Our guns were so closely packed together for the coming offensive that the northern half had to fire for one part of the night and the southern half for the other. It would have been impossible otherwise for the traffic to get through. Daylight movement east of Ypres was impossible – except for individuals. On our divisional front over 2,000 men worked like moles every night burying cables, digging dugouts at Halfway House and carrying stores to forward dumps under almost continuous shellfire.

Every yard of the Menin Road and the Warrington Track was 'taped'. Abandoned wagons, corpses, dead horses and mules lined the roads. Limbs and bodies in the twisted distortion of death festooned the shell-holes. Commanding a working party on these roads was à nightmare. It was usual for over 20 per cent of the men to fail to return.

General Sir Hubert Gough, GOC Fifth Army, planned to attack on a front of seven and a half miles from the Zillebeke – Zandvoorde road to Boesinghe with ten infantry divisions. By early July he had concentrated 752 heavy and medium guns, 324 4.5-in howitzers and 1,098 18-pounders to blast his troops forward two miles by a methodical advance in three stages – to the Blue Line about 1,250 yards distant, the Black Line 900 yards farther on and finally a further 1,400 yards to the Green Line. With communications between infantry and artillery as primitive as they were, this may well seem a clumsy plan. But it should be noted that in March and May 1918 the Germans executed successful attacks along these lines on the Somme and the Chemin des Dames.

About 15 miles west of Ypres a full-scale replica of the German positions we were to attack had been marked out with broad tapes in the standing corn. Every day in hot sunshine, under the eyes of the divisional and brigade commanders, we deployed as if for the real attack, advancing behind an imaginary barrage represented by men with red flags moving forward at the rate of 100 yards in four minutes in 25-yard lifts. We had two companies forward and two companies behind them in depth – each company attacking in two waves. They were all intended to go straight through to their objectives leaving one of their four platoons to follow and deal with enemy over-run. Much emphasis was laid on the need to keep as close as possible to the bursting shells of the barrage. All officers also attended an exposition of the divisional plan on a large-scale relief model. This envisaged an advance on a two-brigade front each with four tanks. Two battalions of each brigade would take the Blue Line. Then the other two would pass through to take the Black Line. A pause would then be necessary while the artillery was moved forward. When this was done the third brigade, supported by 12 tanks, would pass through and capture the Green Line.

It had been intended to launch the attack on 25 July. Accordingly we moved back into the line about Hooge on the 23rd. The preliminary day and night bombardment had reached a crescendo. We now found that the French, who were due to attack in the north, were not ready, so the attack had to be put back to the 31st.

As a result of 1916 experience on the Somme each unit going into action left behind within easy reach a so-called 'battle surplus' or cadre consisting of understudies at every level of command from lance-corporal upwards. There were about a hundred all told. I was left behind with this party as understudy to the adjutant.

On the afternoon of 26 July a signal from brigade HQ ordered me forward at once. It was a scorching afternoon. The road as far as the outskirts of Ypres was choked with transport, raising huge clouds of dust. Just short of the railway station on the western outskirts all traffic stopped. On reaching the Lille Gate I took the Warrington Track. Not a soul seemed to be moving in the wilderness ahead. It was not a pleasant walk. The observer of a German 77 mm battery apparently thought I presented a worthwhile target and sniped at me all the way to battalion HQ by Zillebeke Lake. Here I found utter confusion. The surface shelter which housed the HQ had sustained a direct hit and the adjutant, the Intelligence officer, the signals officer and the chief clerk had all been blown up and killed or evacuated. Even the leather-faced old RSM looked off colour. But he was still able to call my attention to three jars of rum which had been smashed by the explosion – a contingency Higher Authority was likely to treat with suspicion unless vouched for by unimpeachable evidence.

My CO, 26-year-old Lieutenant-Colonel C. G. Buckle, MC, moved the HQ to a vast dugout by the ruins of Halfway House. This shelter was a triumph of engineering under the marsh, designed to hold about 3,000 men before the attack. The greater part of the battalion were already in residence. There was just room for one man to pass another and the floor was a foot deep in grey mud. Pumping went on continuously. The smell was appalling – a delicate blend of marshes, sewage and human sweat. This vast sewer was spasmodically lit by electric light.

The Germans knew all the exits and kept up a continuous bombardment on them. Every visit to the latrines outside was a dash for life; day and night a never-ending stream of men stepped over us *en route* for the hell outside. We remained in these insanitary quarters for four days – jammed shoulder to shoulder. When the light failed and the supply of candles ran out we sat in darkness.

My main worry concerned not the loss of all the paper about the attack but casualties inflicted on the battalion signallers and runners, amounting to 50 per cent a day. When, on my first night, the signal came through postponing the attack for four days I foresaw that we would probably have to start the battle short-handed. In the event the misty weather on the 27th and 28th and rain on the 30th, ominous though they were in other respects, cut down the casualty rate.

A message on the afternoon of the 30th confirmed that zero hour would be at 0350 the next day. On the previous two nights the German artillery had unleashed exceptionally heavy shelling on our form-up area. There was therefore a feeling of acute tension when we all filed out of the great dugout at about 2100 to assembly trenches just north of the Menin Road at Hooge. Just in front of the assembly trenches a party had already laid out the tapes marking the start line. It was a dark and cloudy night.

The CO, the Intelligence Officer and I moved to Birr Cross Roads in the middle of the two rear companies with our little party of signallers trailing D3 cable and carrying some unlucky pigeons in baskets. At 0300 all was quiet; half an hour later all companies had reported that they were formed up on the tapes. Suddenly at 0350 the sky behind and on our flanks erupted. The blast was so deafening that we jammed our fingers in our ears; the ground shook. We could see the flashes of the barrage in the murk ahead. There were just a few silvery streaks in the sky to the east. The swish of the 18-pounder shells tempted us to crouch down. In fact, although we could not see them, the two leading companies advancing on compass bearings were clinging to the barrage and moving forward each time it jumped a further 25 yards. The reserve companies and our own headquarters soon started to move forward in the gloom as well.

We reached what had been the German front line. Here, the wire had been blown to bits by our bombardments of the preceding fortnight. Slowly the light strengthened. We could now see about 100 yards and all around us men moved steadily forward. The going was fairly good at first. Five hundred yards farther on we found the two leading companies on their objective rounding up a number of dazed Germans. The two reserve companies now pressed through towards their objective on the Bellwaarde Ridge and soon struck a ravine of sorts full of water and surrounded by the dead stumps of Château Wood. Here were smouldering dugouts which had been treated to a barrage of Thermite (incendiary bombs) fired from mortars. There were also some pillboxes which had been knocked over by heavy artillery fire.

Ploughing through the mud, the two reserve companies could be seen approaching the crest of the ridge which was our final objective. When the CO and I reached a point on the crest they were mopping up some dugouts running along the northern edge of the wood. It was now quite light. We established HQ in a large shell-hole. I could hear a lot of machine-gun fire 100 yards or so away to our left. Evidently the battle here was not yet over. About 100 ft above our heads an RE8 scout plane was sounding its klaxon horn. Looking up I could see the pilot distinctly. The time had come to put out the ground strips indicating our HQ's position and the capture of our objective. The pilot seemed satisfied, for he put the nose of his aircraft up and made off. One of his friends failed to get back to safety. His aircraft had been caught, probably by our own shells, and was burning a few hundred yards away on our left.

I wrote 'Objective gained' and our map reference on the flimsy message form which the signals sergeant promptly attached to the leg of a pigeon which was released. I could not have said much else at the time. At that very moment Captain T. R. Colyer-Fergusson was winning his Victoria Cross just 200 yards away. As his 'B' Company approached the ridge he found himself in danger of losing the barrage which was already 100 yards ahead. Right in front of him was an enemy trench well wired and occupied by a machine-gun crew which the barrage had missed. Hastily collecting about ten men, amongst whom was Sergeant W. G. Boulding and his own orderly Pte. B. Bell, he rushed forward and gained a footing in the trench which was on the crest of the ridge. Almost at once a German company counter-attacked. Colyer-Fergusson and his little party shot down 20 or 30 of them with rifle fire and the survivors surrendered. The rest of the British company now came up. At the same time a German machine-gun opened fire on them. Leaving his men to hold the trench Colyer-Fergusson and his orderly captured the gun. He then turned the gun on to another group of Germans, killing a large number of them. A few minutes later he was hit in the head by a stray machine-gun bullet and died instantly.

Meanwhile 'C' Company on the right had also had a tough struggle for its objective. Here, Second Lieutenant Frost rushed a post which held a machine-gun which was shooting down men of 1st Battalion, The Worcester Regiment, on our right flank. Frost killed a German officer and 14 men. By now Col. Buckle had gone forward and ordered the two companies to consolidate about 150 yards ahead. The liaison officer from the Worcesters reported that they too were on their objective. It was now daylight. I could now see the 1st Battalion, The Sherwood Foresters, and 2nd Battalion, The East Lancashire Regiment, passing through us and going strong *en route* to the Black Line 1,200 yards ahead on the Westhoek Ridge.

Hours of uncertainty, misunderstanding and confusion descended on the battlefield. It took me a long time to grasp what was actually happening in front and on our flanks. Walking wounded of the Foresters and E. Lancashires said their attack was going well but that they were losing a lot of men from machine-gun fire from their east flank and, surprisingly, from their right rear as well. About 0630 these two battalions were apparently on their objective on the Westhoek Ridge but fighting was still going on. About the same time our own company in Château Wood reported that they were being subjected to very heavy machine-gun fire from their east flank. Looking back I saw our own GOC, Brigadier-General H. W. Cobham, DSO, coming towards us with his brigade major. Suddenly quite close to us the brigade major (Captain A. Holmes Scott, Royal Engineers) was killed by a machine-gun bullet.

On the edge of the tree stumps of Château Wood two tanks were bogged down. They were the only tanks I saw that day. Coming forward from the direction of Hellfire Corner there was a mass of troops from 25th Brigade (Brigadier-General C. Coffin, DSO), destined to carry forward the advance beyond the Westhoek Ridge to the Green Line. About this time my CO, while trying to find out what the situation was on our right flank, was wounded and evacuated. Fortunately Lieutenant-Colonel S. G. Latham, MC, the second-in-command, had found it impossible to restrain himself from coming forward to see if he could be of any help. He never bothered to take cover. We had breakfast – biscuits and cold boiled bacon from our haversacks washed down with cold tea. Latham then went towards the right flank to find out what was really going on there. A lot of machine-gun fire was coming from Nonnebosschen, Glencorse and Polygon Woods. Nobody seemed able to say definitely which group of trees was which. The Worcesters apparently were out of touch with 30th Division which was rumoured to have failed to take Clapham Junction.

The sound of machine-gun fire from this direction continued. About this time our signallers reported that they had line communication with brigade HQ. When I raised the instrument the brigade Intelligence officer's voice seemed far away. I gathered, however, that 30th Division had been checked but were staging another attack on Sanctuary Wood and Stirling Castle. About 1000, the guns on our own front opened up in all-out support for 25th Brigade, now said to be near the final objective for the day – the Green Line on the far side of the Hanebeek stream. Despite the obscure situation on their right flank they seemed to be doing well.

Their progress was a matter of great interest to us as we were due to relieve one of their battalions when it reached its objective. About this time we were heavily shelled. Brigade HQ ordered us to send 60 men at once to Westhoek to act as additional stretcher bearers. A steady stream of walking wounded flowed from the front. They reported that 25th Brigade's three assault battalions were on their objective but had lost a lot of men. Some said they had got their objectives but had been counter-attacked and driven back. Large numbers of Germans had been seen arriving in lorries. By now it was at least clear that they still held Glencorse Wood and Nonnebosschen. The hours dragged by in an atmosphere of continued uncertainty. A wounded officer from 25th Brigade said they were being slowly pushed back to the Westhoek Ridge. Another reported later that Brig.-Gen. Coffin had been forward with his troops all the morning and was now rallying what was left of his brigade on the Westhoek Ridge.

All day the skies had been overcast. At about 1600 it started to rain in torrents. The shell-holes rapidly filled with water. Men were soon sinking knee-deep in the mud. The prolonged preliminary bombardment had shattered the drainage system and the churned-up earth held water like a sponge. The soldiers' ground-sheet capes were poor protection. Very soon we were all soaked to the skin. Only after dark did I fully understand what had happened. The 30th Division on our right, in a maze of shattered tree stumps and wire, had lost the barrage soon after the start. All the tanks supporting them had almost immediately become immobilized in the stinking bog. In the whole day, they had advanced less than 1,000 yards to Stirling Castle after using up all their battalions. For them it had been a nightmare – almost as bad as the first day of the Somme. It was clear that the Germans still held the high ground of the Gheluvelt Plateau at Clapham Junction and Glencorse Wood. The rest of Fifth Army on our left had had better luck and advanced about 2,000 yards.

It rained all night. Soon after dawn 10th Battalion, The Cheshire Regiment (25th Division) arrived to relieve us and we moved back in small parties towards Ypres. For the moment the guns were silent. Stretcher bearers were still bringing back their heavy loads through the all-pervading swamp of glutinous mud. Compared with 25th Brigade's battalions our casualties of 13 killed and 189 wounded had been light. Altogether the division had lost 160 officers and 3,005 men, mainly due to deadly machine-gun fire from the east flank. This was a fifth of the total British loss on 31 July but we had 600 prisoners to show for it. The divisional artillery exposed in the open for six weeks before the attack had lost more men from mustard gas and HE than they had incurred in the whole preceding period from 1914.

We spent the next ten days in comparative comfort in billets in the little town of Steenvoorde near Poperinghe. The Corps commander, after congratulating us on our efforts, informed us that we would have the privilege of continuing the battle in the same area when the weather improved. I do not recall any unbounded enthusiasm at his announcement, but if anyone disapproved he kept his mouth shut. Meanwhile, the rain continued unabated. On 13 August we returned to the line of shell-holes we had captured two weeks previously with two companies forward just short of Westhoek. Conditions had been bad when we left; they were even worse now. All the holes were full to the brim with water. Everywhere it was hard going through the mud. In some places duckboard tracks sank out of sight almost as soon as they were laid. Aerial photographs showed that the Hanebeek, which had been a mere trickle on 31 July, was now a broad stream.

This time the advance to the Green Line which we had captured but failed to hold on the 31st was to be carried out immediately south of the Ypres–Roulers railway on a two-brigade front with Coffin's 25th Brigade on the right. The Northamptonshires were now attached to this brigade as a reserve. On our right Polygon Wood, Glencorse Wood and Nonnebosschen were still in enemy hands. It was abundantly clear that if the 56th Division attacking on our right failed to capture them we would once again be out on a limb and caught under fire as we had been a fortnight earlier.

The battle on 16 August remained imprinted on my mind because it was the only time I ever saw anyone in the act of winning a VC. This time we took into action only 13 officers and 400 men. Zero hour was 0445. The three attacking units of 25th Brigade, 2nd Battalion, The Royal Berkshire Regiment, 1st Battalion, The Royal Irish Rifles and 2nd Battalion, The Lincolnshire Regiment, got off on time despite being shelled when forming up. As the light strengthened, reports passed to us from brigade HQ gave the impression that all was going well and that the Hanebeek had been reached and crossed. Later, however, news came once more that they were being caught in enfilade by machine-guns on right and left flanks. Wounded and stretcher bearers passing by said that Gen. Coffin had gone forward to the hard-pressed front.

In lulls during the bombardment we could once more hear prolonged machine-gun fire from Nonnebosschen and Polygon Wood. Col. Latham therefore ordered Captain C. E. Blake to find out what the situation was there. Working his way to the right, Blake discovered that 56th (1st London) Division had found the tangled mass of dead woods around Inverness Copse and Glencorse Wood concealing considerable numbers of unlocated machine-guns which had been too much for it. There could be no doubt that Coffin's brigade was isolated 1,200 yards ahead with open flanks. The expected counter-attack came at about 0930 under a savage bombardment of shells and machine-gun fire. As the morning dragged on there could be no escaping the fact that 25th Brigade were being shot to pieces and slowly pressed back. A little after noon Gen. Coffin ordered Capt. Blake's two forward companies to come forward at once and our other two companies to join him on the Westhoek Ridge with all speed. When we arrived a terrifying situation prevailed. The German shellfire was hellish. Ours must have been just as bad for them. Our forward observation officers had now brought down a dense curtain of fire across our front. Just behind the Westhoek Ridge the massed Vickers guns of the Divisional machine-gun companies had opened up with good observation and deadly effect. In the din you had to shout to make yourself heard.

On the ridge we found Coffin standing upright in the open. He welcomed us with a smile: 'Those two companies of yours are a fine lot. They got here just in time.' We then discovered that he had led the counter-attack with them and halted the Germans about 150 yards ahead. He and Latham then took the rest of the battalion forward and patched up some sort of line with Royal Berkshire survivors and filled the gap between the right flank and what was left of 167th Brigade (56th Division). Neither Coffin, nor Latham for that matter, showed the slightest inclination to take cover or indeed of being in any way perturbed.

About 1700 quiet descended on the front. It seemed that both sides had had enough for the time being. The sun made a fitful appearance. Three of Coffin's battalions had lost half their strength – the Royal Irish Rifles had only one officer and 60 men left. They were still, however, a disciplined body prepared to fight on. So long as Coffin remained with them they would have gone on to the last man.

Within two weeks my battalion had lost about 330 officers and men. Compared with other 8th Division battalions we escaped lightly. On 16 August our divisional loss came to 81 officers and 2,074 men. When Haig inspected the infantry on 21 August only 3,950 of the 12,000 or so available three weeks previously could be paraded. I do not recollect anything he said. According to the Divisional History, however, he 'gave the division many words of encouragement and thanks, inspiring all ranks by his generous appreciation of what they had done.'

Junior officers in most battles see only the local picture. Historians therefore tend to treat their accounts with caution. Because I had the luck to act as adjutant in both these battles I probably got a broader impression of what went on than most of my fellow second lieutenants. By some fluke, a copy of the three-page report I wrote on the battle a day or so afterwards has survived. I recollect being very proud of this literary effort at the time and feeling somewhat peeved when my CO signed it after only a cursory glance before dispatch to brigade HQ. I realize that my comments are open to the charge of bias. The loss of so many of my friends may well have embittered me. But, I can at least say that in my limited experience the accusation that divisional and brigade commanders ordered their men to face dangers they were not prepared to share themselves is unfair. Even in minor operations they had little scope for initiative and no option other than to obey orders. The casualty rate in battalion commanders (eight out of our 12 on 31 July), company commanders and lieutenants was proportionately far in excess of that of men in the ranks.

What I failed to understand after these two battles was why Haig chose to attack in an area of reclaimed marshland which two years' experience had already shown would revert to bog when it rained. It should have been obvious that this was no place to employ the 136 primitive tanks committed to battle here. Why did he so blatantly advertise his intention of attacking east of Ypres for six weeks before the actual assault by a vast increase in traffic, a gigantic forward build-up of dumps and a fortnight's preliminary bombardment? This mystified me at the time and still does. Having finally shown his hand and staged a fiasco on the 31 July why did he decide to go on with the battle hoping for fine weather? I was even more astonished when we came back to the muddy horror of Passchendaele in November 1917.

Cambrai (1917)

Bryan Cooper

> Accusing as I do without exception all the great Allied offensives of 1915, 1916 and 1917, as needless and wrongly conceived operations of infinite cost, I am bound to reply to the question, what else could be done? And I answer it, pointing to the Battle of Cambrai. *This* could have been done. This in many variants, this in larger and better forms ought to have been done.

Such was Winston Churchill's belief in 1927 and the perspective has only been enlarged since.

At first sight the Battle of Cambrai in November 1917 was no more decisive than most battles fought on the Western Front. Indeed, the initial British advance through the Hindenberg Line that gave such promise of success, and caused church bells in England to ring victory peals for the first time since the Boer War, was repulsed by a German counter-attack that actually took back more ground than had been won. But it was the means of making that original advance, by the first-ever massed attack by tanks with close air-support and an unregistered artillery barrage which established Cambrai as a milestone in the history of warfare. It was a prelude to the tank's decisive role at the Battle of Amiens in August 1918 which signalled the final defeat of Germany.

Although the first, premature and piecemeal use of tanks by the British on the Somme in September 1916 wasted a great chance, it must be remembered that not only tanks were new but also the whole concept of their use. Many Allied commanders continued to disregard their potential but Field-Marshal Sir Douglas Haig, the British C-in-C, made a personal request for 1,000 improved tanks to be built during 1917. It was probably inevitable that the first tanks should be misused in wartime conditions, while those most concerned, crews, designers and commanders, learned from their mistakes. Unfortunately, this was not true of the latter during most of 1917.

The year opened promisingly for the embryo tank force. While a shortage of materials at home reduced Haigh's order, there were some 200 tanks available by March, not only improved Mark Is but also a few Mark IVs. These were similar in outline and armament, but had 50 per cent thicker armor in the vital parts, against German armor-piercing ammunition. The Tank Corps, as it was named in June, became better established with at least a rudimentary training procedure. It had also produced its first master of tank tactics and strategy in the person of Lieutenant-Colonel John Frederick Charles Fuller. As Chief General Staff Officer (GSOI) to Brigadier-General Hugh J. Elles, the Tank Corps' first and 36-year-old commander, he devised many of the principles that were to govern the employment of tanks in battle up to and during the Second World War. Fuller saw the tank primarily as a mobile fortress which could escort the infantry into the enemy's defenses and emphasized the necessity for surprise. He also saw the need to mass not disperse tanks, and preferably on ground that had not been reduced to a quagmire by constant shelling.

Such concepts were too unorthodox for most of the general staff at Haig's GHQ, especially the artillery commanders who believed that only a long and massive bombardment could soften up the enemy and cut his barbed wire as a prelude to any attack, regardless of the warning this gave. The first 1917 use of tanks was in April during the Battle of Arras, in which some 40 took part. Again strung out along a wide front, diminishing their impact, and despite individual successes, most became bogged down in the mud and unable to avoid German shellfire. At Vimy Ridge, eight tanks were to assist the Canadian Corps, but these foundered before they could even fight.

An even greater tragedy occurred at Bullecourt (NW of Cambrai) where 11 tanks were to help the 4th Australian Division. Due to a heavy snowstorm the attack was postponed for a day; the tanks stood out as easy targets against the white background on a bright clear morning. Nine were knocked out before they reached the

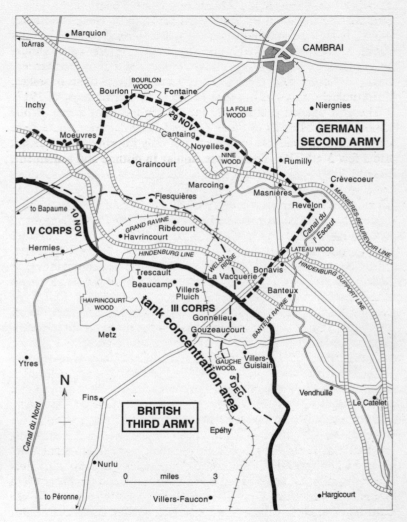

3.8   The Battle of Cambrai, November 1917

Hindenberg Line, and the remaining two were captured, giving the Germans their first chance to examine the new weapon. Australian infantry, following behind the tanks from which they expected protection, suffered appalling losses. They lost their faith in tanks for more than a year.

The worst tank ordeal of all came in Flanders, where the Corps took part in Haig's grand plan to break through the Ypres salient. The start of the offensive, at mine-sprung Messines Ridge on 7 June, was a great success, but 40 new Mark IV tanks were hardly needed, although they gave valuable support to the infantry. It was during the main campaign, begun on 31 July, which resolved itself into the terrible struggle for the village of Passchendaele that tanks, in common with the British Army as a whole, experienced their greatest catastrophe.

The preliminary artillery bombardment reached its highest peak of the war; when in 13 days over four million shells were fired from 3,000 guns, one gun to every six yards of the 11-mile front. This churned the ground into a dreadful condition made even worse by several weeks of non-stop rain and flooding in Flanders. Some 200 tanks were mustered for the Ypres offensive, and when it petered out at the beginning of November, hardly any remained in one piece. Most had sunk deep into the mud and were destroyed by enemy fire, to the point where the Menin Road was known as the 'tank grave-yard'. After three months of bloody fighting, total British casualties were nearly 400,000 men – for the gain of four miles of territory.

GHQ was still unable to see the true value of tanks and held on to an attitude typified by one army commander, who stated after the Ypres campaign: 'One, tanks are unable to negotiate bad ground; two, the ground on a battlefield will always be bad; three, therefore, tanks are no good on a battlefield.' The War Office in London had further doubts about whether to build more tanks. But although few realized it at the time, Passchendaele was the last of the senseless battles of attrition, fought in despair of conducting the war in any other way. For on another part of the front the Tank Corps had quietly been planning an attack in conditions of their own choosing, on dry hard ground, and according to their own tactics, that would show that indeed there was another way.

The town of Cambrai lay seven miles behind the Hindenberg Line, opposite General Sir Julian H. G. Byng's Third Army. It was a region of open, rolling countryside and firm ground covered by uncultivated grass that had seen little fighting during the war. The Germans considered their fortifications to be impregnable and were content to hold them while the Allies wore themselves out in reckless assaults elsewhere. As far back as mid-June, in a paper written on the future employment of tanks, Col. Fuller had suggested the idea of a major tank raid, not to win ground but to destroy or capture enemy troops and guns. One area he thought suitable was the country between St Quentin and Cambrai. The idea was originally turned down at GHQ, but early in August, support for it came from Gen. Byng, already thinking of an attack in the Cambrai area.

Further support came from Haig himself. As it became obvious even to him that Passchendaele was a disaster, he wanted to launch a quick operation with a good chance of immediate success in order to raise morale at home and among his own troops. He believed the Tank Corps plan might work. If it failed, he could always blame the tanks for not fulfilling their earlier promise. In such an event, it was not likely that the Tank Corps could have survived. On 13 October, he gave his approval for the attack to take place on 20 November. Conditions were now not nearly so favorable. Flanders had drained the Army's resources, most divisions were battle-weary and under strength, and on top of that the collapse of the Italian Front at Caporetto on 24 October meant rushing five British divisions to Italy to hold the line, leaving Third Army short of reserves.

Byng's intention was to break through the Hindenberg Line along a six-mile front between two canals, the Canal de L'Escaut (St Quentin) on the right and the unfinished and waterless Canal du Nord on the left. This was to be accomplished by three brigades of Mark IV tanks, followed by six infantry divisions with support from another two and three more held in reserve. While the tanks and infantry captured the two main features of the area, the Flesquières and Bourlon ridges, five cavalry divisions (40,000 horsemen) were to pour through the gap and isolate the town of Cambrai. The German forces would be cut off and rounded up, then the way would be clear to drive NE towards Valenciennes. From then onwards the plan was rather vague, but conformed to Haig's doctrine of attacking the German flanks after a breakthrough and 'rolling up the front'. Supporting the attack would be 1,003 guns, almost a third of 6-in calibre or more, and 14 squadrons (289 aircraft) of the Royal Flying Corps. This novel co-operation between tanks and aircraft was the origin of the German *Blitzkrieg* in the Second World War.

Cambrai itself was an important target, being a major communications center where four railways and a number of main roads and waterways converged, and German defenses were therefore particularly strong. They lay in a wide path, up to five miles deep, between the British front and Cambrai, with three main lines of trenches dug much wider than usual, up to 16 ft and to a depth of 18 ft. Even if tanks were used, the three defending divisions were confident that such vehicles would be unable to cross, and indeed the Mark IV only had a 10 ft trench-crossing capability. Each trench system included concrete dugouts in which were massed batteries of machine-guns and lay behind acres of dense barbed wire, nowhere less than 50 yards thick. British observers had estimated that it would take five weeks of artillery bombardment to cut down this wire in the normal way.

Col. Fuller reckoned that tanks could crush the barbed wire, although there was always a danger of it becoming entangled in their tracks. The sheer size of the trenches was the biggest obstacle. An answer was finally provided by the Tank Corps Central Workshops. Bundles of brushwood of the kind used for road repairs were bound together by thick chains to make huge 10-ft-long fascines, each weighing 1.75 tons. One would be carried on the roof of each fighting tank, to be dropped into the trenches to form a bridge across.

The fighting tanks were to operate an ingenious leap-frogging system, in sections of three. An advance tank would go forward, flatten the German wire for the oncoming infantry, then reaching the first trench would turn left and drive along the edge, firing down at the enemy to protect the two main-body tanks following 100 yards behind. The first of these would drop its fascine in the trench, cross over, and give covering fire in front of the second trench for the next tank. This in turn would cross the second trench and move forward to attack the third and last line of trenches. Meanwhile, the advance tank would have come up to drop its fascine in the third trench, leading its two companions into the open country beyond. Four platoons of infantry were to follow closely (25–50 yards) behind each tank section to capture and garrison the trenches as they were overcome. Finally, 32 special wire-pulling tanks would roll up the flattened wire with grapnels to make broad pathways for the cavalry advance. In addition to these and 378 fighting tanks, there were 54 supply carriers with nine wireless tanks, a telephone cable laying tank and two bridge layers – making a grand total of 476, the largest tank force ever concentrated.

The week before the attack was due to begin, and after ten days training in the technique described above, the tanks were brought up to the front by rail in great secrecy, arriving by night so that even the British infantry did not know of their presence. Late on the afternoon of 19 November, the tanks began to leave their lying-up positions in woods and fields and made their way to the start-line. Dawn came up very slowly, grey and overcast with a fine ground mist. The shapes of the woods and ridges ahead began to emerge out of the darkness. Coveys of partridges sprang up and larks and crows took to the sky as the British infantry began to cut through their own wire, ready for the assault. There was no sign of the Germans, hidden deep in their trenches and dugouts, confident of the protection given by long, dense belts of barbed wire.

At zero hour, 0620, there was a devastating roar as 1,000 British guns opened up, most firing for the first time, having had their targets mapped and not registered by ranging shots, while from out of the sky swept four RFC squadrons, flying low and spraying the German trenches with machine-gun fire. The Battle of Cambrai had begun. And from the beginning it was different from previous battles. The artillery barrage, instead of continuing for days and even weeks, giving the Germans time to bring up reinforcements, almost immediately began to lift towards targets farther on. At the same time, the tanks moved slowly forwards down tape-marked lanes, the sound of their engines hidden by the noise of the guns and their course set by compass. At last they were to be used in a surprise attack as the pioneers of tank development had always intended.

Right in the center and aboard 'Hilda', one of the leading tanks, was Brig.-Gen. Elles, carrying the new Corps flag and insisting on the right to lead his men into the first large-scale tank attack in history. It was one of the very few occasions in the First World War that a general did so. The sight of so many tanks lumbering out of the half-light of dawn, their huge fascines on top making them appear even more like monstrous, prehistoric animals, was too much for many of the German troops, who fled in panic. Those who remained were dismayed to find that their armor-piercing bullets could not penetrate these new Mark IV tanks. And when the tanks opened fire with their 6-pounders and Lewis machine-guns, the demoralization of the enemy was complete. A tank commander called it 'almost a

cake-walk'. And it was recorded that 'the infantry had walked behind
the tanks smoking and with practically nothing to do except mop up
a few dugouts.'

By midday, the tanks had broken through the three trench systems
as planned and advanced nearly five miles on a six-mile front, a
deeper penetration than that achieved after the three months of
fighting just over at Passchendaele. The day had yielded captures
totalling 8,000 men, 123 guns and 281 machine-guns: two divisions
had been annihilated. At HQ German Supreme Command, there
was consternation. An immediate counter-attack was ordered, but
the necessary reinforcements could not be brought up for at least
48 hours. Now the value of a swift surprise attack became evident.

So serious was the situation that General Erich Ludendorff, commanding the German armies, considered an extensive withdrawal of
the whole Cambrai front, one which might have led to a general
retreat. But the attack's success had also surprised British GHQ.
In fact, many commanders refused to believe it and valuable time
was lost while they awaited confirmation of reports from the front.
The morning objectives, with one important exception, had been
taken with such relative ease that some advanced infantry units were
content to remain in the captured German trenches, so much more
comfortable than their own. In some instances the infantry failed
to keep up with the tanks, which later had to withdraw for lack of
support. But there still remained the five divisions of cavalry massed
behind the British lines waiting to advance. They had waited for such
a chance in nearly every other battle previously fought. Now it had
come. The great breakthrough had been made.

Unfortunately, Cavalry Corps HQ was five miles behind the front
line, and local commanders were not empowered to make decisions
on the spot. By the time orders came through to advance, the
momentum of the attack had faltered. And in one vital sector of the
center, at Flesquières, the German 54th Reserve Division was still
holding out. The way should have been clear for 1st Cavalry Division
to pass through the village and move on to the all-important objective
of Bourlon Wood on the ridge covering the approach to Cambrai. But
it was here that the one hold-up of the morning had occurred, largely
due to a lack of co-operation between tanks and the infantry of 51st
Highland Division, for which their commander, Major-General G.
M. Harper, was largely responsible. He did not approve of tanks, just
as earlier he had opposed machine-gun development, and ignored the

instructions laid down by the Tank Corps. Instead of keeping his men in files close behind the tanks, to deal with German artillery, he made them follow in extended order 100 yards or more behind. They had to waste valuable time looking for the paths that the tanks had cut through the barbed wire. Meanwhile, as the tanks pressed on alone towards the crest of Flesquières Ridge, they came under fire from several German 77 mm field-gun batteries. Sixteen were destroyed (a quarter of the figure lost to gunfire), with no survivors among the crews. By the time the Highlanders advanced to this point, the Germans had regrouped and the fighting here lasted until evening. Only then, outflanked on both sides, did the defenders withdraw. But this delay prevented the cavalry advance until next day, and the chance of taking Bourlon without a fight was lost.

By nightfall on the 20th, 179 of the 378 tanks that had moved forward at dawn were out of action. Many of those remaining had fought almost continuously for 16 hours and required maintenance. In spite of the great success achieved, the infantry and cavalry had not taken full advantage of it – perhaps because no one really expected such a breakthrough after the deadlock of earlier battles. Meanwhile, on the German side, five reserve divisions were beginning to arrive around Cambrai. Haig did in fact see the danger. But having provided the British public at home with a victory, the first one for so long, he did not wish to call a halt. The offensive continued.

On the 22nd, the British attack was resumed and very nearly succeeded. With the help of tanks, the infantry managed to fight their way into Bourlon village, while several other tanks almost reached Cambrai itself. But with little by way of reserves to call on, the British offensive lost its impetus. The Germans fought back with grim determination, and for another five days the battle swung first one way, then another. The fighting reached its peak on the 27th in the village of Fontaine, almost within sight of Cambrai. The situation at Bourlon was much the same, with part of the wood and village still in enemy hands. By the end of that day it was apparent to all, even Haig, that the offensive had to be called off. There were just not enough reserves to keep it going.

One week of fighting had achieved little more than the initial success gained in the first few hours, although on the credit side, apart from ground gained, over 11,000 prisoners had been taken, together with 142 guns, 456 machine-guns, 74 trench mortars and large quantities of stores and ammunition. After a hurried conference at GHQ, it was decided to withdraw to a defensive line on Flesquières Ridge, making use of the former German trenches. As far as the British were concerned, the Battle of Cambrai was over. The remaining tanks were pulled back to prepare for entrainment to their winter quarters.

But no one had reckoned with German intentions. On the morning of 30 November, while the British were carrying out an orderly withdrawal, eight German divisions delivered a massive counter-stroke that took 6,000 prisoners and 158 guns on that day, in many ways just as sudden and surprising as the original British attack. The German plan was nothing less than to cut off and destroy all British troops in the salient formed by their advance on Cambrai. Only 63 tanks remained in the area. These were quickly rounded up and sent into action to help the infantry. They made a vital contribution to preventing what could have been a major disaster. Even so, by the time the German offensive ended in a blinding snowstorm on 7 December they had won back as much ground as they had lost and achieved a more or less even balance in casualties and prisoners, which totalled about 45,000 for both sides.

It was by no means the worst British defeat of the year, but after the promising victory of 20 November, the final result seemed just that much more of a bitter failure. There was a public outcry at home and even a Court of Enquiry which whitewashed the generals and put most of the blame on the junior officers, NCOs, and men. But this time, at least, the tanks could not be blamed. No one could deny their brilliant initial success. They suffered for it as well, particularly during the German counter-attack. Of the 4,000 officers and men of the Tank Corps who had taken part in the whole battle, a total of 1,153 were killed or wounded. Less than a third of the 476 tanks returned to base and all of them required extensive repairs. In fact, few saw action again, for the Mark IV was replaced in 1918 by the more efficient and more heavily armored Mark V. Haig had finished his Cambrai dispatch: 'The great value of the tanks in the offensive has been conclusively proved.'

4
Asian Incidents

Shanghai (1937)

Michael Calvert

The weather in Shanghai, the great international seaport by the Yangtze, was threatening. The warnings of the approach of a typhoon had been hoisted, there was low cloud at 1,500 ft with gusts of wind up to 60 m.p.h. It was Saturday morning 14 August 1937 and one of the world's largest cities was about to begin a three-month ordeal.

The start of the Sino-Japanese 'Incident' which was to cost millions of lives, and which might be said to be the start of the Second World War, is traditionally dated to the 'Double Seventh' (when Japanese troops clashed with Chinese at the Marco Polo bridge, just south of Peking, on 7 July 1937). Hostilities near Shanghai began on 13 August. The Japanese had landed about 1,300 sailors and marines to protect their interests in the International Settlement, which included the huge Toyada Cotton Mills. Just over five years before, Shanghai had been the scene of a ferocious month-long battle when a Japanese army had landed to smash a Chinese trade boycott.

General Chiang Kai-shek, eager to involve the Western Powers in the new struggle, and also to gain the attention of the world press, rapidly moved in two of the best of his German-trained divisions, the 87th (involved in the 1932 battle) and 88th. These divisions, part of General Chang Chih-Chung's 9th Army Group, assaulted the Japanese naval forces which were holding bridgeheads along the NW bank of the River Huang-P'u (Whangpoo) on 13 August.

The Huang-P'u, flowing 16 miles north, connected the great port of Shanghai (at that time the fourth largest port in the world with 3.5 million inhabitants) to the Yangtze at Wu-sung near its mouth. Opposite the Japanese warehouses, which were being besieged, and in the middle of the river, was anchored Vice-Admiral Hasegawa's flagship, the old three-funneled cruiser, *Idzumo*. This 9,580-ton warship had been built for Japan in Scottish yards at the turn of the century and had fought in the Russo-Japanese War of 1904–5. Just upstream and in line ahead were also anchored the modern American heavy cruiser USS *Augusta*, and the British *Kent*-class cruiser HMS *Cumberland* flying the flag of the Shanghai-born C-in-C, China Station, Admiral Sir Charles J. C. Little, KCB.

Other naval vessels of the Western Powers in the port included the Royal Navy light cruiser *Danae*, the destroyers *Duncan*, *Delight* and *Duchess* and the sloop *Falmouth*. These were busy ferrying their national troops to reinforce the normal peacetime detachments defending the International Settlement.

On 13 August Vice-Adm. Hasegawa had unilaterally issued an edict that no merchant shipping was to be allowed to enter the Huang-P'u River in case they smuggled Chinese troops ashore in the Japanese rear. Meanwhile several Japanese destroyers were firing broadsides from their 4.7-in guns at point-blank range into the wharves and along the jetties opposite them to hold back the Chinese attackers who had, in places, reached the go-downs (warehouses) on the water front. Chinese snipers in sampans under the wharves succeeded in killing a number of Japanese officers clad in their white uniforms while they controlled the gunfire from the bridges of these destroyers.

In the International Settlement proper, and in the separate French Concession containing most of the more luxurious night clubs, life went on as near normal as possible. At lunchtime, for instance, the European *T'aipans* (heads of thriving business houses) played liar dice in the Shanghai Club's Long Bar on the Bund (a promenade by the Huang-P'u) to decide the final arrangements of contracts and other problems requiring decisions.

With plenty of pink gin and dice, decisions could be reached quickly, saving much time in negotiations. After a Saturday's curry lunch, the Chinese compradores (buyers) and Number Ones of the firms would be telephoned and the decisions would be quickly implemented. Shanghai, in its hundred years of international history, was used to emergencies. For example, permanent steel slots had been installed in the streets so that barbed wire 'knife-rests' could be quickly fixed in to divide the settlement into defensible districts, supported by permanent concrete pillboxes to cover the wire. The only real signs of the times were the very many thousands of Chinese refugees who had fled into the city before the perimeter defenses were manned and who were filling the streets, but were being moved along into the remoter parts of the settlement by the efficient Shanghai Police. Their senior police officers were European, mostly British, while the rank and file were mainly robust Chinese and Sikhs.

On the Huang-P'u Bund European families clustered with their possessions ready to be evacuated to Hong Kong by the warships which were bringing in reinforcements. By the afternoon of the 14th the surge of Chinese refugees had reached Avenue Edward VII, which cut through the French Concession upstream opposite Pu-Tung and south of the International Settlement where the fighting was taking place.

The troops of the main Western Powers manning the perimeter were British soldiers and sailors, US Marines, Dutch Marines and *Savoia* Grenadiers from Italy. The British contingent, besides the sailors and Royal Marines who were later withdrawn, consisted of 2nd Battalion, the Loyal Regiment (North Lancashire) and 2nd Battalion, the Royal Welch Fusiliers (from Hong Kong). They were late reinforced by the 1st Battalion, Ulster Rifles and the Middlesex Regiment, some detachments of Royal Signals and HQ staff. Thirteen stalwart men of the Royal Engineers were to supervise the emplacement of more than one million filled sandbags to form the temporary blockhouses. The watertable was only a foot or two below the pavement gutters, so it was not possible to dig down to find cover from the Japanese and Chinese bombs and shells which missed their targets and landed in the Settlement.

It was agreed that this international garrison, with the exception of the French in their Concession and who liked to be different, was to be under the command of the Scottish Major-General A. P. D. Telfer-Smollett CBE, DSO, MC (later GOC Scottish Command) aided by about ten staff officers who also formed the brigade HQ for the four British battalions. In a very similar situation in Trieste during 1948, the staff was ten times as great for the same size garrison.

Suddenly, at 1600 on Saturday 14 August, a formation of four US-exported Northrop 2E attack aircraft (from 2nd Group of the

Chinese Air Force) emerged out of the 1,500 ft cloud-ceiling and made straight for the *Idzumo*. The pilots had been trained by Colonel Claire Lee Chennault (an American serving as the Inspector of the Chinese Air Force) in level bombing from a height of 7,500 ft on a fixed air speed. As the four aircraft lost height in a shallow dive, the bomb aimers, lying flat on the deck, saw through their sights the three-funneled *Idzumo* and dropped 1,080 lb bombs (which had been sold to them by the British). But they had apparently forgotten to reset their bombsights for the correct speed and lower altitude and, with the gusty air conditions in the prevailing typhoon situation, all the bombs went astray. One fell near *Augusta* damaging her with bomb splinters which killed one sailor. Another two splashed *Cumberland*. But the fourth landed on a road junction off Avenue Edward VII in the French Concession which was teeming with refugees and killed 1,123 persons besides wounding another thousand. Much of the damage was done by falling glass from the tall buildings surrounding the junction.

A second attack on *Idzumo* next day by two aircraft was just as inaccurate and disastrous. One bomb landed in the Great World Amusement Centre and a second on a luxury hotel in the Nanking Road where it killed over 250 people. A total of 1,956 Chinese and Europeans were killed, and 2,426 wounded by these six misplaced bombs. The Avenue Edward VII killing was a record for one bomb for many years to come. It was rumored at the time that Claire Chennault took part in the second raid. But whatever the truth it did not prevent him organizing, and commanding with distinction, the American Volunteer Group (AVG, more popularly known as the Flying Tigers, who fought in an unneutral manner for China in association with the British 204 Mission) from the beginning of 1941, long before Pearl Harbor. In 1943 Claire Chennault was promoted to Major-General commanding the volunteer US 14th Army Air Force in China, and, in spite of shortages of pilots and planes, drove the Japanese air forces from the Chinese skies.

Meanwhile, the Chinese offensive against the Japanese holding out among the wharves and go-downs of Hangkow continued. By 20 August Chiang Kai-shek had committed the equivalent of nine divisions to the Shanghai area, on both sides of the Huang-P'u. In support were 72 guns and 24 light tanks (British Vickers). These ramshackle but numerous Chinese forces threatened to squeeze the thin Japanese bridgehead to death. On the 23rd, Japan's hastily assembled Shanghai Expeditionary Army began disembarking two large divisions with a tank battalion and lavish heavy artillery to save the embattled landing force. It took round-the-clock attacks from 1st Combined Air Flotilla in Formosa (Taiwan) and strikes from four aircraft carriers, backed up by ceaseless naval gunfire, to prevent the multiplying Chinese armies from achieving a dramatic victory.

On 20 September no fewer than 62 'divisions' were in or heading for the theater of war. Meanwhile, three more Japanese divisions and support units had joined the struggle against the 19 Chinese formations in the Shanghai area. General Chang Chih-Chung, commander of four reinforced divisions a month before, now controlled 15 in his Central Group of Armies. Above the ground troops, Chiang Kai-shek's pilots flew up to 142 assorted American and Italian aircraft against twice their number of more modern Japanese machines. Only the introduction of even newer aircraft types began to gain Japan air supremacy in mid-September.

Western warships steaming up the Huang-P'u were surprised to find that Japanese destroyers ceased their bombardment of the Chinese as they passed and gave the usual naval compliments. When that was done they continued their firing. At sea, the concentration of seven cruisers, 17 destroyers and nine gunboats gave General Iwace Matsui (C-in-C Shanghai Expeditionary Army) complete freedom of maneuver.

The British manned two separate sectors of the international perimeter, the most important being in Chapei, north of the Suchow Creek and alongside the Japanese sector where heavy fighting was taking place. On the other side of the sector was the North Station building which had been converted into a Chinese strongpoint. The second British sector, initially manned by the Loyal Regiment, was on the extreme west of the settlement along Bubbling Well Road near Hungjao Airport where a railway bridge crossed the Suchow Creek. A zoo, which was later to be inadvertently bombed, was situated behind the Loyals' position.

The American sector lay between the two British enclaves and was manned by a US Marine Regiment which had last served with the Royal Welch Fusiliers at Peking during the 1900 Boxer Rebellion. The Dutch and Italian contingents closed other gaps in the perimeter while a strong, purposeful French force guarded the French Concession which covered the southern sector near Nantao.

But it was Chapei, where the Fusiliers soon took over from the British Marines and sailors, which was, for some months to come, in the forefront as it constituted a salient between the Chinese and the reinforced Japanese, and acted as a touch-line along which the conflict between these two Oriental countries waxed and waned. Members of the British garrison, with permission, could pay visits to either side and observe the course of the war and the methods used. But Chapei was no pleasure resort. Shells and bombs landing in this sector had caused the inhabitants to evacuate the area north of the Suchow Creek and the mass of derelict brick and black-tiled slums soon became a haunt of rats, flies and maggots as the sewers were destroyed and corpses floated to and fro between the booms in the tidal creek. Some of these unfortunates were suspected saboteurs executed by the Japanese; others were Japanese prisoners executed by the Chinese in retaliation. Between 13 August and November, when the Japanese were enlarging their bridgeheads and obtaining more elbow room, about 20 British troops manning the perimeter of Chapei were killed, mainly by Japanese bombs and shells that were misdirected, or by unexploded bombs that went off later.

Britain's China Command HQ in Hong Kong could not visualize a major war being fought between about half a million Chinese and eventually about 250,000 Japanese in the area between Shanghai and the Yangtze, complete with modern weapons, aircraft and naval support from a fleet anchored in the mouth of the Yangtze. In keeping with the niggardly defense spending of the 1930s, China Command gave orders that it was unnecessary to provide British troops with overhead cover. But Hong Kong had been forestalled in this decision, as Captain (later Major-General) Thomas G. Rennie of the Black Watch, acting Brigade Major, and Captain Howard-Vyse, the Commander Royal Engineers (CRE) had already spent thousands of Chinese dollars buying up 6 in timber struts so that overhead cover, heavily reinforced with sandbags, could be placed over the small redoubts constructed along the dangerous Chapei perimeter. This action undoubtedly saved many British soldiers' lives but, on instructions from the Chief Financial Advisor to China Command, the Hong Kong paymaster refused to pay the bill.

So when the Chief of Staff, British troops in China, Colonel (later Lieutenant-General) Noel M. S. Irwin, DSO and two bars, MC and the Chief Engineer, China Command, Brigadier Geoffrey Cathcart Gowlland, OBE, announced that they would pay Shanghai a visit,

Rennie and Howard-Vyse cooked up a scheme with the Chinese and Japanese commands, neither of which wanted to kill British soldiers, but who fully understood and had suffered from the tortuous minds of accountants in a peacetime army. The Sino-Japanese contestants organized a seemingly furious battle on the perimeter at the wide open space in front of the North Station building. All unwittingly, Gowlland and Irwin, with their solar topees and red tabs in full array, were brought to the scene of action.

At once dozens of shells were plummeted into the area by either side while first Japanese, and then Chinese aircraft bombed and strafed the edge of the perimeter. Armored cars from both sides also roared up and rained tracer bullets vaguely at each other while the infantry and gunners on either side let off their weapons in all directions. The Chinese engineers, not to be outdone, exploded a mine for full measure. Rennie and Howard-Vyse had, over the months, become inured to the sounds of battle. But Irwin and Gowlland had not. These were probably the first shots these two courageous and well-decorated senior officers had heard fired since 1919, 18 years before. Gowlland, now lying in the rubble, gripped the arm of a junior engineer officer and cried: 'This is war! This is war!' After further treatment the two shaken officers got up and were led away to a covered blockhouse where Rennie and Howard-Vyse had the necessary papers ready, complete with the requisite rubber stamps, authorizing the required expenditure. In a daze, Irwin and Gowlland duly signed and then departed back to Hong Kong.

One of the mainstays of the defense of the International Settlement was the Shanghai Volunteer Corps which included a rigorously trained, smart and durable White Russian regiment whose members had escaped from the Soviet regime. The Volunteers mainly consisted of young and energetic businessmen from the great merchant banks and business houses such as Butterfield and Swire, Hong Kong and Shanghai Bank, Jardine Matheson and other British and European firms which had done so much to develop China, taking great financial risks but also gaining great profits. The corps was formed into infantry, cavalry and armored car companies which reinforced the national contingents, especially at night and weekends when businesses were closed. They also supported the very efficient and highly motivated British-trained Shanghai Police. So, in spite of the bombing and after the evacuation of many families, business, trade and life in this city of 3.5 million carried on. But the Chinese had failed as yet to involve the Western Powers in the war. The Europeans were too engrossed nearer home with the Spanish Civil War, Mussolini's invasion of Ethiopia and the threat from Hitler. Soon after the 'Incident' started in Shanghai, Chiang Kai-shek concluded a Non-Aggression Pact with the Soviet Union which brought in a $250,000,000 loan to buy armaments. An unfortunate happening further depressed relations between Japan and Britain. On 26 August, the 6 ft 7 in British Ambassador to China, Sir Hughe Knatchbull-Hugessen (later Ambassador to Turkey and victim of the 'Cicero' espionage case) was returning to Shanghai from the new Chinese capital, Nanking, farther up the Yangtze. In spite of a large Union Jack painted on the roof of his car, a myopic Japanese pilot strafed it, and Sir Hughe was badly injured. As his driver rushed him into Shanghai by way of Chinese-held territory, the car was attacked again. The Ambassador, *hors de combat* for many months, was replaced. The Americans also suffered seven casualties when a US troop transport, the *Hoover*, was bombed and strafed by Chinese aircraft off the mouth of the Yangtze.

These military peccadilloes were bound to occur as long as the Western Powers refused to acknowledge the fact that China and Japan were gripped together in a full-scale war. The Chinese boom at Chiang-yin on the Yangtze, and the subsequent Japanese blockade of the coast, had stopped all trade and traffic up the river. In Nanking the British had stationed the 4,290-ton light cruiser *Capetown*. There were also a number of British and US gunboats which normally protected trade on the river from pirates and bandits. On 19 September a Japanese admiral, who had been trained at Dartmouth Royal Naval College, was piped aboard *Capetown*. His news was that from 0800 on 21 September all foreign nationals were liable to be bombed, as Japan extended her range of attack. The Western admirals decided to ignore the threat and stay put, but arrangements were made to move all Europeans up-river for evacuation to Canton and Hong Kong, via the newly completed Han-k'ou (Hankow)–Canton railway. *Capetown* actually left Nanking on 21 September with a large contingent of refugees for Han-k'ou and only just missed the heavy bombing of the capital the following day.

Meanwhile, the land battle around Shanghai was hotting up. The Chinese defenses between Shanghai and the Yangtze were based on a river and canal line through this low-lying marshy area of the Yangtze Delta, as far as Chiang-yin where the mouth of the Yangtze narrowed. There the Chinese had sunk a number of coasters to form a boom covered by shore batteries to prevent the Japanese Navy advancing up to Chen-chiang, Nanking and beyond (which they were eventually to do). The numerous Chinese divisions, of which there were eventually 33 in six 'army groups' deployed between Hang-chou, Shanghai and Nanking, were now holding the coast south of Shanghai in Hang-chou (Hangchow) Bay.

As the Chinese still wanted to draw the Japanese into the built-up area of Shanghai's outskirts, where street fighting was to their advantage, fierce fighting took place during the hot, steamy malarial months of the remainder of August, September and October. The Chinese lost nearly 80,000 casualties and the Japanese 30,000. While the Japanese developed their base at Wu-sung at the mouth of the Huang-P'u and extended their foothold, fighting spread all along the 70-mile front from Shanghai to Chiang-yin with the Chinese armies fully committed. Ch'ung-ming, an island astride the mouth of the Yangtze, had been captured against quite stiff opposition from the Chinese River Defense Force and was being developed into an advance naval and air base. But the Japanese, in spite of having now landed armor, could make little headway across the flooded paddy area which was intersected with small and large irrigation canals.

The Japanese now took a leaf out of the experience of Major ('Chinese') Charles G. Gordon (of Khartoum). He had successfully fought with his 'Ever Victorious Army' through the same area in 33 actions on behalf of the Chinese Emperor against the T'ai P'ing rebels from 1863–4. Gordon had found that the best method of transport both for his troops and supplies were boats which could easily penetrate land defenses based on water obstacles. The Japanese had developed light, flat-bottomed, shallow-draught landing craft, with armored sides (similar to those developed later by the Western Powers in the Second World War).

These 46 ft vessels could carry 70 men or 10 tons of cargo at 8 knots. As landing craft carriers they used ships modelled on whaling mother ships (in which the whales were normally winched out of the water and cleaned and cut up). The technique was to reverse these ships close to shore from which six to 12 landing craft could be launched to make a simultaneous landing. In this type of operation the Japanese, who had devised these craft specifically for operations on the China coast and in the great Chinese river network, were at least three years ahead of European and American development.

On 5 November 1937 four Japanese divisions (6th, 16th, 18th and 114th), supported by a naval bombardment and carrier aircraft, simultaneously made landings near Fushon, just downstream from the boom at Chiang-yin on the Yangtze and at Cha-pu in Hang-chou Bay, south of Shanghai. They thus formed a pincer movement from either side of the peninsula where the fighting for Shanghai was taking place. Both landings were opposed but the Chinese were overwhelmed. General Matsui's powerful 10th Army heavily outnumbered the defenders in the Hang-chou area.

The Japanese, with their hundreds of landing craft, quickly exploited their success and penetrated inland, relying on rivers and canals for their lines of communication. They were well supported by naval aircraft operating from Ch'ung-ming Island. The Chinese armies around Shanghai were forced to withdraw helter-skelter to avoid encirclement. They split up into two, one half making for Chen-chiang (Chinkiang) and Nanking in the Yangtze valley, and the remainder for Hang-chou, the great seaport to the south. The Chinese set fire to their sectors of Shanghai as they withdrew and destroyed bridges in their rear, but this did not delay the now waterborne Japanese.

By 11 November the Chinese had withdrawn from the environs of Shanghai apart from one unit dubbed the 'Doomed Battalion' by the press, which had been cut off in a five-storey go-down on the Suchow Creek alongside the Royal Welch Fusiliers' sector. It held out for a few days giving the press photographers a field day until arrangements were made for the survivors to be interned in Shanghai. By 12 November the Loyals' sector on Bubbling Well Road was clear of Chinese, who had been replaced by more sinister Japanese units.

During the retreat some shells and bombs had landed in the Zoological Gardens which caused the keepers to open the cages to give their captives a chance to escape. So the Loyals, and the Ulster Rifles manning the perimeter farther to the south, had the eerie experience of finding lions, tigers, bears, elephants, rhinos and wolves prowling around their blockhouses and emplacements. They certainly kept away visitors and most of the press. But the British troops rapidly rounded them up without casualties on either side, and as the fight receded, put them back into their cages or adopted a few as pets.

The Japanese followed up their success by a river assault on the Chiang-yin boom whose land defenses they had captured. At first, landing craft penetrated beyond the boom, and then, after demolitions on the boom had been carried out, Japanese gunboats started to sail upstream, supporting their army which hurried on towards the Chinese capital, Nanking, 145 miles NW of Shanghai. Advancing on a broad front the Japanese captured Su-chou on 20 November. At this stage Germany, through General Alexander Ernst von Falkenhausen (Chiang Kai-shek's military adviser 1934–8), offered to mediate between the contestants, but the Army party in the Japanese government had now begun to sense a great victory.

Japan's terms for peace were so outlandish that Chiang Kai-shek scorned them. He was still intent on carrying on protracted warfare and wearing the Japanese down until Britain and America would come to China's aid. As the Japanese forces approached Nanking and the bombing of the city intensified, clashes occurred with the warships of the Western Powers which were protecting their embassies and consulates in the capital. These culminated in the shelling of the RN gunboat *Ladybird* which rescued survivors from the sinking of the Shanghai-built river gunboat USS *Panay* by Aichi DIAI dive-bombers on 12 December. For a brief period, it seemed that both the US and Britain were on the brink of war with Japan, which was China's one hope. But, after the Japanese had apologized and paid an indemnity for the damage they had caused, both the American and British people suppressed their chauvinistic feelings and the eventual, inevitable war was postponed for another four years.

Khalkhin-Gol (1939)

Alan Lothian

Lieutenant General M. Komatsubara's 23rd Infantry Division had been destroyed utterly – scarcely one man in a hundred escaping – on the empty borderlands of the Khalkhin-Gol river between Outer Mongolia and Manchuria. It was late in 1939, while half a world away Poland bled from the new German *Drang nach Osten* (Drive to the East) and the Western democracies indulged themselves in the 'Phoney War' along the new Siegfried Line, a lonely and disgraced officer of Imperial Japan brought his life to a private end. Komatsubara might now find redemption in the agonizing rite of *seppuku*: only by ripping out his own entrails with his own short sword might he 'prove his sincerity' to the Emperor and his ancestors. But the Khalkhin-Gol disaster was too great to be atoned for by a general's suicide. It was better that it had not happened at all, and the less attention drawn to it the better. Komatsubara, announced Tokyo inscrutably, had died of 'an abdominal ailment'.

The empty steppe country around the Khalkhin-Gol river had represented the farthest fringe of Japanese expansion. China, invaded in 1937, was still unsubdued but the Imperial grip on Manchuria, annexed in 1931, was firm. Here, in the wilderness of the Mongolian Republic, might Soviet strength be tested. Thirty-five years before, Japan's crushing defeat of the old Tsarist armies had astounded the world; now, perhaps, a border pinprick might develop into a deep thrust at the Trans-Siberian Railway, severing Russia's spinal column and allowing the rich Soviet Far East with its port of Vladivostok to fall into the lap of the Emperor.

For years, Japan's highest military councils had been divided into factions advocating either a 'Strike North', at Russia, or 'Strike South', at the western colonies. Emperor Hirohito had already decided upon 'Strike South', which would in the next few years lead to Pearl Harbor, the fall of Singapore, and ultimately Hiroshima. But in the Army many officers still hankered after an attack on Russia, and the High Command of the Kwantung Army in Manchuria was no exception.

'Border incidents' spanning July–August 1938 at Lake Khasan, near Vladivostok, had shown real Soviet weakness after Stalin's terrifying purges of the Red Army. A Russian general, Lyushkov, had defected to the Kwantung Army with details of dispositions and stories of discontent. Acting first without Hirohito's knowledge, and eventually in direct disobedience, the Kwantung command launched an attack on the Russian forces which met with some success until it ran up against superior Soviet armor and airpower. Enraged, Hirohito refused to allow his air force to fly in support of his own disobedient army, and the situation was eventually settled by a diplomatic return to the status quo. But to save his officers from a catastrophic loss of face, the constant problem of the Japanese Imperial regime, he had to let them try again. After a formal cease-fire had been agreed at Lake Khasan, Hirohito approved a General Staff plan for an organized trial of strength farther west, in Mongolia, during the following summer.

The border area chosen by the Japanese staff was beside the Khalkhin-Gol river, for much of its length a frontier between Japanese-occupied Manchuria or Manchukuo to the east and the Outer Mongolian People's Republic, closely bound to Russia by a mutual-assistance pact in March 1936, to the west. At one point, however, the border bulges east of the river around the village and hill of Nomonhan. On this shallow salient, 46 miles wide, the Japanese planned to test the Soviet pledge to defend Mongolia. The country was steppe, blue-green in the summer with sturdy grass, and populated only by a few tribal herdsmen. East of the river it was more broken, with gullies, dunes, and even a few quicksands.

On 11 May 1939, a few hundred Inner Mongolian horsemen under Japanese control and accompanied by 'advisers' from Komatsubara's 23rd Division, crossed the frontier and rode as far as Nomonhan itself

before the villagers alerted their border guards, based in a log fort
five miles away on the west bank of the river. The following day,
the invaders were driven back across the border in an action that
resembled an ancient tribal feud rather than a clash between two
twentieth-century super powers: whooping Tskirik horsemen riding
rings around their Japanese-led Bargut enemies.

But on 14 May the Inner Mongolians reappeared in strength, and
this time they had 300 Japanese cavalry as stiffening. Within a few
hours the Tsiriks had been driven back to their garrison positions,
and that night the local Russian adviser, Major Bykov, was called
in. When he reached the picturesque border fort next morning, he
found that the twentieth century had arrived at last in the shape of
a Japanese air raid which terrified his Mongolian charges and left
the place a ruin. Taking no chances, Bykov at once called in 6th
Mongolian Cavalry Division and the few Red Army detachments
available. But as these troops massed on the Mongolian side of
the Khalkhin-Gol, the Japanese on the east bank melted away.
On the night of 22 May, Bykov made a cautious reconnaissance
in force across the river. In the quiet rough pasture of Nomonhan
the Japanese were waiting. Only after fierce hand-to-hand fighting
was Bykov able to fall back to the Khalkhin-Gol.

The game of cat-and-mouse continued. On 25 May Bykov cautiously moved his full strength forward and over the next two
days cleared the east bank and reoccupied the deserted village of
Nomonhan. By now, about 10,000 men had been involved on the
Mongolian side, mainly 'constabulary' troops with a few specialist
Russian companies. The border incident was rapidly escalating, and
at dawn on 28 May it went a stage further. Five thousand Japanese
regulars, with an accompanying tribal horde, fell on Bykov's troops
before daybreak. Only the veteran Russian's canny dispositions
enabled him to fall back once more to the river without complete
destruction. But the panic button had already been pressed in
Moscow and that same evening troops of the Soviet 149th Motorized
Infantry Regiment began to arrive, to be sent straight into the fight
from their trucks. All that night the battle continued, and the
following morning a Soviet–Mongolian counter-attack pushed the
Japanese back, once more, to the border with a loss of 400 men.

By now, Moscow was feeling real alarm. Despite accurate intelligence from his master spy Richard Sorge in Tokyo on long-term
Japanese planning, Stalin understandably feared the possibility of a

disastrous two-front war with Japan and Germany. Accordingly, no effort was to be spared in crushing this Japanese adventure before it threatened all of the Soviet Trans-Baikal. The first step was to release troops from the interior for the mission, and the second was to appoint a commander, someone new, outstanding, trusted, and with a fighting reputation to make. The man Stalin picked was Corps Commander Georgi Konstantinovich Zhukov.

Zhukov in 1939 was a tough, 43-year-old cavalryman turned 'tankist' and Deputy Commander of the key Belorussian Military District. Squat, barrel-chested, heavy-browed (his name came from the Russian word *zhuk*, meaning 'beetle') he had fought his way up from the ranks of the Red Army in the Civil War to distinction in every peacetime command he had held. He had been in China, perhaps in Spain; he had survived the bloodletting of the 1937 purges unscathed and was already well-known in the Red Army for his short-tempered, no-nonsense thoroughness. As 'the general who never lost a battle' Zhukov was to direct forces and fighting of unsurpassed dimensions in the Russo-German war: 1941 would see him halt Hitler's offensive outside Moscow, in 1942 he would master-mind the Stalingrad campaign, and in 1945 he would meet the Western Allies in the wreckage of Berlin as the epitome of the ruthless, crushing might of the Soviet war machine. But in June 1939, as he flew out with a small staff to Mongolia, his future career and quite possibly his life depended on victory at Khalkhin-Gol. And victory alone would not be enough. Only the utter destruction of the Japanese would satisfy Stalin.

On 5 June Zhukov arrived at HQ, Soviet 57th Special Corps, the only major Red Army formation in the area. There he found little cheer. The command was hopelessly out of touch with the front, there was not so much as a kilometer of telegraph wire in the area, co-ordination of troops was poor and reconnaissance, though inadequate, clearly showed a Japanese build-up far greater than any mere border conflict would require. Furthermore the Japanese were making full use of air superiority, both for bombing and reconnaissance. Zhukov, with papers in his pocket appointing him local C-in-C if need be, at once took charge. The Corps commander was relieved and sent home and Zhukov threw all his characteristic energies into organizing a defense.

By early July, the Japanese had about 38,000 men, 135 tanks and 225 aircraft concentrated on the frontier east of the Khalkhin-Gol.

Soviet and Mongolian forces together amounted to only 12,500 men, though Zhukov had 186 better tanks and 226 armored cars. He would need them. The Japanese plan involved sending a strong force wide around the Soviet left flank, across the river to seize the dominating high ground of Mount Bain-Tsagan. Then, as the main tank-led force attacked along the general front, this outflanking force would surround and destroy the east bank salient from its rear.

According to the Japanese schedule, offensive operations would be over by mid-July and the campaign wound up before the autumn rains. On 2 July, the first attacks pressed into the weak east bank positions and by the end of the day Japanese tanks and infantry were on the river in the Russian third line at some points. But Zhukov was too shrewd a commander to commit his reserves prematurely. Shortly before dawn on 3 July, the Soviet Colonel I. M. Afonin, Chief Adviser to the Mongolian Army, was inspecting Mongolian 6th Cavalry Division defenses on Bain-Tsagin when he stumbled upon Japanese troops who had made a surprise river-crossing by pontoon bridge. The Mongolians, without the training or equipment of their Red Army mentors, were driven off.

As the sun rose the following morning, Zhukov could not fail to appreciate the danger of the situation. The Japanese only had to roll on to the south for the hard-pressed Soviet forces on the east bank to be completely cut off. At once he ordered his armor – practically his only reserve – into action; 11th Tank Brigade was to attack from the north, 7th Mechanized Brigade from the south, and 24th Motorized Infantry Regiment from the NW through the retreating Mongolians. These forces together deployed over 300 fighting vehicles: the Japanese, on both sides of the river, had less than half that. Zhukov wrote in his 1969 memoirs: 'It was impossible to delay a counterblow since the enemy, who saw the advance of our tanks, rapidly began to take defensive measures and started bombing our tank columns. The latter had no shelter whatsoever: for hundreds of kilometres around there was not even a bush in sight.'

The speed of the triple-pronged Soviet thrust first startled, then demoralized the Japanese. From 0700 Zhukov's entire bomber force had been pounding them, and for the first time they felt the weight of the brilliantly organized Russian heavy artillery. By 0900 the advance detachments of Russian armor were arriving in the combat area and at 1045 the full attack went in. The Japanese had had little time to dig in thoroughly; their anti-tank training had always been a weak spot and now they paid the penalty. As the battle raged all that day, it was no longer the Russians who were in danger of encirclement.

An attempt at counter-attack on 4 July was broken up by Red Army aviation and artillery; worse, the single pontoon bridge they had laid across the Khalkhin-Gol was destroyed by Russian bombs. Hundreds of soldiers drowned trying to escape, and Komatsubara was lucky to get across with his HQ. Most of the 10,000-strong Bain-Tsagan assault force lay dead and wounded on the slopes of the little mountain, and when the heaviest fighting ended, on the night of 4–5 July, the Japanese had little cause to celebrate, having lost half the tanks available in Manchuria. And though Soviet 3 July tank losses had been over a hundred, the Red Army had successfully exploited glaring Japanese deficiencies in field and anti-tank (AT) artillery.

But the Kwantung Army was by no means willing to abandon its Mongolian campaign. During the remainder of July, it doubled the force committed, stripping divisions elsewhere of AT units to strengthen the Khalkhin-Gol positions. On 10 August, two full Japanese infantry divisions (7th and 23rd), a Manchukuoan brigade, three cavalry regiments, 182 tanks, 300 armored cars and three artillery regiments with over 450 aircraft were combined into the 75,000-strong Sixth Japanese Army under General Ogisu Rippo. A final general offensive along a 43-mile front was planned for 24 August, after an attack on 23 July got nowhere under Soviet bombardment.

On the Russian side of the hill final victory was far from certain. Powerful reinforcements had to be brought over poor communications from the Soviet heartland. But Stalin knew that Soviet international prestige was at stake and his new negotiations with Hitler, no respecter of weakness, had reached a critical juncture. Neither blood nor treasure would be spared. 'For Stalin,' wrote one former Red officer, 'the losses were of no importance whatsoever.'

Throughout July and August three infantry and two cavalry divisions with seven independent brigades, including five armored, as well as artillery and air force units, were assembled. This was in itself no mean feat. The Japanese, in the year before their attack, had built a railway to within a few miles of the Mongolian border. The nearest Russian railhead from which the new First Army Group could be supplied was 403 miles away. For Zhukov's coming offensive, 55,000 tons of supplies, including 18,000 tons of artillery ammunition, had to be carried along rudimentary Mongolian roads, the overworked trucks and drivers further tormented by late summer heat and the piercing dust storms of Central Asia. Such was the shortage of trucks that gun-towing tractors from the front had to be pressed into service as supply carriers.

So Zhukov laid his plans. The Japanese had attempted a great envelopment; very well, Zhukov would show them how it was done. He organized his new forces into three groups, North, South and Central, with his armored units, ready to move fast and deep, on the wings. He would be ready by 20 August, four days before the enemy. Until then he kept his plans, his troop movements, and thus his future surprise well masked by painstaking and ingenious deceptions. Fake radio signals ordering large quantities of engineering equipment misled the Japanese into thinking the Russians were digging in for the autumn. Sound effects gave the impression of heavy pile-driving work. The night movements of armored and motorized units were covered by air and artillery bombardments. All day a few tanks stripped of their silencers drove up and down until the Japanese got used to the noise. Zhukov even solemnly issued to his troops the official handbook *What the Soviet Soldier Must Know In the Defence*. By Sunday 20 August, unknown to the Japanese, quietly waiting in the jump-off positions were 35 infantry battalions, 20 cavalry squadrons, 498 tanks, 346 armored cars and 502 guns of all types.

The first the Japanese knew of the coming storm was at 0545 when 150 bombers, escorted by 100 fighters, launched a saturation raid on their forward defenses and artillery positions. Before the stunned Japanese had recovered, Zhukov's 250 heavy guns and mortars were playing on their close reserves and at 0845 his yelling infantry were surging forward behind the tanks. All along the front, the Russian waves broke through the Japanese front. The defenders were 'morally and physically suppressed' by the three-hour Red Army artillery bombardment, delivered by twice the number of defending guns which anyhow lacked the wealth of Russian ammunition.

Not that the Japanese crumbled easily. At one point a divisional attack on Japanese fortifications was bloodily repulsed and the division, probably the raw 82nd Infantry sent from the Urals, pinned down under heavy fire. Its commander begged Zhukov for new orders; Zhukov told him to continue his attack. When the divisional commander doubted the possibility, Zhukov said coldly: 'I hereby relieve you of command. Give me your Chief of Staff.' The Chief of Staff agreed to continue the attack, but the attack failed to materialize. Zhukov picked up the telephone once more: 'I hereby relieve you of your command. Wait for the arrival of a new commander.' An officer from Zhukov's own staff was sent over, and with reorganized artillery and air support, the attack succeeded despite appalling losses.

Most successful was Zhukov's Southern group. Its powerful armored forces, which included a battalion of SP guns and a company of flamethrower tanks, swept clear around the left and by 21 August were solidly established behind the Japanese operating south of the Khalkhin-Gol's east–west tributary, the Khailastyn-Gol. Two days later the Northern group, assisted by Zhukov's reserve 212th Airborne Brigade (fighting on the ground) cut its way across the Palets Heights round to join them, and the enemy were surrounded. The fighting was bitter and by no means over. Japanese in dugouts had to be burned out by the flame-throwing tanks, and surrenders were rare. But the Red Army too had a determination which took a heavy toll of 600 dead in the savage hand-to-hand fighting in the dugouts and gullies of the Palets Heights as the pincers of encirclement closed.

After a Japanese relief attempt had been beaten off by 6th Tank Brigade on 26 August all hope for the trapped troops was gone. The growing Russian air superiority alone was enough to prevent the movement of fresh Japanese troops into the battle zone. In the first week the Soviet Air Force flew 474 sorties and dropped 190 tons of bombs, modest by later standards but some of the most intense air fighting since 1918. In the dogfights of the first day five Polikarpov I16 fighters shot down two Mitsubishi A5M fighters with 82 mm RS82 rockets – the first likely instance of air-to-air rockets being lethal against aircraft.

But neither Zhukov nor his government were content with a passive containment. With bloody impatience, he set about planning the liquidation of Japanese units trapped on various patches of high ground within the perimeter. For a week the savage business of mopping up went on. In this phase too, Zhukov demonstrated his tactical skill and the technical superiority of his army. Japanese troops on the Remizov Heights had relied on the muddy bottom of the shallow Khailastyn-Gol to protect their southern flank from attack. But by night Zhukov's engineers reinforced the river bed

and the tanks with their terrifying flamethrowers drove straight
across, as one of the three converging assaults on the last pocket
of resistance.

By the morning of 31 August, any Japanese remaining on Mongolian territory were either dead or prisoners. Of 60,000 troops trapped
in the cauldron, 50,000 were later listed as killed, wounded and
missing. Casualties in the veteran 23rd Division ran as high as 99
per cent. The Russians admitted casualties of 10,000 in killed and
wounded throughout the campaign, but it seems likely that this was
a considerable underestimate. The outnumbered Japanese Army Air
Force claimed to have downed 1,200 Soviet planes (the Russian figure
for their 'kills' was 660) in the four months of hostilities, but in the
days before instant close-support on the battlefield this could not
sway the ground-fighting.

Now, on the last day in August, Zhukov's dog-tired, grimy tank
crews stared east from the border they had regained, waiting for the
order to go on, while the frantic Kwantung Army HQ scraped the
depots of Manchuria to find troops to stem what many feared would
be a Red flood.

That order never came. In that autumn of 1939, Moscow and
the world had other, more urgent problems. On the day Zhukov's
pincers met behind the Japanese, Stalin and Hitler had published
their Non-Aggression Pact: the Soviet dictator now believed, with
unusual trustfulness, that he had bought the time he needed to
prepare Russia against war. On 1 September the German *Panzers*
rolled into Poland and within a few days the victorious Soviet armor
was rattling back across the Trans-Siberian Railway to the new Soviet
frontier in Eastern Poland – just in case.

Hirohito had to face up to more than the shock of military
disaster. The Non-Aggression Pact surprised no one more than
the Japanese, to whom it was a baffling breach of faith. The Prime
Minister resigned in shame. Hirohito would have been more than
just puzzled and disappointed had he heard Hitler ranting to his
generals a few days before. 'The Japanese Emperor . . . is weak,
cowardly, and irresolute. . . . Let us think of ourselves as masters and
consider these people at best as lacquered half-monkeys, who need
to feel the knout.' To Hitler, the Japanese defeat was no surprise.
But thanks to Khalkhin-Gol, the confidence he had in his invasion
of Russia was not shared by the Japanese.

Hirohito was on his own. Yet that was not entirely unsatisfactory.

The 'Strike North' army faction was discredited at last. The Kwantung Army begged to be allowed one more offensive to save its face, but this time the Emperor was firm. In Moscow once more the diplomats took over, and once more the status quo was resumed. A ceasefire was signed on 15 September. In April 1941, a Russo-Japanese Non-Aggression Pact was signed. The Soviet Far East remained safe from Japanese Imperial ambition, and throughout the coming war with Germany, American ships under Soviet flag would sail unhindered from United States arsenals to Vladivostok. Japan would strike south.

5
The Second World War

River Plate (1939)

David Thomas

Commodore Henry H. Harwood, OBE, RN, stabbed a finger on the chart aboard his flagship, the light cruiser HMS *Ajax*: 'That's where she'll turn up next,' he predicted confidently. But he was quite wrong in thinking his quarry was the German pocket-battleship *Admiral Scheer*, nevertheless the chart position was as accurate as a star sight. He further predicted – though with less skill and some luck – that the enemy ship would arrive astride the rich South American trade routes of the River Plate area on 12 December 1939. He was one day out.

The warship was, in fact, the *Admiral Graf Spee* and at the time she was 2,000 miles away celebrating the sinking of the ninth and last victim of her 12-week cruise as a commerce raider. *Admiral Graf Spee* was one of three brilliantly designed German warships: *Deutschland* (re-named *Lützow* in February 1940) was the first, launched in 1931, followed two years later by *Admiral Scheer*, then on 30 June 1934 the garlanded *Admiral Graf Spee* took to the waters of Wilhelmshaven Naval Dock. They were fine ships, and, curiously, they were the direct product of the 1919 Treaty of Versailles which forbade Germany to construct warships of more than 10,000 tons displacement.

German naval architects had evolved an entirely new type of vessel, nominally of 10,000 tons but in the event *Graf Spee* displaced 12,100 tons. A design requirement was to mount guns superior to those of a British heavy cruiser and with protective armor thick enough to withstand such a cruiser's (8-in) shells. By employing welded construction and adopting diesel propulsion in place of conventional steam-turbines, by minimizing thick belt and armor protection, sufficient weight was saved to allow a radius of action of 12,500 miles at cruising speed before the need for refuelling. *Graf Spee*'s 54,000 hp engines gave her a trial speed of 27.7 knots.

The three new warships were armed with a main battery of six 11-in (280 mm) guns in two triple turrets and a secondary armament of eight 5.9-in (150 mm) guns. They could outgun every British cruiser. They could outrun every British battleship. Only three ships in the entire Royal Navy had the speed to catch them and the guns to sink them – the First World War vintage battle-cruisers *Renown*, *Repulse* and *Hood*.

Kapitän zur See (Senior Captain) Hans Langsdorff took command of *Admiral Graf Spee* at the age of 44 in 1938, climaxing a naval career of 26 years; the captain and the ship were well matched but when put to the test of battle it was the man who failed, not the ship. *Graf Spee* sailed from Wilhelmshaven on 21 August 1939, ten days before the outbreak of war, destination mid-Atlantic, and then three days later her sister ship, *Deutschland*, sailed for a similar waiting assignment in the North Atlantic. Each was accompanied by a supply ship, the notorious *Altmark*, later captured as a prison ship, being assigned to *Graf Spee*. The pocket-battleships' tasks had been clearly defined as 'the disruption and destruction of enemy merchant shipping by all possible means.' Action with enemy naval forces was to be avoided at all costs, except to further the primary objective.

Graf Spee entered the sunshine and heat of the South Atlantic and intercepted her first victim, the SS *Clement*, off Brazil on 30 September. But the 5,084-ton ocean-going tramp steamer reported the pocket-battleship as *Admiral Scheer*, a report which confused the eight Raider Hunting Forces formed jointly by the British Admiralty and the French Ministry of Marine. The second victim was the SS *Newton Beech*, one of three ships captured and sunk on the trade routes from the Cape of Good Hope during 5–10 October. *Graf Spee* then rendezvoused with *Altmark* in mid-South Atlantic from whom she fuelled and to whom she transferred the crews of her victims.

A week later SS *Trevanion* was sunk on 22 October, then *Kapitan* Langsdorff rounded the Cape of Good Hope where the 706-ton tanker *Africa Shell* was sunk on 15 November. *Graf Spee* doubled

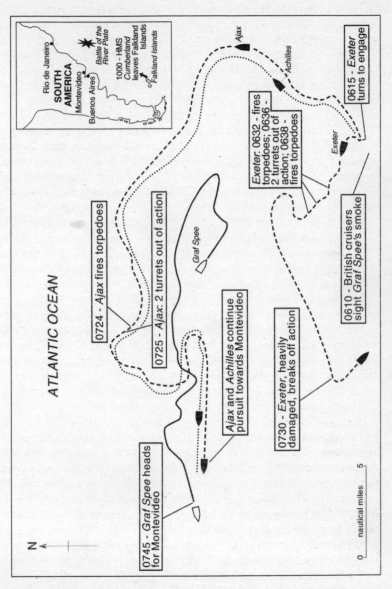

ATLANTIC OCEAN

0724 - *Ajax* fires torpedoes

0725 - *Ajax*: 2 turrets out of action

Ajax and *Achilles* continue pursuit towards Montevideo

0730 - *Exeter*, heavily damaged, breaks off action

0745 - *Graf Spee* heads for Montevideo

Graf Spee

Ajax

Achilles

Exeter. 0632 - fires torpedoes; 0636 - 2 turrets out of action; 0638 - fires torpedoes

Exeter

0615 - *Exeter* turns to engage

0610 - British cruisers sight *Graf Spee's* smoke

SOUTH AMERICA

Rio de Janeiro
Montevideo
Buenos Aires

Battle of the River Plate

1000 - HMS *Cumberland* leaves Falkland Islands

Falkland Islands

N

0   nautical miles   5

5.1   The Battle of the River Plate, 13 December 1939

back, refuelled from *Altmark* on 27 November NE of volcanic Tristan da Cunha island, then a few days later sank the 10,000-ton cargo liner *Doric Star*. Before the end, the liner got away the prescribed distress signal, 'R–R–R', signifying Raider.

The day after the *Doric Star* sinking, SS *Tairoa* was sunk. On 7 December *Graf Spee* sank her last victim, the 3,895-ton cargo vessel *Streonshalh*. This sinking brought her total to nine British ships and 50,089 tons. Not a single life had been lost during these sinkings, a source of great pride to Langsdorff. Many of his prisoners subsequently testified to his courteous firmness, his fairness, distinguished bearing, chivalry and professionalism.

The responsibility for the long and anxious search for the elusive *Graf Spee* in the South Atlantic fell upon Forces G, H and K. Their success depended largely upon attacked merchantmen getting off their R–R–R signal and position. In fact, Langsdorff was better informed about British warship movements. He was aware, for example, that the cruisers *Ajax*, *Achilles*, *Exeter* and *Cumberland* were operating off the South American coast, that the two heavy cruisers *Sussex* and *Shropshire* were off Cape Town and that the battle cruiser *Renown* and aircraft carrier *Ark Royal* were off West Africa.

As Commodore Harwood had predicted, Langsdorff determined to quit the mid-ocean patrol and, as if destiny was directing him to destruction, he set course for the River Plate estuary, attracted by the prospect of rich prizes. Also heading for the estuary was Harwood's squadron, one of the British Raider-Hunting Forces engaged in the ever-changing dispositions, wider-ranging even than the later *Bismarck* pursuit from the wastes of the North Atlantic to the southernmost tip of Latin America.

Early in December 1939, 51-year-old Commodore Harwood, as Officer Commanding the South American Division of the American and West Indies Squadron, flew his broad pennant in the 6,985-ton 6-in gun cruiser *Ajax*, commanded by Captain Charles H. L. Woodhouse. His two heavy 8-in gun cruisers, the 8,390-ton *Exeter* (Captain Frederick S. Bell) and the 9,850-ton *Cumberland* were at Port Stanley in case of an enemy attack to revenge the Battle of the Falkland Islands where Count von Spee's squadron was destroyed on 8 December 1914. The 6-in gun cruiser *Achilles* (Captain Edward Parry), to 7,030 tons and partly manned by 327 New Zealanders, was patrolling off Rio de Janeiro. *Ajax* had recently sailed from Port Stanley for the River Plate.

Harwood calculated after the *Doric Star* sinking that the raider could reach Rio by 12 December and be off the River Plate by the following day. Accordingly, he ordered his cruisers to concentrate. *Exeter* was instructed to leave Port Stanley on the 9th and *Achilles* was instructed to head south from Rio to join the flagship on the 10th. *Cumberland* had to remain in the Falklands to complete an imperative self-refit.

By 0600 on 12 December the three cruisers were in company 150 miles off the River Plate. The Commodore had long considered the tactics his squadron should employ on encountering a pocket-battleship. Undaunted by the greatly superior gunpower of such an adversary, he made his intentions clear in a signal to his three captains, timed 1200, 12 December: 'My policy with three cruisers in company versus one pocket-battleship: attack at once day or night.'

At dawn on 13 December the sea was tropically calm with a light swell. As the light strengthened to promise another beautiful day the three grey British cruisers formed up in line ahead, *Ajax* leading *Achilles* and *Exeter*, 2,000 yards apart, zig-zagging about a mean course of 060° at 14 knots. At 0540 crews stood down from Dawn Action Stations. Visibility rapidly increased with tropical suddenness from a few hundred yards to 20 miles. Twenty minutes before, at 0520, the squadron was in position 34°34′ S, 47°17′ W, 250 nautical miles due east of Punta del Este.

Soon after 0600 Leading Signalman Swanston on *Ajax*'s bridge sighted smoke over the horizon bearing 320°. Harwood ordered *Exeter* to investigate. She swung out of line and at 0616 she signalled by lamp: 'I think it is a pocket-battleship,' and Capt. Bell ordered Flag N hoisted to the yard-arm – 'Enemy in sight'.

Graf Spee, heading 155° at 15 knots, logged an almost identical chart position. Langsdorff held the whip hand. He had sighted the British ships 20 minutes before *Ajax* saw the smudge of smoke. At 0552, fine on the starboard bow, there were first two, then four more thin masts. The stereoptic main range-finder measured a distance of 31,000 metres (33,902 yards = 19.26 miles). By 0600 *Graf Spee* was cleared for action and some of the masts had resolved themselves into the unmistakable superstructure of HMS *Exeter* accompanied by what appeared to be two destroyers.

Now, if ever, was the time for Langsdorff to turn about and refuse action. By maintaining course he committed a cardinal error.

He went even further and decided to attack contrary to Naval Operations Command instructions. Langsdorff's senior navigator, *Korvettenkapitän* (Lieutenant Commander) J. Wattenberg, reminded him of the order to avoid even inferior enemy forces. 'I suspect a convoy.' Langsdorff explained. He ordered full speed to close the range. Phase 1 of the Battle of the River Plate had begun even before the British cruisers had sighted the enemy. At 0615 the pocket-battleship eased to port on to a course of 115° for a running action to starboard with a closing range. By now she had identified the 'destroyers' as *Ajax* and *Achilles*. Her only safeguard now lay in crushing the opposition by destroying it or putting it to flight. At 0618 the two triple 11-in turrets opened fire with a thunderous crash.

When *Exeter* identified the pocket-battleship, Capt. Bell hauled off to the west while Harwood led *Ajax* round to close the range. *Achilles* conformed to the flagship's movements throughout the action enabling the two light cruisers to concentrate their gunfire with great effect. All three ships increased speed, hoisted battle ensigns and fire was opened: *Exeter*'s 8-in guns opened at 0620, *Achilles*' 6-in at 0621 and *Ajax*'s two minutes later. The range was then about 19,000 yards (10.8 miles). Langsdorff had made no effort to maintain his range advantage and he now found himself, as Harwood intended, confronted with two divisions and the problem of whether to divide his main armament to engage them both – or to leave one unengaged. Initially, *Graf Spee* engaged both but very soon shifted fire of all six 11-in guns to *Exeter*. Her accuracy was formidable and remained so throughout the day.

Exeter's 'A' and 'B' (bow) turrets opened fire at 0620 with 'Y' (stern) turret following 2.5 minutes later. She had been steaming on boilers in Boiler Room B only and when the alarm sounded those in Boiler Room A were flashed up and connected. Full speed was ordered at 0620. With his third salvo, the gunnery officer, Lieutenant Commander Richard B. Jennings, straddled *Graf Spee* and prospects looked promising. But *Exeter* herself was under fire and *Graf Spee*'s third main salvo straddled the British ship. A minute or so later – at 0624 – *Exeter* was hit but the 670 lb shell smashed through the deck abaft 'B' turret and passed through the ship's side to the sea without exploding.

A minute later *Graf Spee*'s eighth salvo struck an almost decisive blow: within seconds *Exeter* was transformed from an efficient fighting unit into an uncontrollable machine. 'B' turret took a direct hit between the two gun barrels, putting it and eight of the crew out of action. Splinters swept the bridge killing or wounding nearly everyone there; the wheelhouse was smashed, vital communications cut. Captain Bell, wounded himself, was compelled to retire to the after-conning position where a human chain of command had to be set up.

While the 11-in salvoes were being directed at *Exeter*, Langsdorff employed his eight 5.9-in guns against the 16 6-in guns of the two light cruisers whose accuracy was such that the pocket-battleship shifted fire from *Exeter* to bring her 11-in guns to bear on *Ajax* and *Achilles*.

During this period – at about 0637 – while still under fire from *Graf Spee*'s secondary armament, *Ajax* managed to catapult into the air one of her two 124 m.p.h. Seafox floatplanes, piloted by Lieutenant Edgar D. G. Lewin; a fine evolution considering that 'X' and 'Y' turrets only a few feet away were firing at the time. Lewin and his observer, Lieutenant Richard E. N. Kearney, began their spotting reports at 0654. *Exeter*'s two Walrus seaplanes were damaged beyond repair early in the battle and had to be jettisoned. *Graf Spee*'s Arado 196 floatplane was unserviceable because of a cracked engine block and took no part in the battle.

Exeter's shooting astonished the *Graf Spee*'s officers, both for its accuracy and in particular for the rapidity of each following salvo. Her fifth salvo scored a direct hit but the shell passed through the upper part of the bridge without exploding and caused little damage. Another 8-in shell passed a metre above the armored deck, passing through the 5.5-in (140 mm) armored belt and finally exploding amidships. The ease with which this shell penetrated the armor plate contrary to expectation caused great anxiety aboard *Graf Spee*. Pocket-battleships were not, it seemed, inviolable to 8-in cruisers.

At 0632 the damaged *Exeter*, under severe pressure from the accurate German gunnery, fired her three starboard 21-in torpedo tubes. A few minutes later *Graf Spee* made a heavy alteration of course to port and steered NW under cover of smoke. This change of course prevented a 'crossing the T' situation by *Ajax* and *Achilles*. From this moment on the battle became a pursuit with the light cruisers maintaining contact with *Graf Spee* while the heavily damaged *Exeter* limped along in company. As a parting shot – at 0638 – she fired her port torpedoes, but they too missed.

During this period *Exeter* took two more 11-in shell hits. 'A' turret was damaged and put out of action and a second shell burst in the Chief Petty Officers' flat amidships starting a fierce fire. It was this shell which created the most damage: the 4-in magazine was flooded by burst water mains, all compass repeaters were out of action and Captain Bell handled the cruiser using a whaler's compass. The ship's upperworks were pierced with splinters, dead and dying littered the decks. Lieutenant Commander Jennings, now stationed on the after searchlight platform kept the single remaining 'Y' turret in action under local control. Captain Bell kept adjusting course to keep the turret bearing on the target. *Exeter* took another shell hit under the fo'c'sle, suffered flooding of several compartments and took a 7° list to starboard. Ablaze, she had taken heavy punishment, and was close to being destroyed.

At 0640, when one of *Graf Spee*'s 11-in turrets was being directed against the light cruisers, a shell near-missed *Achilles*, bursting on impact with the sea. Hundreds of splinters penetrated her thin bridge plating and the armor of the Director Control Tower, killing four ratings. Captain Parry and the Chief Yeoman on the bridge were slightly wounded and a splinter severed the halyard for the White Ensign: the battle continued to be fought under the New Zealand flag at the mainmast.

At 0656 Harwood hauled round to the north then west to maintain close range and to keep all guns bearing. He also pursued the tactic of 'chasing salvoes' – sailing towards close splashes and away from distant ones to confuse the enemy spotting. *Graf Spee* also made frequent alterations of course to throw out the British gunfire and from 0700 she made much use of smoke. Despite these tactics she continued to be struck by 6-in shells but these 100 lb projectiles inflicted relatively little damage.

By 0724 Harwood had closed the range to 9,000 yards to deliver a torpedo attack. *Ajax* turned to starboard and fired a spread of four 2-in torpedoes. *Kapitanleutnant* (Lieutenant) Rasenack on *Graf Spee*'s bridge later reported, 'They came right at us. To avoid them our captain again put them under the direct fire of our heavy guns. One of the torpedoes passed only a few metres from our side.' Langsdorff told Captain Patrick G. G. Dove, one of the 62 British Merchant Navy prisoners aboard the pocket-battleship during the battle, 'The *Ajax* and *Achilles* came at me like destroyers.'

But this daring maneuver took an ugly turn for Harwood when *Ajax* received an 11-in shell hit on the after superstructure at 0725; the shell passed through several cabins, wrecking the machinery below 'X' turret and burst in the Commodore's sleeping cabin. Damage was sustained by the 'Y' turret barbette, jamming the turret. Thus one shell effectively put both 'X' and 'Y' turrets out of action, killing and wounding many of the guns' crews. By now *Exeter* was out of the fight, her speed reduced, falling astern of the action, fires raging with 61 officers and ratings killed. *Ajax*, the flagship, had been reduced to only half her main armament. Only *Achilles* remained practically undamaged.

Langsdorff's tactics – British and German naval experts are agreed on this point – are difficult to understand because he should have turned to the southward to finish off *Exeter* before then turning his attention upon the two light cruisers. Yet he deliberately allowed *Exeter* to escape, then pointlessly sought sanctuary in a neutral harbor. Harwood continued to harry *Graf Spee* and by 0728 the range was down to only 8,000 yards (4.54 miles). *Graf Spee* was now being subjected to a deluge of accurate 6-in gunfire and the pocket-battleship even brought into action some of her six 4.1-in (105 mm) AA guns against the cruisers. It was at this stage that the Seafox spotter plane reported torpedo tracks and Harwood altered course to comb them.

Graf Spee, now on a westerly course and clearly heading for the River Plate estuary, was still maintaining accurate fire, one of her last salvoes, at 0738, bringing down *Ajax*'s mainmast with all its radio aerials. Harwood decided to break off the day action, carry out the traditional cruiser duty of shadowing, and close in again after dark. Accordingly, at 0740, 82 minutes since *Graf Spee* had opened fire, the light cruisers turned away to the east under cover of smoke but continued to maintain contact. *Exeter* set course for the Falklands and *Cumberland*, pre-empting a signal from Harwood, sailed at 1000 from the Falklands for the River Plate to take her place.

Langsdorff, who had now recovered from two slight splinter wounds and a bout of unconsciousness from shell blast, made no attempt to pursue Harwood as the cruisers broke off action. He headed for Montevideo in Uruguay at 22 knots and took stock. Senior Surgeon Dr Kartzendorff reported one officer and 35 ratings killed and 61 others wounded. In no way did these casualties reduce the fighting capacity of a ship with a complement of 1,134, but the supply of 11-in shells was only 186–31 per gun.

Damage-control reports revealed a considerable mass of minor damage by 17 6-in shell hits from *Ajax* and *Achilles* and more serious damage by the three 8-in shell hits from *Exeter*. The wireless direction-finding apparatus was damaged and nearly all galleys out of operation. The equipment for purifying lubricating oil was damaged as were the forward ammunition hoists. The armor belt and armored deck had been penetrated: there were 15 holes on the starboard side plating and 12 to port including two in the bows, the largest measuring 6.5 ft wide. Minor items of damage to guns, torpedoes, searchlight and communications was superficial. More important from the point of view of fighting efficiency was slight damage to the main range-finder, foretop, torpedo-ranging device and fire-fighting equipment.

One hit was from a practice shell from *Achilles*, probably loaded in error; it hit aft, killed two ratings, passed through half a dozen cabins and came to rest in the berth of a Petty Officer still identifiable as a drill projectile! It was the large hole in the bows which was serious because *Graf Spee* would ship water in anything for a seaway if she made a dash for Germany. Langsdorff was also worried over the ammunition shortage. He decided, entirely alone and without consultation with his senior officers, to seek shore repair facilities. *Korvettenkapitän* Wattenberg later quoted his captain: 'Our damage cannot be repaired with the means available on board. We must run into port somewhere for repairs.'

Ajax and *Achilles* continued their shadowing for the rest of the day. *Achilles* followed close to the coast. *Ajax* remained to the south to cover a possible doubling back at dusk. At 1915 *Graf Spee* fired two accurate salvoes and at 2048 another three. Sporadic firing finished at 2142 and the pursuit and shadowing phase of the battle ended when *Graf Spee* anchored off Montevideo at 2350.

While the battle and pursuit were in progress the Royal Navy was making dispositions to engage *Graf Spee* whenever she should quit Montevideo. *Cumberland* joined her consorts at 2200 on 14 December after steaming 1,000 miles in 34 hours. The 8-in cruisers *Dorsetshire* and *Shropshire*, carrier *Ark Royal*, battle-cruiser *Renown* and modern cruiser *Neptune* were all directed to the River Plate but this overwhelming strength could not concentrate there before 19 December.

Meanwhile Langsdorff was the center of an unprecedented diplomatic storm in what he later called 'the trap of Montevideo'. He had secured a 72-hour extension over the 24-hour permissible stay of a warship in a neutral port. British objections were more academic than real for they had no wish to force *Graf Spee* to sea before the 19th and the ploy of sailing a British merchant ship each day was adopted. International Law provided that merchantmen leaving port had to be given a head start of 24 hours over an enemy warship.

On 16 December Langsdorff reported to Berlin – erroneously – his belief that the British concentration of warships already lay in wait outside the harbor. *Gross-Admiral* Eric Raeder, C-in-C of the German Navy, discussed this naval dilemma with Hitler that same day and they agreed that an attempted fighting breakout to Buenos Aires was the proper course of action, failing which scuttling would be preferable to internment.

At 1815 on 17 December Langsdorff conned *Graf Spee* out of harbor with a reduced crew aboard: 800 of her company had been transferred to the German tanker SS *Tacoma* which followed close astern. Soon after the ship was outside the three-mile limit she stopped and anchored. Tugs approached. The ensign was lowered. Six fuses were lit. Boats – the last one containing Langsdorff – headed away from *Graf Spee* across the River Plate towards Buenos Aires in Argentina. Six violent explosions shattered the quiet of evening. The pocket-battleship *Graf Spee* exploded like a volcano and settled in the shallows of the estuary, deserving of a more dignified end than a scuttling. She burned like a pyre in position 34°58′ 25″ S, 56° 18′ 01″ W, four miles 117 yards from land.

Langsdorff turned to his senior navigator: 'Pilot, enter in the log book *Graf Spee* put out of service 17 December 1939 at 2000 hours.' *Ajax*, *Achilles* and *Cumberland* steamed by *en route* to Montevideo with Harwood newly knighted and promoted to Rear-Admiral on the bridge of his damaged flagship. Two days later in a suicide letter Langsdorff wrote: 'Now I can only prove by my death that the fighting services of the Third *Reich* are ready to die for the honour of the flag. I alone bear the responsibility for scuttling the pocket-battleship *Graf Spee*. I am happy to pay with my life to prevent any possible reflection on the honour of the flag.'

Lieutenant H. Dietrich found Langsdorff the following morning. He had shot himself in the right temple. He lay in full uniform stretched out on the flag of the German Imperial Navy.

Battle of Britain (1940)

Christopher Dowling

On 30 June 1940 Major-General Alfred Jodl, Hitler's closest military adviser, expressed the view that the final German victory over England was 'only a matter of time'. He had good reason to be confident. Thanks to a run of victories unparalleled since the days of Napoleon, Germany was master of Western Europe from the Arctic to the Bay of Biscay. The much-vaunted French army had been destroyed in a campaign lasting barely six weeks. The British, who had sent a token force to France and Belgium, had been bundled off the Continent. Although the greater part of the British Expeditionary Force had managed to escape, it had been compelled to abandon almost all its heavy equipment and, for the time being, was incapable of offensive action. With the fall of France Britain lost her only ally in Europe. Despite Churchill's defiant speeches, many, including President Roosevelt and his advisers, doubted whether Britain would be able to resist the expected German onslaught.

Paradoxically, the very magnitude of their triumph over France had created intractable strategic problems for the German High Command. No plans had been made for a direct attack on England because the possibility that the Wehrmacht would inflict a decisive defeat on the French army had scarcely been contemplated. At most, Hitler had hoped to occupy bases in the Low Countries and northern France from which a naval and air blockade could be mounted against the British Isles. On 21 May, after the German armour

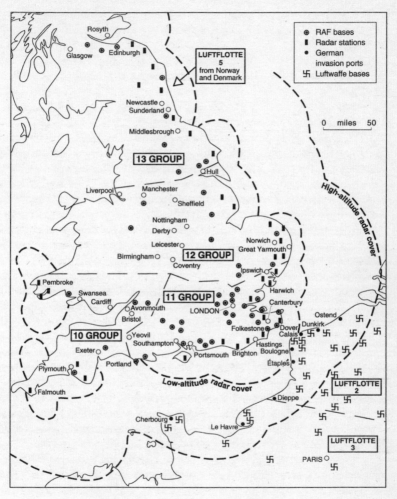

5.2 The Battle of Britain, July–September 1940

had reached the Channel coast, Hitler briefly discussed the idea of invading England with the commander-in-chief of the navy, Admiral Raeder, but he was too preoccupied with the Battle of France (which was far from over) and then with the armistice negotiations to give much thought to the matter. In any case he was convinced that the British, for whom he had a grudging respect, would recognize the hopelessness of their position and sue for peace. He was anxious to bring the war to a Speedy conclusion so that he could fulfil the mission which had always been the ultimate aim of his policy: the carving out of a great land empire in the East.

Hitler's hopes of a settlement with Britain were not finally dispelled until the third week of July, when Churchill contemptuously rejected his ill-conceived 'peace offer'. In the meantime he and his advisers had begun, in a somewhat leisurely manner, to consider possible courses of action should the British refuse to see reason. Britain, with her insular position, her powerful navy and her rapidly expanding air force, was an awkward opponent for the Wehrmacht, which, as the relative size and strength of the three armed services demonstrated, had been designed for Continental warfare. Germany's naval weakness and her lack of long-range aircraft ruled out a strategy of blockade – even if the necessary forces had been available this was bound to be a lengthy process. An invasion seemed the quickest and surest method of bringing Britain to her knees. However, in view of the Royal Navy's overwhelming superiority in surface ships, it was clear that troops could only be landed after air supremacy had been achieved and that even then the operation would be fraught with risk. Unlike some of his generals, Hitler did not regard the voyage across the Channel as merely 'an extended river crossing'. As Raeder was at pains to point out, the navy, which had been decimated in the Norwegian campaign, could provide little or no protection for the invasion fleet. Hitler lent a sympathetic ear to Raeder's arguments and it was agreed that invasion should be a 'last resort', to be launched only when the British had been softened up by air bombardment. If, as its commander-in-chief Hermann Goering boasted, the Luftwaffe was capable of knocking Britain out single-handed, the government might capitulate before the first assault troops crossed the Channel.

On 16 July Hitler announced in a directive that he had decided 'to begin to prepare for, and if necessary to carry out, an invasion of England'. The operation was to be given the codename Sea Lion and preparations were to be completed by the middle of August. The planning for Sea Lion was not marked by the inter-service co-operation and consultation which characterized Operation Overlord, the Allied invasion of north-west Europe in 1944. Goering set little store by Sea Lion and did not attend a single planning session, yet the other two services were relying on the Luftwaffe to establish the conditions for the landing. Disputes between the army and navy over the number of divisions which could be put ashore and the width of the landing front led on 1 August to the postponement of Sea Lion until the middle of September. On the same day Hitler, who was becoming impatient at Goering's dilatoriness, ordered the Luftwaffe to begin intensified warfare against England on or after 5 August. The Royal Air Force was to be overcome as quickly as possible, after which attacks were to be directed against ports; those on the south coast which might be needed for Sea Lion were, however, to be spared. Goering issued his tactical instructions for the air offensive, which he christened Eagle, on 2 August. He had so poor an opinion of the RAF that he allowed only four days for its elimination south of a line from Gloucester to London and four weeks for its total annihilation.

For the coming assault the Luftwaffe could muster some 2,500 serviceable aircraft, of which nearly 1,000 were He 111, Do 17 and Ju 88 medium bombers. In addition there were some 260 Ju 87 dive-bombers – the dreaded Stuka, which, with its menacing silhouette and blood-curdling scream, had come to symbolize the *Blitzkrieg*. The fighters comprised about 800 single-engined Me 109s and 220 twin-engined Me 110s. These aircraft were deployed in three *Luftflotten* (air fleets). *Luftflotte* 2, which was based in Holland, Belgium and northern France, was under the command of Field-Marshal Albert Kesselring, a former artillery officer who had transferred to the Luftwaffe in 1933. His genial manner had earned him the nickname 'Smiling Albert'. Further west lay *Luftflotte* 3 under Field-Marshal Hugo Sperrle, who had commanded the Condor Legion during the Spanish Civil War. It was intended that the 150 or so bombers of *Luftflotte* 5, under General Hans-Juergen Stumpff, should create a diversion by attacking targets in north-east England from their bases in Norway and Denmark. Of the three *Luftflotten* commanders, Sperrle was the only one who had flown in the First World War.

Although the Luftwaffe had officially been in existence for little more than five years it had already acquired a legendary reputation. It had played a spectacular and decisive part in the Polish, Norwegian and French campaigns; in the euphoria of victory the check it had suffered at the hands of the RAF over Dunkirk in May 1940 was soon forgotten and its significance was overlooked. Yet, formidable though it was, the Luftwaffe was in many respects ill equipped for the task which it had been given and which its leaders had embraced so readily. It had been designed not for independent strategic bombing but rather for the tactical support of the army in the field, a role which it had performed with brilliant success. Its organization, the training of its crews and the weapons with which they were provided reflected this purpose. The Luftwaffe lacked the essential instrument for an effective air offensive, a long-range heavy bomber. The medium and dive-bombers which formed its striking force did not have the necessary range, armament or bomb-carrying capacity for strategic operations and were vulnerable to the latest fighters, the dive-bombers particularly so. Had the ambitions of the first chief of the Luftwaffe General Staff, the gifted and far-sighted General Walther Wever, been realized, Germany might by the summer of 1940 have possessed a fleet of heavy bombers capable of reaching every target in the United Kingdom. As early as 1936 – the year in which the British Air Staff first issued the specification for a four-engined bomber – prototypes of the Do 19 and Ju 89 were ready for testing. However, after Wever's death in an air crash both models were scrapped and the heavy bomber programme was given a low priority.

The Luftwaffe was also severely handicapped by the limited endurance (about 80 minutes) of its standard fighter, the Me 109, which in other respects was an outstanding aircraft. The return journey across the Channel took approximately an hour; this left only 20 minutes for combat over England. The longer-ranged Me 110, on which extravagant hopes had been placed, proved incapable of holding its own against the RAF's Hurricanes and Spitfires and had itself to be protected by the faster and more nimble Me 109. As the German bombers were too vulnerable to fly without escort in daylight, their operational zone was necessarily restricted to the Me 109's radius of action – that is, to London and the south-east corner of England, where the British defences were concentrated. Moreover, owing to the comparative neglect of the fighter arm before the war, there were not enough Me 109s to provide adequate cover for the bombers, each of which needed an escort of at least two fighters. This, in effect, reduced the number of bombers that could be launched against Britain at any one time to a mere three or four hundred.

The Luftwaffe High Command was only vaguely aware of these deficiencies. Goering, who was more of a politician than an airman, greatly overestimated the strength of what he fondly regarded as 'his' Luftwaffe. He had been a dashing fighter pilot during the First World War, but he had resigned his commission in 1922 and since then had lost touch with the development of military aviation. Hitler took little interest in air warfare and was content to leave the management of the Luftwaffe entirely to his faithful party henchman. Though he was not without ability, Goering had neither the technical knowledge nor the professional experience to command a modern air force. He lacked the capacity for sustained work and concerned himself only spasmodically with Luftwaffe affairs, preferring to lead a life of self-indulgent ease on his country estate at Karinhall. His chief of staff, the youthful Hans Jeschonnek, was an ardent Nazi and was not disposed to challenge his overbearing superior. In any case, he, like the two field commanders Kesselring and Sperrle, shared many of Goering's illusions about the Luftwaffe's potential.

While the Battle of Britain was, from the Luftwaffe's point of view, an improvised operation hastily mounted with the resources to hand, the RAF had been preparing for it over a period of more than four years. By the summer of 1940 a sophisticated system of air defence had been evolved under the direction of the commander-in-chief of Fighter Command, Air Chief Marshal Sir Hugh Dowding. The cornerstone of this system was the chain of 52 radar (originally called RDF or radio direction-finding) stations which lined the coast from Pembrokeshire to the Shetlands. In the early 1930s the problem of intercepting enemy bombers before they reached their targets had seemed insoluble, since the defending fighters had to be alerted when the raiders were still well out to sea. In 1935, however, Robert Watson Watt demonstrated that radio waves might be used to detect and locate approaching aircraft. His ideas were taken up by another distinguished scientist, Sir Henry Tizard, who harnessed the new device of radar to operational requirements. Although the radar screen was not quite complete when the Battle of Britain began, it was able to provide accurate information on the distance and bearing of hostile aircraft at ranges of 70 miles or more and to give a rough indication of their height and numbers. Once the aircraft had crossed the coast their movements were tracked by the keen-eyed volunteers of the Observer Corps, whose methods Churchill rather tactlessly described as 'early Stone Age'. The Germans were aware of the existence of the radar stations – their towering masts made them an obvious landmark – but they underestimated their efficiency and did not realize how closely they had been integrated into the British defence system. Radar enabled the British fighters to be in the right place at the right time and obviated the need for standing patrols. Without its magic eye Fighter Command would have been at a hopeless disadvantage.

Information from the radar stations and Observer Corps posts was passed by means of an elaborate network of communications to the four groups into which Fighter Command was divided. The most important of these was No. 11 Group, which was responsible for the key area of London and the south-east of England. Its commander was Air Vice-Marshal Keith Park, a New Zealander, who, though very different in personality from Dowding, saw eye to eye with him on the handling of the fighter force. No. 12 Group, under Air Vice-Marshal Trafford Leigh-Mallory (brother of the famous mountaineer George Mallory), covered the Midlands; No. 13 Group, under Air Vice-Marshal R. E. Saul, Scotland and the north of England; and No. 10 Group, under Air Vice-Marshal Sir Quinton Brand, the south-west. Each group comprised a number of sectors. There were seven sector stations in No. 11 Group: Tangmere, Northolt, North Weald, Debden, Hornchurch, Biggin Hill and Kenley. The sector commander ordered aircraft into the air in accordance with the orders he received from group headquarters and directed their movements from the ground by the then advanced method of radio telephone. Although Fighter Command Headquarters at Bentley Priory near Stanmore had a general view of the situation as it developed from minute to minute, the actual conduct of the battle was left to the various groups and sectors. In addition to the radar stations, Observer Corps centres and fighter squadrons, Dowding had at his disposal the 1,500 barrage balloons of Balloon Command, and the 1,300 heavy and 700 light guns of Anti-Aircraft Command.

At the beginning of August the RAF had a front-line strength of 1,200 aircraft, nearly 700 of which were fighters. (The 500 or so bombers were not directly involved in the battle.) All but a handful of the 55 fighter squadrons were equipped with Hurricanes or Spitfires, whose eight wing-mounted Browning machine-guns were capable of destroying a bomber in a two-second burst of fire. The Hurricane has been overshadowed in the popular imagination by the more glamorous Spitfire, and it is not always recognized that it formed the backbone of the fighter defences. It was a steady, robust and highly manoeuvrable aircraft but it was inferior in performance to the Me 109. There was little to choose between the Me 109 and the Spitfire, though the system of direct fuel injection which enabled the German machine to go into a steep dive without any loss of power perhaps tipped the scales in its favour. In terms of the number and quality of their single-engined fighters and the skill and courage of the men who flew them the two sides were evenly matched. The British, however, had the greater reserves and, thanks to the forceful methods of Lord Beaverbrook, the Minister of Aircraft Production, were producing more than twice as many aircraft as the Germans. Between June and September 1940 deliveries of Me 109s averaged only 190 a month, compared with 470 Hurricanes and Spitfires.

The position as far as pilots were concerned was less encouraging. Nearly 300 fighter pilots had been lost during the Battle of France (a third of the total complement), and at the beginning of August Fighter Command was still 154 pilots below establishment, despite the welcome addition to its ranks of trained recruits from France, Belgium, Czechoslovakia, Poland, the United States and the Dominions. On the other hand the British enjoyed the advantage of fighting over their own territory: RAF pilots who baled out or crash-landed could be in action again within a few hours, whereas their opponents were marched off to prisoner-of-war camps. Similarly, many of the British aircraft that were shot down could be salvaged.

Fighter Command was fortunate in being led by men of unrivalled professional ability and experience. Dowding, who but for the outbreak of the war would have been retired in 1939, was a career officer with a keen interest in the application of science to modern warfare. Just as the Grand Fleet of the First World War was moulded by Lord Fisher, so Fighter Command was largely Dowding's creation. Austere, reserved and dedicated, he presented a complete contrast to the flamboyant and vainglorious Goering. By his tenacious opposition to the War Cabinet's proposal to send additional fighter squadrons to France after the German breakthrough in May 1940, Dowding ensured that he had sufficient forces with which to fight the Battle of Britain. Unlike their German counterparts, many of whom had army backgrounds, Dowding and his senior officers had behind them a quarter of a century of continuous service in military aviation.

The Battle of Britain, like the Battle of the Atlantic and the Battle of France, was, strictly speaking, a campaign rather than a battle. In fact it was a campaign within a campaign, for it formed part of a major German air offensive against Britain which lasted from June 1940, when the first bombs fell on British soil, to May 1941, when the bulk of the Luftwaffe was transferred to the Eastern Front in preparation for the attack on Russia. Although there is no agreement about its exact time span, the Battle of Britain consisted in essence of a series of daylight engagements fought in the skies above south-east England between 12 August and 30 September 1940. During these critical weeks the Luftwaffe sought to destroy Fighter Command in order to pave the way for a landing or for the unopposed occupation of a country paralysed by bombing. As Fighter Command could only be engaged in daylight the night raids by unescorted bombers, which began to assume a regular pattern after 24 August, cannot properly be regarded as part of the Battle of Britain, except perhaps for those that supplemented the daylight attacks on London during the last three weeks of September. After September the daylight fighting gradually died down and the Battle of Britain merged imperceptibly into the Blitz.

The prelude to the battle was an attempt by Goering early in July to wear down Fighter Command by attacking ports and shipping in the Channel. Neither side was at full strength, for the Luftwaffe had not yet completed its redeployment after the French campaign, and Dowding prudently refused to commit more than a small number of squadrons in conditions which usually favoured the enemy. The *Kanalkampf*, as the Germans called it, continued with mounting intensity until well into August. The results of these preliminary skirmishes were inconclusive. The Germans sank 30,000 tons of shipping and succeeded in establishing air superiority over the Straits of Dover in daylight, but their losses in aircraft were twice those of the British.

The Battle of Britain proper can be said to have begun on 12 August, when the Luftwaffe struck its first real blows at the RAF's fighter airfields and radar stations. Of the six radar stations attacked, one, Ventnor on the Isle of Wight, was so badly damaged that it was out of action for ten days, though this was skilfully concealed from the Germans. The Luftwaffe, however, failed to follow up the limited success it had achieved. Owing to faulty planning and slipshod staff work the long awaited Eagle Day on 13 August, which was to herald the opening of the main air assault, proved to be a flop. No attempt was made to repeat the attacks on the radar stations, and the aerodromes at Eastchurch, Detling and Andover were heavily bombed in the mistaken belief that they were fighter stations.

On 15 August the Luftwaffe made its greatest effort of the battle, flying no fewer than 1,786 sorties. Every available fighter was thrown in and for the first and last time all three *Luftflotten* were committed. The outcome was a notable victory for Fighter Command, which shot down 75 German aircraft at a cost of 34 of its own. The weakly escorted bombers of *Luftflotte* 5 came in over the North Sea expecting to encounter little or no opposition. They were set upon by fighters from Nos 12 and 13 Groups when they were still some distance from land and suffered such crippling losses that they took no further part in the battle. There was heavy fighting on 16 and 18 August before a spell of cloudy weather brought the first phase of the struggle to an end.

Although Fighter Command was putting up stiff resistance, Goering, whose wishful thinking was reinforced by wildly inaccurate intelligence estimates, believed that Dowding had only about 300 fighters left – this was less than half the true figure. By concentrating his attacks on Fighter Command's vital airfields in south-east England he hoped to draw the British into an all-out fighter action in which Dowding's remaining squadrons would be wiped out. Hitherto, on Park's instructions, the British fighter pilots had engaged the bombers and avoided combat with the Me 109s. This had driven the Germans to employ their fighters in a close escort role rather than in the offensive sweeps for which they were best suited. In order to provide the strong escorts which Goering demanded for the bombers, almost all the Me 109s in Sperrle's area were transferred to Kesselring. The Ju 87s, which had been severely mauled, were withdrawn. Further attacks on the radar stations were discouraged by Goering, who considered them a poor investment, and after 18 August they were left unmolested.

The second and most crucial phase of the battle opened on 24 August with a devastating raid by *Luftflotte* 2 on No. 11 Group's forward aerodrome at Manston, which was so badly knocked about that it had to be evacuated. During the next fortnight the Luftwaffe began for the first time to gain the upper hand. The new German tactics of maintaining continuous patrols over the Straits of Dover and of delivering feint attacks across the Channel confused the British defences. Park's fighters found it difficult to get to grips with the German bombers, which were now protected by swarms of Me 109s. The disparity in losses narrowed sharply. From 31 August to 6 September the Luftwaffe lost 225 bombers and fighters, the British 185 fighters. As bombers accounted for about half of the German figure the British losses in fighters were considerably higher. Of even greater concern than the dwindling reserves of aircraft was the wastage of trained pilots: weekly casualties were running at more than 10 per cent of Fighter Command's total combat strength and the strain of almost daily action was beginning to tell. The Luftwaffe was also causing serious damage on the ground. At Biggin Hill, which was raided six times in three days, the operations room was wrecked, hangars, workshops and barracks destroyed and nearly 70 station staff killed or wounded. Early in September the Luftwaffe was close to winning some measure of air superiority over Kent and Sussex. This would have forced Park to withdraw his squadrons to airfields north of the Thames, from which an effective defence of south-east England would have been impossible.

But on 7 September Goering relaxed the pressure on Fighter Command's ground organization by switching the main weight of the offensive to London. Shortly after 5 p.m. over 300 bombers escorted by some 600 fighters converged on the capital and dropped a hail of bombs and incendiaries on the East End and the London docks, kindling numerous fires. Fighter Command was taken by surprise and the German bomber losses were comparatively light. The blazing warehouses and oil refineries acted as a beacon for a further 250 bombers, which continued the work of destruction during the night. When dawn rose over the smoke-laden city 306 civilians were dead and 1,337 seriously injured.

There were two reasons for what, in the event, proved a disastrous change of strategy: one military, the other political. The time of decision for Sea Lion was fast approaching. Already, in the first week of September, hundreds of barges and tugs had begun to creep round the North Sea coast to the ports of embarkation in the Channel, yet the Luftwaffe had still not achieved the necessary degree of air superiority to justify launching the invasion. Goering and Kesselring, though not the more realistic Sperrle, were convinced that Fighter

Command was on its last legs and that mass daylight raids on a target as important as London would hasten their victory by forcing Dowding to expend his few remaining fighters. The possibility that ruthless bombing of the civilian population might break the British will to resist was an added inducement. The political reason for the assault on London was Hitler's demand that reprisals should be carried out for British raids on Berlin, which had themselves been ordered as reprisals for the accidental bombing of London by the Luftwaffe on the night of 24 August.

Because of unsettled weather and the growing fatigue of its aircrews the Luftwaffe was unable to sustain its daylight offensive against London. In the week that followed the big attack of 7 September there were only three days – 9, 11 and 14 September – when sizeable forces were sent over London, though it was heavily bombed every night. The raid on 9 September was a failure, but two days later the Luftwaffe inflicted greater losses than it incurred, while in the fighting on 14 September honours were even. The opposition was patchy and it seemed to the Germans that the British fighter defences were at last on the point of collapse. Encouraged by Goering's jubilant account of the Luftwaffe's recent achievements, Hitler determined to wait until 17 September before making a final decision about Sea Lion. In the meantime the raids on London were to continue.

The weather on the morning of 15 September was clear and sunny. Sensing that the day would not be devoid of incident, Winston Churchill paid one of his periodic visits to No. 11 Group's headquarters at Uxbridge. As Park accompanied the Prime Minister and his wife down to the operations room, 50 feet below the ground, he remarked: 'I don't know whether anything will happen today. At present all is quite.' Shortly after 10.30 a.m. radar plots revealed that enemy aircraft were massing over the Pas de Calais, and it soon became apparent that a major attack was imminent. The Germans neglected to carry out their usual feints and Park was able to deploy his forces to the best advantage. When the German bombers crossed the English coast at about 11.30 a.m. they were engaged by successive squadrons of British fighters and harried all the way to London. Although a considerable amount of damage was done few of the bombers succeeded in reaching their targets. After a two-hour interval, which gave the British fighters an opportunity to rearm and refuel, a second and heavier attack was launched. It too was repulsed.

One of the features of the day's fighting was the timely intervention of a wing of five squadrons from No. 12 Group, aggressively led by Squadron Leader Douglas Bader. Park, who believed in using his squadrons singly or in pairs rather than in the large formations advocated by Leigh-Mallory and Bader, had, on previous occasions, complained bitterly about the lack of support from No. 12 Group.

As the German bombers straggled back to their bases, many with their wings and fuselages riddled with bullets and with dead or wounded men on board, it became clear that the Luftwaffe had taken a severe beating. The British thought that they had shot down 185 German aircraft, and on the strength of this grossly inflated estimate 15 September has come to be celebrated as Battle of Britain Day. The actual German losses were about 50 – fewer than on 15 and 18 August. Even so, the two actions on 15 September, if not particularly significant from a tactical point of view, were strategically decisive. The German fighters had once again held their own but they had been unable to protect the bombers. There was no disguising the fact that Fighter Command, which had lost only 26 aircraft, was still very much in being and that air supremacy was as far away as ever. Furthermore, since 4 September Bomber Command had been mounting nightly attacks on the Channel ports and had sunk or damaged more than a hundred barges and transports. On 17 September Hitler postponed Sea Lion indefinitely. Two days later, after Bomber Command had struck further damaging blows, he ordered the invasion fleet to be dispersed.

The abandonment of Sea Lion (formally cancelled on 12 October) did not, as might have been expected, bring the Battle of Britain to an end, for Hitler was anxious to keep up the threat of a landing and Goering, who was not one to admit defeat, still nourished the hope that his stubborn adversary might yet be vanquished. After 15 September the Luftwaffe turned increasingly to night bombing – a tacit acknowledgement that it had failed to win the daylight battle – but daylight attacks on London and other targets by mass formations of bombers continued for another fortnight. The fighting did not go in the Luftwaffe's favour and at the beginning of October, in order to avoid further bomber losses, Goering resorted to the use of fighter-bombers, which relied on speed and altitude to evade the British defences. These raids were mere pinpricks compared with what had gone before and they served no real strategic purpose. Nevertheless the battle dragged on, its finale being the belated intervention of the Italian air force, which made two gallant but ineffectual raids on 29 October and 11 November. The crew of one of the antiquated Fiat BR20 bombers which was shot down over East Anglia presented an incongruous spectacle: they wore steel helmets and were armed with bayonets.

There were many reasons for the Luftwaffe's defeat in the Battle of Britain: Goering's muddled strategy and his boundless capacity for self-delusion; the failure of the Germans to destroy or neutralize the British radar screen; the shortage of Me 109s and their unsuitability as bomber escorts; the high courage and superb morale of Fighter Command's pilots and ground crews, whose belief in ultimate victory never wavered; and, not least, the resolute strategy and skilful tactics pursued by Dowding and Park. Ironically, their conduct of the battle, in particular their reluctance to employ their fighters in big wings, earned official disapproval, and both were removed from their commands before the year was out. Few battles of comparable importance in world history have been won at such a small cost in human life: between 10 July and 31 October 1940 (the official British dates for the Battle of Britain) Fighter Command's casualties were only 449, though these were nonetheless grievous losses. In the course of the battle Fighter Command lost 915 aircraft, the Luftwaffe 1,733. Tactically the fighting was inconclusive, since neither air force was able to do irreparable harm to the other. At the end of the battle Fighter Command's strength in aircraft was greater than it had been at the beginning. The Luftwaffe took longer to recover, largely because of Germany's low rate of aircraft production, but it had made good its losses both in aircraft and in personnel by the spring of 1941, and its operational efficiency was not noticeably impaired. Its leaders, however, failed to take action to remedy the shortcomings which the Battle of Britain had exposed. Little attempt was made, for example, to step up aircraft production, or to expand the woefully inadequate training programme, or to accelerate the development of a four-engined bomber. It is a remarkable fact that the only major new aircraft type introduced into service in Germany between 1939 and 1944 was the Focke-Wulf 190. In so far as the Luftwaffe never again enjoyed the prestige or the relative striking power that it had possessed in June 1940, the Battle of Britain marked the beginning of its decline.

Dowding's victory in the Battle of Britain was no less significant than Nelson's at Trafalgar, with which, indeed, it has sometimes been compared. Yet in many ways Lord Howard of Effingham's victory over the Spanish Armada in 1588 affords a closer parallel. The defeat of the Spanish Armada was the first great naval battle of modern times, the Battle of Britain the first (and almost certainly the last) great air battle. Like the Battle of Britain, the duel between the English fleet and the Armada was not a setpiece encounter but a string of engagements of varying size and intensity. Both were successful defensive battles, though neither decided the issue of the war. Nor was the disparity in strength between the respective fleets and air forces nearly as wide as was thought at the time: the two battles were more akin to the combat between Hector and Achilles than to that between David and Goliath. Like some of the German generals, notably Field-Marshal von Rundstedt, the Duke of Parma, whose troops were to carry out the landings, was indifferent to the invasion project. The antipathy which existed between Drake and Frobisher finds some echo in the clash between Park and Leigh-Mallory over tactics. Just as Howard was criticized for failing to annihilate the Spanish fleet, so it was argued in some quarters that Dowding and Park could have inflicted greater losses on the Luftwaffe by adopting a more aggressive policy. There, however, the parallel ends, for whereas the defeat of the Armada led to a revival of Spanish naval power, the defeat of the Luftwaffe, as we have seen, was one of the signposts on the road to its ultimate demise.

The failure of the Luftwaffe to destroy Fighter Command in the summer of 1940 had far-reaching strategic consequences. It was the first setback suffered by the Wehrmacht in the Second World War and it dented the myth of German invincibility in much the same way as Napoleon's repulse at Aspern-Essling in 1809 had shown a demoralized Europe that the all-conquering Grand Army could be mastered. Furthermore, it shattered Hitler's hopes of a swift victory and ensured that the struggle would be a protracted one; Germany, whose economy and armed forces were geared to a *Blitzkrieg* strategy, was ill-equipped to fight this kind of war. Hitler realized that in view of Britain's rapidly growing military strength an invasion in 1941 would not be feasible. Germany was thus forced to seek alternative avenues to victory, which involved her in costly campaigns in the Mediterranean. Although the frustration of the German attempt to conquer Britain had nothing to do with the attack on Russia, planning for which had started several weeks before Eagle Day, operations in the East seemed to offer a solution to the stalemate in the West. Hitler was obliged to embark on the invasion of Russia with an unsubdued enemy in his rear. The threat of British intervention on the Continent pinned down more than 35 divisions, thereby reducing the forces available for Operation Barbarossa. Perhaps the last word should be given to von Rundstedt. Shortly after the war he told a group of Russian officers that had the Luftwaffe won the Battle of Britain Germany would have defeated Russia in 1941. The Russians had come to ask him which he considered to be the decisive battle of the war, expecting him to name Stalingrad. When he replied, 'The Battle of Britain', they closed their notebooks and went away.

Keren (1941)

John Strawson

'Am concerned at check developing at Keren. Abyssinia might be left, but had hopes Eritrea would be cleaned up' – read the telegram to Cairo of a worried Winston Churchill on 20 February 1941. The mountainous escarpment of Keren formed a natural fortress barrier shielding the coastal province of Eritrea from the interior of Africa. Italy had annexed Eritrea in 1890 and from there Mussolini's armies had overrun Ethiopia (Abyssinia) in 1935–6. Now, five years later, they had made Keren the bastion of *Il Duce*'s East African Empire against British invasion from the Sudan. Keren was to be a soldier's battle in the grimmest imaginable conditions and terrain and here as nowhere else in the Second World War Italian soldiers of all types were to belie the belief that they were a pushover in battle.

As early as August 1939, General Sir Archibald Wavell, British Commander-in-Chief in the Middle East, concluded that there were four things he must do in the event of Italy going to war alongside Germany. These were to secure the Suez Canal base by acting boldly in the Western Desert; get control of the Eastern Mediterranean; clear the Red Sea; then develop operations in south-east Europe. After Mussolini's entry into the Second World War in June 1940 Wavell wrestled to achieve these objectives. What he had not foreseen was that he would be required to do all four simultaneously with inadequate resources. Yet in spite of some nasty shocks he managed the first of these tasks and was wholly, startlingly, successful in the third. It is of this campaign, the clearing of East Africa and the Red Sea, that Keren formed a part.

Wavell's strategic dilemma is admirably depicted and the one bright spot on an otherwise dark canvas is suitably illuminated by his cable to Winston Churchill in the last week of March 1941, after Keren had been captured. It was in reply to a message from the Prime Minister expressing alarm at Rommel's advance to El Agheila, and it helps to set the battle in its proper context:

> I have to admit taking considerable risks in Cyrenaica after capture of Benghazi in order to provide maximum support for Greece . . . Result is I am weak in Cyrenaica at present and no reinforcements of armoured troops, which are chief requirement, are at present available . . . Have just come back from Keren. Capture was very fine achievement by Indian divisions. Platt will push on towards Asmara as quickly as he can and I have authorised Cunningham to continue towards Addis Ababa from Harrar, which surrendered yesterday.

Wavell had four campaigns on his hands – Cyrenaica, Greece, Eritrea and Ethiopia. It was essential to get the East African battles over and done with. Ethiopia had to be dealt with quickly in order to send the much-needed troops back to the Western Desert where the dangers were so much greater – point which Rommel was shortly to rub home. But before this could be done, before troops and stores could be sent via the Red Sea port of Massawa to Egypt and so on to Libya and Greece, the Asmara–Addis Ababa road had to be captured. And in the way stood the fortress of Keren.

On 19 January 1941, Lieutenant-General William Platt advanced from the Sudan into Eritrea, while a few days later Lieutenant-General Sir Alan Cunningham set out on his march from Kenya with African and South African troops. Platt quickly reached Keren but the battle for it, the most severe of the whole East African campaign, lasted nearly two months. After its capture Platt soon took Asmara and Massawa, thus opening the vital route to the north. Cunningham's successes were equally astonishing in speed and distance. By 25 February he had taken Mogadishu together with a huge petrol dump, and a month later, having advanced 1,000 miles, reached Harrar. By 5 April he had captured Addis Ababa and then the two forces, Platt from the north, Cunningham from the south, converged on Amba Alagi. It was here that the Duke of Aosta, Italian Viceroy of Ethiopia, had concentrated what was left of his armies. By 16 May all was over. The extent and totality of the victory were summed up by Wavell in his despatch: 'The conquest of Italian East Africa had been accomplished in four months . . . in this period a force of 220,000 men had been practically destroyed with the whole of its equipment, and an area of nearly a million square miles had been occupied.'

It was that rare thing – a complete victory, a battle of annihilation since none of the enemy escaped. The fighting was unlike any other in the war. Great mountain barriers had been stormed. In Ethiopia the operations, among which Orde Wingate's Gideon force ranks high, had been largely guerrilla, and had succeeded in tying down large numbers of Italian troops which were thus unable to concentrate against the advancing British columns. Yet these columns had been small and this was their strength, since supply problems, although formidable, had been surmountable. Mobility had been everything, while for the Italians the very size of the huge Empire they tried to protect had paralyzed them. How did the situation appear to the Italian Viceroy?

Despite the Italians' early and relatively insignificant successes of July 1940 when they captured frontier posts in Kenya and Sudan and invaded British Somaliland, Aosta's strategy was essentially defensive. By the beginning of December 1940 he was already expecting British offensives from the Sudan against Eritrea, particularly from Kassala towards Keren, and from Kenya against Italian Somaliland and Ethiopia. Because of fuel and vehicle shortages it was difficult to ensure that his centrally held reserves would be sufficiently agile to reinforce a threatened area rapidly. He therefore decided to send some of these reserves forward, especially in the north towards Eritrea where he rightly thought that the first blow would fall.

In Eritrea itself he ordered the local commanders to organize areas of resistance which were to be firmly held while mobile reserves, mainly colonial brigades, would be prepared to operate between these areas and attack an advancing enemy's flanks. Eritrea contained three colonial divisions and three colonial brigades plus garrison troops. These native troops, *Askaris*, would be peculiarly susceptible to reverses and their loyalty would be unlikely to survive serious setbacks. In the north, where Generale di Corpo d'Armante Luigi Frusci commanded, the Viceroy foresaw grave difficulties in countering the British mechanized forces which would advance across flat country near the Sudan–Eritrea frontier, and on 11 January 1941 he therefore sought Mussolini's agreement to the evacuation of Kassala, Tessenei and Gallabat-Metemma. *Il Duce* agreed. On the other hand, Aosta decreed that there would be no withdrawal from Agordat and Barentu, both south-west of Keren, and that Keren itself would be strengthened by a regiment of the elite *Savoia* Grenadier Division. In this way they would help 'to close the gap absolutely.'

Such was the situation shortly before Platt began his advance. He had two very famous Indian Divisions under his command – the 4th (which Wavell had sent from Libya in January thereby taking the sort of risk he pointed out in his telegram to Churchill) and the 5th stationed in the Sudan since September 1940. These divisions were made up largely of Indian troops, ideally suited to the mountain warfare which they were about to wage, but there were British battalions and other units too. Platt had also formed the 1,000-strong Gazelle Force partly from units in 5th Indian Division, notably the renowned Indian cavalry regiment, Skinner's Horse, and from the Sudan Defence Force. The group included machine-gun, artillery and supporting units and was commanded by the dashing Colonel Frank W. Messervy. While Platt was still on the defensive, Gazelle Force had been used to harass and ambush Italian troops in and near Kassala. So successful were they that the Italians withdrew from Kassala by mid-January.

General Platt's task was clear. He must advance from Kassala into Eritrea and take Massawa, a distance as the crow flies of about 230 miles. There were only two ways of getting there and both routes led through Agordat to Keren. The northern route, a poor and narrow dry-weather road, was via Sabderat and Keru; the southern one was a better road but less direct and went through Tessenei and Barentu to Agordat. A well-surfaced road ran from Agordat to Keren and then on to Asmara and Massawa. The whole country was in one sense ideal for war. Except for the few towns, roads, railways and bridges, there was, as in the desert, little made by man to be destroyed. Yet curiously enough the place was alive with game. For the soldiers themselves it was less hospitable – mountainous, arid and rough. 'The plains and valleys', wrote Lieutena-General Sir Geoffrey Evans, 'were a mixture of jungle or open spaces dotted with outcrops of rock, stunted trees, palms near water and scrub, the mountains, strewn with boulders of immense size, spear grass and thorn bushes, were extremely arduous to climb in the heat, particularly when the troops were loaded with a full pack, ammunition and often an extra supply of water since there was none on the slopes.'

Fifth Indian Division was to advance to Agordat by Tessenei and Barentu, while 4th Indian Division with two of its brigades made for the same objective via Keru. The third brigade of 4th Indian Division was to move to Keren from Port Sudan. The whole advance began with Gazelle Force in the lead on the northern route. There was a certain amount of excitement before they reached Agordat. On 21 January, as a divisional history has recorded,

> while Messervy was engrossed with the situation at Keru, a nearby patch of scrub erupted. With shrill yells a squadron of Eritrean horsemen, 60 in number raced on the gun positions in front of Gazelle Force Headquarters. Kicking their shaggy ponies to a furious gallop, the cavalrymen rose in their stirrups to hurl small percussion grenades ahead of them. With great gallantry they surged on, but the gunners brought their pieces into action in time to blow back the horsemen from the muzzles of the guns.

There could have been few such bizarre actions during six years of war. The intrepid horsemen, led in by an Italian officer on a white horse, left 25 dead and 16 wounded on the field of battle.

More serious business confronted Gazelle Force. The battle for the heights to the south of Keru Gorge required the combined efforts of 4th Battalion, 11th Sikh Regiment, Skinner's Horse and 2nd Cameron Highlanders against firm Italian resistance. Even then it was more the danger of being outflanked and cut off from the south by 10th Brigade of 5th Indian Division than direct frontal pressure which caused the Italians to abandon their positions. By 25 January 4th Indian Division had closed up on Agordat, had cut the Barentu road and faced their first real obstacle. Meanwhile 5th Indian Division was ordered to take Barentu. Italian resistance there was stubborn, and just as 10th Brigade's advance had helped 4th Indian Division to capture the Keru Gorge heights, so 4th Indian Division's subsequent success at Agordat allowed the 5th to overrun the Italians at Barentu on 2 February.

The battle for Agordat resolved itself into a struggle for Mount

Cochen, described by those who saw it as 'a steep and involved ridge system which sprang to a height of 1,500 ft, its rugged barrier extending into the east until it ended above a defile four miles long through which the road to Keren passed.' The Agordat and Mount Cochen position was held by the Italian 4th Colonial Division, which was then attacked by two brigades, the 5th and 11th, of 4th Indian Division. The gallant actions of Indian and British infantry were greatly assisted by four 'I' (Infantry) tanks whose job it was to knock out the Italian armor. Lightweight Bren-gun carriers were used to lure the Italian tanks out of their hides. 'The bait was taken with a vengeance. Eighteen Italian tanks burst from cover and raced to destroy the flimsy intruders. Then the "I" tanks barged into the open, their guns playing on their Italian adversaries at point-blank range. Six medium and five light tanks went up in flames. The survivors scuttled frantically into cover.'

On the crests of Mount Cochen itself the final action had been dramatic and bloody. The Italian commander then had dispatched a company of Eritrean infantry to contain Indian troops advancing on the peak itself so that he could withdraw his main body to new positions. But the Eritreans encountered a covering force of some 40 Rajputana Rifles and Pathan Sappers and Miners who 'fell on the Eritreans like furies, plying the steel and leaving a wake of dead and wounded behind them. The survivors scattered in frantic flight. Over 100 bodies were counted along the slopes after. No further resistance was met as 11th Brigade advanced along the heights and made good the eastern end of the Cochen ridge system overlooking the Keren road.' It seemed at this moment as if the road to Keren itself was open. The cost had not been high. Fewer than 150 casualties had been suffered by Major-General Sir Noel M. Beresford-Peirse's two brigades while the Italian 4th Colonial Division had disintegrated, losing over a thousand prisoners.

Yet the road to Keren was not open. Demolition of the Ponte Mussolini, a great bridge 12 miles east of Agordat on the Via Imperiali autostrada, plus heavy mining of the deviation, bought the Italian rearguards precious time. The retreating enemy were able to pass through the Dongolaas Gorge, 40 miles farther east, and then to prepare another far more formidable demolition. On 2 February the vanguard of 4th Indian Division, advancing along the Ascidera valley, were within two miles of the Gorge's entrance:

From the canyon came dull booms, clouds of smoke and dust curled upwards in the still, hot air. The last Italian rearguards had passed through, and on a stretch of several hundred yards demolition squads were blowing away the retaining walls which pinned the road to the cliffsides. Two tanks crossed the valley to reconnoitre and reported the ravine to be blocked by barricades of huge boulders covered by anti-tank and machine guns. The eastern gateway of the Eritrean fortress was bolted and barred.

The Keren position, to those who first saw it, looked almost impregnable. Fifty-three days were to elapse before the fortress itself was passed by British troops. Either side of the Dongolaas Gorge 11 great peaks rose steeply to a height of more than 2,000 ft above the valley. To the west were Sanchil, Cameron's Ridge, Brig's Peak, Saddle, Hog's Back, Flat Top and Samanna; to the east Fort Dologorodoc, Falestoh, Zeban, Acqua Col and Zelale (the Sphinx), overlooking what was ironically named 'Happy Valley'. Sanchil and Brig's Peak afforded observation of Keren itself and were therefore particularly important. On this naturally powerful position the Italians deployed the best part of 30,000 men, some 40 infantry battalions, supported by 144 guns. Most of the troops were colonial, but the regular Italian battalions included some of their finest fighters – *Savoia* Grenadiers, *Alpini* and *Bersaglieri*.

The two Indian divisions – and because of transport shortages it was impossible to maintain both divisions complete in battle simultaneously – were faced with the disagreeable prospect of a frontal assault. There was simply no other way to open the road through the Dongolaas Gorge and thus achieve the objective of reaching Asmara and then Massawa. The battle can be divided into three phases. The first phase from 3 to 7 February was conducted by Brigadier Reginald A. Savory with his 11th Indian Infantry Brigade. He attempted to capture Brig's Peak and Sanchil. His troops reached both summits, but lost them again to *Savoia* Grenadier counter-attacks, while hanging on to Cameron's Ridge, won by the Scottish regiment of that name. The great difficulty facing the British and Indian infantry was that to reach their objectives at all demanded intensive physical effort. Artillery bombardment could normally reach only the forward slopes and had to be lifted before a final assault. On reaching their objective the exhausted infantry, already depleted in numbers by casualties and by having to use as much as a quarter of each battalion as supply porters, were terribly vulnerable to immediate counter-attack by the protected defenders who were supported by accurate mortar fire.

In the next phase Maj-Gen. Beresford-Peirse used both 5th and 11th Brigades, this time attacking farther east against the Acqua Col where desertions by colonial Italian troops were encouraging, with a view to outflanking the more formidable defenses to the west and pushing straight down the track to Keren. In spite of great efforts by the 4/6 Rajputana Rifles who gained the objective, a counter-attack pushed them off again. Severe fighting by isolated units was the pattern of the battle as this account shows:

> The leading Rajputana Rifle company had reached the haunches of high ground which rose on both sides of the entrance to the gap when heavy mortar and machine-gun fire opened. The company commander fell wounded, but Subedar Richpal Ram sprang to the front and headed the rush which carried the leading platoons over the crest. . . . In the next four hours five counter-attacks were smashed by the bombs, bullets and bayonets of this dauntless handful. An hour before dawn, their last cartridges expended, the gallant Subedar with nine survivors fought back through an enemy block in the rear and rejoined the main body of the battalion, which had dug in under the shelter of a low crest afterwards known as Rajputana Ridge.

Beresford-Peirse abandoned his plan. Next he decided to renew the attack on 10 February in both areas. It was a further story of great gallantry and prizes won only to be lost again. Eleventh Brigade was to capture Brig's Peak and 5th Brigade Acqua Col. Brig's Peak was taken twice, as were Saddle and Hog's Back. None were held. Acqua Col was almost reached – Subedar Richpal Ram of the Rajputana Rifles won a posthumous Victoria Cross in the battle – but his battalion suffered 123 casualties. Such losses could not be sustained. Platt and Beresford-Peirse, while still acknowledging that their main effort must be made at Keren, began to cast about for means of diverting some of the enemy to deal with threats elsewhere.

Thus 7th Indian Infantry Brigade under Brigadier Harold Briggs made its way south from Karora and was supported by the Free

French *Brigade d'Orient* made up of the 14th Foreign Legion Battalion (containing Italians who fought against their own countrymen) and 3rd Battalion of the Chad Regiment. Brigg's force fought a successful engagement against the enemy on 23 February at Cub Cub which was only 45 miles north-east of Keren and began to distract Italian reserves from the Keren front.

Meanwhile, preparations for the next main assault, the third and final phase, went on. They were enormously assisted by British aircraft. Heavy air attacks were made on Italian airfields between mid-February and mid-March and so successful were they that the Italian air force was virtually inactive. By 22 March the *Regia Aeronautica* could only muster 37 serviceable aircraft in the whole of East Africa. Additionally the Italian defenses themselves received repeated attention. By the beginning of March Platt had completed his planning even to the point of briefing his commanders on a sand-model. Fourth Indian Division was to attack to the west of the Dongolaas Gorge taking all the peaks from Sanchil to Samanna, while Major-General Lewis M. Heath's 5th Indian Division, fresh from a mountain warfare refresher course at Tessenei farther east, would capture Fort Dologorodoc and exploit to Falestoh and Zeban. Yet it was still 19 battalions against 42 defending and the attackers were slogging uphill in a temperature of 100°F. Meanwhile Briggs' force, now only about 15 miles distant from Keren to the north-east, would advance.

On 15 March, with maximum air support from some 50 bombers and an artillery bombardment by 96 guns, 4th Indian Division attacked. The 2/5 Mahratta Regiment seized and held Flat Top while 1/6 Rajputana Rifles took Hog's Back for the loss of half their number. But by 1600, after eight hours fighting and climbing, the Cameron's three rifle companies were down to 30 fit men in front of Brig's Peak, having lost 288 men in the effort to capture it. During the night these meager gains were just retained against three Italian counter-attacks. The following night 10th Brigade was thrown in against the two untaken peaks. Its two battalions were so savagely mauled that they were withdrawn to 'Happy Valley'. By the time the attack was called off on the evening of 17 March the division had sustained 1,100 casualties in three days.

On the other flank 5th Indian Division had better luck, taking Fort Dologorodoc on the first night, principally because, unlike the other Italian defenses, it was not overlooked by a high ridge behind.

Its capture proved to be a turning point, for the fort dominated the town and plateau of Keren behind the mountains, thus providing a superb artillery observation post for the British guns. Nevertheless, exploitation of the success to Falestoh and Zeban ended as so often before with the troops pinned down on the forward slopes; this time they even had to be air-supplied before being withdrawn at night.

The two-division offensive had one other positive result – it enabled engineers to examine the original Italian roadblock in the Dongolaas Gorge. They found that the boulders and craters extended back 100 yards, but estimated that a 48-hour clearance would enable tracked vehicles to get through. Furthermore on the west side of the block the railway line to Keren ran under Cameron's Ridge through a barricaded tunnel. Once cleared this offered a covered way approach for armor to get through the Gorge and advance to Keren. No wonder General Heath declared, on receiving this information, that 'Keren is ours!' His division's second effort was fixed for 25 March, giving a week for preparations and the resting of units.

Meanwhile, between 18 and 22 March, the Italians made seven desperate attempts to recapture Fort Dologorodoc during which they suffered many casualties. Among the dead was General Lorenzini, a bold inspiring leader, nicknamed by his men, the Lion of the Sahara. His 4th Italian Division of regular troops had been the mainstay of the defense.

By 20 March Italian units had lost a third of their strength. On 25 March the 9th and 10th Brigades of 5th Indian Division attacked on both sides of the Gorge and seized it, taking some 500 prisoners including many *Bersaglieri* and two batteries of artillery. The following afternoon Sappers and Miners had blasted a way through the road block. This meant that before long the 14 infantry tanks and 50 Bren carriers of Fletcher Force would get behind the main Italian positions. On the night of 26 March the Italians skillfully withdrew leaving only light covering forces. Next morning white flags fluttered from Sanchil and Brig's Peak. Fourth Indian Division advanced and tanks entered Keren by 0800 on 27 March. Asmara, capital of Eritrea, fell on 1 April and Massawa, the Red Sea port, a week later.

The battle was best summed up by General Platt, talking to his officers on 14 March before the final phase started: 'Do not let anybody think this is going to be a walk-over. It is not. It is going to be a bloody battle: a bloody battle against both enemy and ground.

It will be won by the side which lasts longest. I know you will last longer than they do. And I promise you I will last longer than my opposite number.' That Platt was right about the bloodiness of the action needs but statistics and the memory of those present to endorse. The British lost 536 killed and 3,229 wounded. Three thousand Italians, according to their commander, General Frusci, were killed.

Without the determination, devotion to duty and sheer bravery of the regimental soldiers, the battle could not have been won. The magnificent efforts of the logistic planners and producers were also vital, for no troops, however courageous, can win without food, fuel, ammunition and water. The Italians on Mount Sanchil had a piped water-supply – their assailants had to carry two-gallon petrol tins up the heights. Major-General G. Surtees, then a Brigadier in charge of administration for the campaign, did much to win what he called the 'Q' (Quartermaster's) war. He recorded that speed, simplicity, common-sense, improvisation and imagination were the watchwords. But, Surtees continued, none of these would have been any good without the men who carried out the plans – driving the vehicles, humping the stores and evacuating the wounded. 'British, Indian and Sudanese', Surtees wrote, 'grumbling, cursing and laughing, swept by sand storms, soaked in tropical rain, they sweated it out in the heat, they froze in the heights. Unexciting, if not uninteresting, was much of their back area toil, often imposing endurance and struggle against shortage of sleep. At any heroics on devoted service to the fighting men, they would have scoffed and sworn. Yet the urge was there.'

So too was the will to win in the higher commanders. Wavell, despite all his lack of resources and mounting commitments, had had the foresight and boldness to commit the right troops to the right place at the right time. After Keren, 4th Indian Division hastened back to the Western Desert. Eritrea gone, the Duke of Aosta concentrated his dwindling strength in one more great fortress at Amba Alagi. There he was stalked and harried and, eventually, forced to surrender by the converging columns of Platt and Cunningham. Mopping up, interrupted by the rainy season, finished in November 1941. Of all the East African battles Keren was the bloodiest and longest. It had been besieged for nearly eight weeks and was held by nearly four divisions of Italian troops. It was a battle partly won by the skill and perseverance of the British, Indian and French troops and partly lost by the Italians in their reckless but valiant attempts to retake Fort Dologorodoc. The Italians could rightly be proud of their record at Keren, even though, as Brigadier Savory said, 'No enemy but the Italians would ever have allowed us to take the place. It was practically impregnable and even with Italian defenders we suffered heavily and at times began to wonder if we ever would succeed.' For the great 4th and 5th Divisions of the British dominion of India, the battle remains a shining star in their histories.

Kiev (1941)

John Strawson

Hitler hailed it as 'the greatest battle in the history of the world'. For on 16 September 1941 the German *Panzergruppen* of Colonel-Generals Heinz Guderian and Ewald von Kleist had joined hands in the Ukraine at Lokhvitsa, 125 miles east of Kiev. The Soviet commander in the Ukraine, Marshal Semyon Mikhailovich Budenny, had just been sacked by Stalin, but his army group was encircled. Within ten days the Germans captured 655,000 prisoners, 884 tanks, 3,718 guns and 3,500 motor vehicles. Colonel General Franz Halder, Chief of the German General Staff, called Kiev the principal strategic blunder of the Russian campaign. His view seems irreconcilable with Hitler's. How had it all come about?

The answer lies in the planning and aims of Hitler's invasion of Russia. As early as 1924, Hitler's book *Mein Kampf* was explicit: 'We stop the endless German movement to the south and west, and turn our gaze towards the land of the East. If we speak of new territory in Europe today, we can primarily have in mind only Russia and her vassal border states . . . This colossal empire in the East is ripe for dissolution.' Hitler's foreign policy was not just to abolish the Treaty of Versailles and extend the *Reich*'s frontiers to include all Germans. These aims were virtually achieved by 1939 without recourse to war. But *Lebensraum* (living space) demanded far more than what was 'rightly' Germany's. It needed Russia for ideological as well as strategic reasons.

Despite all the campaigns in the west and the south, it can be argued that Hitler concentrated three-quarters of his forces with his prime object clearly in view – the defeat of Russia. Only then could he settle 100 million Germans of pure Aryan stock on lands east of Germany to ensure that the New Order would last for a thousand years.

Hitler knew that the establishment of a German empire in the East, would, sooner or later, mean war with Russia. Even in 1934 he was telling Hermann Rauschning: 'We cannot in any way evade the final battle between German race ideals and pan-Slav mass ideals. Here yawns the eternal abyss which no political interest can bridge . . . We alone can conquer the great continental space, and it will be done by us singly and alone.'

It might be necessary to make arrangements with the Soviet Union along the way, but only the more quickly to erase Russia completely for 'it will open to us the mastery of the world.' In July 1940, with France crushed but England defiant, Hitler turned his arguments inside out when trying to persuade his Commanders-in-Chief about how to defeat England. England's hope lay in Russia and the United States. If Russia dropped out of the picture, America would too, for Russia's elimination would make America think only of Japan's threat to themselves. 'Decision: Russia's destruction must therefore be made part of this struggle. The sooner Russia is crushed the better. The attack will achieve its purpose only if the Russian state can be shattered to its roots with one blow . . . if we start in May 1941, we will have five months in which to finish the job.'

In December 1940 Hitler's War Directive No 21, *Case Barbarossa*, sent a shiver down the spines of those first privileged to read it. 'The German Armed Forces must be prepared, even before the conclusion of the war against England, to crush Soviet Russia in a rapid campaign.' The bulk of the Red Army stationed in Western Russia would be encircled and destroyed by deeply penetrating armored forces. Above all, any Soviet forces still able to fight would be prevented from withdrawing into the depths of Russia. Herein lay the reason for the battle of Kiev. Hitler's directive gave a broad outline of the conduct of operations and the final objective – the creation of a barrier against Asiatic Russia on the general line of the Caspian Sea at Astrakhan to Archangel in the Arctic. It did not say how and where the Soviet armies were to be destroyed. This failure to draw up an absolutely clear and realizable master plan for the Red Army's annihilation ensured that the astonishingly successful Kiev battles made no difference to the final outcome of the war.

Hitler had always maintained that 'we have only to kick the door in and the whole rotten structure will come crashing down.' In order to foment this instant collapse three Army Groups were assembled. Army Group North would strike for Leningrad. Army Group Centre with the two main *Panzergruppen* (1,770 tanks) was aimed at Smolensk. Field Marshal Karl Gerd von Rundstedt's Army Group South was to deal with the enemy west of the Dnieper river in the Ukraine. Throughout planning, Hitler constantly reiterated the need to wipe out, not just put to flight, the main enemy forces. But he consistently failed to lay down any absolute strategic plan or objective to which all operations would contribute and be subordinate.

As *Barbarossa* developed, the Führer constantly chopped and changed, or worse still, vacillated. In spite of rapid advances and huge bags of prisoners, there was little sign of the whole Soviet structure crashing down. Army Group North got to Leningrad, but was repulsed before the city itself and had to be content with investing it. Field Marshal Fedor von Bock's Army Group Centre executed a great pincer movement converging on Minsk and by 10 July, 20 days after the start of the campaign, claimed 300,000 prisoners. The battles around Smolensk started a week later and lasted for three more. They produced a comparable number of prisoners, but took such a toll of von Bock's armies that the advance towards Moscow from Smolensk was not resumed until 2 October. It was this lack of a conclusive decision in the north and center, combined with Hitler's constant change of heart over what constituted decisive objectives, which led to glittering but illusory success in the Ukraine.

On 19 July Hitler issued his War Directive No 33. This directive (and its supplement on the 23rd) caused furious controversy between the Führer and his generals. In the first place Army Group Centre was instructed to keep advancing on Moscow, while its vital *Panzer* formations were hived off. *Panzergruppe 3* was to join in the battle for Leningrad. Guderian's *Panzergruppe 2* would attack the Ukraine in conjunction with von Kleist's *Panzergruppe 1* from Army Group South. Hitler made it clear that the priorities were the capture of Leningrad whose fall, he believed, would lead to the collapse of the regime it politically symbolized, and the Ukraine, an economic objective to be denied to Russia and used by Germany.

Col. Gen. Halder, Chief of the General Staff, argued that the whole campaign was endangered by the lack of a clear aim. Were the Führer's aims military conquest or economic exploitation? Hitler replied that both were equally important. But when Halder supported by von Bock, von Rundstedt, Field Marshal Walther von Brauchitsch (C-in-C of the Army) and Guderian insisted that a final autumn thrust must be made on Moscow, Hitler simply lectured his Commanders on the economic aspects of conducting war. Hitler only conceded Army Group Centre a defensive role after losing its *Panzergruppen*. It would not have to push on to Moscow with infantry alone. A 12 August supplement to Directive No 34 made it plain that the new offensives would be directed north on Leningrad and southwards to the Crimea, Kharkov, the Donets river basin and the Caucasus mountains. Large enemy forces on the flanks of Army Group Centre, especially the Soviet Fifth Army in the Pripet Marshes north of Kiev, were to be destroyed. This was the foundation of the great Kiev battles.

Among those who attempted to dissuade Hitler was the very man who did most to make the Kiev battles a stupendous triumph. In a last-ditch attempt to overturn the decision, Guderian obtained an interview with Hitler in the *Wolfsschanze* ('Wolf's lair' HQ at Rastenburg in E. Prussia) on 23 August. He pointed out that Moscow was the objective which ordinary soldiers understood. It was also a vital communication center, the political solar plexus of the Soviet Union, industrially important and psychologically perhaps conclusively so. He maintained that to capture Moscow first and destroy the Russian forces defending it (half a million men had escaped from the Smolensk encirclement) would make the subsequent overrunning of the Ukraine easy. To go for the Ukraine first would rob the *Wehrmacht* of the chance to take Moscow before winter came.

Guderian heard what was planned for his own *Panzergruppe* – movement to the Ukraine and back involving more than 600 miles – he commented, 'I doubt if the machines will stand it, even if we are unopposed.' But having been told by Hitler that Moscow must wait and the Ukraine offensive go ahead, Guderian assured the Führer that he would do his best. Hitler used Guderian's acquiescence to parry the continued doubts of Halder. He was always dividing and ruling his servants. But whatever the decision-making process, the outcome was that the main striking power of the German Army went north and south, not east to Moscow.

If there was discord among German military leadership about where to continue the offensive, there was just as much discord in STAVKA, the Soviet High Command, about how to stem its seemingly invincible advance. Colonel General M. P. Kirponos's SW Front had been pushed back into the Ukraine, while Hitler's Rumanian satellite armies from the Balkans begun to move into Bessarabia and towards Odessa. The Soviet problem here was the unenviable one of trying to defend a broadening front with disintegrating forces. STAVKA decided to amalgamate Southern and SW Fronts into one SW Theater. Stalin appointed as its Commander his old crony, Marshal Budenny. The Commissar with a main job of evacuating industry was none other than the 47-year-old Lieutenant General Nikita S. Khruschev. The 58-year-old Budenny, having held no real field command for 20 years, had little to recommend him save political 'reliability' against the German professionals, von Rundstedt and von Kleist.

As if choosing so questionable a commander was not enough, Russian strategy itself was soon a matter of violent disagreement. At a meeting in Moscow on 29 July, General Georgi K. Zhukov, Chief of the General Staff, urged that Kirponos's SW Front be withdrawn from the Dnieper river-line, even though this meant giving up Kiev. Stalin angrily rejected such a course, and instantly accepted Zhukov's offer to resign. Zhukov therefore went off to command the Reserve Front. The ailing Marshal Boris M. Shaposhnikov became Chief of the General Staff again. In any event, Stalin's decision to fight on the line of the Dnieper prevailed. Kiev, capital of the second most important Socialist Republic, was to be held at all costs.

Marshal Budenny's army group was positioned in an enormous salient about 150 miles wide, stretching from Trubchevsk in the north to Kremenchug in the south with Kiev as the apex of the salient sticking out to the west. The opportunity for encirclement and annihilation was therefore present from the outset. Budenny had the best part of 1.5 million soldiers in his area, about eight armies, mainly at Uman and Kiev itself.

The German recipe for annihilation was *double* encirclement. The first and *inner* ring would be drawn by three infantry armies; the Second moving SE from Gomel, the Seventeenth striking north from

Kremenchug and the Sixth keeping Russian attention riveted on Kiev itself. Meanwhile the *outer* ring would be closed by Guderian's *Panzergruppe* driving south with some 500 tanks from Trubchevsk to meet von Kleist's 600 tanks striking north from Kremenchug, at a point some 125 miles east of Kiev. It was the strategist's dream, a re-creation of the unique victory won by Hannibal over Rome at Cannae in 216 BC. The Carthaginian military genius had destroyed 70,000 out of 86,000 Romans for a cost of only 5,700. His infantry had lured 16 legions into the heart of their concave formation while the cavalry smashed the Roman wings and enveloped the infantry – to charge into their rear.

While the German plan unfolded, the Russians seemed to be paralysed and incapable of decisive action. Had Budenny had any inkling of the scope of German plans, he might have reversed his troop concentrations to withdraw behind the Dnieper. But having no notion of the kind of battle about to be fought, he reinforced those very areas, like Uman, which were to be engulfed even before the main battle was launched. While Uman was being reinforced, von Kleist's three *Panzer* Corps were dashing eastwards roughly between the two main Soviet concentrations at Uman and Kiev. By the end of July the *Panzers* were more than 100 miles SE of Budenny's main forces. The noose east of Uman was looped by Eleventh Army infantry crossing the river Bug and pushing on to Novo Ukraine where they joined up with 14 *Panzer* Corps from the north. Uman was a foretaste of greater things to come – by 8 August 103,000 prisoners had been taken from 21 divisions of three encircled Russian armies. The week's reduction of the pocket yielded booty totalling 850 field guns, 317 tanks, and 242 AT and AA guns. One German artillery battery pounding these targets fired more ammunition in four days than it had in the entire six-week 1940 campaign in France.

At this point in the Russian campaign – it was still only August – seven weeks after the start, the morale of the *Wehrmacht* was at its peak despite checks at Leningrad. In the south they were advancing fast without too much opposition. When the Russians did counter-attack, they usually signalled their coming by a lot of radio conversation *en clair* and then stuck to their normal pattern of a short artillery bombardment followed by wave after wave of infantry. Sometimes they were supported by tanks or trucks crammed with soldiers which simply drove straight at the German positions until inevitably knocked out. These were halcyon days and it was as well that the Germans enjoyed them for there would not be much more to enjoy after the autumn. This gallop across the Ukraine was recalled by C. Malaparte:

> During the night-time all fighting ceases. Men, animals, weapons rest. Not a rifle shot breaks the damp nocturnal silence. Even the voice of the cannon is hushed. As soon as the sun has set, and the first shadows of evening creep across the corn field, the German columns prepare for their night's halt. Night falls, cold and heavy, on the men curled up in the ditches, in the small slit trenches which they have hastily dug amid the corn, alongside the light and medium assault batteries, the anti-tank cannon, the heavy anti-aircraft machine-guns, the mortars . . . Shielded from sudden attack by the sentries and patrols the men abandon themselves in sleep. There in front of us, concealed amid the corn and with the solid dense mass of the woods – over there beyond the deep, smooth, bleak fold of the valley, the enemy sleeps. We can hear his hoarse breathing. We can discern his smell – a smell of oil, petrol and sweat.

By 7 September German operations were crystallizing. During a visit to von Rundstedt's Army Group South HQ, Halder agreed final details of the plan involving both this army group and Army Group Centre by which all enemy in the Kiev–Dnieper–Desna bend would be destroyed and Kiev itself taken. From Army Group Centre, Guderian would continue his 12-day-old thrust southwards from Starodub to Romny and Priluki with Second Army covering the right flank of the *Panzer* advance. From Army Group South, Seventeenth Army would pin the Soviet forces on the Lower Dnieper below Cherkassy and get a bridgehead over the river at Kremenchug. Then von Kleist could drive northwards from it to link up with Guderian in the general area Romny–Lokhvitsa thus cutting off some six Soviet armies. Field Marshal Walther von Reichenau's Sixth Army would cross the 700-yard wide Dnieper opposite Kiev and attack the encircled Soviet forces there.

Within a few days the German armies had made great strides. Seventeenth Army crossed the Dnieper on 11 September and von Kleist was packing his tanks into the bridgehead. To counter these moves, Budenny's only recourse was a desperate appeal to Stalin on 11 September for permission to withdraw.

It is possible, when we remember that he had given Budenny over a million men, to sympathize even with Stalin's exasperation and his refusal to authorize retreat to the east. Instead the Party slogan was 'Stand fast, hold out, and if need be die.' But by this time it was virtually too late. From the outset Russian leaders just could not believe that Hitler would abandon Moscow as his prior target when it looked as if he could reach it even earlier in the year than Napoleon (14 September 1812) – so while Guderian was seen to be heading south, it was thought that he was only trying to dodge round the strong Soviet forces barring the direct route to Moscow. Russian mobility, despite mechanization tied essentially to the foot soldier, could never hope to match that of the German *Panzer* troops who roamed more or less at will, at least six times as fast.

What is more, after von Kleist's breakthrough, there was nothing to stop them. Indeed with his *Panzers* ranging as far east and south as Dnepropetrovsk, Krivoi Rog and Nikolayev, von Rundstedt's difficulty was not so much that he could not gain his objectives, but to know what these objectives were. All southern European Russia, including the whole of the Donets basin, was his for the taking. There was nothing to stop him swarming on into Asiatic Russia except possibly a shortage of petrol. What should he aim for, what objective was there that would actually finish off the Russians? Their scorched-earth policy, emphasized by the blowing up of the Zaporozhe Dam which supplied power for the Dnieper bend industries, was hardly encouraging or likely to lead to realization of Hitler's prediction that the whole rotten structure would come crashing down. Von Rundstedt, therefore, in keeping with the broad directive of the whole campaign to prevent large bodies of Russian troops from retiring into the hinterland, had switched his *Panzers* back north in order to meet Guderian's drive south and so close the door on the huge prize of Kiev and nearly 750,000 Red Army troops.

Guderian's 24 *Panzer* Corps was being led by two *Panzer* divisional commanders, both wounded in the battle, who subsequently achieved fame. Lieutenant General (later Field Marshal) Walther Model of 3rd *Panzer* Division became known as the Führer's 'Fireman' of 1944 because of a knack for putting out fires, that is, of restoring collapsing fronts both east and west. But now the future 'Lion of the Defence' was displaying the dash and elan of a Rommel. General Ritter von Thoma, the Spanish Civil War tank expert who commanded 17th *Panzer* Division, was later to take over the *Afrika Korps* and be captured by the British at El Alamein. Once Model took the Desna bridges at Novgorod-Severskii, there would be no proper terrain obstacle between Guderian and Kleist. On 26 August Model's division punched into the town on the north bank of the marshy river. The Russians blew the small pedestrian bridge, but a headlong scramble by a special engineer assault detachment secured intact the vital 750-yard wooden road bridge. Lieutenant Störck calmly dealt with the final obstacle – an adapted aerial bomb planted right in the middle of the bridge – by unscrewing the detonator.

Model poured men and equipment along the vital artery to carve out a bridgehead that was to be proof against eight days of Soviet counter-attacks. Thoma's division made a crossing higher up the Desna and led a flank cordon that stretched and stretched to a N–S length of 155 miles but always just held against piecemeal Russian assault. On 9 September, despite late summer torrential rainstorms that churned roads into quagmires and dwindling fuel supplies, 3rd *Panzer* Division captured Romny, the last town before the pincers' rendezvous.

Meanwhile Kleist was about to join up with Guderian. His pincer had been held back so long lest the Russians recognize the threat of double envelopment too soon. On 12 September, the day snow first fell on the Eastern front, 16th *Panzer* division sliced 43 miles north after breaking out of the bridgehead at Kremenchug. The division's infantry needed a day and a half to master Lubny, fiercely defended by workers' militia and NKVD secret police. The closing pincer spearheads were still 60 miles apart. By the 15th, 3rd *Panzer* Division was down to ten battle-ready tanks but under Guderian's stimulus had struggled on beyond Lokhivitsa while the bulk of its units were still mudbound along the road back to Romny. Reconnaissance parties from *Panzergruppen* made contact and on the 16th the greatest encirclement of the entire Russo-German conflict was achieved. Twenty-two days after the opening of the battle 50 Soviet divisions had been trapped. Three days earlier Budenny, specially flown out, had finally been relieved of his command and Marshal Semyon K. Timoshenko, Stalin's indispensable 'rescue' general, appointed in his place.

From 16–19 September the Second and Seventeenth German infantry armies closed in on Yagotin, target of the inner ring of encirclement, while Sixth Army took Kiev on 20 September. For the next week what became known as the Kiev cauldron – originally about 130 miles wide and deep – which for all its efforts outside the Red Army was not able to burst into and meet the belated breakout efforts begun during the night of the 17th–18th, was broken up by the Germans. Some six Soviet armies (5th, 21st, 26th, 27th, 38th and 40th) were either wholly or partially destroyed. One army commander extracted just 500 survivors. Besides having no proper direction, the Russian soldiers simply had not enough ammunition or fuel – two indispensable commodities of modern war – to conduct a co-ordinated battle of any sort. Courage they did have and in a series of fanatical and desperate counter-attacks made by men down to five bullets apiece were simply annihilated.

During the fighting the words of Stalin, magnified to gigantic proportions by the loudspeakers, rain down upon the men kneeling in holes behind the tripods of their machine-guns, din in the ears of the soldiers lying amid the shrubs, of the wounded writhing in agony upon the ground. The loudspeaker imbues that voice with a harsh, brutal, metallic quality. There is something diabolical, and at the same time terribly naive about these soldiers who fight to the death, spurred on by Stalin's speech on the Soviet Constitution. By the slow deliberate recital of the moral, social, political and military precepts of the Commissars, about these soldiers who never surrender; about these dead, scattered all around me; about the final gestures, the stubborn, violent gestures of those men who died so terribly lonely a death on this battlefield, amid the deafening roar of the cannon and the ceaseless blaring of the loudspeaker.

The killing went on for the best part of a week, and then the surrenders began. Once they started they went on and on until over 600,000 Russian soldiers were prisoners. A colossal part of the Red Army, perhaps a third of its June 1941 strength, had been removed from the battle. It was not enough. No matter how many times Hitler might trumpet that 'The Russian is finished,' he obviously was not. The Russian Bear refused to lie down and expire. He insisted on fighting on. And within three months of their fantastic Kiev victory, something like despair was to grip leading German formations as they stumbled to a halt before Moscow and then began to withdraw.

For irony of all ironies, having condemned his generals' notions of capturing Moscow in no moderate terms – 'Only completely ossified brains, absorbed in the ideas of past centuries could see any worthwhile objective in taking the capital' – Hitler insisted Moscow be captured. But he still made the fatal mistake of trying to go for Leningrad and the Caucasus as well. Soon after resuming his advance in the center, *two months* since halting after the Smolensk battle, von Bock had taken another 600,000 prisoners and by 15 October his spearhead was at Mozhaisk, a mere 65 miles from the capital. If even at that point Hitler had gambled all, concentrating the dwindling tank strength of all four *Panzergruppen* on the drive for Moscow, while merely defending the northern and southern fronts, then surely victory – if by that we mean destruction of the Soviet armies defending Moscow and capture of the city itself – would have been within his grasp. Instead he failed to observe the never-to-be-forgotten principles of singleness of purpose and concentration of resources to that end. By the time he had realized it, the chill breath of winter and defeat was breathing down the necks of ordinary soldier and High Command alike.

From the Russian point of view the greatest numerical military catastrophe of their history was caused by Stalin's refusal to give up his regime's tenuous ideological grip on the Ukraine without a fight. Surely in this he may be judged right for to have chucked his hand in there would simply have given the Germans more time and resources to finish off the job in the center. Moscow's loss might well have brought about a total collapse of the Red Army's will to continue as opposed to the willingness of hundreds of thousands of its soldiers to surrender. The same sort of ideological and military question mark had also been half-posed in 1919 during the Russian Civil War when anti-Bolshevik forces were converging on Moscow from all points of the compass. But given that the Ukraine was to be defended in 1941, Budenny's defense ensured that had the Germans been allowed to choose their enemy's response they could not have done better. For the Germans indeed the battle was a brilliantly executed operation of war – the technical and tactical highpoint of the *Blitzkrieg* era.

Yet strategically it was a flop. All the slaughter, all the advances, all the planning and controversy and triumph went for nothing. The magnitude of Russia's resources proved equal to the enormity of the loss. Four million out of her 10 million military casualties occurred in the first six months of almost four years' fighting, but in 1941 alone four million reserves were mobilized. Kiev was a second Cannae – but, as after the first, the losing side would fight on to eventual and total victory.

Leningrad (1941)

Alan Clark

What brought the *Wehrmacht* to a halt at the very gates of Leningrad in 1941? Was it the indomitable spirit of a beleaguered citizen army? Could it have been a breaking from within the German impetus in its thrust forward into Russia's vitals? Or was it the desperation of a population caught frighteningly between a German hammer and the anvil of Communist political oppression?

The three primary objectives for the Germans in their invasion of Russia on 22 June 1941 were the coal and iron fields of the Donet basin in the south, the capital, Moscow, in the center, and the city of Leningrad at the extreme northern point of the front. And to each of these objectives the Germans had assigned a separate army group concentrating their tanks in *Panzer* groups. These were to clear the way and weld the chains of encirclement around the more cumbersome Soviet forces, whose surrender would be forced by the slower moving infantry divisions that followed in the *Panzers'* wake. In their advance, the Luga River was the last major obstacle facing the German army before the city of Leningrad. But on 8 August 1941 the Russian armies collapsed and the 41st *Panzer* Corps, commanded by General Georg-Hans Reinhardt, broke into open country. The German tanks had already travelled nearly 500 miles on their own tracks and the motorized equipment was overdue for servicing after six weeks of continuous use in the dust and summer heat of Northern Russia. The soldiers themselves were exhausted.

They had had only four to six hours sleep a night: but morale was at its height. Now, they felt certain, there would be nothing to stop them capturing Leningrad, the ancient Tsarist capital.

The situation was severe enough for the Russian Chief of Staff, Major General D. N. Nikishev, to report two days later to Marshal Boris M. Shaposhnikov, the Red Army Chief of Staff: 'The difficulty of restoring the situation lies in the fact that neither divisional commanders, army commanders, nor front [army group] commanders have any reserves at all. Every breach down to the tiniest has to be stopped up with scratch sections or units assembled any old how.'

In the city itself, citizens were being conscripted ruthlessly into the *Opolchenye* (militia). But this was little more than an enthusiastic rabble, indifferently armed, without signals or communications equipment, and whose training had been confined to weekends in local Party camps. A contemporary Russian account says that 'in addition to some rifles and machine-guns . . . the workers were armed mainly with Molotov cocktails and hand-grenades; they also had 10,000 shotguns and about 12,000 small calibre and training rifles donated by the city's population.'

Gloomily, and with the threat of a firing squad hanging over him, Lieutenant General M. M. Popov, the Russian Commander in Chief of the Northern Front, reported to his superiors in Moscow: 'To suppose that opposition to the German advance can be resisted by militia units just forming up, or badly organized units taken from the North-Western Front command after they have been pulled out of Lithuania and Latvia . . . is completely unjustified.' And yet even at this moment a plan to storm Leningrad was not part of the German strategy. As early as 8 July Colonel General Franz Halder, the German army's Chief of Staff, had noted that: 'It is the Führer's firm decision to level Moscow and Leningrad and make them uninhabitable, so as to relieve us of the necessity of feeding the population during the winter. The city will be razed by the Air Force. Tanks must not be used for the purpose.' And on 15 July the German Commander of Army Group North, Field Marshal Ritter von Leeb, was given express instructions that 'the immediate mission is not to capture Leningrad but to encircle it.'

It is possible that Gen. Reinhardt's corps could have driven without a halt to the Nevsky Prospect in those early August days; that the SS could have set up their headquarters in the Winter Palace. But the spirit and enforced discipline of the Soviet citizens

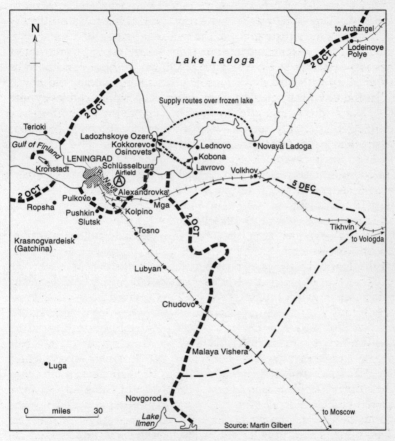

5.3　*The Siege of Leningrad, October 1941–January 1944*

was so different from that of their Western Allies that it is unlikely the German army's tactics (which succeeded the previous summer in France) would have brought lasting victory in Russia.

Then, between 14 and 18 August, all the Russian forces in the area, at the urgent prompting of Moscow, began to advance. And this counter-offensive – uncoordinated, extravagant, tactically inept, with masses of cavalry and unarmored lorries, with soldiers making costly frontal charges – did, nonetheless, have the effect of diverting General Erich von Manstein's 56th *Panzer* Corps, which should have been reinforcing Gen. Reinhardt's 41st *Panzer* Corps. For three critical weeks Gen. Manstein's corps marched and counter-marched across the dried-out marshes of the upper Illmen river, further exhausting its men and machines. It was not until September that *Panzer* Group IV could again contemplate the problem of Leningrad.

Within the city the activities of the Communist Party became ever more frenzied: 'Comrade Leningraders! Dear friends! Our dearly beloved city is in imminent danger of attack by German Fascist troops. The enemy is striving to penetrate into Leningrad . . . The Red Army is valiantly defending the approaches to the city . . . and repelling his attacks. But the enemy has not yet been crushed, his resources are not yet exhausted . . . and he has not yet abandoned his despicable plan to capture Leningrad.'

Marshal K. E. Voroshilov and Lt. Gen. A. A. Zhdanov organized a 'Military Soviet for the defense of Leningrad' – an independent move which even at this time of acute danger was bitterly resented by Marshal Josef Stalin who expressed his 'extreme dissatisfaction'. Voroshilov's answer was that 'it corresponded to the actual requirements of the situation.' But Stalin brushed this aside and demanded 'an immediate review of the personnel', and both Voroshilov and Zhdanov were dismissed.

In order to assert the Party supremacy over the Army, Foreign Ministers Vyacheslav M. Molotov and Georgi M. Malenkov were sent from the Committee for the Defense of State to replace them. A special order was issued to the troops:

Individual soldiers, commanders, and political workers are forgetting . . . their pledge and are revealing in battle a criminal absent-mindedness, faint-heartedness, and cowardice. Not only are there commanders and political leaders who do not set an example of courage and audacity and do not carry along their soldiers by their example, but there are also loathsome self-seekers who hide in fox-holes and do not lead the fight. Such disgraceful individuals cannot be tolerated in the Red Army. Those who fail to perform their duties have no place in our ranks.

The rattle of firing-squads could stiffen discipline, but Party theorists were of small value in handling men in battle. And at the end of the month Stalin sent General Georgi K. Zhukov, who was given absolute power. In his day, Zhukov was to visit and stabilize in turn every dangerous sector of the Eastern Front. Few commanders, with the possible exception of Montgomery before Alam Halfa in North Africa, can have arrived at their headquarters with so little time to spare.

On the German side, Wilhelm Ritter von Leeb was clear about his personal ambition – to seize Leningrad, the most prestigious prize of the campaign, by force, thus confirming entitlement to his field-marshal's baton. But Hitler had different ideas. His imprecise instructions were: 'to level the town, make it uninhabitable and relieve us of the necessity of having to feed the population through the winter.' The German High Command were against getting involved with the civilian population at all. One of them, Lieutenant General Walther Warlimont, prepared a memorandum. 'Normal' occupation was rejected. It might be acceptable to evacuate the children and the old people 'and let the remainder starve,' but this could lead to 'new problems'. Perhaps the best solution, said Lt. Gen. Warlimont, would be to seal off the whole town, and surround it with an electrically charged wire fence, guarded by machine-guns. But there remained the danger of epidemics spreading to the German front.

In case Warlimont's proposals should be adopted, corps commanders were alerted to the need for using artillery against civilians trying to break out of the city. It was thought 'doubtful whether the infantry will shoot at women and children trying to break out.'

There was also the possibility of the Germans making propaganda capital out of the affair. It was suggested that an approach be made to: 'the philanthropist Roosevelt to send either food supplies to the inhabitants not going into captivity, or to send neutral ships under the supervision of the Red Cross, or to ship them off to his continent.'

Naturally, any response to this which threatened to assume real shape would not have been accepted.

The proper solution was to: 'Seal off Leningrad hermetically, then weaken it by terror [air raids and artillery bombardment] and growing starvation. In the spring we shall occupy the town . . . remove the survivors into captivity in the interior of Russia, and level Leningrad to the ground with high explosives.'

But first the Russian defenders had to be put to rout. Unfortunately for von Leeb's plans, Führer-Directive No 35, issued on 6 September, ordered the diversion of the whole of General Erich Hoepner's *Panzer* Group IV to Army Group Center, where it was to participate in the attack on Moscow. The 8th Air Corps, of close-support dive-bombers, was to co-operate. But Leeb ignored this signal. His plans for a final assault were already complete. By taking advantage of a provision in the Directive that the redeployment be subject to 'first achieving a close encirclement' he staged what was, in effect, a full-scale assault on the city's defenses, with the 1st *Panzer* Division following the left bank of the Neva and 6th *Panzer* straddling the main railway to Leningrad from the south.

Both divisions were soon enmeshed in a net of anti-tank ditches and straggling earthworks which had been thrown up by the construction battalions and *Opolchenye* during the previous weeks. These defenses were often poorly sited and crudely finished, but they were extensive. The Russians were seriously deficient in artillery, and indeed in all arms not produced on the spot at Leningrad and its environs. But they had a large number of medium and heavy mortars whose weight of fire, at the ranges of the first day's battle, was nearly as effective as regular field artillery.

On the coastal sector, between the sea and Krasnoye Seloe, the 12-in guns of the Baltic fleet pounded away at the German rear. Over the battlefield, massive KV tanks roamed singly and in pairs, manned sometimes by civilian testers and mechanics from the Kirov factory where they were still being produced at the rate of about four a day. This was the kind of close in-fighting where Russian courage, obstinacy, cunning in camouflage and ambush more than counterbalanced the deficiencies in command and technique which had crippled them in the open battlefields on the frontier and on the Luga.

The *Panzers*, in contrast, were suffering as armored troops always do when they encounter close defenses after weeks of mobile fighting. Like the British 8th Army when it hit the Tunisian mountains after months in Libya, the tank commanders took fearful punishment as they sought to adapt their tactics in an unfamiliar element. In the first day of the assault four successive commanders of 6th *Panzer* were casualties.

By the evening of 10 September the Germans had penetrated as far as the last line of Russian defenses, which ran along the crest of some shallow eminences known as the Dudergof heights – about six miles to the south-east of Leningrad. During the night many of the tanks of the leading division, 1st *Panzer*, lay out on the battlefield, forward of the main German positions, and fought throughout the hours of darkness to beat off the succession of counter-attacks which the Russians always put in during the night.

By the glare of blazing petrol bottles and sodium flares the Germans broke up one Russian formation after another as they assembled to charge the positions captured during the day. At first light, the *Stuka* dive bombers returned to the battlefield and 41st *Panzer* Corps braced itself for 'one last heave'. The 1st *Panzer* had lost so many tanks that there was only one battalion left with over 50 per cent effective strength, yet they gradually inched their way forward during the day and by 1600 had scaled 'Height 167', a hill 450 ft high, the topmost point in the Dudergof ridge to the south-east of the city.

'In front of the victorious troops stood the city of Leningrad in the sunlight, only 12 kilometres away, with its golden cupolas and towers and its port with warships that tried with their heaviest guns to deny us possession of the heights.'

On the left flank of the *Panzer* corps the infantry were slowly edging their way across the valley, and once the Russian guns and observers had been cleared off Height 167 the Germans were able to make better progress, entering the suburban districts of Slutsk and Pushkin, and, on the evening of 11 September, Krasnoye Seloe.

By 12 September, the fourth day of the assault, it was painfully obvious to the *OKH* that a full-blooded engagement was raging in an area from which they were trying to draw reinforcement. Col. Gen. Halder ordered F. M. Leeb that the city 'was not to be taken, but merely encircled. The attack should not go beyond the Peterfog–Pushkin road.' For another five days close fighting continued although at a diminishing tempo. The German resources were not enough to cope with the dilution of their technical superiority which street fighting imposed.

The only alternative to closing down the operation was massive reinforcement on a scale which, one year later, was to be granted to Field-Marshal Friedrich Paulus at Stalingrad. Halder wrote the epitaph of the battle in the *OKH* diary: 'The ring around Leningrad has not yet been drawn as tightly as might be desired, and further progress after the departure of 1st *Panzer* and 26th Motorized from that front is doubtful. Considering the drain on our forces on the Leningrad front, where the enemy has concentrated large forces and great quantities of material, the situation will remain critical until hunger takes effect as our ally.'

The weight now shifted from the Red Army's soldiers in Leningrad's defenses to the civilian population, although the Communist Party continued for some months to direct its energies at 'stiffening' the army in case a further assault should develop. A 'letter campaign' from schoolchildren mailed every infantryman with a stilted request that 'you at the front must strike harder at the enemy who had the gall to attack our great cities and villages,' and resolutions were constantly sent out from the factory workers to the soldiers in the field:

With great pain and bitterness we hear that among you there are sometimes cowards and deserters . . . The coward and deserter thinks that he will succeed in hiding from the people's censure and anger. He is mistaken. He will be cursed by his own mother, his wife will turn from him, his name will be spoken with loathing by his own children. With hatred and contempt – that is how his friends and comrades will greet him. A bullet in the head is what such a scoundrel and self-seeker will get.

September passed, and October, and with the leaves stripped from the trees along the Neva came the first frosts, followed by snowfalls. Food was already short, for supplies had not been stockpiled in the town. The German advance to Schlusselburg had occurred so suddenly and the demand for purely military items such as ammunition had been so acute that very little had been brought into the town before the ring of encirclement was sealed.

In two months, and before the ice on Lake Ladoga began to harden, everything that was edible in the city was consumed. Rats were considered a great delicacy. So too was the earth that came from near the Badaev warehouses where the sugar and chocolate had been stored and which had been burned down in one of the *Luftwaffe* raids. As winter tightened its grip, fuel became as scarce as food.

One Leningrader remembered:

First, the feeling of being cold. One gets up with it, one walks with it, one goes to bed with it. It seems to wander around somewhere under the skin; it penetrates the bones and sometimes it seems as if it even enters the brain. One can't escape from it. It penetrates under all shirts, sweaters, and jackets, no matter how many one puts on. The second is the feeling of hunger. This feeling has many shadings – from a dull, painful, sharp, unbearable one, which appears as soon as one has eaten one's ration of 125 grammes, to being tortured by fantasies.

Soviet records show that of the 26,600 persons who took the basic civilian military training course (the *Vzevobuch* programme) in the month of November over 6,000 were too ill or weak to finish the course. Of these 800 died of starvation while under training. Another 10,000 were so frail that they could only be given a short course. Trainees were very reluctant to fail as an allocation to the front-line units meant a different and improved ration scale. As fuel ran out so was electricity power confined to military use from emergency generators. In the short days of November and December, Leningrad must have seemed a city of the dead, shrouded in snow and freezing mists from the Baltic, without light or movement. In the factories, starving and frozen workers toiled for 14 hours a day making armaments, many dropping dead at their lathes.

Medical attention for civilians was virtually nil. In hospitals

the absence of electricity, heat, and water made work extremely difficult. The temperature in the wards usually stood between 30° and 35° Fahrenheit. The patients lay fully clothed, with coats and blankets, and sometimes even mattresses, piled on top of them. The walls were covered with frost. During the night water froze in pitchers. The hunger had the effect of causing diarrhea among the patients, many of whom from weakness were unable to use the bedpans. Sheets on the beds were filthy – no water for laundering. The only medicine available was sodium bromide, which the doctors prescribed under various names.

The only hope for Leningrad was to bring supplies across the ice on Lake Ladoga from the harbors of Lednevo and Kabana to Osinovets. The lake was not smooth ice. October gales had made the ice pile up in irregular heaps and there were always some crevasses that never froze. On 18 November, when the ice was only 5 in thick, a small reconnaissance party made the crossing on foot followed by a man on horseback, and for a few days supplies were brought in by ponies drawing sleds with light loads. The first truck column on 24 November lost nine of its vehicles crashing through gaps in the ice into the water. Only two of the drivers survived. But by the end of November there were 500 trucks in use, battling against arctic blizzards, mechanical breakdowns and constant strafing by the *Luftwaffe*.

It was not until January that the ice was thick enough to allow trucks to carry full loads. Few survived more than three journeys on the ice and over 1,000 trucks were lost before the middle of January when the ice was 3 ft thick and could bear almost any load. Yet, in spite of the efforts on the 'ice road', Leningrad never had more than one or two days of food in hand. Even during the previous October the bread ration had been reduced to 400 grammes a day for workers and 200 grammes for other categories and on 20 November these were reduced to 250 and 125 grammes. Under these conditions it was simply a matter of waiting for death by starvation. A schoolgirl, Tania Savich, kept a diary:

Jenia died on 28 December, 1941, at 12.30 a.m.
Grandmother died on 25 January, 1942.
Lena died on 17 March, 1942.
Uncle Lesha died on 10 May, at 4.00 p.m.
13 May, at 7.30 a.m. darling Mama died.

Then Tania herself died.
A Leningrad doctor describes his experiences:

I entered without knocking. My eyes beheld a horrible sight. A dark room, the wall covered with frost, puddles of water

on the floor. Lying across some chairs was the corpse of a
14-year-old boy. In a baby carriage was a second corpse, that
of a tiny infant. On the bed lay the owner of the room, K. K.
Vandel – dead. At her side, rubbing her chest with a towel,
stood her eldest daughter, Mikkau. . . . In one day Mikkau lost
her mother, a son, and a brother who perished from hunger
and cold. At the entrance, barely standing on her feet from
weakness, was a neighbor, Kizunova, her horrified gaze fixed
on the dead. She, too, died the next day.

Had the Germans been as skilled at offensive warfare under winter
conditions as the Soviet Army it is possible that a surprise assault in
that first bitter winter of 1941–2 might have overcome its emaciated
garrison and populace.

The awful winter passed, and during the spring and early summer
of 1942 the reinforcement of Leningrad by the sea route across Lake
Ladoga gathered momentum. Freight steadily increased from 1,500
tons in May to 3,500 tons in June, and the ships took out wounded
and non-combatants instead of returning empty. It gradually became
apparent to the Germans that Leningrad was threatening their
extreme northern flank, and plans were laid for a full-scale assault.

For this, Manstein's 11th Army, which had by now fought a successful Crimean campaign culminating in the capture of Sevastapol,
was given the support, once again, of the 8th Air Corps. In addition,
a special siege train of 800 heavy artillery pieces was concentrated
round the city. But the German plans were foiled by a series of
spoiling attacks which the Russians launched at the end of August.
Before Manstein had completed the deployment of his forces most
of the German resources were used up in preventing the rupture of
their corridor to Lake Ladoga.

At the beginning of 1943 the siege was lifted when the Red Army
succeeded in forcing a narrow passage about five miles wide along
the southern shore of Lake Ladoga and a rail link was established.
From then – although the siege of Leningrad was effectively over –
the city's fate was ultimately dependent on the outcome of the great
battles that raged in southern Russia.

With hindsight we can see that the Germans might have rushed the
city in August of 1941. Had the Germans been able to fight aggressively in the depths of winter their best chance would have been at
Christmas 1941 when the citizens and the soldiers' spirits were at

their lowest. But the intractable problem remained: highly trained and disciplined troops lose their advantage when dispersed over acres of rubble. Street fighting places a premium on numbers and tenacity. It is unlikely that the Germans could ever have succeeded in storming Leningrad any more than (with much greater resources) they could have been successful at Stalingrad the following year.

But they did come very near to starving the city out. Was it the iron discipline and terror of the Communist Party system that kept it alive?

Pearl Harbor (1941)

Paul Hutchinson

'All hands, general quarters! Air raid! This is no drill!' The alarm sounded for an attack that was to kill 2,403 American citizens as well as cripple her Pacific Fleet. But the Japanese attack on Pearl Harbor on 7 December 1941 was the key that released the unrivalled military might of the US. The eventual fate of the fascist powers – both east and west – was sealed.

Japan's strike at Pearl Harbor is often presented as a surprise attack on the US Navy, yet relations between the two countries were so strained because of Japan's colonizing policies it was practically inevitable that, for Japan to get her expansionist way in Asia, she would have to use force against the US.

In May 1940 the US Pacific Fleet was moved from San Diego to Pearl Harbor. The Fleet had been taking part in maneuvers off Hawaii the previous month and was ordered to stay in Pearl Harbor by Roosevelt when the exercises were finished. This decision did much to spur Japan into signing the Tripartite Pact with Italy and Germany the following September.

By mid-1940 it seemed that the fascist powers were everywhere triumphant. Nazi Germany controlled the better part of Europe and looked menacingly towards Britain from the coast of France. Meanwhile, Imperial Japan was locked in her expansionist war with China – a conflict of almost unsurpassed brutality. America was deeply involved in the fight against the aggressors in both

theaters and short of military intervention was giving all possible help.

Public opinion in the US was deeply split over whether or not
to go to war, with the majority firmly in the isolationist camp. But
President Franklin D. Roosevelt saw clearly enough that unless
the dictatorships were defeated the US's own independence would
eventually be threatened.

On 27 September 1940 Japan joined the Axis when she entered
into a tripartite pact with Germany and Italy. Under the terms of
this agreement 'the leadership of Japan in the establishment of a New
Order in Greater East Asia' was acknowledged. By this time Britain
had been pressured into closing an important life-line to China –
the Burma Road. America imposed a partial embargo on exports to
Japan. This embargo was later intensified and anything regarded as
a strategic war material was included in the restrictions.

It soon became painfully clear in Tokyo that Japan's empire-
building conquests in Asia could not possibly continue for much
longer without the raw materials of war – especially oil.

Relations between America and Japan continued to deteriorate
into 1941 and an armed clash appeared increasingly likely. But US
naval strategists did not think an attack on Pearl Harbor at all likely.
According to them, such an action would be an impressive but rather
pointless piece of sabre rattling – yielding Japan no great benefits. It
was for the same reason that the Japanese rejected the idea when it
was proposed by Admiral Isoruku Yamamoto in September 1941. Its
lack of any military value apart, an attack on Pearl Harbor would snap
the already strained relations between the two countries and all-out
war would result.

Yamamoto – himself opposed to war with America – kept his
faith in the viability of his plan. He had put the finishing touches
to this as early as the spring of 1941. But for the attack to succeed,
Yamamoto realized that absolute security was essential. There was in
existence a cryptographic code which enabled Japanese naval officers
to communicate with no risk of American interception reading their
messages. Another risk to security in a venture of such importance
was the inevitable prolonged argument and counter-argument within
the Japanese High Command. The chances of a 'leak' were enormous, so Yamamoto bypassed the High Command altogether and
approached Emperor Hirohito's brother Prince Takamatsu, then
a navy staff officer based in Tokyo. He was intrigued and told

his brother, who gave the go-ahead for the idea to be studied in secret.

As relations between Japan and the US went from bad to worse, Yamamoto trained his men. The harbor at Kagoshima was chosen for dummy dive-bombing and torpedo dropping because the lie of the land was similar to that of Pearl Harbor.

In late July the French were pressured into handing over Southern Indochina to the Japanese. America retaliated promptly. Japanese assets in the US were immediately frozen and the partial embargo already imposed on strategic material was made total. Britain and Holland joined in the economic boycott. The stark choice facing Japan was certain economic collapse or an armed clash. War with the US was no longer a question of 'if' – only 'when'. Unless the flow of oil was swiftly resumed Japan would have to abandon the Chinese mainland – an intolerable loss of face for the military. The absolute deadline for a solution was October.

Talks were held throughout the summer and autumn of 1941. Cordell Hull, American Secretary of State, made his country's position clear – all sanctions would be lifted only if Japan took her forces out of China and Indochina. But the negotiations were nothing but a device for buying time. Hull knew perfectly well that Japan would never accede to such a demand. Despite the pleadings of the Japanese Prime Minister, Prince Fumimaro Konoye, the Emperor and War Minister General Hideki Tojo refused to countenance any compromise. They were convinced of Japanese invincibility against all comers. 'The day after war begins we will have to issue an Imperial Declaration of War. Please see to it, Emperor Hirohito told his Lord Privy Seal, Koichi Kido, on 13 October.

Also in October, the US was warned of a planned strike on Pearl Harbor by an unusual source. Richard Sorge, Moscow's master spy in Tokyo, had passed the information to Josef V. Stalin, who in turn had informed Washington. But American naval strategists still considered an attack on Pearl Harbor unlikely.

Anxious for a peaceful settlement with the US, but outnumbered in the cabinet and overruled by his emperor, Prince Konoye resigned as Prime Minister on 16 October 1941. The extreme hawk Gen. Tojo took his place. At this point the Japanese Ambassador in Washington, Kichisaburu Nomura, asked Tokyo to recall him. His request was refused and the expert diplomat Saburo Kurusu was dispatched to buy time by supervising yet another round of 'negotiations'.

At this point it is worth speculating whether President Roosevelt was really ignorant of Japan's aggressive intentions. Apart from Richard Sorge's warning, the President also had access to *Magic* information – the decoded transcriptions of Japanese secret messages. It has also been suggested that Churchill thought that a Japanese attack on Pearl Harbor would demolish the case of the isolationists and bring America into the war and that Roosevelt agreed.

On 5 November Japan decided to make one more diplomatic approach to Washington before unleashing the now fully rehearsed attack on Pearl Harbor. This approach was sure to fail and was not intended to succeed – merely to give Japan the international veneer of 'peacemaker'. Presuming the breakdown of the talks, the Japanese Supreme Command's operational orders ended with: 'War with the Netherlands, America, England inevitable; general operational preparations to be completed by early December.'

Also on 5 November, the US Chiefs of Staff (Army and Navy) met Roosevelt to discuss the Far East. A month before, Generalissimo Chiang Kai-Shek, the Chinese Nationalist leader, had pleaded with America and Britain for help. US Secretary of State Cordell Hull feared that any further aid to China would provoke Japanese retaliation and General George Crook and Admiral Harold R. Stark urged the President to tread carefully. But it was resolved that if Japan undertook any military action against British, Dutch or US territory, America would intervene militarily.

After this decision the November talks between the two sides had no meaning whatever. Japan demanded a totally unacceptable retreat from America's stated position and tied her diplomats to a deadline of 29 November. This came and went with nothing resolved.

The force destined to attack Pearl Harbor had left Japan almost a fortnight before the 29th and congregated at Tankan Bay in the Kurile Islands. It was a powerful force – six aircraft carriers and nine destroyers, with tankers and supply ships, two cruisers and two battleships in support. Twenty ocean-going submarines acted as an advanced guard. Five of these were equipped with two-man midget subs. This force, commanded by the brilliant Vice Admiral Chuichi Nagumo, was the cream of the Imperial Japanese Navy.

On 26 November, the strong armada left the Kuriles and set

course for Pearl Harbor – adopting a route that would bring them towards the US Pacific Fleet from the north. Japanese met forecasters had told the task force that the weather was expected to be bad in the regions it would pass through. This would make the necessary refuelling tricky, but if they approached from the north there was less chance of being spotted by the Americans.

By 6 December, American naval strategists were still saying an attack on Pearl Harbor was most unlikely. Their grounds for such confidence were the unequivocal reports from US and British reconnaissance planes that Japan was launching a full-scale amphibious operation in the south, and Japanese ships laden with soldiers were reportedly entering the Gulf of Siam. American opinion could not accept the idea that Japan was capable of mounting two naval operations at the same time.

As dawn broke on 7 December, the Japanese carrier force had reached a position 275 miles north of Pearl Harbor. Fifty-one Aichi 'Val' dive-bombers, 43 Mitsubishi Zero-Sens 'Zeke' fighters, 40 Nakajima B5N2 'Kate' bombers with shallow-running torpedoes and 50 high-level 'Kates' left the decks at 0600. Eighty Vals, 54 Kates and 36 Zeros followed up.

The ships lying at anchor at Pearl Harbor were charged to keep a 'Condition 3' state of preparedness. Every fourth gun was supposed to be manned. But as America still regarded herself precariously at peace, none of the main guns was manned and the ammunition for the machine-guns was in locked boxes. The keys were in the charge of officers – some of whom were not even on duty.

A boatswain's mate saw between 20 and 25 aircraft approaching at 0730 but he could not see who they belonged to. All doubt was dispelled when the first bomb dropped just before 0800. Pearl Harbor's naval commander, Admiral Husband E. Kimmel, got the news of the attack three minutes later. Naval air commander, Rear-Admiral Bellinger, broadcast the words that were to smash the isolationist grip on America: 'Air Raid, Pearl Harbor, this is no drill!'

Even the ambitious Yamamoto could scarcely have hoped for a more total surprise attack. The US Pacific Fleet was caught with its pants well and truly down. Blunders and bad luck brought about this American debacle. One certain blunder was when two NCOs, manning a radar station, saw Japanese planes closing in and watched them for 40 minutes. They tried to raise the alarm by telephone, but failed to contact anybody who believed their report. USS *Ward* gave another warning at 0645 when she sank a midget submarine at the mouth of Pearl Harbor. This too was ignored.

'Tora–Tora–Tora!' (Attack, attack, attack!) Commander Mitsuo Fuchida, in charge of the first wave, signalled to his airmen at 0749. Six minutes later the bombs began to fall. Their target was Battleship Row – eight battleships at the SE of Ford Island. Low-flying torpedo Kates roared in on the hapless ships. Four of them were holed or damaged in five minutes. While the Kates punished the vessels below the waterline, Vals were busy smashing decks, bridges and gun turrets. Other Kates were finishing off the job with high-level bombing.

The initial attack inflicted shattering losses on the Pacific Fleet. USS *Arizona* (32,600 tons) blew up and snapped in two. More than 1,000 men were drowned. The carnage continued when three torpedoes smashed into *Oklahoma* (29,000 tons). She turned over – imprisoning what was left of her crew below decks. When holes were later cut in her bottom only 32 survivors crawled out. A total of five hits – four torpedo, one bomb – put paid to the 31,800-ton *West Virginia*, while the *California* (32,600 tons) blazed for three days after fires reached her fuel tanks. Then she sank.

USS *Nevada* (29,000 tons) tried to steam out of the harbor, but Japanese bombers caught her and she finally beached on a mudflat at the entrance to the harbor. *Maryland* and *Tennessee* escaped relatively lightly. They were shielded from torpedoes by *Oklahoma* and *West Virginia*, which were moored on the seaward side. The 33,100-ton flagship of the US Pacific Fleet, *Pennsylvania*, was in drydock and was more or less unscathed at the end of the attack.

The old battleship *Utah* had been in use as a target ship for some time before the Japanese attack. Denuded of her superstructure, from the air she looked like an aircraft carrier. Japanese pilots expended valuable torpedoes on this worthless relic.

At the NW shore of the harbor Japanese aircraft damaged the light cruiser *Helena* and the seaplane tender *Curtiss*, while the light cruiser *Raleigh* was crippled. The minelayer *Oglala* was sunk. The destroyers *Shaw*, *Cassin* and *Downes*, the light cruiser *Honolulu* and the repair ship *Vestal* all suffered damage.

While the Pacific Fleet in the harbor was being pulverized, the airfields on the mainland were also taking a hammering. At the US Marine Corps' Ewa Field were 49 airworthy planes. By the time the

Japanese were through with them only 16 remained intact. Kaneohe was a flying-boat base equipped with 36 Catalinas. After the attack an incredible 27 were complete write-offs while six others were severely damaged. This was one of the most punishing attacks on air bases in the Second World War. Of 148 first-line naval aircraft, at least 112 were destroyed, as were 52 out of the 129 Army planes. Thirty-eight American planes did take off. Ten of them were shot down.

The first Japanese wave then departed. Its attack had lasted 25 minutes. In that time thousands of American lives had been lost and millions of dollars worth of strategic weaponry destroyed. But there was more to come.

At 0845, 36 Zekes, 54 torpedo Kates and 80 high-level Kates provided Japan's second wave. But now the Americans had woken up and were a little more prepared. Shore batteries opened up as did still-serviceable ships' guns. Japan lost only nine planes in the first wave. In the second the score rose to 20 in return for little effect – its value being confined to finishing off already crippled installations. The submarine base escaped unscathed as did the fuel depot. Here was stockpiled almost as much oil as Japan had in her entire reserves.

President Roosevelt spoke of the 'day that shall live in infamy.' If it was, it was also a day of appalling military cost to the United States. The Japanese had lost 29 aircraft and 55 men. For this meager expenditure 2,403 soldiers, sailors, airmen and civilians had been killed, 164 planes destroyed and six battleships and three destroyers sunk, while a number of others had been badly damaged. Apart from the dead, the Japanese left 1,178 wounded Americans in Pearl Harbor. The only section of the US Pacific Fleet to escape damage was its carrier force. It was not at Pearl Harbor at the time of the attack.

If the Japanese had sent in a third wave – as Cdr Fuchida wanted – there is little doubt that they could have totally devastated Pearl Harbor. But Fuchida did not have his way. Vice-Adm. Nagumo, the task force commander, believed that he and his men had done more than a good day's work and the effectiveness of the strike had certainly surpassed all expectation. His force turned tail and settled down to a quiet journey home to Japan.

At 1347 Washington time, news of the attack reached Cordell Hull. Abruptly breaking off the now pointless diplomatic wrangle he unceremoniously dismissed Nomura from his presence.

The isolationist grip on America was at last smashed and she was now at war with Japan. The attack on Pearl Harbor, while brilliantly successful in itself, unleashed the might of the US military machine against Japan, as well as her German and Italian partners. For Japan the end would not come until she was utterly demoralized and Hiroshima and Nagasaki had been flattened by the atom-bomb. The entry of America into the war ensured the eventual defeat of fascism in both theaters.

Singapore (1942)

C. C. M. Macleod-Carey

It was Friday 13, February 1942 and I was watching the sun rise from my Command Post on top of Mount Faber, Singapore. The rays from the red orb of the sun radiated in ever widening shafts of red; just like the old 'Rising Sun' flag of Japan used to be.

I remember that I was feeling pretty gloomy at the time but this evil omen gave me an uncomfortable sense of impending doom. Singapore at that time was obviously in its death throes and there seemed to be very little future in it. The Japanese Army had driven right down the length of Malaya and the city was closely besieged by a ruthless and efficient enemy.

About midnight the following night, a signal came from HQ at Fort Canning saying an unidentified ship had been located just outside the minefield covering the entrances to Keppel Harbour and that no British ship was in the area. I was at that time second-in-command of the 7th Coast Artillery Regiment covering Keppel Harbour with its powerful armament of 15-in, 9.2-in, 6-in and a host of other smaller weapons. There was another similarly equipped regiment defending the Naval Base at Changi. I rang up the Port War Signal Station, our line with the Navy, which was manned by sailors. There was no reply and we discovered later that it had been evacuated but for some reason no one had informed us. I then ordered the 6-in batteries at Serapong, Siloso and Labrador to sweep the area with their searchlights. Almost immediately a ship

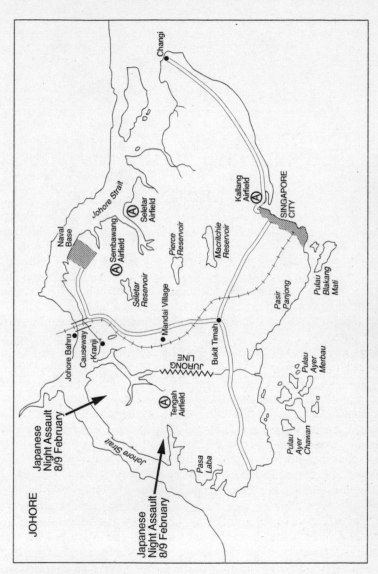

5.4 *The Fall of Singapore, February 1942*

which seemed to be of 8,000 tons was illuminated at a range of 7,000 yards, just outside the minefield. We challenged the ship by Aldis lamp but the reply, also by lamp, was incorrect.

Fortunately, in order to assist in this sort of situation, the Navy had posted an excellent rating who was standing by my side. We had a copy of *Jane's Fighting Ships* and the rating pointed to a photograph of a Japanese landing craft carrier and said, 'I reckon that's it, sir.' I gave the order 'Shoot' and within seconds all six 6-in guns opened up with a roar. The guns had been permanently sited, and even without radar, which had not been installed, their instruments and range-finding gear were so accurate that preliminary ranging was unnecessary. Direct hits were scored at once. Flames, sparks and debris started flying in all directions. The crew could be seen frantically trying to lower boats but it was all over in a matter of minutes, after which the ship just disappeared into the sea.

This action was reported to Fort Canning but it is strange that it has never, so far as I know, been mentioned in an official account. Most likely the record was lost together with a good many other documents in the subsequent events after the surrender of Singapore.

Next morning we were ordered to fire the guns at the very large number of oil tanks situated on the islands around Pulau Bukum about 3.5 miles from Keppel. Something like 200,000 tons of oil were set on fire. After that we were ordered to blow up all the guns. This was achieved by placing a charge of gelignite in the breech of each gun and another in their magazines. Time fuses were lit and the resulting explosions were pretty impressive.

Singapore in its death throes has been described in all its harrowing details by a good many writers. It is not a pretty story but the overriding factor of which everyone was painfully conscious was that the supply of water had just about dried up. In fact, troops were having to break into houses to get at the water remaining in the cisterns.

On the evening of 15 February, the gunners manning the Command Post on Mount Faber had been joined by a small Indian Commando unit and were holding a line across the main road near Keppel Golf Course below Mount Faber. At about sunset we distinctly heard Japanese troops farther up the road shouting 'Banzai!' 'Banzai!' 'Banzai!' Shortly afterwards orders were received from Fort Canning that we were to cease fire and we were informed that the great fortress of Singapore had surrendered. The Coast

Artillery had done its best and the fact is that the power and efficiency of its armament had the effect which it was designed for. It was exceedingly unlikely that the Japanese naval forces would be so rash as to make a frontal attack on Singapore because it is doubtful if they would have survived the encounter.

The plans for countering the expected invasion of Malaya by the Japanese were based on this factor and they were well conceived. The 11th Indian Division was poised on the frontier of Malaya and Thailand in December 1941, and Operation Matador was to send 11th Indian Division into Thailand and occupy the beaches at Singora and Sungei Patanie before the Japanese landed. British officers dressed in plain clothes and riding bicycles had been sent into Thailand to reconnoiter the area, where they met Japanese officers doing precisely the same thing. Air reconnaissance had reported large numbers of Japanese transports heavily escorted by warships and yet Operation Matador was called off for political reasons. So we got off to a bad start and our troops were caught on the 'wrong foot'. It soon became apparent that Japanese methods of warfare were totally different from ours and we had an awful lot to learn.

Part of my job was to direct the fire of the coast guns on to landward targets. It was mostly harassing fire, sometimes at the request of the Army and sometimes at targets picked at random, such as likely landing places on the north and west side of Singapore Island. There was no possible means of observing and correcting the fall of shot at 27,000 yards (15.3 miles) or more, so what the results were, goodness only knows. The only live Japanese I saw was a little perisher perched on top of a telescopic mast where he was probably spotting for his own guns. He was about three miles from where I was watching with my binoculars and just behind the grandstand of the racecourse near Burkit Timah. I turned the Connaught 9.2-in battery on to him and fired about 30 rounds. The little man disappeared in a cloud of smoke, dust and debris most of which came from the grandstand. Coast Artillery was not designed for this job but it certainly made a lot of noise, particularly the 15-in guns, whose flashes at night were quite spectacular. It was all a matter of firing at map references and hoping for the best.

I am anxious to dispel the myth that the Coast Artillery did not turn round and shoot at the enemy, so I propose to deal with each of the main batteries in turn.

The searchlights were manned by locally enlisted Malays who

deserted overnight the day before the surrender. They just vanished – with one exception. He was a half-caste whom we promoted to Bombardier because he spoke English and Malay fluently and was very useful. He stayed and the curious thing is that he reported to me a month later in Colombo (Ceylon) and asked me if he could be sent back to Malaya. Intelligence grabbed him, gave him a course of training and, eventually landed him with a wireless set on the coast of Malaya. I hope he survived.

The following is an account of the actions of the Coast Artillery batteries.

Faber Fire Command

Pasir Laba Bty.   Fired at the Japanese crossing Johore Strait in boats but the battery was a sitting duck for the Japanese who brought up mortars and lobbed bombs from concealed positions until the battery was put out of action. The guns were blown up and the detachments withdrew.

Buona Vista Bty.   When Vickers installed the two 15-in guns in 1938 they fitted Magslip cables that were too short for all-round traverse. These cables carried an electric impulse from the Plotting Room to actuate the dials on the guns. The result was that stops were put on the traversing arcs of the guns which prevented them from pointing inland. The Japanese broke into the battery area but were driven out by the gunners and Australian infantry. The guns were then blown up and the personnel marched to Mount Faber and next day were attached to an infantry battalion with their battery CO Major Phillip Jackson.

Siloso and Labrador Btys.   Both batteries fired a good deal of HE at Japanese troops advancing along the coast road through Pasir Panjang. It was reported to me by an infantry sergeant that the guns had caused a lot of Japanese casualties.

Serapong and Silingsing Btys.   Owing to hills and buildings, they were not well sited to fire inland and I do not know whether they actually fired or not. It is possible that they fired counter-battery programs.

Connaught Bty.   The three 9.2-in guns fired a considerable amount of ammunition including all their 90 HE rounds. Targets which I know were engaged included Johore Bahru, right across Singapore Island, where the Japanese had their HQ, possible landing places on the south bank of Johore Strait, a tank attack on the Bukit Timah road, Tengah Airfield, Jurong road and the Japanese artillery spotter already mentioned. Also counter-battery programs.

Changi Fire Command

Most of the action took place on the western side of the island. It is difficult to obtain accurate information on this Fire Command but it is obvious that the guns could only in many cases have been fired at extreme range.

Johore Bty. I do know that the three 15-in guns fired a great deal of their AP ammunition, notably at Johore Bahru and the reservoir area. They had all-round traverse but they had to knock down some of the concrete emplacements in order to get the shields round. Colonel Masanobu Tsuji, Chief of Staff Japanese Twenty-Fifth Army (Lieutenant General Tomoyuki Yamashita), records coming under their fire on the newly captured Tengah Airfield (11 February). Abandoning his car, he was blown into a ditch and watched the 50-ft-wide shell-holes appear around the drainage pipe he crawled into.

Tekong Bty. The three 9.2-in guns fired at several targets including the 400 Japanese landing on Pulau Ubin island.

Counter Battery An organization was hastily set up with OPs (observation posts) on the tops of high buildings such as the Kathay Building and other places. Bearings of enemy gun flashes were fed into an operation room, probably in Fort Canning.

There must have been plenty of enemy batteries to neutralize. The Japanese did not make great use of their artillery in their advance through Malaya, relying mostly on their infantry guns and mortars which they were very expert at handling. For the final assault on Singapore Island they deployed a very large concentration of artillery which they managed somehow to transport all the way down the peninsula. Japanese Army engineers excelled in repairing broken bridges. They brought up a considerable amount of heavy artillery which, judging by the effect of their shells, must have been up to 6-in caliber. Their preparatory bombardment (from 440 guns) before crossing Johore Strait was almost of First World War proportions.

One was constantly aware that once the small supply of HE was used up the guns could only fire armor-piercing (AP) projectiles.

These are made with very thick, hard steel walls and nose, designed to penetrate the thick armor-plate of a warship without collapsing. They have a delay-action fuse fitted to the base of the shell. The effect is that the shell detonates inside the ship and, as the quantity of ammatol or lyddite explosive is comparatively small, due to the thickness of the walls, the shell casing breaks up into very large chunks of steel. These smash up boilers, steam pipes, electric cables and machinery and generally create havoc inside the ship. As a man-killing instrument of warfare AP ammunition is not very effective. I expect the shells with a high angle of descent drilled a hole about 20 ft deep and there was none of the fragmentation which is essential for antipersonnel requirements.

It is interesting to indulge in that well-known pastime of hindsight and wisdom after the event. The lessons of Singapore were learnt and applied with considerable urgency in Ceylon. Colombo and Trincomalee were the last remaining bases for the Royal Navy in the Far East and were vitally important. The following measures were taken and, had they been applied in Singapore, it is reasonable to suppose that the Coast Artillery could have been more effective.

1 The post of C-in-C and Governor-General was created and ably carried out by Admiral Sir Geoffrey Layton. This ensured there was little likelihood of politics rearing its ugly head and cramping the style of the Service Chiefs in the way that it did in Malaya. The atmosphere in Ceylon was electric – 'There is not going to be another Singapore here.'

2 Both Colombo and Trincomalee had quite powerful Coast Artillery of modern 9.2-in and 6-in guns. All guns were given all-round traverse and overhead cover against air attack.

3 Each Fire Command was given an armored, tracked vehicle which was fitted with a No. 19 wireless set, to act as a mobile OP for co-operation with the field army.

4 Permanent OPs were established round the perimeter of each port. These OPs had a permanent telephone line to an operation room.

5 Each coast bty had its own 40 mm Bofors AA gun manned by coast gunners.

6 Each Fire Command had on its establishment a fully equipped eight-gun 25-pounder field battery. This had the good psychological effect of identifying the coast gunners

with the field army instead of being out on a limb as they were in Singapore.

7 An expert in counter-battery work was sent down from India who organized a workable counter-battery organization. He also instructed the officers in that important aspect of artillery work.

8 The proportion of HE ammunition was augmented.

In conclusion it can be stated that the coast artillery did its job just by being there. Singapore was one of the most heavily defended ports anywhere and the existence of its enormously powerful artillery dictated the strategy of the war in those parts. The Japanese were fully aware of this and we knew that they knew, so the campaign started more or less exactly as it was expected it would. The Coast Artillery locked the front door and it was up to the field army to bolt the back door.

Santa Cruz (1942)

Michael Orr

In 1942, the seemingly unstoppable expansion of Japanese imperialism threatened to engulf the whole of SE Asia and even Australia. American forces in the Pacific fought desperately to stem the tide. The Battle of the Santa Cruz Islands was of vital importance. There was no clear victor at the time but it was to significantly affect the war in the Pacific. Why?

Between May and October 1942 a series of four naval/air battles in the western Pacific established that the aircraft carrier had replaced the battleship's supremacy in the world's fleets. The battleship era was by no means completely finished and a number of vital battleship actions were still to be fought, but the aircraft carrier had become the linchpin of the fleet. The battleship and every other type of warship were now its subordinates. This change vastly increased the potential of seapower. The ability of the battleship to influence a war directly was limited to a score of miles – the range of its guns. But the carrier was a far more flexible weapon – able to strike over hundreds of miles and influence events over huge areas.

The strategic problems which the two sides faced were very similar. Guadalcanal lay at the end of a long and difficult line of communication and competed with other areas for scarce resources. The Japanese were very slow to realize the island's importance, giving more priority to the war in China and the threat of a war with Russia. The Imperial Navy therefore was forced to make do with the troops already in the SW Pacific. On the American side, Guadalcanal had to compete with the Battle of the Atlantic and the need to supply Russia. And preparations were reaching a climax for the Operation Torch landings in North Africa. It was not surprising that the Marines on Guadalcanal were soon thinking of themselves as a forgotten army.

After several months of fierce fighting neither side wanted to risk their depleted fleets without the certainty of decisive victory. The Japanese chose to wear their enemy down until they could re-establish an effective superiority. The waters between the American base at Espiritu Santo, in the New Hebrides islands, and the Solomons were so heavily patrolled by Japanese submarines that the area was dubbed 'Torpedo Junction'. Henderson Field, near Lunga Point, was in the possession of the Americans. They took advantage of this to control the waters around Guadalcanal during daylight.

A pattern of operations was soon established. American convoys delivered supplies from Espiritu Santo to their garrison while day lasted, but withdrew at nightfall. Under the cover of darkness the 'Tokyo Express' of Japanese troop-carrying destroyers and cruisers would rush down 'the Slot' to land stores and reinforcements or bombard the American positions. But they would have to leave in a hurry in order to be out of range of avenging aircraft from Henderson Field before daybreak. Thus neither side was able to achieve a superiority in ground forces on the island. The Japanese were particularly short of supplies, rather than men. They had few landing craft and had to rely on fast destroyers and small boats. The Americans found fuel for Henderson's aircraft their greatest problem.

A series of skirmishes and minor battles established the Japanese superiority in night fighting and turned the water north of Guadalcanal into a wreck-strewn 'Ironbottom Sound'. An attempt by the Japanese to force through a larger convoy than usual resulted in another carrier battle on 24 August.

The honors of the Battle of the Eastern Solomons were fairly evenly shared. A Japanese light carrier, the *Ryujo*, was lost. The American carrier *Enterprise* was damaged and had to return to Pearl Harbor. The next weeks saw several successes for the Japanese policy of attrition. The carrier *Wasp* was sunk, and the carrier *Saratoga* and the battleship *North Carolina* damaged. At one time the Americans had only one carrier in the Guadalcanal area. Better news for the Americans came with the Battle of Cape Esperance on 11 October when a Japanese cruiser force was severely damaged in a night action.

By this time the Japanese had decided to break the stalemate on Guadalcanal, which was also delaying the progress of the New Guinea campaign. In mid-September Imperial Army and Navy Staffs agreed that: 'After reinforcement of Army forces has been completed, Army and Navy forces will combine and in one action attack and retake Guadalcanal Island airfield. During this operation the Navy will take all necessary action to halt the efforts of the enemy to augment his forces in the Solomons area.' The capture of the airfield was left to the Army. After its experience at Midway, the Navy was apparently chary of risking a major battle while the enemy had the use of an 'unsinkable aircraft carrier' – Henderson Field. During October the 'Tokyo Express' increased its work, with heavy bombardments of Henderson Field and other American positions. It brought the Japanese strength on the island up to 20,000 men.

The Americans were fully aware of their own danger. On 15 October Admiral Chester W. Nimitz, C-in-C in the Pacific, considered that his forces could not control the sea. Supplying American positions could be done, but only at great military cost. By 18 October Vice Admiral William F. Halsey had been appointed to succeed Vice Admiral Robert L. Ghormley as Comsopac (Commander, South Pacific Area). Halsey's reputation in the Pacific was second to none. He had commanded the carrier task forces which had first struck back at the all-conquering Japanese and in particular had commanded the group from which the Doolittle Raid on Tokyo was launched. His strategy was 'Kill Japs! Kill more Japs!' At last, with the Torch convoy on its way, Washington was prepared to increase its support of the South Pacific operations.

The Japanese had planned to capture Henderson Field on 21 October, but the unexpected strength of the American garrison (which rose to over 23,000 Marines and GIs) caused them to postpone the attack until 23 October. The delay did not do them much good. They lost over 2,000 men and all their tanks. However, on the 24th Admiral Isokuru Yamamoto, the Japanese naval C-in-C, warned his military colleagues that the fleet, which had been at sea since 11 October, was running dangerously short of fuel and would soon have to withdraw. The attacks on Henderson Field therefore continued and a false report of victory in the early hours of 25 October brought the Japanese fleet hurrying south, only to reverse their course as soon as the report was denied. At 1200, two Japanese carriers were spotted by a Catalina flying boat but they immediately turned away and so avoided the search aircraft of the American carriers.

Another night of doubt and indecision followed for both fleets. On land the Japanese mounted another attack, but were eventually forced to admit defeat. The first part of the Japanese plan had failed. The outcome of the land attack was so uncertain that the units of their fleet had been drawn much farther south than intended. On the night of 25/26 October elements of the Japanese navy were twice sighted and attacked by Catalinas. In his headquarters at Noumea, in New Caledonia, Admiral Halsey was in no doubt what his orders to his commanders at sea should be: 'Attack – Repeat – Attack!'

Task Force 64, led by Rear Admiral Willis A. Lee, in *Washington*, was responsible for protecting Guadalcanal from night bombardments and operated independently throughout the battle. During the night of 25/26 October, the battleship *Washington* was patrolling west of Savo Island. Task Force 16, under Rear Admiral Thomas C. Kinkaid, was based on the carrier *Enterprise*. Rear Admiral George D. Murray commanded Task Force 17 from the carrier *Hornet*.

Enterprise and *Hornet* were sister-ships, completed in 1938 and 1941 respectively. In October 1942 they were the last word in carrier design and represented the fruits of the USN's inter-war experience of aircraft carriers. With a displacement of 19,000 tons (*Enterprise*) and 20,000 tons (*Hornet*) they were capable of speeds up to 34 knots and could operate between 80 and 100 planes. Both ships were veterans of the Pacific war, having worked together on the Doolittle Raid to Tokyo and at Midway.

The battleship *South Dakota* of Task Force 16 was one of a new generation of fast ships. With a displacement of 35,000 tons, she was capable of 28 knots and had a main armament of nine 16-in guns. She was fresh from Pearl Harbor where her AA guns had been increased to include 68 of the new 40 mms in quadruple mounts and 78 20 mm guns. Captain Thomas L. Gatch, her commander, neglecting the conventional 'bull', had concentrated on gunnery practice. The battle that followed proved that he had made a trained and efficient fighting team of his inexperienced ship's company.

The Japanese divided their fleet into a number of smaller units as well, but on principles which differed significantly from those of the Americans. The two main elements were the Advance Force,

under Vice Admiral Nobutake Kondo, in *Atago*, and the Striking
Force under Vice Admiral Chuichi Nagumo. The Advance Force
was intended for the close support of the troops on Guadalcanal
and had been responsible for most of the night bombardments
of the American positions during October. On 26 October it
consisted of two battleships, four heavy cruisers and a destroyer
screen. Originally two carriers had provided air cover, but *Hiyo*
had developed engine trouble and had been forced to return to Truk
on 22 October. This left only her sister ship *Junyo*, completed as
recently as May. Both ships were converted passenger liner hulls.
For their size, 24,000 tons, they carried a small complement of
aircraft, just over 50, and were underpowered, being capable of
only 25.5 knots.

The Striking Force to deal with any major interference by
the American fleet, was sub-divided into a Carrier Group, under
Nagumo, of three aircraft carriers and their screen, and a Vanguard
Force, under Rear Admiral Hiroaki Abe, of two battleships, three
heavy cruisers and a destroyer screen. The carriers *Shokaku* and
Zuikaku were sister-ships, designed as fleet carriers to work with
the *Yamato*-class super-battleships. They displaced 25,000 tons,
but with engines capable of 160,000 SHP they had a speed of
34 knots. Able to handle air groups of over 80 planes, they had
operated together at Pearl Harbor and the Coral Sea. Damage
in the latter battle ensured that they missed Midway. *Zuiho* was
a light carrier, originally designed as a submarine tender. Dis-
placing 11,000 tons, she could reach 28 knots with up to 30
aircraft.

The Japanese practice of dividing their fleets into sections has
been criticized. The fault lay not so much in the division itself but
the way in which it was done. By separating the individual parts too
much and dividing their carriers between the parts they generally
ensured that only a fraction of their available carrier strength would
be able to intervene in any battle. This happened at Midway and,
to a lesser extent, at Santa Cruz. Within the main divisions of the
fleet, the carriers operated as a unit, but without the support of
other types of ship, save destroyers. Although this made it easier
to co-ordinate aircraft operations, it meant that the carriers were
exposed to air attack.

Once their carriers were sighted, all the Japanese eggs were in one
basket. And they lacked the fearsome AA fire of the Americans.

At Midway four Japanese carriers were caught together and three were sunk. The fourth escaped temporarily because of a fortuitous rainstorm. On the other hand the Japanese, although they sighted one American carrier group at Midway, remained ignorant for a long time of the presence of another, stronger, group. A further Japanese disadvantage was that their carriers had restricted bridges and limited radio facilities. This made them unsuitable as flagships, yet they had to be used as such.

First light on 26 October came shortly after 0500, revealing a fine day, with just enough cloud in the sky to conceal a dive-bomber attack. The American carriers were by then north of the Santa Cruz Islands. They chose to approach Guadalcanal from that direction rather than risk encountering Japanese submarine patrols in Torpedo Junction. Their course was north-westerly and less than 200 miles ahead of them were the Japanese forces in a triangular formation. The Vanguard Group of the Japanese Striking Force was leading the carriers by 60 miles. One hundred miles to the west was the Advanced Force, with the carrier *Junyo* maneuvering independently even farther west. The Japanese forces were all steering northwards. Both sides were aware that the enemy's carriers were at sea, but neither knew the other's exact location. Delays in transmission meant that Kinkaid had not received the report of the Catalina which had attacked *Zuikaku* during the night. This was unfortunate because the overwhelming advantage in carrier battles went to the side which struck first. Kinkaid ordered an aircraft search from *Enterprise*. Sixteen Dauntless dive-bombers took off. Each was armed with a 500-lb bomb. They fanned in pairs to the north and west. One group saw a 'Kate' torpedo bomber on a similar mission and at 0617 the Vanguard Group, led by Admiral Abe, was sighted. There was no sign of the carriers until 0650. The first pair of scouts could not break through the fighter patrols. Then at 0740 another pair, having heard the sighting report and altered course, made an unobserved approach. They attacked the light carrier *Zuiho* and both scored a hit. A 50 ft hole in the flight deck made the carrier useless. But it was too late to prevent a strike taking off.

The 'Kate' spotted by *Enterprise*'s aircraft had identified a carrier task force at 0658. At 0700 a 65-strong force of 'Zekes', 'Kates' and 'Vals' flew off and another group was soon being ranged. The American carriers did nothing about their sighting reports until 0720. Even then, the attack was not co-ordinated. At 0730, 15 Dauntless, six Avenger torpedo bombers and eight Wildcat fighters left *Hornet*. *Enterprise*'s first strike consisted of eight Avengers and eight Wildcats and only three Dauntlesses. The carrier was by now critically short of dive-bombers. Six had not returned from the previous evening's attempt to find the Japanese carriers, six more were on anti-submarine patrol, and the 16 scouts had not yet come back. The *Enterprise*'s strike flew off at 0800 and was followed at 0815 by *Hornet*'s second strike – nine Dauntlesses, nine Avengers and seven Wildcats. With their targets nearly 200 miles away there was neither time nor fuel for the aircraft to circle the carriers until a concentrated strike could be built up. Squadrons flew in a long-drawn-out gaggle. As they flew they passed the incoming Japanese strike. Some Japanese fighters left their convoy to attack the *Enterprise* group. Four Wildcats and four Avengers were either shot down or severely damaged and forced back to the carrier. The size of the *Enterprise*'s strike had been halved at a cost of only three 'Zekes'.

The American fleet was expecting the Japanese strike. Every possible step was taken to avoid a disastrous carrier fire, such as that which had destroyed the *Lexington* at the Coral Sea. Aircraft were secured in the hangar deck, aviation fuel lines were filled with carbon dioxide, and damage control parties were on constant alert. Speed was maintained at 28 knots and around the carriers their escorts were poised to provide massive AA fire.

The first line of defense was the 38 Wildcats of the combat air patrol (CAP). This was directed from the *Enterprise*. But the officer in charge was new to his job, having recently replaced a Midway veteran whom Halsey had taken to Noumea. For some time the fighter-direction team could not distinguish between the American and Japanese air groups on their cluttered radar screens. It was 0857 before a clear picture emerged. The CAP was too near the fleet, and too late – only 10 miles out at 0906. Although the Wildcats claimed some victims, neither they nor the American gunners could break the co-ordination of the Japanese attack.

At about 0900 *Enterprise*'s group was hidden by a rain squall. This left *Hornet* – lacking the close support of a battleship like *South Dakota* – to face the full might of the Japanese attack

alone. 'Val' dive-bombers began the assault, scoring one hit and
two near-misses. The squadron commander, his plane having been
hit, made no attempt to drop his bombs but kept on diving. The
'Val' bounced off the carrier's funnel and burnt through the flight
deck. The dive-bombers suffered heavily, but their attack covered
the approach of a squadron of 'Kate' torpedo bombers from astern.
Two torpedoes crashed into *Hornet*'s engine-rooms and she slowed
to a halt under a pall of black smoke. A sitting target, *Hornet* was
hit by three more bombs and then a burning 'Kate' made a suicide
run into the ship's port side. It was all over in 10 minutes. The
Japanese had lost 25 planes, but the once-formidable *Hornet* was a
listing, blazing wreck.

Meanwhile the American air groups were approaching the Japanese
fleet. But their straggling formation had been disturbed by the
fighters. They were unable to deliver a united attack, or even
find the same target. Fifteen Dauntlesses from *Hornet* led the
attack. The first wave of defending fighters was kept at bay by
their escorting Wildcats but the Dauntlesses were then left without
protection. At 0930 *Shokaku* and *Zuiho* appeared below and the
main Japanese CAP above. Even so, 11 bombers got through and
scored between three and six hits on *Shokaku*. The 1,000 lb bombs
tore her flight deck apart and started a tremendous blaze in the
hangar. But there were no torpedo bombers to finish the job.
Hornet's Avengers had lost touch with the rest of the strike and
so *Shokaku* and *Zuiho* went unmolested as they limped towards
Truk. The Avengers made contact with Abe's Vanguard Group,
but they were so short of fuel that they could not continue to
search for the carriers. At 0930 they made an unsuccessful attack
on the cruiser *Suzuya*. The rest of the American aircraft also
missed the carriers and attacked Abe's group. *Hornet*'s second
wave damaged the cruiser *Chikuma* but *Enterprise*'s aircraft had
no luck at all.

As the American aircraft turned for home the result of the battle
was still very much in the balance. Two Japanese carriers were out
of action, but the second strike from *Shokaku* and *Zuikaku* had
not yet attacked. *Zuikaku* was ready to gather up the survivors of
all three carriers and prepare another strike. *Junyo* was hurrying
westwards and, as Nagumo's flagship *Shokaku* was out of action, he
transferred command of flying operations to Rear Admiral Kakuji
Kakuta on board *Junyo*. She was still more than 300 miles from

the American task forces. Even so, Kakuta ordered a strike to commence. Her aircraft were to land on *Zuikaku* or *Shokaku* after the attack.

On the American side, *Hornet*'s fires had been brought under control, although at one stage the order to abandon ship had been given. By 1005 the 9,050-ton cruiser *Northampton* was ready to begin towing the carrier when an unsuccessful attack by a stray 'Val' disrupted operations.

Although Task Force 16 had not yet been attacked, it was the scene of increasing confusion. Overhead were stacked the surviving aircraft from both carriers. They were by now nearing the end of their fuel. At 1002 the destroyer *Porter* was torpedoed by a Japanese submarine while picking up the crew of a crashed aircraft. The *Porter* was so badly damaged that she had to be sunk by gunfire, her crew transferring to another destroyer, *Shaw*. A submarine was the last thing which any carrier wanted to encounter while forced to keep a straight course for aircraft to land.

Then (almost as soon as the landings started) the second Japanese strike was detected on the *South Dakota*'s radar. *Enterprise* suspended operations and prepared to defend herself. Fortunately this attack was not so well co-ordinated as that on *Hornet*. The dive-bombers arrived 20 minutes before the torpedo-bombers and were met by the heaviest AA fire yet seen in the Pacific War. *South Dakota*, only 1,000 yards from *Enterprise*, showed to perfection her crew's gunnery skills. She shot down 26 'Vals', *Enterprise* claimed another seven. But two bombs found their mark, damaging the flight deck and starting fresh fires in the hangar. But the torpedo-bombers were too far behind to deliver the final blow.

When they finally arrived they were attacked by the combat air patrol. One Wildcat pilot, Lieutenant Vejtasa, shot down six before he ran out of ammunition. About 14 'Kates' got through to the Task Force. Five of these were destroyed by AA fire. Then the surviving Japanese moved in on the luckless *Enterprise*, attacking on both sides. Full-speed maneuvering by her captain once more saved the carrier. One 'Kate' did not even try to launch its torpedo, but dived straight onto the forecastle of the destroyer *Smith*. The blazing ship used *South Dakota*'s wake to douse her fires and so survived the battle.

On board *Enterprise*, the ship's company worked with disciplined but feverish haste to clear the flight deck and complete the recovery of the circling aircraft before they ran out of fuel. The appearance of a submarine periscope made things more difficult. Then at 1101 *Junyo*'s aircraft appeared on *South Dakota*'s radar screen. Alerted by this, her gunners opened fire on six unidentified aircraft at 1110. These proved to be returning Dauntlesses. By the time that this mistake had been sorted out *Junyo*'s aircraft were hidden in the cloud over the Task Force. Twenty attacked in a two-minute flurry, but achieved only one near-miss on *Enterprise* and lost eight planes. At 1127 two isolated 'Vals' dived on *South Dakota* and the AA cruiser *San Juan*. One bomb exploded on *South Dakota*'s foremost turret, without penetrating the armor. But Captain Gatch was wounded by splinters and for a moment the battleship was not under command.

As *South Dakota* headed towards *Enterprise, San Juan* was hit astern and her rudder jammed. The tight formation of Task Force 16 was shattered as the ships maneuvered out of the way of their careering consorts. Both ships were soon under control and *Enterprise* was able to land aircraft again. But with her forward elevator out of action the carrier was slow in getting aircraft below and several planes were forced to ditch before their turn came. *Enterprise* launched a CAP, but did not attempt to renew the battle. All morning the carrier had been steering south-eastwards into the wind, but at 1400 she turned east. Admiral Kinkaid had decided that with only *Enterprise*'s limited capacity to operate aircraft he could not risk an offensive against an unknown number of Japanese carriers.

The Japanese still had two carriers left in the battle, but had lost over 100 aircraft. *Zuikaku* and *Junyo* collected the mixed assortment of aircraft and sent them off in penny packets. Kondo and Abe also increased the speed of their battleship squadrons, hoping to finish off the crippled American ships after nightfall.

The cruiser *Northampton* was inching *Hornet* to safety when they were spotted at 1515 by Japanese aircraft. *Northampton* cut her tow, leaving the stationary carrier an easy target for the approaching torpedo planes. One hit was enough to seal her fate. The order to abandon ship was given, but three more Japanese formations attacked before all the survivors had been taken off. Then *Hornet* showed the same endurance as her sister-ship *Yorktown* at Midway. Destroyers fired nine torpedoes into her and over 400 5-in shells.

But *Hornet*, burning from stern to stern, was still afloat when she was sighted by Abe's ships at 2120. The Japanese at least had the satisfaction of avenging the Doolittle Raid by giving the *coup de grâce* to the ship which launched it.

During the night, the Japanese carriers were once again attacked by Catalinas. It was not until the afternoon of the 27th that the Combined Fleet began its withdrawal to Truk.

At the end of the battle neither side had suffered decisive losses. The Americans had lost *Hornet* and a destroyer. *Enterprise, South Dakota, San Juan* and a destroyer had been damaged. No major Japanese unit had been sunk, but two carriers and a destroyer had been damaged. *Shokaku* was out of action for nine months. The Japanese also lost 100 aircraft, against American casualties of 20 planes destroyed in action and another 54 missing or damaged.

What was the final result of the battle? Admiral Samuel E. Morison claims in the Official History of the battle, 'The Struggle for Guadalcanal', that 'Measured in combat tonnage sunk, the Japanese had won a tactical victory; but other losses forced them back to the Truk hideout.' This is less than fair to the Japanese. Truk was no more a 'hideout' than Noumea, and the American fleet turned for home first. The real reason for the retirement of the Japanese fleet was the failure of their army to capture Henderson Field. The struggle for Guadalcanal reverted to its former pattern: supply runs by day and night and a long, hard fight on land. Eventually the Americans won the reinforcement battle and in February 1943 Japan evacuated the survivors of her garrison.

With the advantage of hindsight it would be easy to argue that the Battle of Santa Cruz made little difference to the final result. But this is to ignore the question of what might have been. After Santa Cruz the Japanese had four undamaged carriers and the Americans had only the damaged *Enterprise* and the escort carrier *Long Island* in the Pacific. Japan had the opportunity to exploit her carrier superiority and win the decisive victory which had escaped both sides. She failed to do so because, although she had the carriers, both aircraft and pilots were lacking.

The Japanese fleet, lacking both air cover and the striking power of the carrier, could not check the American daylight convoys. By the time the Japanese carrier fleet had been repaired and re-equipped it was too late to save Guadalcanal. When the two fleets next met, in the Philippine Sea in June 1944, Japan could send only nine carriers and 430 aircraft against 15 carriers and 891 aircraft. Whether or not Santa Cruz was a setback for the Americans it bought them enough time to ensure final victory.

Kokoda Trail (1942)

John Laffin

One of the least known of all the campaigns of the Second World War is that of the Kokoda Trail over the Owen Stanley Mountains in Papua New Guinea. But among land battles it ranks with Stalingrad and the Burma Campaigns for sheer toughness, and with Stalingrad, Alamein and the Normandy landings in importance.

A no-holds-barred fight between the Australians and Japanese, the Kokoda Trail campaign – sometimes called the Battle of the Ranges – lasted seven months and put an end to the myth of Japanese infantry invincibility. It also saved Australia from invasion – with the naval battle of the Coral Sea – and gave Australian military history a name to place alongside Gallipoli and Tobruk.

After their attack on Pearl Harbor in December 1941 and their steam-roller successes in the Pacific and SE Asia, the Japanese turned their eyes to Australia. No matter how successful a landing on the Australian mainland might be, they first had to capture the islands to Australia's north. Lightly defended, New Britain and New Ireland quickly fell. Next on the list was New Guinea, whose northern part was Australian mandated territory, while the southern part, Papua, was Australian soil.

The capital, Port Moresby, was the Japanese target. On the southern coast of the island, it was the most vital supply link with Australia. A second force would take Milne Bay at the eastern end of

New Guinea and a third would menace the Bulolo Valley and another key settlement, Wau, in the north.

The first people to know of the Japanese arrival off the north coast, 63 air-miles from Moresby, were a lieutenant and a sergeant at Buna Government Station, who, on 21 July 1942, watched an enemy cruiser shell shore targets. The sergeant ran to the radio hut and on emergency frequency sent off his report:

A JAPANESE WARSHIP IS SHELLING OFF BUNA, APPARENTLY TO COVER A LANDING AT GONA OR SANANANDA. ACKNOWLEDGE, MORESBY. OVER . . .

Over and over again, the message was repeated, but Moresby did not acknowledge.

Soon it was too late to matter. The Japanese had landed their vanguard of 2,000 troops to begin a thrust across the forbidding mountains. There was little that generals in Port Moresby or their leaders in Australia could do.

The elite divisions of the volunteer Australian Imperial Force were not available at the time. The 6th and 7th were either on their way back from fighting German, Italian and Vichy French troops in the Middle East or regrouping in Australia, the 8th had been lost in the lightning Japanese conquest of Malaya and the 9th was Eighth Army's trump card in the first Battle of Alamein. Until the 6th and 7th Divisions could be brought in, the defense of Papua depended on militia battalions. The militiamen had not volunteered for service outside Australia, most were city conscripts and many considered they had been 'shanghaied' to Port Moresby without being told where they were going.

The men of the Australian Imperial Force (AIF) – volunteers to a man – despised the militiamen as 'chokos', chocolate soldiers. With some outstanding exceptions, morale was low in the militia units. In Moresby many were unloading stores from ships, digging slit trenches for air-raid defense and guarding airfields. Virtually untrained in jungle warfare, the most arduous of fighting, they rotted in tropical heat.

Meanwhile a formation known as 'Maroubra Force' (after a famous Sydney beach) commanded by Lieutenant-Colonel W. T. Owen was trying to stem the Japanese advance. The striking unit of this 'force' consisted of one grossly understrength battalion – the 39th – formed of a few hundred militiamen and stiffened by AIF reinforcements. Their average age was 18. If the Japanese could defeat them and take Kokoda airfield – the only way the defenders could receive adequate reinforcements and supplies – they might well be in Port Moresby before the AIF veterans could arrive.

The battle developing was to be fought in a terrible climate in jungles, swamps and mountains. The Owen Stanley range, which reaches a height of 13,000 ft, is a maze of ridges, spurs, valleys and rivers. Each big river is laced like a shoe with numerous small ones. The northern coast has flat and perpetually swampy ground, blanketed with dense and smelly rain forest which the sun never penetrates. The mountain jungles drip water continuously. Such tracks as exist are steep, muddy and treacherous. In places the jungle is thick with vines and creepers armed with spikes the size of fingers. Paths had to be hacked with machetes.

Vast areas are infested with malarial mosquitoes, leeches and other insects which burrow into the flesh and cause painful, itchy swellings. Here and there the jungle is broken by clearings of *kunai* – elephant grass. But because these were ideal for ambush, troops learned to avoid them.

Much fighting took place on a one-man front – the width of the track. Many Australians were killed or wounded by Japanese snipers, tied into position high up in the trees. They would allow perhaps a hundred troops to pass while they waited to pick off an officer or NCO. As a precaution the Australians abandoned badges of status and nobody was addressed by rank. Even senior officers were known by a makeshift codename. A CO might be 'Dick' or 'Curly' to his troops. The Japanese sniper who waited so patiently for a target was nearly always killed – as he knew he would be – by the troops he had allowed to pass.

The Japanese who landed at Gona and Buna trapped many Europeans at the plantations, missions and hospitals. Only a few escaped and crossed the mountains to safety. Most of those captured were murdered. In front of terrified natives, an Anglican mission party – two ministers, two women, two half-caste mission workers, a six-year-old boy and an army officer – were beheaded one by one with a sword – the boy last of all.

After several aggressive rearguard actions Col. Owen's battered battalion was forced back. When the forward Japanese troops met opposition they deployed and engaged while support moved in with machine-guns and mortars. With probing attacks the Japanese found out the width and depth of the defenses by drawing Australian fire. Stronger support units would then move around the Australian flanks to force a withdrawal or to wipe out the enemy by a rear attack. The Japanese often shouted, fired furiously, blew whistles and pulled noisily at the jungle in attempts to frighten the Australians into withdrawal. They sometimes shouted orders or requests in English to lure them into ambush, but without mastery of the Australian accent or slang this rarely worked.

The administration post of Kokoda – 1,200 ft above sea level and 45 miles from Port Moresby – possessed the only airfield between Port Moresby and the northern coast. To defend this vital place Col. Owen had about 80 men in all – 60 young soldiers and a handful of Papuans from the Papuan Infantry Battalion under Major Watson. This small exhausted force cheered mightily when they saw aircraft approaching with reinforcements. Then the planes sheered off, climbed steeply and vanished. Word had been flashed to them from Army HQ in Melbourne, 2,000 miles away on the mainland, that Kokoda had fallen. Had those planes landed the epic of the Kokoda Trail might never have happened.

That night 500 Japanese attacked Kokoda. In this first pitched battle on Papuan soil, attackers and defenders became mingled in the confused fighting. Col. Owen was mortally wounded. Maj. Watson, assuming command, extricated the survivors and withdrew to the native village of Deniki.

For several days the 39th, under Major Alan Cameron, fought a savage rearguard action. With malaria and dysentery adding to their casualties, the battalion was in poor shape by the time it reached Isurava. Here on 16 August, what was left of Maroubra Force was taken over by an AIF veteran officer, Lieutenant-Colonel Ralph Honner, who had been ordered hurriedly to the crumbling front.

Honner, with service in Libya, Greece and Crete, looked at his thin, gaunt and tattered men. They had been unable to change their clothing for weeks. Their boots were rotting on their feet. Despite great care, their Bren light machine-guns and Lee-Enfield rifles were rusting. When it got through, their food was bully beef and biscuits. They lived in continual rain without shelters or groundsheets. At night they shivered, blanketless, in the cold. Supplies were dropped from aircraft but much was lost in the jungle. Yet these men could still fight and Honner decided on a stand at Isurava. He had a few hundred men and his largest weapons were 3-in mortars firing a 10 lb shell. Against this puny force were three battalions of the Japanese 144th Regiment, with another full regiment, the 41st, coming up fast. Supporting them were a mountain artillery battalion and two engineer units – about 4,000 men in all.

Despite these odds, the Australians fought the Japanese hand-to-hand in a series of ambushes and raids for two weeks. One group of 39th sick and wounded were on their way down the trail to Moresby. Upon hearing that their battalion was fighting for its life they disobeyed orders, turned round and hurried back into action.

Another battalion placed under Honner's command, the 53rd, was not so valiant. Slow to move forward and reluctant to fight, it was removed from an offensive role after its CO was killed. Its men were made carriers and porters on the Kokoda Trail.

On 25 and 26 August, Major General Horii, the Japanese commander, launched a full-scale offensive. On the 28th the Japanese, shouting 'Banzai!' made frontal attacks on Australian positions. Violent hand-to-hand fighting followed. Horii did not know it then but he was too late to win the campaign.

The AIF had arrived at Isurava.

The 150 survivors of the 39th had left Isurava the day before the battle, fighting their way out down the trail. They were young, tired veterans who had held on for as long as they had been asked. The Japanese now faced men of the first AIF battalion to reach the battle – the 2/14th, soon joined by part of the 2/16th, both part of the 21st Brigade. On 29 August, Gen. Horii concentrated five battalions in a narrow valley for a decisive blow against the still heavily outnumbered Australians. Along the entire 350-yard Australian front he unleashed a storm of artillery shells, mortar bombs and continuous machine-gun fire; then wave after wave of infantry went in. The Australian veterans fought off every attack. One platoon repulsed 11 attacks of 100 or more men. It lost its commander and every NCO. A private soldier took command, with other privates acting as NCOs.

During the fighting on this day Sergeant R. N. Thompson led a fighting patrol of seven men to push the enemy back along the track. One of his men was 24-year-old Private Bruce S. Kingsbury, armed with a Bren and grenades. Seeing that the Japanese were getting ready for a fresh assault, Kingsbury charged them. Japanese machine-gunners opened fire on him from farther back but Kingsbury ran on, sweeping the enemy positions. The patrol finished what Kingsbury had begun and regained 100 yards of track – considerable in jungle warfare. While Thompson was preparing a holding position a Japanese sniper killed Kingsbury. He was awarded a posthumous VC. At another point Acting Corporal Charles McCallum – wounded three times – killed 40 Japanese in a brief, furious action while extricating the survivors of a forward platoon from a dangerous position. He won the Distinguished Conduct Medal.

The Australians held Isurava for four days before Japanese pressure became too great. The Australian commander, Brigadier A. W. Potts, could not challenge Horii's control of the upper spurs and ridges without weakening the defense of the main track, the Australians' lifeline route to Moresby. The 2/14 and 2/16th Battalions made a slow, deliberate withdrawal. A bloody bayonet charge checked the Japanese but their outflanking movements isolated parties of Australians. Those captured were killed on the spot.

Others finally reached safety after such privations that only a tropical, mountainous jungle can inflict. One badly wounded soldier crawled for three weeks on his hands and knees. Most wounded men were luckier, being carried to medical help by native porters – lauded by the Australian public as 'the Fuzzy-Wuzzy Angels'.

At Iora Creek an ever-thinning line of Australians killed 170 Japanese and kept their line intact before withdrawing to Imita Ridge, the last defensible point of the Owen Stanleys. Here they held while the Japanese dug in on the facing ridge – Iorabaiwa. Horii had a chance to smash through but again he was too late. The three battalions of a fresh AIF Brigade, the 25th under Brigadier K. W. Eather, relieved the exhausted 21st Brigade.

While the Japanese were striking for Port Moresby over the mountains a linked action was developing at Milne Bay, 200 miles to the east. The Royal Australian Air Force (RAAF) had established Kittyhawk fighter-squadrons there in July 1942 and the 7th Infantry Brigade (militia) and 18th Infantry Brigade, AIF – both under Major-General C. A. Clowes – were moved in to defend them. A few hundred Americans had also arrived. On 24 August a Japanese invasion got under way and troops and tanks landed from barges the following day.

On 4 September the first VC of the New Guinea campaigns was earned at Milne Bay by Corporal John Alexander French. When

Japanese machine-guns held up the advance, Corporal French ordered his section to take cover and with grenades rushed the first of a group of three machine-guns. He silenced the first, returned for more grenades and put paid to a second. Firing a Thompson sub-machine-gun he rushed the third gun and killed its crew. He died from wounds on the edge of the gunpit.

By 7 September, after much patrol fighting, Japanese naval attacks and RAAF strikes on enemy troop barges, the Japanese had lost the battle and at least 1,000 dead – mostly elite marine assault troops. Fighting was invariably savage. One Australian was found dead with 30 Japanese corpses around him. The heads of two had been smashed in with the butt of the Australian's sub-machine-gun.

Crackers with a slow-burning wick led a few Australians to their deaths. A Japanese would creep through the long grass, place a lighted cracker and then steal away and position himself. When the cracker exploded, an Australian would turn towards the sound and perhaps advance towards it. The Japanese sniper would see the sudden movement and have time to aim and fire. Here, as elsewhere in New Guinea, men often died without ever seeing the enemy in the impenetrable jungle darkness.

Milne Bay was the first clear-cut land victory over the Japanese anywhere in the war. Strategically it confined the main Japanese operations in Papua to the Buna–Kokoda area and spelt failure for the Japanese plans to capture Port Moresby.

This was not clear at the time and in the Owen Stanleys the Australian 25th Brigade was preparing for the counter-attack which would push the enemy out of the mountains. These men had already beaten the Foreign Legion in Vichy French Syria.

Using the Australian-made Owen gun, a 9 mm light sub-machine-gun for close quarter fighting, the Australian infantry soon dominated the valley between the Imita and Iorabaiwa ridges. For the first time the Australians had artillery – two 25-pounders painfully dragged up the tracks. Australian aircraft, for the first time able to help their infantry, destroyed the bridge over the wide, treacherous Kumusi River – cutting Horii's supply lines. On 26 September Horii, obeying an order from his HQ at Rabaul, began a withdrawal. Men too sick or weak to keep pace were simply left to die.

The Australian pursuit was governed by the ability of the RAAF to drop supplies. Ground troops rarely recovered more than 30 per cent of a drop. The track was so bad that, even without enemy opposition, a battalion would sometimes cover only a mile a day. Every day at noon, rain fell in solid sheets over the mountains, turning the tracks into narrow streams of black and yellow mud. Hidden in this mud were countless tree roots to catch the boots of tired soldiers. Steps cut into the track deteriorated into mudpools.

On one spur of Imita Ridge engineers cut and blocked with logs 2,000 steps – ironically nick-named the Golden Stairway. This was not the record number; Maguli Ridge had 3,400 steps.

The track was disheartening. For every 1,000 ft of altitude the troops climbed they dropped 600 ft to the start of the next ascent. Between Uberi and the crest of the Owen Stanley range the track climbed more than 20,000 ft in this switchback fashion. It crossed many rivers by log or vine bridges. At times it climbed or skirted precipices.

The temperature lurched from humid, oppressive heat to bitter cold. When not rain-drenched the soldiers were sweat-soaked. In these conditions a man was too old for jungle warfare at 30. The Japanese were so hungry that they frequently ate flesh cut from Australian or their own dead. But they often turned and fought back – on one occasion holding the Australians for eight days. Beheading or bayoneting captives, the Japanese remained a disciplined and formidable foe. Cleverly concealing their weapon pits which they made proof against mortar fire, they had to be prised out of every position.

Their food supply improved as they fell back to their bases. They could also use artillery, which the Australians were denied. The guns could not be taken across the ranges. But the Australian advance was irresistible and, on 3 November, they re-entered Kokoda.

To commemorate the recapture the Australian commander, Major-General G. A. Vasey, raised the Australian flag and presented medals to five natives for loyal and meritorious service. A great crowd of carriers assembled for the ceremony – the first of its kind in the campaign. 'Without your help', Vasey told the natives through an interpreter, 'we would not have been able to cross the Owen Stanleys.' All the carriers received gifts of knives and rami – the native kilt-skirt.

Vasey might have added that without Dr G. H. Vernon and Captain Herbert Kienzle the natives would not have been an effective force. Vernon had fought in the First World War as Regimental Medical Officer to the 11th Light Horse Regiment and had returned to Australia with the Military Cross. Stone deaf – from a bursting shell at Gallipoli in 1915 – he was working in Papua as a government medical officer when the war with Japan broke out. The Australian Government evacuated the women, children and older men. Although Vernon was 60, he refused to leave, even when threatened with arrest. Instead, he took upon himself the medical care and much of the organization of the native carriers between Owen's Corner – at the end of the motor road from Port Moresby – and on to Kokoda. His first dramatic act was to post himself to the 39th Battalion when he heard that the unit was temporarily without its medical officer. In this way he served through the first battle of Kokoda, patching up many wounded and treating the dying Col. Owen. He was one of the last four men out of Kokoda.

Resuming his work with the natives, Vernon – himself a strong mountain walker – kept the carrier line working. Everything that went up to the troops was carried on the backs of these natives. Unavoidably loaded and worked to the limit they came to love Dr Vernon. He saw to it that they had proper rest periods and treatment. Having taken supplies up, the natives became stretcher bearers and brought out many badly wounded men. On those tortuous tracks and crossing rushing rock-strewn rivers, eight men were needed for each human load. Carrying a stretcher in these conditions was an appalling task. Sometimes it had to be held at arm's length above the head. Yet the bearers always managed to be gentle and careful.

Herbert Kienzle – a rubber planter when war came – was also responsible for organizing and maintaining much of the native line of communication across the Owen Stanleys.

Strangely, Vernon got no official recognition for his extraordinary labors, which contributed in no small measure to his death in 1946, aged 64. Kienzle received an MBE, the lowest class of the Order of the British Empire.

From Kokoda, the Australian infantry pushed on steadily. At Gorari on 11 November two battalions of the 25th Brigade – 2/25th and 2/31 st – made fierce bayonet charges, killing 580 Japanese in fighting that lasted five days.

This action – by jungle warfare standards a major battle with serious casualties – demonstrated Gen. Vasey's tactical skill. By clever maneuvering he had caught the rarely surprised Japanese off guard. The victory precipitated the collapse of organized resistance outside the Buna–Gona beach-head. The able, determined Gen. Horii, in an effort to evade capture, tried to cross the white-water Kumusi River on a raft and was drowned when it overturned.

The last bitter phase of the fighting was fought at Buna, Sanananda and Gona in a vast morass of swamp, mud and battle-torn jungle. Many Australians, exhausted by combat, fever, lack of sleep and poor food went out on patrols with high temperatures. In November 1942 alone the evacuations numbered 1,500, but by now American troops were reinforcing the Australians. Their numbers and weight of firepower were decisive. In other parts of northern New Guinea fighting would go on until 1944 but the Battle of the Ranges was over.

The 39th Battalion, which had begun the Battle of the Kokoda Trail, was in at the end. Colonel Honner led it back over the mountains to victory in action at Gona.

On 23 January 1943, the Kokoda Trail campaign completed, the battalion held a roll call. Its strength amounted to seven officers and 25 men – out of a normal 800.

Stalingrad (1942)

Peter Young

By the end of 1941 the Russians, it is estimated, had already suffered about 4,500,000 casualties. It is idle to pretend that their long retreat was part of a subtle master-plan, though this myth was an article of faith to all good Bolsheviks while Stalin lived. Even so their heavy sacrifices had won the Russians time to organize new armies and by December 1941 the Germans had identified 280 rifle and cavalry divisions and 44 tank or mechanized brigades.

The great Russian winter offensive, designed to encircle the German Army Group Centre, had lost its momentum by mid-February. Fresh German divisions arrived to fill the gap torn by the Russians between Army Groups Centre and North, and the Germans, clad in the furs and winter clothing produced by Goebbels' appeal, made a gradual recovery. Then came the spring rains, and, both sides being stuck in the mud, there was a temporary halt.

On the ground the great Russian offensive had been indecisive, but in people's minds it had a tremendous importance. The veteran Russian generals, January and February, had lost none of their old skill; the new ones Zhukov and Koniev had also proved their worth. The myth of Teuton invincibility was exploded. Everywhere the men who were to face the German armies in the years ahead took heart. But despite all this Hitler himself had strengthened his personal position. His will-power, he could boast, had saved the day, when his staff-trained generals had wanted to take refuge in retreat. The

Führer was now his own Commander-in-Chief. General Halder, chief of the OKH, was no more than his personal chief of staff. By remote control this semi-educated former corporal conducted the operations involving millions of men, from his Headquarters, the *Wolfschanze*, at Rastenburg in East Prussia. On 5 April 1942 he issued Directive No 41 in which he outlined his plans for his summer offensive. His aim was 'to wipe out the entire defence potential remaining to the Soviets, and to cut them off, as far as possible, from their most important centres of industry.' All available German and allied forces were to take part in this task, but the security of occupied territories in western and northern Europe, *especially along the coast*, was to be ensured in all circumstances.

The plan was for Army Group Centre to stand fast while the armies in the north were to capture Leningrad and link up with the Finns, while those in the south were to break through into the Caucasus. Hitler considered that these aims could only be achieved one at a time and therefore meant to begin in the southern sector by 'destroying the enemy before the Don'.

The Russians too were thinking in terms of the offensive and, as preliminary operations, meant to launch local attacks at Leningrad, Demyansk, Orel, Kharkov, in the Donetz bend, and in the Crimea. On 12 May Marshal Timoshenko (South-West Front) began with a thrust near Kharkov, only to find that he had run into the main German striking force. With the concurrence of his political commissar, Nikita S. Krushchev, he asked Stalin to let him call off the offensive. This permission was refused, and when on 17 May the Germans struck back, his force in the Izyum bridgehead south of Kharkov was seriously compromised. On 19 May Stalin gave Timoshenko his belated permission to extricate his men, but the trap had sprung. In the fighting that followed 240,000 Russians were taken. And that was the end of Stalin's summer offensive.

For the Germans this was a great start to the campaigning season, but there was now a delay of two months while they overran the Crimea. Sevastopol, which had held out for eight months, fell to the Eleventh Army on 1 July.

It was not until 28 June that the main German summer offensive was begun by Army Group B. By 6 July the Second and Fourth Panzer Armies had taken Voronezh. Meanwhile, on 30 June the Sixth Army had pushed eastward from Kharkov to act as the southern jaw of a giant pincer movement. The bag produced by

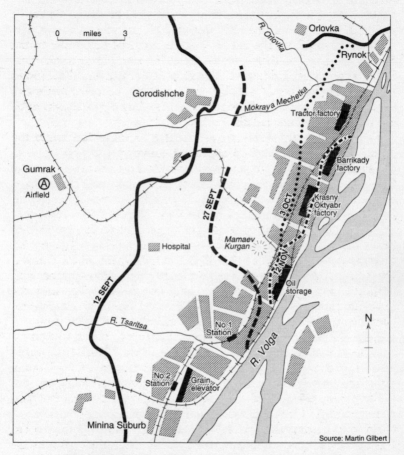

5.5   The Battle for Stalingrad, September 1942–February 1943

this encirclement fell short of 100,000 prisoners, and Hitler, so far from being grateful for a respectable victory, sacked von Bock and on 13 July gave command of Army Group B to Field-Marshal von Weichs. On the same day Hitler ordered Army Group A, with Fourth Panzer Army attached, to turn south, cross the lower Don and drive the Russians into a pocket round Rostov. The town fell on 23 July, but once again the Führer got less prisoners than he had bargained for. It was at this juncture that, most unwisely, he removed about half of the Eleventh Army for his Leningrad offensive. As in 1941 he was flouting the principle of concentration of force.

The early summer of 1942 had seen some revival of the old German successes – the rapid overrunning of the Crimea; the capture of Tobruk (21 June); the air offensive which seemed to be starving Malta into submission. Certainly Hitler had reason to be pleased with these successes, but they deluded him into believing that his strategic situation was rather better than was actually the case. On 21 July, in Directive No 44, Operations in Northern Finland, he stated his view that:

> The unexpectedly rapid and favourable development of the *operations against the Timoshenko Army Group* entitle us to assume that we may soon succeed in depriving Soviet Russia of the Caucasus, with her most important source of oil, and of a valuable line of communication for the delivery of English and American supplies.
>
> This, coupled with the loss of the entire Donetz industrial area, will strike a blow at the Soviet Union which would have immeasurable consequence.

He went on to say that the time had come to cut the northern supply route, the Murmansk railway, by which the Anglo-Saxon powers were supplying Russia. He assumed that Leningrad would be captured 'in September at the latest'.

In his next Directive (No 45), which dealt with the Caucasus offensive, he alleged that only weak forces from Timoshenko's Army Group had got back across the Don. 'We must expect them to be reinforced from the Caucasus.' In a perceptive moment he added: 'A further concentration of enemy forces is taking place in the Stalingrad area, which the enemy will probably defend tenaciously.'

The German successes continued in August, but already the troops were showing signs of tiredness and their tactics were becoming stereotyped. Marshal Chuikov (64th Army), who had his Second World War 'baptism of fire' on the Don Front in July, has some comments on their performance.

> Observing how the Germans carried out their artillery preparation against the 229th Infantry Division's sector, I saw the weak points in their tactics. In strength and organization this artillery preparation was weak. Artillery and mortar attacks were not coordinated or in depth, but only against the main line of defence. I saw no broad manoeuvre with artillery cover in the dynamic of battle.

He goes on to say:

> I was expecting close combined operations between the enemy's artillery and ground forces, a precise organization of the artillery barrage, a lightning-fast manoeuvre of shell and wheel. But this was not the case. I encountered the far from new method of slow wearing down, trench by trench . . .
>
> The German tanks did not go into action without infantry and air support. On the battlefield there was no evidence of the 'prowess' of German tank crews, their courage and speed in action, about which foreign newspapers had written. The reverse was true, in fact – they operated sluggishly, extremely cautiously and indecisively.
>
> The German infantry was strong in automatic fire, but I saw no rapid movement or resolute attack on the battlefield. When advancing, the German infantry did not spare their bullets, but frequently fired into thin air.

On the other hand the thoroughly efficient co-operation of the *Luftwaffe* showed the familiarity of the pilots with the tactics of both sides.

> In modern warfare victory is impossible without combined action by all types of forces and without good administration. The Germans had this kind of polished, co-ordinated action. In battle the different arms of their forces never hurried, did not push ahead alone, but fought with the whole mass of men and

technical backing. A few minutes before a general attack, their aircraft would fly in, bomb and strafe the object under attack, pinning the defending troops to the ground, and then infantry and tanks with supporting artillery and mortar fire would cut into our military formations almost with impunity.

Meanwhile, on the Leningrad front the Russians had made an unsuccessful attempt to break the German siege, but had at least forestalled the German attempt to capture the city.

In the south Army Group A (Field-Marshal von Kleist) had taken Maikop, but too late to prevent the complete destruction of the oilfield. German Jäger planted the Swastika on Mount Elbrus, but the Russians still held out in the passes of the Caucasus. By 21 August the Führer was already 'very agitated' by the lack of progress on that front. The Sixth and Fourth Panzer armies closed in on Stalingrad, but being compelled to detach troops to guard their flanks, were gradually brought to a halt by 6 September. At last the Russians seemed to be getting the measure of the invaders. Their losses in men and territory, though grievous, had been far less serious in 1942 than in the previous year. In terms of attrition the German position was by no means brilliant. Hitler's armies on the Eastern Front numbered some 3,138,000, excluding the Finns, while Stalin had 4,255,000 men in the field. Behind the German front the partisans were active, as Hitler tells us in Directive No 46 of 18 August.

In recent months *banditry in the East* has assumed intolerable proportions, and threatens to become a serious danger to supplies for the front and to the economic exploitation of the country.

By this time he had evidently resigned himself to the thought that the war was not going to be won that year:

By the beginning of winter these bandit gangs must be substantially exterminated, so that order may be restored behind the Eastern front and severe disadvantages to our winter operations avoided.

He expressed the pious hope that the confidence of the local population in German authority could be gained by handling them strictly but justly – a notion that would probably not have worked in the summer of 1941, and was certainly unrealistic in the autumn of 1942.

As the situation worsened, Hitler resorted to his old remedy of sacking generals. List was the first to go (9 September), and for two and a half months the Dictator actually commanded Army Group A in person: an extraordinary arrangement. The fact that his HQ, Vinnitsa in the Ukraine, was 700 miles in the rear of his front might have daunted a more professional soldier, but in Hitler's fantasy world such considerations went for little. On 24 September, after a series of fearful scenes, Halder was relieved as chief of OKH by General Zeitzler. Warlimont, whose position as Deputy Chief of the OKH staff gives his evidence considerable weight, assesses the Führer's state of mind at this period. He tells us of a briefing conference:

> Hitler fixed me with a malevolent stare and suddenly I thought: the man's confidence has gone; he has realized that his deadly game is moving to its appointed end, that Soviet Russia is not going to be overthrown at the second attempt and that now the war on two fronts, which he has unleashed by his wanton arbitrary actions, will grind the Reich to powder. My thoughts ran on: that is why he can no longer bear to have around him the generals who have too often been witnesses of his faults, his errors, his illusions and his day dreams; that is why he wishes to get away from them, why he wishes to see people around him who he feels have unlimited and unshakeable confidence in him.

Colonel-General Halder was a typical German General Staff officer of the old school, a thorough professional soldier. Dismissed by Hitler he wrote in his diary 'My nervous energy is used up and his is not as good as it was. We must part.' No doubt it was a relief to go. Hitler now prepared to run the army on his own lines. It was 'necessary to educate the General Staff in fanatical belief in an ideal.' The Army 'rather than relying on technical competence . . . must be inspired by the fervour of belief in National-Socialism.'

For a time the new chief of staff, Zeitzler, enjoyed great popularity with Göring and the rest of Hitler's courtiers. He certainly began well, with an address to the officers of OKH in which he said:

I require the following from every Staff Officer: he must believe in the Führer and in his method of command. He must on every occasion radiate this confidence to his subordinates and those around him. I have no use for anybody on the General Staff who cannot meet these requirements.

This was to be the atmosphere at HQ during the siege of Stalingrad, in that winter when the tide of war had at last reached the turn.

November was a black month for Hitler. The news of El Alamein, followed by that of Torch, made it clear that sooner or later the Axis forces in North Africa were going to be crushed. This news came when Hitler was on his way to address the 'old comrades' of the Nazi party in the Munich Beer Cellar. By way of offsetting the bad tidings he could think of nothing better than to assure the veterans that he was now master of Stalingrad, where the doubtful battle had been raging since early September. On 19 November the Russian Fifth Tank Army broke through the Roumanian Third Army North of that city. By the 22nd the Sixth German Army and about half of General Hoth's Fourth Panzer Army were encircled; 280,000 men were in mortal peril.

This was indeed a reversal of fortune, for in the September days there had been desperate fighting at Stalingrad, and the Russians had barely clung to the west bank of the Volga. Marshal Chuikov, who bore much of the responsibility, had decided, as a result of his experiences against 'the Whites' in the Civil War and his study of enemy tactics,

> that the best method of fighting Germans would be close battle, applied night and day in different forms. We should get as close to the enemy as possible, so that his air force could not bomb our forward units or trenches. Every German soldier must be made to feel that he was living under the muzzle of a Russian gun, always ready to treat him to a fatal dose of lead.

They reduced No Man's Land to the throw of a grenade. Strongpoints were fortified in the centre of the city and garrisoned by 50 or 100 men. Buildings changed hands not once but many times. From 17–20 September, for example, there was a fierce struggle for an enormous building on the southern outskirts of the town, the grain elevator. Colonel Dubyanski (OC Guards Infantry Division) reported by telephone to Chuikov: 'The situation has changed. Before, we occupied the upper part of the elevator and the Germans the lower part. Now we have driven them out of the lower part, but German troops have penetrated upstairs and fighting is now going on in the upper part.'

Stubborn fighting marked the resistance of improvised fortresses without number. Archetype of these was the defence of 'Pavlov's House', a key strongpoint in the central district held by a handful of men belonging to Rodimtsev's 13th Guards Infantry Division. Sergeant Jacob Pavlov and two of his men, Alexandrov and Afanasiev, were Russians. The rest of his garrison were Subgayda and Gluschenko from the Ukraine; Mosiyashvili, and Stephanashvili, both Georgians; Turganov, an Uzbek; Murzayev, a Kazakh; Sukba, an Abkhazian; Turdiev, a Tajik; and Ramazanov, the Tartar. It was a roll call of the nationalities of the USSR! Chuikov tells us that the Germans 'unleashed a torrent of bombs and shells on to the house', which was held for more than 50 days, without sleep and rest, and remained impregnable to the end. For his dogged defence Pavlov became a Hero of the Soviet Union.

All through October the struggle went on. Those were the darkest days. But somehow the Russians hung on. Reserves were fed in across the Volga as they reached the front and eventually Paulus' seemingly inexhaustible reserves could do no more. On 29 October the battle began to die down, and the next day, apart from exchanges of firing, there was no action. On the 31st the 62nd Army counter-attacked from its narrow strip of land along the banks of the Volga. Advances were measured in yards, but the attack was a great success and retook part of the Krasny Oktyabr factory.

Early in November the temperature dropped sharply and ice began to appear on the river. On 11 November Paulus launched a new attack, but this too was held in two days of stubborn fighting. The *Luftwaffe*, which in October had been flying as many as 3,000 sorties a day, could no longer manage more than 1,000.

And thus it came about that when on 19 November the Russians counter-attacked on three fronts at once a trap closed behind the Germans which cost them 22 divisions.

Hitler entrusted to Field-Marshal von Manstein the task of rescuing Sixth Army, but he refused Paulus permission to try and break out. The supply difficulty became acute. Petrol, shells, and firewood were hard to come by. After Christmas the bread ration was cut by half to 50 grammes a day. Many of the men existed on watery soup fortified with the bones of horses they dug up. Colonel Dingler tells us that 'As a Christmas treat the Army allowed the slaughtering of 4,000 of the available horses.' This was no help to the armoured and motorized Divisions.

The cold was bitter in December and the ground was too hard to dig. Aeroplane tyres stuck to the runways. If a position was abandoned the soldiers found themselves without dugouts or trenches when they got back to their new line. Without petrol the armour could not manoeuvre to repulse the Russian attacks. The apertures of tanks became blocked with ice. Men froze to death in their vehicles.

But all hope was not yet gone. On 9 December it was announced that Fourth Panzer Army, which had been reinforced, would start its relieving attack next day, and by 16 December distant gunfire could be heard. Plans were made to break out as soon as Colonel-General Hoth's spearhead should be within 20 miles.

The plans for the relief were carefully examined by Field-Marshal von Manstein. It was decided that Hoth, himself 'an officer with an excellent reputation', should make his thrust from the direction of Kotelnikovski some 60 miles SE of Stalingrad. At Nizhna Chirskaya on the Chir the Germans were only 25 miles away, but an attack from this direction would involve a crossing of the Don, which von Manstein rightly rejected as too hazardous an operation.

From the first Hoth met with furious opposition from strong Russian forces of armour and infantry under General Vatutin. It took the Germans a week to fight their way forward 30 miles, but at the end of it they succeeded in capturing two crossings over the river Aksay by a *coup de main*. They were still 45 miles short of the beleaguered army.

At this moment Marshal Zhukov launched a massive offensive on the middle Don, tore a 60-mile gap in the front of the Italian Eighth Army, and thrust southwards towards Rostov, threatening the communications of Field-Marshal von Kleist's Army Group in the Caucasus. Von Manstein had nothing up his sleeve. To check the Russian flood he was compelled to take 6th Panzer Division from Hoth's army. On paper the latter still had two panzer divisions, though their tank strength was now down to 35. Desperate fighting during the next week brought no real progress, partly perhaps because Paulus himself remained inactive. Had he also attacked, the Russians might not have been able to concentrate against 57th Panzer Corps, Hoth's spearhead. Again lack of petrol may have been the key to the tactical situation.

On Christmas Eve the Russians counter-attacked the Aksay bridgehead in great force, and, keeping up the pressure night and day, had retaken both bridges by the 26th. The decimated Germans withdrew southwards.

> The characteristic features of this dramatic battle were mobility, quick reaction and utter perseverance on both sides. Tanks were the main weapon used and both sides realized that the main task of the armour was to destroy the opposing tanks.
>
> The Russians did not stop their attacks when darkness fell, and they exploited every success immediately and without hesitation. Some of the Russian attacks were made by tanks moving in at top speed: indeed speed, momentum and concentration were the causes of their success. The main effort of the attacking Russian armour was speedily switched from one point to another as the situation demanded.

Von Mellenthin concedes that 'the tactical conduct of the battle by the Russians was on a high level.' By 26 December, 57th Panzer Corps had 'literally died on its feet'.

No power on earth could now save the Sixth Army, least of all the *Luftwaffe*, which Göring had promised would keep Paulus supplied. On 15 January the Hungarian Second Army disintegrated, and far away in the north on that same day the German siege of Leningrad was broken. On the 22nd General Zeitzler, urged on by von Manstein, plucked up his courage to ask Hitler whether Sixth Army should now be authorized to capitulate, only to be told that the army should fight to the last man. But Sixth Army had reached the end of its tether. On 31 January Paulus, who had been promoted Field-Marshal only the previous day, surrendered. Hitler had lost 20 German divisions, of which three were armoured and another three motorized, besides two Roumanian divisions – whom their allies had struck off the ration strength a fortnight before the end!

The Germans lost 60,000 vehicles, 1,500 tanks and 6,000 guns. Of the 280,000 men encircled 42,000 wounded, sick and specialists were evacuated by air; 91,000 surrendered. Of these, it is thought only 6,000 lived to see their homes once more.

It has often been suggested that Hitler should have given Paulus permission to break out. But had this been attempted it is difficult to imagine it being successful. We know that petrol for the six mobile divisions was lacking. The remaining 16, with the possible exception of the Roumanian cavalry division, were comparatively slow-moving and had eaten most of their horses by the end of December. If Hitler and his entourage had withdrawn Sixth Army at the end of October, when it was clearly stuck, a large part of it might have made a reasonably orderly retreat. By the time von Manstein tried to break through, there was really very little hope of pulling Paulus back, even had Hitler consented to such an attempt. Mussolini, more clear-sighted about other people's troubles than his own, commented that Stalingrad 'makes clear to the minds of the masses the great attachment of the Russian people to the regime – a thing proved by the exceptional resistance and the spirit of sacrifice.'

No disaster suffered by the Allies in a war where disasters had not been lacking could be compared with the blow Hitler received at Stalingrad. And he was soon (13 May) to receive another at least as costly in Tunisia. Truly the tide had turned in those November days of 1942 when Montgomery emerged victorious from the field of El Alamein; when Eisenhower's host set foot on the shores of North Africa; and when, after an epic defence, the Russians encircled their besiegers on the banks of the Volga.

El Alamein (1942)

J. F. C. Fuller

The first three weeks of July, 1942, on the El Alamein line [in North Africa] were devoted to attack and counter-attack. Rommel's one aim was that the front should not become static, and Auchinleck's aim was to make it so. The latter won the tussle and the outcome of the campaign became a question of reinforcements and supplies.

Faced with this situation, Rommel calculated that up to mid-September the advantage would be his; but in this he was badly deceived, because from the end of July on Auchinleck switched the main weight of his air offensive from the forward positions to the ports of Mersa Matruh, Bardia, and Tobruk, which left Rommel with Benghazi – 680 miles away – as his nearest secure base of supply. The results were that by the middle of August he was still short on establishments of 16,000 men, 210 tanks, 175 troop carriers and armoured cars and 1,500 vehicles; his army consumed double the amount of supplies that crossed the Mediterranean, and had it not been for the vast enemy dumps captured in Marmarica and western Egypt, 'it would', as he says, 'never have been able to exist at all.'

Rommel was severely criticized for not halting on the Egyptian frontier after he had taken Tobruk. True enough, had he done so he would have curtailed considerably his communications, but this in itself would not have solved his supply problem, because, as long as Malta remained in British hands in the long run it was impossible

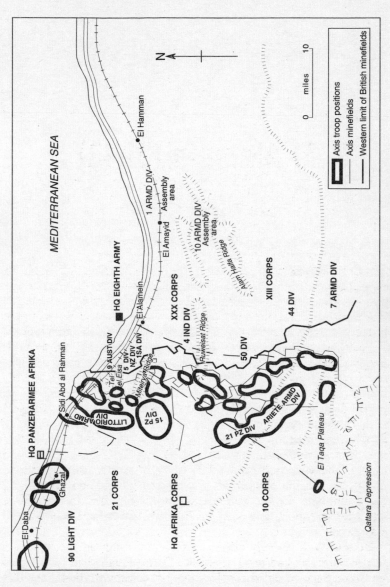

5.6 *The Battle of El Alamein, 23 October 1942*

for him to out-stockpile his enemy. Further, once his attempt to rush
the Alamein position failed, he could not fall back on a rear position
because he had not sufficient transport simultaneously to supply his
forward position and build up a position in rear. Since to remain
where he was could not solve the problem of driving his enemy out
of Egypt, he realized that he would have to attack, not when he was
fully ready – that he could never hope for – but before his enemy's
deficiencies had been made good.

It should be remembered that because Rommel was nominally
subordinated to Marshal Bastico, Marshal Cavallero, the Italian
Chief of Staff, whom Ciano calls 'that crook' and 'this charlatan,'
was responsible for the supply of Rommel's army. In order to clarify
the supply situation, Rommel asked Cavallero and Field-Marshal
Kesselring to meet him in Egypt. This they did on 27 August,
and when they guaranteed to supply him with 6,000 tons of petrol,
one-sixth of which Kesselring promised to deliver by air, Rommel
decided to attack. But to be doubly assured, he turned to Cavallero
and said that the outcome of the battle would entirely depend on
its receipt, to which the latter replied: 'You can go on with the
battle, it is on its way.' Unfortunately for Rommel, Kesselring
failed to mention the recent arrival in Malta of Spitfire aircraft,
which profoundly altered the situation.

When Rommel was thus engaged, General Alexander arrived at
Cairo on 8 August, and four days later he was joined by General
Montgomery, who at once assumed command of the Eighth Army.

Montgomery was a man of dynamic personality and of supreme
self-confidence. Known to his officers and men as 'Monty', he
was a past-master in showmanship and publicity; audacious in his
utterances and cautious in his actions. Though at times smiled at by
his officers, his neo-Napoleonic personal messages – 'I am proud to
be with you' . . . 'YOU have made this Army what it is. YOU have
made its name a household word' . . . 'YOU and I together will see
this thing through,' etc., etc., interlarded with 'The Lord Mighty in
Battle' and 'hitting the enemy for six,' electrified his men. He was the
right man in the right place at the right moment; for after its severe
defeat the Eighth Army needed a new dynamo and Montgomery
supplied it.

As soon as he arrived at his headquarters he summoned a meeting
of his staff and said that his mandate was to destroy the Axis forces in
North Africa, and if anyone doubted this he had better clear out. He

added that he had ordered all withdrawal plans to be burnt; that the defence of the Delta meant nothing to him; and that in a fortnight he would welcome attack, but he did not intend to assume the offensive until he was ready to do so. In order to carry it out, it was essential to have a *corps d'élite*, like the Afrika Korps; therefore he would at once create one out of two armoured and one motorized divisions. Further, it was also essential that Army and RAF headquarters should live in close proximity, so that the planning of the great offensive he had in mind might be a joint effort from the start.

Except for the Wadi Akarit position north of Gabes, the El Alamein Line was the only one in North Africa that offered no flank that could be turned from the south. Rommel's tactical problem was how to penetrate this position, and because of his enemy's minefields and the tactical features in rear of them, it was by no means easy to solve. The former ran from Tel el Eisa, close by the Mediterranean, to Hunter's Plateau, which fringed the Qattara Depression, the northern border of which was girt with precipitous cliffs; and the latter comprised two ridges, the Ruweisat, about 200 ft above sea level, which ran from the centre of the front eastward, and the Alam el Halfa, to its south-east, which at its highest point was a little over twice the height of the former, and which extended in a north-easterly direction towards El Hamman on the Alexandria–Mersa Matruh railway.

Auchinleck's plan, which Alexander and Montgomery accepted as the basis of their own, was to hold as strongly as possible the area between the coast and the Ruweisat Ridge; lightly to hold but heavily to mine the area south of it to Hunter's Plateau; and to hold in strength the Alam el Halfa Ridge so that, should the enemy's mobile forces penetrate the front either north or south of the Ruweisat Ridge, they could be counter-attacked in flank, and should they break through along the ridge itself, then they could be met frontally.

When Montgomery assumed command of the Eighth Army he found the front held by the XXXth and XIIIth Corps, the former north of the Ruweisat Ridge and the latter south of it. The former consisted of the 9th Australian, 1st South African and 5th Indian Divisions and the 23rd Armoured Brigade; the latter of the 2nd New Zealand and 7th Armoured Divisions. Alexander had in reserve the 8th and 10th Armoured and the 44th and 51st Infantry Divisions, also the 1st Armoured and 50th Infantry Divisions, both refitting. At once Montgomery asked for the 44th and 10th Armoured Divisions, the one to hold the Alam el Halfa Ridge and the other to occupy its western extremity as a mobile striking force.

Rommel's army was disposed as follows: In the north the German 164th Infantry Division, then the Italian XXIst Corps, which consisted of the Trento and Bologna Divisions and Ramcke's German Parachute Brigade, and lastly the Brescia Division of the Italian Xth Corps; all these formations were in front line. As his striking force Rommel had the Afrika Korps, which consisted of the 15th and 21st Panzer Divisions; the German 90th Light Division (motorized infantry); and the Italian XXth Mobile Corps, which comprised the Ariete and Littorio Armoured Divisions and the Trieste Division. In rear, at Mersa Matruh and Bardia, were the Italian Pavia, Folgore, and Pistola Divisions in reserve.

Rommel's plan was to make a feint attack in the north, a holding attack in the centre, and the main attack in the south. On the night of August 30–31, lanes through the southernmost sector of his enemy's minefields – which he believed to be weak, but which were strong – were to be cleared by German and Italian infantry. Next, at dawn on the 31st, the Afrika Korps was to follow through, take the Alam el Halfa Ridge and make for the area south-west of El Hamman. In the meantime the 90th Light Division and the Ariete and Littorio Armoured Divisions were to break through to the north of the Afrika Korps and cover the left flank of its advance. His idea was to cut off his enemy from his supply depots, while the 90th Light Division and XXth Mobile Corps held the enemy, and then annihilate him. He sought a decisive battle, and for its success it was imperative that the Alam el Halfa Ridge should be overrun early on the 31st.

According to General Alexander, the opposing forces were evenly matched on the southern half of the front. Both had about 300 field and medium guns and 400 anti-tank guns; Rommel had 500 medium and light tanks, and the XIIIth Corps 300 medium and 80 light tanks and 230 armoured cars. Besides these, 100 tanks with the 23rd Armoured Brigade constituted a reserve. Though numerically evenly matched, Rommel was badly outclassed, because half his tanks were Italian and they were very indifferent machines.

For Rommel, the battle of Alam el Halfa was a desperate gamble because the plan on which it was based was the only one feasible with the means at his disposal, and precisely because of this Montgomery expected Rommel to adopt it. For Montgomery, whose intention it was to maintain a firm defensive until he was fully prepared to attack, it was a heaven-sent opportunity; not only did it enable him to rebuild the morale of his army, but at the same time it enabled him to weaken that of his opponent and thereby doubly assure the success of his eventual offensive. In order to impede an attack on the southern sector of his front Montgomery considerably added to its minefields that on the night of August 30–31 when the Germans and Italians began to clear lanes through them, they were greatly delayed. To add to this difficulty, General von Bismarck, commander of the 21st Panzer Division, was killed by a mine, and the commander of the Afrika Korps, General Nehring, was severely wounded. Further, Rommel was so sick that he was unable to leave his truck. This, Desmond Young considers, was 'perhaps the greatest handicap of all', because Rommel – like Charles XII – 'relied much more on his personal observation and judgement during the progress of a battle than on a preconceived plan.'

The results of these misfortunes were that there was no surprise; the advance of the Afrika Korps was delayed; that of the 90th Light Division still more so; and the Ariete and Littorio Divisions could not penetrate the minefields. Rommel, bereft of half his striking force, was compelled to abandon his sweep to the north-east and restrict the attack of the Afrika Korps to the western end of the Alam el Halfa Ridge. But its advance was so impeded by soft sand and by air attacks that at 4 p.m. it had to be called off.

During the night of 31 August – 1 September the Italo-German forces were so pounded by the RAF that, on 1 September, Rommel was compelled to abandon any attempt to carry out a major operation, and only desultory fighting on the Alam el Halfa Ridge followed. In the meantime Montgomery, when he saw that the battle was in his hands, switched the 10th Armoured Division from the south to the west of the ridge preparatory to carrying out a counter-attack southward with the 2nd New Zealand Division directly he had exhausted his enemy's offensive.

On 2 September, still under constant air attack and desperately short of petrol, Rommel renewed his offensive, but with so little success that he ordered a withdrawal for the morning of the 3rd. Montgomery then launched his counter-attack, and at the same time ordered his 7th Armoured Division to harass the enemy's southern flank. After stiff fighting he drove him back to the minefields, and at 7 a.m. on 7 September called off the battle. Rommel's losses were nearly 3,000 men killed, wounded and missing, 50 tanks, 15 guns, 35 anti-tank guns and 400 lorries lost; and Montgomery's losses were 1,640 killed, wounded and missing, and 68 tanks and 18 anti-tank guns put out of action.

Kesselring's opinion is that if Rommel had not been sick he would never have pulled out of the battle because he had 'completely encircled his enemy.' This is a fantastic statement, and more especially as it is made by a highly experienced soldier. There was no encirclement, and once the battle had opened Rommel was under no illusion that his enemy's command of the air predoomed his defeat. He has much to say on this question, and among other things that,

> Whoever enjoys command of the air is in a position to inflict such heavy damage on the opponent's supply columns that serious shortages must soon make themselves felt. By maintaining a constant watch on the roads leading to the front he can put a complete stop to daylight supply traffic and force his enemy to drive only by night, thus causing him to lose irreplaceable time. But an assured flow of supplies is essential; without it an army becomes immobilized and incapable of action.

This should be remembered when we come to the part played by Rommel in the Normandy campaign of 1944.

'With the failure of this offensive,' writes Rommel, 'our last chance of gaining the Suez Canal had gone.' He knew that the battle for supplies was irretrievably lost, if only because the large convoy of 'well over 100,000 tons, laden with the very latest weapons and war material for the Eighth Army', which he expected 'would arrive at Suez at the beginning of September,' arrived there on 3 September with Roosevelt's gift of 300 Sherman tanks. He knew that his enemy would attack, and in all probability under a full moon. Kesselring remarks: 'Was it right under these circumstances to wait for the British offensive?' and adds that neither OKW nor the Comando Supremo would have objected to a withdrawal. Although this assumption is highly improbable, possibly the reason why Rommel stayed where he did was that either a voluntary withdrawal was repugnant to him, or that he had not the petrol and vehicles to carry it out. This latter reason is supported by Ciano, who, on 2 September, entered in his diary: 'Three of our tankers have been sunk in two days,' and on the 3rd, 'Rommel's pause continues, and, what is worse, the sinking of our ships continues.' But had Rommel fallen back shortly before the next full moon, he would have disrupted his enemy's plans.

Whatever his reasons, he decided to stand and accept battle. His plan was to hold with outposts only his forward belt of minefields, in which some 500,000 mines and vast numbers of captured British bombs and shells had been sunk, and to fight his defensive battle in a mined zone 1,000 to 2,000 yards behind. On his northern flank he posted the German 164th and 90th Light Divisions in depth; allotted to the Italians the defence of the front south of them; and divided his armoured divisions into two groups, the 15th Panzer and Littorio Divisions in the north, and the 21st Panzer and Ariete Divisions in the south. Tactically this was a faulty distribution and unlike any Rommel had hitherto adopted; possibly it was forced upon him through lack of petrol. In all he had 300 Italian tanks of little fighting value and barely fit for action, and 210 German tanks, of which 30 were Panzer IVs armed with 75 mm guns, and the remainder Panzer IIIs with 50 mm guns.

As he was then a very sick man he decided to return to Germany, and on 22 September he handed his command over to General Stumme, an experienced tank officer, and informed him that should the enemy attack he would at once return. This was not a very satisfactory arrangement. Back in Germany, on 10 October he was presented with his Field-Marshal's baton, which had been awarded to him immediately after the fall of Tobruk.

While Rommel was engaged on his unenviable task, his opponent, General Alexander, prepared for an all-out offensive. On 10 August Mr Churchill had handed to him a directive to annihilate the German–Italian Army 'at the earliest opportunity', but the date was governed by certain factors. Firstly, Operation Torch had been scheduled for 8 November; and it was considered of vital political importance, in order to win over the French in Morocco and Algeria, that the Axis forces in Egypt should be decisively defeated before the invasion was launched. Secondly, because the 300 Sherman tanks would not arrive until early in September, and when they did several weeks' training with them was imperative, as well as a full moon under which to attack, the date fixed upon was the night of 23–24 October.

The next problem was one of grand tactics: where should the

decisive blow be struck on the 40-mile front? Although in the
front's southern sector the minefields were less extensive than in
the northern, because a successful penetration in the south would
drive the enemy northward towards his communications – the coastal
road – it was decided to deliver the main blow in the north, to gain
an outlet on to the coastal road, and to cut off the bulk of the enemy
forces south of it. This settled, the next problem was one of minor
tactics.

Because minefields can no more be rushed by tanks than wire
entanglements can be rushed by infantry – and in the northern
sector they were from 5,000 to 9,000 yards in depth – it was agreed
that the initial advance would assume the form of an old-fashioned
infantry attack accompanied by mine clearing parties and covered
by artillery and bomber aircraft, with tanks in rear.

On 6 October, Montgomery issued his plan. The main attack
was allotted to the XXXth Corps (Lieutenant-General Sir Oliver
Leese) on a four divisional front of six to seven miles in width. Its
task was to cut two corridors through the minefields; the northern
south of Tel El Eisa, and the southern across the northern end of
the Miteiriya Ridge. Once this had been done, the Xth Corps
(Lieutenant-General Sir Herbert Lumsden) which comprised the
1st and 10th Armoured Divisions, was to pass through and engage
the enemy's armour. In the meantime, to mislead the enemy and
pin down the 21st Panzer Division in the extreme south, the
XIIIth Corps (Lieutenant-General Sir B. C. Horrocks) and the
7th Armoured Division were to carry out two subsidiary attacks
against the enemy's right flank. In all Montgomery had seven
infantry divisions, a formation of Free French, a Greek brigade,
three armoured divisions and seven armoured brigades; a total
of 150,000 men and 1,114 tanks, of which 128 were Grants and
267 Shermans, both armed with 75 mm guns, and 2,182 pieces
of artillery, of which 1,274 were anti-tank guns of various types.
The battle was to be opened by a short intense counter-battery
bombardment, to be followed, once the infantry advanced, by a
bombardment of the enemy's defences. From 6 October to the night
of the 23rd the RAF (500 fighters and 200 bombers) was to intensify
its attack on the enemy's communications and transport, next, to
support the artillery bombardments, and finally to concentrate on
the areas in which the enemy's armour was located.

In addition, there was an elaborate cover plan, the aim of which was to make good lack of strategical surprise by deceiving the enemy. The first task was to conceal the various concentrations as much as possible, and the second, by means of dummy hutments, dumps, tanks, vehicles, gun emplacements, water installations and a pipeline, to mislead the enemy about the probable date, and direction, of the attack. Until the invasion of Normandy, it was the most elaborate fake undertaken, and its principle was – hide what you have and reveal what you haven't.

At 9.40 p.m. on 23 October, under a brilliant moon, the whole of the artillery of the Eighth Army, nearly 1,000 guns, simultaneously opened fire on the enemy battery positions. Twenty minutes later the infantry advanced, and on the XXXth Corps front by 1 a.m. on the 24th the enemy forward defences were captured without serious loss. Half an hour's halt was then made in order to reorganize, after which the advance was resumed and met with stern opposition. Nevertheless, by 5.30 a.m. the Australians had secured most of their final objective, and the New Zealanders the whole of theirs; but in the centre the 51st Division was held up by strongpoints in the middle of the northern corridor some 1,500 yards from its final objective, and in the south the 1st South African Division was held up for several hours.

The Xth Corps crossed its starting line at 2 a.m., but the engineers, who worked behind the infantry, were so greatly delayed in lifting the mines that it was not until 6.30 a.m. that the southern corridor was sufficiently cleared to permit the 9th Armoured Brigade, followed by the 10th Armoured Division, to move forward. When the latter did go ahead it gained a footing on the eastern slope of the Miteiriya Ridge, but came under such heavy fire that it could proceed no farther. In the meantime, the 2nd Armoured Brigade and the 1st Armoured Division had been seriously delayed by mines and artillery fire in the northern corridor, and it was not until 3 p.m., after an intense artillery bombardment and a combined attack by the 51st Division and the 1st Armoured Division, that the corridor was finally established. These delays put back the timetable and prohibited a break-out on the 24th.

In the south the operations of the XIIIth Corps met with so limited a success that Montgomery instructed Horrocks to press the attack no farther, but to resort to 'crumbling' action – local attacks of attrition – without the 7th Armoured Division being involved.

On the Axis front the situation rapidly deteriorated, for although the outposts had fought staunchly, the terrific enemy bombardment so smashed the network of communications that command was paralysed. General Stumme went forward at dawn on the 24th to find out what was happening, and shortly after had a heart attack and died. When this became known hours later, General von Thoma, Commander of the Afrika Korps, assumed the chief command.

When the battle opened, Rommel was in hospital at Semmering, and on the afternoon of the 24th he was telephoned by Field-Marshal Keitel, who inquired whether he would be well enough to return to Africa. He replied that he was, and at 7 a.m. on the 25th took off for Rome. When he arrived there at 11 a.m. he was met by General von Rintelen, the German military attaché, who informed him that only 'three issues of petrol remained in the African theatre,' which was equivalent to '300 kilometres worth of petrol per vehicle between Tripoli and the front'. As experience had shown that one issue of petrol was required for each day of battle, it was obvious to Rommel that the battle was as good as lost, for without petrol the army could no longer react to the enemy's movements.

That evening Rommel learnt from von Thoma that ammunition was so short that Stumme had forbidden the bombardment of the enemy's assembly positions on the night of 23–24 October, and that on the 24th and 25th the petrol situation had so deteriorated that major movements were no longer possible, and that only groups of the 15th Panzer Division had been able to attack; that they had suffered frightful casualties; and that the division was now reduced to 31 effective tanks.

In spite of this crippling shortage of means, the Axis forces put up so determined a defence that Montgomery realized that his 'crumbling' attacks were too costly. He decided to switch the axis of the offensive more to the north, and instructed the XXXth Corps to order the 9th Australian Division to direct its offensive toward the coast, to cut off the enemy in the salient which had been created north of the Tel el Eisa Ridge. At the same time the 1st Armoured Division was ordered to fight its way westward toward what the British called Kidney Ridge and the Germans Hill 28. These attacks resulted in the most savage fighting of the battle. The Australian advance was successful, but the 1st Armoured Division made no appreciable progress until nightfall, because Rommel brought forward the 90th Light Division, elements of the 15th Panzer and Littorio Divisions, and a battalion of Bersaglieri. He writes: 'Rivers of blood were poured out over miserable strips of land,' and after it had grown dark: 'Never before in Africa had we seen such a density of anti-aircraft fire. Hundreds of British tracer shells criss-crossed the sky and the air became an absolute inferno of fire.' At length, during the night, the 1st South African and 2nd New Zealand Divisions gained 1,000 yards more depth on the Miteiriya Ridge, and the 7th Motor Brigade of the 1st Armoured Division established itself on Kidney Ridge.

On 26 October it became apparent to Montgomery that the momentum of his attack was on the wane, and that his break-in area was still hedged in by a strong anti-tank screen. He decided to assume a temporary defensive, and to regroup his forces and build up fresh reserves for a renewal of the offensive in the north. He ordered the 2nd New Zealand Division to be relieved by the 1st South African Division and brought into reserve, and the front of the latter to be taken over by the 4th Indian Division, which was placed under the command of the XIIIth Corps. Further, he instructed the XIIIth Corps to send north the 7th Armoured Division and three brigades of infantry.

While these moves were under way, on the night of 26–27 October Rommel moved the 21st Panzer Division north, and on the 27th violently attacked Kidney Ridge, but was repulsed at such heavy cost that Montgomery was able to withdraw the 1st Armoured Division and the 24th Armoured Brigade into reserve. At the same time he ordered the 9th Australian Division to attack the enemy in the coastal sector on the night of the 28th–29th. Apparently Rommel expected this attack, and in order to reinforce his left he was compelled to denude his southern front of practically all heavy weapons and German units and to replace them by part of the Ariete Division which had been engaged in the north.

The Australian attack was launched under cover of an intense bombardment at 10 p.m. on the 29th in the direction of the coastal road between Sidi Abd el Rahman and Tel el Eisa. For six hours the battle raged furiously, and 'again and again', writes Rommel, 'British bomber formations flew up and tipped their death-dealing loads on my troops, or bathed the country in the brilliant light of parachute flares.' So intense was the fighting that, on the morning of the 30th, Rommel began to consider a withdrawal to the Fuka position, which ran from the coast 50 miles west of El Alamein southward to the Qattara Depression. This is the first intimation of a contemplated retreat which, irrespective of the severity of the fighting, was being pressed to the fore by petrol shortage. On 27 October only 70 tons had been delivered by the *Luftwaffe*, and on the 29th Ciano entered in his diary: 'Another oil tanker was sunk this evening . . . Bismarck has learned from Rintelen that Rommel is optimistic about the military quality of the troops, but that he is literally terrified by the supply situation. Just now not only is fuel lacking but also munitions and food.'

During the morning of 29 October Montgomery became aware that the 90th Light Division had been moved into the Sidi Abd el Rahman area, and as this indicated that Rommel had reacted to his intent to break out along the coastal road, he decided to shift the axis of his break-through attack southward so that it would fall mainly on the Italians. In order to cover this operation and pin down the 90th Light Division, he ordered the 9th Australian Division to resume its attack on the night of the 30th–31st. In the meantime the 2nd New Zealand Division was to be brought up in readiness to force a gap through the enemy's front a little to the north of the existing northern corridor, and once it had been made the Xth Corps with the 1st, 7th, and 10th Armoured Divisions was to pass through it into the open desert. This operation was code-named 'Supercharge'. Montgomery writes: The operation

> was to get us out into the open country and to lead to the disintegration of Rommel's forces in Egypt. We had got to bring the enemy's armour to battle and get astride his lines of communication. Second New Zealand Division's tasks involved a penetration of some 6,000 yards on a 4,000 yards front. I made it clear that should 30 Corps fail to reach its final objectives, *the armoured divisions of the 10th Corps were to fight their way through*.

On 30 October, Rommel had the Fuka position reconnoitred, and although he realized that because the Italian infantry had practically no transport they would be no more than a dead weight in the open desert, he nevertheless planned to load as many of them as he could on his transport columns and withdraw them under cover of night, after which his remaining motorized forces were, on a wide front, to beat a fighting retreat to the west. 'But first,' he writes, 'we had to wait for the British move, to ensure that they would be engaged in battle and could not suddenly throw their strength into a gap in our front and then force a break-through.'

It came that night, when the Australians resumed their attack toward the coast and, after they had reached it, they turned eastward and cut off the Panzer Grenadiers of the 164th Division in the northern salient. But most of the grenadiers, helped by counter-attacks delivered by elements of the 21st Panzer Division and the 90th Light Division, effected their escape.

Montgomery's original intention had been to launch 'Supercharge' on the night following this attack, but the situation compelled him to postpone it for 24 hours, and it was not made until 1 a.m. on 2 November, after an intense artillery bombardment, reinforced by relays of bombers. Under cover of a creeping barrage two brigades of the 2nd New Zealand Division, supported by the 23rd Armoured Brigade, moved forward on a 4,000-yard front; their task was to drive a lane 4,000 yards in length through the enemy's position, clear it of mines and open a path for the 9th Armoured Brigade, which before dawn was to push forward another 2,000 yards to the track which ran south from Sidi Abd el Rahman, and establish a bridgehead from which the 1st, 7th, and 10th Armoured Divisions could debouch into the open desert and bring on a decisive armoured battle.

The lane was successfully cleared, but when a little before daylight the 9th Armoured Brigade reached the track, it ran into a formidable anti-tank gun screen and suffered a loss of 87 tanks – over 75 per cent of its strength. In the meantime the 1st Armoured Division debouched and was at once engaged by the Afrika Korps. A fierce tank battle followed around Tel el Aqqaqir. Although Rommel's tanks were outclassed by his enemy's, and their 50 mm and 49 mm (Italian) guns could make little impression on the British Grant and Sherman machines, the attackers were brought to a halt and the penetration sealed off. Nevertheless, Rommel was under no illusions; he realized that the battle was lost. Not only were there signs of disintegration – units of the Littorio and Trieste Divisions streamed to the rear – but the supply situation, he writes, was 'absolutely desperate'. During the day his army had expended 450 tons of ammunition, and only 190 tons had been brought to Tobruk by three destroyers. He also states: 'The Afrika Korps had only 35 serviceable tanks left.'

'This then', writes Rommel, 'was the moment to get back to the Fuka line,' and especially as 'the British had so far been following up hesitantly and that their operations had always been marked by an extreme, often incomprehensible caution.' He then made what he acknowledges was a crucial blunder. Early on the morning of 3 November he sent his ADC, Lieutenant Berndt, to report direct to Hitler and to ask him for full freedom of action. He did not doubt that it would be given and ordered part of the Italian formations to retreat. At 1.30 p.m. he received Hitler's answer: stand fast and yield not a yard of ground. 'As to your troops,' it read, 'you can show them no other road than that to victory or death.' Rommel then halted the withdrawal, and in the evening sent Berndt back to Hitler with a message to inform him that to stand fast meant annihilation.

Early on 4 November Kesselring arrived at Rommel's head-quarters and, according to Rommel, said to him, 'that the Führer had learnt from his experiences in the East that, in circumstances like these, the front must be held at all costs.' In his *Memoirs* Kesselring contradicts this, and writes that he told Rommel, 'there could be no question of any such folly, that Hitler's order must be ignored,' and that he would accept full responsibility for ignoring it.

When on the morning of 3 November Montgomery learnt of his enemy's withdrawal westward, he asked the Desert Air Force to switch the whole of its weight to the retreating Axis columns. But it was not until nightfall that he ordered the 51st Division and a brigade of the 4th Indian Division to move forward on a four-mile front and to break through the southern sector of the enemy's anti-tank screen and win a gap through which he could pass his three armoured divisions. This was successfully done by the morning of the 4th.

Of this, the final action of the battle, Rommel supplies the following dramatic description:

Enormous dust-clouds could be seen south and south-east of headquarters, where the desperate struggle of the small and inefficient Italian tanks of XX Corps was being played out against the hundred or so British heavy tanks which had come round their open right flank. I was later told by Major von Luck, whose battalion I had sent to close the gap between the Italians and the Afrika Korps, that the Italians, who at that time represented our strongest motorized force, fought with exemplary courage. Von Luck gave what assistance he could with his guns, but was unable to avert the fate of the Italian Armoured Corps. Tank after tank split asunder or burned out, while all the time a tremendous British barrage lay over the Italian infantry and artillery positions. The last signal came from the Ariete at about 15.30 hours: 'Enemy tanks penetrated south of Ariete. Ariete now encircled.'

By nightfall the XXth Italian Corps had been destroyed; the Afrika Korps on its left had been broken through and its commander, General von Thoma, captured; a 12-mile gap had been driven through the Axis front; and Rommel had no reserves and no petrol. In spite of Hitler's insane order, retreat became compulsory, and Rommel tried to save what he could of his army. Next morning a message arrived from Hitler's headquarters to authorize the withdrawal.

That Rommel was ever able to withdraw even his motorized units was firstly because of Montgomery's instinctive cautiousness, and secondly because of the reluctance of the RAF to engage in low flying attack, as it had done so successfully after the battle of Vittorio-Veneto. According to General Alexander, the Eighth Army could still muster 'very nearly six hundred tanks against eighty German'; it needed only a modicum of audacity by Montgomery to turn his enemy's retreat into a rout. On the second point, de Guingand writes:

> With the virtual air superiority we possessed, and the state of disorganization of the enemy, it looked to us in the Army that here was the 'dream target' for the RAF. In the event, the results appeared very disappointing. When setting out along the road between Alamein battlefield and Daba, I had expected to see a trail of devastation, but the visible signs of destroyed vehicles were few and far between. After Daba much better results had been obtained but even here a lot of the vehicles we found had stopped through shortage of petrol.

This he rightly attributes to the RAF's trust in high-level bombing instead of low-level machine-gunning, with the consequence that training in low flying attack had been neglected. Had it not been for this, his opinion is that Rommel's withdrawal would have been paralysed.

The crux of Rommel's retreat was the pull-out on the night of 4–5 November, when chaos reigned, but fortunately for him his methodical opponent, fearful of the difficulties of a night pursuit, halted his forces. 'On 5 November', Montgomery informs us, 'I regrouped for the pursuit.' Thus he lost some 18 invaluable hours. When he had regrouped he decided that the Xth Corps (1st, 7th Armoured and 2nd New Zealand Divisions) were to lead the chase; the XXXth Corps was to come into reserve between El Alamein and Mersa Matruh; and the XIIIth was to clear up the battlefield. In spite of this delay, by an outflanking movement through the desert he nearly cut off his enemy at Mersa Matruh. But on 6 November the van of the 1st Armoured Division was brought to a halt through lack of petrol and Rommel succeeded, as he says, 'in forming a fairly firm front and beat off all enemy attacks.' He adds that his enemy 'still continued to operate with great caution.'

It is also stated that 'conditions on the road were indescribable. Columns in complete disorder – partly of German, partly of Italian vehicles – choked the road between the minefields [south of Mersa Matruh]. Rarely was there any movement forward and then everything soon jammed up again. Many vehicles were on tow and there was an acute shortage of petrol, for the retreat had considerably increased consumption.'

To add to the difficulties of both sides, and more particularly to the pursuers, on the 6th torrential rain made the desert tracks impassable. For 24 hours the pursuit was bogged down. According to Montgomery the rain saved Rommel 'from complete annihilation.'

Bou Arada (1943)

Donald Gurrey

When the Allies landed in Algeria in November 1942 it was hoped that a quick dash up the 400-mile road to Tunis might enable the latter to be seized and Rommel's line of retreat from Libya cut off. The speed with which the German High Command rushed *ad hoc* formations over from Italy and Sicily thwarted this pious hope. A set-piece drive up the Medjerda valley from Medjez-el-Bab on Christmas Day 1942 had to be abandoned when torrential rains made the going impassable. With stalemate at Medjez and in the broken mountainous terrain to the north the German forces were quick to probe the open flank to the south, up till then only guarded by long-range patrols of 1st Derbyshire Yeomanry, the British 6th Armoured Division's armored reconnaissance unit. German pressure along the Pont-du-Fahs/El Aroussa road, 20 miles to the south, began to mount.

Leaving 78th Infantry Division to hold the Medjez sector, the British First Army's only other division, 6th Armoured, accordingly moved down in early January to the Bou Arada area. The aim was both to block any German advance and to see if a drive towards Tunis might be forced up this axis. From this time until late in February the Bou Arada–Goubellat plain area became the division's main 'stamping ground'.

The 6th Armoured, under 41-year-old Major-General Charles F. Keightley, was short in experience but high in training and morale;

its formation sign was a mailed fist (referred to in later months by nurses from a neighboring field hospital as 'the sign of the disengaged hand'). The division's tanks were in 26th Armoured Brigade (16th/5th Lancers, 17th/21st Lancers, 2nd Lothian and Border Horse with 10th Rifle Brigade as their battalion of infantry). The Derbyshire Yeomanry had armored cars for scouting. The 38th (Irish) Infantry Brigade (6th Royal Inniskilling Fusiliers, 1st Royal Irish Fusiliers, 2nd London Irish Rifles) provided the main infantry element (to be replaced, later in the campaign, by 1st Guards Brigade, which had come out to North Africa as an independent brigade). The artillery support was provided by 12th Royal Horse Artillery Regiment (RHA), 152nd Field Regiment (The Ayrshire Yeomanry), both with 24 25-pounder field guns; 72nd Anti-Tank Regiment (48 6-pounders) and 51st Lt AA Regiment (54 Bofors 40 mm). Extra artillery was borrowed from 5th Corps to 'thicken up'; 17th Field Regiment and one troop of 14th/16th Medium Regiment with four 5.5-in guns.

Bou Arada itself and the foothills south of it were held by a motley but enthusiastic French force designated Groupement Tremeau: 4ème Chasseurs d'Afrique, three companies of Algerian *tirailleurs*, 1ère Bataillon, 1ère Régiment Etrangère (French Foreign Legion), two companies of colonial infantry and a squadron of mounted *Spahis*. For artillery support they had 12 75 mm guns – the famous *soixante-quinze* of 1914–18 vintage. To the SE, British 1st Parachute Brigade fought a difficult running battle in the broken scrub-covered hills between Bou Arada and the Djebel Mansour, a critical feature which dominated a mountain road giving access to Bou Arada from the south.

The terrain presented interesting tactical problems. The Plain of Goubellat, halfway between Medjez and Bou Arada, was flattish rolling farmland, intersected by occasional wadis; it was dominated by higher ground on all sides and was therefore untenable (even if sufficient troops had been available). The high ground to the NE of it, close to Medjez, was held by units of 78th Division; but to the west and SW of it ran a high ridge, the Djebel Rihane, rising to 2,500 ft at its maximum and running southwards to within a mile or so of the El Aroussa–Bou Arada road. This ridge was covered with dense *maquis* scrub, making it impossible to defend, since there was no field of fire in any direction. In consequence the whole ridge was unoccupied for some 10 miles of its length except for some Derbyshire Yeomanry posts on the main tracks and for a standing patrol of 24 *Spahi* cavalry. Yet immediately to the west of it ran the main Medjez–El Aroussa road, carrying heavy military traffic.

By day, the Goubellat plain slumbered in apparent peace, empty of life; but at night there was heavy patrolling by both sides, and Royal Engineer (RE) detachments from 6th Armoured Division's 5th Field Squadron were quickly active in setting a colorful selection of booby traps in and around Goubellat village. One variety was sunk into the earth surface of paths and tracks, and fired a bullet into the foot of anyone unlucky enough to step on it. The main struggle quickly concentrated, however, on a long bare stony ridge which ran along the south side of the plain, some four miles north of the little village of Bou Arada. The Germans, with their experienced military eye, had quickly identified this as the key to this sector, just as Longstop Hill was to the Medjez–Tunis axis. In the fighting of early January 1943 the Irish Brigade managed to grab a feature on this ridge, lying just on the west side of the Bou Arada–Goubellat–Medjez road and christened 'Grandstand Hill'. The Germans held onto a rather high 'pimple' known, for self-evident reasons, as 'Two-Tree Hill'. Between these two features, 1.5 miles apart, a First World War-style trench system quickly developed, wired-in and with only a few hundred yards separating the two front lines.

Between this ridge and Bou Arada village stretched flat open wheatfields, the main road through them being fully visible to the Germans on Two-Tree Hill. A couple of small woods on the east side of the road gave admirable cover for 72nd AT Regiment's 6-pounders in enfilade positions, but by day there were no infantry positions along some two miles of this road, although 38th Brigade were responsible for providing standing patrols at night to protect the guns. The main 25-pounder gun positions lay in masked ground to the west of the road. On the German side, 75 mm PAK 40 AT guns concealed in wadis along the south flank of the ridge, together with deep minefield belts among the wheatfields, foiled any easy British tank attack eastwards across the open ground.

Overall, the British and German forces facing each other were virtually equal in the early weeks. The British infantry were more numerous, but the Germans opposite them had vastly more battle experience and, with 54 MG42s per battalion, far more firepower. The British had many more tanks, but the 6-pounders and the 2-pounders of their Crusaders and Valentines were well outgunned by the fewer *PzKpfw III*s and *IV*s, especially over the long ranges of this open terrain. Only in artillery were the British greatly superior. Time and again in the Tunisian campaign it was the concentrated fire of well-drilled 25-pounder and 5.5-in guns, controlled by Forward Observation Officers with a clear view of the enemy over the open ground, which brought menacing German attacks to a standstill.

But in the air, through January and February, the *Luftwaffe* held the whip hand. Their airfields were only 35 miles away, with concrete runways, permanent hangars and workshops, whereas the RAF were 80 miles back at Souk-el-Arba, flying off PSP (Pierced Steel Planking) runways laid on a sea of mud, the aircrews and fitters living in tents, cold and wet. For the 10-mile road from El Aroussa to Bou Arada the term 'dead straight' had a nasty ambiguity to it unless one kept a nervous eye open for 'Gert and Daisy' the pair of Me109s which would swing suddenly over the crest of nearby hills. A squadron of Ju87s put in frequent appearances, travelling majestically in tight formation just out of Bofors range, to peel off and swoop down on forward positions or on supply dumps in El Aroussa.

We have already listed the Allied troops engaged, who were they up against? Facing Medjez itself was 86th *Panzergrenadier* Regiment, of 10th *Panzer* Division. The principal infantry force south of this, manning positions down the east edge of the Goubellat plain, on the Two-Tree ridge and covering the Pont Du Fahs axis, were three battalions of the *Hermann Goering Jäger* Regiment. This was a crack formation, originally airborne, often referred to as 'Division Koch' after its paratrooper CO, a 29-year-old *oberstleutnant* (Lieutenant Colonel) with the Knight's Cross. Also on this sector was one of the several improvised infantry units quickly assembled by the Germans to meet the sudden Tunisia crisis, a *Marschbataillon* designated A/24, under *Oberleutnant* (First Lieutenant) Helmcke. This had been formed in Hamburg in November from men wounded on the Russian Front; it had left by train on 9 December for Naples and Palermo, arriving in Tunis on Christmas Day aboard two Italian destroyers. Its unusual organization consisted of four companies of four platoons, the fourth platoon in each company being a heavy platoon with six heavy machine-guns and two 81 mm mortars.

Armored support was provided by 1st and 2nd Battalions of 7th *Panzer* Regiment; each battalion consisted of three companies of 12 tanks with an HQ of five, giving a battalion total of 17 *PzKpfw II*s and 24 *PzKpfw III*s or *IV*s (1st Battalion for example had 21 Mark IIIs and 3 Mk IVs). The 2nd Battalion had suffered badly on the way over; both 5th and 8th Companies lost all their tanks and drivers when the MV *Menes* was sunk off Bizerta on 3 December. The survivors benefited to some extent, since 8th Company was subsequently re-equipped with 12 brand-new *PzKpfw IV Ausf F2*s with the more powerful long-barreled 75 mm gun. Artillery support was scant; 90th Artillery Regiment, of 10th *Panzer* Division, had to spread itself widely over the whole sector and suffered badly from lack of ammunition. It had 24 105 mm guns and 12 150 mm howitzers, plus one battery of 88 mm AA guns and one of self-propelled 75 mm *Sturmkanone*.

The *Hermann Goering (HG) Jägers* were 6th Armoured's principal adversary. The 1st Battalion was commanded by *Hauptmann* (Captain) Jungwirth, 2nd Battalion by *Hauptmann* Becker; a third battalion was created, early in December, by *Hauptmann* Schirmer withdrawing companies from the other two battalions. These battalions had three companies apiece, armed with 18 MG42s (double the normal establishment) and three 50 mm mortars, plus a heavy company of 12 HMGs of 4–6 81 mm mortars. The 2nd Battalion had some 4–6 75 mm AT guns under command; doubtless the other battalions were similarly supported. An illustration of the stop-gap arrangements forced on the German High Command by the Allied landings is that 14th Company of 104th *Panzergrenadier* Regiment, nominally a unit of 21st *Panzer* Division and about to join it in Libya, was diverted from Italy to Tunisia on 11 November and operated from the outset as a unit of the *HG Jägers*.

By any standards these were first-class troops; most of them had considerable battle experience and were adept at holding defensive positions. Their officers were good leaders and courageous; by 20 March, for example, no company of 3rd Battalion had any officers left alive apart from the company commander.

After the initial clash with 38th Infantry Brigade early in January all further attempts by British infantry to capture Two-Tree Hill and advance east along the ridge were beaten off. Two-Tree Hill remained a real thorn in the flesh; it dominated the British forward defense lines both by observation and by the fire of well dug-in machine-guns. Already by 13 January the *HG Jägers* were demonstrating their aggressiveness when they struck across the Bou Arada–Grandstand road with two night raiding parties of 12 men each. These surprised 'D' Troop 12th RHA, which had just moved in that night, taking prisoners and blowing up guns and tractors with satchel charges. A couple of weeks later they again showed initiative when a gunner observation post, established high up on the Djebel Rihane with a clear, if distant, view of the whole Two-Tree ridge, was taken out by a patrol which crept up the mountainside at night and killed the subaltern and sergeant sleeping there.

By mid-January, however, 6th Armoured Division were firmly installed; 38th Brigade holding the Grandstand Hill feature, 26th Armoured Brigade just behind them on the plain, ready to block any breakthrough by the German armor. It was just in time. On 18 January *Generaloberst* (Colonel General) Jürgen von Arnim (commanding Fifth *Panzer* Army in Tunisia since 9 December) launched Operation *Eilbote I* (special messenger), an operation aimed at driving back the French (who had been advancing from Robaa towards Pont du Fahs) while holding back 6th Armoured by a diversionary attack. The latter was so fierce that many considered it at the time to be the main attack.

The *Jägers* had taken the brunt of the early fighting for Grandstand Hill on 11–12 January; so this time it was *Marschbataillon A/24* that led the attack, with 1st and 3rd Companies moving at first light against the British positions in front of Grandstand, supported below the hill by 2nd Battalion, 7th *Panzer* Regiment. The positions attacked were held by the Royal Irish Fusiliers and the Inniskillings, and although A/24 once gained a footing on Grandstand Hill, it was forced eventually to withdraw, suffering heavy casualties from artillery fire. By nightfall it was back to its start lines. During the morning a dive-bombing attack was made by 12 Ju87s on El Aroussa, repeated at 1600 against Bou Arada.

More unusual was the first attack, outside Russia, by the new

Henschel 129B 'tank-buster' aircraft, armed with one 30 mm and two 20 mm cannon as well as machine-guns (8 *Staffel*, II *Gruppe*, *Schlachtgeschwader* 2 operated seven Hs129s from El Aouina airfield, north of Tunis, at this stage). Three of these attacked Bou Arada during the morning, probably believing it to be infested by British armor. One was shot down by 51st Light AA's Bofors, crashing close to the crossroads and yielding valuable technical intelligence; both the others were hit and damaged, one possibly crashing behind the German lines.

During this time 7th *Panzer*'s 2nd Battalion, under *Hauptmann* Burk, attacked west astride the Pont du Fahs–Bou Arada road at first light, using some 25 tanks, including four *PzKwpf IV*s and 17 *PzKwpf III*s from 7th and 8th Companies. Three miles from Bou Arada they swung half right and made across the wheatfields for the Bou Arada–Grandstand road, apparently not suspecting the presence of 17th Field and 72nd AT Regiments, the latter hidden in the outskirts of Bou Arada and in the woods east of the road. Fire was opened at 800 yards and three Mark IIIs and four Mark IVs were quickly put out of action. Half of the remaining tanks swung north behind a feature called Mehalla, while the rest withdrew behind a farm a mile to the east, whence they engaged our guns with direct fire, using HE. Both these groups of tanks were pounded repeatedly by the divisional artillery, immobilizing another Mark III. By 1400 the *Panzers* were withdrawing under continuous shellfire, followed up at dusk by two squadrons of Lothians and Border Horse, who harbored as night fell some 4 miles farther east, in an area held by 10th Rifle Brigade. During the night Royal Engineers went out and blew up the eight immobilized German tanks to prevent their removal and repair.

The next morning, 19 January, started quietly, disturbed only by a low-level attack on Bou Arada at 1100 by three Focke-Wulf 190 fighter-bombers, but during the afternoon 6th Inniskillings carried out a sweep of the Point 286 feature and prisoners were taken. While this was in progress the usual dozen Stukas bombed Royal Irish Fusilier positions just east of Grandstand, and there was unusually heavy shelling of the area by the German 90th Artillery. There was welcome support for the hard-pressed Irish Brigade that evening when 3rd Grenadier Guards Battalion, detached from 1st Guards Brigade, arrived to relieve 2nd London Irish of its position just south of Bou Arada, thus allowing them to reinforce their brigade up at Grandstand.

January 20 saw a renewed Stuka attack on 12th RHA and 152nd Field gun positions, but this time two were shot down by Bofors fire, which was improving with so much practice. When the attack was repeated at 1315 a timely radio intercept was received to the effect that the Stukas were expecting to have their targets indicated for them by smoke shells. The smoke which the German mortars fired shortly afterwards onto the British positions was puny compared with that which 12th RHA quickly fired onto the German infantry positions, so that it was these latter which received the full weight of the Stuka attack, to the delight of the British forward troops.

That night an assault was launched in the moonlight by 38th Infantry Brigade to secure Points 279 and 286; in spite of a sharp counter-attack by A/24 the next morning the positions ended up in the hands of the London Irish. Two out of the four German tanks which attempted to intervene were destroyed by indirect artillery fire, together with two SP guns. Prisoners from A/24 said that they had never experienced artillery fire like this before, even in Russia; at least two of their companies had been halved in size during the previous 72 hours.

There was then a lull in the sector, broken only by an unusual night tank attack by 7th *Panzers*. This broke through across the Bou Arada–Grandstand road, causing some of the Irish to abandon their positions; the 6-pounder AT gunners stood firm, but were unable to fire for lack of any target illumination. After milling around somewhat inconclusively in the darkness, on the edge of the field gun positions, the *Panzers* withdrew before dawn, having caused little damage but a good deal of alarm.

In mid-February, 26th Armoured Brigade, 12th RHA and 1st Guards Brigade were all withdrawn from the sector in order to rush back to block Rommel's Kasserine Pass attack, leaving the Bou Arada valley only thinly held. This led to some excitement on 26 February, when von Arnim launched Operation *Ochsenkopf* (oxhead) to aid Rommel in the south. The main weight of *Ochsenkopf* was directed against 46th (North Midlands) Infantry Division at Sidi Nsir, north of Medjez; but pressure was exerted all along the front and included a well-executed raid in force right across the Djebel Rihane, to cut the El Aroussa–Medjez road at a point known as 'Steamroller Farm'.

Two battalions of *HG Jägers*, with seven tanks under *Leutnant* Beisbarth from 6th Company, 7th *Panzer*, four armored cars and ten lorries, moved by night south of the Mahmoud Gap – the shallower part of the Djebel Rihane – and set up road blocks with tanks and machine-guns. The raid was commanded by *Hauptmann* Schirmer himself, and had been begun on 24 February by advance parties of the German battalions 'lying up' just short of the main road and observing British movements. The Intelligence Officer (IO) of 'Y' Division – a special force consisting of little more than the bulk of 38th Irish Brigade and half the 6th Armoured's divisional artillery, left to hold the Bou Arada sector – had already learnt of this, both from interrogation of prisoners and from an Arab who had been bribed by the Germans to lead them across the Djebel Rihane by a little-known track, but who had thereafter reported in to the nearest French troops.

An SOS to First Army for extra troops resulted in the only reserve available – No. 6 Commando, withdrawn only the day before after some vicious fighting on Green Hill, near Beja – being sent forward on 25 February, bivouacking just north of Steamroller Farm. The 'Y' Division IO, Captain Noel H. Burdett, went up that night to brief them of the danger of their situation, and recommended an immediate offensive patrol. Lieutenant-Colonel Mills-Roberts, the 500-strong Commando's CO, was sympathetic but considered, perhaps understandably, that his men needed a night's rest first. By dawn on 26th it was too late: the *Jägers* had seen the Commando arrive, surrounded it during the night and opened fire from higher ground and Steamroller Farm at first light. A sharp battle developed, but when the first *Panzers* appeared towards midday the Commando, having no AT weapons, could only run for it. They lost a number of killed and badly wounded, and over 50 prisoners, including six officers – one being the unfortunate Capt. Burdett (who later, however, escaped from POW camp and got away safely to Switzerland).

Next day a squadron of Churchill tanks – its first action in Tunisia – arrived in El Aroussa via Teboursouk and moved up towards Steamroller Farm. The unit was shelled with fearsome accuracy by an 88 mm gun brought across the Rihane by the Germans, who seemed content to hold their position without ranging further afield. The British artillery now set to work, both from the El Aroussa and Medjez sides, and began to plaster the farm with shellfire. By dawn on 28 February the Germans had evacuated it for more discreet cover on the hillsides, but many of their vehicles were hit and 'brewed up' across the landscape. *Hauptmann* Schirmer was soon calling up on the radio for Stuka attacks to be made on the British troops now closing in on him. In this wild country, with no front line easily identifiable, some of the bombing almost inevitably fell on the German troops themselves. By the next night a German withdrawal back to the far side of the Goubellat plain was in full swing (after an epic Churchill tank attack), and the crisis was over; the sector was to remain thereafter relatively quiet until the final attacks towards Tunis were launched from here some six weeks later.

Kursk (1943)

Alan Wykes

The German armies in Russia were prepared for a massive offensive to reverse the disaster of Stalingrad. The finest divisions of both the *Wehrmacht* and the *Waffen SS* were gathered in an enormous concentration of men and armor. Armed with the latest tanks, their morale high, they expected to be unstoppable, even if the Russians were ready. But 'Whenever I think of this attack', said Hitler, 'my stomach turns over' – and his queasiness was understandable. For now, in the spring of 1943, both he and his generals knew that only a decisive victory over the Red Army could ease the relentless, threatening pressure on the Eastern Front.

The cracks in the wall of Axis domination were becoming ever more numerous and more apparent. The Allies were beginning to overcome the efforts of the U-boats. Italy was in a more parlous state than ever before. Japan's advances in Burma and the south-west Pacific had been stopped, and were going into reverse. The bombing of German industrial centers was disrupting essential war supplies. The hit-and-miss methods of the Red Air Force were being offset by increasing numbers of planes and the increasing skill of the Russian air crews. And the threat of a Second Front kept many German divisions tied up in Europe, reducing the possibility of any major effort on the Russian front.

Then, in March, came Field Marshal von Manstein's great victory at Kharkov for Army Group South and it seemed for a moment as

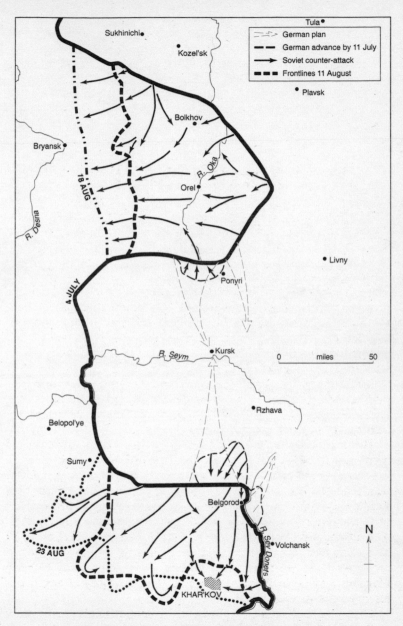

Tula●

Sukhinichi●

Kozel'sk●

Plavsk●

Bolkhov●

Bryansk●

R. Oka

18 AUG

Orel●

R. Desna

Livny●

Ponyri●

4 JULY

R. Seym

Kursk●

| | German plan |
| 0 | miles | 50 |

Rzhava●

Belopol'ye●

Sumy●

Belgorod●

R. Sev Donets

23 AUG

Volchansk●

N

KHAR'KOV

Legend:
- ⤳ German plan
- – – – German advance by 11 July
- → Soviet counter-attack
- ▰▰▰ Frontlines 11 August

5.7 The Battle for the Kursk Salient, July–August 1943

if the tide was turning. But it was a short-lived hope. The victory, so far as the restoration of the German initiative was concerned, was incomplete. A great Russian-held salient remained – a bulge roughly semi-circular in shape, driven some 75 miles westward into the German lines at Kursk, with its base measuring more than 100 miles from north to south. Within the salient were said to be a million men, and armaments in proportion. Clearly, a pincer movement thrown across the base of the salient would cut off and destroy the forces contained in it and considerably weaken the total power of the Soviet army, and von Manstein planned such a movement to clinch his victory.

As so often before, however, the weather took a hand. The spring thaw turned vast tracts of frozen ground to mud, rivers rose, swamps appeared, ruined villages were mirrored in the desolation of floods. There was nothing von Manstein could do but withdraw his armor to save it from getting bogged down, and leave the infantry in possession while a plan was worked out. But there was a catch: the longer the Germans remained purely on the defensive, the sooner there would be an attempt by the Russians to widen the salient and breach the German front completely.

At a time when speed and decisiveness of action could have produced results, the Germans vacillated. Hitler changed his mind. His generals feuded among themselves. And there were conflicting interpretations of the demands of the situation in Europe. Even the promise of a new assault on the Don and an advance towards Moscow after the salient had been pinched out could not bring the Führer to decide. Tanks and other heavy assault weapons – particularly the Tigers and Panthers – were not reaching the army in the expected numbers. It was 11 April before the semblance of a design was arrived at, and it was in essence the same design that von Manstein had been unable to fulfill after Kharkov. It was indeed the obvious plan – and its obviousness was now appreciated equally by the Russians, who made haste to improve their defenses round Kursk. Any chance of surprise had been lost. Now, the only possibility lay in an assault so tremendous that no defenders could resist it.

Such an attack meant risking far more armor than the Germans could afford to lose, and if infantry support was to be forthcoming for the tanks it also meant imprudently weakening the front both north and south of the salient.

Hitler was himself caught in a pincer movement of commitment.

On the one hand he had the conflicting views of his advisers as to the possibility of success. Field Marshal von Kluge, the Army Group Center commander, and Generals Keitel and Zeitzler of the Army General Staff were in favor; Colonel-General Guderian, the Inspector-General of Armored Troops and, by this time, von Manstein himself were equally strongly against. On the other hand, there was the assurance of Speer, Minister of Production, that the necessary tanks would be available, and the certainty that without a German offensive the whole weight of the Soviet forces would come crashing against the over-stretched *Wehrmacht*.

While Hitler hesitated, General Vatutin and the Red Army went ahead – not merely with defenses as impenetrable as they could be made, but also with the preparation of a large-scale counter-attack. The news filtered back to Hitler intelligence reports and alarming air photographs that indicated the withdrawal of the Russian mobile forces from the area west of Kursk in obvious preparation for a counter-attack. But at last, on 10 May, Hitler gave his consent to the plan – it was to be called Operation Zitadelle – emphasizing his underlying reluctance with the words 'It must not fail.'

The forces were decided. Colonel-General Model's Ninth Army, with seven *Panzer*, two *Panzergrenadier*, and nine infantry divisions was to attack from the north. Colonel-General Hoth's Fourth *Panzer* Army, with ten *Panzer*, one *Panzergrenadier* and seven infantry divisions would sweep up from the south. The two arms of the pincer would meet east of Kursk, thus enclosing the salient and cutting off huge Russian forces. But, although the plan and deployment were decided, Hitler continued to hesitate.

Knowing that the Russians were building up their defenses, he postponed the first mooted date for the start of Zitadelle from 13 June until the beginning of July so that an extra couple of battalions of Panthers could be sped off the production line and allotted to Model's northern pincer. The opening of what was to become known – justifiably – as the greatest tank battle in history was finally fixed for 1500 on 4 July, despite continued proposals for abandonment from von Kluge, von Manstein and Guderian.

Opposing the 36 German divisions was a force of 11 Russian Armies, including the crack Sixth and Seventh Guards Armies that had fought so well at Stalingrad and the First Tank Army. Each Russian 'army' corresponded approximately with a German corps in size. In terms of manpower there was little to choose between the conflicting forces, but the Russians had reinforced the north corner of the salient, which would bear the brunt of Model's attack, with thickly sown minefields – so dense that, according to Marshal Rokossovski, who was the joint commander on the Kursk front with Vatutin, 'you could not have put one of Goering's medals between them.' There were 2,200 anti-tank and 2,500 anti-personnel mines per mile of the defensive front, four times the density at Stalingrad. In addition there were no fewer than 20,000 guns of various kinds, including 6,000 76.2 mm anti-tank guns and more than 900 *Katyusha* rocket guns. For attack they had the famous T34 tank – one of the best armored vehicles to be produced during the war – with its long-range 76 mm gun and great reliability.

The German attacking force was largely based on the new Panther D, a fine tank in many ways but with numerous technical faults caused by hasty production. But the Germans still had considerable superiority in the air, as was to be proved by the squadrons of Stuka dive-bombers.

But if the opposing forces were fairly matched there were other factors that would determine the course of the battle – not least the lost element of surprise, which had been frittered away in argument and indecision.

The ground over which the battle was to be fought was reasonably good for tank warfare. Kursk lies in the basins of the Don and Dneiper and the countryside which surrounds it and formed the salient is characterized by low hills and wide-ranging plains of fertile arable land. The ground is watered by numerous brooks and tributary rivers – one of them, the Pena, being a swift stream running between steep banks. Cornfields stretch for unbroken miles across the landscape. Such roads as there are are for the most part sandy cart-tracks that become unusable by wheeled traffic during heavy rain. Numerous scattered villages lie in the shallow valleys and small thickets bristle on the low hills. To the north of the village of Beresowka there is a thickly wooded area, roughly circular in shape and some four miles in diameter.

Along the southern front of the salient, Hoth's Fourth *Panzer* Army was lined up along a slight curve extending some 30 miles from west to east. First the 3rd and 11th *Panzer* divisions and the *Gross Deutschland* division (a *Panzergrenadier* unit with a high complement of tanks under 48 *Panzer* Corps); then the three SS divisions, *Leibstandarte Adolf Hitler*, *Totenkopf* (Death's Head) and

Das Reich in the SS *Panzer* Corps; and on the right wing the 6th, 19th and 7th *Panzer* divisions of 3 *Panzer* Corps. There had been the closest co-operation between ground and air forces and the utmost care had been taken to get the huge force of tanks into position under cover of darkness. 'Morale', according to Model, 'was high' – and was raised even higher by a message from the Führer:

> Soldiers of the Reich! This day you are to take part in an offensive of such importance that the whole future of the war may depend on its outcome. More than anything else, your victory will show the whole world that resistance to the power of the German army is hopeless.

Unfortunately the message arrived during a four-hour intense artillery bombardment from the Russians which confirmed that the defenders were well aware that the attack was about to be launched. The intensity of the bombardment inevitably had its effect on the striking power of the attackers, but the attack began as planned at 1500 after a return bombardment by German artillery and some devastating strikes on the forward Russian lines by dive-bombing Stukas.

By 1900 advance infantry and grenadiers of the three divisions on the German left flank of the southern pincer had thrust into the Russian forward line at Luchanino, Alexejewka and Sawidowka – three villages only lightly held by the defenders. The ease with which they were taken was characteristic of the tactic, much used by the Russians throughout the battle of Kursk, of luring the attackers into a position that subsequently proved to be untenable.

Model's northern pincer managed to break into the salient on a 15-mile front and 47 *Panzer* Corps pushed forward about five miles during the next 30 hours, but at great cost in huge Porsche Ferdinand (or *Elefant*) assault tanks. These lacked machine-guns and, as Guderian had warned long before, quickly proved vulnerable. As their escorting light tanks were knocked out, they found themselves at the mercy of infantry who dashed out from slit trenches and directed flame-throwers into the engine louvres, thus setting the fuel systems alight and forcing the crews to either be roasted alive or to bale out into captivity. The Model thrust was to gain only five more miles to south and west during the next week. Engineers who tried, under covering fire, to clear lanes through the minefields found that this only aided the Russians, who deftly scored many hits with rockets and 76 mm guns as the tanks passed through.

'For all our bitter struggling in the north', one young officer wrote subsequently, 'we moved virtually nowhere – we stood still. It was like Verdun in 1916. There was a little village called Teploye. We saw it first on the second day and we never saw it more clearly than then. Thick black smoke from brewed-up tanks blew about and each time the smoke cleared away we saw Teploye again, but it was like a mirage. We never got any nearer.'

In the south, Hoth's forces gained ground by advance detachments of infantry and grenadiers, but only at great cost. During the night the defenders withdrew and the front line was shelled throughout its length. Paul Hausser, commander of the three SS divisions *Leibstandarte*, *Totenkopf* and *Das Reich*, wrote afterwards: 'Again and again we showed this weakness of tactics that made us insist on holding ground that had been too easily gained. Having chased Ivan out, we should have withdrawn ourselves and let him bombard the place out of existence. Then we could have moved the armor forward relatively safely.'

This lack of imagination, which was characteristic of German planning, in this particular case won an undeserved reward. During the night a cloudburst caused an immediate overflowing of the Pena and its tributary streams and turned the ground into an impassable morass. But for this, all the tanks would have been moved up into the line of bombardment. Even as it was, the losses were considerable because of the difficulty of taking up camouflaged positions, so that when daylight illuminated the swamped valleys the Red Air Force easily picked out the stranded tanks and attacked.

Luftwaffe Stukas attacked too and had considerable success in demolishing Russian artillery batteries, but as one pilot, Hans Rudel, has recorded, 'The Russian guns were almost as numerous as their mines, and the camouflage was masterly . . . you had to assume that every copse was a gun battery and dive down to treetop level . . . four times out of five you found you scored a hit on a 76 . . . if it didn't get you first.'

This success, however, did little to neutralize the trouble that faced the tanks on the morning of 5 July. The whole of 48 *Panzer* Corps – 3rd and 11th *Panzer* divisions and *Gross Deutschland* – were ordered to move up from the bombarded villages to the next Russian line of defense and capture Ssyrzew and Ssyrzewo, which lay beyond the

Pena river, and wheel round to the north-west to capture the wood at Beresowka and the three small hills that lay beyond it. The floods from the cloudburst, however, made this impossible without the aid of engineers to bridge the river and the flooded cornfields on either side of it, and the engineers were continually harassed by snipers and Soviet planes. As the grey day advanced, the dense formation of tanks along 48 Corps' entire front was seen to be extremely vulnerable – many of them bogged down because they had approached too near the swamped ground round the Pena, and all of them on open ground that made them easy prey for aerial attack.

The three SS divisions on 48 Corps' right were more fortunate. The ground over which they attacked was slightly higher and much of it was outside the cloudburst area, so that the hazard of swampy ground was considerably reduced. Sepp Dietrich of SS *Leibstandarte*, a commander of great skill and daring, forced his tanks forwards some seven miles during the day, knocking out 27 T34s in his advance. By late afternoon his patrols reported the village of Gremutshy clear of enemy, but Dietrich was not to be caught in the lure of a deserted objective. He halted his tanks, got them hull down in folds in the ground and saw that they were well camouflaged. His cunning was rewarded. At sunset the bombardment of Gremutshy began and continued till midnight. Then the whole of the *Leibstandarte* moved forward – without having lost a single tank in the baited trap. Gremutshy had been reduced to a smoking ruin by shelling. Its thatched cottages still blazed fiercely and dust rose in clouds from the rubble as, in the moonlight, Dietrich's tanks skirted the razed village and got into position for a dawn attack.

Dietrich supposed, rightly, that the Russians believed their bombardments had disabled or destroyed many German tanks and that they were therefore unprepared for the attack. But, since surprise was of the essence, there was no time for such refinements as the clearing of minefields, and there were a good many casualties as SS *Leibstandarte* pressed on. But by midday the huge Panthers, which were impervious to 76 mm fire except at point-blank range, had penetrated the Russian defensive positions south of Werchopenje and were making for Hill 260 a mile south of Nowosselowka – one of the objectives that had been unattained by 48 Corps. Their losses had been heavy, however – as much from breakdowns as from Russian attacks. The day ended with stalemate on that middle section of Fourth *Panzer* Army's front.

It was in fact only on the third day, 7 July, that any real success was achieved by the southern pincer. By that time the sun had dried out the swampy ground and the battlefield presented a different, though equally desolate, appearance: miles of devastated cornfields, hundreds of burnt-out tanks of both sides, and the bodies of the dead already swelling obscenely in the heat. A soldier's diary records, 'One man had been caught by bomb blast while squatting in a ditch with his trousers down. It seemed the ultimate in humiliation.'

The minefields had created great devastation and the blackened flesh and bones of those who had been blown up were strewn grotesquely over the battlefield:

> Coming stealthily upon a small copse I looked warily up to meet the face of a sniper poised in a tree. Panic-stricken I fired my pistol up at him before he could get me; but it was just a head, a blown-off bodiless head, still – it seemed to me – smiling craftily, that had lodged in the branches there. When I climbed up I dislodged it and it fell to the ground with a thud, the crafty smile undisturbed.

By this time, the Russians had moved back into the ruins of Gremutshy in preparation for a counter-attack. While they were forming up for this, 48 *Panzer* Corps launched their delayed attempt to make their two-pronged wheel to the north-west. They caught the enemy by surprise, broke through on both sides of Ssyrzew in great force and caused havoc among the assembling Seventh Guards Army, which fled in disorder to shelter behind Hill 243 beyond Werchopenje, losing 70 tanks and artillery pieces in the carefully timed and aimed German barrage.

With the ground clear before them, *Gross Deutschland* now gained momentum and wheeled round to Ssyrzewo with only the most minor casualties. The Russians seemed for the moment nonplussed. But by afternoon they had recovered and launched their counter-attack on Ssyrzewo. It resulted in a head-on collision in which 500 tanks simply faced each other and went on firing until, after several hours, the reverberation of guns along the steep banks of the Pena diminished and night fell on the still-blazing hulks.

No ground had been gained by either side, and it became clearer than ever that the chief characteristic of the Battle of Kursk – which town, though less than 40 miles to the north, remained to the Germans as remote as the moon – was the huge wastage of men and arms in a fight that lacked any subtlety of direction. Mass was posed against mass in a conflict that, in theory, should have been brief and sharply decisive, but in five days showed no sign of reaching a climax.

Dietrich, one of Hitler's oldest friends, said in one of his rare criticisms of the Führer:

Perhaps the feeling of failure had permeated the troops on the Russian front since Kharkov. Not to be able to clinch the victory then was a bad thing. Then Hitler's uncertainty was a sign. The conflict between the top commanders was another. There were personal feuds. Kluge and Guderian hated each other; they nearly came to blows once. Hitler's intuition was always right, and he should have allowed it to overcome the pressure of the generals who wanted Zitadelle to go on for their share of the glory. Also, the way the Russians poured men and machines into the fray was absolutely unlimited. They simply had a disregard for numbers. It didn't matter to them that they were losing a million. Another million were packed behind them ready to be fed into the battle machine.

It was true, although it could hardly be said that Hitler was sparing in his expenditure of men and machines either. But his was the expenditure of desperation, and the Russian High Command knew this very well. Viewing the battle in retrospect Stalin declared to the Supreme Soviet: 'We were an immovable mass against which the Fascists tried to pitch an irresistible force. A scientific impossibility in any case. But they were out-maneuvered by our generals also. They never had a chance.'

That was untrue. There were a number of occasions when Russian tactics were as unimaginative as the Germans', and many more when the jaws of the pincer seemed to be closing. But it was always a piecemeal closure by isolated units, never a concerted forward movement. The shoulder-to-shoulder positioning of Hoth's entire Fourth *Panzer* Army within a 30-mile front had packed a punch that could hardly have failed. Yet it was a punch that was weakened by circumstances that should have been anticipated. Such simple devices as the lure of the abandoned village were overlooked, and the enemy's ability to contain Model's northern force in, so to speak, a salient within a salient was not appreciated. This last factor dealt the death blow to the whole operation. With every abortive attempt Model made to press southward it became increasingly difficult for Hoth to link up with him. 'The Russians have learnt a lot since 1941,' he told Manstein, 'They are no longer peasants with simple minds. They have leant the art of warfare from us.'

Wherever they had learnt it, their knowledge was nowhere more apparent than in the intense fighting that took place around the railway junction of Orel, north of the salient. The Russian Third Army had forced its way forward with the object of encircling Model's Ninth Army in a sweep to the south-west. In that objective it failed, but it did keep most of Model's infantry and artillery engaged in defense instead of attack. The German infantry were thus unable to lend support to the southward armored thrusts that were meant to link up with the Fourth *Panzer* Army on the heights east of Kursk. For three continuous days and nights from 9 to 11 July, Orel in the north and Belgorod in the south – where the Seventh Guards Army was attempting a similar tactic to split the SS divisions from their supporting battle group in 48 *Panzer* Corps – were subjected to bombardment after bombardment. 'It was a continual earthquake,' one eye-witness put it, 'The ground just split asunder and any tank on the move would tip into the fissure.'

Yet another blow was delivered by the Red Air Force, which succeeded in bombing the German supply base at Poltava and destroying the railway line to Kharkov, making lengthy and delaying engineering work necessary. There was no doubt that, whether newly learnt or not, the art of warfare was much in evidence in the Russian designs.

By the time both German pincers had been fighting uninterruptedly for a week, they were showing signs of exhaustion. A shortage of supplies and ammunition, abetted by the cutting off of the railhead, was also making itself felt. But on the left flank of the southern pincer they managed to drive the enemy off the main road from Rakowo to Kruglik and head for the Beresowka forest. Once that objective was attained there was a good chance of capturing Hill 247 with the help of the north-west sweep of the SS division on the right flank, which was intended to wheel round from Hill 260 south of Nowosselowka and make a synchronized attack on Hill 247 from the east.

During the night of 9 July the 3rd *Panzer* Division entered the village of Beresowka from the west, much reduced in numbers – at least a third of its heavy tanks lay burnt out on the battlefield – but tenaciously holding on to every inch of ground it had fought for up the Kruglik road. Help was on its way in the form of one regiment of SS *Leibstandarte* that was making its way unopposed across open country from Werchopenje. Rudolf von Ribbentrop, son of the German Minister, was in command and reported later that he had got to within half a mile of the woods north of the village when a strong Russian counter-attack met them. 'Russian tanks of all sizes came streaming out of the forest and fanned out to meet us,' he said, 'Visibility was bad because of the cornfields, but there was a battle royal and we shot up two of their big mobile guns before the *Luftwaffe* came in to help.'

As one of the pilots described it: 'In the first attack four tanks explode under the hammer blows of my cannon; by evening, after four more sorties, the total rises to 12. The evil spell is broken, and in the Stuka we possess a weapon which can speedily be employed everywhere and is capable of dealing successfully with the formidable numbers of Soviet tanks.'

This was wishful thinking on his part, however. Nothing could deal wholly successfully with the huge number of Soviet tanks. On every section of the battlefield those that were destroyed or immobilized were replaced with seeming magical rapidity. Supplies were endless 'and appeared from nowhere,' as Manstein told Hitler at a conference at the Führer's headquarters on 12 July. By that time the railhead at Poltava was operating again, but there were no endless supplies coming from Germany. The enormous force of fighting vehicles with which Manstein and Kluge had opened the battle to close the Kursk salient had been depleted by more than half. There was continual activity at the repair shops to get into some sort of fighting order those tanks – especially Panthers and Tigers – that had been retrieved from the battlefield. An equally continual effort was made to overcome the successes of the Soviet aircraft in attacking the ammunition trains for which every German tank still left in the field was desperately waiting.

It was now being proved only too clearly that Hitler had indeed put in hazard far more armor than he could afford to lose. Although no resolution of the Kursk conflict could yet be seen, developments in Europe were calling for a speedy conclusion of the offensive and the transfer of forces to the western theater. For, by 12 July, the Allies had landed in Sicily.

The climax to the battle of Kursk was reached during the two days 12 to 14 July, although it amounted to only the fadeaway ending of a battle of attrition. For nine days the two contestants had been slugging at one another like heavyweights swinging giant blows that consistently failed to achieve the knockout.

Early on the morning of 12 July, Hoth summoned his corps commanders and planned for a breakthrough before the Russians could intensify their defenses between Kruglik and Nowosselowka and build up their forces for a big push southward. He had received intelligence reports indicating that the extreme southern tip of Army Group South's fortified line along the Donetz and Mius rivers, between Taganrog and Stalino, was under the threat of a Russian attack. 'We shall be needed there,' he told Hausser, commander of the SS Corps. 'Let us finish the issue of Kursk once and for all.'

Brave words. His armored strength consisted now of only 600 operative tanks to spearhead the attack. Every man in Fourth Army was suffering from battle exhaustion, and ammunition was at a premium. In contrast, Vatutin had new machines, including the new 85 mm SU85 self-propelled gun, and men fresh to the front. He also had the entire Fifth Armored Army in reserve and ready for action. It was not difficult to see where the advantage lay. This climactic action came to be known as 'The Death Ride of Fourth Panzer Army.'

'It's a fine day for a joy ride,' Sepp Dietrich said laconically to the driver of his command tank. 'It won't rain.'

Nor did it. It was a day of intense dry heat. The interiors of the tanks were like ovens despite the air induction systems and fan coolers. The high speed traffic of heavy vehicles over the sandy roads threw up clouds of dust that made it virtually impossible for the *Luftwaffe* to pick out their targets. On one occasion, according to Dietrich, a T34 and a Panther collided head on as they rolled through the dust. 'Ivan had broken through our anti-tank screen and his progeny were streaming like rats all over the battlefield.'

The 'all over' certainly suited the situation. The Fifth Armored Army had come charging into action with all the zest of experienced troops who had waited too long in reserve positions. As the spearhead of the SS *Panzer* Corps rolled towards Prokhorovka it met the full force of this fresh and eager force. Slightly outnumbered, but with more heavy tanks, Hausser's exhausted tank crews met their match. The thick dust prevented the Tigers from making full use of their superior range, and many fell prey to the T34s. The battlefield was littered with burning wrecks – more than 300 tanks were lost by each side. But it was the Germans who could least afford such heavy losses. The onslaught of the *Panzers* was over. By evening the Russians had recaptured Berezowka and cut off 3rd *Panzer* Division and a large wedge of *Gross Deutschland* that had forced its way through the woods to the rescue.

For the Germans, the battle was clearly lost. All the open country between Belgorod, where Seventh Guards Army had broken through as far as the rear echelons of the SS corps, and Orel to the north was possessed by the Russians. Only isolated pockets of Germans were evident in the villages.

From the three hills so fiercely fought for and now relinquished by the Germans, the Russians had a straight line of fire down on to the irrepressible attackers, whose commanders were continually reminding themselves of the Führer's words: 'It must not fail.'

Nevertheless it did fail. The immediate cause of failure, or anyway of termination, was the Führer's own order, relayed through Manstein and radio link to Army Group South's headquarters: 'Operation Zitadelle is cancelled forthwith.'

It is of course impossible to stop a raging battle instantaneously unless both sides are given the same order. A withdrawal meant fighting a rearguard action, and it was two weeks before Hoth's forces got themselves back to their original positions on the starting line – with further considerable losses. In the north, Model's Ninth Army, having advanced so little, had correspondingly little to cover in retreat. The situation at Orel was still critical, however, and Manstein had to order two *Panzer* divisions north to help deal with this threat. He sent two more to the south, where the Taganrog–Stalino sector was also being increasingly threatened.

During the whole of the operation, from H-hour to cancellation, the advances made by the two jaws of the pincer, collectively or by individual units, had never reduced the breach across the base of the salient to less than 60 miles. Twenty *Panzer* divisions, the pride and joy of the *Wehrmacht*, had been bled white, and although on the credit side could be counted the huge number of Russian prisoners and the vast booty and destruction of the battlefield it was only too clear that with Allied assistance the Russians could afford losses on this colossal scale far more easily than the Germans could.

The Death Ride of the Fourth *Panzer* Army signaled the approaching end of the German struggle for Russia. By December, the reconstituted Ninth and Fourth *Panzer* Armies had been pushed back to, and beyond, the Dneiper. The whole of the Eastern Front from Nevel in the north to Kirovograd in the south reflected the turning of the tide, for it had been subjected to unremitting Soviet attacks against the weakening power of Hitler's armies. Now, not even a stalemate could be achieved. The Kursk gambit had been played and had failed.

Sicily (1943)

Hubert Essame

The invasion of Axis-occupied Sicily, Operation Husky, in July 1943 was the greatest seaborne assault of the Second World War. Almost eight divisions – 181,000 troops – were simultaneously put ashore along a hundred mile stretch of the island's coastline. Backing the men was an array of technological expertise and military might that from then on was the hallmark of the Western Allies at war: 14,000 vehicles; 600 tanks; 1,800 guns; 750 warships (including six battleships, 15 cruisers and 128 destroyers) and 5,000 aircraft. For Sicily, the United States contributed her latest inventions – the 'walkie-talkie' radio, and the versatile DUKW six-wheeled amphibious truck. By contrast, in the invasion of Normandy a year later, only 133,000 men were landed over the 45-mile stretch of D-day beaches. Husky marked not only the return of the Allies to the mainland of Europe, but also signalled their determination to knock Mussolini's Italy out of the war.

By January 1943 it was apparent that the Axis forces in Tunis were trapped in the vice being closed by the Allied armies from west and east, and that their destruction was only to be a matter of time. Field Marshal Albert Kesselring, Axis Supreme Commander in the Mediterranean, predicted that the Allies would soon be 'in possession of a jumping-off base for an assault on Europe from the south'. There was an urgent need, therefore, for President Franklin D. Roosevelt and Prime Minister Winston Churchill to meet with their Chiefs of

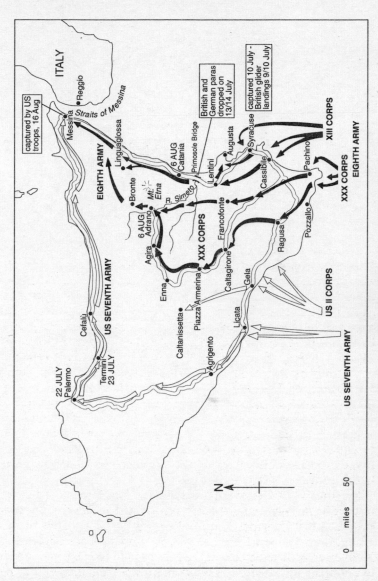

5.8 *The Invasion and Conquest of Sicily, July–August 1943*

Staff to decide the next move. They met on 14–23 January 1943 in French Morocco for the Casablanca Conference, with Major General George S. Patton, commanding the United States forces in Morocco, as host.

After discussing – and discarding – the possibilities of a second European front to take the strain off the hard-pressed Soviet Armies, the conference decided that when the North African campaign was over, the Allied forces, under General Dwight D. Eisenhower, should stage Operation Husky – the invasion of Sicily by two armies, one American, under Patton, and one British, led by General Sir Bernard Montgomery, both under command of General Sir Harold Alexander. It was hoped to placate Stalin by drawing German forces away from the Russian front; to open up the Mediterranean to Allied shipping; and to give the war-weary Italians an excuse for overthrowing Benito Mussolini and getting out of the war.

Sicily is about the size of the state of Vermont, and a little larger than Wales. The terrain generally favors the defense. Inland, the ground is rugged and mountainous, with Mount Etna, in the north-east corner, rising to 10,000 ft. Good roads ran along the east and northern coasts; elsewhere they were few, badly surfaced and with many sharp corners and steep gradients. Deployment off the roads would inevitably be difficult. Only in the Plain of Catania could armor move with any degree of freedom. The Allied plan made the capture of the 30 Sicilian airfields a priority, for it was these bases that posed such a threat to Allied shipping in the Mediterranean. They had also sustained the Axis defense in Tunisia. The airfields fell into three groups: the Gerbini group in the Plain of Catania; the Castelvetrano group south-west of Palermo; and the Conte Olivio Comiso group near the south coast ports.

Combined operations were still in their infancy. No one knew to what extent it would be possible to maintain the invading forces over the beaches with the DUKWs, LSTs, LCMs and LCIs. It was therefore considered vital to gain possession of the major ports as soon as possible. Messina, the largest of these, was out of fighter range and known to be strongly defended. Palermo, Trapani and Marsala, also out of fighter range, could maintain about half the invading force; Catania, Augusta and Syracuse, within range, would supply the other half. Operation Husky was proving as formidable to prepare as Operation Torch, the previous (and first) Anglo-American amphibious landing of the war.

For the assault the admirals stressed the advantages of dispersed landings from the naval point of view. The airmen, their case forcibly put by Air Chief Marshal Sir Arthur Tedder, demanded the neutralization of the airfields on the island as a first priority: both British and American logistic staffs insisted that they must have the use of Palermo and the southern and south-eastern ports at a very early stage. After seven invasion plans had been discussed, Eisenhower gave the final decision: the two armies would land side by side, the Seventh US Army about Gela and the Eighth British Army in the south-east corner of the island. July would be the deadline for the landings.

Most post-war comment gives the impression that the Americans and British in the Mediterranean were continually at loggerheads. But the reverse was the case, due largely to the magnanimity and vision of Eisenhower, the Supreme Commander. Seldom did the Allies work together so cheerfully and unselfishly. Eisenhower had in Alexander the most experienced and tactful commander in the British Army to handle his two brilliant but brittle Army commanders – Patton and Montgomery. Finally in Vice Admiral Sir Bertram H. Ramsay, his Deputy Commander, he had the admiral who had organized the largest evacuation in history – Dunkirk – to help him execute the largest combined operation in history.

The air strength of Tedder and Lieutenant General Carl Spaatz (USAAF) was formidable – 267 squadrons, 146 of which were American and the rest British, totalling over 5,000 aircraft and thus outnumbering the 520 Axis planes by ten to one. Immediately after the fall of Tunis, the Allies turned to the task of securing the air dominance over Sicily which must be gained before a single ship could safely approach it or one soldier step ashore. First, the Allied aircraft ranged far and wide against strategic targets in Italy. Then they began an intense bombardment of the enemy airfields and radar stations within striking distance of Sicily and the proposed routes of the convoys. Tedder interrupted the first stage of his air plan to seize Pantellaria; the island fortress Mussolini had constructed as rival to Malta.

Starting in May, the bombardment of this island gradually increased in intensity till 7 June. Thereafter for four days it rose to a crescendo: over 5,000 tons of bombs were dropped. On 10 June, the third anniversary of Italy's entry into the war, a force from 1st British Division approached the island covered by a precision attack by American flying Fortress B17 bombers. The garrison of 4,600 surrendered without a struggle. For the first time victory had been gained by air power alone.

At the end of June, Alexander's plans for the assault were complete. Montgomery and Eighth Army, embarking at ports between Syria and Sfax were to land on a 30-mile front with two corps, 13th Corps (Lieutenant General Sir Miles C. Dempsey) just south of Syracuse and 30th Corps (Lieutenant General Sir Oliver Leese) astride the Pachino peninsula to capture the airfield there. Patton planned to land his Seventh Army on a 70-mile front in three simultaneous seaborne assaults; two on the east flank by Major General Omar N. Bradley's 2nd Corps with 45th Division at Scoglitti and the 1st at Gela, and 3rd Division (Major General Lucian K. Truscott), directly under his own command, at Licata. As a floating reserve he had 2nd Armored Division and part of 9th Division. All were battle-hardened with the exception of 45th Division.

Initially Alexander prescribed the establishment of beach-heads and the early seizure of Syracuse, the Pachino and Ponte Olivo airfields and the port of Licata. Thereafter Montgomery was to seize Augusta, Catania and the Gerbini group of airfields. Patton planned to advance about 15 to 20 miles inland on the first day. Both armies were to link up on a common boundary – the Yellow Line. But what was to be done thereafter was, unfortunately, not clear. Patton suspected (with good reason) that the major role of exploitation would be given to Montgomery. He protested to Alexander but when overruled, like a good soldier for the moment raised no further objection. Both British and American landings were to be preceded by airborne assaults: the British 1st Airborne Division in gliders and the 82nd American Airborne Division parachuting.

Meanwhile, in early June, Generale d'Armata Alfredo Guzzoni had assumed command of the Italian forces on the island with his Sixth Army headquarters at Enna. He found, even by Italian standards at this stage of the war, an appalling situation. There was a total Italian garrison of 30,000 men and 1,500 guns but only four divisions out of 12 were relatively mobile. The rest were scattered in low-grade coast defense units on the scale of 41 men to the mile. Many of them were of local origin and virtually untrained; the standard of their officers was exceptionally low. Most of their arms and equipment were obsolete and the coast defenses, except near the ports, were either perfunctory or non-existent. One Corps headquarters presided over the destinies of these depressing troops at the east end of the island and another at the west. Only German assistance gave cause for any hope.

Guzzoni had attached as adviser Major General Fridolin von Senger und Etterlin, a Bavarian who had distinguished himself at the head of a *Panzer* Corps in Russia. Detached from 14 *Panzer* Corps on the mainland were 15th *Panzer Grenadier* Division under Major General Eberhard Rodt and *Hermann Goering Panzer* Division under Lieutenant General Paul Conrath, a former Nazi police chief, making a total of about 30,000 troops and including a Tiger tank company of 17 Mark VI tanks and approximately 90 Mark IIIs and IVs.

Anticipating landings at opposite ends of the island, as the Allies had originally planned, Guzzoni and von Senger deployed 15th *Panzer Grenadier* Division in the west and the *Hermann Goering* Division in two battle groups; one near Caltagirone about 20 miles north of Gela and the other under Colonel Schmalz in the Catania Plain. With these troops and the *Livorno* Division, south of Caltanisetta near the Ponte Olivo airfield, the Axis counted on holding the ring by rapid counter-attack until reinforced by the rest of 14 *Panzer* Corps from the mainland.

The day before the invasion, 9 July, started hot with scarcely a ripple on the sea. Rear Admiral Louis Mountbatten, the British Director of Combined Operations, with Adm. Ramsay on board the command ship *Antwerp*, watched the six invasion convoys as they passed on their way to the rendezvous south of Malta. Seven and a half divisions, totalling 160,000 men, were afloat in 2,760 ships and landing craft. They came from the Clyde, from Norfolk, Virginia; and ports along the African coast from Beirut to Algiers. Incredibly there was not a single enemy aircraft in the sky.

At noon, a light breeze sprang up from the west; by mid-afternoon it was blowing Force 7. Almost all the troops in the smaller craft were sick. As the British came under the lee of the land, conditions for them improved but for the Canadians and Americans there would be no respite. They would have to land sick to death and soaked to the skin. But the rough weather was not an unmitigated disaster. Most of the defenders of the Sicilian coast retired to bed, deciding that no man in his senses would attempt to land in such conditions.

First to land in the blackest hours of the night were the British 1st Air Landing Brigade in Waco and Horsa gliders. Their target was the Ponte Grande area near Syracuse. But it was disastrous.

Partly owing to the lack of experience of the pilots of their towing aircrafts and due also in part to the high winds their landing was widely scattered. Seventy of the 134 gliders were released too soon and lost in the sea. Only eight officers and 65 men out of a total 2,075 emplaned in Africa, reached their objective. But they managed to hang on until relieved by the 5th British Division. The 82nd Airborne Division (for the same reason) had an equally difficult landing. About 200 paratroopers of 505th Parachute Regiment managed to seize the vital high ground near Piano Lupo to set up and defend road blocks. They were to prove of great value when the expected counter-attack came later that day. Others roamed far and wide, cutting communications and generally spreading despondency and alarm amongst the Italians, rudely wakened from their slumbers.

On the Eighth Army front the guns of the four supporting battleships quickly silenced any coastal batteries and field guns that dared open fire and the landing proceeded smoothly, partly owing to the thorough training the troops had received and partly to the absence of Italian resistance. At one stage, Montgomery received a report that the Royal Marines had been charged by cavalry! In fact they had inadvertently stampeded the horses of the Italian 206th Coastal Division. These they rounded up, mounted and themselves charged inland. By nightfall the British had taken Syracuse and all their objectives for the day.

On the American front, 45th Division at Scoglitti, although delayed for an hour by the gale, had similar good fortune. At Licata, 3rd Division, in the new beaching craft (LSTs, LCIs and LSTs), landed on time and almost without a hitch. Mountbatten was impressed by the coolness, discipline and efficiency of the US Navy crews and the rapid organization of movement inland. By 0830, guns and tanks were freely coming ashore. Only at Gela was there serious opposition.

As Force X, a special force of Rangers attached to 1st Division, approached the shore, the enemy blew up the pier. Simultaneously the coast defense guns opened up. But they were quickly silenced by devastatingly accurate fire from the 5-in and 6-in guns of the destroyer *Shubrick* and the cruiser *Savannah*. As the Rangers touched down they dashed forward into Gela with the leading troops of 1st Division close on their heels. By 1000 Patton, in the headquarters ship *Monrovia* with Vice-Adm. Hewitt, had 3rd Division holding eight miles of coastline and forces moving rapidly inland. At Gela

1st Division held the road junction of Piano Lupo, the town itself and the airfield. The 45th Division reported that its leading troops were five miles inland.

Now that the Allies had shown their hand, Gen. Guzzoni's reaction was prompt but ill-starred. Clearly there was no risk of a landing at the Palermo end of the island. *Kampf Gruppe Schmaltz* could be relied upon for the moment to guard the Gerbini group of airfields. The major threat was posed by the Americans at Gela. Guzzoni therefore set the 15th *Panzer Grenadier* Division in motion towards Enna, thus creating a reserve under his own hand, and ordered the *Livorno* Division, plus two mobile groups and the *Hermann Goering* Division, to make a co-ordinated attack on Gela and drive the Americans into the sea. The orders for the *Hermann Goering* Division went astray: in consequence the Italians attacked on their own at 0830 with infantry and about 20 light tanks. They struck the 16th Regimental Combat Team supported by the guns of the Navy who were in no mood to be pushed aside. Their attack was a costly fiasco.

The German counter-attack during the early afternoon came with greater vigor, accompanied by heavy shelling of the beaches and determined low-flying attacks by the *Luftwaffe* on the mass of shipping now lying offshore. Despite the courage of the Germans it was a muddled affair and came to nothing. About an hour later they renewed the attack, this time supported by Tiger tanks. This too petered out in confused fighting which continued till nightfall, leaving the Americans in possession of all their first day's objectives except the Ponte Olivo airfield.

To Patton it was evident that 11 July would be the crucial day and that his army would have to bear the brunt of a full-dress counterstroke by the bulk of the German armor. To the consternation of the staffs, he therefore scrapped the pre-arranged landing schedules and ordered 2nd Armored Division and the 18th RCT ashore with all speed. Disembarkation proceeded at a frantic rate throughout the night. He was thus ready to meet the thrust on Gela soon after dawn by the *Hermann Goering* Division who attacked in three columns from the east and by the *Livorno* Division from the west. When he disembarked from Adm. Hewitt's barge at 0900, German 88 mm guns were pounding the beach. When his scout car had been de-waterproofed he set off into Gela for the headquarters of the 1st Division. On the way he decided to look in on the HQ of Colonel Darby, one of the Rangers.

It was a lucky decision. In fact, the *Hermann Goering* Division had cut off the 1st Division from the Rangers and a confused battle was raging along the eastern outskirts of the town. From an observation post close to the front, Patton was able to watch a battle between the Rangers, using a captured battery of Italian 77 mm guns and *Livorno* Division. Every gun the enemy could bring to bear was used. They turned Gela into a shambles. In the nick of time, ten Shermans joined in the fray, having driven all the way from Licata. Deadly and accurate fire from the 6-in guns of the *Savannah* was brought to bear on the *Livorno* Division. By mid-morning they had had enough and retired badly mauled.

Patton now moved on to the 1st Division's front which only had two tanks ashore. Outside the town Conrath had flung in all his 60 tanks with orders to hurl the Americans into the sea. Burning tanks soon littered the Gela Plain. The 32nd Field Artillery Battalion, disembarking their guns from DUKWs, went straight into action and engaged the German tanks over open sights. The infantry of the 1st Division stood like a rock. Three miles inland, the Germans reeled back before the 16th Infantry at Piano Lupo. Meanwhile, the tanks of 2nd Armored Division, struggling through the sand of the beaches, roared into action. Deadly and accurate fire from the Navy added to the inferno. The German tanks faltered and then turned back leaving over half their number behind in flames. Patton then got through to Major General Terry de la Mesa Allen, commander of the 1st Division, to congratulate him and at the same time remind him that he still had to take his D-day objective, Ponte Olivo airfield, four miles inland. Meanwhile, farther to the east, the paratroops had put up a magnificent resistance on Biazzo Ridge and disembarkation had continued. By nightfall the bridgehead at Gela was secure. As Patton had foreseen, this was the bloodiest day of the campaign.

An unfortunate incident that night marred a story of outstanding success. Patton had arranged for 504th Parachute Regiment, consisting of two battalions of parachutists, to be dropped on the Gela airfield and had taken every precaution to warn his own troops of the operation. He and his staff were assured that all the anti-aircraft gunners of the huge supporting fleet had also been told. Regrettably, and perhaps due to the 550 Axis air sorties in two days, enemy AA guns in the fleet opened up against the aircraft carrying the parachutists. As a result, the men were dropped far and wide. When daylight came, out of 2,000 men and equipment, all that could be mustered at the landing zone were a scratch company and a few light howitzers.

With both Eighth and Seventh Armies firmly ashore, the first phase of Operation Husky was nearing its end. By the evening of 12 July Montgomery had captured Augusta and was on the point of advancing on a front of four divisions into the Catania Plain. Patton had linked up with him and was nearing the Yellow Line 20 miles inland which was his first objective. Meanwhile, Guzzoni had been moving his armored forces into the Catania Plain and reinforcements from 14 *Panzer* Corps were arriving opposite the British front. The time had clearly come for Alexander to decide which line of advance the Allied armies should take. It seemed obvious to the Americans and others that Patton rather than Montgomery was better sited to strike due north on Enna and the north coast.

On 14 July, Montgomery, in his drive towards Catania, found himself held up by 29th *Panzer Grenadier* Division and two regiments of parachutists flown in from Avignon as well as Battlegroup Schmalz. General Hans Valentine Hube, of 14 *Panzer* Corps, a one-armed veteran of the Eastern Front, had taken charge. Montgomery, without even mentioning the fact to Patton (but apparently with Alexander's acquiescence), now set in motion a left-hook round the foot of Mount Etna on Route 124, which was within the American area of operations. Of the three good roads running north he now had two. That evening, to the consternation of Patton and Bradley, a directive arrived from Alexander allotting to Montgomery the main effort against Messina, on both sides of Mount Etna.

The Americans, cramped for space and resentful of the fact that they had not even been consulted, found themselves relegated to the invidious task of guarding the British left flank. Later, they were to have the consolation prize of a ride to Palermo, when Messina was in Montgomery's grasp. Stung, Patton took off for Tunis to see Alexander and to express his disappointment. Only now did Alexander realize how deeply Patton felt the affront. But it was too late to halt Montgomery. Alexander therefore gave Patton a free hand in advancing towards Palermo and the north coast.

Released from his strait-jacket Patton launched his spectacular all-out drive on Palermo. To this end he created a provisional Corps under Major General Geoffrey T. Keyes, his Chief of Staff. The 82nd and 3rd Divisions were to make for Palermo from the south and south-east, with 2nd Armored Division in their wake for the final advance on the city. Meanwhile Bradley's Corps was to strike due north and cut the coast road. During a six-day lightning campaign in torrid heat Keyes' Corps, with the infantry riding on the tanks, thrust forward 100 miles and took 53,000 prisoners. On 22 July Patton, with 2nd Armored Division, entered Palermo in triumph to the plaudits of the inhabitants and took up his quarters in the Royal Palace. Next day Bradley's Corps reached the north coast at Termini Imerese.

After the war attempts were made to detract from Patton's achievement. It was claimed that, before the campaign started, contact had been made by Intelligence officers through 'Lucky' Luciano, head of the Mafia in the United States (and serving a 30-year prison sentence), with his opposite number in Sicily, Don Calogero Vizzini, to ensure that the Italian troops put up no resistance to the invaders. In particular, it was alleged that Mafia agents persuaded Colonel Salemi's battle group (consisting of a battalion, some field guns and several Tiger tanks) holding a very strong position in the mountainous Cammarata area which dominated the two roads to Palermo, to let Patton's columns through on 20 July. That there were contacts with the Mafia in Sicily is probably true – they would have been almost impossible to avoid – but to suggest that their influence was in any way decisive is ludicrous.

With every justification the Press were jubilant. The Americans now had a deep-water port capable of handling ships coming direct from the United States and were no longer dependent on supply over beaches; the 9th US Division landed at Palermo. Magnanimously Patton restored his Sicilian prisoners to their families, which reduced the demand on Allied food supplies. Alexander now directed Patton to swing along the north coast towards Messina. Montgomery was to make a short hook with the Canadians about Regalbuto to give Bradley room to maneuver. Thus the so-called inter-Allied race for Messina.

Although the Allies had not secured a military decision in Sicily their progress now finally precipitated the fall of Mussolini and his government. Hitler was still sane and the time had not yet come when a policy of 'No withdrawal' would be his strategic panacea. The disasters at Stalingrad and in Tunisia, and now his appalling losses in his Russian summer offensive, Operation Zitadelle, at last brought home to him that his manpower resources were running down. On 26 July, the day Marshal Pietro Badoglio arrested Mussolini, Hitler gave Kesselring permission to abandon Sicily, before the Allies made their invasion of Italy.

Next day Kesselring, ignoring Guzzoni, told Hube to prepare for evacuation. The chances of success must have seemed slim, for he gave orders that men rather than equipment were to have priority. Hube accordingly planned a slow withdrawal to a series of five defensive positions across the Messina peninsula. The rugged country was in his favor: it gave him magnificent artillery observation; the roads were narrow and winding, often passing through defiles which were easy to block. The anti-aircraft defenses at Messina under Colonel Ernest Guenther Baade were very strong and Captain von Liebenstein of the German Navy had an excellent ferry service across the three-mile-wide straits.

When Patton and Montgomery resumed operations at the end of July they found themselves condemned to attack side by side against a series of excellent defensive positions held by first-class troops, whose morale remained unshaken. For neither the British nor the Americans was there great scope for maneuver: German mines and demolitions harassed their every move. Montgomery had 13th Corps on the right and 30th Corps on his left. In Seventh Army, 45th and 1st US Divisions led first, later giving way to 3rd and 9th Divisions. The weather was hot and the dust appalling. There were many casualties from malaria. Patton, determined at all costs to reach Messina before Montgomery ordered 'a sustained relentless drive until the enemy is decisively defeated'. Inevitably the terrain channelled the advance along narrow lanes or on to ridges and up valleys devoid of cover and in full view of the enemy's artillery observers. Air co-operation on the fronts of both armies left much to be desired. There were far too many incidents of friendly aircraft bombing their own troops.

At Troina, the 1st Division, slogging along rugged hillsides to outflank immensely strong German positions, fought for four days the bitterest battle of the campaign. Allen and his deputy commander were at loggerheads; their men were tired and beginning to feel that they were being called upon to shoulder more than their fair share of the fighting, having been through the whole Tunisian campaign. When Troina finally fell, on 6 August, Patton had to take the decision to relieve both the divisional commander and his deputy.

Exasperated by the delay and worried by the increase in the numbers of men evacuated with battle neurosis, Patton staged three amphibious hooks. But incredibly only enough landing craft could be provided to lift a battalion group. The first run was abortive. The second landed at Brolo on 11 August just behind 29th *Panzer Grenadier* Division's position on the north coast road. It was not strong enough to cut off the battlegroup opposing 45th Division but, helped by the fire of American warships, accelerated the German withdrawal by 24 hours. Regrettably the *Panzer Grenadiers* made up lost time by hanging on to the next position for an extra day. For the night of 15 to 16 August Patton staged a further end run, this time of regimental size. It was a blow in thin air. The Germans had fallen back to the next position and the amphibious force waded ashore not behind the Germans but to meet the leading infantry of 3rd Division.

A similar landing by No. 40 British Royal Marine Commando, just south of Scaletta on the same night, found nothing to stop it except demolitions. But so impeded was their advance into Messina that when they entered the town on the morning of 17 August they found that the 7th Infantry Regiment of 3rd US Division had arrived ahead of them, and Patton had won the race to Messina. He had already accepted the surrender of the city at 1015. There was an element of anti-climax in these last days of the campaign. Despite the overwhelming strength of the Allies in the air and on the sea, Hube had succeeded in evacuating nearly 40,000 German troops with 9,605 vehicles, 47 tanks, 94 guns and 17,000 tons of ammunition. It was a miniature German version of Dunkirk in which typically they had saved a much greater proportion of their heavy equipment than the British. In addition some 62,000 Italians had escaped across the straits.

Baades' 350 dual-purpose anti-aircraft guns had maintained a barrage described as 'heavier than the Ruhr', over the four evacuation routes starting on 11 August, along which 140 small craft plied. From 13 August, von Liebenstein decided to risk working by daylight as well as by night. Losses were remarkably light. Surprisingly, the Allies did not realize until 14 August that the Germans were pulling out. Judged objectively by professional standards, Hube and von Liebenstein were the winners of the race to Messina.

Kesselring was astonished that the Allies should have failed to secure an overwhelming victory, in the last week of the campaign, by landing another amphibious force on the toe of Italy, seize the ferry terminals at Reggio and hamstring the withdrawal across the Straits of Messina. The Allies had ample reserves of troops in North

Africa. Their navies could have provided the landing craft if they had been asked and would not have hesitated to bring their big ships within range of the coastal batteries if ordered. They had unchallenged superiority in the air which they failed to concentrate over the straits.

Finally, Adm. Cunningham was not prepared to risk his warships in the straits at night; the only other foolproof method of disrupting the frantic Axis ferry service. There was no capitulation in Sicily because, before the landing, no agreement had been reached as to whether or not Husky should be followed by the invasion of Italy. It was therefore left to Eisenhower to exploit his victorious landing as he thought fit. As operations progressed, Alexander failed to use his initiative, awaiting orders which never came.

Nevertheless, the campaign had achieved its major objects. It had unseated Mussolini. It had set in motion the negotiations, through the British embassies in Lisbon and Madrid, which would soon result in the Italians abandoning their German Allies and surrendering their fleet. The Mediterranean was at last freed for Allied shipping and in particular for tankers from the Persian Gulf.

Much battle experience had been gained and many good commanders, notably Bradley, had come to the fore. Casualties, at 9,000 British and 8,735 American, were remarkably light. The Germans had lost 32,000 and the Italians 132,000, mostly prisoners of war. And the threat the Allies now offered to 'the soft underbelly of Europe', although it did not swing Turkey over to the Allied side, undoubtedly induced Hitler to call off the ghastly battle of Kursk (Zitadelle) on 14 July and to divert reserves from the Russian front in order to retain his grip on the Italian mainland. The experience gained in the invasion of Sicily, especially in amphibious operations, ensured the success of Overlord, the invasion of North West Europe, less than a year later.

Admin Box (1944)

Patrick Turnbull

In the latter half of 1943, Lieutenant General Renya Mutaguchi, Japanese Fifteenth Army commander, and his divisional commanders, were summoned to a series of conferences at Lieutenant General M. Kawabe's Burma Area Army HQ in Rangoon. They were there to discuss operations for the coming year. The outcome of these meetings – held under considerable strain, since Tokyo had impressed on Kawabe the necessity for speedy victory in Burma to boost flagging morale at home – was the plan for an offensive – Operation *U-Go* – on the central Assam/Manipur front by Fifteenth Army. Its objective was the destruction of 4th Indian Corps, and an advance to the Bengal frontier. It was somewhat optimistically reckoned that success – and it was stressed that failure could not even be contemplated – would spark off a general uprising in India against the British Raj, and what Japanese propaganda was to refer to as 'The March on Delhi'.

But it was not until the general outline of *U-Go* had been approved by Southern Area Commander, Field Marshal Count Hisarchi Terauchi, that a rider for a preliminary, diversionary, operation in Arakan – code name *Ha-Go* – was added. To be carried out by 55th and elements of 54th Divisions under the recently arrived Lieutenant General Tadashi Hanaya, the object of this limited offensive was to pin down, and draw off, British-Indian reserves from the main central front.

Japanese hopes of a resounding victory in Burma seemed justified. Early in 1943, an attempt by 14th Indian Division to recapture the Arakan port of Akyab ended in ignominious failure. Though eventually expanded to six brigades, 14th Division had failed to break through the Japanese defenses on the Donbaik Chaung. This was at no time manned by more than two battalions and by as little as two companies to begin with. Finally, in early April, the recently arrived Japanese 55th Division staged a brilliant counter-attack, driving 14th Division and its replacement 26th Indian Division back well beyond their starting point.

At his Ranchi HQ, Lieutenant-General Sir William J. Slim, commanding 15th Indian Corps, who had been called to take charge of the Arakan battle too late to do other than convert a threatened rout into an orderly withdrawal, was one of the very few not afflicted by the wave of pessimism following this disaster. The jungle, he insisted, was the reverse of the desert – infantry, not tanks and fighter-bombers dominated the battlefield. Therefore until the British copied the Japanese, and made the infantry the *corps d'élite*, there could be little or no hope of victory. Acting on his own theory, Slim devoted the Monsoon period to the intensive battle training of his reconstituted Corps, 5th and 7th Indian Divisions, commanded by Major-Generals Harold R. Briggs and Frank W. Messervy, both veterans of East Africa and the Western Desert, and Major-General C. G. Woolner's 81st West African Division. The Bihar jungle was the scene of tough exercises under active service conditions. Non-combatants – clerks, storemen, wireless operators, cooks – had to join in, warned by Slim that 'in the jungle every man, whatever his job, is likely to find himself engaged in hand-to-hand fighting with the enemy.'

When the 1943/44 dry season operational plans were made known, 15th Corps was gratified to learn that it was to be given the opportunity for a 'return match'. While in Manipur, 4th Corps' activities were to be confined to 'a limited offensive up to the Chindwin', 15th Corps was entrusted with the job of clearing the enemy forces from Arakan, and (possibly) to follow up with the capture of Akyab.

As the Monsoon abated, 15th Corps left Ranchi *en route* for Arakan, but within a few days of setting up his HQ at Bawli Bazar, Slim was called upon to command the newly created Fourteenth Army. His place was taken by Lieutenant-General Philip Christison from 33rd Corps in Southern India.

Arakan's terrain, as 14th Division had found to its cost, heavily favored the defense. A narrow strip oriented north–south, it is bounded on the east by almost trackless jungle-covered hills, the Arakan Yomas and Arakan Hill Tracts, on the west by the Bay of Bengal. What flat ground there is consists of *padi* fields and swamps, furrowed by wide, swift-flowing rivers, and tidal creeks. The Mayu Peninsula, ending at Foul Point opposite Akyab Island, is bisected by a dragon-crested spine of hills, the Mayu Range. Its precipitous jungle slopes rise to 2,500 ft in places, crossed east–west by only three passes. The Goppe and Ngakyedauk Passes were barely fit for mules. But the Tunnels Road was suitable for mechanical transport. This was formerly the track of a narrow-gauge railway connecting the little port of Maungdaw on the west, at the mouth of the Naf river, with Buthidaung on the east, at the point where the tidal Mayu River became the Kalapanzin, and cutting through the range by two short tunnels. This road – 16 miles in length – was the line on which Lt. Gen. Hanaya had chosen to base his main defenses, giving the whole area the picturesque name of 'The Golden Fortress'.

Since the destruction of the Japanese, rather than territorial gain, was Christison's objective, this concentration of enemy forces suited him. Advance was on a two-divisional front, 5th Division to the west, 7th Division to the east of the Mayu Range. After making a wide sweep to the east the West Africans were moving on a pack basis down the Kaladan Valley, acting as a flank guard. Christison had met with only token resistance. By the New Year of 1944, he was poised for the first phase of his main attack; an assault on the Golden Fortress's western bastion, Razabil, just south of Maungdaw. The choice of Razabil as the first objective was dictated by the urgency of securing Maungdaw with its harbor facilities, since, till the port became operational, 15th Corps had to rely on a single supply line. This was a road on the west, coastal, side of the Mayu Range – built the year before by 14th Division's engineers.

In the first week of January, 161st Brigade (5th Division) began to probe the outer edges of the Razabil defensive network. They met such determined opposition that what was hoped would be the decisive blow could not be delivered until 26 January. Though preceded by heavy aerial and artillery bombardments, and supported by the Corps' armored unit – the 25th Dragoons in Lee-Grant medium tanks – hardly any progress was made. After three days of abortive assaults, heavy losses – the Sikh company of 1st Battalion,

1st Punjabi Regiment was reduced to 21 men, while the 4/7th Rajputs lost 27 killed and 129 wounded – Christison had to call a halt.

He planned to switch the main weight of his renewed offensive to 7th Division's front. With this in mind he ordered 25th Dragoons to move to the eastern side of the Mayu Range via the Ngakyedauk Pass, by then capable of taking heavy vehicles, thanks to superhuman efforts on the part of the engineers, since the track included a rise and fall of 1,000 ft in three miles. It was renamed, and since immortalized, as the 'Okey-doke' Pass.

At the same time the eastern exit in the neighborhood of Sinzweya was converted into an administrative area, with petrol and ammunition dumps, vast stores of rations, spare parts, and medical supplies, manned by Ordnance, Service Corps, Transport and Medical units. Its defense against possible tip-and-run raids was entrusted to the 24th Light Anti-Aircraft/Anti-Tank Regiment, commanded by a peace-time solicitor, Lieutenant-Colonel R. B. 'King' Cole.

By 3 February the redeployment was almost complete. The offensive was fixed for 7 February. But unimpressed by the fact that he was outnumbered, and anxious to repeat his division's earlier triumph, Hanaya struck first.

For the tactical execution of *Ha-Go* he detailed a force of roughly 8,000 men under the command of Major-General T. Sakurai (commander of 55th Divisional Infantry Group; an appointment without equivalent in the British Army) which was split into three columns. Though the main striking force of these three was designated *Sakurai* Column, it was in fact led by Colonel S. Tanahashi. He was a dynamic officer who had played a major role in 14th Division's discomfiture. At the head of his own 112th Infantry Regiment, supported by an artillery and an engineer group, his task was to pass through the advanced posts of 114th Brigade (7th Division) strung out on the eastern bank of the Kalapanzin, capture Taung Bazar, then, crossing to the west bank, swing left and 'destroy the enemy forces between the Kalapanzin river and the Mayu Range' – the bulk of 7th Division.

While this was in progress, a smaller column of only one battalion under Colonel Tai Koba, marching rapidly north, was to make a left-wheel near the Goppe Pass, cross the Mayu Range, and establish a road block across 5th Division's lifeline – the Bawli Bazar–Maungdaw road. To pin down forward troops while these outflanking movements were being performed, two battalions, under

Colonel Doi, were to mount a series of holding attacks along the entire front from the Kalapanzin to the sea.

Relying on the element of surprise, *Sakurai* Column took almost suicidal risks when it set out from Kindaung at 2300 on 3 February. In a solid phalanx, 16 men abreast, together with their mules, 112th Regiment marched down a narrow valley, barely 400 yards wide, knowing that units of 114th Brigade were in positions on the ridges on either side. The gamble paid off, helped by the fact that the night was moonless and by a thick mist blanketing the valley. Brigade HQ reported hearing the sound of movement, of muffled voices and the clanking of mule accoutrements, but assumed that the sounds came from Royal Indian Army Service Corps supply columns taking advantage of the cover of darkness. As a result, the few troops installed in Taung Bazar were taken completely by surprise at first light, and wiped out.

By evening most of 112th Regiment had crossed to the west bank. There were indecisive skirmishes with elements of 89th Brigade, divisional reserve, the next day, but by 7 February Col. Tanahashi had reached the Ngakydeauk Pass. Meanwhile Col. Koba had descended on the coastal road near Briasco bridge, spanning the widest of the tidal *chaungs* (Burmese name for watercourses), and overrun a Field Park and a Workshops Company. With only a weak battalion, Koba could not hold his ground. A morning counter-attack beat him back to the foothills after he had set fire to most of the vehicles and damaged the bridge. The vital road was soon reopened, even though convoys were often under fire. Tanahashi on the other hand was soon firmly astride the Ngakyedauk, successfully separating 5th and 7th Divisions.

Christison appreciated from the start the primary importance of retaining the Sinzweya administrative area – from then on referred to as the 'Admin Box'. Having first directed 26th Indian Division, then in reserve at Chittagong, to move forward with all haste, he telephoned Maj.-Gen. Briggs of 5th Division instructing him to order 9th Brigade commander, Brigadier Geoffrey C. Evans, to move immediately with all his spare troops to the Box, and hold it to the last.

Even with the reinforcements Evans could count on in the next hour or so, the chances of holding out against attacks by crack Japanese troops, with a garrison composed mostly of non-combatants, seemed slender. Furthermore all advantages of the terrain lay with the attacker. Never foreseeing that it would become the scene of a major battle, it had been chosen for its flatness and absence of scrub and jungle. Even so, the clearing measured a bare 1,200 yards in diameter. This meant that not a square inch would be out of range of small arms fire. It was a tactical trap; a bowl, the bottom naked, the sides and encircling rim densely covered in jungle. Ammunition dumps piled up at the foot of the western face of a central 150 ft hillock – 'Ammunition Hill' – were particularly vulnerable.

Evans realized that the defenders would be under direct observation, while the enemy could approach unseen to the edge of the perimeter from any direction. Again, although every man from storeman to cook and muleteer would have to take his place in the defenses, there would still not be enough to provide an unbroken line. Concentrating, therefore, on the most likely lines of enemy attack, Evans was obliged to leave the eastern and north eastern sectors dangerously open, counting on his mobile reserve – the veteran 2nd Battalion, The West Yorkshire Regiment, commanded by the experienced Lieutenant-Colonel 'Munshi' Cree, and two squadrons of the 25th Dragoons under their second-in-command, Major Hugh Ley.

Frantic digging was in progress when at 1430 on 6 February, a ragged group appeared from the jungle to the east. It was Maj.-Gen. Messervy, with a number of his staff. His 7th Division HQ had been overrun that morning. Throughout the afternoon more stragglers arrived, giving hair-raising accounts of their escape. By evening Messervy, in touch with his brigades, had resumed command, but had also made it clear that the defense of the Box was to remain in Evans's capable hands. At 1700 the latter called a conference of his commanders, to issue his orders. His instructions were brief – 'Stay put and keep the Japanese out.'

By evening the garrison had been strengthened by the arrival of two companies of the 4/8th Gurkhas – the other two temporarily lost in the jungle – a mortar battery of 139th Field Regiment RA, and a battery of 6th Medium Regiment. A troop of the 8th (Belfast) Heavy Anti-Aircraft Regiment, and two batteries of the 24th Mountain Regiment were ordered to abandon their positions to go to the Box immediately.

During the afternoon there was a low-level attack by Zero fighters, causing a number of casualties, but it was not until midnight that a first assault was delivered at a sector held by an Indian mule company. The muleteers – many of them Pathans – showed exemplary fighting discipline, holding their fire, unflustered by streams of tracer, until the yelling Japanese were almost on top of them. No determined attempt was made to press home the attack – possibly because no serious opposition had been expected.

The next day, the 7th, started badly. A patrol up the Ngakyedauk Pass was ambushed – making clear the fact that the Japanese had severed communications with 5th Division. Then, the two companies of the 4/8th Gurkhas, ordered to occupy a low jungle-covered hillock dominating the 'eastern gate' of the Box (Point 315), were violently attacked before reaching their objective. Forced to give ground, their retreat was followed up by the Japanese who smashed through the perimeter – only to be halted by fire of the 25th Dragoons' 37 mm and 75 mm tank guns, then hurled back in confusion by 'D' Company of the West Yorkshires. The Gurkhas were later able to seize and dig in on part, but not all, of Point 315.

The afternoon and evening were quiet, but in the early hours, Evans heard 'rifle and automatic fire . . . accompanied by screams and cries for help.' A Japanese raiding party had infiltrated the forward positions and entered the Box hospital. This had been set up in three widened and deepened dried-up *chaung* (watercourse) beds, at the foot of a hillock known as MDS Hill. The raiders' first act was to bayonet a number of the badly wounded as they lay helpless on their stretchers. Six doctors were then lined up and shot. An Indian doctor, Lieutenant Basu, escaped by smearing himself with blood and feigning death. When, at dawn, a counter-attack was organized, the survivors, wounded and medical staff alike were used as human shields to protect the retreating Japanese, only to be later murdered in cold blood.

Another crisis developed at first light on 9 February. During the night before, the Japanese manhandled their 70 mm infantry howitzers to the crest overlooking Ammunition Hill, and opened up on the ammunition dumps. Fires were soon raging and crates of .303-in and 25-pounder shells exploding with much the same effect as if the enemy had reached the center of the Box. Having recovered from the surprise, the Dragoons and the Belfast Heavy AA troop engaged the Japanese guns in an extraordinary artillery duel over open sights. As the Lee-Grant's 65 mm (2.56-in) armor was proof against 70 mm shells, it was not long before the enemy batteries were silenced and the surviving crews killed by the West Yorkshires' bayonets. But the burning dumps continued to explode. It was not until late afternoon that the last fires were extinguished.

Early the next morning a partial revenge for the hospital murders was exacted. Regimental Sergeant-Major J. Maloney, 'B' Echelon, 9th Brigade, with a handful of HQ clerks, normally considered too old for combat, held a trench overlooking a dried-up *chaung*. At around 0200 the sound of approaching footsteps and voices was heard. Seconds later, about 50 Japanese headed by an officer came into view. Maloney held his fire until the enemy was level with his trench. Then, at his word of command, a volley of grenades and Sten submachine-gun bursts at point blank range wiped out the entire party. It was a minor victory all the more appreciated when it was found that the dead men's packs were stuffed with hospital rations.

The first phase of the battle was over by 11 February. The Japanese had failed to destroy 5th and 7th Divisions. They had not even thrown them into confusion. On the other hand, rather than mopping up the Golden Fortress, 15th Corps was grimly battling for survival. Yet Christison had sound reason for optimism. Convoys, though sometimes under fire, flowed down the vital coastal road. The isolated *Koba* Force, driven back to the foothills, faced starvation. The Box, despite furious onslaughts, showed no sign of being swamped or running short of supplies. From the 10th the defenders were receiving all they needed, not only in the way of vital rations and munitions, but also such comparative luxuries as toothpaste, mail, rum and spare clothing, by air. Allied Troop Carrier Command's Dakota transports flew a total of 714 sorties, dropping 2,300 tons of supplies without which, starving, their guns silent, Evans's men might well have suffered the fate of Dien Bien Phu.

Over the rest of 7th Division area, the three brigades – 114th, 33rd, and 89th – had dug themselves into subsidiary boxes, and though individually cut off were holding fast and hitting back hard. The advanced elements of 26th Indian Division were in contact with detachments of *Sakurai* Column north of Taung Bazar, while the army reserve, 36th Indian Division was at sea, *en route* from Calcutta to Chittagong.

At this stage, common sense dictated that Hanaya withdraw what was left of Sakurai's original force to the still intact Golden Fortress. His offensive had been halted. Soon his badly mauled regiments would be faced by no fewer than four divisions, two of them fresh to the battle. He had no armor, and the enemy was master of the skies. But he suffered from the besetting Japanese military sin – inflexibility. Once having issued an order, he could not tolerate the thought of modifying it. Furthermore his overconfident dispatches had encouraged Tokyo to broadcast – 'It's all over in Burma.' Sakurai was ordered to press home his attacks with even greater vigor, an order with which he endeavored, loyally, to comply. From 10–18 February the fate of the Box often hung in the balance.

A major onslaught was directed at 'Artillery Hill', held by 24th LAA/AT Regiment, a bare 200 yards from Evans's HQ. Hidden by the jungle, the Japanese advanced to within yards of the gunners' trenches. Their first charge swamped the position, and a hastily organized counter-attack was thrown back.

By then Evans and his commanders had devised a plan for tank/infantry co-operation. It was to prove brilliantly successful. As the infantry left their starting position, the tanks saturated their objective with high explosive, until when, within assaulting distance, the infantry commander fired a Very light. This was the signal for the tanks to switch from HE to solid shot. The Japanese were still forced to keep their heads down, but as they pushed forward the attacking infantry were not exposed to fragmentation. The tanks were, therefore, able to keep up their fire until the leading sections, as close as 15 yards to the enemy, could make the final charge with grenade and bayonet, before the stunned Japanese had time to react. Employing these tactics, 'A' Company of the West Yorkshires, supported by a squadron of the Dragoons, retook 'Artillery Hill' by evening. Only 24 hours later this maneuver was repeated with equal success, after the Japanese had overrun 'C' Company Hill, overlooking the eastern exit of the Pass.

After ten days of ceaseless harassment, Evans could congratulate himself that not one of the Box's main positions had fallen. But casualties were mounting alarmingly. Continuous night attacks, though not on a major scale, were achieving the dual purpose of stopping the exhausted defenders gaining any proper rest and necessitating a frightening expenditure of ammunition.

Efforts were also made to knock out the tanks which at night moved into laager – their machine-guns dismounted and laid on fixed lines. The most determined attack was launched at daybreak from Point 315. Caught in the open by the combined fire of tank guns and machine-guns, the Japanese were all slaughtered before covering half the distance.

Outside the Box, there were setbacks. On the 13th, the 2/1st Punjabis and 4/7th Rajputs (123rd Brigade of 5th Division) overran the key to the Ngakyedauk Pass – the fortified hill feature Point 1070. It seemed the relief of the Box could be only a matter of hours. But during the night, the company of the 1/18th Royal Garwhal Rifles, ordered to hold the position, was subjected to continual *kamikaze* attacks. At dawn the survivors were hurled back down the slopes, leaving the feature firmly in enemy hands. On 10 February a gallant attempt by three companies of the 1st Lincolnshire Regiment (26th Division) failed to clear Point 315 overlooking the 'eastern gate'. One of the company commanders, Major Ferguson Hoey, earned for himself a posthumous VC in this clash.

By the 19th, though the garrison had been strengthened by the 4/8th Gurkhas and the 2nd King's Own Scottish Borderers, general conditions in the Box were deteriorating. The hospital was a shambles as the wounded piled up. Flies by the million infested the primitive wards where the two surgeons labored without rest in the most unhygenic surroundings imaginable. Ammunition proved a constant source of anxiety. Dumps were repeatedly hit. In trying to put out a fire threatening to destroy the entire stocks, 'King' Cole was badly wounded. He refused to leave his post till the siege ended.

On 21 February, however, Point 1070 fell at last to the 2/1st Punjabis, led by Major Sarbjit Singh, holder of the DSO and Bar. This successful assault opened the way to the Box, and 123rd Brigade moved steadily down the Pass, mopping up isolated posts. At last forced to admit failure, Hanaya was obliged to cancel *Ha-Go* while 7th Division's brigades, breaking out of their individual boxes, fanned out into the jungle in an attempt to cut off Sakurai's withdrawal.

But the ordeal of the Admin Box was not over. Night attacks redoubled in their ferocity. On the night of 21/22 February the Japanese broke through to within 20 yards of 9th Brigade HQ. The morning revealed 30 enemy dead ringing the officers' mess. That same morning, a suicidal charge came near to swamping Cole's HQ. But for the murderous volume of fire the Box could then command, it might well have succeeded.

dawn on 24 February Maj.-Gen. Briggs, who had spent the 123rd Brigade HQ, climbed into a Lee-Grant. The last

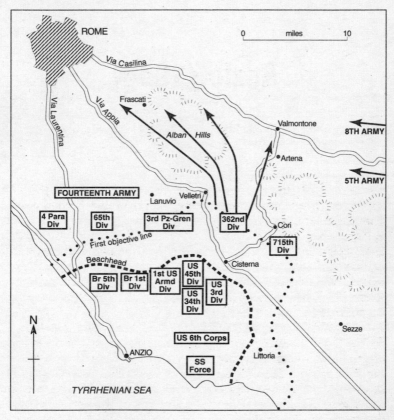

5.9   The Battle for Anzio, May 1944

also presented problems – there were more of them than the Allied High Command had anticipated and they had built a belt of fortifications, the Gustav Line, which, with the advantages of climate and geography, gave a coherency to their defensive line.

The only progress made by the Allies' two armies, the American Fifth on the Mediterranean coast and the British Eighth on the Adriatic, was by set-piece assaults on strongly defended river lines. These were time-consuming to prepare and costly to execute. Since they had run up against the heavily fortified and well-manned Gustav Line, in early November, they had made virtually no progress at all.

It was against this background that plans for a seaborne invasion behind enemy lines were formulated. The Allied High Command realized that their earlier belief that the Germans would withdraw into northern Italy if heavily pressed was mistaken. General Dwight D. Eisenhower and General Sir Harold Alexander concluded that the enemy's current strategy of making the Allies win Italy inch by inch could be countered only by a seaborne landing in their rear. Alexander, in a directive dated 8 November 1943, laid down a timetable for such an operation: it entailed a triple offensive, first by the Eighth Army to attract German reserves onto the Adriatic coast, then by the Fifth to set the campaign again in motion towards Rome and finally by an amphibious force, landing near Rome, and linking up with the Fifth across the river lines of the Mediterranean coastal plain.

The plan was orthodox – but the means to execute it were not immediately available. The plan demanded ships – but shipping was needed for the coming Normandy invasion and had been directed to leave the Mediterranean forthwith. Troops were needed – but the necessary divisions were also wanted for Normandy. They had begun to leave and had not yet been replaced by the Free French Army which was training in Africa. The plan, code-named Operation Shingle, was, after a feasibility study, therefore shelved. But it was not forgotten. As the winter fighting increased in severity, and apparent futility, the idea of a seaborne descent near Rome came to appear more and more attractive to the protagonists of the original plan, notably Alexander and the British Prime Minister, Winston Churchill.

On 22 December, Shingle was officially canceled; but on the following day Churchill insisted that it be reconsidered. As the author of the heart-breaking Gallipoli failure of the First World War, Churchill's credentials to oversee a revived Shingle did not bear close examination. But he could well argue, if anyone had drawn the parallel, that the Allied position in the Mediterranean was far more favorable in 1944 than in 1915, and that while the objectives Shingle proposed were more limited than those intended at Gallipoli, the investment required was proportionately more limited.

He could and did argue that Shingle made excellent military sense – if only by contrast with the fighting along the narrow mountain roads and hidden defiles to which their current strategy condemned the Allies. There they were unable to disguise either the timing or the direction of their strokes and could gain little advantage from their air superiority. A seaborne movement offered the chance to surprise the enemy both in space and time, and to force him into battle on the naked plain, while supplying themselves plentifully along the broad highway of the Mediterranean. If the enterprise were successful, moreover, it would give them Rome, put the Balkans under threat and perhaps – and here the argument became speculation – even make Operation Overlord, the invasion of Normandy, unnecessary.

It was vital, if Shingle was to work at all, to delay the transfer out of the Mediterranean of the necessary shipping. By direct intervention with President Roosevelt, Churchill secured the retention, first until 15 January, then until 5 February, of 68 Landing Ship Tanks (LSTs), the basic requirement of a seaborne landing. As planning proceeded, Churchill made further requests for logistic supplies and secured them. At the same time he ensured that there was no wavering in the enthusiasm of Gen. Alexander, Army Group Commander, and of Lieutenant General Mark Clark, the American Fifth Army Commander, two of the three men who had chosen Anzio for the invasion point.

In fact, this was unlikely for both had strong, if different, personal motives for wishing the operation well. Alexander, disappointed that Eisenhower, rather than himself, had been appointed Supreme Commander, was resolved that the struggle for Italy should not become a stalemated sideshow – and, without Shingle, it threatened to become just that.

Gen. Clark, who felt that his Fifth Army had not been given the credit its achievements deserved, ached for the glory of capturing Rome. His American and British divisions, now pinned to the river valley floors by fire from the heights of the Monte Cassino range, were 100 miles short of the capital. He counted on Shingle to release them from the stalemate of the plains below Monte Cassino. Seventy miles separate Anzio from Cassino, and Clark thought that, given determination, the launching of concentrated offensives from the two spots should break the German defense on the west coast and lead him into Rome.

This was Churchill's hope and, having secured the necessary equipment for his commanders, he left them to put the plan into action. But the translation of military decisions into effect always reveals unanticipated difficulties. The preparation of Shingle was no exception. Further staff study suggested that the Germans would probably react strongly to the initial landing, and that a two-division landing, for which Churchill had had to commit his personal prestige to find the shipping, might not survive the onslaught. Further shipping, and more men, had to be found to land with three divisions.

The final order of battle, therefore, included, besides the British 1st and American 3rd Divisions, the American 45th Infantry and 1st Armored Divisions, as well as members of American Parachute and Ranger and British Commando battalions. The whole was to be subordinate to a Corps headquarters – the US 6th Corps. This was debatably too small to handle the operations of a force though it had grown from the initial planning figure of 24,000 to a final 110,000. Doubts also emerged about the efficiency of the force itself. At a dress-rehearsal in Naples Bay, both the 1st and 3rd Divisions mishandled their equipment, losing 40 DUKWs (the amphibious lorry on which cross-beach mobility depended) and two batteries of 105 mm howitzers; while the naval parties operating the landing craft made a series of unnerving mistakes. It was not a happy augury.

These events badly worried the already anxious commander of 6th Corps, Major General John R. Lucas. An experienced and respected soldier, Lucas was not happy with the Anzio idea and expressed his doubts strongly and continuously in the pages of his diary. He described himself as unusually tender-hearted for a general in an army which traditionally took a blood-and-guts attitude to the prospect of casualties and he feared he was leading, or worse, sending, his men to their deaths.

Hence his growing obsession, which the weeks of preparation made more and more apparent, with reinforcement and re-supply considerations. It was vital, in his view, that the men in the beach-head should have ashore with them the largest possible quantity of armored vehicles and artillery pieces as well as ammunition and petrol. Given these, and air support, the beach-head troops would be able to repel a counter-attack, which Lucas expected to come swiftly and in strength, despite the different story from Allied Intelligence.

His superior, Mark Clark, an abler man than his posturing suggested, was sensitive to Lucas's anxieties, which to some extent he shared. Consequently, he refrained from giving Lucas the additional responsibility for a decisive breakout from the bridgehead. The orders Clark issued to 6th Corps were for 'an advance on' the Alban Hills – the feature which commands the land between Anzio and Rome – not for an advance 'onto'. This ambiguity gave Lucas the option of halting his troops short of the objective if he felt that the strength of enemy reaction threatened his beach-head.

The Germans were also making their plans. The *Luftwaffe* Field Marshal Albert Kesselring had been preferred to Field Marshal Erwin Rommel for the post of Commander-in-Chief in Italy because of his optimistic and generally correct forecasts of the way events would go in the peninsula. Kesselring was aware that, over a distance of several hundred miles, both his flanks were vulnerable to amphibious assault. He suspected, however, that the coast near Rome was the most likely spot for the Allies to choose, and he accordingly kept two divisions in reserve nearby. They were divisions he could hardly spare, for his armies were at full stretch on the Gustav Line, the cross-peninsula German defense line from which, Hitler had ordered, there was to be no retreat. He was aware, moreover, that even this reserve might not be sufficient to contain a landing, for the Allies might outnumber it before reinforcements, which could only come from southern France, the Balkans and the far north of Italy, had arrived.

On 18 January, and only after receiving the firmest assurances of the unlikelihood of an Allied landing in the near future, from his own and higher Intelligence sources, he agreed to send his two reserve divisions from Rome to Cassino, where Clark's Fifth Army had just succeeded in forcing the line of the Garigliano. General Heinrich von Vietinghoff, commanding the Tenth Army, had represented this breach of his sector of the Gustav Line as potentially catastrophic, for it threatened to outflank the Monte Cassino position on which the whole line hinged. Kesselring was persuaded by his entreaties. What neither appreciated was that Clark, though delighted by this local success, had planned it precisely as a means of clearing the Anzio area of anti-invasion forces. Once Lucas was ashore Clark then intended to launch a major offensive from the Garigliano bridgehead, directed towards Anzio, the Alban Hills – and Rome. The Germans in between, if the strategy proved right, would flee, or surrender to the pincer attack.

Thus Lucas, thanks to an excellent stroke of strategic deception by his own commander, and to the enemy's faulty Intelligence, was to enjoy the most precious advantage an amphibious force leader can obtain – total surprise. His fleet of 240 landing craft and 120 warships made an undetected overnight passage northwards from Naples. In the early morning of 22 January 1944, they began to unload the two assault divisions – 1st British, 3rd US – on beaches left and right of Anzio without interruption from the enemy, apart from some light, uncoordinated cannonading by a few, soon-silenced, batteries. By midnight nine-tenths of the assault force (36,000 men and 3,000 vehicles) had come ashore for a loss of 13 dead, and had established a perimeter between two and three miles inland. The Allied air forces had flown 1,200 sorties, but had not been opposed. The port had been captured intact and was now ready to receive supplies from the fleet which swung untroubled at anchor offshore.

Lucas felt, and rightly felt, that he had done well. Indeed as landings go, the first day at Anzio must be regarded as an impeccable exercise in that particular tactical form. But success did not dispel Lucas's anxieties, for he now feared a major enemy counter-blow. Rather than cripple the expected counter-attack by seizing commanding terrain features and communication centers inland, he redoubled his concentration on building up his base and perimeter defenses. For the next few days the American 3rd Division pushed cautiously inland, the British 1st Division, on its left, rather more boldly. But both failed to reach their obvious objectives, Campoleone and Cisterna, from which an advance on the Alban Hills must start; and neither was urged onward with any fervency by Lucas. He was now directly under the eye of Clark, who had come to see the bridgehead for himself. But even the presence of his superior could not stir him to action, though his diary reveals that it rattled him. When he was ready, he wrote, he would move. He thought he would be ready by 30 January.

Unfortunately for the Allies, the Germans were ready also. If there was one thing at which their staffs had always excelled, it was the rapid improvisation of defense and counter-attack, and this war had given them all the practice they needed at perfecting their procedures. The landing had badly frightened them – Vietinghoff was so alarmed that he had begged Kesselring for permission to withdraw from the commanding Cassino position. But *Oberbefehlshaber* (CinC) Kesselring was not prepared to fall for Clark's ploy and had kept his nerve. He called up his *Alarmeinheiten* and settled down to win the build-up. *Alarmeinheiten* were 'paper' units, formed from clerks, drivers and men returning from leave and all German headquarters had plans to form such units in an emergency. German headquarters in Rome sent several of these units to the beach-head in the first day.

Meanwhile Kesselring called for better units to replace them. From the north of Rome came the 4th Parachute and Hermann Goering *Panzer* Divisions, from southern France the 715th Division, from the Balkans the 114th, from northern Italy the 92nd, 65th and 362nd Divisions and the 16th SS *Panzer* Grenadier Division. From the Gustav Line, which Kesselring insisted should be thinned out, came the 3rd *Panzer*, the 1st Parachute and the 71st Divisions. Not all of these were destined for Anzio. Kesselring had two crises on his hands, the Anzio beach-head and Cassino, and needed a surplus of units with which to juggle his way to stability. By 30 January, he had extracted sufficient force from these newly liberated reserves to have sealed off the Allied bridgehead and to be contemplating his own counter-offensive, which he had scheduled for 2 February.

Lucas's methodical preparation of his offensive had thus ensured the conditions which would bring about its failure. For his postponement of the capture of Cisterna and Campoleone had not only allowed the Germans to build up opposition on the commanding ground of the region; it had also betrayed to them what would be the thrust of his eventual attack. If he had taken these two places, his forces could have moved north-west, north or north-east. Cramped within his original bridgehead, with the coast on his left and the impassable inundations of the Pontine Marshes on his right, he could only attack straight ahead, due north. There the Germans sat and waited for him.

Lucas planned his H-hour, the attack time, for 0200 on 30 January. This timing gave his infantrymen some advantage for darkness covered the movements of the Ranger force he sent along the dry bottom of the Pantano ditch towards Cisterna. But it also concealed the Germans assembling stealthily to ambush them. Of the 767 Rangers who set out on this commando penetration only six returned to the Allied lines. Their comrades of the 1st and 3rd Armored Divisions, following up in a conventional assault, suffered fewer casualties but nevertheless met desperate resistance and, after an advance of three miles in three days, which brought them near to the vital Highway 7, were forced to a halt. Only in the British sector was there promising progress. Here the veteran 1st Division had launched its attack from the positions it had won a week before near Aprilia. (These were 'The Factory', as the Allies termed the Fascist model farm at Aprilia, and 'The Flyover', a road bridge which carried a minor road over the Anzio–Campoleone road.) But it was made at a dreadful price.

The countryside beyond the roads was a maze of gullies or 'wadis', and these denied protection to the flanks of 3rd Brigade, attacking up the Anzio–Campoleone highway. Its three battalions suffered crippling casualties as a result; one, the 2nd Sherwood Foresters, was almost completely destroyed in the final assault on Campoleone. 'There were dead bodies everywhere,' wrote an American visitor to the scene, 'I have never seen so many dead men in one place. They lay so close I had to step with care.'

Though the offensive of 30 January to 3 February was a failure, in that it cost much for little, fell short of a break-out and further depressed Lucas at a time when buoyant leadership was becoming vital to the beleaguered invaders, it did achieve some positive gains for the Allies. It had inflicted heavy losses on the Germans, who had no way of suppressing the fire of the Allied fleet or of chasing off the Allied air force, and had no real answer to the enormous weight of artillery the Allies could always deliver. Both the British 1st and American 3rd Divisions had penetrated Kesselring's main line of resistance; and the upset they had inflicted forced him to postpone the planned 2 February offensive.

The Allied assault had averted a German offensive designed to obliterate the Anzio beach-head and sweep the Allies into the sea. But if it had avoided another Dunkirk, Colonel General Eberhard von Mackensen, whose Fourteenth Army Headquarters Kesselring had brought down to oversee German operations at Anzio, was determined not to let the Allies consolidate. He inaugurated the first of a series of minor attacks, beginning on 3 February, and chiefly aimed at the British Campoleone salient. All of these were designed to win the ground necessary for a major counterblow. He was unable to shift the British on 3 February but kept them subjected to fierce pressure which, the next day, drove them out of most of their salient. On 7 February, Mackensen attacked towards 'The Factory' and nearly took it. On 9 February he got possession of Aprilia village but failed to take 'The Factory'. It fell next day, was retaken by the British in a counter-attack, and only passed finally from their hands on 11 February.

The British 1st Division had now lost half its strength, which, as always in a stricken infantry formation, meant much more than half its infantrymen. A fresh British division, the 56th, had landed but it was needed elsewhere in the line and could not relieve the 1st and much of its front was, on Lucas's orders, taken over by the American 45th Division with the aim of fighting the Germans out of Aprilia. Lucas seemed to have little fight left in him. Badgered by his superiors, Mark Clark and Alexander, who were frequent visitors to the beach-head; menaced by the appointment of a deputy commander, Major General Lucian K. Truscott, whom he suspected of being kept ready to supplant him, and more distressed than ever by the losses his men were suffering, Lucas busied himself in supervising the preparation of a 'final beach-head line' of strongpoints, roughly following the perimeter of 24 January.

In the coming days the men at the front, who were also frantically strengthening their tactical positions, were to feel grateful for the sense of refuge the final beach-head line offered, for on 16 February Mackensen unleashed his long-prepared offensive. There were two thrusts to the assault. The first, against the British 56th Division on the west bridge-head, was by 4th Parachute and 65th Divisions. The other, and main attack, by 3rd *Panzer* Grenadier, 114th and 715th Divisions, with 29th *Panzer* Grenadier and 26th *Panzer* Divisions in support, was down the now dreadfully familiar axis of the Campoleone–Anzio road. It was spearheaded by a unit chosen specially for the task by Hitler – the *Infanterie Lehr* Regiment. Successor to the *Lehr* Regiment of the Kaiser's Guard, and brother to the mighty *Panzer Lehr* Division, the regiment looked, and thought itself, invincible. In fact, the only activity it was accustomed to were military displays and demonstrations in Germany. It was inexperienced and overconfident. Exposed to the defiant resistance of the American 45th Division, astride the main road, the Nazi regiment suffered heavy casualties and its discipline broke.

Equally disappointing – for those like Hitler, who believed in fancy solutions to old-fashioned military problems – was the performance of the 'Goliath', a remote-control miniature tank. Each of the 13 such tanks used in the attack carried 200 lb of explosive at 6 m.p.h. for a maximum distance of 2,000 ft. It was supposed to open a cheap way into an enemy position. All bogged down on the approach; Allied fire destroyed three, the rest were dragged ignominiously back to base.

But these two reverses were compensated by substantial German successes on 16 February. Although unable to deploy their tanks off the road, just as the Allies had been unable to do during their offensive, Mackensen's divisions had inflicted substantial loss on the British 56th and American 45th Divisions and driven both back. Behind one of their rare air bombardments they continued their attacks during the night, and attacked again early next morning down the main road. A further air raid in mid-morning aided their advance, and by noon they had secured a salient two miles deep and one mile wide in the 45th's front. They were now only a mile from Lucas's 'final beach-head line'. But the Germans could get no farther. Lucas found reinforcements, which included the battered British 1st Division, and with the help of these troops the 45th held out.

The Germans, by the end of the day, had suffered such heavy losses in their engaged infantry battalions, which were down to a rifle strength of 150 to 200 men, that Mackensen persuaded Kesselring that he could only continue if allowed to commit his *panzer* reserve – 26th and 29th Divisions. Kesselring, though not optimistic, agreed. They attacked next day, 18 February, and managed to enlarge the breach considerably. Then they ran into a carefully prepared fire-trap laid on by a 'grand battery' of 200 Allied guns. Five times the Germans tried to break through the barrage that the battery laid around the Flyover on the Anzio road but each time their formations were broken up and driven back. Still they rallied to attack again in the afternoon and only the committal of final Allied reserves from Anzio, and more self-sacrifice by the 45th and 56th Divisions, turned back the assault.

The Germans had very nearly broken through on the afternoon of 18 February and Mackenson continued to attack, at a lower intensity, for the rest of the month. But after 18 February both he and Kesselring accepted that their offensive must end. With the cessation of the great Allied attack on Cassino on 13 February, the reason for the German offensive had gone. They had also, with 5,000 casualties in five days, run out of troops and supplies were low.

The Allies too had suffered heavy losses in men. But their supply line, though occasionally interrupted by the new German radio-controlled glider bomb – most spectacularly when the ammunition-ship *Elihu Yale* was blown up – was never broken and continued to provide ammunition in a quantity the enemy could not hope to match. Profusion of ammunition, after stark bravery, was the principal reason for the Allies' survival in the beach-head. After 20 February the German commanders tacitly accepted that the continued existence of the beach-head was a situation they would have to live with.

For the Allies, however, mere survival fell rather short of a victory. It was enough to satisfy Lucas, but not his superiors who, in the aftermath of the German winter-offensive, promoted him out of his command and into obscurity. With his departure, and the Germans' exhaustion, the beach-head relapsed into a lethal slumber. Maj. Gen. Truscott, who could have won the ground Lucas dared not grasp for, was ironically compelled to oversee a prolonged period of siege-warfare – something for which his predecessor was perfectly fitted.

Yet perhaps it was still not Lucas's sort of battle. For despite the lack of movement on either side, Anzio remained a place of death, the death of young soldiers whom Lucas had cherished more deeply with each day of battle. And the deaths they were to suffer, in this gentle Italian landscape, warming to the spring, were those of a different war in another country – the deaths of soldiers of the First World War in the trenches of Flanders. For at Anzio, as at Ypres, the lines ran within grenade-throwing distance of each other, and men spent their days, throughout the 'lull' of March, April and May, pressed against the earth walls of their bunkers, listening for the distinctive discharge noises of short-range weapons and bracing themselves to withstand the shock of the explosion. Rest, when it came, took tired units no more than three or four miles from the line where shelling, which at least they were spared 'up front' by their proximity to the enemy, was a constant harassment and killer.

There was also the German propaganda barrage. Its message meant nothing to many soldiers; to others it was demoralizing and provocative. Radio broadcasts from Rome warned of the danger and horror of further fighting and encouraged desertion. Leaflets fired over in shells alleged unfaithfulness on the part of wives and girlfriends at home – leaflets for the British troops spoke of English girls enjoying themselves with the Americans encamped in 'Merry Old England' while, for the American soldiers, the villain was the archetypal Jew. One of the most effective leaflets carried the chilling legend, 'The Beachhead has become a Death's Head' and showed a map of Anzio over which a skull was superimposed.

All who survived the 'lull' at Anzio testify to the tension, caused by constant alarms and persistent sense of claustrophobia, they experienced within the perimeter. When orders came, on 23 May, to break out and meet the spearhead probing north from Monte Cassino, they were greeted with the sort of genuine enthusiasm soldiers rarely accord the prospect of risk. The Allies had been too long at Anzio. It had proved no short-cut from the path to Rome.

Ought Anzio to have worked? Mark Clark thought so; Alexander thought so; Churchill continued to think so, long after the war's western focus of effort had moved out of the Mediterranean. Were they all wrong? It depends whether one wants a tactical or strategic answer to the question. Tactically, there seems little doubt that Lucas might have seized the high ground between the beach-head and Rome – the Alban Hills – had he pressed on hard from his perimeter in the first three or four days after the landing. But equally there seems little doubt that to have pressed on farther, to Rome itself, would, even though the city lay temporarily undefended, have resulted in the destruction of his Corps.

Hitler's snap judgement about Anzio was that it betrayed an Allied reluctance to risk a cross-channel invasion and he was willing in consequence to release reserves from much farther afield than usual to crush the landing. Given this reaction, Lucas's caution looks justified. But, his critics argue, bolder action would have frightened the Germans into thinning out the Cassino front which, in turn, would have heightened the chance of the Allies breaking the Gustav Line and dashing to his rescue.

That argument shifts the debate from the tactical to the strategic level. Its validity is dubious also – Cassino and Anzio are so far apart (about 70 miles) that the two Allied forces, given their strength relative to each other and to the enemy's, could not mutually assist each other. A much stronger punch at Cassino, a much bigger landing at Anzio, a weaker Tenth Army, a slower, smaller reinforcement by

Hitler – any of these would have turned the trick for Mark Clark, Alexander, Churchill, perhaps even for the depressive Lucas. But these alterations in the strategic equation presuppose a major revision of priorities in the Allied plans for the conduct of the war in 1944. Not only was there no such revision but American opinion, at the highest level, was rockfast against it.

Roosevelt and Marshall were determined to transfer the focus of Allied war-making out of the Mediterranean and into Normandy, agreed to Anzio with bad grace and resolved to concede it with no more than would pacify Churchill. Given their attitude, the 70 miles between Cassino and Anzio were unbridgeable by any Allied effort. Hitler's hopes and fears – fears that he might be about to lose both the Balkans and Italy; hopes that a brutal extinction of the Anzio beach-head might deter the Allies from risking a landing elsewhere – determined that the Germans would give Lucas and Mark Clark no help either. It was this combination of enemy determination and Allied lack of enthusiasm which robbed the Anzio operation of its chance of success and made the subsequent battle so terrible.

Monte Cassino (1944)

E.D. Smith

When I first saw the monastery it was intact, an ancient and magnificent building set on the top of the steep slopes of Monte Cassino. It dominated the surrounding countryside. As we drove towards the battlefield, at every turning, at the top of every crest, there was the monastery getting bigger and clearer. On a cold February morning in 1944 it presented a noble sight with the pale winter sun shining on the glass of its windows and the great towers and dome outlined against the grey sky.

During the next two weeks, at a comparatively safe distance from the monastery and the town of Cassino, I acted as a supernumary liaison officer, and was a spectator, removed from the fierce struggle that was taking place on the hills across the Rapido valley. Some two or three miles away from our vantage point we could see and hear the battle being waged in the ruined town, among the rocks and scrub on the ridges under the shadow of the monastery, against the background of Monte Cassino, and, to the north, the towering snow-capped peak of Monte Caira where the French wrestled with the elements as well as stubborn German defenders.

Under a clear sky on the morning of 15 February and with token opposition only from the Germans, an armada of bombers made their appearance over the monastery and for four hours wave after wave of bombs pulverized the building; the planes dropped their bombs from heights between 18,000 ft and 10,000 ft. It was an impressive and awe-inspiring spectacle. Even from our remote vantage point we found it difficult to envisage anyone surviving the punishment being meted out. Then, to add to the destruction, the Allied artillery began to batter away as soon as the bombers had returned to their bases. By now the monastery looked like a gigantic decayed tooth and in our innocence most of us thought it would never dominate the valley again. We were wrong. Without scruple, the Germans were now able to use the ruins for defense.

German paratroopers constructed loopholes in the ruined walls from where they could fire in several directions. Artillery and mortar observers kept a ceaseless watch from posts that gave them a perfect view over the terrain below, the ground over which Americans, British, Indians and Poles hurled themselves against defenses until the monastery was abandoned on 17 May 1944.

On 7 March the call came for me to join my battalion, 2/7th Gurkha Rifles, which was holding a position on the hills north of Monte Cassino. The journey forward was on foot and it is etched clearly in my memory. The track up the hills, little used by day, was the life-line of the battalions from 4th Indian Division that were holding the sector around Snakeshead Ridge. Up and down this crude path worn out of the mountainside, went everyone and everything. New, clean soldiers going up, prematurely old bedraggled men returning; some wounded, others acting as escorts to mules. The mules were moving in both directions, being urged on by Italians, Indian and the occasional British voice. How we depended on those mules in Cassino! There was no other way of getting rations, ammunition and other stores up the mountains to the forward positions. It was a dangerous, uncomfortable walk.

The noise of gunfire never stopped. Far behind Mount Trochhio, on the south side of the valley, we could see the flashes of the Allied guns. Ahead we could hear the thump of the German artillery replying, and the sound of tearing silk as the shells flew above our heads in both directions. Occasionally a shell or mortar exploded on the rocks nearby or in a ravine which magnified the noise: no wonder that the climb seemed an eternity though probably it took us less than three hours to reach battalion HQ.

Mules and men, eventually we arrived at our various destinations. The journey up was over. Little did I guess that it would be five weeks before I walked down that trail, all hope of victory gone, our battalion having suffered many casualties, and not one inch nearer

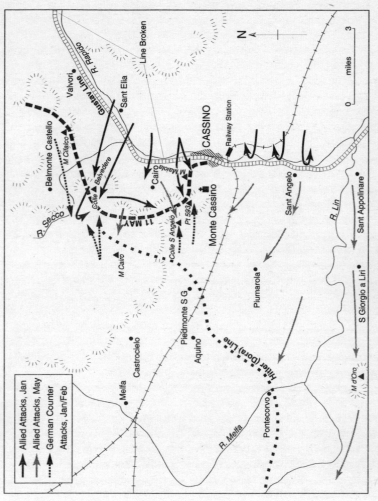

5.10 *The Battle for Cassino, January–May 1944*

that battered hulk of a monastery. Within those five weeks, two fine and experienced Divisions, one from New Zealand and the other, the 4th Indian, were to take such a hammering that neither formation ever reached maximum effectiveness again. Fortunately the future was not to be disclosed to us when I joined 'A' Company which was then in a reserve position.

The Company was not holding or defending any ground. The Gurkha soldiers were sheltering in holes behind rocks or beside man-made stone 'sangars' from the snow, sleet, winter wind and the equally unwelcome shelling. It was not long before I had constructed my own stone shelter, my place of refuge, and thus we stayed seemingly forever, though my diary tells me it was only a week. Rarely did we move far from our cramped shelters unless for the call of nature or for some pressing military chore.

Visits to toilets had to be postponed until evening. Then, at dusk, it was a common sight to see small groups of bare hindquarters in the semi-darkness, their owners fervently praying that they might be allowed to complete the proceedings in peace before the shelling started.

Our tactical role was to be ready to move up to reinforce any one of the three forward companies which were in position on the early slopes of the hill. Fortunately no one attacked those localities while I was serving with 'A' Company. This was just as well, because a move forward in full view of the monastery by day would have been impossible and by night the path would have been difficult.

We had been told that a third attempt to capture Monte Cassino was to be launched under the code name 'Bradman', but winter struck with all the violence of a fresh enemy so that the attack was postponed from day to day because there was no chance of aircraft even flying, let alone carrying out pinpoint bombing against Cassino town. Friend and foe, German, British and Indian, clung to exposed positions on those mountains during the worst storm in an Italian winter which held us all in its icy grasp. Long-drawn-out days, followed by nights of activity meant that the morale and physique of our Gurkhas was severely tested. I wrote in my diary:

Each night we pray that the following morning will bring a change in the weather, a respite from the rain and snow and the endless vigil that is never a quiet one because the whine and crump of the guns and mortars continue by day and night.

As day succeeds day, anxiety about the next attack has changed into a desperate longing to do anything rather than sit for ever undergoing an ordeal that tests minds and bodies alike.

Such a winter could not go on for ever, even at Cassino, and on 13 March the sky began to clear and the prospects looked brighter. We were told that the long-postponed attack was due to begin on the 15th morning: it was to be preceded by a bombardment of Cassino town by over 500 bombers. Next day dawned clear and at 0830 wave upon wave of bombers arrived, to begin pounding the town which was soon shrouded in billows of smoke and dust. It was a terrifying exhibition, even to us cowering down in our foxholes below Point 569. After a few minutes I felt like shouting – 'That's enough!' but it went on and on until our ear drums were bursting and our senses befuddled. Several bombs fell astride the company position and I found myself shouting curses at the planes.

It's no fun being bombed by anyone, but the feeling of bitterness at being bombed or shelled by your own side is beyond description; the sight of friends killed or mangled by the mistakes of friendly supporting arms arouses the deepest of emotions in the hearts of front-line soldiers. That evening I wrote in my diary: 'What an inferno is Cassino now! Dear God – take pity on those men, if there are any survivors in the town, which I doubt.'

In spite of that terrible ordeal, many German paratroopers survived amongst the collapsed walls and the deep craters caused by the bombs. The German High Command decided to stand firm and, although casualties were heavy, they had been less than expected in proportion to the damage caused by the aerial bombardment. The battle went on. Next day, Maj. Beckett would not let us carry out the mission which had been given us by brigade HQ. Already he had seen too many costly attacks, all of which had ended in failure. Moreover, he was deeply concerned about the safety of Castle Hill itself: an active fighting company of Gurkhas near at hand and ready to help his defenders would be of far more use than another broken band of men who, he knew, would eventually trickle back like their unfortunate predecessors. He refused to let us commit suicide and told brigade HQ accordingly. As a consequence, I lived to write this story.

Later that afternoon a direct hit by a heavy German shell caused one of the castle walls to collapse, engulfing and burying several

Essex soldiers under the rubble. Without hesitation their comrades, British, Indian and Gurkha, began tearing at the stones in an attempt to save their lives. After a few minutes came German paratroopers from foxholes, some only 75 yards away, to join in the rescue operations side by side with our soldiers. In the middle of the Cassino battle there began an unofficial and very local 'ceasefire'. Friend and foe worked together, talked and exchanged cigarettes. My company commander spoke German fluently and he learnt that the enemy's view of Cassino was very similar to ours – it was Hell, the weather bloody, and the end impossible to predict.

It is not surprising that this incident remains clearly in my mind, truly an extraordinary commentary on the senselessness of war. My Gurkha orderly summed it up by saying that the 'Dushman' (enemy) were so like 'our Sahibs' that he wondered if there had not been a mistake somewhere! Why were we not all fighting the Japanese instead? However, his comments and the rescue operations were brought to an abrupt end by the Allied artillery which, for some inexplicable reason, opened up: the German snipers scuttled back and almost as if someone had said 'Let battle commence,' we were shooting away at one another once more. A few men were never released from the rubble.

I was ordered to return and brief 'A' Company who were still waiting at the foot of Castle Hill. Not wishing to retrace my steps along the slippery path at the top of the deep ravine, I sought another route. I met four Indian soldiers, Sikhs, who were hiding behind some rocks on the stony hillside. Their faces reflected fatigue and cold. I greeted them cheerfully, even jauntily, but their hearts were heavy. I asked them the quickest way down to the bottom of the hill. One huge Sikh replied that there was a short cut along the ridge but on this they had lost several men from accurate sniper fire. The alternative path that would take longer, was the slippery precipitous mountain track that I had used before. 'One way you get shot, Sahib, the other you slip to your death.' And he grinned without humor.

Being impetuous and wishing to carry out my mission as soon as possible, I decided to take a chance and dash down the track that snaked its way along the ridge to the base of the hill. I waited and waited. All was quiet. Nothing moved on the path below. Nothing appeared to be moving in the town – indeed there had been a lull in the fighting for some time although, behind me, the sound of battle around the castle continued as fiercely as ever. I rose to my feet at the top of the hill and charged down the track: nothing mattered but to get to 'A' Company. It seemed as if I was going to be lucky when something flicked off my black side-cap as I threw myself behind a rock. I lifted my head and saw the bullet mark. The bullet had only just missed my head. Something had prompted me into diving for cover. It was a cold day, but in a second I was covered in sweat. Cold sweat. Everything seemed to stop: the noise of battle, the guns. Probably less than a minute or two passed. It seemed like an age. I crawled forward and willed myself to make another dash. I prayed with great sincerity, prayed for speed. I prayed that the sniper would think I had already been hit. Into the open, zigzagging down the track at the fastest speed I had ever attempted. Once again the crack, crack, a blow on my haversack and then the safety of another rock. Breathless, I lay as dead until a glance at my watch spurred me on, this time to safety. The Gurkhas welcomed me, surprised to find that I was alive because they had seen me drop twice on the track above.

It had been an exciting day, but it was not yet over. While the company remained at the foot of Castle Hill in close support of the besieged garrison, I was told to make my way through the town and report to brigade HQ to act as liaison officer and, possibly, return with fresh orders. After dark my Gurkha orderly, Rifleman Rambahadur Limbu, accompanied me as we scrambled a way down to the battered Cassino below us. It was not long before I realized that the landmarks that had appeared to be so prominent in fading daylight, from an observation point on the hill, were not nearly so easy to find in pitch darkness among rubble and ruins. After about 10 minutes I was convinced that we were lost. Unfortunately, Rambahadur and I could not agree on the direction we should be taking. We appeared to have gone round in a complete circle but Rambahadur had no doubts whatever: he was sure he knew the way and so, against my better judgement, I agreed to let the Rifleman lead. The town, or the remains of it, was strangely quiet after a day of close-quarter fighting when the noises of machine-guns and grenades had continued to pay testimony to the bitter struggle that was being waged in Cassino.

The two of us shuffled and groped an uncertain way around walls, skirting bomb craters, and scrambling over piles of stones. Occasionally we heard voices or smelt cooking which wafted out of the darkness from improvised cellars and hiding places. It was quite impossible to tell who was friend and who foe: occasionally we saw movement at a distance. Suddenly a dark form appeared in front of Rambahadur and challenged him – in German. As Gurkha and German stood frozen in mutual surprise, I fired at the enemy sentry with my tommy-gun, saw him drop, hit by the burst of fire. We dashed down the remains of an alleyway to throw ourselves behind a wall. Within seconds, several Germans, who had been cooking or eating their evening meal below ground, were shouting furiously at each other and shooting at random. Fortunately no one came to look for us and after about five minutes all was quiet.

This time I took the lead and soon we recognized one of the lost landmarks and, without any further incidents, located brigade HQ. Here we were told to rest but although I was near the end of my tether, the clamor of battle and the nervous strain was too much for me: I could not sleep so back I went to the improvised Operations room where the brigadier informed me that 'A' Company would be returning before dawn. I was to guide them to a quarry nearby which was to be our temporary position until further orders. Rambahadur and I spent some considerable time searching for the best route before meeting them at the outskirts of the town. There was no sleep for any of us that night.

'A' Company had been withdrawn into reserve because a German force had infiltrated its way down the large ravine behind Castle Hill in an attempt to isolate the British defenders by cutting off supplies of food and ammunition. The quarry afforded us some protection from intermittent shelling and mortaring which increased in intensity during the afternoon. As darkness fell, the Germans rushed up to hold a sector and, for the rest of the night, both sides fired indiscriminately at one another without any apparent gains in territorial possession. The next day, 21 March, proved to be just as dangerous – the pressure never relenting for one moment. Throughout the morning the Germans kept up their shelling of our position while we tried to construct stronger defenses and to cover any gaps with mines. By now we were so exhausted that even sleep became impossible. I have never been a good sleeper and I was so wound up that I thought madness was close at hand even if I managed to survive German fire and bullets. Nature eventually saved me when I was going round the company's positions after three sleepless days and nights. My legs buckled under, I hit my head and passed out. At the Regimental Aid Post, the Indian doctor who had already supplied sleeping pills without success, soon diagnosed my comotose state. Events did not let me sleep for more than six hours, but I was restored to sanity again.

So it went on, the merciless shelling and mortaring that claimed many victims. 'A' Company was near the end of its tether. Our Gurkhas' normal resilient cheerfulness, their toughness, their fatalistic attitude towards life generally, all these admirable qualities that make them such magnificent soldiers had evaporated. This was not their kind of soldiering. It provided no opportunities for them to get to close grips with the enemy: for hour upon hour they were targets for mortars, shells and the banshee screams of the *nebelwerfers*. In retrospect, I wonder if we could have held on for another 24 hours, but fortunately our ordeal was nearly over.

During the morning of 22 March, the shelling of our positions became more intense and accurate. It was an inferno all day but early in the evening came the news that saved the lives of the survivors – and our sanity. Later that night we were to move back to rejoin our own battalion which had been resting while we were being hammered.

For five hectic days and nights we had been on detachment away from the 7th Gurkhas. My chief recollection was the noise that never stopped. It was to be two days before we recovered our spirits. Fortunately our colonel decided to send us back to act as reserve company again, while the other three rifle companies held the front line near the Snakeshead Ridge.

Unbeknown to us, however, the generals above had realized that 4th Indian Division was exhausted and would have to be withdrawn. We had shot our bolt and had little to show for our efforts. Our friends of the 1/9th Gurkha Rifles, still clinging to the isolated position on Hangman's Hill, were ordered to begin their withdrawal after dark on 25 March. By a miracle they made their way down the hillside and through German outposts without any major incident. Eight officers and 170 Gurkha ranks abandoned Hangman's Hill without relief: later the Germans claimed to have counted 185 dead Gurkhas in and around their old position, the price that battalion paid for the nine days spent under the walls of the monastery.

And our turn was soon to come. In the early evening of 25 March, an advance party from the Lancashire Fusiliers arrived to begin the take-over of our positions. For me the relief could not have been delayed because by that time I was suffering from a nasty bout of diarrhea. In my diary I wrote: 'Now very weak – how long can I continue?' Next morning brought confirmation that we were to be relieved by 78th British Division during that night, a complicated and dangerous operation of war because the German outposts were, in some places, less than 100 yards from ours. And then we faced a long march back across the valley of the Rapido to our waiting transport.

The distance was probably less than five miles, but during the time in the front line many men had hardly walked at all for six weeks. We had been cramped in foxholes, we were unfit, mentally exhausted, and many of our soldiers had lost their willpower. Even though the ordeal was nearly over, the fact did not seem to be understood. The Germans did little to hamper or harass us – indeed I believe they were relieving their own units but this was not known at the time. All we knew was that our group of dejected, tired soldiers, had to be across the valley before the sun rose the next morning. No one looked back. They just stared ahead with eyes that seemed to see nothing and kept on following the man in front, trying to force one foot past the other.

Never will I forget that nightmare of a march. Officers, British and Gurkha, shouted at, scolded, cajoled and assisted men as they collapsed. At times we had no alternative but to strike soldiers who just gave up; all interest lost in everything, including any desire to live. By dint of all the measures we could think of, most of our battalion reached the waiting transport and survived to fight another day, elsewhere, in Italy.

Cassino for us was over – a few weeks later it was to be over for the Germans as well. The third battle had been a grim struggle with few prisoners being taken, by either side, with every yard contested and no quarter given. Like many others who fought at Cassino, I remember how the decencies of war were observed to an astonishing degree. There were many examples of feelings, akin to comradeship, recounted by soldiers who fought at Cassino. Many wounded men survived because stretcher bearers were allowed to carry out their missions of mercy under the Red Cross flag in the forward areas: the contestants had a mutual respect and understanding of each other's problems. The German High Command's cautious claim to a victory was a true assessment because their defenders had won the battle: it was a victory, however, dearly bought because their losses were as distressingly high as ours.

When we left Cassino, the monastery still glowered down at us, an impregnable fortress. The ruins did not fall to any direct assault or succumb to the heaviest weapons available to the Allies. Monte Cassino continued to dominate the lives of the soldiers that fought under its shadow.

Omaha Beach (1944)

Nigel Bagnall

'You guys going to stay here until you're all dead? Like to see me attack alone?' The American lieutenant rushed towards the barbed-wire entanglement and blew a hole in it with an assault charge. 'Come on, let's go!' Three hundred exhausted men of the 1st US Division, 5th Corps, death staring at them on their bitterly contested toehold of Nazi Europe, flung themselves after the lieutenant. At last the Americans began to move forward from the slaughter of 'bloody Omaha' beach on D-day 6 June 1944, the first day of the Allied invasion of Europe.

At 2130 on Sunday 4 June Group Captain Stagg, senior meteorologist, reported to General Dwight D. Eisenhower, Supreme Commander Allied Forces, and his senior commanders that the bad weather, which had already forced one postponement of the Allied invasion, was improving.

A rain front over the planned assault area was expected to move in two or three hours and the clearing would last until Tuesday morning. Stagg expected the high winds to moderate and cloud conditions to permit bombing during Monday night and Tuesday. But a heavy sea would still be running and the cloud base might not be high enough to permit spotting for naval gunfire.

Eisenhower faced a critical decision. Such weather conditions would be barely tolerable but to decide on another postponement meant that the invasion would have to wait until 19 June before the right conditions of moon, tide and daylight returned. The choice was between a risky disembarkation of troops or postponement – and the longer the delay, the shorter the likely duration of good campaigning weather on the Continent. Admiral Sir Bertram Ramsay, Commander-in-Chief Allied Naval Forces, reminded the Supreme Commander that he had to make a decision within half an hour for by then, if the invasion were to go ahead, orders must be given to the first convoys to sail. Turning to General Sir Bernard Montgomery, Ground Force Commander, Eisenhower asked, 'Do you see any reason for not going on Tuesday?' 'I would say Go,' replied Montgomery. At 2145 Eisenhower announced his decision. 'I am quite positive we must give the order . . . I don't like it, but there it is . . . I don't see how we can do anything else.'

With the decision taken, the detailed plans that had been prepared over the years began to unfold. The invasion would take place along the 40 miles of coastline between the Vire Estuary and the River Orne in western Normandy. This area offered several advantages – it was near the ports in southern and south-western England, the beach-heads would be within Allied fighter range, it was near the major port of Cherbourg which, hopefully, would be captured early, and Allied air attacks on railways and bridges might be able to isolate the assault area and slow up the arrival of German reinforcements and supplies.

The initial assault landings were to be carried out by 21st Army Group, under Montgomery's command, consisting of six reinforced infantry divisions landing from the sea, and three airborne divisions. On the east was the British 2nd Army and on the west the United States 1st Army. Five beach-heads had been selected – 'Utah' and 'Omaha' for the United States 1st Army; 'Gold', 'Juno' and 'Sword' for the British 2nd Army.

A number of factors governed the selection of D-day. A long period of daylight would enable maximum advantage to be gained by Allied air power. The moon should be nearly full to aid the airborne troops and the tide should be strong. Beach obstacles would thus be fully exposed at low water and vehicle landing craft could ground, unload and withdraw on a rising tide. The requirements of the actual timing of the landing, H-hour, also entered into the calculation.

The Allies had learnt several lessons from previous amphibious operations and these had to be considered in selecting H-hour. At Tarawa, the Americans learnt that naval fire support could not be

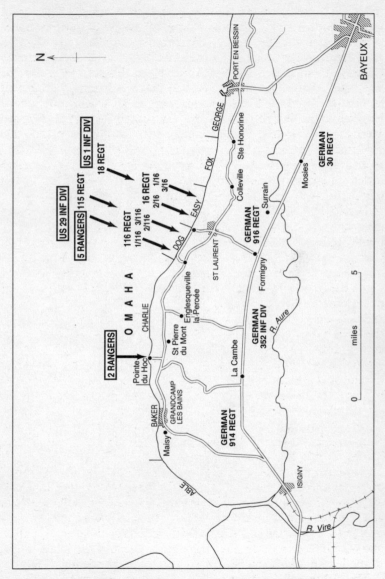

5.11 *The Invasion of Normandy – Omaha Beach, 6 June 1944*

relied on to neutralize beach defenses, unlocated gun positions, or to provide close fire support for the assaulting troops. Admiral Ramsay studied the full report and observed that 'the heaviest casualties were caused by the failure to neutralize enemy positions during the period immediately before and after the touch down of the assault.'

The final period selected for D-day was between 5 and 7 June and H-hour was to be staggered, varying by about an hour from the easternmost British and westernmost American landings, because of the different tidal and beach conditions.

On the German side, an invasion in the west had been expected since 1942. To protect the 3,000 miles of coastline Germany controlled, an 'Atlantic Wall' was planned. This fortification existed largely in Hitler's mind and though it was good propaganda it was never completed. Their manpower situation was also discouraging. On paper there were between 50 and 60 German divisions in the west but they rarely had more than 25 efficient, full-strength field divisions available at any one time.

The 5th Corps assault at Omaha was planned to extend over 7,000 yards of beach which curved landward in a slight crescent, flanked at both extremities by 100-ft-high cliffs rising almost directly out of the sea. Above high-water mark there was a sloping bank of shingle, in places 15 yards wide, which extended into sand dunes on the eastern two-thirds of the beach. On the remaining western third of the beach, the shingle butted against a sea wall, between 4 ft and 12 ft high.

Behind the dunes, which formed an impassable barrier to vehicles, was a shelf of sand some 200 yards wide in the center but narrowing sharply at either end. Beyond this sand shelf, the grass-covered ground rose sharply to between 100 ft and 180 ft before opening on to a plateau of rolling farm land. Four small wooded valleys extended inland from the beach area to provide natural corridors onto the plateau. Near the eastern end, there was a fifth, less distinct, exit.

Below the high-water mark the beach sloped very gently but with an 18 ft tidal range, some 300 yards of firm sand would be exposed at low tide. Here the Germans had built three bands of obstacles which would be concealed at high tide. None of the bands was unbroken but together the three formed one continuous obstacle over 100 yards wide and 250 yards out from the high-water mark at its seaward edge. The first two belts consisted of waterproofed Teller mines fixed to iron frames and upright logs and the third comprised a series of metal 'hedgehogs' designed to hole assault craft that had avoided the mines.

The German shore defenses at Omaha were based around 12 strongpoints though not all of them had been completed by June. Each of these strongpoints was a small complex of pill boxes, gun casements and firing trenches, surrounded by minefields and wire. Only two of the complexes were bomb-proof. Deep trenches or tunnels connected the various components and there were underground living quarters and ammunition stores. The strongpoints were mainly sited to block the valley exits from the beach though they could also cover the tidal flat and the whole beach with both flanking and direct fire. Machine-gun emplacements, weapon pits, barbed wire and minefields fortified the areas between the strongpoints. In all there were 35 pill boxes with artillery pieces of various sizes and/or automatic weapons, four artillery batteries, 18 anti-tank guns, six mortar pits, 35 rocket-launching sites, each equipped with four 38 mm rocket tubes, and 85 machine-gun nests.

There was no heavy coastal artillery in the Omaha sector and only two batteries of mobile field guns in the immediate vicinity, but there were about 60 light artillery pieces within the strongpoints. The Allies had been informed that the defensive positions were held only by a reinforced infantry battalion, 800 to 1,000 strong, belonging to the 716th Infantry Division. Fifty per cent of these were supposed to be non-Germans. But this intelligence assessment was wrong.

Field Marshal Erwin Rommel, Army Group B Commander-in-Chief, and responsible for coastal defenses between Denmark and the Pyrenees, knew from his experience in North Africa that it was folly to use massed armor against an enemy who had air superiority. If the German army could not fight the Allies on something like equal terms, then its only chance of offering a successful defense was to fight from the strongest natural positions. The battle for the West, Rommel considered, would be decided at the water's edge, and the decision would come within the first 48 hours of the Allied landing. He therefore wanted to move the German armored divisions forward into the coastal areas, so that at least elements of them could intervene.

But Rommel was overruled by von Rundstedt. He was only permitted to make a few moves forward nearer to the coastline. This proved to be very fortunate for the Allied troops at the Omaha beach-head. Allied intelligence estimated that the nearest German reserves to the Omaha sector were two more battalions of the 716th Division, but they judged that it would take them two to three hours to arrive, and then they would be able to do little more than help contain the Allied landings. A full scale counter-attack would have to await the arrival of the 352nd Infantry Division, thought to be in the St Lo–Caumont area some 20 miles farther inland, and the Allies believed that it was not capable of delivering such an attack until the afternoon of D-day.

The objectives of 5th Corps were then laid down with the aim of gaining an adequate foothold or lodgement area as quickly as possible. The assault echelons (an echelon is a formation of troops in parallel divisions, each with its front clear of the one ahead) were to break through the beach defenses within two hours of landing, and then clear the exits leading out through the valley by H + 3 hours. This achieved, 5th Corps' D-day objective was to advance four miles inland and secure the plateau up to the river Aure, where the Corps was to be prepared to repel German counter-attacks. Later 5th Corps was to push southwards towards Caumont and St Lo, conforming with the British 2nd Army on its left flank.

Fifth Corps consisted of three infantry divisions; the 1st Division, which had seen action in the Mediterranean, and the 2nd and 29th Divisions. Since the Corp's subsequent operations were to develop on a two-divisional frontage, it was necessary to land elements of both divisions in the assault echelons, so as to avoid having to pass one formation through another within the restricted bridgehead. There was neither sufficient shipping nor room on the beach to allow both formations to assault at once.

The Corps would then conduct its landing in four basic echelons, the two assault ones each consisting of some 15 waves of landing craft. The first echelon (Force O) and the second echelon (Force B) were commanded by the headquarters of the 1st and the 29th Divisions respectively but were made up from elements of both formations. The 2nd Division formed the third echelon, and a miscellany of units the fourth and last.

Embarkation of Forces 'O' and 'B' began on 31 May and 1 June and both were completed by 3 June. The numbers of men and vehicles involved was enormous – for Force 'O', the first assault echelon, 34,000 men and 3,300 vehicles were loaded into 300 landing craft. Two battleships, three cruisers, 12 destroyers, 33 minesweepers and 105 other ships supplied the escort, minesweeping and fire-support requirement. In addition, 600 vessels of different types were ready for a variety of support and service work. The main convoy of Force 'O' left Portland harbor in Dorset on the afternoon of 5 June and made an uneventful crossing of the English Channel under continuous Allied air cover.

At 0300 the armada arrived at a point 12 miles off Omada. The wind gusted between 10 and 18 knots and waves were 3 ft to 4 ft high. Into this swell the assault craft were unloaded from larger ships. Some were winched down fully loaded, but to get into others soldiers had to scale the scramble nets over the sides of the parent ships. This was a hazardous operation as the craft were tossing and bucking in the heavy sea. The men were heavily laden – each soldier was equipped with weapons, a rubber life-preserver, a gas mask, a first-aid kit, entrenching tools, a canteen, knives and rations and extra ammunition and explosives.

Ten small craft sank almost at once, throwing 300 heavily laden men into the sea. The assault craft circled the transport area, getting into formation. As dawn lightened the sky, the craft edged towards the beaches. Discomfort followed the soldiers as waves sloshed over the blunt bows of the landing craft and they had to bail out with their helmets. Seasickness added to the misery.

The sea also took a toll of the guns and armor that were to follow the assault craft. Thirty-two amphibious tanks were launched too early into the swell and sank within minutes. Some crews escaped, others drowned in their vehicles. Ninety-six tanks were planned to follow the soldiers onto the beaches – a third of that number had now been lost without ever coming under fire. The DUKWs that were to ferry support artillery ashore also ran into difficulties. The small, heavily laden craft foundered – the 111th Field Artillery Battalion lost all but one of its 105 mm howitzers and the 16th Infantry Cannon Company and the 7th Field Artillery fared little better.

With 40 minutes to go to H-hour, when the troops would reach the beaches, the Allied aerial and naval bombardment of the enemy defenses reached a climax. The Allies had a massive air superiority on D-day. A total of 3,467 heavy bombers, 1,645 medium, light and torpedo bombers, 5,409 fighters and 2,316 transport aircraft were stationed in England on 6 June. Against this the Germans could muster only 319 aircraft, of which 100 were fighters. Field Marshal Hugo Sperrle, Commander of *Luftwaffe* Air Fleet III, had requested more aircraft before D-day – the *Luftwaffe* simply could not spare any from the defense of Germany's industrial centers. German naval patrols had been canceled on 5–6 June because of bad weather and the ships stayed in port. In fact the German navy did not consider the weather suitable for an invasion and, because they had no weather stations in the west, they were unable to detect the improvement in the weather noted by the Allies. German E-boats did approach the Allied fleet by accident but the mighty steel shield of warships that protected the invasion force was impenetrable. One German rating, on seeing the Allied force, said in astonishment that 'It's impossible. There can't be that many ships in the world!'

At Omaha, 500 heavy bombers of the US 8th Air Force mounted a concentrated attack on the German defenses. The US battleships *Texas* and *Arkansas* poured 3,500 shells into the enemy positions from their total of ten 14-in, 12 12-in and 12 5-in guns. A variety of fire-support craft softened up the landing areas. But even this did not convince German High Command that the invasion point was between Cherbourg and the Seine and not the Pas de Calais area which, to strengthen the illusion, the Allies had bombed extensively in the days leading up to 6 June.

In the assault craft the cold and miserable vanguard of the invasion, bailing frantically to remain afloat, paused to look up and cheer the flying shells that were to destroy the German coastal defenses. The landing craft moved closer and closer to the shore of occupied Normandy and still no response came from the enemy defenses.

It was a silent prelude to disaster. The naval bombardment had overshot many of the front-line enemy positions. Some had been neutralized but only temporarily. The final aerial bombardment did not deliver a single bomb on the beaches – for fear of hitting their own men the aircraft crews had delayed a few seconds in dropping their bombs. They fell three miles inland. The landing craft, in a strong lateral current, had tended to drift eastward: the landmarks, seen so often in aerial photographs and in training exercises, were shrouded in smoke and dust and early morning mist. And so the troops, trained for specific tasks in their planned landing areas, found themselves in a confused and unexpected situation.

But this was the least of their immediate problems. The German shore batteries opened up, crashing into the bobbing, awkward landing craft. Artillery, mortars and machine-guns thundered all along the four-mile stretch of Omaha beach. Those units whose job it was to ensure that the successive waves of assault craft could beach safely and disembark their men and equipment on the rising tide suffered badly. The special Engineer Task Force was responsible for clearing gaps through the belts of obstacles during the first half-hour of the landing. Only five of the 16 assault ferries carrying the Engineers landed in the correct sectors and of these, three of the teams had no infantry or tank support. Sixteen bulldozers were to have come ashore with the task force – only six reached the beach and three of these were quickly disabled by artillery fire. Much of the equipment needed to mark lanes through the obstacle belts was lost or destroyed.

To add to the Engineers' problems they came in behind schedule and became mixed up with infantry, some of whom sought shelter behind the obstacles the Engineers were intended to blow. The Germans singled them out for special attention, with sniper fire detonating the mines fixed to the obstacles while the Engineers were working on them and mortar fire detonating rows of mines. At the end of the day there were 50 per cent casualties among this special unit.

Despite the difficulties, the Engineers managed to clear six lanes through the belts of obstacles before the incoming tide submerged them. Four of these lanes were in the 16th Regiment's sector and two in that of the 116th Regiment. But only one of these lanes could be marked and this created casualties and confusion as waves of assault craft, unaware of the situation, approached the areas. One craft struck a mine and disintegrated, showering the Engineers with debris and spreading blazing fuel over the water.

On 5th Corps' right flank, the invasion plan was for the 116th Infantry Regiment to land four companies in the first assault wave on each of their four beaches – code-named Dog Green, Dog White, Dog Red and Easy Green. A Ranger Company was to land slightly farther to the right on Charlie beach and from there it was to assault a strongpoint just to the west of Vierville. The 16th Infantry Regiment should also have landed four companies in the first assault wave in Easy Red, Fox Green and Fox Red.

Because of the general eastward drift of the landing craft few touched down in the correct sectors and sub-units became hopelessly mixed. Few landing craft made dry landings, most of them grounded on sandbanks up to 100 yards from the beach and in some places troops were disembarked into water that was neck deep.

F and G Companies came ashore on Dog Red and Easy Green.

Although under heavy fire and disorganized by landing in the wrong place, many of them crossed the 200 yards of tidal flat to shelter behind the sea wall and shingle. Those who stopped at the water's edge were under direct German observation and suffered casualties. The right wing of 5th Corps' assault wave had practically disintegrated and the four companies of the 116th Infantry Regiment were no longer a fighting force. A Company had been cut to pieces on the shore line, F Company was disorganized by heavy casualties, scattered sections of G Company were trying to find their correct sector and E Company had veered widely off course, landing on the eastern extreme of the 116th Regiment, on the left flank.

To the west of the 116th Regiment, on the extreme right flank of Charlie beach, the 2nd Ranger Battalion had suffered severely. Their objective was an enemy strongpoint to the west of Vierville. One of their two landing craft was sunk by artillery fire and the other came under direct machine-gun fire as soon as the ramp was lowered. By the time the soldiers had reached the base of the cliff, 200 yards from the water's edge, only half the 65-strong unit was still alive. By nightfall, only 12 remained.

There were heavy casualties on the left flank, in the 116th Regiment's sector, but the majority of the supporting tanks had got ashore. Four tanks landed on Easy Red, a mile-long beach marking the junction point of the 116th and 16th Infantry Regiments, but only about 100 men landed with them – unfortunate for the Allies, for here enemy resistance was light. E and F Companies were scheduled to land on Easy Red but the bulk of both companies drifted too far to the east. The result was that only elements of these companies, together with part of E Company of the 116th Regiment, came ashore in the right sector in the first assault wave and these were bunched on the extreme eastern part of the beach.

Some of the troops were disembarked in waist-high water but then had to cross a deep channel to get to the beach. This pulled them even farther to the east and though casualties were light, with only two men killed, most of their heavy equipment such as flame throwers and mortars and some personal weapons were lost. Others landing slightly farther to the east were less fortunate – not only were they disembarked in deep water but they came under heavy fire. Only 14 men reached the shingle.

Stiff enemy resistance, faulty navigation and delays contributed to the critical situation that was now developing on Fox Green.

Two companies from the 116th Infantry were scheduled to land in the first assault wave but the bulk of four companies, including elements of E Company of the same regiment, landed hopelessly intermixed in a comparatively restricted sector. Few casualties had been incurred in the final approach to the beach but as soon as the leading landing craft lowered their ramps and disembarkation got under way interlocking enemy machine-gun fire swept the water and inflicted heavy casualties. The survivors struggled to the water line and here, with most of their officers dead or wounded, they stopped.

I and N Companies of the 16th Infantry Regiment, which should have formed the first assault wave on Fox Green, were delayed – and they missed the disaster. I Company drifted widely off course and were an hour behind schedule. N Company was 30 minutes late and landed beyond the eastern limit of Fox Green. The company lost a number of men at sea and during the landing but it disembarked at a point where the tidal sand reached almost to a steep escarpment. This was the only company, of the nine that formed the first assault wave, that was ready to act as a unit.

At 0700, 30 minutes after the first assault wave had landed, a second group of five follow-up waves approached the beaches. These included the support battalions of the two leading regiments and was timed to go ashore at 0740. None of the follow-up assault waves arrived under the conditions that were expected. The tide had risen nearly 8 ft and now covered most of the beach obstacles. Only six lanes through the obstacles had been cleared and these were still not properly marked. The initial assault waves had not advanced beyond the sea wall or shingle and neither the surviving tanks nor the infantry from the first wave were in a condition to provide more than spasmodic covering fire. Nowhere had the enemy defenses been neutralized.

The troops in the second wave were organized, briefed and equipped to do no more than mop up any enemy positions that had been by-passed by the first wave. They were then to move inland, by boat loads, to their respective battalion assembly areas. Only a few sections of the second waves had special assault equipment – flame throwers, demolition charges and bangalore torpedoes for clearing lanes through minefields once ashore.

The troops in the second waves, as they approached the shore, could see the carnage wrought among the first wave. Debris from

sunken assault craft bobbed among half submerged bodies and struggling survivors. Broken or discarded stores, weapons, lifejackets,
equipment of every kind littered the shore line. Silent, wounded
soldiers were grouped among the desolation, many in severe shock.
One sergeant recalled a 'terrible politeness among the more seriously
injured' and a soldier of the 741st Tank Battalion saw a man sitting at
the water's edge, oblivious to the machine-gun bullets that spattered
about him, 'throwing stones into the water and softly crying as if his
heart would break.' Medical orderlies, there to treat the wounded,
did not know 'where to start or with whom'.

On the right wing, in the 116th Infantry Regiment's sector, the 1st
Infantry Battalion had landed only A Company in the initial assault
wave; the other three companies in this wave belonged to the 2nd
Infantry Battalion. The 1st Battalion's three remaining companies
were to come ashore in the second wave on Dog Green in echelon
formation at ten-minute intervals. They assumed that A Company's
assault wave had cleared most of the enemy positions.

At 0700, B Company started to come ashore but it was badly
scattered over an area extending to nearly a mile on either side of
its intended sector. A few assault craft beached in the correct area but
were subjected to the same heavy fire that had decimated A Company
30 minutes earlier. The survivors of B Company struggled ashore to
mingle with those of A Company along the shore line. Only three
widely dispersed groups on the flanks played any effective part in
the subsequent battle.

C Company was scheduled to land directly behind B Company at
0710. A major navigational error prevented it from doing so – and
it was saved the disastrous fate of B Company. The company came
ashore 1,000 yards to the east on Dog White beach. One of its six
assault craft became entangled on the mined obstacle belt and it took
20 minutes of gentle maneuvering before it got free. The remaining
five assault craft approached the shore in reasonably good order but
the vessel carrying the special assault equipment capsized in the
surf when its ramp jammed and the entire load was tipped into
4 ft of water. The unit recovered from this set-back and suffered
only six casualties in disembarking and crossing the sand, largely
because smoke from grass fires in the escarpment obscured enemy
observation. C Company moved up to the sea wall and started to
reorganize.

At 0720 D Company began to disembark having lost two assault

craft, one swamped and the other hitting a mine. The remainder
of the company got no farther than the shore line, having come
under fire as soon as they disembarked. Most of the heavy support
weapons were lost. To add to the disruption, the three assault craft
carrying the battalion command group, the Headquarters Company
and the Beachmasters party for Dog Green were widely scattered
several hundred yards to the west. They came in directly under the
cliffs and suffered heavy casualties in doing so. They stayed in the
same position for most of the day and played no part in co-ordinating
the scattered remnants of the battalion.

The 2nd Infantry Battalion had landed three of its companies
in the initial assault wave – now only G Company survived as
a fighting unit. Machine-gun fire ripped into the ranks of the
supporting H Company and of the battalion headquarters as the
ramps were lowered. Men scrambled for shelter behind disabled
tanks near the water's edge. The battalion commander, together
with his command post and elements of H Company, braved the
fire, running up the open beach to the shingle bank where they joined
the leaderless survivors of H Company. Because of the faulty radio
communications it was over an hour before further progress could
be organized. Eventually an attack by about 50 men was mounted
against the enemy positions in and around Les Moulins, but it was
beaten back to the crest of the shingle bank.

While this was in progress, the four sections of G Company, trying
to move along the beach to get near their objectives on Dog White,
gradually lost cohesion. One by one individuals or small groups
stopped to take cover, only to become mixed and separated as they
progressed westwards along the shingle bank crowded with survivors
of other companies. By the time the remnants of G Company had
reached their correct sector at about 0830, the main action was
already over.

The 3rd Battalion of the 116th Infantry Regiment was scheduled
to arrive directly behind the 2nd Battalion on Dog White, Dog Red,
and Easy Green between 0720 and 0730. But the battalion was ten
minutes late and came in well to the east on Easy Green and Easy Red
along a thousand-yard frontage. Only a few scattered elements of the
first assault wave had landed in this sector. K and I Companies came
in behind them in close formation on Easy Green, and suffered only a
handful of casualties in crossing the tidal flat to the shingle, but having arrived there safely they appear to have become immobilized.

L Company disembarked on either side of the junction between Easy Green and Easy Red, where they met only light enemy fire, which many men seem not to have noticed. M Company landed farther to the east on Easy Red and, encountering enemy fire on first disembarking, they stopped at the water's edge. Eventually, when the rising tide began to push them forward, the whole Company moved to the embankment as a body and, as one of them later remarked, 'the Company learned with surprise how much fire a man can run through without getting hit.'

Although the enemy defenses had not been breached, the second assault group suffered much less severe casualties than the initial one. Altogether five of the eight companies of 116th Infantry Regiment were capable of developing and holding a precarious toe-hold which they had established. Troops who were demoralized and lacked inspired leadership found this supplied when, at 0730, the Command Group of the Regiment, which included the assistant divisional Commander Brigadier General Cota and Colonel Canham began to land on Dog White. Both men were fearless soldiers and could not have arrived at a more opportune moment nor at a better place to influence events. To their left troops were crowded along the embankment of a few hundred yards, while the main Ranger contingent was about to land in the same area. Ahead of them, behind the embankment, smoke from burning grass obscured the enemy's view and rendered his fire largely ineffective.

The experience of the 16th Infantry Regiment was similar to that of the 116th. Although the initial assault wave all landed on Fox Green, leaving the large 2,000-strong force on Easy Red beach with only a handful of infantry operative, the second group started to land, and casualties were high. The main problem was the dislocation of command posts, faulty landings, casualties, the loss of radio sets and the physical difficulty commanders experienced in imposing control. Except for those immediately around them, they could exert little influence over the many men lying against the sea wall – a shelter they were all too reluctant to leave. Behind them the troops could see successive waves battling through the same fierce defense they had been through and the bodies of dead and dying comrades, and in front of them lay the enemy and a beach flat littered with minefields and wire obstacles.

The situation looked critical and further vehicles and support weapons could not come ashore until the exits had been cleared.

But slowly, desperately slowly, inspired leadership and individual heroism began to turn the tide. General Cota and Colonel Canham, the latter already wounded, walked up and down the beach oblivious to enemy fire and bluntly directed officers and NCOs to get their men moving. Slowly groups of men, often from different units, and in other places units of company size, started to move forward supported by the few remaining tanks. Behind Easy Red beach an engineer lieutenant and a wounded sergeant walked forward under fire to clear a lane through the wire obstacles. Their task done they returned and looking down in disgust at the men huddled behind the shingle, exhorted them to get forward before they were killed where they lay. Advances were made in a world of smoke and confusion, each group isolated from its neighbors. An impetus developed, however, as successive penetrations brought a slackening of enemy fire.

The most significant advance in the 116th Regiment's sector came from Dog White beach. Here C Company and the 5th Ranger Battalion were spurred forward by General Cota at about 0750.

German defenses in this area consisted of lightly manned weapon pits connected by deep trenches sited just on the crest of the escarpment. The machine-guns were mainly sited to provide flanking fire down other sectors of the beach, rather than to deal with a direct assault. On the opposite side of the sea wall there was a double apron wire obstacle which had to be breached before the infantry could get through. After an initial setback, a gap was eventually blown by a bangalore torpedo and the infantry started to filter through under cover of heavy smoke from the grass fire drifting eastward along the face of the escarpment.

The leading infantrymen were joined by others who had cut their way through the wire and together they moved forward to the high ground giving access to the plateau. Progress was slow here through fear of mines, and the company advanced in column following an indistinct track. On gaining the top of the escarpment the enemy positions were found to be unoccupied and, after suffering only six casualties since leaving the shelter of the sea wall, the advance was resumed for a farther 200 yards when, still moving in column, the company encountered machine-gun fire from a flank and went to ground.

At 0810 the 5th Ranger Battalion, without knowing exactly what C Company was doing ahead of them, crossed the beach flat after blowing four lanes through the wire and started to climb the escarpment. Heavy smoke forced some of the men to put on their respirators and contact was lost between the various sub-units. However, for the loss of only eight men, the few enemy positions still holding out on the edge of the escarpment were overrun, and, after pausing to reorganize, the Rangers resumed their advance.

By 0830 a penetration 300 yards wide had been made and the last groups of infantrymen were leaving the sea wall. It was not in itself an advance of great significance but similar actions, frequently on an even more reduced scale, were being conducted all along the beaches. These isolated penetrations were then gradually linked together, expanding the bridgehead laterally and, what was of equal importance, giving it some depth so that further reinforcements of both men and equipment could be brought ashore as the beach exits were first cleared and then developed.

On the 16th Regiment's front, a gap opened up by G Company became an exit for movement off the beach during the remainder of the morning. The Regiment's command group landed in two sections at 0720 and 0815. The second section included Colonel Taylor who got his disorganized and leaderless men moving with terse instructions: 'Two kinds of people are staying on this beach, the dead and those who are going to die – now let's get the hell out of here!' As soon as the engineers had cleared gaps through the wire obstacles and scattered minefields, the infantry were organized into haphazard groups and sent forward under the command of the nearest available officer or NCO. As they moved forward through the gap, there was intermittent enemy fire from both flanks and the already congested route became a scene of even greater confusion as leaderless groups stopped to shelter below the crest.

Strenuous efforts by the officers who had landed with the various command groups in the later waves encouraged the troops forward onto the plateau and gradually the bridgehead was extended. Progress inland was aided by a few isolated but determined groups of Rangers who had landed to the flanks of the main assault, and then fought their way forward unaware of what was happening elsewhere. As the penetrations which had been made between 0800 and 0900 started to link up, a new but still fragmented phase of the battle began. German defenses along the immediate coastline had begun to crumble and there were no significant reserves available to the enemy in the Omaha sector. A more immediate threat to the Germans came on the flank of 5th Corps attack. Here the British 2nd Army had broken through the German defenses in a number of places, and to the west, the American 7th Corps was firmly ashore with men and vehicles pouring across the beaches almost unhindered.

The inland battle behind Omaha developed into three generally unconnected and largely uncoordinated actions around Vierville, St Laurent and Colleville. Although there was only scattered resistance from small but determined enemy groups, seldom as much as company strength, progress was slow for a variety of reasons. Little fire support was available since most of the tanks and heavy support weapons had been lost during the landings, vital communication links were missing, units were frequently still hopelessly mixed, and control amongst the thick hedgerows was extremely difficult.

By 1100, however, Vierville had been cleared after a frontal attack by two battalions of the 116th Regiment, who then tried to extend the bridgehead laterally to link up with the Rangers who had landed farther to the west. By late afternoon this advance had been halted and Colonel Canham decided to withdraw and concentrate on the defense of Vierville, where the scattered Engineers, with only a quarter of their equipment, struggled to open up the beach exit giving access to Vierville. East of the Les Moulins valley, the 3rd Battalion of the 116th Regiment fought their way forward in small groups until they were stopped just short of St Laurent. Farther to the east, two battalions of the 16th Regiment fought a series of confused and fragmented actions in an advance towards Colleville, which was halted short of the town by a local German counter-attack.

At sea, the 115th Infantry Regiment had been held as a floating reserve only to be committed if the situation became critical. The desperate situation which had developed during the 116th Regiment's landings on the right wing of 5th Corps assault demanded their committment so the 115th Regiment was ordered to land at H+4 (1030) to give immediate support. The same eastward drift which had disrupted the earlier assault waves dislocated the landings of the 115th Regiment. Pulled eastward by the incoming tide sweeping up the English Channel, the Regiment landed on top of the 18th Infantry Regiment in the process of disembarking east of St Laurent. It was not until early afternoon that the confusion on the congested beaches could be sorted out and the 115th Regiment headed for its assembly area south-west of St Laurent. After an unsuccessful attempt to take the town, the regiment halted short of the St Laurent–Colleville road.

The 18th Infantry Regiment, whose disembarkation had been disrupted by the unscheduled arrival of the 115th Regiment in their rear, was tasked with taking over the 16th Regiment's D-day objectives. However, because of delays and enemy resistance, their orders were changed and it was directed onto the high ground beyond the St Laurent–Colleville road to fill a gap between the 16th Infantry on the right, but at dusk it had not managed to reach the road.

At the end of the day 5th Corps had established two footholds, the first in a narrow sector between St Laurent and Colleville, nowhere more than a mile and a half deep; the second, slightly farther to the west, around Vierville. The cost of these modest gains had mounted to 2,000 killed, wounded and missing, together with the loss of a large amount of equipment which included about 50 tanks and 26 artillery pieces. The whole of the landing area was still under enemy artillery fire and of the 2,400 tons of supplies planned to be onloaded during D-day, only about 100 tons had actually arrived. Beach obstacles were only about a third cleared, even after a low tide during the afternoon had enabled the Engineers to resume work on them; beach exits had not been developed, nor had the essential beach organization, necessary to ensure the orderly handling of successive landings, been properly established.

The principal cause of 5th Corps' setback was the unexpected degree of enemy resistance. Not only were prisoners taken from the 726th Regiment which was known to be in the area, but also from the fully combatant 352nd Division whose presence on the coast came as a complete surprise. How much of the 352nd Division was actually in the Omaha area is not known – certainly not the whole formation, since elements of it were encountered as far east as Bayeux in the British 2nd Army sector. The division appears to have been moved into the area between Grandchamp and Arromaches – in order to stiffen the second-line coastal formations deployed within the immediate beach defenses. In this manner, all the prepared strongpoints and their various interconnecting weapon pits were fully manned and the artillery of the 352nd Division, consisting of three field and one medium battalion, was at least in part able to support the German troops confronting the Omaha landings.

Had it not been for the massive assistance of the Allied navies and air forces during this critical period of 5th Corps' landing, it is doubtful whether the shaken and depleted troops of the assault waves would have been able to recover, reorganize and then develop an offensive which was to deepen and widen their bridgehead in the succeeding days.

Omaha is a story of near disaster but no shame. Largely unseasoned troops, subjected to all the hazards of a vast and complex amphibious operation, further compounded by unfavorable weather conditions and stubborn opposition, were initially near paralysed by shock but, under the shield of fire provided by the allied navies and air forces, rallied and resumed a dogged offensive.

Aachen (1944)

Hubert Essame

The greatest US involvement in ground fighting during the Second World War was not in the battle of the 'Bulge' nor the recapture of the Philippines, but in the little-known battles of Aachen in the autumn of 1944. They were in some respects akin to the Meuse–Argonne offensive of 1918 which holds a similar place in the First World War, but the Aachen battles were not ultimately successful. After three months two US armies only penetrated 22 miles into Hitler's Reich at a cost of 140,000 casualties, then they were subjected to a totally unexpected German winter counter-offensive in the Ardennes. Allied hopes of victory in 1944 died with the protracted and frustrating campaign on the Siegfried Line.

Back in the heady days of the Normandy breakout, comparatively little stress had been laid on the spectacular success of Lieutenant General Courtney H. Hodges ' First US Army in their helter-skelter advance from the Seine, in accordance with General Dwight D. Eisenhower's 'Broad Front' policy, towards the Aachen Gap and Cologne. Hodges, in the last days of August, advancing on a three-Corps front with Major General 'Lightning Joe' Lawton Collins' 7th Corps on the right flank suddenly swung it NE towards Mons. Approaching this area were disjointed elements of 20 routed German divisions flushed out of Normandy by the British. Neither had been forewarned of the other's approach and both stumbled into an impromptu battle which ended in more than 2,000 Germans being killed and another 30,000 POWs being rounded up. First Army in fact had destroyed the last reserves of both Seventh and Fifteenth Armies leaving the way ahead to Liege and Aachen virtually open. It was this little-advertised victory which enabled US patrols to be first across the Belgian border into Germany west of Aachen on 11 September. The First Army closed up on the west bank of the river Wurm.

Thereafter Eisenhower gave priority for supply to Field-Marshal Sir Bernard Montgomery's airborne carpet thrust towards Arnhem. Hodges closed down offensive operations on 22 September to shorten his front and bring forward another Corps to fill the gap in the Ardennes between his army and Patton's. Ahead on either side of Aachen from Geilenkirchen to the Huertgen Forest stretched one of the strongest parts of the West Wall. Hodges also knew that whatever its military value Hitler would not lightly let Aachen go. The days when cities could be carried at a run in the confusion of the pursuit were over. First Army would once more have to face new problems demanding novel techniques. In Normandy it had been hedgerows, now it would be concrete pillboxes, minefields and all the bedevilments of fighting in a densely populated industrial area. Inevitably success would depend more on the courage and skill of the individual infantryman than on air support or armored strength.

On purely military grounds retention of Aachen had little to recommend it, surrounded as it was by hills and lying within two defensive belts of the West Wall. The city's roads were relatively unimportant as First Army had already found adequate ones leading towards the Rhine both north and south of the city. Over a millennium before, however, in the days of the Emperor Charlemagne, Aachen (Aix-la-Chapelle) had been capital of the Holy Roman Empire and thus had become identified with the mythology of National Socialism. To strike at Aachen was to strike at a symbol of Nazi faith. Hodges therefore decided to encircle it using 30th Division and 2nd Armored Division of 19th Corps to strike south to link up with 7th Corps NE of Aachen near Wuerselen and thereafter reduce the city at leisure. West and north of Aachen lay a densely built-up urban area. Major General Leland S. Hobbs, commander of 30th Division, therefore chose to make the first penetration of the West Wall on a narrow front along the Wurm nine miles north of Aachen where the country was more open.

On 26 September over 300 guns began a systematic attempt to

knock out all the pillboxes on the divisional front; results were disappointing. Heavy bomber support was arranged with the proviso by 30th Division that the USAF should avoid bombing them instead of the enemy as they had done with disastrous results at St Lo in Normandy – 75 men killed and 505 wounded by American bombs. Bad weather resulted in the attack's postponement until 2 October. When the air strike went in, many of the medium bombers missed their targets – one group bombed a town in Belgium 28 miles away! The fighter-bombers, although they found their target area, failed to knock out a single pillbox. The 117th Infantry Regiment had to fight its way forward supported only by its own artillery, mortars, heavy machine-guns and tanks. There followed a day of small battles amongst the houses of Marienberg and Palenberg.

A volunteer flame-thrower operator of Lieutenant Robert P. Cushman's platoon, Private Brent Youenes, advanced within 10 yards of the first of two pillboxes and squirted two bursts into the embrasure. Private Willis Jenkins then shoved a pole charge into it. Out came five badly shaken Germans, lucky to be still alive. The platoon next shot up a machine-gun crew in a trench outside the pillbox and, creeping round the back of another, tossed hand-grenades through the embrasure. Pte Youenes squirted it with flame and the garrison surrendered. The platoon then dealt with three more pillboxes in like manner. An observer's comment, 'These infantrymen have guts' erred on the side of understatement. Meanwhile the Engineers worked on treadways across the quagmires of the Wurm to enable the tanks to cross; none, however, could get into action before nightfall.

On the next day house-to-house fighting in Palenberg often lapsed into hand-grenade duels. One rifleman, Private Harold G. Kiner, spotted a hand-grenade that landed between him and his fellow riflemen, threw himself upon it and saved his companions at the cost of his own life. He was posthumously awarded the Medal of Honor. On the right flank of 117th Infantry, the 119th Infantry Regiment established a shallow bridgehead along the Wurm in the face of intense artillery fire.

Close infighting like this characterized the struggle among concrete and wire for the next three days. On 4 October the Germans staged a full-dress counter-attack with tanks and assault guns supported by well-directed artillery fire: even the *Luftwaffe* made an appearance. They got nowhere despite goading by Field Marshal Walther Model.

By the 6th, superior American morale and armament swung the issue in their favor. On the left, 2nd Armored Division attacking SE carried all before it; on their right. 30th Division, despite fatigue, burst into the ghost town of Arlsdorf and the squalid streets of Merkstein. It was here that Private Salvatore Pepe refused to take cover but, rushing forward alone firing his rifle and tossing hand-grenades, wounded four Germans and caused 50 more to surrender. The 30th Division was now only three miles from Wuerselen, the planned point of junction with 7th Corps attacking from the south. Inch by inch the advance continued. By the evening of the 7th, Hobbs, justifiably exuberant, could report to his Corps Commander, 'We have a hole in this thing big enough to drive two divisions through . . . this line is cracked wide open.' His division and 2nd Armored had literally ruptured the West Wall in the face of a surprisingly large concentration of heavy and medium artillery and over 50 assault guns. Both divisions had taken in their stride the shock of the abrupt change from exhilarating pursuit to a grim battle in fortified zones.

It was now the turn of 7th Corps to strike north with 1st Division and complete the encirclement of Aachen by advancing to Wuerselen. Major General Clarence R. Huebner of 1st Division planned to do this with the 18th Infantry Regiment. Only a two-and-a-half-mile advance was involved, but it would take them through a dense maze of pillboxes and over exposed hill crests. To take these hills was no easy task; holding them thereafter under heavy artillery bombardment would be even more difficult. In Aachen itself there were about 12,000 Germans. Furthermore, unknown to the Americans, Field Marshal Gerd von Rundstedt had promised to provide 3rd *Panzergrenadier* Division and 116th *Panzer* Division under 1 SS Corps for counter-attack when the situation was ripe. Huebner's preparations included the provision of special pillbox assault teams equipped with flame-throwers, Bangalore torpedoes and pole and satchel charges. A battery of 155 mm guns and a company of tank destroyers were also provided to hurl point-blank fire against the pillboxes.

Attacking at night on 8 October and again on the 9th, the 18th Infantry fought their way forward to Verlautenheide, halfway to Wuerselen. Here they had to endure the most intense artillery fire yet encountered in the campaign. Despite fatigue, the 18th Infantry faced the prospect of a counter-attack with determination. It came in full force during 15–16 October. German losses were heavy; over 250 dead were counted in front of 16th Infantry Regiment. Altogether a third of the attackers were killed to no avail.

Meanwhile, from the north, 30th Division had turned southwards to meet 1st Division, in the process attracting particularly vicious attacks by 1 SS *Panzer* Corps. Amidst the slag heaps and pit heads around Bardenberg the reserve battalion of the 120th Infantry Regiment knocked out six tanks and 16 half-tracks, the CO, Major Howard Greer, personally accounting for two with his bazooka. Almost hourly fresh German units were fed into the struggle. But divisional morale remained unshaken, despite 2,020 casualties sustained in the past ten days. All efforts on their part to get forward still continued to meet vicious and obstinate resistance. The pressure on Hobbs from his superiors to close the now mile-wide gap and get on to Wuerselen became almost unendurable. On 16 October he struck again with 119th Infantry as his spearhead against the dug-in tanks and pillboxes blocking the way forward. In the mid-afternoon, 18th Infantry in the south spotted American troops on the ridge SW of Wuerselen. They were the two survivors of a patrol of 119th Infantry, Privates Edward Krauss and Evan Whitis. At 1615 these two, quickly reinforced, had the honor of closing the ring around Aachen.

Aachen itself, already a wilderness of rubble as a result of RAF attention earlier in the year, now found itself the target of 7th Corps artillery and fighter-bombers of 9th Tactical Air Force. An ultimatum to surrender delivered under a flag of truce, broadcasts on Radio Luxembourg and leaflets shot into the ruins by artillery on 10 October were all scornfully rejected by the garrison commander, Colonel Gerhard Wilck. Huebner had to commit 25th Infantry to a tedious battle within the ruins 'from attic to attic and sewer to sewer'. German resistance, reinforced by SS Battalion *Rink*, continued obstinate to a degree. Methodically, 26th Infantry inched their way forward. Outside the perimeter all attempts by 1 SS *Panzer* Corps to re-establish contact with the encircled garrison came to nought. Finally on the 19th Model abandoned the city to its fate.

But Col. Wilck issued an order of the day, 'The defenders of Aachen will prepare for their last battle. Constricted to the smallest possible space we shall fight to the last man, the last shell, in accordance with the Führer's order.' Over the air he continued to affirm his 'unshakeable faith in our right and our victory'. By the night of 20 October, 26th Infantry, reinforced by two battalions of tanks, had corralled his few remaining soldiers into the western and SW suburbs. Next morning, Lieutenant Colonel John T. Corley's battalion, supported by a 155 mm gun, approached a big air raid bunker at the northern end of the city. Faced by the threat of being blasted into eternity, Colonel Wilck surrendered. He had fought to a finish. The battle for Aachen was over; the once proud city, the first city of the Reich to be captured, lay in utter ruin. Burst sewers, broken gas mains and dead animals raised an overpowering stench.

It had been a costly battle. The 30th Division lost over 3,000 men, the two battalions of 26th Infantry 498. Throughout the armor had been forced to fight in penny packets cheek by jowl with the infantry. It had been a soldiers' battle in which Allied air power and material superiority counted for less than the fighting spirit of the infantry and the tank crews. Between them 1st and 30th Divisions had taken some 12,000 prisoners. What was surprising was the skill with which the German commanders had handled the many miscellaneous elements thrown piecemeal into the fighting as the days went by. Even more surprising was the tenacity with which their troops continued to fight.

Long before the battle it had become evident that Model, commander of Army Group B, whose frontage coincided almost with that of General Omar N. Bradley's 12th Army Group, had succeeded in establishing a well-organized defense of the West Wall astride the Aachen Gap. The morale of his troops was high, and even his second-class troops, established in fixed defenses, built-up areas and woods, could be formidable. Stolberg's 4,000 defenders put up a week's street fighting. Much bitter fighting in ever-shortening hours of daylight and deteriorating weather would have to be faced before the line of the river Roer, 12 miles ahead, let alone the Rhine, could be reached.

It is an indisputable fact that on the whole the German Army still outclassed the Allies in the flexibility and simplicity of its organization and in the professional skill of its battle-experienced corps and divisional commanders and their staffs. In the debacle at the end of August and the first week of September, although the Seventh and Fifteenth Armies had been reduced to skeletons, most of their staffs had survived and still continued to function. With the aid of Military Police and *Waffen* SS detachments they succeeded in regaining a measure of control. Hitler rushed forward First Parachute

Army to fill the gap between what remained of Seventh and Fifteenth Armies.

Heinrich Himmler, commanding the Home Army in addition to his duties as Minister of the Interior, Chief of Police and Head of the SS, had put all his weight behind the drive to fill the ranks of 43 *Volksgrenadier* (the People's Grenadiers) Divisions now being formed. To supplement the artillery Hitler ordered 12 motorized brigades (about 1,000 guns), 10 *Werfer* Brigades, 10 assault-gun battalions and 12 machine-gun battalions to be raised. Himmler diverted the best of the manpower and equipment into the *Waffen* SS which now composed one third of the *Panzer* and one fourth of the *Panzergrenadier* divisions. The great strength of these divisions lay in their young officers – Nazi to a man, coarse, arrogant and cruel, but well trained and ruthless in battle. From them Hitler planned to produce a new generation to replace the regular officers of the *Wehrmacht*.

'Unconditional surrender' and the announcement of the Morgenthau Plan on 24 September, which revealed the Allied intention of turning Germany into a third-class agricultural state, reinforced Joseph Goebbel's propaganda appeals to the German people. Now that the enemy stood on the sacred soil of the Fatherland a deeply felt, instinctive love of country prompted all, soldiers and civilians alike, to fight on in the belief that the Führer in some mysterious way would emerge finally triumphant like Frederick the Great when all seemed lost in the Black Year of 1759. Behind the ramparts of the West Wall and depths of the Huertgen Forest they would fight on as the nights grew longer and the autumn rains slowed down the Allied armies and diminished the threat from the air.

As a matter of strict nomenclature, defined by the US Army Military History Department, the battle of Aachen ends with the fall of the city. Popularly, in the Allied Armies of the time and in European eyes, especially German, it also embodies all the operations of First and Ninth Armies east and west of Aachen in November and the first half of December.

At Brussels on 18 October Eisenhower revealed to the Army Group commanders his intention of continuing the battle on the Aachen front with First and Ninth Armies as a first step towards enveloping the Ruhr. He made it clear that serious logistic difficulties must first be overcome. Until the mouth of the Scheldt was cleared, enabling the port of Antwerp to be opened, no large-scale offensive could be sustained. Two other serious supply problems were causing him great anxiety. Surprisingly, US factories had failed to keep up with the Army's needs and an acute shortage had developed, which would take some time to make up. Eisenhower broadcast a personal appeal to the United States. Casualties, especially infantry riflemen and tank crews, had been much heavier than anticipated. Drastic steps had to be taken to comb out and retrain as infantry men from other arms. For these reasons and the vagaries of the weather affecting air support a resumption of the battle was deferred for nearly a month. If there was no fog over the airfields in Great Britain there was always fog over the target area and vice versa. As a result, autumn, with overcast skies, damp depressing fogs, persistent rain and ever shortening hours of daylight, was already far advanced when on 16 November Bradley renewed his offensive towards the Rhine.

Immediately south of Aachen, First Army, now numbering 12 divisions, was to make the main effort. In particular it was to take the seven Roer dams at Schmidt, so that Eisenhower's future plans for the Second British and Ninth Armies could be implemented. North of Aachen the Supreme Commander brought in the Ninth Army, fresh from America, to advance simultaneously and protect First Army's northern flank. Some seven miles ahead and almost parallel to the front lay the river Roer, initial objective of both Armies. To reach it First Army would have to fight its way through the dense Huertgen Forest, three miles deep, flanked by extensive built-up areas. On Ninth Army's front the country was more open for tanks and for controlling the large forces now to be engaged.

By this time, although the Allies had not an inkling of his intentions, Model's plans for an Ardennes counter-offensive in December with Fifth and Sixth *Panzer* Armies and Seventh Army were already far advanced. Facing First and Ninth Armies he had Fifth *Panzer* Army and Seventh Army; in their immediate rear Sixth *Panzer* Army had already started to assemble. Altogether some 30 divisions would be concentrated here and large stocks of fuel and ammunition built up. Model had over 1,000 guns centrally controlled and plenty of ammunition. His losses of the early autumn had been replaced and his intentions were crystal clear – to fight the Americans in the Devil's Garden of the West Wall and Huertgen Forest; under no circumstances would he allow the Americans to cross the Roer. Furthermore, the Sixth *Panzer* Army, destined to execute the main effort in the Ardennes, must be kept out of the battle on the Aachen front but look like joining it.

Bradley imagined that an overpowering aerial bombardment would shatter German morale and then he intended to blast his way through with massed artillery. Over 1,200 heavy bombers of 8th USAAF and RAF Bomber Command were to 'take out' the towns of Duren, Julich and Heinsberg on the Roer. The forward troops would have 750 fighter-bombers on call. Late on the morning of 16 November vast fleets of aircraft passing over First and Ninth Armies signalled the start of Bradley's offensive. Results were disappointing – the 9,400 tons of bombs, for safety reasons, were dropped so far behind the German forward troops that they almost completely missed them. The attacking troops, four divisions on a 25-mile front, although supported by 1,000 guns, found themselves greeted by deadly small arms, artillery and mortar fire. It was small consolation and no help to them that six miles ahead three towns on the Roer had been destroyed in the heaviest tactical air bombardment yet launched.

Thus inauspiciously began the month-long battle of attrition which occupies a place and significance in the history of the American Army similar to that of Verdun for the French and Passchendaele for the British. In the end it absorbed some 17 divisions, resulted in severe casualties both from enemy action and sickness and severely tested the morale of the troops. It was fought in vile weather – damp grey mist alternating with heavy downpours reduced the battlefield to a ghastly quagmire and precluded effective air support. Everything favored the enemy. In the Huertgen Forest, First Army plumbed the depths of misery. Here, hidden from view amongst the closely planted trees, protected by barbed wire, anti-personnel mines, log bunkers, log-covered foxholes and machine-gun emplacements, a few men could hold up whole battalions. There were so many mines that the attackers were reduced to using pitch forks to uproot the new wooden and glass types. Charles B. Macdonald, American Official Army Historian, vividly recorded the fighting in *The Siefried Line Campaign*:

It was attrition unrelieved. Overcoats soaked with moisture and caked with freezing mud became too heavy for men to wear. Seeping rain turned radios into useless impedimenta. So choked with debris was the floor of the forest that men broke under the sheer physical strain of moving supplies forward and evacuating the wounded. The fighting was at such close quarters that hand grenades were often the decisive weapon. The minefields seemed endless. A platoon would spend hours probing, searching, determining the pattern, only to discover after breaching one minefield that another just as extensive lay 25 yards ahead. Unwary men who sought cover from fire in ditches or abandoned foxholes might trip over lethal booby traps and turn the promised sanctuary into an open grave.

The swollen bodies of the dead in grotesque positions added to the general horror. So bitter was the fighting that the village of Huertgen changed hands 14 times and the village of Vossenack eight times. Inevitably there were unfortunate incidents in which both officers and men cracked under the strain. More than 24,000 killed, missing, captured and wounded fell a prey to the fighting here; a further 9,000 succumbed to the misery of the forest itself, the wet and the cold, trench foot, respiratory diseases and combat fatigue. To some extent, too, the torpor which comes from prolonged exposure without relief to shellfire and bad weather was reflected at command level.

In the more open country on the northern part of the front Ninth Army had better fortune and reached the Roer from Julich to Linnich on 28 November. Thanks to realistic training in the United States and the support of more lavishly supplied British artillery, the army stepped off on the right foot in this its first battle. It would be another two weeks, however, before First Army was able to close up with the river opposite Duren. The testimony of British officers who saw the American troops at this time should also be recorded. During the battle many officers and men of Guards Armoured Division were exchanged with the Americans. Their impression was that 'their methods might be somewhat curious and unorthodox, but there could be no doubt about the excellent results when put into practice. Divisions such as the 29th and 30th Infantry who fought in this battle could have challenged comparison with the finest of our own.' Lieutenant-General Sir Brian Horrocks, commanding the British 30th Corps on the extreme left flank of the offensive, and with the 84th US Infantry Division under his command, was most impressed by their performance in their first battle, their bravery, initiative and ability to learn from experience.

The first snow fell on 9 December; thereafter the days were chill and the sky overcast. By 15 December First and Ninth Armies, having advanced eight miles in a month, had reached the high ground overlooking the river Roer. But three miles to the south the Germans still held Schmidt and the vital dams despite persistent attack. Attempts by the RAF to burst them with their heaviest bombs had failed. On their right, on a 100-mile front in the Ardennes, Bradley only had some four divisions, two new to battle and two badly mauled in the Huertgen Forest. The Germans, fighting what was an essentially defensive action, had reinforced the front with 11 divisions including two *Panzer*. Of these, however, only one, 10th SS *Panzer*, was scheduled to take part in the now imminent Ardennes offensive. American losses, mostly in front-line units, in killed, wounded or missing in the Aachen battles since September now totalled 68,000, plus over 70,000 sick as a result of fatigue, exposure, accidents and disease.

Fifty years later it is fair comment to say that First Army fought in the wrong place. They would almost certainly have had greater success if they had advanced in September, as originally planned, south of the Ardennes in conjunction with Patton's Third Army. Better still, they could have been sent through the Ardennes, which, as the Germans had proved in 1940 and would soon confirm, were not the barrier to large-scale military movement they had traditionally been assumed to be.

At 0530 on 16 December in darkness and fog from south of Monschau came the rumble of 2,000 German guns, their heaviest artillery barrage of the whole campaign. Model launched 13 infantry and seven armored divisions, followed by a further ten, a thousand tanks and 250,000 men into the Forest of the Eifel. The battles of Aachen were over. Another had begun.

Ardennes (1944)

Peter Young

Not since Pearl Harbor had the Americans received so rude a shock as when the dawn of 16 December 1944 was broken by the thunder of a thousand guns: German guns, heralding a most determined onslaught.

Ever since July, Hitler, with a strategic sense which one is compelled to admire, had been building up a reserve, a *masse de manoeuvre*, of 250,000 men. It was little enough for a two-front war, nor were they the soldiers of 1940, but it was still a force capable of delivering a heavy blow. And it was commanded by von Rundstedt, a man of whom miracles could still be expected. He had already performed one when he stabilized the German line on the Western Front after the débâcle in Normandy. Now he performed another by concentrating Hitler's last army (Model's Army Group B) in the Eifel area without attracting the attention of the American High Command. How did the Allied intelligence fail to see a quarter of a million men, their vehicles and 1,100 tanks? They saw what they wanted to see. The Germans, they thought, were licked – and anyway who would think of mounting an offensive in the Ardennes in the middle of winter? A certain number of suspicious troop movements were reported by prisoners, civilians, and by airmen, but their significance was discounted. As the Germans hoped, these were thought to be reinforcements for the fighting round Aachen.

Although von Rundstedt was to command the offensive, he did

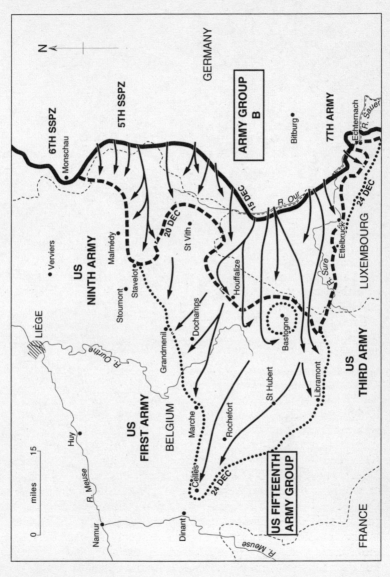

5.12 *The Battle of the Bulge, December 1944*

not favour it. It was Hitler's own brain-child. Physically the Führer was not the man he had been before the bomb attempt of 20 July. Lt-General Hasso von Manteuffel saw him as 'a stooped figure with a pale and puffy face, hunched in his chair, his hands trembling, his left arm subject to a violent twitching which he did his best to conceal, a sick man apparently borne down by the burden of his responsibility. When he walked he dragged one leg behind him.' But this miserable, shambling creature could still make himself obeyed. Whatever his physical condition his willpower was unimpaired. Temperamentally unstable, he was incapable of playing a waiting game. He deliberately sought a decision. Moreover, that acute if unbalanced mind could detect certain factors in favour of his plan.

In 1940 the Ardennes had been the weak link in the French chain. Now the Monschau–Echternach sector was the weakest part of Eisenhower's front. Lt-General Courtney H. Hodges (First Army) was holding 85 miles with only five divisions and three of them (2, 4, and 28) had suffered heavily in the recent fighting round Aachen. Only about 100 miles to the NW was Antwerp, the great Allied supply base, which had recently been opened to seaborne traffic. The German commanders knew the narrow roads of the Ardennes with their hairpin bends and steep hillsides very well. They had come that way in 1940. Bad weather could be expected to nullify the Allied air superiority. Otto Skorzeny's Panzer Brigade 150, disguised in American uniforms, would cause confusion behind the lines.

Von Manteuffel had a conversation with Hitler on 2 December, when the latter admitted that there was

a certain disparity between the distant objective of Antwerp and the forces which were to capture it. However, he said, this was the time to put everything on one throw of the dice, 'for Germany needs a pause to draw breath.' Even a partial success, he believed, would retard the plans of the Allies by eight to ten weeks . . . Temporary stabilization on the Western Front would enable the Supreme Command to move forces from there to the threatened central sector of the Eastern Front.

The German generals were not unnaturally concerned about the question of air cover. After the Berlin conference Manteuffel told Hitler that 'in our sector of the front we never saw or heard a German aeroplane these days.' He received this curious reply: 'The *Luftwaffe* is being deliberately held back. Göring has reported that he has three thousand fighters available for the operation. You know Göring's reports. Discount one thousand, and that still leaves a thousand to work with you and a thousand for Sepp Dietrich.'

.When the attack came the SS General Sepp Dietrich with the Sixth SS Panzer Army fell upon the US V Corps (Major-General Leonard T. Gerow) and thrust towards Liège. The Americans were driven back to the Eisenborn Ridge, but in three days' desperate fighting they denied the enemy the direct road to Liège, the main communications centre of Bradley's Twelfth Army Group. A German armoured column did succeed in thrusting forward through Malmédy, Stavelot, and Stonmont, but as luck would have it narrowly missed not only the Allies' main fuel dump but Hodges' HQ at Spa. By 19 December it had been brought to a halt.

Fifth Panzer Army, though weaker than Sixth, made much more progress. Von Manteuffel achieved tactical surprise by attacking without a preliminary bombardment, relying on close co-operation between his armour and his infantry. His onslaught shattered the US VIII Corps (Major-General Troy H. Middleton), which was strung out upon a long front. On Manteuffel's right a corps cut off two regiments of the inexperienced US 106th Division in the Schnee Eifel. On his left two panzer corps broke through the US 28th Division, and reached the outskirts of Houffalize and Bastogne.

Seventh Army (General Erich Brandenberger) was supposed to cover Manteuffel's left flank by thrusting forward towards the Meuse. It made some progress at first especially on the right, but after a few days was held up by the US 4th Infantry Division and elements of the 9th Armoured Division.

Dietrich's failure meant that the Germans were not going to retake Antwerp. Hitler determined nonetheless to exploit Manteuffel's narrow breakthrough.

In 1940 Gamelin had had no theatre reserve, no *masse de manoeuvre*. Eisenhower had the XVIII Airborne Corps; this he now sent to General Hodges.

Eisenhower ordered General Omar N. Bradley (12th Army Group) to attack each flank of the German breakthrough with an armoured division. But he saw that if Model succeeded in widening the shoulders of the breakthrough Bradley's army group might be split right down the middle. Practical as ever, he placed all the US forces north of the breakthrough (First and Ninth Armies) under

Montgomery (21st Army Group), leaving Bradley in command of the forces to the south.

Like Joffre in 1914, Eisenhower was willing to give up ground rather than let his line break. Patton (Third Army) was to disengage, make a tremendous left wheel, and drive northwards. The 6th Army Group in Alsace would have to take over Patton's sector in the Saar even if this meant giving ground in Alsace and perhaps abandoning Strasbourg. General de Gaulle was *not* pleased. But in fact the Germans were in no position to mount another offensive, and although the northern corner of Alsace was evacuated, Strasbourg itself was saved.

While Eisenhower was taking a grip on the situation, his front-line troops, though hard-pressed, were putting up a fight which compared more than favourably with the resistance of the French IXth Army in 1940. The unfortunate Corap had had few if any tanks. It was the American armour that won time for Eisenhower's measures to take effect. The 7th Armoured Division denied St Vith to the enemy until 21 December. Part of the 10th Armoured Division delayed von Manteuffel just long enough to allow 101st Airborne Division to establish itself in Bastogne.

Bastogne stood like a rock. Fifth Panzer Army, unable to drive through, had to go round, shedding considerable forces to contain the improvised fortress. Summoned to surrender 22 December Brigadier-General Anthony McAuliffe, a modern Cambronne, curtly answered 'Nuts'.

The Germans had not quite shot their bolt. Sixth Panzer Army got going again and Manteuffel's two panzer corps drove on westward and on Christmas Eve his 2nd Panzer Division was in sight of the Meuse, near Celles, three miles east of Dinant. But the attack had lost its momentum.

Meanwhile, the Allied counter-attack was getting under way. The weather had cleared and 5,000 Allied planes were strafing the transport strung out nose to tail all the way to the German frontier. In the words of General Arnold 'We prepared to isolate the battlefield.' Moreover it was air supply that saved Bastogne, while Patton pushed up from the south to its relief.

In the line north of the gap Montgomery had three American corps under Hodges (V, XVIII Airborne, and VII) with the British XXX Corps in reserve on the Meuse. Hodges' centre was still vulnerable and to shorten it Montgomery evacuated a salient round Vielsalm – *reculer pour mieux sauter* is no bad tactical axiom.

The US 2nd Armoured Division (VII Corps) cut off and destroyed Manteuffel's spearhead at Celles on Christmas Day. Next day the US 4th Armoured Division broke through to Bastogne. Thus ended the first phase of the battle.

By Christmas Day von Rundstedt realized that the battle had been lost, but Hitler was not the man to admit defeat or to cut his losses. Instead he thought up a new double offensive. He would begin by taking Bastogne and then, wheeling north, would take the First Army in flank while a secondary attack engaged it from the direction of Roermond. In the New Year he would mount yet another offensive in Alsace.

At the same time Eisenhower was planning a counter-offensive which had rather more substance. Bradley and Montgomery were to strike simultaneously.

Bastogne was still the storm centre. The corridor to the town was only a mile wide in places. Patton was determined to drive off the two German corps that were squeezing its lifeline. At the same time Manteuffel was concentrating for the attack which would rid him once and for all of this thorn in his flesh. On 30 December they met head on, and locked in a deadly winter battle which ranged blindly and fiercely through the snow-clad woods and ravines of the Ardennes.

By the time the battle died down the Germans were spent. On 8 January 1945 Hitler reluctantly agreed to limited withdrawals, and next day Patton broke out of Bastogne. Model, helped by a break in the weather, began to disengage his forces. On the 13th, owing to the Russian winter offensive, the German Supreme Command withdrew Sixth SS Panzer Army from the Ardennes battle, and permitted a general retreat. Patton and Hodges joined hands at Houffalize on the 16th and Bradley was able to resume command of his army and restore his original line. By 28 January it was all over.

The battle cost the Allies 76,980 casualties, but it ruined Hitler's last reserve army both morally and physically. The Germans lost 70,000 casualties and 50,000 prisoners, besides 500–600 tanks and 1,600 planes. The Russians had launched their great winter offensive on 12 January, and Hitler no longer had his *masse de manoeuvre* to meet it: a terrible price to pay for the six weeks delay it imposed on the Western Allies.

It was a great victory. Even so the Germans, though less well trained than three years earlier, had hacked a wound 50 miles deep in the American line. They had fought with all their old devotion. The more credit to the Americans who beat such men.

The part of the air forces must not be underrated. The *Luftwaffe* was still able to send over 700 aircraft on New Year's Day, 1945, to attack Allied airfields and to destroy nearly 200 planes on the ground. On 22 January the Anglo-American air forces claimed to have destroyed 4,200 pieces of heavy equipment; railway engines and trucks, tanks, motor and horse-drawn vehicles.

There are those who regard General Eisenhower as a very indifferent general, little more than a sort of Grand Liaison Officer. It is true that in the battle of the Ardennes his original lay-out was faulty. Major-General Fuller even goes so far as to say: 'The enormity of Eisenhower's distribution can be measured by supposing that it had been made in May, 1940. Had it been, then there can be little doubt that his armies would have suffered a similar fate to Gamelin's.' But this is going altogether too far, and ignores the fact that up to mid-December 1944 Eisenhower had had the initiative on the Western front, and was not simply sitting waiting to be attacked. Once the battle began he made the right decisions and he made them in time. In the event his 33 divisions mauled 26 German divisions. One can only judge a general by his works, good or ill, and it seems to the present writer that Eisenhower's stature is greatly enhanced by this macabre winter battle.

> *Few, few shall part where many meet*
> *The snow shall be their winding sheet*
> *And every turf beneath their feet*
> *Shall be a soldier's sepulchre.*
> (Thomas Campbell, *Hohenlinden*)

Berlin (1945)

John Strawson

In all the talk that went on in the last months of the Second World War about strategy and objectives and partitioning Europe, one vital point was overlooked by everyone. It was that the only military objective whose capture or elimination could actually bring the war to an end lay in the person of one man – Adolf Hitler. It was Hitler's will alone which kept the German people on their dreadful path to destruction. He had made his intention clear to his generals on the eve of the Ardennes offensive in December 1944: 'We must allow no moment to pass without showing the enemy that, whatever he does, he can never reckon on a capitulation. Never! Never!' Indeed he had already said it countless times – in *Mein Kampf* and in his endless table talk years before. 'We shall not capitulate – no, never. We may be destroyed, but if we are, we shall drag a world with us – a world in flames.'

The battle for Berlin turned this reckless prophecy into the reality of *Götterdämmerung*. Albert Speer, technocrat, and Minister of Armaments and War Production, described the helplessness to which Hitler's miscalculations had reduced the once mighty Reich: 'Howling and exploding bombs, clouds illuminated in red and yellow hues, droning motors and no defence anywhere – I was stunned.'

Before 1945, when it was hard to see how it could be done, both the Russians and the Western Allies had repeatedly named Berlin as their goal. But such definitions made little sense unless it was possible

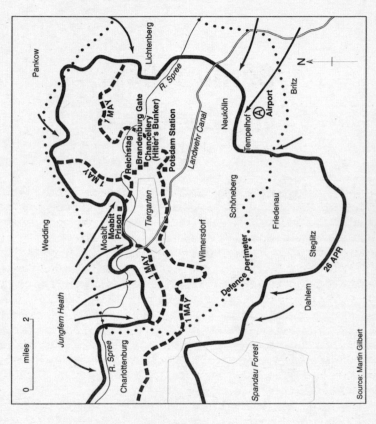

5.13   The Fall of Berlin, April–May 1945

to make a proper plan to capture the city. This was not feasible until the beginning of 1945. Once the *Wehrmacht* had at last recognized that there was nothing left but a strategy of defense, in the East on the Vistula and in the West on the Rhine, once Germany itself was on the point of being invaded, that is in January 1945, the battle for Berlin – then only a few hundred miles away from each main enemy army – was on.

Planning the final battle of the war began in the Soviet High Command in October 1944. It was intended to advance from the Vistula to Berlin and beyond in six weeks. The offensive was to start on 20 January 1945. Later the date was brought forward to 12 January. Three army groups or 'fronts' were to attack – 1st and 2nd Belorussian commanded respectively by Marshals Georgi K. Zhukov and Konstantin Rokossovski, and 1st Ukrainian under Marshal Ivan S. Koniev – 2.5 million men against fewer than a million Germans. The Russians' material superiority was even greater. When the attack started it had immediate and startling success. The Eastern Front collapsed, as Colonel General Heinz Guderian, Chief of the German General Staff, had forecast, like a house of cards. By early February the Red Army had reached the River Oder opposite Berlin. They were only 40 miles from the city. Here they paused.

Why did Stalin not push on after his first brilliant success? Was it simply that with Berlin virtually in the bag he wanted to get his hands on as much of SE Europe as he could? Still more interesting is the question he put to his generals: 'Who is to capture Berlin, we or the Allies?' – and this at a time when it had already been agreed with the Americans that they would halt their armies well to the west of the city.

Zhukov maintained that because of so many casualties to men and equipment suffered during the January battles, difficulties of supply and air support, as well as the German counter-attack capability, further advance was impossible. Colonel General Vasili I. Chuikov, on the other hand, commanding 8th Guards Army under Zhukov, claimed that the war could have been ended in February. He also recorded that when on 4 February the advance on Berlin was being discussed, Stalin telephoned Zhukov and told him to halt the advance on the city and attack the German forces in Pomerania instead.

The result was that the final thrust on Berlin did not start until 16 April. Broadly, Zhukov was to take the city while Koniev would cut off the German Army Group Vistula from Berlin and secure Zhukov's southern flank. Zhukov had no illusions about the problems facing him:

> The unusual and highly complex offensive against Berlin required the most careful preparation at all front and army levels. Troops of the 1st Belorussian front were expected to break through a deeply echeloned defense zone extending from the Oder River all the way to heavily fortified Berlin. Never before in the experience of warfare had we been called upon to capture the city as large and as heavily fortified as Berlin. Its total area was almost 350 square miles. Its subway and other widespread underground engineering networks provided ample possibilities for troop movements. The city itself and its suburbs had been carefully prepared for defense. Every street, every square, every alley, building, canal and bridge represented an element in the city's defense system.

Yet four days after the attack started, his artillery opened up on Berlin and on 21 April the leading troops of three armies, 3rd Shock, 2nd Guards Tank and 47th broke into the outskirts of the city. The last phase of the battle had begun. Eleven days later on 2 May, General Helmuth Weidling, Berlin Commandant, surrendered. It was all over. The battle between 16 April and the German capitulation had cost the Red Army a terrible 300,000 casualties.

'How pitiful is their Berlin!' announced Marshal Zhukov after his troops had captured it. It was the Red Army and Allied bombing which had made it so. Yet the courage and perseverance of the Berliners themselves should not be forgotten. The long road to Berlin had cost the Russians 20 million men since that day almost four years earlier when the two great armies had clashed head on. And all of it had been brought about by the man who at the height of the fighting for Berlin conducted, or thought he conducted, the battle which he claimed would cause the Russians to suffer their bloodiest defeat.

That it was the Russians and not the Americans who reached Berlin first was because of decisions and actions taken during the first two weeks of April 1945. Lieutenant General William H. Simpson's US Ninth Army crossed the Elbe astride Magdeburg on 12 April, and reached Tangemunde – only 50 miles from Berlin. The Russians' next offensive was not planned to start for another four days, 16 April, and they were at this time 40 miles from Berlin on the Oder. The day before, Simpson asked General Omar N. Bradley to let his troops expand the Elbe bridgehead and push on in force for Berlin. That he would have got there seems more or less certain for he had suffered very few casualties and opposite him were only scattered, ill-equipped and untrained formations of General Walther Wenck's Twelfth Army which had no air support at all. Wenck commented: 'If the Americans launch a major attack they'll crack our positions with ease. After all what's to stop them? There's nothing between here and Berlin.' But Eisenhower vetoed the idea.

On the same day Stalin sent a message to the American Ambassador in Moscow to the effect that the Red Army was about to renew the offensive. The main thrust would be on Dresden with a subsidiary one on Berlin. This information was hardly accurate. The main Russian forces were directed at and astride the German capital. Could the *Wehrmacht* withstand the forthcoming Russian steamroller? Colonel General Gotthard Heinrici in command of Army Group Vistula (still called this although it had long since left the Vistula far away) had two armies – General Theodor Busse's Ninth Army, directly in the path between the Red Army and Berlin, and General Hasso von Manteuffel's Third *Panzer* Army which was on the Oder 30 miles NE of the city and was deployed as far north as Stettin. He would be attacked by three Russian Fronts – Rokossovski's aimed at Stettin, Zhukov's at Berlin and Koniev's at Dresden.

It took the Red Army only ten days from 16 April to surround Berlin. But it was by no means a walkover for them. The battle for the Seelow Heights, a critical position, was hard and costly. Despite all their superiority in artillery, the Russian troops came under heavy AT and machine-gun fire which took such a toll of the advancing troops that they were stopped. This caused Stalin to order Koniev to direct his armored forces on Berlin so that on 17 April two Soviet fronts were making for the city. This was too much for Busse's Ninth Army, and by 20 April the Germans defending the approaches to Berlin were overrun. One Russian witness, Konstantin Simonov, saw the remnants of a German battle group:

In front of us lay Berlin, and to our right a forest clearing, now a chaos of jumbled tanks, cars, armored cars, trucks,

special vehicles and ambulances. They had uprooted hundreds
of trees, probably in an attempt to turn round and escape. In
this black, charred confusion of steel, timber, guns, cases and
papers, a bloody mess of mutilated corpses lay strewn along
the clearing as far as the eye could see . . . Then I noticed
a host of wounded men lying on greatcoats and blankets or
leaning against tree trunks; some of them bandaged and others
covered in blood, with no one to tend to them.

Before the Russian attack on the Oder position started, Heinrici
had explained to Speer that there would be no proper battle for
Berlin because the two wings of Army Group Vistula would simply
withdraw respectively north and south of the city. But when it was
clear to him that Zhukov had broken through, Heinrici did make an
attempt to organize the *Volkssturm* (home guard) battalions to establish some defenses to the east of the city. But *Volkssturm* battalions
without transport and with inadequate supplies of ammunition could
never stop the Red Army.

On 20 April Soviet artillery began to shell Berlin. Next day 2nd
Guards Tank, 3rd Shock and 47th Armies – all Zhukov's formations
– reached the outskirts of the city. At the same time Koniev was
moving forward with 3rd Guards Tank Army. Then with two huge
pincer movements, the Russians encircled the German Ninth Army
to the SE of Berlin and Berlin itself, while their spearheads pushed
on to the Elbe. By 25 April the Russians had surrounded Berlin and
contacted US forces at Torgau. Now there was only one thing left to
do – take Berlin and finish the war in Europe.

Col. Gen. Chuikov has left his recollections of it all:

A battery of heavy howitzers was stationed on an open grassy
space beside a wood. Dark, ragged clouds were sailing across
the sky. The earth seemed to doze, shivering a little from
time to time from shellfire in the distance. The gun crews
had already run out the howitzers, and were awaiting the
command to fire. The muzzles were trained on Berlin . . .
on the fortifications of Fascist Berlin – 'Fire!' The heavy
shells flew up, cleaving the air with a whistling sound. The
path had been opened. In the morning I went up to my
observation post. It was in a large five-storeyed building
near the Johannisthal aerodrome. From a corner room here,

where there was a jagged hole in the wall, one got a view of the southern and south-eastern parts of Berlin. Roofs, roofs without end, with here and there a break in them – the work of landmines. In the distance factory chimneys and church spires stood out. The parks and squares, in which the young leaves were already out seemed like little outbreaks of green flame. Mist lay along the streets, mingled with dust raised by the previous night's artillery fire. In places the mist was overlaid by fat trails of black smoke, like mourning streamers. And somewhere in the center of the city ragged yellow plumes rose skywards as bombs exploded. The heavy bombers had already started their preliminary 'working-over' of the targets for the forthcoming attack . . . Suddenly the earth shuddered and rocked under my feet. Thousands of guns announced the beginning of the storming operation.

The 'Fascist beast' himself had made much of making *Festung Berlin* an impregnable fortress. It was a myth. In March 1945 a 'Basic Order for the Preparations to Defend the Capital' had been signed and issued, but little had been done to turn Berlin into a proper defensive position. The city was defended more by words than deeds. The battle for Berlin would decide the war, Hitler claimed. So it did, but not in the way he meant. The Basic Order envisaged an outer perimeter about 20 miles out, another one 10 miles out, a third following the S-Bahn (the railway serving the suburbs), and a final citadel around the government buildings.

A plan was all it was without troops and weapons, ammunition and supplies or a proper command system to control everything. The battle for the city itself never really developed. It was simply a gigantic mopping-up operation. The Red Army isolated Berlin with overwhelming numbers. Then it slowly crushed the city's life. It was impossible to fight a full-scale battle there with nearly two million inhabitants, mostly old men or women and children living in shelters. Allied bombing had forced them below ground. In any event the military organization defending the city was a lame skeleton. So-called *Panzer* divisions had a mere dozen or so tanks and armored vehicles. After engaging the advancing Russians, they inevitably retreated, leaving the dead and wounded lying in the streets. The fighting itself was done in the midst of civilians who had themselves either been killed by rockets and shells, were cowering in cellars or desperately trying to find further cellars behind the retreating soldiers in order not to fall into Soviet hands. The streets were littered with bodies. Yet in some extraordinary way the spirit of the Berliners survived. They scrawled defiant messages on walls, proclaiming ultimate victory in spite of retreat. It was not the *Götterdämmerung* that Hitler had foreseen. But it had its moments of glory.

Up to 22 April Hitler was still nominally in charge of operations. One day earlier he directed his last battle. How did he conduct himself? First, he gave exact instructions to General Karl Koller, a *Luftwaffe* officer and Goering's Chief of Staff. When Goering had left the Bunker, Koller stayed. Like so many others he was unable to stand up to Hitler. Earnest and fussy, he would accept the Führer's raving invective and threats with misgiving but without dissent. Instead he would wring his hands and examine his conscience. On this occasion, as so often before, Hitler's orders were given in the greatest detail. He selected precisely which troops were to be brought back into reserve from the northern part of the city in order to launch a counter-attack on the Russians in the southern suburbs. He laid down exactly which ground units of the *Luftwaffe* were to be employed and in what way. The attack would be an all-out and final attempt to turn the tide. Every man, every gun and every tank would be committed, the *Luftwaffe* would put every available plane into the skies. All would be staked on a final desperate blow. An SS general, *Obergruppenfuehrer* (Lieutenant General) Felix Steiner, would command the operation.

The tactical plan for Steiner's attack was that it would be launched from the Eberswalde into the gap between von Manteuffel's Third *Panzer* Army and Busse's Ninth Army, so smashing the spearhead of Zhukov's drive on the city. But Army Group Steiner was a figment of Hitler's imagination. It had nothing like the strength required to mount an attack of the sort envisaged. Nonetheless Hitler told Steiner on the telephone to withdraw every man available between Berlin and the Baltic up to Stettin and Hamburg. The order was absurd. Steiner had no communication with any of these troops. Even had he the means of giving orders, there was no transport to move them. Yet when Steiner protested, Hitler broke in with an assurance that the Russians would suffer their bloodiest defeat before the gates of Berlin.

The shortage of troops was made up for by an abundance of

threats. Commanding officers who did not thrust home would not live to tell the tale. Steiner's written instructions contained a specific promise that he was answerable with his life for the execution of his orders. 'The fate of the Reich capital depends on the success of your mission.' Koller too was assured that his own head would guarantee both the vigilance of the effort to be made and the success that would result. All was in vain. Hitler's granite willpower was powerless now. Skeleton German battalions could never hold back the fully manned and equipped Russian divisions. The attack never came off. It did not even cross the start-line. German withdrawal in the north simply allowed Russian tanks to stampede through to the center of Berlin. The Steiner attack had made a desperate military position still more hopeless.

Weidling, on the other hand, who became Commandant of Berlin on 25 April, knew the city was almost surrounded. That evening on reporting in the Bunker to the Führer and his entourage, he showed them from a sketch map that the ring around the city would soon be finally closed. In fact the ring was already closed. After explaining the dispositions of enemy and German forces, Weidling gave his view that despite the defenders' efforts, the Russians were slowly and surely advancing to the center of Berlin. The encirclement involved eight Soviet armies. On the same day, 25 April, Hitler ordered the *Wehrmacht* to re-establish contact with Berlin by attacking from the NW, SE and south – so bringing the battle of Berlin to 'a victorious conclusion'. The only troops Weidling had, would ever have, were some *Volkssturm* battalions, *Luftwaffe* ground personnel and Hitler Youth units, and the remainder of his own 56 *Panzer* Corps. These he organized into defense sectors.

Despite all these difficulties Weidling made a plan which he put to the Führer on 26 April for effecting Hitler's escape from the city. Hitler rejected it. He was not prepared to be caught wandering about somewhere in the woods: 'I stay here to die at the head of my men. But you must continue to defend the city.' While inspecting defenses that day Weidling saw little to comfort him:

The Potsdamer Platz and the Leipziger Strasse were under strong artillery fire. The dust from the rubble hung in the air like a thick fog . . . shells burst all round us. We were covered with bits of broken stones . . . The roads were riddled with shell craters and piles of brick rubble. Streets and squares lay deserted. Dodging Russian mortars we made our way to the underground station by jumps. The roomy underground station was crowded with terrified civilians. It was a shattering sight . . . Colonel Barenfanger, who commanded in this sector, pressed me for more men and more ammunition. I could promise him neither. Most of his men were *Volkssturm* troopers who had been sent into the exceptionally severe fighting with captured arms . . . No ammunition for these guns could be found in the whole of Berlin.

Exactly how Berlin would finally fall remained to be seen. Lieutenant Colonel Pavel Troyanovski, a 'Red Star' correspondent, was there on the same day as Steiner's abortive attack:

It seemed as though we were confronted not by a town, but by a nightmare of fire and steel. Every house appeared to have been converted into a fortress. There were no squares or gardens, but only gun positions for artillery and mine throwers . . . Our guns sometimes fired a thousand shells on to one small square, a group of houses or even a tiny garden. Then the German firing points would be silenced, and the infantry would go into the attack . . . From house to house and street to street, from one district to another, mowing their way through gunfire and hot steel, went our infantrymen, artillery, sappers and tanks . . . On 25 April the German capital was completely encircled and cut off from the rest of the country. At the height of the street fighting Berlin was without water, without light, without landing fields, without radio stations. The city ceased to resemble Berlin.

On 23 April Stalin laid down the boundary between Zhukov and Koniev. The *Reichstag* (Parliament Building), where the Soviet flag was to be raised, was given to Zhukov. His soldiers captured the *Reichstag* and ran up the Red flag at about 1430 on 30 April – an hour before Hitler committed suicide. But German resistance, recalled one German soldier, continued in the hands of an SS officer:

The close combat boys went into action. Their leader was SS-*Obersturmführer* [First Lieutenant] Babick, battle commandant of the *Reichstag*. Babick now waged the kind of war he had always dreamed of. Our two battery commanders, Radloff and Richter, were reduced to taking orders from him. Babick's command post was not in the *Reichstag* itself but in the cellar of the house on the corner of Dorotheenstrasse and the Hermann Goring Strasse, on the side nearer the Spree. There he ruled from an air-raid shelter measuring some 250 sq ft. Against the wall stood an old sofa and in front of it a dining table on which a map of the center of Berlin was spread out. Sitting on the sofa was an elderly marine commander and next to him two petty officers. There were also a few SS men and, of course, SS-*Obersturmführer* Babick bending over his map. He played the great general and treated everyone present in the dim candle-lit room to great pearls of military wisdom. He kept talking of final victory, cursed all cowards and traitors and left no one in any doubt that he would summarily shoot anyone who abandoned the Führer.

Babick was tremendously proud of his successes. He was hoping for reinforcements. From somewhere or another, marines had come to Berlin on the night of 28 April, led by the very Lieutenant-Commander who was now hanging about the cellar with nothing to say for himself. Babick never moved from his map, plotting the areas from which he expected reinforcements and even the arrival of 'Royal Tigers' [heavy tanks]. Babick was still bubbling over with confidence. For one thing, he thought himself perfectly safe in his shelter. SS sentries were posted outside, others barred the corridor to the *Reichstag*, and Royal Tigers, our finest weapons, were apparently just around the corner. He had divided his men into groups of five to ten. One group was commanded by SS-*Untersturmführer* [Second Lieutenant] Undermann; he was posted south of the Moltke Bridge in the Ministry of the Interior (the building the Russians called 'Himmler's House') and the bridge itself lay in his line of fire.

Then an SS ensign, aged about 19, came to Babick with the report that Undermann and his men had come across some alcohol and that they had got roaring drunk. As a precaution he had brought Undermann along; he was waiting outside. Babick roared out the order: 'Have him shot on the spot!' The ensign clicked his heels and ran out. Seconds later we heard a burst of fire from a submachine-gun. The boy reappeared and reported:

'Orders carried out.' Babick put him in charge of Undermann's unit. Our ranks in the *Reichstag* got thinner and thinner. Part of our battery gradually dispersed, and by the night of 30 April, no more than 40 to 50 people, soldiers and civilians, were left in the cellar. This remnant was now busy looking for the safest possible hiding-places. There we intended to sit tight until the Russians came. But they kept us waiting for another 24 hours. At dawn on 1 May, we heard over our portable radio that the Führer had 'fallen in the battle for the *Reich* Capital,' his wife at his side. Goebbels and his family had gone the same way. We were our own masters, at long last.

The only thing still to be done was to negotiate with the Russians in order to surrender what was left of the city. By this time all that was left in German hands were the Government buildings, part of the adjoining *Tiergarten* and the area between the Zoo and the Havel river. Hitler had forbidden Weidling to capitulate but he had authorized a break-out. After Hitler's death Martin Bormann, the Deputy Führer, had sent a telegram to Admiral Karl Dönitz in Plön, appointing him as Hitler's successor. Dönitz, not realizing that Hitler was dead, replied: 'My Führer! My loyalty to you will be unconditional. I shall do everything possible to relieve you in Berlin. If fate nevertheless compels me to rule the Reich as your appointed successor, I shall continue this war to an end, worthy of the unique, heroic struggle of the German people.' But Goebbels and Bormann were trying above all to put an end to the pointless bloodshed. They therefore made contact with the Russians who agreed to receive a German representative.

This was Lieutenant General Hans Krebs, Chief of the General Staff since Guderian's dismissal on 28 March, who spoke Russian and had been in Moscow as Military Attache. He met Gen. Chuikov, Commander of the 8th Guards Tank Army, at Schulenburgring near Tempelhof Airport, at 0400 on the morning of 1 May. He had been authorized to negotiate only a truce or armistice, but the Russians, despite suspicions that the Western Allies were contemplating a separate peace with the German armies in the West, refused to consider anything except unconditional surrender. When Krebs referred to 1 May as a day which their two nations shared as a holiday, Chuikov drily observed that it might be a fine day in Moscow, but he could not say the same for Berlin. Thus Krebs

failed and he committed suicide after returning to the Bunker. Next
Weidling tried to negotiate. On the following morning he crossed the
line dividing the two armies and surrendered the Berlin garrison with
its 70,000 troops. The battle for Berlin was over. The question now
was how would the Russians behave?

Rape, looting, burning and murder became commonplace. Hitler's
very last War Directive of 15 April had made it clear what fate
threatened a defeated Germany: 'While the old men and children will
be murdered, the women and girls will be reduced to barrack-room
whores.' Even at the end Hitler's reliance on propaganda and
foresight did not desert him. But better things were on the way
for Berlin. The Red Army positioned more disciplined regiments
there: American troops reached the city on 1 July; the British arrived
next day.

Iwo Jima (1945)

Paul M. Kennedy

Iwo Jima made an unremarked appearance on the island-littered map of the Pacific when, over 70 years ago, an underwater volcano spewed out ash and mud. The eight square miles of barren ash and soft, freshly formed rock might have remained in obscurity but for the strategic significance of this speck of land in the battle for the Pacific in the Second World War. Vital to the American campaign of rolling back the newly acquired Pacific empire of the Japanese to attack the enemy homeland, the grim battle for the tiny island lasted over a month and at the end 5,800 Americans and nearly 22,000 Japanese lay dead. Seizure of the island would deny the Japanese an excellent strategic base and give the Americans a bomber base only 660 nautical miles from Tokyo. Previous bombing missions had flown from the Marianas, 2,800 miles from Japan – a range which precluded fighter escort and led to heavy B29 Superfortress casualties. Iwo Jima was also a necessary link in the air defenses of the Marianas and it had to be captured, not merely isolated. There was a final consideration – the island was traditionally Japanese territory, administered from Tokyo, and its fall would be a severe psychological blow to the enemy.

Such blows were important. The Japanese had expanded their empire at a phenomenal rate. In the first five months of 1942 they had captured territory stretching from Burma in the west, through the Malay archipelago, to the central Pacific island groups of the

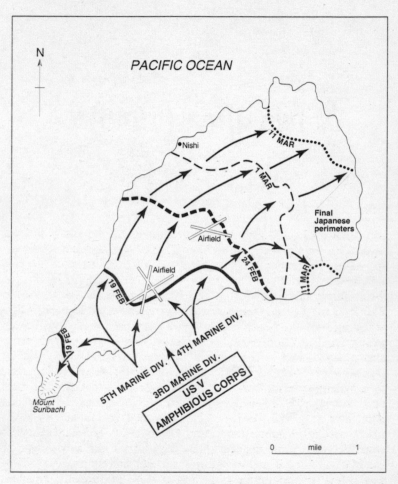

N

PACIFIC OCEAN

•Nishi

11 MAR

7 MAR

Final
Japanese
perimeters

Airfield

24 FEB

11 MAR

Airfield

19 FEB

19 FEB

Mount
Suribachi

5TH MARINE DIV. 4TH MARINE DIV.

3RD MARINE DIV.

US V
AMPHIBIOUS CORPS

0   mile   1

5.14   *The Campaigns in the Pacific, 1943–5*

Gilberts and the Marshalls. Control of these islands, small in size, gave them air command of the surrounding area, and command of the skies was vital to control of the seas.

The Americans responded in two ways. They built up fast carrier-based forces which could gain command of the air in disputed areas, from which land and sea control could follow. To gain land control they devised sophisticated amphibious assault techniques to capture island bases. The land targets were so small that such invasions were, in reality, direct attacks on fortified positions and the landing was not an orthodox preliminary move, it was the battle itself.

Naval victories at the Coral Sea on 7 May 1942 and a month later at Midway, on 4–5 June, started the American comeback. On 7 August, 19,000 Marines under Major General Alexander A. Vandegrift landed on the island of Guadalcanal in the southern Solomons. The move took the local Japanese commanders by surprise and there was no need for an amphibious assault. On the nearby island of Tulagi, however, the Marines had a grim struggle with the local garrison and learned their first lesson – that the Japanese soldier, even if his position was hopeless, would fight to the death rather than surrender.

The next step in the Pacific re-conquest was a two-pronged assault. General Douglas MacArthur thrust into the south-west Pacific, taking the Solomons, isolating Rabaul on the island of New Britain, and 'hopping' along the northern coast of New Guinea. Admiral Chester W. Nimitz's central Pacific forces captured the Gilbert, Marshall and Mariana groups, and isolated the Carolines. So swift was the American drive that on 20 October 1944 the re-conquest of the Philippines began, against which the Japanese could offer only sporadic resistance after their naval defeat at Leyte Gulf.

The US Marines played a decisive part in the drive across the Pacific, particularly in the central Pacific advance. In their first attack, against the Gilbert Islands in November 1943, the Corps suffered heavy losses in the confused and bloody assault on Tarawa. Yet they learned a lot from the assault and in later and larger operations in the Marshalls and Marianas the benefits of earlier experience were clearly revealed. Now, at the beginning of 1945, with Japan pushed almost back to her national boundaries, the Marines were preparing for their toughest assignment yet – the assault on Iwo Jima.

The Japanese were also aware of Iwo Jima's importance and

began speedy reinforcement towards the end of 1944. A garrison of 23,000 men under Lieutenant General Tadamichi Kuribayashi was sent to the island with orders to hold out as long as possible – American air and naval superiority ruled out further reinforcement. Kuribayashi was a courageous and dedicated soldier, described by Tokyo Radio as one whose 'partly protruding belly is packed full of strong fighting spirit.'

The Japanese took with them 120 big guns of over 75 mm caliber, 300 anti-aircraft guns of over 25 mm, 20,000 small guns, including machine-guns, 130 8 cm and 12 cm howitzers, 20 20 cm mortars, 70 20 cm rocket-guns, 40 47 mm and 20 37 mm anti-tank guns, and 27 tanks. The building of pillboxes began in October 1944 and five months later 360 were complete. A superb network of deep, interconnected caves, which were almost impervious to naval bombardment, was built. All this on an island of eight square miles.

Adm. Nimitz entrusted overall control of the Iwo Jima operation to Admiral Raymond Spruance's Fifth Fleet which, with its fast carrier and battleship units supported by a mobile fleet train, was the most powerful naval body in the world. Its role was to give distant cover against enemy air or naval attack and to participate in the bombardment of the island. Rear Admiral Richmond Kelly Turner, probably the most experienced leader of amphibious operations during the Second World War, was given command of the landings. The US troops, 84,000 in all, were to come from 4th and 5th Marine Divisions, with 3rd Marine Division in floating reserve, along with Major General Harry Schmidt's 5th Marine Amphibious Corps.

Major General Groves B. Erskine's 3rd Division had fought at Guam and Bougainville and the 4th Division, under General Clifton B. Cates, had seen action at Saipan and Tinian. Major General Keller E. Roche's 5th Division did not have combat experience but they were trained and strengthened by many veterans. Lieutenant General 'Howlin' Mad' Smith, the vigorous leader of the Marine Division at Guadalcanal and now commander of the Fleet Marine Force, Pacific, was the commanding general of the Expeditionary troops. With such a tried team of commanders and good calibre soldiers, there was little doubt about the eventual outcome of the invasion. The question was, how easy – or difficult – would the Marines find the assault?

From late 1944 the most intensive softening up yet of the Pacific War began. Army bombers flew raids by day, Marine ones by night with ever-increasing intensity in the weeks leading up to the invasion, which was scheduled for 19 February 1945. Three days before the landings, Admiral William Blandy's Amphibious Support Force, which included five battleships, began an intensive bombardment of the island. At the same time, Spruance supervised carrier forces in their aerial attacks on Honshu to prevent any possible Japanese air strikes against the invasion fleet.

The shelling of Iwo Jima proved completely inadequate, as Schmidt had forecast in repeated requests for a longer, ten-day bombardment. The Americans received a shock on 17 February when 11 of 12 gunboats supporting beach demolition teams were sunk by enemy fire. Blandy realized from this that the island's defenses were far heavier than had been expected and accepted Schmidt's advice to concentrate bombardment on the beaches and nearby areas. Iwo Jima, like Tarawa, was so small that it was virtually all beach – unless enemy fire could be neutralized before the assault the Marines would be completely exposed.

The 'gunboat incident' benefited the Americans in two ways. It forced a reassessment of the enemy defenses and also exposed many Japanese gun positions. It seems unlikely that the orders to open fire came from high-ranking commanders – the first of Kuribayashi's 'Essential Battle Instructions' demanded that 'while the enemy bombardment is going on, we must take cover in the dugouts and we must keep our casualties to a minimum.' Kuribayashi was swift to order redeployment of the guns that had opened fire.

With a broad rocky plateau in the north and the extinct volcano of Mount Suribachi at the southern tip of the pork-chop shaped island of Iwo Jima, the only place a full-scale invasion could be mounted was on the black cinder beaches along the south-east coast. From this point it was only a short distance to airfield No. 1; but a landing here also meant that the open beaches would be subjected to an intense fire from higher ground to the north and the south.

At 0640 on 19 February, just before sunrise, Blandy's ships, now reinforced by two battleships and 13 cruisers from Spruance's fleet, opened up with a stupendous close-range bombardment of the island. The astonishing number of 450 ships ringed the island. Blasted by shells ranging from five-inch to 16-in in diameter, the beaches seemed to be torn apart. Shortly afterwards, rocket-firing gunboats attacked the Motoyama plateau while other gunboats lobbed mortar rounds at Mount Suribachi. Then, as the firing was temporarily checked and the various ships moved into their final positions, carrier aircraft and

heavy bombers from the Marianas showered the areas surrounding
the beaches with rockets, napalm and bombs. After a further ten
minutes the naval shelling recommenced, joined by ten destroyers
and over 50 gunboats which steamed as close inshore as possible
in an effort to screen the approaching invasion armada. The whole
co-ordinated action was immensely impressive – one history of the
battle describes the bombardment as 'a power-laden deployment
packing the utmost momentum yet devised by the mind and
engineering of man. This was the acme of amphibious assault.'

As the naval bombardment, now a creeping barrage, reached its
crescendo, the landing-ships lowered their ramps and the first of the
five assault waves emerged, 5,500 yards from the shore. Each wave
consisted of 69 amphtracs, armored amphibian tractors which could
take 20 troops each right onto the beach and scramble over coral reefs
if necessary. The first wave, the 4th Marine Division on the right,
the 5th on the left, moved virtually undisturbed towards the shore.
At 0902, after 30 minutes' steaming, the amphtracs hit the beach,
spewing out their men and the armored mortar and rocket-firing
vehicles.

They were immediately up against two unexpected physical
obstacles – black volcanic ash into which men sank up to a foot
or more, and a steep terrace 15 ft high in some places, which only a
few amphtracs managed to climb. Most stayed on the beach, getting
in the way of oncoming waves, while the troops jumped out and
struggled through the ash. One Marine described how he 'tried to
sprint up the terrace wall but my feet only bogged in the sand and
instead of running I crawled, trying to keep my rifle clean but failing.'
Fresh waves of assault troops arrived every five minutes and soon
10,000 men and 400 vehicles were on the beach. Despite inevitable
confusion the first combat patrols pushed 150 yards inland, then 300.
And then the enemy opened up.

From rabbit-holes, bunkers and pillboxes, small arms and machine-
gun fire crashed into the Marines. Heavy artillery and mortars, from
deep emplacements and caves on Suribachi and the Motoyama plateau, and trained exactly on the beaches well in advance, thundered
out, destroying men and machines. The Japanese garrison, true to
their orders, had withheld fire during the landings – only five
amphtracs were lost from the early waves. As the momentum of the
assault slowed at the terrace and the creeping barrage out-distanced
the Marines, the defenders nearest the beach were able to recover

and man their weapons. The ash on the beach cushioned all but direct blasts from the mortars and artillery – but one war correspondent stated that 'nowhere . . . have I seen such badly mangled bodies.' It soon became clear that to stay on the beach was near-suicide – but to move off it meant moving into fire from the well-developed defense system.

At this point – and probably only here – the outcome of the battle was in doubt. If the Japanese had mounted a counter-attack, they might have routed the disorganized Marines. But the lessons of Tarawa, Roi-Namur, Saipan and Guam were that furious counter-assaults upon the invaders simply exposed the defenders to the overwhelming American firepower. Kuribayashi's task was to deny Iwo Jima to the enemy for as long as possible and his troops were ordered to stay strictly on the defensive. Many of the guns were firing only sporadically to conserve their ammunition, although no one at the beach-head would have believed this. The initiative still lay with the Marines – they and their equipment were successfully ashore. Now they could, they *must*, go forward.

Slowly, desperately slowly, the Marines pushed inland, a confused collection of small groups rather than a united force. Each bunker, each rabbit-hole meant a fight to the death. Each enemy position was supported by many others – the Japanese would disappear down one hole and pop up at another, often behind rather than in front of the advancing Marines. The Marines struggled on, pouring bullets, grenades and flame into enemy positions. Flail tanks rumbled forward with the Marines, detonating land mines, tank-dozers carved channels through the terrace and ordinary tanks relieved the pressure on the Marines by knocking out machine-gun nests and pillboxes. But it was no pushover, even with the armor. Facing 4th Division's lines, for example, were ten reinforced concrete blockhouses, seven covered artillery positions and 80 pillboxes. A battalion commander asserted that 'whenever a man showed himself in the lines it was almost certain death.' By mid-afternoon the reserve battalions of four regimental combat teams and two tank battalions had been committed to the battle to relieve the pressure on the leading units.

As dusk fell on this first, bloody day of the campaign, the numbers of Marines had risen to 30,000, with the committal ashore of the reserve regiments for both divisions. On the left flank Colonel Harry B. Liversedge's 28th Regiment had pushed across to the ridge which overlooked the beaches on the south-west; but fierce enemy opposition had halted its progress towards its main target, Mount Suribachi. Next in line was Colonel Thomas A. Wornham's 27th Regiment, which had similarly been brought to a halt in its efforts to overrun airfield No. 1. Farther to the right were the two regiments of the 4th Division, Colonel Walter W. Wensinger's 23rd Marines and Colonel John R. Lanigan's 25th Marines; both had come under extremely heavy fire from the entire Motoyama plateau area, and the 25th Regiment, being farthest on the right, suffered many casualties – one battalion had only 150 men left in the front line.

Although the Marines had failed to reach their first day's objectives, they had secured a foothold and, aided by the inflow of reserves, were digging in to await the expected counter-attack. It didn't come. Instead, the Japanese kept up a deadly accurate mortar and artillery fire against the beaches, causing great damage and loss of life. Most feared of all were the 60 kg and 250 kg bombs which the Japanese had converted into rockets, which came screaming out of the blue to burst upon impact. 'A nightmare in hell' was one description of the scene.

On the second morning, after a 50-minute naval bombardment, the Marines moved on again. But progress was, if anything, even slower than on the previous day. Liversedge's 28th Regiment, making repeated attacks upon the approaches to Mount Suribachi with the aid of artillery, half-tracks and destroyers positioned nearby, advanced only 200 yards that day. To the north the 4th Division reached their objectives on No. 1 airfield and then swung right to face the rising ground that constituted Kuribayashi's first major defense line. Here, too, early progress soon petered out. On the next day this line remained virtually static but the 28th Regiment, again assisted by naval and aerial bombardment, penetrated almost to the foot of Suribachi.

The rugged volcanic mountain, rising steeply out of the sea to a height of 556 ft, was not of central importance to the defense of Iwo Jima. Yet it offered fine observation and artillery siting positions and, because of its imposing appearance, control of it tended to symbolize mastery of the island. Recognizing that it would soon be cut off, Kuribayashi had allocated only 1,860 men to its defense; but to its natural advantages had been added several hundred blockhouses, pillboxes and covered guns around its base together with an intricate system of caves in the slopes. As always, each position had to be taken separately, using a variety of weapons: mortars, tanks, rockets, flame-throwers and dynamite. When the Marines reached the caves, they went in with knives to kill the Japanese in close combat. Some of the defenders, out of ammunition, were reduced to rolling stones down the slopes, but still they fought on. By the morning of 23 February, the Marines were approaching the summit and 40 men under Lieutenant Harold Schrier carried an American flag to signify their victory. At 1020 it was raised amid cheers while fighting was still going on in the vicinity; and at noon it was replaced by a much larger flag. The planting of the second flag was photographed by Joe Rosenthal of Associated Press and the picture became probably the most famous of the entire war.

The end of the campaign was far from in sight – the worst had yet to come. Anticipating a fierce struggle, the Americans had committed the 3rd Marine Division on the same day to the middle of the front line, with the 4th on the right and the 5th on the left, and General Schmidt had come ashore to take direct control of what was the largest group of Marines yet to fight under a single command. Only 2,630 yards of island were left but it was obvious that every one was to be paid for dearly.

Kuribayashi had systematically turned the plateau region into an armed camp. Rockets, artillery and mortars, one a 320 mm weapon that lobbed 700 lb shells, were in good supply and blockhouses and pillboxes were numerous. Caves were elaborate and well fortified – one could hold 2,000 troops and had 12 exits – and the defenders were well trained and in high morale. They were prepared to hold a position to the death, infiltrate Marine lines, or throw themselves under an enemy tank with a bomb strapped to their backs. It was all deadly, frighteningly inhuman. Admiral Turner called it 'as well defended as any fixed position that exists in the world today.'

Fortunately this kind of operation was exactly what the Marines were trained for. During the Pacific War, as they fought from one atoll to the next, the Marines endured a much more personal and individual form of combat than that seen in actions in Western Europe or North Africa, and against a fanatical enemy who would not surrender.

To reduce the casualties of the attacking force, weapons of modern military technology were brought to their aid. The Japanese positions were bombarded by the guns of warships, they were battered by heavy bombers, the rockets and machine-guns of fighters, as well as dive-bombers. Tanks, artillery, mortar and rockets hammered the positions, flame-throwers scorched them, and dynamite blasted them. But the Marines knew, as they looked ahead over the next ridge, along the next gully, that the capture of virtually every position also involved close-in fighting – with machine-gun, pistol, grenade, knife, digging-tool, even hands – before the defenders were fully overcome. This was how the hell on earth of Iwo Jima had to be taken.

The battle for the second airfield, sited almost in the dead center of the island, was typical of this form of fighting. There the Japanese had constructed hundreds of pillboxes, rabbit-holes and concealed emplacements, which defied the concentrated American firepower for two days. On 24 February, the two battalions of the 21st Marine Regiment rushed forward to take the enemy lines with bayonet and grenade, the terrain being too difficult for tanks. Not only did the Japanese fire upon them from all their entrenched positions, but many rushed into the open and engaged in a struggle reminiscent of some medieval carnage, with the bayonet as the key weapon. Casualties rose steeply on both sides. The Marines, thrown back by this fierce counter-attack, re-formed and charged again. By nightfall of the next day, they had captured the airfield and were pressing towards Motoyama village, with only the prospect of another bitter struggle ahead: to the right of them lay the formidable Hill 382, a position which became so difficult to secure that the Marines referred to it ominously as 'the Meat Grinder'.

The fighting in the days following was the same. The Americans had to take the higher, central part of the enemy's lines first, for whenever the 4th and 5th Divisions pushed ahead on their respective flanks they were heavily punished by the Japanese who overlooked them. The problem was that it was this middle zone where it was hardest to deploy tanks and artillery, or to direct the naval support fire with accuracy. Although the elements on the flanks helped, the Marines had the main job, the slow and deadly job, of clearing the area. By the tenth day of the fighting, though, the supporting fire for the 3rd Division had been substantially increased and the forward battalions found a weak spot in the Japanese line, and poured through. By evening Motoyama, now a heap of stones and rubble, was taken and the Marines could look down upon the third airfield. Once again, though, further momentum was broken by Kuribayashi's second major defense line, and there remained many areas to wipe up. Hill 382 was fiercely held by its defenders for two more days, and Hill 362 in the west was equally difficult. The whole operation was taking much longer than the ten days Schmidt had estimated for it, and the Marines were tired and depleted in their ranks: some units were down to 30 per cent of their original strength.

On Sunday 5 March, the three divisions regrouped and rested as best they could in the face of Japanese shellings and occasional infiltration. On that day, too, the Marines had the satisfaction of seeing a B29 with a faulty fuel valve returning to Tinian from a raid on Tokyo make an emergency landing on airstrip No. 1. Iwo Jima was already fulfilling its function.

For the Japanese, the situation was serious. Most of Kuribayashi's tanks and guns and over two-thirds of his officers had been lost. His troops were in a serious position, reduced to such desperate measures as strapping explosives to their backs and throwing themselves under American tanks. The Marines were moving relentlessly forward, however slowly, and this forced a gradual breakdown in Kuribayashi's communications system. This meant that, left to their own devices, individual Japanese officers tended to revert to the offensive. This may have been more appealing to the Samurai but it exposed the greatly depleted Japanese forces to the weight of American firepower. One attack, by 1,000 naval troops on the night of 8–9 March, was easily repulsed by 4th Marine Division with Japanese losses of over 800 men. The pressure on the defending forces was starting to tell; they were losing their cohesion.

On the afternoon of 9 March, a patrol from the 3rd Marine Division reached the north-eastern coast of Iwo Jima and sent back a sample of salt water to prove that the enemy's line had been cut in two. There was no stopping the American advance but even now there was no sign of Japanese surrender – the only indication of their desperate condition was the increasing number of 'banzai' charges. Kuribayashi's reports, however, describe the deteriorating situation: 10 March. American bombardment 'so fierce I cannot express nor write of it here'; 11 March. 'Surviving strength of northern districts (army and navy) is 1,500 men'; 14 March. 'Attack on northern district this morning. Much more severe than before. Around noon one part of the enemy with about ten tanks broke through our left front line and approached to 220 yards of divisional HQ'; 15 March.

'Situation very serious. Present strength of northern district about 900 men.'

On 14 March the Americans, believing all organized resistance to be at an end, declared Iwo Jima occupied and raised the Stars and Stripes. Yet underground, in their warren of caves and tunnels, the Japanese lived on. Kuribayashi told the survivors on 17 March: 'Battle situation come to last moment. I want surviving officers and men to go out and attack enemy until the last. You have devoted yourself to the Emperor. Do not think of yourselves. I am always at the head of you all.'

Clearing out pockets of organized resistance with tanks, demolition teams, rifle fire and flame-throwers took until 26 March. On this day the Japanese staged their last desperate fling when 350 troops rushed an Air Force and Seabee (Civil Engineers of the US Navy) construction camp. They were destroyed by a Marine pioneer battalion after a day of wild fighting. Kuribayashi committed suicide in the northern corner of Iwo Jima in the last few days of the battle. He promised that to help revive the Japanese army after his death, 'I will turn into a spirit.' One US Marine hoped that 'the Japs don't have any more like him.'

Only 216 Japanese had surrendered by 26 March; 20,000 were dead. In the following two months 1,600 Japanese were killed and another 370 captured as sporadic resistance was crushed. The American casualties, considering their air and sea control and their superior firepower, were equally daunting. A total of 275 officers and 5,610 men of the Marine Corps were killed and 826 officers and 16,446 men were wounded. Thirty per cent of the entire landing force and a staggering 75 per cent of the infantry regiments of the 4th and 5th Divisions were battle casualties. So depleted were some units during the action that one battalion commander commented that 'the appearance of a war dog and its handlers seemed like heavy reinforcements.' Twenty-four Medals of Honor were awarded and there were 2,648 'combat fatigue casualties' – both facts telling evidence of the gruelling nature of the battle for Iwo Jima.

Iwo Jima soon justified the strategic value which the Joint Chiefs of Staff and, in particular, the Air Force had attached to it. Before the end of the war against Japan, more than 20,000 crewmen in crippled planes had landed upon the island's airstrips; and from 7 April onwards, thanks to the efforts of the Seabee construction units, Mustang fighters were able to escort the daylight raids of the Superfortresses against Tokyo and other Japanese cities.

General Smith called the battle 'the toughest we've run across in 168 years' but also insisted that 'When the capture of an enemy position is necessary to winning a war it is not within our province to evaluate the cost in money, time, equipment, or most of all, in human life. We are told what our objective is to be and we prepare to do the job.' Admiral Nimitz summed up the achievement of the assault troops: 'Among the Americans who served on Iwo Island, uncommon valor was a common virtue.'

6
The Korean War

Inchon (1950)

Sydney L. Mayer

The Inchon landings of September 1950 were to prove the turning point of the war in Korea. General Douglas MacArthur conceived of the landings as a way of breaking the Communist stranglehold on the South. When UN forces had succeeded in taking Inchon they were to push on to the main prize – the South Korean capital, Seoul. The struggle for the control of this city was to prove the most savage of the whole war.

On Saturday 24 June 1950 United States President Harry S. Truman heard some grim news. Secretary of State Dean Acheson telephoned – the North Koreans had invaded South Korea. He advised the President to call on the United Nations Security Council to declare that an act of aggression had taken place. The following day Acheson called again. There was no doubt that a full-scale invasion had taken place but the United Nations was unlikely to do more than call for a ceasefire – and the call would probably be ignored. The United States therefore had to decide what degree of support, if any, it would give to South Korea.

The Japanese surrender in August 1945 left the US and Russia in Korea and they decided on the 38th Parallel as a purely military demarcation line between their two forces. In September 1947 the US turned the Korean problem over to the UN. By this time Korea had become a pawn in the rivalry between the two major world power blocs. A UN call for all-Korean elections was ignored by

the Russians and elections were held in the South only. In August
1948 the Republic of Korea (ROK) was established in the south
under the veteran nationalist Dr Syngman Rhee. In September
the Democratic People's Republic of Korea was created in the
north, with former guerilla leader Kim Il Sung as premier. There
were now two mutually antagonistic Korean regimes, each claiming
rights to the whole country and each backed by one of the two world
power blocs. Sporadic fighting took place along the 38th Parallel
and though the US believed an invasion of the south was possible,
Acheson admitted that 'its launching in the summer of 1950 did not
appear imminent.'

Despite appearances, it had happened. President Truman, like
most Americans, was acutely aware of the dangers of appeasement.
The dictators had not been stopped in 1931 when Japan invaded
Manchuria; in 1935 when Mussolini invaded Abyssinia or in 1938
when Hitler marched into Austria. The result was a massive and
bloody war. If the US did not react to the agression, so the reasoning
went, the Communists would seek to extend their conquests and this
would inevitably lead to a third world war. There were pressing
domestic considerations too – failure to act would encourage the arch
witch-hunter of Communists, Senator Joseph McCarthy, to charge
the government with appeasement, possibly fostered by subversives
within the President's own staff.

In Washington, the State and Defense Departments presented
joint recommendations. General Douglas MacArthur, then stationed
in Japan, was ordered to evacuate all Americans from Korea but to
attempt to keep the key airports open. The US air force was to
remain south of the 38th Parallel and ammunition and supplies
for the South Korean army were to be delivered by air drop and
other means. The Seventh Fleet was to sail to the Formosa Strait
to prevent any possible conflict between the nationalist Chinese on
Formosa and the Chinese Communist mainland. American policy
had altered – Korea and Formosa now fell within the US defense
perimeter.

To MacArthur, news of the invasion was like a nightmare, a
repetition of Pearl Harbor. As soon as he received orders from
Washington he sent aircraft to evacuate Americans from Korea but
did nothing else. But soon, orders came to commit US troops to the
field and MacArthur took immediate action.

Events had given MacArthur a new role. After a successful military

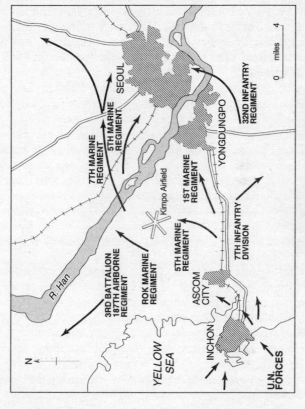

6.1 *The Inchon Landings, September 1950*

career in the Second World War and a smoothly run administration of post-war Japan, MacArthur had little more to look forward to than an honored retirement. Now, as commander of US, and later UN, forces in Korea he had another chance of glory and fame in the field. Thrilled by the challenge, MacArthur prepared his staff for his last great military campaign.

In the meantime, the UN voted to support American operations in Korea. MacArthur was now leader of a nominal UN force – nominal because, especially at the start, the only active participants were the retreating South Koreans and whatever American forces could be shipped or flown from Japan.

By the start of July, North Korean forces had crossed the Han river, pushing streams of dispirited ROK forces before them. At the same time, the first US combat troops arrived in Korea. MacArthur's arrogant hope that the North Koreans might 'turn round and go back when they found out who was fighting' came to nothing and on 19 July North Korean tanks smashed through American defenses at Taejon and rolled towards the Naktong river, the last major natural obstacle guarding the Pusan perimeter.

The Pusan perimeter was a 140-mile line running west and north of Pusan, from the Korea Strait to the Sea of Japan. Organized by Lieutenant General William Walker, commander of the US 8th Army in Korea, the Pusan perimeter held out against intensive North Korean pressure while US tanks, artillery and troops arrived through the port to reinforce the bridgehead. UN aircraft flew sorties against North Korean supply lines and the enemy's failure to mass forces for a decisive penetration at one point along the perimeter also contributed to the Americans' ability to hold the line.

By September 1950, the situation was deadlocked along the Pusan perimeter. Although North Korean forces seemed unable or unwilling to launch a major attack against the perimeter line, ROK and American forces were not of sufficient strength for a land assault on the enemy lines.

MacArthur considered that the only way out of the impasse was to attempt an amphibious landing behind enemy lines. The risks involved in such an action were enormous. Failure would result in irreparable damage to UN credibility in Korea and devalue the stature of the organization. Its ability to effectively intervene in any crisis situation would be greatly impaired.

The idea of landing at Inchon dated back to MacArthur's first visit to Korea following the start of open war between North and South. North Korean supply lines were stretched to the limit. A landing at Inchon would force the enemy to fight on two fronts. The result of this, MacArthur calculated, would be the total breakdown of enemy supply lines. As a result, they would be forced to withdraw from the Pusan perimeter within weeks.

If a landing at Inchon was successful the UN would enjoy a considerable propaganda boost. It would also make possible the recapture of Seoul, the South Korean capital, 18 miles to the east.

Codenamed Operation Chromite, plans for the Inchon landings went ahead. Meanwhile, thousands of reservists were sent from the West Coast of the United States to Japan. The first objective was to capture the island of Wolmi-do, at the entrance to the port of Inchon. Once taken, large numbers of troops could be brought forward, and the island would act as a springboard for the invasion proper.

The next step was to capture the city of Inchon itself. The prime objective – the recapture of Seoul – would now be in the UN forces' grasp. To make this possible, Kimpo – Seoul's major airport – had to be taken. At the same time as preventing the North Koreans from bringing in reinforcements, control of the airport would allow the UN to do just that.

MacArthur fervently believed that the North Koreans would be forced to retreat. He thought that, while fleeing, they would be trapped between the UN troops controlling Seoul and the forces heading north – freed from their 'prison' behind the Pusan perimeter.

Once the plan for the Inchon landings had been constructed, it was necessary to select the right personnel to head the operation. It was decided that the 10th Corps, commanded by General Almond, would be landed at Inchon by Rear Admiral James H. Doyle. Doyle was Amphibious Group Commander of the Pacific Fleet. His flagship, *Mt McKinley*, was anchored at Tokio. The landing force was to be in two groups – a marine division to push south and the 7th Division to cover their flank. Both these divisions would then form a defensive buffer against the North Koreans as the 8th Army moved north from the Pusan perimeter.

From the moment the idea of an amphibious landing had been mentioned, the Joint Chiefs supported it. But they were not so keen about the choice of Inchon as a landing place. Their reasoning was that because Inchon was far to the north and so near Seoul, the

North Koreans would almost certainly put up a savage defense. Also, Inchon's unusually high tides would make a quick and easy landing very difficult. UN casualties could be enormous before they even reached dry land. There was little room for failure. In contrast to the attitude of the Joint Chiefs, MacArthur had supreme confidence in his own judgement.

After much pressure, the Joint Chiefs finally gave MacArthur the go-ahead on 28 August, and the plan was finally ready for operation on 4 September. The assault on Inchon was set for 15 September. This date was chosen because the tide would be at its highest. Some doubts were voiced by navy and marine personnel – and rightly so. On that day the morning tide was at 0659 and the evening tide at 1919. A tide of at least 23 ft was necessary to enable the LSTs to navigate their way to the narrow peninsula of Wolmi-do, from where the landings were to be staged.

It was planned that a Battalion Landing Team (BLT3) of the 5th Marines would land at Green beach. This was to take place at 0630 with the morning tide. The sea front of Inchon itself, *Red beach*, was to be taken by BLT-1 and 2 at 1730. Back-up forces bringing tanks, bulldozers and engineers in eight LSTs would be brought forward. The 25 ft of tide would be just enough. Three heavily armed battalions would be landed at Blue beach simultaneously. Their task was to be the most demanding of all – to move forward and seize the main road and rail links between Inchon and the capital Seoul. Precise timing was vital for this operation. No margin of error could be afforded. Because of the tide, landing craft had to arrive and depart within a strictly laid-down timetable. Otherwise they ran the risk of being stranded on a sand bar.

MacArthur suspected that the Marines would have to use ladders to go into Inchon. This suspicion was confirmed when Lt. Eugene Clark was sent to inspect the beaches in the landing zone. He discovered that the mud was waist-deep at the harbor wall.

To complicate matters still further, the North Koreans launched an offensive against the Pusan perimeter in early September. General Walton Walker, in the perimeter, feared that if the Marines left for Inchon the North Koreans would have taken over Pusan by the time the landings took place.

MacArthur insisted that his plan to land at Inchon was the only way to avoid a protracted conflict, as well as a likely UN defeat in

Korea. So, after further argument and appeal to President Truman for confirmation, MacArthur had his way.

About 70,000 men had to be transported from Japan and Pusan to Inchon. An armada of 260 ships from the United States, France, Britain, Canada, New Zealand and Holland was formed. They were to link with support units at a prearranged series of points.

Things seemed to be going smoothly when a typhoon blew in from the Pacific with wind speeds of up to 125 m.p.h. The ships held their course. Any delay would have wrecked the whole plan. Remarkably, the typhoon passed – causing little harm.

The flagship *Mt McKinley*, with MacArthur aboard, arrived off Inchon on 14 September. By this time the coast had been under almost continuous bombardment for five days. Wolmi-do was singled out for the heaviest of the fire in order to clear the way for one of the three planned landings.

A thin causeway linked Wolmi-do with the mainland. If one of the mainland landings failed, UN troops could defend the island for some time while awaiting reinforcements. But for this to be feasible, Wolmi-do had to be captured swiftly.

The 5th Marines started to land on Green beach, on Wolmi-do, at 0633 on the 15th. It was held lightly and they encountered only scattered resistance. The total enemy presence on the island was around 350 men. By 0655 the 'battle' was virtually over and UN forces raised the flag on Radio Hill – the highest point on the island. This first step in the Inchon plan which had caused the Chiefs of Staff so many sleepless nights, was completed by 0800. Wolmi-do had been captured without a single fatality.

UN forces bombarded Red beach from sea and air for the rest of that day. But the landing had to wait for the evening tide, 1730, and as the tide flowed in the landing operation began. This time, things did not go so easily for the UN forces.

There was a fierce battle for the control of Cemetery Hill in the city of Inchon itself. A North Korean bunker held down the Marines below a sea wall. But by midnight the Marines had established a firm line across Observatory Hill – and had complete control of Red beach. Within six hours, UN forces had entered the very heart of Inchon.

So far, things seemed to be running smoothly and to plan. A number of landing craft became stuck in mud some 300 ft out from Blue beach, forcing Marines to wade ashore, and some vehicles stalled when a road collapsed. After a sea wall was dynamited, however, the landings at Blue beach were made easier. The Marines reached their objective by midnight and by the following day the North Koreans had fled Inchon.

Inchon had been taken at the cost of 196 casualties, including about 20 dead. The Joint Chiefs' fears had been proved unfounded and MacArthur's stock had never been higher. But it still remained to capture Kimpo airfield and Seoul itself. This had to be done quickly, but it was not going to be so easy.

The North Koreans had decided to abandon Inchon to avoid unacceptably high losses. However, they intended to dig in their heels at Seoul. The capital was turned into a virtual fortress.

Once Inchon was theirs, MacArthur, Almond and Admiral Struble visited the battlefields. MacArthur believed that he could take Seoul within five days. Almond thought it would take almost a fortnight. Almond was right.

The first target – Kimpo airfield – was captured on 18 September. As it happened, Kimpo was hardly used at all by the North Koreans, but within days it became one of the world's busiest airports as the Americans airlifted in reinforcements. It seemed inevitable to the Americans that Seoul must fall very soon. But they had reckoned without the ferocity of the North Korean defense of the city. The Americans had to bombard the city with all the firepower they possessed. Many civilians were trapped and burnt to death in an inferno from which there was no escape.

MacArthur was a great respecter of the virtues of technology. He believed that tanks, artillery and aircraft should be used to the full in order to save lives. The North Koreans, however, were not equipped with so much sophisticated hardware and, consequently, thought quite differently. Almost all they had was men. They were to fight to the last.

To the Americans, Seoul was a political symbol of the first importance. If this had not been the case, it would have been possible – and certainly wiser – to by-pass the city and join up with the northward bound 8th Army. MacArthur, however, was determined to capture the city and had to pour in more and more forces in the attempt to do so. In Seoul itself there were 20,000 North Koreans who were determined to fight it out until every one was dead.

This was unfortunate for the citizens. Living in Seoul soon

became a nightmare. Prior to the Marines moving into the city, aerial bombardment had devastated whole districts. The badly built wooden dwellings of most of the people were burnt to the ground. Often, their owners went with them. North Korean suicide squads threw themselves at the advancing tanks but failed to slow them in any way.

When the Americans finally entered the city, most of the defenders were dead. Thousands of civilians – men, women and children – had been slaughtered and many more were horribly maimed by fire. Panic-stricken homeless refugees were everywhere.

The situation was made still worse as the surviving North Koreans fought a last-ditch, street-by-street battle with the Americans. This fighting was desperate and vicious. Intense heat from the burning buildings added to the horror. The fighting continued until 27 September when the Marines reached the 'Capitol of the Republic of Korea' and raised the American flag above it. By the time the North Korean defenders were finally overcome, more than 130,000 prisoners had been taken.

On 29 September MacArthur entered the shattered city and in the South Korean National Assembly pronounced that Seoul was restored as the seat of government. On that same afternoon he returned to Tokio. As a city, Seoul suffered one of the greatest hammerings to be perpetrated in modern warfare. Thousands of its people were dead or homeless. Its buildings were mostly rubble. MacArthur had confounded his critics and scored the greatest triumph of his military career.

Imjin River (1951)

A. H. Farrar-Hockley and E. L. Capel

The Stalinist regime of North Korea launched a major offensive in the Korean War on 22 April 1951, breaking through the line held by the United Nations west of Chungpyong Reservoir. The situation was only saved by the stand of the Gloucestershire Regiment at Imjin River against a much larger enemy force, composed mostly of Chinese communists. The Glosters' action was later termed 'the most outstanding example of unit bravery in modern warfare' by the UN Commander in Korea, General James Van Fleet. A. H. Farrar-Hockley, the co-author of this account of the Glosters' stand was the Adjutant of the regiment during the Imjin River battle.

The battalion moved back towards the battle line on 21 March 1951, a monumental date for the past and, did they but know it, for the future. But the first step towards the Imjin river was neither very demanding nor challenging: Colonel Carne was ordered to site and dig a battalion position covering Uijongbu. The sector belonged to the 3rd United States Division and its Commander was anxious to have a long stop on the road leading south from the river through the hills at this point. Though little more than a rough track it had been used successfully by the Chinese less than three months previously as a main thrust line to Seoul. It was, indeed, an ancient invasion route by the armies of Imperial China. So the Glosters dug and wired, grumbling cheerfully as British soldiers do when they are obliged to prepare defences without an enemy in sight.

Even when, at the beginning of April, they moved north through the hills along this route to the Imjin itself, there was no sign of the enemy, and this was in many ways a comfort; for though the river formed the front edge of the UN defensive line 'Kansas', there were so few troops to man it that the gap between the Glosters' left and the nearest ROK unit was three miles. On the right, the nearest friendly element was a company of the Fifth Fusiliers, almost two miles distant. Thus isolated, the battalion was required to deny to the Communist Forces the use of the road running south.

The Glosters relieved the PEFTOK (Phillipines Expeditionary Force, Task Organization Korea) and these small, brown, friendly men withdrew to the south. They had been in the position only a few days and had very little intelligence about enemy locations or strengths. It seemed to Colonel Carne that he had better do something to remedy this lack of knowledge as soon as his companions had settled. 'A' Company, under Major Pat Angier, was left forward on the old Castle Site, a high point (148) west of the village of Choksong. 'D' under Major 'Lakri' Wood, were on the hill feature south-east of the village. 'B' Company, commanded by Major Denis Harding, somewhat to the east guarded the right flank approaches. 'C' (Major Paul Mitchell) lay in reserve on the high ground directly above battalion headquarters. The headquarters site was at a point where the road running south entered the hills and swung across a shallow stream. The open valley mouth towards the river was held by the Drums. Troubled by a triangular-shaped height immediately to the west overlooking this site, the colonel put out on it his only uncommitted force, the assault pioneers under Captain 'Spike' Pike.

It was a carefully considered deployment which made the best of a frontage of seven miles and depth of five. Any enemy approach would lie through the small arms fire of at least two companies, and two sections of the Vickers machine-guns. The guns of 45 Field Artillery Regiment, backed potentially by the United States 3rd Divisional artillery, the mortars of 'C' Troop, 170 Mortar Battery and the Glosters own 3-inch mortar platoon were able between them to cover both companies and approaches with shell or bomb. The difficulty was to detect enemy movement by night. A change in darkness to a tight defensive position was not practicable because of the shortage of

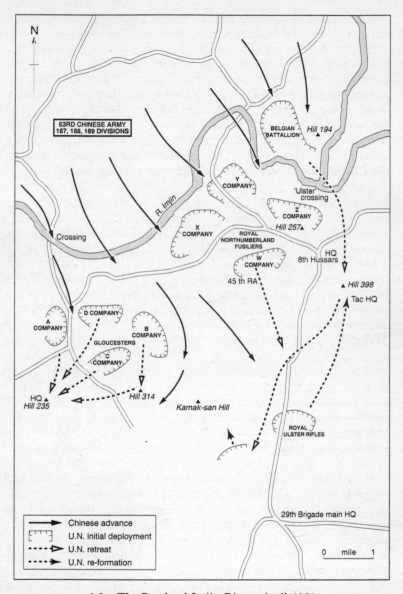

N

63RD CHINESE ARMY
187, 188, 189 DIVISIONS

BELGIAN BATTALLION   Hill 194

Y COMPANY

'Ulster crossing

R. Imjin

Z COMPANY

X COMPANY

Hill 257▲

Crossing

ROYAL NORTHUMBERLAND FUSILIERS

W COMPANY

HQ 8th Hussars

45th RA

▲ Hill 398

Tac HQ

A COMPANY

D COMPANY

B COMPANY

GLOUCESTERS

C COMPANY

HQ ▲ Hill 235

Hill 314▲

Kamak-san Hill▲

ROYAL ULSTER RIFLES

29th Brigade main HQ

→ Chinese advance
�... U.N. initial deployment
⇢ U.N. retreat
⇢ U.N. re-formation

0   mile   1

6.2   *The Battle of Imjin River, April 1951*

defence stores. It took eight days to get the first truckload of barbed wire and the second did not reach the battalion until it had been in position for 17 days. Much had happened in that time.

An active patrol programme confirmed that the ford across the Imjin river, carrying the road from Seoul northwards, was intact and the enemy defences covering it on the far bank empty. But there had been movement in the high ground immediately to the north amongst a series of bunkers. 'A' and 'D' Companies combined in a night operation to close on these and sweep them at dawn. Apart from a radio mishap at the outset, this was most successful, though when the troops searched the bunkers these were also found to be abandoned. Where had the enemy gone?

A major sortie followed in daylight: two company groups and Major George Butler's squadron of the 8th Hussars moved north across the Imjin to a distance of seven miles in an operation named 'Cygnet' – young swan. At last a few half-starved and very miserable Chinese soldiers were captured. Was this the rearguard of the mighty Chinese Peoples' Volunteers?

As a matter of fact it was. Weakened by the severity of the winter and defeated by the advancing United Nations forces, the mass of Chinese divisions had broken away from their pursuers during March. There had thus been no pursuit into the heart of North Korea as in 1950. General Ridgway had now replaced General MacArthur as Supreme Commander, Allied Powers, and his orders were to hold on or about the line of the 38th Parallel of latitude – the old demarcation line between north and south – which, in this sector, was roughly along the course of the Imjin. A few exhausted Chinese and North Korean units had been left to hold an outpost line while, 20 miles to the north over a period of six weeks, the Chinese commander-in-chief, Peng Teh-Huai, refreshed, replenished, and reinforced his armies. Then, with the winter finally past, he gave orders on 13 April for a fresh offensive. Small reconnaissance parties were sent south to discover and infiltrate between the UN positions, travelling only by night, resting and watching by day. On the night of the 21st, the mass of the attacking armies began to march south after them, amongst them the 63rd Army of three divisions* – the 187,

---

* A Chinese Communist Forces (CCF) Division was about 9,000 strong, mostly infantry with six to eight batteries of light artillery and about twice this number of medium and heavy mortars.

188, 189 – with orders to force open the ancient route to Seoul.

Various sources of intelligence had disclosed to the United Nations commander in Korea, General James van Fleet, that an offensive was impending. All units were ordered to be ready and thus all were watchful. A little after midday on 22 April, the Glosters' artillery observation posts saw 20 enemy moving south in file . . . dressed in dark uniforms. A larger body of moved round behind hill . . . immediately north of the Imjin ford known as Gloster Crossing. Air recce began to search as Colonel Carne accompanied a patrol to a vantage point close to the river from which to observe. The adjutant joined the colonel and the intelligence officer, Lieutenant Henry Cabral, on the bank. Five more enemy parties between 10 and 20 strong were observed occupying the old positions on the high ground immediately to the north, in which they were severely shelled. But otherwise the colonel's orders, sent back to the adjutant, were clear: the companies were to take pains to lie low and conceal themselves from what were obviously enemy scouting parties. A fighting patrol was to be prepared in 'C' Company – one platoon – to lay an ambush on the south side of the ford as soon as it was dark. Meantime, 'A' Company's observation post was to watch this sensitive point until dusk and to shell and mortar any attempt to seize it in daylight.

The afternoon passed in an atmosphere of excitement. Everyone in the battalion sensed that a major clash was imminent. Men rested in all positions. At 5 p.m. the hot evening meal was eaten and before dusk a comprehensive check of weapons and ammunition had been completed. Half the reserve ammunition was brought forward from 'A' Echelon to the headquarters site. As the light waned, the ambush party from 'C' Company, Lieutenant Guy Temple's platoon, came down from their hilltop and made their way to the river and ford.

The task of the 'C' Company platoon was to surprise and destroy the enemy attempting to cross to the south of the Imjin. It was only partially successful for two reasons. First, because the weight of the enemy seeking to cross were far greater than had been expected from air reconnaissance and ground observation reports during the afternoon and evening. At dusk on the 22 April, the main body of the enemy were not within 12 miles of the river. They closed on the Imjin in a forced march of three hours carrying all their battle gear. Lieutenant Temple's platoon destroyed the enemy's advanced party attempting to seize the crossing by *coup de main* early in the night but were then pressed by a battalion backed by two more. Seventy

Field Battery, 'C' Troop of 170 Mortar Battery, the mortar platoon and the small arms of the ambush fired continuously for some hours but they could not stem indefinitely the flood of Chinese soldiers.

Meantime, unknown to the Glosters, a second enemy brigade was crossing the Imjin at another ford, of which they were unaware, one-and-a-half miles downstream. This was the second reason for the limited success of the ambush and a consequence of the excessive frontage held by the battalion. Even while the ambush held the enemy to its front in check, a strong assault was being launched against 'A' Company on the Castle Site by about two battalions while a third crossed the road to the east to attack 'D' Company.

Upstream, the left flank company of the Fifth Fusiliers holding a ridge overlooking the river and lateral road had been attacked and forced to withdraw. A battalion from this area moved south to attack 'B' Company of the Glosters. Not long after midnight, therefore, the three forward rifle companies of the Glosters were in action, 'A' Company being critically pressed by an enemy outnumbering them by six to one.

At battalion headquarters, Captain Reeve-Tucker, the signals officers, entered the command vehicle with a message from the ambush party.

'They're still trying to cross in hordes, sir,' he said to the colonel. 'In another five minutes, he [Temple] reckons they'll be out of ammunition.'

The colonel looked across at Major Guy Ward, the battery comander, and the adjutant.

'Tell him to start withdrawing in three minutes,' he said to the adjutant. 'Guy, I'm going to ask you for one last concentration, and then start dropping them short of Gloster Crossing as soon as the patrol is back at the first cutting south of the river.'

The advantage of the United Nations' Forces as their line was, almost everywhere, assailed that night was in the power of their weapons, particularly artillery, to drop destructive fire accurately into the enemy masses. Their weakness lay in the length of front which resulted in numbers of fragmented battles, each of which needed to be won by the defence if Line Kansas was to be held. The artillery could not engage so many targets adequately. The morning light would permit the UN air forces to add their weight of firepower. The question was, would it be enough?

At a number of points, air strikes forced the enemy to withraw temporarily by 9 a.m. on the morning of the 23rd but there were none available to the Glosters.

Before dawn on the 23rd the battalion Command Post had moved up to the ridge held by 'C' Company. From there, in a bunker constructed under RSM Jack Hobbs' supervision some days before, the colonel could overlook the battle on the two hill positions to the north. The desperate nature of the struggle was manifest before the morning sun rose. By night, the calls for fire support, each fresh report from 'A', 'B' or 'D' Company headquarters and the artillery radio links had made it all too clear that the attack was in strength. Just after dawn, in the command post, Corporal Walters told the adjutant that Major Angier, commanding 'A' Company, wished to speak to him.

'I'm afraid we've lost the Castle Site. I'm mounting a counter-attack now but I want to know whether to expect to stay here indefinitely or not. If I am to stay on, I must be reinforced as my numbers are getting very low.'

When the message was passed to the colonel he was already considering what his options were now that daylight had come. Two questions were in his mind: would the Chinese continue to press their attack in daylight with the threat of intervention by UN aircraft; and, secondly, how long would it be before the Chinese discovered that both battalion flanks were completely open and encircle his battalion?

He questioned Major Angier briefly and then gave his orders: 'You will stay there at all costs until further notice.'

At all costs and until further notice . . . The need for 'A' Company to hold its position was this: notwithstanding the loss of the highest point of their position, they had still observation over the approaches to 'D' Company as well as forward to the two river crossing points. If the company was precipitately withdrawn, the Chinese would reinforce freely the force on the south bank, overwhelm 'D' Company, and in turn, 'B'.

The adjutant sent forward a supply of ammunition in a pair of Oxford carriers under Lieutenant Cabral.

'Don't worry about us,' said Major Angier on the radio; 'we'll be all right.' He returned to the fight. The counter-attack was in progress to regain the Castle Site on which, in one of the company's bunkers, the Chinese had installed a medium machine-gun. Lieutenant Philip Curtis led his platoon forward as the guns of 70 Field Battery fired in support. But the overhead cover in the bunker protected the enemy machine-gun crew and they fired freely into the attacking platoon, driving them back within half a minute. Amongst the wounded dragged into cover was Lieutenant Curtis. Corporal Papworth of the Royal Army Medical Corps began to attend to the injuries. Curtis did not wait for his attention.

'We must take the Castle Site,' he said.

'Just wait until Papworth has seen you, sir,' said a soldier at his side. But he would not wait. Alone he ran forward painfully, a pistol in one hand, a grenade in the other. Possibly waiting until this single figure advancing reached point-blank range the Chinese machine-gunners held their fire. Curtis pulled the pin from his grenade and threw it. As it flew through the air, the Chinese opened fire and killed him; but were themselves killed a few seconds later as the grenade landed directly in the bunker opening and blew away the muzzle of their gun. Then, as Major Angier was directing a platoon to close upon this key point, he was killed and command of the company passed to the only surviving officer, Lieutenant Terry Waters. By the time he came up to take over, the opportunity to recover the Castle Site had passed.*

To the east, 'D' Company was under command of Captain M. G. Harvey.† By about 0830 on that morning, 23 April, it was apparent that neither 'A' nor 'D' Companies could hold against the weight of successive attacks unless air support was available. At 0730, the brigade commander had given permission to Colonel Carne to withdraw his forward positions. When it became clear about 50 minutes later that the Glosters' request for air strikes would not be satisfied, the colonel gave the order to withdraw. 'A' and 'D' Companies were brought into positions immediately north-west and west of battalion headquarters and 'B' Company to a hill feature below the great height of Kamak-San to the east of the road.

In breaking away from the enemy, the whole fire potential of the battalion, Captain Frank Wisbey's heavy mortar troop and the three batteries of 45 Field Regiment was used against the enemy of the 187 CCF Division. Their dead and wounded lay in heaps on the hill slopes they had occupied and in the gulleys along which they

---

* Lieutenant Curtis was to receive a posthumous Victoria Cross for his gallantry.

† Major W. A. Wood was away with a leave party in Japan.

had sought to infiltrate past the main position. With 'A' and 'D' Company positions in their hands, they had had enough and by noon the battlefield fell quiet.

The adjutant recalled a series of incidents of that day, 'clear in themselves but joined by a very hazy thread of continuity.'

Colour Sergeant Buxcey organizing his Korean porters with mighty loads for the first of many ascents to the new 'A' company positions . . . When Buxcey's anxious face has left my mind, I can still see Captain Bob Hickey, the doctor, working at the Regimental Aid Post, one hand still wet with blood as he turns round, pausing for a moment to clean himself before he begins to minister to yet another wounded man. The ambulance cars are filled; the jeep that Bounden drives has been out time and again with the stretchers on its racks. Sergeants Baxter and Brisland, Corporal Mills, the whole staff of the RAP is hard at work with dressings, drugs, and instruments . . . I remember watching the slow, wind-tossed descent of a helicopter that came down for casualties to whom the winding, bumpy road back south would have meant certain death . . . Shaw, my driver, and Mr Evans, the Chief Clerk, went off to Seoul . . . Captain Carl Dain, the counter-mortar radar officer came in to say, 'I'm sending my vehicles back, except for my jeep. I've decided to stay with you to make up your numbers of Forward Observation Officers . . . Lieutenant Donald Allman, the assistant adjutant, was sent to reinforce 'A' company, now under its second-in-command, Captain Anthony Wilson . . . That morning the Padre, Sam Davies, said a funeral service for Pat Angier, whose body had been brought back on one of the Oxford carriers by Lieutenant Cabral. Pat's body was the only one to which we could pay our last respects – but we did not forget the others. Three of us stood by while the solemn words were said: then we saluted and walked away, each busy with his own thoughts. Pat lay at rest beside the soft-voiced stream, quiet in the morning sunlight.

Later that morning, the battalion second-in-command, Major Digby Grist, came forward to see what was to be done by way of support for the battle which must surely come to life again as soon as darkness fell. While discussing the prospect, news came that rear battalion headquarters ('A' Echelon) five miles back, had been attacked and forced to withdraw: the enemy had infiltrated strong patrols this far south. The colonel said, 'I think you'd better go back at once, Digby, to see what is happening.' Well aware that he was almost certainly about to run a gauntlet of fire, the second-in-command set off calmly with his driver, Bainbridge. Thirty minutes later, they were driving for their lives through an enemy ambush.

On the right flank, Major Harding had managed to withdraw from his former position secretly and his new site was unknown to the enemy. He was determined not to reveal it until compelled to do so. When observers reported the approach of enemy patrols, Sergeant Pethrick was sent out to lay an ambush on the most likely approach. Not long after he had settled, expecting to catch a patrol, about 200 Chinese obligingly entered his position and a fire fight began. The Chinese, part of 188 CCF Division, reinforced and began to work round the flanks of the ambush. Sgt Pethrick was ordered back while other detachments from his company went forward, greatly assisted by medium and heavy mortar fire, to hold the enemy off the main position. Backwards and forward, all among the little knolls that lay below the peak of Kamak-San, engagements flared up and died, only to be renewed elsewhere.

Notwithstanding the capture of the forward company positions of the Glosters, the commander of 63 CCF Army was dissatisfied, as we are now aware, with the progress of his force after 24 hours of attack. The 187 Division had failed to destroy the battalion holding the old road running south through Solma-ri. On the night of 23/24 April, it had been planned that 188 Division should march down this road to cut in behind the bulk of the British 29th Brigade and the 3rd United States Division. Due to the casualties inflicted on the 187 Division, the 188 had now to complete the elimination of the Glosters though, as the battle line stood, the tactical opportunity seemed still to be open to the 63rd Army. The 29th Brigade and 3rd Division were fighting in positions east-north-east of the Glosters: if the latter could be disposed of during the first hours of darkness of that night, it should prove possible to march rapidly down the road to Uijongbu. For this reason, Chinese patrolling and probing attacks began early in the evening, particularly against 'B' Company, with the aim of finding a route into the heart of the battalion's position and a bypass along which part of the division might slip to the south.

Under the arrangements of Sergeant Smythe, the signal sergeant, telephone cables had been run to all new company positions. At ten minutes to midnight on 23 April, Major Denis Harding telephoned the battalion command post.

'Well, we've started. They're attacking Beverly's [Lieutenant Gael's] platoon now – about 150 I should think.'

This explained the noise from this direction. Captain 'Recce' Newcome, the artillery FOO, was directing defensive fire from the guns. From 'C' Company came similar news. The 188 Division was attempting to force the right flank of the battalion while simultaneously making for the highest ground in the area, the peak of Kamak-San. In character, the assaults on the rifle companies followed the pattern of the previous night: wave after wave of men armed with grenades and sub-machine-guns stormed the positions under cover of medium machine-guns and mortar fire, were halted by the fire of the defence – small arms, mortars, guns – and driven back with heavy loss.

At the outset of the engagement on the night of 23/24 April, the Chinese were at a disadvantage. The information gained by their patrols was faulty largely due to Major Harding's deceptive tactics: they attacked late and obliquely the battalion right flank, so that the assaults, pressed blindly for the first few hours, were struck by enfilade fire. Some time after two o'clock in the morning of the 24th there was a lull during which it seems probable that a fresh regiment came forward, with a truer idea of the Glosters' positions.

About a quarter to three, intense enemy mortar and machine-gun fire fell among 'B' and 'C' Companies. The soldiers waiting – regulars, national servicemen, recalled reservists; west country-men predominantly, with a scattering from London and almost every other county of the British isles; but long since moulded in comradeship by the fortunes of war – stood to their weapons to face another onslaught. Despite the slaughter inflicted on the enemy by their courage and skill, the Glosters' numbers were dwindling. There seemed to be no limit to the casualties the Chinese commanders were prepared to sacrifice to their aim. There was a limit to the casualties that the British battalion could accept if it was to sustain an effective defence.

At three o'clock the telephone from 'C' Company rang in the

command post. Major Paul Mitchell spoke to the adjutant. 'I'm afraid they've overrun my top position and they're reinforcing hard. They're simply pouring chaps in above us. Let me know what the colonel wants me to do, will you?'

The colonel had no doubt as to what had to be done. With the enemy in strength on the commanding ground of 'C' Company's ridge, the right half of the battalion had been cracked open. Below this lay the headquarters site with the radios connecting the battalion to brigade headquarters and the guns, the regimental aid post with the wounded sent down during the night, the battalion 3-inch mortars and the artillery heavy mortars.

'Pack the headquarters up,' the colonel said to the adjutant, 'and get everyone out of the valley up between "D" Company and the anti-tank platoon position. I'm going to withdraw "C" Company in ten minutes; and I shall move "B" over to join us after first light.' The withdrawal of 'C' Company was an extremely difficult operation in darkness, and as a result only one-third of the Company eventually joined the battalion on Hill 235 – the final position.

By dawn, all but 'B' Company were on the high ground overlooking the valley from the west. The next problem was to disengage 'B' Company and bring them into the main position; a taxing problem because they were still under attack. By fortunate chance, the local Chinese commander decided to concentrate his force against one platoon, Lieutenant Geoffrey Costello's, and no less fortunately Costello's platoon held firm, the wounded standing with the unwounded. Across the valley in the main position, Captain Dain was able to bring shellfire down amongst the Chinese infantry scrambling up the hillside and Sergeant Syke's section of Vickers opened fire effectively into this target at 2,000 yards range. At first slowly and painfully, Major Harding managed to draw away what remained of his company. With the rearguard of Lieutenant Arthur Peal's platoon, Harding himself broke away at last. A group of the enemy followed them, closing as they approached the foot of the Glosters' hill but were driven back as Private 'Lofty' Walker of 'C' Company, entirely of his own initiative, ran down to meet them, firing a Bren light machine-gun from the hip into the approaching foe. Twenty of 'B' Company survived the journey. Colonel Carne combined them with the remnant of 'C' Company under Major Harding's command.

During and after the movement of 'B' Company, three important matters had to be attended to: the detailed knitting together of the defences in the new position on Hill 235* against renewed attack; the clarification of the battalion's position in relation to the remainder of the battle in the sector; and a check of physical resources in weapons, ammunition, radio batteries, water, medical supplies and food. The colonel was engaged in the first between seven o'clock on the morning of the 24th, when the sun broke through a haze of grey clouds, and 0845. His round of the battalion was not without incident. Prior to 'B' Company's move he came across a group of Chinese infiltrating forward and, supported by two of the regimental police and his driver, he drove them back with the loss of two dead.

'What was all that about, sir?' asked his adjutant as he came back over the ridge.

'Oh, just shooing away some Chinese.' He continued on his way. A few minutes later, the brigade major† came on to the radio to answer the adjutant's request for information about tactical intentions. He had cheering news. PEFTOK – the Filipinos – were on their way forward to reinforce the battalion and on 25 April armour and infantry in brigade strength would come up in relief. The battalion should be back in reserve by the evening of the 25th.

Meantime, it had to maintain its powers of defence. An expedition was arranged to descend the steep path to the headquarters site to collect ammunition and all the other supplies which were needed. RSM Jack Hobbs and CSMI 'Muscles' Strong of the Army Physical Training Corps assembled men and porters. Major Guy Ward got together a parallel party of gunners to pick up batteries for their radios. Captain Dain screened the sortie with smoke shells and discouraged Chinese intervention by an occasional salvo of shrapnel. By nine o'clock all had safely scrambled back, heavily laden.

Through the morning and afternoon came several reports about the progress of the relief column. They were not encouraging: Chinese forces were said to be blocking the southern entrance to the hill road. Tanks of the 8th Hussars were sent to help them but in the afternoon the news was that the latter had lost its leading troops in an ambush. The tank carcasses were blocking the road in a gorge. But this was

---

* Later to be called Gloster Hill.
† Major Jim Dunning, who was acting in place of Major K. R. S. Trevor, on leave.

not all. The brigadier came on the radio to say that the unrestricted passage of the Chinese past the Glosters would lead to the remainder of the 3rd Division, including the 29th Brigade, fighting to the east, being cut off from their withdrawal route. Though unlikely now to be reinforced on 25 April, it was essential for the Glosters to remain in position.

The colonel had been studying his map as he listened to this statement. When Brigadier Brodie had finished he put his map on top of the radio and replied.

'I understand the position quite clearly,' he said. 'What I must make clear to you is that my command is no longer an effective fighting force. If it is required that we shall stay here, in spite of this, we shall continue to hold. But I wish to make known the nature of my position.'

It was a plain statement of fact. The numbers in the position capable of fighting were about 350, many of whom were wounded. A lot of weapons had been smashed. There had been no resupply of ammunition since the 22nd. Radio batteries might last a further 12 to 15 hours. Once darkness fell, the battalion had no means of stopping the enemy from using the road below.

The brigadier recognized this but stressed that by remaining in position the battalion must pose a threat to the Chinese. They would be obliged to keep attacking and thus retain forces close to the Imjin which would otherwise be used to the south against division and corps.

Seen from the view of the commander of the 1st United States Corps, Lieutenant-General Frank W. Milburn, it was essential for the battalion to remain. This did not ease Colonel Carne's difficulties of holding fast against a third night of attacks. Yet with a calm face he set off up the hillside to the topmost ridge to consider night positions while the adjutant settled arrangements for emergency resupply by Auster aircraft and a full supply by Fairchild Packets the next day. There would be no helicopter for the wounded that night, but perhaps that also might manage to reach the Glosters' hill next morning. For the moment, a night battle had to be reckoned with: dawn on the 25th was 12 hours distant.

The remainder of the afternoon passed. Colonel Carne arranged to draw in his force tightly round spot height 235, the centre of the feature: on the north-west, 'A' Company; to the east, 'D' Company; south, 'B' and 'C'; south-west, Support Company, now grouped together under their commander, Major Sam Weller. Battalion headquarters was to be sited between 'A' and Support Companies. At dusk, when the Chinese could no longer see their movement, the Glosters moved together, carrying their wounded among them.

The ridge was generally bare apart from patches of sere dwarf oak and a copse of scrubby trees. The ground was rocky; tools were few. But none doubted the need to dig and, where this was impracticable, rock sangars were raised. By 2000 hours all was quiet.

It was a time for contemplation among the defence. Some of those awaiting the enemy attack were fearful and all were apprehensive of a series of desperate battles ahead. Yet there were no signs of panic or recrimination; none of despair. A sense of determination to fight the battle out successfully was manifest. It was a mood which owed a good deal to individual valour but stemmed, too, from the immense confidence all felt in their commanding officer. He had been amongst them a good deal that day, making the occasional, quiet remark as he was apt to do, neither purveying false confidence nor betraying fears. He gave the impression of being unshakeable and they believed that he was.

By the night of the 24th/25th, according to Chinese prisoners-of-war, the 188 Division had lost over 4,000 killed and wounded since it had cross the Imjin. 189 Division began to cross the river at dusk with orders to clear away the Glosters once and for all. Commanders of the leading regiment had crossed earlier in the day to study the ground and plan the night attack. It was to begin quite silently, the assault companies creeping forward to a range at which they might effectively throw grenades – say, 25 yards. So six companies marched from their assembly area behind the Castle Site to the foot of Hill 235 as soon as it was dark and began stealthily its ascent.

The Glosters had put out trip wires with tins to rattle. These warnings revealed the enemy's approach at 2045 and within a few minutes the faithful guns of 45 Field Regiment were firing into the densely packed enemy. Even so, several hundred Chinese got right up to the Glosters' defences, blowing trumpets and whistles, calling commands shrilly as they sought to overwhelm their dogged foes. Gradually, they were driven back until 2300 hours when all became quiet once more. The Glosters set aside their dead in hollows and sent back the wounded to Captain Bob Hickey in his makeshift RAP.

Three hours later, the Chinese returned. Again the guns, the rifles and machine-guns fired, grenades were exchanged, the battle swayed to and fro. Towards dawn fresh numbers began an ascent across the little valley to the east with many trumpets directing them.

'It will be a long time before I want to hear a cavalry trumpet playing after this,' said the colonel to the adjutant.

'It would serve them right, sir,' said the adjutant, 'if we confused them by playing our own bugles. I wonder which direction they'd go if they heard Defaulters played!'

'Have we got a bugle up here?' asked the colonel. The adjutant called down the question to Drum-Major Buss on the eastern slope.

'Got one in my haversack,' came the reply.

'Well, play it, Drum-Major,' said the adjutant.

'What shall it be, sir?'

'It's getting towards daylight; play Reveille – the Long and the Short. And play Fire call – in fact, play all the calls of the day as far as Retreat, but don't play that!'

There were a few preliminary peeps from the Drum-Major as he tried out his lips and then his calls rang in the morning air: Reveille, Defaulters, Cookhouse, Officers Dress for Dinner, Orderly NCOs and many more. When the last sweet note died away there was silence. Certainly surprised, perhaps confused and apprehensive of a counter-attack, the Chinese stopped their movement for a while.

The attacks began again after dawn, principally from the north, assault after assault. 'A' Company were driven back from their position, being reduced to one officer, CSM Gallagher and 27 soldiers. The adjutant took them back in a counter-attack and remained to command. He asked the guns of 54 Field to fire deliberately on the restored company position when a Chinese assault flowed into it. This ejected them but they massed again. The forward observation officer with the company, Captain Ronnie Washbrook, brought in with great skill a series of air strikes using napalm against those on the northern slopes. It was a joy to the defenders to see six more pairs of F 80s attack concentrations of troops from Hill 235 to the Imjin. Daunted at last, the Chinese drew back. It was 0610 on the morning of 25 April.

The morning news came from brigade headquarters. Pressure on the route to the east had become so great that all forces were falling back towards Uijongbu. There were no troops available to fight a way forward to the Glosters. The battalion was to fight its own way back, given maximum support from the guns. Orders were passed to Major Weller, the adjutant, Captain Harvey, Lieutenant Temple representing Major Harding, Henry Cabral, Major Ward of 70 Battery and Captain Wisbey of the heavy mortar troop. Captain Hickey was present from the RAP. After pointing out the route to be taken and giving orders for tactical movement, the colonel paused and looked at the doctor.

'Bob, I'm afraid we shall have to leave the wounded behind.'

'Very well, sir. I understand our position.'

Ten o'clock was to be the hour of disengagement from Hill 235. In each defensive location beforehand, everything of value was destroyed, to prevent it falling to the Chinese. At 1000, the colonel met the adjutant.

'Let Sam Weller know that I have just been told by the brigadier that the guns are unable to support us – the gun lines are under attack themselves. Our orders are quite simple; every man to make his own way back.'

Word was hastily passed: soon officers and men were hurrying down the hillside in the warm sunlight. The adjutant passed the RAP. 'Come on, Bob,' he called to the doctor. 'The colonel will be off in a moment and that will be the lot.'

'I can't go,' he said. 'I must stay with the wounded.'

Soon none of the battalion was left on Hill 235 but the dead, the wounded and the gallant RAP staff, Padre Sam Davies amongst them.

The long ridge two miles to the south of Gloster Hill was held in strength by the Chinese and thus blocked the attempts of the Glosters to break out. Some of those running and marching away were shot down and some were captured by the enemy sallying down from the hilltops or advancing to occupy the abandoned hill.

A group under Captain Harvey took fortuitously a route first north and then west and some of this number survived a hail of fire to reach friendly lines (a total of 46 all ranks).

By the evening of the 25th, about 350 of the battalion and its supporting Arms were being marched north across the Imjin River as prisoners of war. So too were the 63 CCF Army which had been so mauled that its remnants were withdrawn over the river to recover.

At brigade headquarters, Brigadier Brodie had written in the operations log his own documentary: 'No one but the Glosters could have done it.'

So passed Lieutenant-Colonel Carne's battalion of the 28th/61st

Foot from view – at least for a time. But almost at once a new battalion came into being. The remaining fragment of the Glosters was ordered to the rear until a decision could be taken as to the future. This disposal reckoned without the character of Major D. B. A. Grist who had assumed command. He gathered in every officer and soldier, including those who had just escaped from the line, returned from leave or arrived from the reinforcement camp and formed them into a fighting body. Replying to a special message of encouragement from the Colonel-in-Chief, he signalled, 'we are already operational again.' Thus continuity was maintained. As it happened, the main battle was fast waning: the Chinese strength was insufficient to carry the battle across the Han and CCF units north of Seoul began to draw back on 30 April.

From 26 April to 23 May, the Glosters with the remainder of the 29th Brigade were deployed on the Kimpo Peninsula, watching the right flank of the UN line. It was a quiet sector and here all units were reinforced and equipped anew. Major Grist was promoted to lieutenant-colonel and confirmed in command of the battalion. Officers, warrant officers and NCOs of the regiment came from far and wide to fill out the companies; many had hastened to return of their own volition as soon as they heard the news of the battalion's loss. Comrades old and new shared a unique occasion when, on 8 May, General James van Fleet, presented a Distinguished Unit Citation to the battalion and 'C' troop, 170 Heavy Mortar Battery, by command of the President of the United States.

In the last week of May, once more at full strength, the British brigade returned to the Imjin, the Glosters holding the reserve position but taking an active part in patrolling north of the river. Those who had been there before were happy to see tons of defence stores arrive. The front was covered with wire; trenches were properly revetted and covered. In August, the battalion moved forward from reserve into many of their old positions and, finally, in September, to a sector north of the river where a new line, 'Wyoming', was dug and wired. From its place in this sector, the battalion was relieved by 1st Battalion, The Welsh Regiment, in November 1951.

A year and a month after leaving, the 28th/61st returned to England. Despite the pleasure of being safely at home once more, the thoughts of many of its members were often with those left behind in the prison camps.

Two main columns of British prisoners had been formed up at

the end of April from those captured out of the British 29th Brigade. Amongst them were a few members of the United States Air Force shot down in the same battle area. As they marched, certain individuals and small groups escaped but the majority were secured effectively by the Chinese guards as the columns marched nightly in stages of 12–15 miles until a point was reached beyond the range of day-fighter/ground attack aircraft of the United Nations. Thereafter the marches were made by day. Some of the prisoners were passed over to the North Koreans for intelligence interrogation at the notorious 'Pak's Palace' at Pyongyang, in which conditions were so bad that hundreds of UN prisoners died. The majority were marched to Chiangsong on the Yalu river where a dull life was not enlivened by daily political lectures aimed at subverting the loyalties of United Nations prisoners.

In the officers' camp, Colonel Carne was singled out for pro-longed isolation and beatings due to his immense prestige. Many of his officers and soldiers were also confined and beaten, and some were tortured for escape or defiance of Chinese demands for information. Less than one per cent of the British prisoners co-operated with their captors against their own country or fellow prisoners.

With the failure of their offensive in the spring of 1951, the Chinese had abandoned the hope of driving the United Nations Forces from Korea. Their problem was how to end a war which they saw they could not win, and which was unduly expensive in war material, without sacrificing all political prospect for the communist camp. Armistice negotiations dragged on from May 1951 until August 1953. Only then, at last, were the prisoners-of-war able to move south to be exchanged at Panmunjon, close to the 38th Parallel. Amongst the whole body of prisoners origi-nally taken, many had died of neglect or starvation. Among the 33 dead of the Glosters' group none had died more honourably than Lieutenant Terry Waters, attached to the 28th/61st from the West Yorkshire Regiment, who had chosen to die of his wounds rather than make propaganda broadcasts against his own nation.*

In the autumn of 1953, what remained of Colonel Carne's battalion sailed back into Southampton water. Sirens and hooters sounded as

---

* Lieutenant Waters was posthumously awarded the George Cross.

they came ashore to be reunited with wives and families. They were astonished and a little embarrassed to find themselves famous as men who had made history. Such is the way of the British soldier: may it always be so.

7
Vietnam

Dien Bien Phu (1953)

Charles Mey

Dawn is about to break over the North Vietnamese airfields of Gia-Lam and Bach-Mai, just outside Hanoi in the north-east corner of Vietnam. Over 1,800 French and South Vietnamese are ready in full fighting kit, tense and waiting to go into battle. With them are their three commanders, Major Marcel Bigeard, Major Jean Brechignac and Major Jean Souquet, all seasoned veterans of the Indo-China war. On the runway, 67 C47 Dakotas sit, their crews ready to take off. It is 20 November 1953.

Another Dakota, 190 miles away, is circling over a valley shrouded in mist and drizzle. Three French officers, Lieutenant General Pierre Bodet, Brigadier General Jean Decheaux and Brigadier General Jean Gilles, are aboard. They will soon give the go-ahead for the dropping of three parachute battalions who are waiting to attack a small village held by the Viet Minh. It is the village of Dien Bien Phu.

Suddenly, at 0700, the sky clears. An order goes to the parachute battalions outside Hanoi. It is the beginning of Operation Castor. Over Dien Bien Phu, the swarming Dakotas fill the air with their roar and thousands of Thai peasants stare up in surprise. The planes discharge their cargoes of men, and hundreds of white parachutes blossom against the blue sky. Viet Minh soldiers rush to their battle stations. On the dropping zone (DZ) Natasha, a Viet Minh company on exercise has already skirmished with Maj. Bigeard's paratroopers of the 6th Colonial Parachute Battalion. The DZ covers a large area and already the recovery of the tons of equipment parachuted into it is becoming difficult. Machine-guns, 81 mm mortars and radio sets litter the ground. But many of the radios have not survived the drop. Worse, some of the mortars cannot be found.

Farther to the south, on DZ Simone, Maj. Brechignac's paratroopers, from the 2nd Battalion of the Parachute Chasseurs Regiment, have been dropped in difficult conditions and it is proving difficult to rally the soldiers and get them into action as a concerted force. Without waiting for support, Bigeard has left the DZ to attack the village of Dien Bien Phu with three of his four companies. But the Viet Minh regular soldiers defend doggedly. At 1500, Souquet's 1st Colonial Parachute Battalion, who have jumped in support of Bigeard, arrive to take part in the mopping-up action. The 148th Regiment of the People's Army withdraws in good order and the villagers flee into the mountains. French losses are only 13 dead and 40 wounded. It is confirmation of the value of surprise blows struck by well-trained parachute units.

On the second day, 21 November, a second force of paratroopers jumps into the valley of Dien Bien Phu. These are the legionnaires of the 1st Foreign Legion Parachute Battalion and the soldiers of the 8th Vietnamese Parachute Battalion, with their commanding officers, Lieutenant Colonel Pierre Charles Langlais – who breaks a leg on landing – and Gen. Gilles, commander of the whole Dien Bien Phu operation. Heavy supplies are now dropped on DZ Octavie, but one of two bulldozers parachuted in buried itself in the ground after its chute had failed to open fully. The French forces on 22 November are 4,560 men, after a fresh battalion of Vietnamese had arrived. It was time to begin the construction of defensive positions.

After the airborne landing of 20 November, Dien Bien Phu is soon to be a fortified zone, capable of holding 12,000 soldiers. Why is it sited in such an area? Because the French High Command's patience is wearing thin. Embroiled in a war with Ho Chi Minh's revolutionary army since 19 December 1946, a spectacular victory is badly needed. And with Gallic daring, they have chosen to occupy Dien Bien Phu, a base 200 miles inside the enemy's territory.

The French High Command at Saigon is not sure about the role which Dien Bien Phu is being called upon to play. Is it a rallying point for the Lai Chau garrison? A 'hedgehog' in an essential strategic position? Or a start point for an offensive, as Major General Renee Cogny declares? Perhaps it is a trap sprung for the army of General

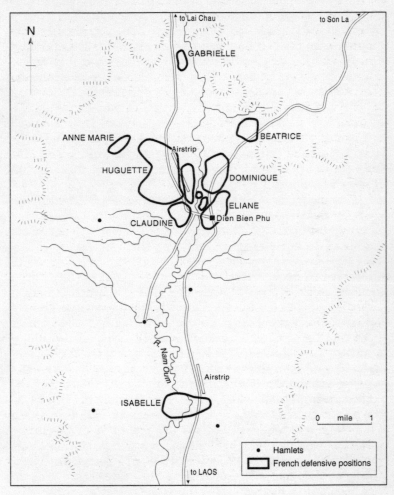

7.1   The Siege of Dien Bien Phu, March–May 1954

Vo Nguyen Giap, of the Vietnamese People's Army. Or could it be a diversion in anticipation of an attack on the Red River Delta?

Before being replaced by General Henri Navarre, General Salan, Chief of Staff of the French Expeditionary Force in Indo-China, said that Laos could only be defended by holding Dien Bien Phu, as well as Na-San and Lai-Chau. Navarre will come under severe criticism for his action here in establishing Dien Bien Phu as a fortress, sited as it was in the bottom of the valley. But he saw the ten-mile-long and six-mile-wide valley floor as an ideal base. From it he could make sorties to attack the Viet Minh. He felt that the enemy could not surround his fortification, nor could they effectively use artillery against the airstrip from the hills ten miles away.

For some time, Dien Bien Phu is almost a tourist venue for many high-ranking French officers and politicians, together with their Government's military visitors. The fortress is praised from all sides, although one man, General Blanc, has his criticisms about the area in times of monsoon. His warning is not heeded. Among the visitors are General Spears, British Military Attache and High Commissioner Malcolm McDonald, many American Generals including John ('Iron Mike') O'Daniel, US Army Commander in the Pacific. But none of these highly expert people question the ability of Dien Bien Phu to withstand attack.

There is a collective blindness on the part of senior French officers. And this notwithstanding the fact that the archives hold details of defense preparation, backed by information from the Deuxième Bureau on the movement and capability of the enemy forces.

But from December 1953, events will show that if Navarre has set the scene, it is Giap who will script it. The situation created by the French airborne landings at Dien Bien Phu on 20 November is analyzed by the Viet Minh Council of War. Orders are given to the 316th Division to attack Lai-Chau so that it will be compelled to fall back to Dien Bien Phu. But in December 1953 the French forestall the Viet Minh plans. The Lai-Chau garrison is evacuated in 183 sorties by air transport four days before the arrival of the North Vietnamese troops. Over 2,000 men who had to be left behind have to try to make the 60-mile jungle journey to Dien Bien Phu on foot. But only 175 T'ai soldiers make it. The rest die in ambush. Many desert.

With the Viet Minh fallen back from Dien Bien Phu, the offensive and reconnaissance missions ordered by Gen. Cogny immediately begin to be costly. Two missions, Operations Ardèche and Régate, are undertaken by a paratrooper task force commanded by Lt. Col. Langlais. They leave the base to link up with the Laotian light infantry and Moroccan *Tabors* from Laos. The rendezvous is to be in the Sop Nao region, a mountainous area with thick jungle, providing perfect ambush sites. The task force is harried by a mobile enemy and the losses make it necessary to abandon these long-range penetrations and to concentrate efforts on the mountains that surround Dien Bien Phu itself.

In the fortress, information from French intelligence is that the 351st, 308th and 312th Divisions are moving towards Dien Bien Phu. Soon Giap is mobilizing his forces and the French are preparing for a siege. Their engineers calculate that enormous quantities of equipment will be needed – 36,000 tons. This would take an impossible 12,000 Dakota trips from Hanoi. All the engineers get is 4,000 tons – and 75 per cent of that is barbed wire.

There is another battle between the French and the Viet Minh. It is one of logistics. And the French will lose this one too. All their fortification work is accurately mapped. It can be seen clearly from the surrounding high ground. The smallest trench stands out clearly in the bare earth. As for the French, they see nothing of the enemy's movements in the dense jungle. They do not know that 55,000 regular and locally raised troops surround them. Giap's forces open five routes through the jungle towards Dien Bien Phu. They are used by 600 Russian-built 2.5-ton lorries which travel by night with all lights extinguished. The French air attacks on the passes of Lung Lo and Phadin cause sections of these precarious roads to slide into ravines, and torrential rains make fords impassable and turn valleys into marshes.

But traffic is never interrupted for more than a few days. Thousands of coolies work day and night maintaining the Viet Minh supply routes. In addition, on the narrow tracks pack-horses, mules and convoys of bicycles, each one laden with 220 lb, head towards the battlefield. Nothing can stop this conveyor belt of human ants. But the fortress can count only on transport aircraft. Everything has to come from Hanoi.

Ten M24 Chaffee tanks stripped down (each requiring five C47s and two Bristols to lift them), 105 mm and 155 mm guns, rations for 11,000 men, generators, water-purifiers. But French airpower, even with the help of a squadron of C119s supplied by the Americans, could not meet the demands of Dien Bien Phu.

Even before the real trial of strength begins the French have lost the logistics battle. When the airstrip is destroyed and the parachute is the only means of supply, the consequences will be disastrous for the French.

Gen. Giap's artillery strength around Dien Bien Phu is impressive. On the day before the attack the besiegers have 144 field-howitzers (American 75s and 105s), 48 120 mm heavy mortars, 30 75 mm recoilless guns and 36 37 mm AA guns. And during the course of the battle 12 siz-barrel Katyusha rocket-launchers will come into action. The physical effort of dragging these guns into place over wet and slippery slopes by human muscle power must have been enormous.

On D-Day, Giap has at his disposal stocks of shells far greater than the French thought possible. From 13 March to 8 May 1954 his guns will fire about 150,000 shells, about 30,000 of them from the 105s. And the French artillery will need an airlift of incredible proportions to keep the guns firing. A total of 95,000 rounds of 105 mm and 8,500 rounds of 155 mm ammunition are parachuted into the base. But a quantity falls beyond the ever-shrinking perimeter into Viet Minh territory.

The besieged French have six batteries (24 guns) of 105 mm, one battery of four 155 mm howitzers and 32 120 mm heavy mortars. Colonel Piroth, who commands the base artillery, considers they can stop any enemy infantry attack, and are good enough for effective counter-battery work. He said: 'No Viet Minh gun will fire three rounds without being destroyed.' The French have underestimated the enemy's artillery strength, the supply of ammunition, the skill of his gunners and the effectiveness of his camouflage.

Bur Dien Bien Phu's firepower inferiority is also the result of other factors. Contrary to expectations the Viet Minh guns are served by excellent crews, trained in camps in south China. Their fire is directed and controlled by observers with uninterrupted views of the airfield and the unprotected French batteries. From the first day of the attack their power and their precision will come as a bitter shock. The French counter-battery work is random and will have no effect.

The Viet Minh 105s, in fact, are undetectable and practically invulnerable, because they are well dug-in, though this is at the expense of wide fields of fire and large handling crews. Dummy guns are used by the Viet Minh to deceive the French spotters in the base. And so the battle of Dien Bien Phu was going to start under unfavorable conditions for the defenders. Their officers either know or sense it and it seems that Navarre and Cogny have their doubts. But by this time the die has been cast.

'Gentlemen, it is at 1700 tomorrow.' Colonel Christian de la Croix de Castries had just completed his briefing on the evening of 12 March 1954. The unit commanders have been waiting this moment for several weeks. Less than six miles away, Giap issues his final orders for the attack. He knows the importance of the battle and its cost: 'We will have to sustain losses in the course of the battle. Victory is bought at the price of blood and paid for, like all revolutionary conquests, with sacrifices.'

At D-day the attackers have a superiority of eight to one: there are only 6,500 French front-line troops against the 50,000 seasoned combat troops of the elite 308th, 312th, 316th, 304th, the 351st (engineers and artillery) divisions and the 148th local regiment. The French have five Foreign Legion battalions, but eight others are composed of Algerian and Moroccan riflemen, Thais, Vietnamese, Montaguards and mobile police. On 13 March Viet Minh movements are spotted around Beatrice and Gabrielle strongpoints, as two regiments of the 312th Division move up to their start-lines less than 100 yards from the French defenses. Two C47s and a fighter are destroyed by artillery fire on the airstrip.

At 1715 the first 105 mm shells land on Beatrice which is held by 3rd Battalion, 13th Demi-Brigade of the Foreign Legion. Two 105 mm guns in the position are destroyed and Colonel Gaucher, the commander, killed. The Viet Minh infantry attack in the failing light after sappers have blown paths through the wire. Regardless of casualties the enemy move forward, overrunning bunkers and dug-outs. Hand-to-hand fighting with grenades occurs in the trenches and amongst the ruins. At 2100 only one strongpoint is still holding out. Shortly after midnight a heavy silence settles over Beatrice. The garrison of legionnaires has lost 75 per cent of its numbers and fewer than 200 men regain the main French lines.

In the entrenched camp the French are dumbfounded. A strong-point, defended by the Legion, overrun in six hours! Thousands of men look towards the lost position and try to understand. Col. de Castries, who has sat up all night by his telephones and has lived out the agony of Beatrice, alerts his HQ in Hanoi. He is promised reinforcements and air support. The airfield is all but closed and enemy shelling forces those fighter-bombers still intact to escape to Laos. In addition a quarter of the French 105 mm ammunition has been exhausted in one night.

On the next day, 14 March, the 5th Vietnamese Parachute Battalion is dropped in reinforcement and de Castries contemplates a counter-attack on Beatrice. But low cloud and a violent storm make close air support impossible, besides which it is known that Giap's next objective will be Gabrielle. At 1800 the Viet Minh batteries begin their shelling of the strongpoint, which is held by a battalion of Algerian riflemen and eight Foreign Legion 120 mm mortars. The Viet Minh send in 88th and 165th Regiments of the 308th Division to the attack. It is eight battalions against one. Benefiting from their in-depth defense the Algerians resist the first onslaught. But by dawn on 15 March only one redoubt is still in French hands and awaiting a promised counter-attack by the main part of the garrison.

The counter-attack consists of two companies from the Legion and one battalion of Vietnamese paratroopers supported by six M24 tanks. It fights its way to within 1,000 yards of the position and enables 150 men to regain the French lines before the thrust is called off. The second outlying strongpoint has gone. Within two days of the start of Giap's offensive the French illusions have been shattered. Dien Bien Phu is a trap. Gén. Navarre is directing the battle from his office in Saigon, more than 1,000 miles from the fighting. Gen. Cogny, installed in Hanoi, has the immediate responsibility for the battle. Knowing of the setbacks of 13 and 14 March and realizing what they portend, another battle is to be fought in secret between these two officers.

Navarre finally arrives at Hanoi where a message signed by Cogny awaits him: 'One has to envisage the possibility of a defeat at Dien Bien Phu with the attendant loss of our personnel who are at present located there.' Cogny, having recognized inevitable defeat, wishes to make certain that responsibility for it does not fall on him. Henceforth, relations between the two generals conducting the same battle will be restricted to exchanges of written notes. But this does not stop them trying to find scapegoats – the engineer officers who designed the fortifications, the photographic interpreters, the transport and ground-attack crews, and – of course – the French civilian government.

At this point both Navarre's and Cogny's responsibilities are crushing and it is made worse by the fact that knowing the enemy's capabilities, they themselves chose the ground on which the battle is being fought. In 1953–4 the Vietnamese People's Army is a well-balanced force of divisions, regiments, battalions and companies, all well-equipped with up-to-date weapons and well led and disciplined. In addition it is fighting for its own country and for a cause in which it passionately believed. To present this modern army as a collection of rebel bands was perhaps necessary for propaganda's sake but to believe it was absurd.

By 15 March morale in the Dien Bien Phu garrison is at its lowest ebb. During the night Col. Piroth, unable to face the defeat of his artillery, takes a hand-grenade and kills himself in his dug-out. In the command post, several officers have cracked. And de Castries hesitates, overwhelmed and overtaken by events. He lacks neither courage nor panache but rather the qualities needed to direct a battle of this magnitude. Later he will be taken to task for his passivity. But it must be remembered that he was ordered to defend Dien Bien Phu after several generals and colonels had 'declined the honor'.

A soldier of much sterner stuff is the hatchet-faced Langlais, commander of the airborne troops. On 24 March de Castries effectively hands over command of the entrenched camp to him with the exception of Isabelle which is put under the control of Colonel André Lalande. It is an unofficial transfer of authority and a tacit recognition of the plight of the garrison. Langlais is also aided by Bigeard, sent back to the valley some eight days earlier with his battalion. Bigeard is to be Langlais' adjutant. Ultimately the paratroop 'Mafia' will take over the defense of the base.

Taking advantage of several days rest from shelling, all those capable of wielding pick and shovel have been put to work reinforcing the dug-outs and bunkers. But on 16 March the 3rd Thai Battalion on Anne Marie sense that things are going against them. They decide to leave the field and return to their villages. And several hundred North African and Vietnamese desert and go to ground in the dug-outs on the banks of the Nam Yum.

Giap and the Front Military Committee have considered the lessons of the first phase of the offensive. Losses have been very heavy and it is decided to pursue the policy of strangling the base. In ten days his front-line troops will dig more than seven miles of trenches and approach routes. A 50-yard tunnel will be dug to place an enormous explosive charge under the position known as Eliane. On the night of 30 March, after a violent preliminary artillery bombardment, the 312th and 316th Divisions launch their attack on the five hills that make up Dominique and Eliane. The battle rages for four days with hand-to-hand fighting for positions that are lost, recaptured and lost again. On one day, the defenders fire 13,000 rounds of 105 mm ammunition. This is largely responsible for the enemy's terrible losses and their failure to take their objectives. But they have made some progress and continue to erode the defended area.

The situation becomes critical on 2 April after units from the 308th Division are thrown against Huguette. At this point Bigeard scrapes together forces for a counter-attack and Viet Minh units break off the action, leaving 800 dead on the wire. The morale of the besieged forces soars and is maintained when Bigeard and his paratroopers recapture one of Eliane's lost strongpoints. Into a harrowing battle, Giap throws four battalions but in vain. Overall, the French position has not improved. Several thousand men are still isolated and trapped. There is little they can do but delay defeat. The Viet Minh divisions have been exhausted by their efforts. Giap is forced to launch a campaign for the 'mobilization of morale and rectification of right-wing tendencies.'

But on 1 May he orders a general offensive to begin at 2200. On that day there remains for the garrison three days' rations, 275 rounds of 155 mm, 14,000 rounds of 105 mm and 5,000 rounds of 120 mm mortar ammunition. Two strongpoints fall in the first assault, but Langlais and Bigeard hope to be able to hold on with reinforcements of men, supplies and ammunition parachuted into the base.

But the advantage of the attackers is overwhelming. Towards midday on 6 May Giap orders his Katyusha rocket-launchers, the 'Stalin Organs', into action to blow up the dumps and spread terror in North African and Vietnamese ranks. By dawn on 7 May the base has been reduced to a rectangle of half a square mile. Incredibly Bigeard mounts another counter-attack with two companies supported by the last Chaffee tank. By 1800 all firing had ceased. The base does not surrender, it is simply overwhelmed.

The price paid in the 56-day defense of Dien Bien Phu is more than 2,000 French dead, 7,000 wounded and missing, and 7,000 prisoners *en route* for the death camps. And it has cost Giap 8,000 lives and 15,000 wounded to secure his 'revolutionary conquest'.

The French High Command was relying heavily upon the firepower of its medium and fighter-bombers to destroy the supply lines of Giap's divisions and to smash those artillery batteries which had escaped the fire of the base's 155 mm guns. It was mistaken reliance. In fact, the French Expeditionary Corps' air support is ridiculously weak, no more than a hundred strike aircraft, of which three-quarters are committed to the battle at Dien Bien Phu. More pitifully still, there are only 80 transport planes and too few pilots.

Dive-bombing attacks on the supply lines, just as those on the edges of the entrenched camp, have only a limited effect because of the meticulous camouflage of the Viet Minh. Napalm, which had been used with devastating effect two years earlier at Vinh Yen, on the edge of the Red River defenses, is rendered less effective by the different thicknesses of vegetation in the dense forest. On the other hand, the Viet Minh anti-aircraft weapons (36 37 mm cannon and 50 12.7 mm machine-guns) are very formidable. It is soon obvious that French airpower cannot change the course of the battle.

In December 1953 Navarre had studied the operation which, coming from Laos, would crush the Viet Minh army brought to Dien Bien Phu. He had given this the name Condor. By April this was to be the last hope of relief for the defenders of Dien Bien Phu. Three thousand men, two-thirds of them Laotian Light Infantry, would march on the base to attack the Viet Minh's rear areas. At the same time the guerillas of Colonel Trinquier's Mixed Airportable Commando Group would be mobilized, together with Mollat's commandos and all those groups of irregulars fighting in the Viet Minh areas. And an airborne task force would be sent as reinforcement in good time.

But on 22 April Navarre cancels the promised reinforcements and leaves the units already engaged freedom of action to continue or break off. These troops will get close to the perimeter and recover the 78 men to escape from the valley but on 7 May they will receive the order to pull back.

A breakout and withdrawal of the Dien Bien Phu garrison towards Laos would have been, without any doubt, fraught with danger. But it was the only chance to escape annihilation. Capture of all the garrison, if it remained where it was, appeared inevitable. There was a possibility of trying to break out on 3 May under the code name Albatross. But the breakout, covered by all the guns and combat aircraft, would only have been towards the south-east by those still capable of carrying four days' rations and their personal weapons. In the effort to save some of the 6,000 men still able to fight, the wounded would have to be abandoned. But HQ in Hanoi vetoed the plan as being dishonorable. The forces inside the entrenched camp were left to their fate, to fight on heroically without hope until overwhelmed.

The debacle of Dien Bien Phu was due to a number of grave errors in the siting, supply and quality of the French defensive positions. Its ultimate destruction was due to the inability of the French to sustain an adequate supply of men, ammunition and provisions for the besieged garrison. To this must be added the brilliance of General Giap's powers of leadership and the unexpectedly high quality of his battalions.

The loss of Dien Bien Phu was not only the end of a battle, it was the first time an Asian subject people had beaten their European masters in battle. And it was the finish of France as a colonial power in Indo-China.

Ia Drang (1965)

Ian Westwell

On 22 October 1965 Major-General Harry W. O. Kinnard, Commanding General of the 1st Cavalry Division (Airmobile), received the message he had been anxiously waiting for. Short and to the point it stated: 'Commencing first light 23 October First Air Cav deploys one Bn TF [Task Force] minimum 1 Inf Bn and 1 Arty Btry to PLEIKU, mission to assist in defense of key US/ARVN [Army of the Republic of Vietnam] installations at PLEIKU or reinforce II Corps operations to relieve PLEI ME CAMP.' Since the division's arrival in South Vietnam it had had a few brushes with small bands of local Viet Cong guerrillas and, although Kinnard knew his men had performed well, he remained aware that they had yet to face the cream of the North Vietnamese Army.

Kinnard was a great believer in the value of airmobility and had been involved with the division from its early days. Indeed, as a brigadier-general, he had led the 11th Air Assault Division, where his enthusiasm and firm but relaxed style made him popular with the men. Close attention had been paid to their training and he felt sure that the successful completion of an operation lasting more than a few days would silence those critics who complained at the cost of the division.

Kinnard knew the men of the 1st Cavalry were special. They had to be: helicopters were temperamental beasts. A large part of the division would be used to keep them in the air. Pilots needed the skill to fly at tree-top level at over 100 m.p.h. The division's strength was speed and firepower. Eagle Flights, the basic tactical unit, consisted of six UH-1C Hueys, armed with 2.75-in rockets and a minigun capable of saturating an area the size of a football pitch in a few seconds, and seven UH-1Ds for carrying combat troops. Going into action they flew in a V-formation to give all-round vision and mutual protection. It worked in theory – would it work in practice?

Good up-to-the-minute intelligence on the strength and position of the enemy would be essential to the mission. A few days after the initial attack on the Plei Me Camp Captain William P. Gillette, the Air Cavalry Squadron intelligence officer, was able to give a full and remarkably accurate report. It was clear that the NVA assault on the camp, 40 km south-west of Pleiku, was meant to be the beginning of a full-scale offensive aiming to cut South Vietnam in two. Two enemy regiments were in the area: the 33rd around Plei Me and the 32nd, lying in ambush ready to destroy any ground force attempting to relieve the camp. The month-long battle that was to follow became known as the Battle of the Ia Drang Valley. It was to be a major test for the 1st Cavalry Division and was the first time that regular NVA troops controlled by a divisional headquarters fought a conventional battle against US forces.

Initially the 1st Cavalry Division acted in support of the South Vietnamese Army. The Cav's 1st Brigade, ordered to secure Pleiku, to provide artillery backup and to furnish a reserve force, was soon in action. At 1730 hours the NVA hit a relief column at two points and the air cavalry was called up. The brigade was quick to respond – its helicopters were in the air in 10 minutes – and the firepower it deployed was widely recognized as the decisive factor in the defeat of the enemy. Plei Me camp was relieved on 25 October.

It soon became clear that a major opportunity for the full deployment of the air cavalry was unfolding. The NVA was pulling back after receiving a bloody nose and a quick response might give them a further mauling. General William C. Westmoreland, Commander of the US Military Assistance Command, Vietnam (MACV), flew up to the front and after a brief conference ordered the cavalry in pursuit. For Kinnard it was the chance he had long waited for. He was given a free hand and his job was no longer just reinforcement and reaction but unlimited attack. A pattern for future actions was being born: the division was to engage in hard-hitting search-and-destroy missions against NVA forces operating in the difficult terrain of Vietnam's Central Highlands.

It was not just the enemy that caused problems. Much of this part of South Vietnam consisted of dense vegetation, and jungle composed of 30 m high trees. Rocks hidden by man-tall elephant grass could flip a helicopter on its side. Most clearings were too small for even a single Huey, but by using the tail-rotor as a chain-saw – strictly against regulations – pilots could hack a way to the ground. A slight error of judgement, all too easy after six hours in the saddle, would be costly, and maybe fatal.

For the next 12 days much of the 1st Brigade was deployed to the west of Pleiku. Most of their operations involved fierce fighting and most of them proved successful. On 1 November, for example, a routine reconnaissance patrol flying 12 km west of Plei Me spotted some unusual ground activity beneath the jungle canopy and ordered in units of the 1st Brigade. The enemy had no time to melt back into the undergrowth. Seventy-eight were killed and 57 captured. More damaging was the capture of a complete field hospital – dozens of cases of essential medical supplies, including morphine and penicillin, were stacked to chest height over a large area.

The 1st Squadron, 9th Cavalry, again drew blood two days later in a perfectly executed ambush on an enemy unit of company strength moving along an east–west trail just north of the Chu Pong mountains. The troopers had to wait an agonizing 90 minutes before the unit entered the ambush zone, but their training taught them to wait until the leading elements had gone by. With a deafening roar eight claymore mines were exploded and then the cavalrymen fired continuously for two minutes. There was no return fire. But the Cav did not have things entirely their own way this time. Back at base they came under sustained, almost fanatical, attacks from three companies of NVA regulars and by midnight their perimeter was in grave danger of being overrun. Now, however, the advantages of airmobility became apparent. Help was soon at hand, as Company A, 1st Battalion, 8th Cavalry, located 20 km to the north, flew in. The first platoon was on the ground and in combat 40 minutes after midnight.

These first sustained combats by units of the 1st Brigade though small in scale were, for Kinnard, ample justification of the airmobile concept. Scout ships were regularly finding enemy forces. Highly mobile rifle units were then being flown in to fix the enemy before massive air and ground firepower was used to inflict maximum damage. Many lessons were learnt through combat experience.

In their first skirmishes many cavalry troopers were disconcerted by the suicidally close ranges at which they came to grips with the enemy. Several units were almost dropped into the laps of the NVA and firefights often took place at ranges of less than 20 m, where the firepower of Soviet and Chinese-built assault rifles could be devastating. It was often difficult to organize artillery support and the emergency medical evacuation of casualties was delayed because of the lack of equipment to clear landing zones.

The early encounters of the Ia Drang campaign were also remarkable for the successful deployment of airborne units at night. The battle of 3 November, for example, was the first time a defensive perimeter under heavy fire was reinforced in the dark by airborne toops flown into an unfamiliar landing zone. It was also the first time that aerial rocket artillery was used at night and as close as 50 m to US troops.

Basic training taught the pilots to fly low and fast – they would be away before the enemy could get them in their sights. That was the official line, but most pilots took it as a sick joke. Fully laden they had to fly low, but there was no way they could fly fast.

Flying at night or dropping into a vicious firefight from 500 m was every pilot's nightmare. No amount of training could prepare them for it. The enemy always knew they were coming. Helicopter engines were noisy and in the jungle-quiet could be heard several miles away. Over the drop zone tracers would shoot up out of the undergrowth. Beautiful but deadly, a 0.5-in calibre round would go through anything. If the enemy were lucky they might hit the 'Jesus nut' that held the rotor blades in place. There would be no survivors after a hit like that.

On 9 November the 1st Brigade was withdrawn from the Ia Drang battles. Its deployment had clearly been a major success and some 200 North Vietnamese soldiers were killed and an estimated 180 wounded. More importantly it had destroyed over 100,000 rounds of 7.62 mm ammunition, two 82 mm mortars and three 75 mm recoilless rifles and captured over $40,000 worth of medical supplies.

The 1st Brigade was replaced by the 3rd, consisting of the 1st and 2nd Battalions, 7th Cavalry. For the battles in Ia Drang it was supported by the 2nd Battalion, 5th Cavalry. By this stage Kinnard's major concern was that the NVA might slip away and that the cavalry would fail to capitalize on its earlier successes. He ordered Colonel Thomas W. Brown, the 3rd Brigade commander, to initiate patrols south and south-east of Plei Me. Colonel Brown, well versed in airmobile techniques, started a vigorous hunt for the enemy. Intelligence reports suggested that the 33rd NVA Regiment was reorganizing between the Ia Drang river and the Chu Pong mountains. It was also believed that the 32nd Regiment was nearby and that other reinforcements had arrived.

On 14 November the 1st Battalion, 7th Cavalry, commanded by Lieutenant-Colonel Harold G. Moore, began a sweep along the base of the Chu Pong range. The battalion was, however, short of helicopters, only 16 UH-IDs were available. Fire support, the most essential part of any airborne assault, was to be provided by two 105 mm batteries located at landing zone (LZ) Falcon, 9 km east of the search area. Like the senior officers of the 1st brigade, Moore was conscious that his men had yet to be tested against a large NVA force.

LZ X-Ray, 10 km west of Plei Me, and capable of taking up to ten UH-IDSs at one time, was chosen by Moore as the best place for the opening air assault. The co-ordination of all arms was of crucial importance in the early phases. At 1017 hours a preliminary bombardment by 105s began and was quickly followed by an aerial attack. The LZ was saturated with fire – helicopter gunships fired 50 per cent of their rockets in 30 seconds. Company B of the 1st Battalion was the first to drop. On landing the troops spread out to secure a perimeter around the LZ, and Companies A and C quickly followed.

By 1330, however, the North Vietnamese had made further reinforcement extremely hazardous. At ground level the LZ was ringed by sparse bush which, with elephant grass and anthills, provided ideal cover for the enemy who were able to pin down the cavalrymen. Several Hueys carrying the leading elements of D Company were hit and, though none was shot down, Colonel Moore forbade a further eight from landing. A and B Companies were ordered to pull back and prepare a tight defensive perimeter for the night. Of the two, Company B was in the worse position. One of its platoons had become separated and could not be precisely located.

LZ X-Ray was hot. Sitting in a pilot's seat, the target of all surrounding hostile fire, the men who flew the helicopters were desperate for the troopers to get out of the craft as quickly as possible; and then there was the agonizing wait as the wounded were loaded aboard. Crews counted themselves lucky if they got back into the air in under a minute. It was a hell of a long time to wait. A pilot who was present recalled the atmosphere of tension:

'Orange One, abort your landing. Fire on the LZ is too heavy,' a pathfinder called from X-Ray. Orange flight turned and we followed. There was a whole bunch of yelling on the radios. I heard two ships in the LZ call out they were hit badly. What a mess. Finally we heard Yellow One call to take off, and we saw them emerge from the smoke on the left of the LZ, shy two ships. They had waited in the heavy fire while the crews of the two downed ships got on to other Hueys. One crew chief stayed, dead. One pilot was wounded.

By mid-afternoon on 14 November Moore knew he was in a major battle and his men were fighting for their lives against the 66th and 33rd NVA regiments. It seemed obvious to Colonel Brown at Plei Me that the enemy were intent on destroying the 1st Battalion, 7th Cavalry. He prepared to send in reinforcements to strengthen the landing zone. Company B of the 2nd Battalion, 7th Cavalry, arrived at X-Ray by 1800 hours, and night landing facilities were set up.

The situation around the perimeter was by this stage less dangerous and it was only the isolated platoon of Company B that was causing concern. Although reports suggested it was holding its own with morale still high, eight men had been killed, 12 had been wounded in action and only seven remained unhurt. The platoon faced several attacks but all were beaten off by small arms and artillery fire. Dawn revealed dozens of enemy dead around their position. Savage close fighting went on inside the perimeter. The 1st Platoon leader of C Company was found dead with the bodies of five NVA soldiers around his foxhole and one trooper was found with his hands locked around the throat of an adversary. By 1000 hours on 15 November air strikes and aerial rocket artillery units firing 2.75-in rockets and miniguns had blasted the North Vietnamese out of their positions.

Moore was confident that the enemy was no longer capable of attacking the landing zone in any strength and at 1330 ordered his tired men to pull out. The troopers were quick to realize they had inflicted a heavy defeat on the enemy. Many bodies littered the battlefield, and heavily bloodstained bandages suggested that far more had been very badly wounded. By noon a relief force, the 2nd Battalion, 5th Cavalry, reached Moore's position and the relief of the isolated platoon was little more than a formality. The troops at LZ X-Ray were ordered to sit tight and await the arrival of the 2nd Battalion, 7th Cavalry, who had been detailed to act as a relief force. By 0930 hours on 16 November its leading elements began to arrive and Colonel Moore's men were airlifted out.

The two-day battle around LZ X-Ray was the high point of the 1st Cavalry campaign in the Ia Drang Valley. Colonel Moore's men suffered nearly 200 casualties but the NVA lost many more: 634 known dead, 581 supposed dead and six taken prisoner. Large amounts of their equipment fell into the cavalry's hands. It was clear to both sides that there would now be no full-scale offensive in South Vietnam's Central Highlands. The 3rd Brigade continued to sweep the Chu Pong area until 20 November and the 2nd was withdrawn on the 26th.

The 1st Cavalry Division fought in the Ia Drang Valley for 35 days and during that time changed the nature of the war in Vietnam. No longer would US forces have to footslog through dense undergrowth in search of an elusive foe. Air cavalry units could respond to any situation in a short time and maintain contact with the enemy for longer than was previously possible. Commander-in-chief General Westmoreland was full of praise. 'The ability of the Americans to meet and defeat the best troops the enemy could put into the field of battle was once and for all demonstrated beyond any possible doubt as was the validity of the Army's airmobile concept.'

Hamburger Hill (1969)

John Pimlott

In the aftermath of the Tet Offensive in early 1968, the Americans and their allies in South Vietnam enjoyed a distinct military advantage. Despite the failure of the Communists to trigger a countrywide revolt, by the end of February the Communists had suffered grievous manpower losses and had been forced back to their border bases. With half a million troops in-country, the Americans could contemplate offensive operations into such bases, inflicting yet more casualties while impressing upon the North – about to engage in peace negotiations in Paris – that the costs of continued aggression would be crippling.

General Westmoreland, in his last weeks as MACV commander, looked particularly toward the A Shau valley on the far western edge of Thua Thien province in ICTZ. About 28 miles long and up to 2 miles wide, this 'slash in the mountains', close to the Laotian border, had long been a natural route for NVA troops and supplies entering South Vietnam. Surrounded by towering, jungle-covered mountains, the valley was isolated and exceptionally difficult to penetrate, especially during the monsoon with its torrential rain and thick fog.

US and South Vietnamese Special Forces had established camps at A Loui, Ta Bat, and A Shau village, but the first two were abandoned in December, 1965, and the third was overrun by the NVA in a bruising battle the following March. Since then, the A

Shau valley had been abandoned to the Communists, something that Westmoreland found deeply frustrating. In April, 1968, he ordered the 1st Cavalry Division to mount an offensive – codenamed Delaware – to reassert Allied control.

US aero-rifle teams entered the valley on 14 April, intending to seize the former Special Forces camp at A Loui in the northern sector. They encountered a wall of anti-aircraft fire which 200 B-52 and 300 fighter-bomber sorties failed to quell; and, although battalions of the 7th Cavalry did take A Loui, conditions were appalling. Low cloud and rain effectively negated the advantages of airmobility; Delaware was called off on 11 May.

This pattern was repeated in August, when the 101st Airborne Division entered the valley in Operation Somerset Plain. The only answer seemed to be the construction of a road from the coast into the A Shau, reducing the dependence on helicopter resupply. By the end of 1968, this had been pushed to the eastern edge of the valley, but if it was to go further, operations would have to be carried out to clear the way.

These began in January, 1969, with Operation Dewey Canyon – a Marine assault south through the Da Krong valley into NVA Base Area 611 astride the Laotian border. It enjoyed a degree of success, persuading the new MACV commander, General Creighton Abrams, to order a follow-up offensive.

In March, the 2nd Brigade, 101st Airborne, air assaulted the central sector of the valley in Operation Massachusetts Striker. It culminated in a three-day battle at Dong A Tay ('Bloody Ridge'), in which the 1/502nd Infantry lost 35 men killed and over 100 wounded. The NVA were clearly prepared to fight.

Massachusetts Striker forced the NVA back toward the north-western sector of the valley, around a mountain (Dong) known as Ap Bia, but marked on US maps as Hill 937. Situated close to the Laotian border, 937 and its neighboring ridges – Hills 900 and 800 to the south and Hill 916 to the south-west – were covered in thick jungle, tangled vines, and impenetrable bamboo. In residence since 1964, the NVA had fortified the area, building log-covered bunkers and camouflaged spiderholes to protect all avenues of approach. By May, 1969, when the A Shau valley was chosen as an objective of the 101st in Operation Apache Snow, Ap Bia was being held by over 1,200 men of the crack NVA 29th Regiment.

Apache Snow began on 10 May with helicopter assaults by five

Allied battalions (three from the 101st Airborne Division and two from the 1st ARVN) into the northern A Shau. At LZ2, about 2,000 yards north-west of Hill 937, Lieutenant Colonel Weldon Honeycutt's 3/187th Infantry landed without incident and began to conduct RIF (reconnaissance-in-force) operations toward the mountain and Laotian border. A more permanent LZ and battalion command post was set up closer to 937 and, with no reaction from the NVA, Company B was ordered to seize the summit.

Starting out at 1640 hours, the paratroopers followed a trail to the south-east of the new LZ which took them into thick jungle, enclosed by tall trees, matted vines, and bamboo. Moving forward over fallen trees, the lead scouts trod warily while their comrades, sweating in the dank, humid air, plodded behind. As they crossed a low saddle, the NVA struck, firing RPGs (rocket-propelled grenades) and AK-47s into the American column. Airstrikes were called in, and, as dusk was gathering, the company pulled back into an NDP (night defensive position).

With only three men wounded, the skirmish was hardly significant, but when another ambush was sprung in the same area the following morning, killing three Americans, it was obvious that the enemy had been found. This suited Honeycutt, who immediately revised his plan. Recalling Company C from its RIF along the Trung Pham River, he ordered it to attack, parallel to Company B, along a ridge that ended between Hills 900 and 937, while Company D worked around the northern edge of the mountain. The aim was to have all three companies in position to assault the summit by first light on 13 May. It did not work.

The companies moved out at 0830 hours on 12 May, after intense air and artillery 'prepping' fire. They entered a nightmare of close-quarter fighting that was to continue with little respite for eight days. During that time, the 3/187th was to be shattered, both mentally and physically, as enemy resistance hardened and conditions deteriorated. On Company B's line of advance, the NVA drew the Americans closer to the mountain, into a clearing that sheltered line after line of bunkers, each of which seemed impervious to airstrikes or artillery strikes.

Day after day, the company moved up, attacking the bunkers with grenades, recoilless rifles and machine-guns, only to be forced to pull back, dragging their wounded to safety. By 15 May, Company B was exhausted and had to be replaced by Company D, itself less than strong after terrible experiences farther north. On 12 May, the company had found its way blocked by a steep-sided ravine. On reaching the bottom 24 hours later, they had been ambushed and forced to reverse their journey, in the dark and under torrential rain, manhandling seven of their wounded (including the pilot of a downed medevac helicopter) up a virtually sheer slope. They had then returned to recover seven dead, killed in the initial ambush.

Horrific as all this was, it did not match the experiences of Company C as it pushed along its designated ridge. Once again, the NVA drew the Americans closer to the mountain before springing a carefully prepared ambush on 13 May. The company lost two dead and 35 wounded in a matter of minutes: Honeycutt had no choice but to withdraw the survivors to his command post, sending Company A to take their place. It fared no better, stalling in front of a line of bunkers which defied all efforts at destruction. Meanwhile, the 1/506th, ordered to move from the south toward Hills 916 and 900, made little progress amid a maelstrom of enemy fire and violent thunderstorms.

By 16 May, all attacks had ground to a halt, and soldiers were beginning to react to the appalling strain of the situation. Honeycutt, with his repeated demands for action, became the focus of the men's discontent: 'If that sonofabitch wants to take this . . . mountain so bad, why don't he do it himself?'

But the fighting did not end. On 17 May, the 1/506th edged closer to Hill 900 and, 24 hours later, the weary assault companies of the 3/187th made enough progress to suggest that one final effort would take the summit of 937. They were blocked, not by the enemy, but by one of the most spectacular thunderstorms yet experienced. As visibility declined to zero, the rain turned the slopes of 937 – by now devoid of vegetation – into a sea of sticky mud. The attack was called off.

During the night of 18/19 May, Major General Melvin Zais, commanding the 101st, ordered three fresh battalions – the 2/501st, 2/506th, and 2/3rd ARVN – to join the battle. They landed without incident on the 19th, taking up blocking positions to the south-east and north-east of Ap Bia. On 20 May, all five battalions attacked, surrounding the NVA and cutting them off from their bases in Laos.

As the 2/501st and 2/3rd ARVN climbed the precipitous north-eastern and eastern faces of 937, respectively, the 1/506th put in a three-company assault across Hill 900 and into a deep draw – the major NVA escape route – to the south-west. At the same time, Honeycutt's men continued their attacks over familiar ground, gradually clearing the bunker lines and reaching desperately for the summit.

Enemy fire did not slacken, even when small groups of Company C scrambled onto the western edge to set up a defensive perimeter. But once they were joined by squads from Company A, the paratroopers were able slowly to clear the mountaintop. By 1655 hours, the fighting was dying down.

In any other war, the Battle of Dong Ap Bia – soon to be dubbed Hamburger Hill by the 3/187th, 'because they say this mountain turns men into hamburgers' – would have been hailed as a great victory. Despite heavy casualties – the Americans lost 70 killed and 372 wounded in the ten days of fighting – over 630 enemy bodies were found, and a well-defended base had been taken. But Vietnam was different, and, as news of the battle filtered out, controversy began.

Publicly condemned by Senator Edward Kennedy as 'senseless and irresponsible', the action fueled the anti-war lobby, particularly when, on 5 June, the 101st abandoned Ap Bia and allowed the enemy to return. Military arguments that the strategy was to impose casualties, not occupy real estate, cut little ice, especially when, on 27 June, *Life* magazine ran a misleading feature on 'The Faces of the Dead in Vietnam. One Week's Total.'

Many readers imagined that the 241 photographs shown were all of men killed at Ap Bia. Under considerable political and public pressure, President Nixon ordered Abrams to cease offensive operations in NVA-controlled territory, accelerating the process of Vietnamization to allow US troops to be withdrawn. US involvement in Vietnam was drawing to a close.

8
The Six-Day War

Jerusalem (1967)

Ashley Brown

Shortly after 0930 hours on the morning of Tuesday, 6 June 1967, Colonel Mordechai Gur, commander of the Israeli 55th Parachute Brigade, spoke on the radio net to his waiting paratroopers. 'We stand on a ridge overlooking the Holy City. Soon we will enter the city, the Old City of Jerusalem about which countless generations of Jews have dreamed, to which all living Jews aspire. To our brigade has been granted the privilege of being the first to enter it.'

The capture of Jerusalem was the most potent symbol of Jewish victory in the Six-Day War of 1967, for the control of the Holy Places, such as the Temple Mount and the Wailing Wall, was enormously important to the young state of Israel. The honour of being the troops who would physically take possession of this great prize had been earned by Gur's men, who had shown great courage and skill over the past two days. In particular, they had wrested control of northern Jerusalem from the experienced and well dug-in forces of the Jordanian Army in the early morning of 6 June.

Tension had been building between Israel and her Arab neighbours for some time when, on the morning of 5 June, the Israeli Air Force launched a sudden strike against the Egyptians. This was totally successful, but in the confusion of that morning's events, King Hussein of Jordan was led to believe that the Israelis had themselves been hard hit, and agreed to send his forces in to attack Israel. At 1100 hours a bombardment began from the Jordanian side of the

heavily fortified border, and the Jordanian Air Force flew sorties
into Israeli air space. This was a foolhardy move that Hussein was to
regret bitterly. Within hours, the rampant Israelis had put his entire
air force out of action, and Major-General Uzi Narkiss, in charge of
Central Command, was putting into operation his contingency plans
for an offensive against Jordanian territory.

The Israelis had to cope with an unpromising strategic situation.
Their main problem was that a long, narrow finger of land, inviting
attack or artillery barrage from the Jordanian territory on either
side, was the only link with the Israeli-held areas of Jerusalem.
This corridor had to be made secure, and so Narkiss used the
tanks of Colonel Ben Ari's 10th Mechanized Brigade to push
north of the corridor and seize the ridge linking Jerusalem with
the important centre of Ramallah; at the same time, Latrun was
attacked and overrun. Meanwhile, to the south of the corridor, the
16th Jerusalem Brigade launched a series of attacks that cut the main
Jordanian communications with their forces in Hebron. The success
of these two sets of operations, greatly helped by the command of the
air that the Israeli Air Force was now exerting, gave the situation a
new complexion. Far from being the side with the strategic initiative,
the Jordanians were now vulnerable, and their position in Jerusalem
under threat.

Within Jerusalem, the possibilities and prospects for either side
were complicated by two factors. First, there was a substantial Israeli
enclave within Jordanian territory on Mount Scopus, comprising the
Hadassah Hospital and the Hebrew University. A prime Israeli goal
was to relieve this enclave (which had been maintained, under United
Nations auspices, since 1948) while the Jordanians in turn wished
to overrun the position. The second factor affecting operations in
the city was that in the two decades since the establishment of
the existing frontier, both sides had built up complex sets of
fortifications. These networks of deep concrete bunkers, carefully
sited linking trenches, mines and barbed wire promised to make a
frontal offensive a difficult, if not impossible, task.

The main Jordanian force in the city was the 27th Infantry Brigade,
under Brigadier Ata Ali. Further brigades were in support to both
north and south, while a tank battalion was stationed behind the
main built-up areas in the Kidron valley. The Israeli Air Force made
every effort to cut the communication lines of these forces with the
Jordanian concentrations further to the north and east, but Ali was

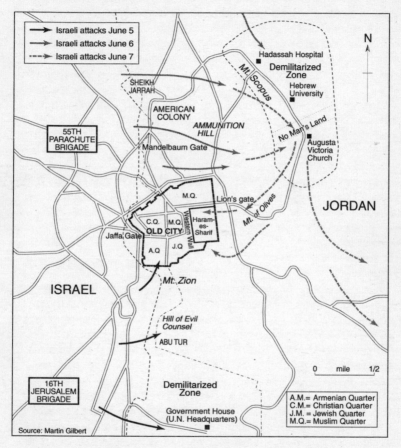

8.1   *The Capture of Jerusalem, 5–7 June 1967*

a competent officer and he had been reinforced. His men, basically the former Arab Legion under a different name, were well trained and confident of the strength of their defensive positions. Against them, the Israelis decided to throw in one of their crack formations – the 55th Parachute Brigade.

The 55th Parachute Brigade was a body of men trained to expect shock action and to be in the forefront of any Israeli offensive. Under its experienced commander, Colonel Mordechai Gur, were many veterans of raids on Arab territory, although some of the most senior officers had not yet seen action. Raised to a fever pitch by the days of waiting before the air strike that marked the beginning of the Six-Day War, the paras had expected to be used against the Egyptians in the Sinai, and at noon on the 5th were told to prepare for a jump against El Arish, to give impetus to the northern axis of advance. However, such was the pace of the Israeli success that by 1600 hours the decision was taken to use the whole brigade against the Jordanians in Jerusalem.

The basic plan was for the 66th and 71st Battalions of the 55th Brigade to attack along a front running from the Mandelbaum Gate to a point opposite the Jordanian-held Police School building. When a breakthrough had been made, the 28th Battalion would push through to exploit southwards, towards the walls of the Old City. Some support would come from the tanks attached to the Jerusalem Brigade, but the paras would have to fight their way through an awesome set of obstacles with only minimum support before the attack could gather momentum.

The staff of the 55th Brigade urgently prepared for the assault. It was due to go in as soon as possible, but in the event, the battalions would not be ready before 0215 hours on the 6th. The crews manning the 81 mm mortars were especially concerned, because the shells they needed were very slow in arriving. They were anxious to start rangefinding, but could not risk running short of ammunition. Units were getting lost as they struggled to find their place in the line and Jordanian shells, falling at random, were causing casualties. In addition, the deputy commander of B Company, 71st Battalion, had mistakenly attached his men to the convoy of buses carrying mortars forward, and with him was all the communications equipment for the battalion. But eventually all was just about in position and, at 0215 on 6 June, the barrage began.

With buildings on the Jordanian side bursting into flame and lines of tracer flicking through the darkness, the first Israeli platoons approached the Jordanian positions. They thrust bangalore torpedoes below the coils of barbed wire, and then hastily pulled back and hit the deck. The 71st Battalion in particular had trouble in their sector: bangalore torpedoes were not exploding, and then further wire obstacles were looming up after the first breach had been made. The delays meant that men moving forward to exploit the expected breach caused overcrowding, and the milling soldiers could have been very vulnerable to Jordanian shells. Eventually the way through was cleared. Waving green torches (usually the recognition signal for assembly after a night jump) to indicate that the path was open, officers led the platoons through into the next phase of the assault.

Once through the wire, the 66th Battalion was to exploit north-wards, through the Police School, taking the important position of Ammunition Hill, while the 71st Battalion was to move through the Sheikh Jarrah area and the American Colony towards the Wadi El-Joz. The men of the 66th knew that they would face enormous difficulties. Ammunition Hill was a vital point, and the Police School itself was well fortified. The paras were heavily laden, carrying extra magazines for their Uzi sub-machine-guns and knapsacks stuffed with grenades. In some cases, men were unable to get up when they fell over, and in one narrow trench Israeli troops got stuck because they were too bulky to pass along.

Giant searchlights illuminated the white walls of the Police School; Jordanian flares suddenly lit up the whole scene. Blazing houses made the darkness around them seem even darker, and the constant explosions of tank, mortar and Jordanian 25-pounder shells provided a deadly backdrop as the paras pushed ahead. It was impossible to see exactly where the enemy small arms fire was coming from. If a trench or emplacement was seen, then it could be attacked and wiped out, but the main priority was to push on to the important objectives. In spite of their loads, and in spite of the fire, the men of the 66th Battalion kept going.

First into the Police School was A Company, cutting a way through a cattle-fence outside. The long passages inside were completely dark, a darkness rendered even more impenetrable by the sudden shell flashes outside. Groups of four men cleared the rooms, two throwing in a grenade and then spraying a room with fire, while the other two moved on to the room next door. But the paras kept tripping and falling in the pitch blackness; in the end, the officers had no option but the dangerous one of using torches. When they had taken the school, A Company moved on towards the Ambassador Hotel, together with D Company; B and C Companies moved towards Ammunition Hill.

As dawn broke (at about 0340 hours) the paras were engaged in a deadly, exhausting fight for the hill. In the trenches and bunkers it was often very difficult to tell friend from foe, and the fighting was further confused by Jordanian sniping from hills to the north. Tanks came up in support, but close-quarters fighting against prepared positions is a tanker's nightmare, and they needed infantry protection against bazookas and recoilless rifles. Soon, the paras had emptied the spare loaded magazines they had brought with them, and had to refill magazines by hand from ammunition boxes – a tiring, fiddly task when under fire. But gradually, the hill was cleared, and the final, so-called 'great bunker' was taken at 0515.

Meanwhile, the 71st Battalion was also meeting stiff resistance in its attack. Having had the most problems in assembling for the assault, this battalion also had difficulty in finding its way once it was into the Jordanian lines. The difficulty of finding the right road in the darkness with only photographs to guide them was magnified by the need to clear hidden Jordanian positions. Dropping grenades into emplacements, and carefully moving along the sheltered sides of streets, the Israelis began clearing the area between the frontier and the Nablus Road, and had a stroke of luck when the Jordanian defenders of the street leading to Wadi El-Joz were taken by surprise. A company of paras moved rapidly down the street to set up positions at this important intersection.

Although the advance was generally going well, the Jordanian support weapons soon picked out the assembly area of the Israelis, and the brigade's mortar crews and recoilless rifle operators suffered casualties as artillery fire began to zero in on them. The breaches in the front-line defences were soon being crossed by the wounded returning from the fight up ahead, some stoical but others screaming with pain. The medical resources of the brigade were becoming dangerously stretched by the mounting casualties in the attacking battalions and among the support units that were under artillery and machine-gun fire.

One heavy machine-gun in particular had caused great concern as it swept the breaches with fire before it was knocked out by a bazooka; and in spite of many efforts, a light machine-gun proved endlessly troublesome. It would stop as soon as a shell burst near it, then open up again. A group of staff officers from the 28th Battalion volunteered to finish it off; but when they tried to approach it they were caught in a trap, and the commander of the support company, leading the attempt, was seriously wounded.

With bullets flying and shells bursting around them, the men of the 28th Battalion moved off to begin their part of the assault soon after the 71st Battalion had gone through the breach in the wire. One shell chanced to injure the deputy commander of D Company, while there were serious officer casualties when a Jordanian 25-pounder struck lucky and hit battalion headquarters. After a seemingly interminable wait, it was dawn before the first members of the 28th Battalion had got to the Jordanian side of the wire, and then they had to fight their way south.

Fighting in the daylight proved, in some ways, worse than the night fighting. Now, snipers could fire without the flash of their muzzles giving away their position, and Jordanian artillery observers had a better view of events. Some of the districts through which the men of the 28th were moving were supposed to have been cleared, but the Israelis soon found that enemy troops could easily infiltrate back into good positions. The building of the Moslem Council had to be cleared three times to make certain that a single shot, or a carefully lobbed grenade, would not take its toll of the advancing Israelis.

The task of moving down Saladin Street was given to C Company but, unable to identify the area properly, it went down Nablus Road. Here the paras had to flush out the YMCA building, from which there was considerable fire. Entering it cautiously, they found most of it empty, finding only the base of a machine-gun mounting. Suddenly the squad that was investigating the situation was fired upon, and men went down wounded. Time was too short to waste it on just one obstacle, and a hand-to-hand combat would have resulted in further casualties. The squad pulled out, and a supporting tank put two shells into the upper stories; the advance went on.

About 0500, there was a lull and the men of the 28th Battalion were ordered to halt. This was a nerve-racking moment, because the risk of a sniper's bullet, or of a well-aimed salvo of artillery shells was as great as ever. Then the advance began again with more tank support. The main task now was to get to the Rockefeller Museum, an imposing new building that dominated the approaches to the north-east corner of the Old City. The roar of the tank guns when they fired almost deafened the paratroopers as the sound echoed between the high buildings. The paras also found it difficult to communicate with the tank crews because the cables for the external telephones had been cut by shrapnel, or were turned off so that the tankers could listen to the stream of orders they were getting on their radio net. But in spite of these problems, the tanks were a real boon, for they drew fire away from the men on foot and they certainly gave the Jordanian defenders second thoughts about opening up at short range.

By 0800, the 55th Brigade had performed brilliantly. All its objectives were secured, and it had set the scene for further advance. From Ammunition Hill in the north through Sheikh Jarrah, the Ambassador Hotel, and down to Wadi El-Joz, a line had been established that gave contact with the slopes of Mount Scopus and promised imminent relief for the besieged garrison; while in the south, the capture of the Rockefeller Museum made an assault against the Old City a practical possibility. Indeed, paras of the 28th Battalion had set themselves up in the Rivoli Hotel opposite Herod's Gate, and when they were not engaging the defenders of the walls of the Old City they were able to sample the delights of the hotel's kitchens, and have a bath.

The casualties sustained by the brigade in reaching these objectives had been horrific – but the achievement had been immense. Gur visited the troops at the Rockefeller Museum. Although many had no previous experience of real action, he noted that already they were comporting themselves like veterans; they knew exactly where enemy fire might come from, and where to find precisely the safest places to sit and relax.

The ranks of the three battalions were thinned by the pounding they had taken during the assault, but there was no shortage of volunteers to replace the dead and wounded. The mortar crews and anti-tank personnel were now anxious to get into the front line – especially as the Old City was beckoning. Morale was sky-high, and Gur prepared to move the 66th Battalion further south for another day's fighting.

Narkiss, desperate to finish things off and to get into the Holy City, ordered Gur to concentrate on taking the last Jordanian strongpoint in the region, the Augusta Victoria Hospital on a ridge to the south of Mount Scopus, and then to prepare an encirclement of the Old City. The plans for the assault were swiftly drawn up, and it was decided to wait until after 1930 hours, when darkness fell, before attacking.

The assault on Augusta Victoria Hospital got off to a bad start, when some troops strayed too close to the walls of the Old City and were fired on from there; and then, at 2140, Gur was informed that 40 Patton tanks of the Jordanian Army had been seen on the reverse side of the slope his men were to attack. With only four Shermans as support, Gur could not risk the assault. He decided to wait until the next day, when aerial support could be called in. Anti-tank dispositions were made and then the soldiers tried to sleep.

Gur's new plan was to attack at about 1130 hours on 7 June, by which time the Israeli Air Force should have dispersed the Pattons. The Israeli high command decided, however, that the attack should go in much earlier in the morning, at 0830. Again, there was frantic haste to reschedule operations, for the new attack was to be mounted from Mount Scopus as well as from across the Kidron valley.

Had the Israelis known it, such frenzied preparations were hardly necessary. Far from being able to bring up substantial armoured reinforcements, Brigadier Ata Ali had been completely cut off by the success of Israeli moves to north and south, and by the Israeli Air Force's devastating attacks on Jordanian road convoys. His troops began a skilful withdrawal in the early hours of 7 June.

At 0804, just before his attacks were to start, Gur was at last given the order that he was so anxious to receive: he was told to take the Old City. Immediately after the air attacks on the Augusta Victoria Ridge, his men stormed over it, and at 0930 he was able to give the historic order to his brigade that the time for waiting was past.

The entry into the Old City was to be via the Lion's Gate, which was the only one able to take tanks, and as the armoured support of the paratroopers approached this point of entry, there was some sporadic defensive fire. Gur himself led the entry into the Old City, and his troops met only light resistance from isolated snipers. At about 1000, he reached the Wailing Wall. The brigade's ordnance officer produced a bottle of whisky, and passed it round. The 55th Brigade had won a victory that no one in Israel would ever forget.

9
The Falklands War

Wireless Ridge (1982)

John Frost

The British Army's Second Battalion of the Parachute Regiment fought in all the major battles of the 1982 land war between Britain and Argentina for the Falkland Islands (Malvinas). After spearheading the landings at San Carlos on 21 May, the battalion fought its way to Port Stanley against determined Argentinian resistance, via Bluff Cove, Goose Green and Wireless Ridge. The most famous of these battles is undoubtedly Goose Green (where 2 Para commander, Lieutenant-Colonel 'H' Jones, won a posthumous Victoria Cross for his charge against an enemy position), but the engagement at Wireless Ridge on 13–14 June was no less dramatic and arguably more decisive. The Ridge, a spur on the north side of Port Stanley, was heavily defended by troops from the Argentine 7th Infantry Regiment and the Argentine 1st Parachute Regiment.

The origins of the Parachute Regiment lie with an initiative of Winston Churchill who, after noting the success of German paratroop operations during Germany's invasion of Holland and Belgium, suggested the formation of a British airborne elite force. The first units began training in June 1940, with volunteers from the units forming the Parachute Regiment in August 1942.

2 Para's task was to capture the Wireless Ridge features, keeping

west of the telegraph wires, and Colonel Chaundler's plan called for a two-phase noisy night attack. In Phase 1, A Company would take the northern spur where the ponds were, C Company having secured the start-line. Once this was secure Phase 2 would come into operation, and B and D Companies would pass through from the north to attack the main Wireless Ridge feature itself. B Company would go to the right (the western end of the ridge), while D Company attacked the rocky ridge-line east of the track.

The mortars would move forward from Mount Kent to a position in the lee of the hillside south of Drunken Rock Pass, and this would also be the site for a static Battalion Headquarters during the attack. H-hour was to be at about 0030. The importance of digging in on the objectives was emphasized once more, since Wireless Ridge was dominated by both Tumbledown and Sapper Hill, and if enemy troops should still be there at dawn they could make 2 Para's positions untenable.

The orders were straightforward, and the plan simple, involving the maximum use of darkness. As the 'O' Group ended the company commanders were told that they would now fly up to Mount Longdon to look at the ground over which they would operate.

The CO went on ahead with the Battery Commander to meet Lieutenant-Colonel Hew Pike, CO of 3 Para, and Major William McCracken, RA, who controlled the artillery 'anchor' OP on Mount Longdon. They discussed and arranged for co-ordinated fire support, with 3 Para's mortars, Milan teams and machine-guns all ready to fire from the flank, and Major Martin Osborne's C Company, 3 Para, in reserve.

Back at the gully all was peaceful in the bright sunshine. Suddenly this was shattered as nine Skyhawks appeared further to the north, flying very low in formation and heading due west towards Mount Kent. The effect was electric, for no one expected that the Argentines could still flaunt their air power in this way.

At 'A' Echelon, behind Mount Kent, there was no doubt as to who the jets were aiming for. As they came screaming up over the col and rose to attacking height, the formation split: three went for the area where the artillery gun-line had recently been, three went for 3 Commando Brigade HQ, and three attacked 'A' Echelon. All the machine-guns opened up, claiming one possible hit as the bombs rained down. Amazingly, there were no casualties from this minor blitzkrieg. But the accuracy of the attack, and

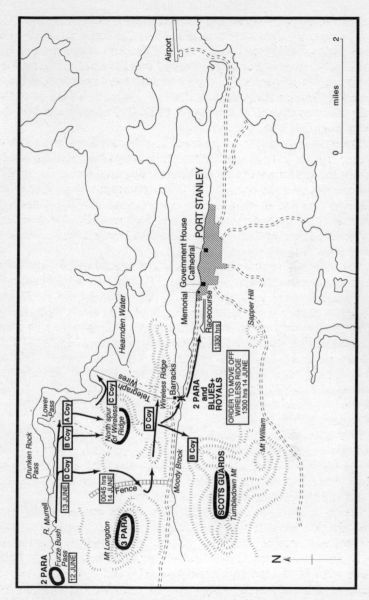

9.1   *The Capture of Wireless Ridge and Port Stanley, June 1982*

its obvious definiteness of purpose, left people wondering if the enemy had left concealed OPs behind, watching Mount Kent, or if satellite photography had shown up the various targets or, possibly, if Argentine electronic-warfare equipment had picked up radio signals from Brigade HQ.

The air raid created delays to all helicopter movement, but eventually the CO was able to fly on to Brigade HQ, while the company commanders were dropped on to Mount Longdon for their own recces. Colonel Chaundler had already been updated on the actual strength of the enemy, which was greater than had been thought, and a new Argentine position had been detected to the east of the pond-covered spur, on a knoll overlooking Hearnden Water and the mouth of the Murrell River.

While the CO was at Brigade HQ, the company commanders were able to study Wireless Ridge in detail from the commanding position on Longdon. It at once became obvious that much of the information so far given to them was inaccurate. What was thought to be C Company of 3 Para proved to be nothing of the sort: Major Dair Farrar-Hockley noticed that it was an *enemy* position of about company strength, situated dangerously on the flank of the 2 Para axis of attack, west of the northern spur. It was also clear that Wireless Ridge proper was heavily defended, with positions which stretched a long way to the east beyond the line of telegraph poles that marked the 2 Para boundary. Strangely, no harassing fire was being brought to bear during the day on any of the Argentine positions, and their soldiers were free to stand about in the open.

The company commanders flew back to Furze Bush Pass, but clearly a major change in plan was necessary. The CO returned from Brigade HQ as evening approached and was told of the situation. 'Go away and have your supper. Come back in 45 minutes and you will have a new set of orders,' he said. Meanwhile the move-up of mortars and the adjustment of artillery had been delayed, and as a result the changes to the fire-plan had to continue into the night, directed by the OP on Longdon and using illuminating rounds.

Unfortunately for the company commanders, normal battle procedure had already ensured that relevant details of the first plan had permeated to the lowest level. Platoon and section commanders had had time to issue clear and well-constructed orders to their subordinates, but now their efforts were all useless, for by the time the company commanders returned with the CO's revised plan, it was too late to go into new details. Such a sudden last-minute change did little for the men's faith in the system, but it was unavoidable and, in any case, the soldiers had by now become stoical, while the cynics among them were not disappointed by this evidence of fallibility at higher levels. Nevertheless, the battalion was able to adapt and change its plans and moved off on time. But Phil Neame had his misgivings about what the SAS to the east of his line of advance was *meant* to be doing, and there was no knowledge of what the SAS was actually *going* to do. Furthermore, no one really knew what was beyond Wireless Ridge to the south, in the Moody Brook area, and everyone would have liked to have known exactly when the 5 Brigade attack on Tumbledown was timed to begin.

The battalion's new plan was for a four-phase noisy night attack. In Phase 1 D Company would capture the newly discovered enemy position west of the northern spur; A and B Companies would then assault the pond-covered hilltop; Phase 3 called for C Company to take the knoll to the east; and finally D Company would roll up the enemy on Wireless Ridge itself, with fire support from A and B Companies, starting in the west and finishing at the telegraph poles.

Fire support was to be lavish in comparison to Goose Green: two batteries of 105 mm guns, HMS *Ambuscade* with her one 4.5-inch gun offshore, and the mortars of both 2 and 3 Para, totalling 16 tubes. Ammunition was plentiful, and the battalion's mortars had been moved complete from Mount Kent by helicopter, and were thus fresh for action. The Machine-Gun Platoon had also been flown forward. Between the six guns they had enough ammunition to provide a massive weight of fire, and the men were fresh and rather proud of their earlier achievement behind Mount Kent against the Skyhawks. The Milan Platoon was already forward with the battalion – the experience of Goose Green had demonstrated the capability of this precision guided missile against static defences. Finally the light tanks of the Blues and Royals would be there, Scimitars with their 30 mm automatic cannon and Scorpions with 76 mm guns, and both equipped with very high quality night-vision equipment and having superb cross-country performance. All available support was allotted first to D Company, then to A and B in their assault, and finally to D Company again as it traversed the ridge.

As night closed in the tanks, the mortars and the Recce Platoon, which was to secure the start-line, moved up. By now the promise of the day had vanished and snow and sleet were falling, considerably limiting the effectiveness of all the gun-sighting equipment, and reducing visibility.

At about 0015 a storm of fire from the supporting artillery and mortars was unleashed upon the Argentine positions. A and B Companies passed by, led by C Company patrols to the new start-line secured by Corporal Bishop's patrol in the relatively safe ground overlooking Lower Pass. At 0045 hours on Monday 14 June, D Company moved over its own start-line further to the west, and headed towards the identified enemy position.

As the company moved forward, the tanks of the Blues and Royals and the machine-guns provided fire support while the artillery increased its rate of fire. Enemy mortar fire in retaliation became heavy. In the rear of the company, Private Godfrey of 12 Platoon had a near miss as a piece of shrapnel cut through his windproof and dug into his boot. He dived for cover – straight into an Argentine latrine!

The weight of supporting artillery and mortar fire was singularly effective, for the enemy on the D Company objective could be seen running away as the company pushed forward, although 155 mm air-burst shelling increased as the Paras began to clear the Argentine trenches, now abandoned except for a few enemy killed by the barrage. The darkness of the night and the extent of the enemy position caused the company to spread out, creating problems of control. Lieutenant Webster of 10 Platoon counted up to 20 trenches on his right, with more over to the left, where 2nd Lieutenant Waddington's 11 Platoon found the other half of the assault formation.

Occasionally as they moved forward, men would suddenly disappear into the freezing water of an ice-covered pond. Privates Dean and Creasey of 11 Platoon went in up to their necks, and had to tread water to stay afloat until their platoon sergeant, Sergeant Light, dragged them out.

Fire support for the company was immaculate. The tanks used their powerful image-intensifier night-sights to pinpoint targets. Once enemy positions were identified, they fired. As soon as the battalion's machine-gunners saw the strike they, too, opened up. Occasionally the machine-gun fire was too close for comfort, even for D Company, and in the end 10 Platoon Commander called for it to stop.

The opposition had fled, and D Company took its first objective in record time, remaining *in situ* while A and B Companies began their part of the battle. Enemy artillery fire was increasing, however, and Neame therefore decided to push forward for another 300 m into relative safety, to avoid the worst of the barrage.

Several of those waiting to move on the A and B Company start-lines were reminded of scenes they had seen from films of the First and Second World Wars. As shells landed all around, men lay huddled against the peat, with bayonets fixed. There could be no denying that, for the soldiers, fear of the known was in this case worse than blissful ignorance of the unknown. In the shelter of the peat bogs some smoked, watching the display of illuminants above.

Just as the time came to move, the shelling claimed its first victim, for Colour Sergeant 'Doc' Findlay was killed in the rear of A Company, and soldiers from Support and HQ Companies were also wounded. The advance began, the two companies moving southwards parallel to each other, on either side of the track. The men crossed the stream in the valley north of their objective with the tanks firing over their heads. The effect upon the enemy was devastating. In their night-sights the tank crews could see Argentine soldiers running or falling as the accurate fire took effect. The boost to morale that this form of suppressive fire gave was considerable; fundamentally, the battle was being won by supporting arms, the infantry being free to do their own job, which is actually clearing and securing the ground.

On the left, all was going well with A Company. Command and control had been well practised back at Goose Green and now the junior officers and section commanders were quite expert in maintaining direction. Silence was unnecessary and orders were shouted backwards and forwards. The enemy were still shelling as the companies advanced, but now counter-battery fire was being provided by our own artillery. From his own position the CO could see the two companies in extended formation, moving quickly up the hill, the whole battlefield brightly lit by starshell.

Co-ordinating the two assaulting companies' advances was difficult, however. The track provided a boundary of sorts, but controlling upwards of 200 men during a noisy battle over difficult terrain is not easy. Colonel Chaundler had another worry. Earlier, before the battalion had moved up, he had been shown a captured Argentine map which indicated a minefield directly in the path of the assaulting companies. There was only 15 minutes to go before 2 Para set off – far too late for a change of plan. The CO only had time to brief OC B Company, while John Crosland had none in which to warn his men, and in any case was told to push on regardless, since there would be no time to clear the mines. Only afterwards did Major Crosland tell his men that they had actually moved directly through the minefield without knowing it. Miraculously, no one was blown up on the way.

The ponds on the spur claimed a victim, however, when Private Philpott of 5 Platoon suddenly plunged into over 6 ft of water. He was dragged out and his section commander, Corporal Curtis, immediately organized a complete change of clothing from the other men in the section, which probably saved Philpott's life.

The two companies consolidated on the objective. There was some firing from the trenches, swiftly silenced as the men of both companies ran in to clear them. Once more the enemy had fled, leaving only 20 or so of their number behind, quickly taken prisoner as they were winkled out of their holes. Radios were still switched on, and several dead lay around the positions. As the men dug in, the enemy shelling increased and it was to continue for the rest of the night at the same level of intensity. Most thought it was worse than Goose Green, but fortunately the abandoned enemy bunkers provided reasonable shelter, although a number of casualties occurred in A Company.

It was now C Company's turn. Already they had had a minor scare on the A and B Company start-line when a Scorpion tank had careered towards Company Headquarters in the darkness. It was hopelessly lost and its commander had to be evacuated after a dose of 'hatch rash' – the effect of placing the head in the path of a rapidly closing hatch. The confused vehicle was soon heading in the right direction, but now under the command of Captain Roger Field, who had seized this opportunity to revert to a more honourable role than foot-slogging.

With A and B Companies now firm, C Company was ordered to check out the Argentine position further to the east that had been spotted from Mount Longdon on the previous day. Major Roger Jenner was glad to be moving again, for it seemed that the supporting artillery battery had developed a 'rogue gun' and every sixth round meant for the enemy was coming in uncomfortably close to his company. He and his men set off, taking cover occasionally on the way as shells fell close by. There had been no firing from the company objective during the battle, and soon the platoons were pushing round the side of a minefield on to the knoll.

As the Recce Platoon advanced, they could hear noises of weapons being cocked. The bright moonlight left them uncomfortably exposed on the hillside. On the forward edge of the slope were two parallel lines of rock, and on the second line the platoon found a series of shell scrapes, suggesting recent occupation by a body of troops. Once again it seemed that the enemy had left hurriedly, leaving tents and bits of equipment behind in the process. Away over to the east Jenner's men could see the bright lights of Stanley airfield, and could hear a C-130 landing. The company was ordered to dig in, but since an enemy attack on this feature was extremely unlikely the CO changed the orders, and C Company moved up to the pond-covered hill.

If any particular group deserves special praise for what was done that night, then it must be the tanks of the Blues and Royals. Their mere presence had been a remarkable boost to morale during all the attacks that had taken place, and the speed and accuracy of their fire, matched by their ability to keep up with the advancing Paras, had been a severe shock to the enemy. Lance-Corporal Dunkeley's tank, which Captain Field had taken over following the injury to its commander, had alone fired 40 rounds from its 76 mm gun.

2 Para was performing superbly, its three first objectives taken with great speed and a minimum of casualties, despite heavy and accurate enemy artillery fire. Whenever the enemy in trenches had sought to return fire they had been met by a withering concentration of fire from the rifle companies' weapons which, coupled with very heavy support, had proved devastating. It is not known whether the Argentines had gathered that they were facing the men from Goose Green, but there can be no question that 2 Para knew.

D Company was now ready to go into the final phase of the attack and began moving forward again to the west end of Wireless Ridge. The tanks and support weapons moved up to join A and B Companies on the hilltop overlooking the D Company objective, and endured the artillery fire as well as anti-tank fire from Wireless Ridge to the south.

12 Platoon was now in the lead. Lieutenant John Page, who had taken over from the tragically killed Jim Barry, looked for the fence, running at right-angles to the ridge, that would guide him to the

correct start-line for the assault. Unfortunately there was little left of the fence marked on the maps, and Corporal Barton's section, at the point of the platoon, could only find a few strands of wire to follow. The number of ice-covered ponds added to the difficulty and the intense cold was beginning to affect men's reactions, as they worked their way south to the western end of Wireless Ridge.

Once more, massive fire-power began to soften up the enemy, who apparently still had no intimation that they were about to be rolled up from a flank. The initial idea had been for D Company simply to sweep eastwards along the ridge without stopping, with 11 Platoon on the left, 12 Platoon on the right and 10 Platoon in reserve. There was still uncertainty as to whether Tumbledown to the south had been taken or not, and clearly a battle was still in progress on that mountain as the Scots Guards fought to drive out the Argentines on its summit. But Neame and his D Company had no intention other than to push on regardless, although they knew that if Tumbledown was still in enemy hands by daylight then 2 Para would be extremely vulnerable.

The bombardment of the western end of the Wireless Ridge continued as the platoons advanced. It seemed to have been effective, since no enemy were encountered at all, although, to be certain, 11 Platoon cleared any bunkers they came across on the reverse slope with grenades.

The first part of Wireless Ridge was now clear and across the dip, where the track came up, lay the narrower rocky outcrops of the remainder of the objective. Fire was concentrated on these areas from A and B Companies as tanks, Milans and machine-guns provided an intense concentration on to three enemy machine-gun posts that remained.

Efforts to switch artillery support further forward and on to the area of Moody Brook had unfortunate results. Five rounds of high explosive crashed on to the ridge around and very near the leading D Company platoons. 3 Section of 11 Platoon was caught in the open and, despite screams to stop the firing, it was too late. Private Parr was killed instantly, and Corporal McAuley was somersaulted into some rocks, completely dazed, and had to be picked up by a stretcher party.

There was a considerable delay while a livid Major Neame tried to get the gunners to sort themselves out. It seemed that one gun was off target, as C Company had noted, but at the gun-lines they

did not know which, since in the dark it was impossible to note the
fall of shot, even if there had been time, and the other battery was
not available owing to shortage of ammunition. In the meantime
the CO was growing increasingly impatient, urging the D Company
commander to press on.

As soon as the gunners could guarantee reasonable support, and
with increased efforts from the Blues and Royals, Neame was off
again. All through the wait constant harassing fire from the enemy
had been landing around the company, so none were sorry to
move. Despite the fire pouring on to the ridge-line ahead, enemy
machine-gunners continued firing from well-sited bunkers, and were
still staunchly in action as the platoons advanced.

They moved with 11 Platoon on the left, 12 Platoon ahead on
the ridge itself, with the company commander immediately behind
and, in the rear, 10 Platoon. 12 Platoon came across an abandoned
Argentine recoilless rifle, an anti-tank weapon, as they crossed the
start-line, which may well have been the weapon that had earlier
been engaging the tanks on the A and B Company positions. The
platoon moved down into the gap between the two parts of the
ridge line, but as the soldiers passed by some ponds, very heavy
machine-gun fire began from their front and illumination was called
for as the platoon answered the firing. Corporal Barton came across
some orange string, possibly indicating a minefield, but his platoon
commander urged him on regardless.

The enemy appeared to be surprised by the direction of the assault,
and as the Paras advanced, they could hear an Argentine voice calling
out, possibly to give warning of this sudden attack from the west. 10
Platoon came across a lone enemy machine-gunner who lay wounded
in both legs, his weapon lying abandoned beside him.

Corporal Harley of 11 Platoon caught his foot in a wire, which
may have been part of a minefield, and, fearing that it might be
an Argentine jumping mine, unravelled himself with some care.
The platoon pushed on, skirmishing by sections until they met a
concertina of wire. Fearing mines, Sappers were called for from
Company Headquarters, but these could do little in the darkness
except tape off the suspect area. In fact channels could be discerned
between the concertinas, and these were assumed, correctly, as it
turned out, to be safe lanes.

While 11 Platoon was extricating itself from the minefield, Neame
pushed 12 Platoon on and brought 10 Platoon out to the left to

maintain the momentum. Suddenly an intense burst of firing brought the company to a halt. It was a critical moment. For a short time, *all* commanders had to do everything in their power to get things going again, with platoon commanders and sergeants and section commanders all urging their men on. It was a real test of leadership as several soldiers understandably went to ground.

A brief fire-fight ensued, with 12 Platoon engaging the enemy as they pushed forward on the right overlooking Moody Brook below, where lights could be seen. The moment of doubt had passed, however, and once more the men were clearing bunkers and mopping up with gusto. 10 and 12 Platoons now moved on either side of the company commander. Maximum speed was needed to keep the enemy off balance as they fell back, conducting a fighting withdrawal along the ridge. The tanks continued to fire, directed by the company commander. Unfortunately his signaller had fallen into a shell-hole and become separated, thus creating considerable frustration for the CO, who wanted to talk to Neame about the progress of his battle.

During 12 Platoon's brief fight Private Slough had been hit and died later in hospital, and another soldier was wounded.

Enemy artillery fire continued to make life uncomfortable. Fortunately D Company's task was no longer difficult, as most of the enemy bunkers had now been abandoned. 12 Platoon reached the telegraph wires and consolidated there, while the other platoons reorganized further back along the ridge. Shellfire intensified and snipers began to engage from enemy positions further to the east along the ridge.

Neame went up to see the platoon commander, Lieutenant Page. Snipers in the rocks were still firing on the platoon and it seemed that the enemy might be about to counter-attack from the direction of Moody Brook, to the right.

On several occasions the company commander was nearly hit, and his perambulations began to be the cause of some comment. Sergeant Meredith shouted to him, 'For God's sake push off, Sir – you're attracting bullets everywhere you go!'

A hundred metres or so to the east, Argentines could be heard shouting to each other, as though rallying for a counter-attack. John Page called for fire support, and then ordered his own men to stop firing, for by so doing they were merely identifying their positions. They felt very isolated and vulnerable.

For two very long and uncomfortable hours the company remained under pressure. Small-arms fire mingled with all types of HE fell in and around 12 Platoon's position as the men crouched in the abandoned enemy sangars and in shell-holes. John Page continued to move around his platoon, organizing its defences, and suffering a near-miss in the process. He was hit by a bullet, which passed between two grenades hanging on his webbing and landed in a full magazine in his pouch. He was blown off his feet by the shock. 'It was like being hit by a sledge-hammer and having an electric shock at the same time,' he later described the moment. As he lay there a round exploded in the magazine, but fortunately the grenades remained intact, and he was soon on his feet.

Meanwhile the CO was still trying to get in touch with Neame to know the form. Lieutenant Webster, OC 10 Platoon, was momentarily elevated to commanding the company since he was the only officer left near Company Headquarters. As he talked to the CO, voices could be heard below in the direction of Moody Brook. Corporal Elliot's section opened up and automatic fire was returned by perhaps ten to fifteen men. 11 Platoon moved forward to join 10 Platoon in a long extended line along the ridge, the men firing downhill towards the enemy position. Eventually the CO got through to the company commander, who had had a hair-raising time walking along the ridge to discover what was happening. He now informed the CO of his fears of imminent attack.

Sporadic enemy fire from Tumbledown added to D Company's danger, and all the earlier fears of the consequences of delay to the 5 Brigade attack came to the fore. The CO offered to send tanks up but Neame declined, since they would be very exposed on the forward slope fire positions they would be forced to adopt. He would have preferred another company to hold the first part of Wireless Ridge, which as yet remained undefended.

The company reorganized, leaving Corporal Owen's section forward as a standing patrol while 10 and 11 Platoons found dug-outs on the reverse slope. 12 Platoon stayed in its positions near the telegraph poles.

There was little more that the Companies on the northern spur could now do to support D Company. Two of A Company's trained medical orderlies had been wounded by the shelling that still continued, so the platoons had to look after their own casualties – once again the value of the medical training for all ranks was

Full refund issued for new and unread books and unopened music within 30 days with a receipt from any Barnes & Noble store.
Store Credit issued for new and unread books and unopened music after 30 days or without a sales receipt. Credit issued at <u>lowest sale price</u>.
We gladly accept returns of new and unread books and unopened music from bn.com with a bn.com receipt for store credit at the bn.com price.

Full refund issued for new and unread books and unopened music within 30 days with a receipt from any Barnes & Noble store.
Store Credit issued for new and unread books and unopened music after 30 days or without a sales receipt. Credit issued at <u>lowest sale price</u>.
We gladly accept returns of new and unread books and unopened music from bn.com with a bn.com receipt for store credit at the bn.com price.

Mistory of Warfare   15.00N
0679730826
Mammoth Book of Battles   11.95N
0708706899

SUB TOTAL   26.95
TOTAL   26.95
AMOUNT TENDERED
MASTERCARD   26.95
CARD #:   ************4903
AMOUNT   26.95
AUTH CODE   009758

TOTAL PAYMENT   26.95

vindicated. Fortunately the helicopters in support that night were fully effective, evacuating casualties with minimum delay, and other casualties were taken back to the RAP on one of the tanks. The enemy artillery fire gave the remainder every incentive to dig, and the possibility of being overlooked by Mount Tumbledown in the morning was an additional spur.

For A and B Companies it was now a matter of lasting the cold night out, which was not without incident. Privates 'Jud' Brookes and Gormley of A Company's 1 Platoon had been hit by shrapnel. The rule was to switch on the injured man's easco light, normally used for night parachute descents, to ensure that he would not be missed in the dark. Sergeant Barrett went back to look for Brookes, whose light was smashed.

'All right, Brookes – me and the Boss will be back to pick you up later.'

'Ee, Sarge,' he replied in a thick Northern accent, 'Ah knows tha f— will.'

Unknown to them, the men of 3 Platoon were actually sitting next door to 13 Argentine soldiers, who were taking cover from their own shellfire. Only later in the morning were they found and taken prisoner.

In B Company, the state of Privates Carroll and Philpott of 5 Platoon was a cause for concern, since both were now suffering from hypothermia after being immersed in one of the ponds. Their section commander, Corporal Steve Curtis, decided to tell the platoon commander. As he ran out into the shelling, a round exploded close by, shredding his clothes almost completely yet, amazingly, leaving him unharmed.

The mortar teams had been busy all night. By now they had moved on to the side of the A and B Company hill to avoid shelling, which had been uncomfortably close at their first position in the bottom of the valley to the north. Improvised bins had helped to reduce the tendency of the mortar tubes to bed into the soft peat, although not completely, and another problem was that tubes would at times actually slip out of their base-plates under recoil. To prevent this, mortarmen took turns to stand on the base-plates as the tubes were fired, and by the end of the night four men had suffered broken ankles for their efforts. The fire they had been able to provide was very effective, however, and all concerned had been determined that, this time, there would be no question of running short of ammunition or of being out of range. The 3 Para mortars on Longdon did sterling work providing illumination.

The Machine-Gun Platoons, too, had been hard at work, their six guns providing intense heavy fire throughout the night. Re-supplied by the tanks and by the splendid work of WO2 Grace's Pioneer Platoon, they had had no worries about ammunition. But gradually the guns broke down, and by dawn only two of the six were still in action.

In Battalion Headquarters the second-in-command, the Operations Officer and Captain David Constance had taken turns at duty officer. At one point the second-in-command, Major Keeble, had been able to see the flashes of the enemy 155 mm guns as they fired, but no amount of reporting back produced any counter-measures. Once the drone of a low-flying Argentine Canberra jet was heard, and amidst the din of artillery even larger thuds reverberated as the aircraft dropped its bombs. Private Steele of the Defence Platoon was unlucky: as he lay on the ground a piece of shrapnel caught him in the back. He hardly felt it, thinking that it was only a piece of turf from the explosion – only later did he discover a rather nasty wound where the metal had penetrated.

The CO's party had not escaped either. A stray round hit Private McLoughlin, a member of the Battery Commander's group, and actually penetrated his helmet at the front. The helmet deflected the round, however, and McLoughlin walked away unharmed.

The snipers were in great demand. Their night-sights enabled them to identify the enemy infra-red sights and to use the signature that then appeared in the image intensifier as an aiming-mark. The Commando Sappers had had a relatively minor role to play in the battle, since there were no mines that it was imperative to clear. But, as at Goose Green, they provided a very useful addition when acting as infantry.

On Wireless Ridge at first light, 12 Platoon was still being sniped at from behind and to the right. Further back along the ridge, Corporal Owen had searched a command post. While rummaging in the bunker, he found a map showing all the details of the Argentine positions, as well as some patrol reports. These were quickly dispatched to Company Headquarters and on to Brigade.

Private Ferguson, in Owen's section, suddenly noticed four or five men below them. The corporal was uncertain as to who they could be – possibly 12 Platoon – and told Ferguson to challenge. The latter yelled 'Who's there!' and was instantly greeted with a burst of fire that left them in no doubt. Grenades started to explode around Owen and his men as the enemy counter-attacked. The section opened fire, and Corporal Owen shouted for the machine-guns to engage.

10 Platoon meanwhile were firing on either side of the section, and Owen himself blasted away with eight M-79 rounds. The section was soon short of ammunition, and the men began to ferret for abandoned Argentine supplies. Just then the remainder of the platoon moved up to join the section; though uncertain as to exactly where the enemy were, they were determined to prevent the Argentines from regaining the ridge.

Private Lambert heard an Argentine, close in, shouting, 'Grenado, grenado!'

'What a good idea,' he thought, and lobbed one of his own in the direction of the voice. There were no more shouts.

11 Platoon also saw a group of four men to its front. 2nd Lieutenant Chris Waddington was unable to make out who they were and, thinking they might be 10 Platoon, shouted to them to stop. The four men took no notice, so he ordered a flare to be put up – the figures ran off as the platoon engaged with small arms and grenades. The orders not to exploit beyond the ridge-line meant that not all the enemy positions had been cleared during the night, and it seemed that some stay-behind snipers had been left there, and it was probably these that had given 12 Platoon so much trouble. But the counter-attack, such as it was, had fizzled out. Artillery fire was called down on Moody Brook to break up any further efforts at dislodging D Company. Down below the ridge a Landrover could be seen trying to get away. Lance-Corporal Walker fired at it and it crashed.

11 Platoon now came under extremely accurate enemy artillery fire, possibly registered on the flashes of their weapons. Major Neame therefore ordered them to cease firing with small arms, intending to continue the battle with artillery alone. Moody Brook was deserted, however. In the distance the men of D Company noticed two Argentine soldiers walking off down the track as if at the end of an exercise.

In the light of dawn it appeared to the Paras on the ridge that a large number of enemy troops were moving up to reinforce Sapper Hill to the south-east. Neame called for artillery with great urgency, but no guns were available. After a further 20 minutes or so, by which time the enemy had reached the top, the target was engaged. Meanwhile other Argentines could be seen streaming off Tumbledown and Harriet – 5 Brigade had won its battles.

As D Company began to engage this new target the CO arrived. He confirmed Neame's orders to fire on the enemy retiring towards Stanley, and the company now joined in with machine-guns in a 'turkey shoot'. John Greenhalgh's helicopters swept in and fired SS-11 rockets and, together with two other Scouts, attacked an Argentine battery. The enemy AA was still active, however, and all the helicopters withdrew.

The retiring Argentines on Tumbledown had made no reply to the helicopters, and their artillery had stopped. It was obvious that a major change had occurred. The news was relayed to the Brigadier, who found it difficult to believe what was happening. But the CO realized how vital it was to get the battalion moving into Stanley before the enemy could rally, and A and B Companies, together with the Blues and Royals, were ordered to move as fast as possible up on to Wireless Ridge. The Brigadier arrived, still disbelieving until Colonel Chaundler said, 'It's OK, Brigadier, it's all over.' Together they conferred as to what to do next. D Company ceased firing on the fleeing enemy on the far hillside, and the order was given that men were only to fire if fired upon first. Permission was then given for the battalion to move on.

B Company, by now on the ridge, was ordered down into Moody Brook. Corporal Connors's section of 5 Platoon led the way, still expecting to come under fire from the 'Triple As' on the race-course. The other two sections covered him forward. He cleared the flattened buildings of the old barracks and Curtis's section took over, clearing the bridge over the Murrell River and the building on the other side, while all the time their platoon commander was exhorted, 'Push on, push on!' They remained cautious, fearing booby traps or a sudden burst of fire.

A Company now took the lead as B Company, covering A's advance, moved south on to the high ground on the far side of the valley, above the road, passing through three abandoned gun positions on the way. The tanks of the Blues and Royals moved east along Wireless Ridge to give support if it should be necessary. A Company was well on the way down the road into Stanley, with C and D Companies following, when Brigade announced a cease-fire. Cheers went up, and red berets quickly replaced steel helmets.

Bottles of alcohol miraculously appeared to celebrate with. Relief, elation, disbelief – all in turn had their effect.

Major Dair Farrar-Hockley led his men towards the race-course, past the abandoned guns that had been spotted so many hours earlier yet had remained operational in spite of requests for artillery fire. According to civilians afterwards, the Argentines still on the outskirts of Stanley simply broke and ran when they heard that 'the Paras' were coming. The leading elements of the battalion arrived in Stanley at 1330 hours, on Monday, 14 June some five hours before the official cease-fire, with 2nd Lieutenant Mark Coe's 2 Platoon the first into the town. They were the first British troops into the capital.

Eventually all the companies were brought into the western outskirts, finding shelter amongst the deserted houses, a few of which had suffered from stray shells. One or two dead Argentine soldiers still lay in the street where they had been caught by shellfire. On the race-course the Argentine flag was pulled down and Sergeant-Major Fenwick's Union Jack once more served its purpose.

10
The Persian Gulf War

Desert Storm (1991)

Jon E. Lewis

In the vast winter silence of the desert night the ominous keening of aircraft high overhead could be heard. Everywhere along the Saudi–Kuwaiti border troops looked anxiously skywards from their foxholes. The jets were flying east, and mud soldiers of the Coalition shivered a sigh of relief. Ours. At the wet, temporary HQ of Britain's First Armoured Division a single voice rang out clear into the sandy darkness: 'Yellow Alert. We are at war.'

It was 11.30 p.m. on the evening of 16 January 1991. Operation Desert Storm, the effort to remove Saddam Hussein from his occupation of Kuwait, and the biggest concerted military action since the Second World War, had begun – just five months and 13 days after the Iraqi dictator had sent his tanks rolling across the Kuwaiti border. If the invasion of Kuwait had been a military success, it had also proved to be the biggest political mistake of Saddam's career.

No sooner had Saddam ordered his 500,000 victorious invasion troops to dig-in along the Kuwaiti–Saudi Arabian border, than the Americans had, under the flag of the United Nations, garnered together a considerable Coalition of anti-Saddam forces dedicated to ejecting him from Kuwait. Wars are seldom fought for moral principle, and the war which would be fought in the Persian Gulf was no exception. Though politicians would declare that force was necessary to deal with the 'bully' Saddam (while ignoring similar illegal occupations of smaller neighbours by Israel and Turkey, among other nations) the truth was always more prosaic: Saddam's occupation of Kuwait threatened to restrict the free access of the major economic nations to its huge subterranean seas of oil, as well as upsetting the area's fragile Arab balances of power.

As the US had taken the diplomatic lead against Iraq, so the US provided the overwhelming bulk of men, women and arms which would fight Operation Desert Storm; nearly 450,000 troops. In recognition of this, an American, General H. Norman Schwarzkopf, was appointed Commander-in-Chief of Coalition forces in the Gulf. (As a courtesy to the host country, Schwarzkopf was officially subordinated to the Saudi defence Minister, General Prince Khalid, but in practice operational command remained wholly with Schwarzkopf and his US CENTCOM; the only non-American on Schwarzkopf's central planning staff was Britain's Lieutenant-General Sir Peter de la Billiere, an acknowledgement of the fact that Britain provided the second largest troop contingent, 40,000 soldiers.) 'Stormin' Norman', as he became dubbed, was a 56-year-old Vietnam veteran, of some irascibility. Whether by luck or design, in him the Americans had appointed a commander who was a canny user of the media – many American officers still blamed TV for defeat in Vietnam – and a master of the soundbite. At the end of the campaign, Schwarzkopf was asked by a journalist what he thought of Saddam Hussein as a military strategist. Using the fingers of his left hand to count off Saddam's 'attributes', Schwarzkopf replied: 'As far as Saddam Hussein being a great military strategist, he is neither a strategist, nor is he schooled in the operational arts, nor is he a tactician, nor is he a general, nor is he a soldier. Other than that, he is a great military man. I want you to know that.'

Schwarzkopf himself, however, was all the above. A near-genius at battlefield strategy and tactics, his Operation Desert Storm would draw comparisons with Cannae and El Alamein.

Following his arrival in Saudi Arabia in August 1990, Schwarzkopf had initially been concerned only to secure the east Saudi border (Operation Desert Shield) against Iraqi incursions. Two months later Washington, mindful that economic and diplomatic sanctions might well fail to persuade Saddam to withdraw his forces from Kuwait, directed the general to prepare contingency plans for an offensive.

On paper, at least, the Iraqi Army was a formidable opponent and CENTCOM planned for the worst. Intelligence suggested that the

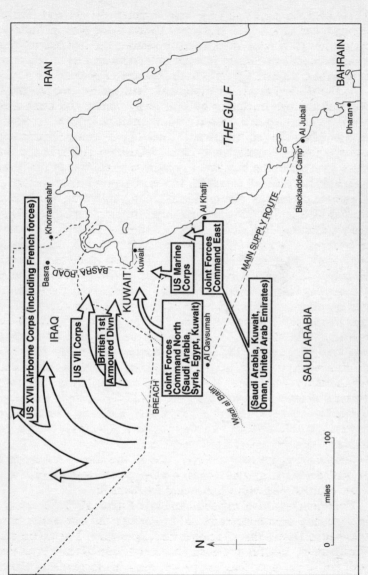

10.1 *The Liberation of Kuwait, February 1991*

Iraqi Army was as big and as dangerous as Saddam Hussein himself claimed. It contained over a million men, and possessed a devil's feast of modern weaponry: around 6,000 tanks (including a number of Soviet T-72s), 4,000 armoured personnel carriers, between 800 and 1,000 combat aircraft and 3,200 artillery pieces, including some which could outgun those of the Coalition. Moreover, the Iraqi Army was reputed to be battle-hardened after its grinding 1980–8 war with Iran, and extremely adept at defence. It had already fortified the border with Saudi Arabia with a continuous belt of obstacles, including sand berms and oil-filled trenches which could, with the touch of a torch, be turned into a wall of fire. Most dangerous of all the Iraqi forces were the armoured divisions of the 'elite' Republican Guard, held as a theatre reserve in southern Iraq and northern Kuwait. Uncomfortable at not having the classic three to one ratio of advantage that military wisdom says an attacker should have in order to guarantee victory, and worried that an offensive might break down into an attrition battle or *slugfest*, Schwarzkopf decided to exploit the Coalition's huge air force to reduce Saddam's military capability, especially in the Kuwaiti Theatre of Operations (KTO). This would be the preliminary to a ground offensive with air support (in line with the AirLand Battle Doctrine adopted by the Pentagon in 1982) which would outflank the main Iraqi defences in the west beyond the point at which the Iraqi, Saudi and Kuwaiti borders meet – and where the Iraqis had failed inexplicably to build fortifications. This massive outflanking drive into the KTO from the west would be accompanied by direct attacks from the south and a feint amphibious landing from the east, where 17,000 US Marines were waiting offshore. The Iraqis would be crushed and caught in a massive envelopment. Though it was apparently bitterly contested by some of his staff, Schwarzkopf stuck to the essentials of his plan, finally getting it approved in mid-January 1991.

The plan was no sooner approved than it was called into use. The deadline for the implementation of United Nations Resolution 660 (Iraqi withdrawal from Kuwait) expired on midnight 15 January. The first Coalition aircraft were in the air twenty-four hours later, flying the first of a total of 110,000 sorties against targets across Iraq and Kuwait. Radar-guided American Stealth bombers executed pinpoint attacks with so-called smart bombs, accurate enough to be deposited down the airshafts of Iraqi bunkers. Other planes, wave after wave of them, F-15Es, F-A18 Hornets, A-6E Intruders and RAF Tornadoes bombed Iraqi military and communications targets and destroyed much of Saddam's air force before it could leave the runway. In the first day of the air campaign, US warships in the Gulf launched more than 100 Tomahawk Cruise missiles (each armed with half a ton of high explosive); observers in the Iraqi capital, Baghdad, watched in wonder as the Cruise missiles flew between buildings and turned corners before hitting their targets. Baghdad shook under the weight of the bombardment. Iraqi anti-aircraft fire turned the sky white.

Over the following weeks the air campaign drastically degraded Saddam's ability to fight a battle, destroying his highly central- ized communications and command system, his arms and his army's morale. The Coalition achieved complete air supremacy. In Schwarzkopf's phrase, the removal of the Iraqis from the skies 'blinded' Saddam. For this, the Allies were to lose a total of 67 aircraft.

The one black cloud in the Coalition's silver-lined air campaign was Iraq's Scud missile capability. Saddam began firing his Soviet-built Scud missiles on the second night of the air war, the first targets being Tel Aviv and Haifa in Israel. Although the six missiles which landed in Israel killed no one, and did not contain the feared chemical or nuclear warheads, the impact was psychologically and politically explosive. Israel threatened to take unilateral retaliatory action, something which would have wrecked the anti-Iraqi alliance, even perhaps starting a new Arab–Israeli war. Frantic diplomacy by the Americans, together with the dispatch of Patriot ground-to-air missile systems to shoot down Scuds, managed to persuade Israel from immediate punitive measures. The Patriots, though, were only of minimal effectiveness, failing even when they intercepted incoming Scuds always to destroy the warhead. Covert operations by British SAS and US Special Forces teams, dropped behind Iraqi lines, and the hunting of mobile Scud launchers by the Coalition air force did better. In the end, the Israelis suffered only 13 fatalities from Scuds. The Iraqis' most effective Scud launch was one of those aimed at Saudi Arabia. In the dying hours of the war a Scud landed on a US barracks in Dhahran, killing 28.

Such was the effectiveness of the air campaign that senior Coalition air force officers began to question whether a ground offensive was necessary. Schwarzkopf, however, along with the army and the Marines, was mindful that a war has never been won by airpower alone. Consequently, as the air campaign continued its attrition of enemy units, Schwarzkopf continued the deployment of the coalition army, most crucially of all the move west of the bulk of his forces: the US XVIII Airborne Corps, including the French Light Armoured *Division Daguet*, farthest west, its task a lightning drive to the Euphrates which would simultaneously protect the left flank of the invasion and cut off an Iraqi escape; then, to the right of XVIII Airborne, VII Corps, including British 1st Armoured Division, the steel *schwerpunkt* of the offensive which would smash north and then north-east towards Kuwait, hitting the Republican Guard in the flank. This remarkable movement of XVIII Airborne and VII Corps to their start positions was accomplished across several hundred miles of desert by thousands of tanks, trucks and other support vehicles. In order both to tie down Iraqi troops and confirm Iraqi expectations of a frontal attack on Kuwait City, Coalition Arab forces and the US 1st and 2nd Marines, together with the 1st (Tiger) Brigade of the US 2nd Armoured Division were deployed in the south of the battlefield, along the Kuwaiti–Saudi border.

While Schwarzkopf made ready, time was trickling away for Saddam Hussein. If the air war had degraded his military capacity it had done nothing to diminish his rhetoric or his will to hold onto Kuwait, promising the Coalition 'the Mother of All Battles' should it try to force him out. A Soviet attempt to broker talks failed. On 22 February US President Bush gave Saddam the ultimatum to withdraw from Kuwait or face the consequences. In the best fashion of the Western, Bush's deadline expired at noon – noon (EST) on Saturday 23 February. Saddam refused to blink. That night, with singular appropriateness, American Forces network radio in the Gulf played 'Saturday Night's All Right (For Fighting)'. As Elton John sang, soldiers along the front line were making ready for combat, Marine bulldozers breaching Iraqi defences. Sand berms were demolished, trenches filled with oil burned off, and minefields cleared.

As Saturday night edged into Sunday morning, Coalition air force and navy began a massive bombardment of the Iraqi lines. It started raining. And then at 4 a.m., US and Saudi Marines in the coastal area that was the easternmost point of the battlefield began moving forward through the Iraqi defences, the vaunted 'Saddam Line'. The ground war had begun.

The Marines breached the Iraqi barriers with relative ease, the minefields posing fewer problems than expected: many mines had become exposed by shifting sand, while some Marines crossed the minefields by walking on anti-tank mines, knowing that they could not be detonated by the weight of a man. By the end of the first day of the ground war (G-Day) the 1st Marine Division had secured Al-Jaber airfield, halfway to Kuwait City, having bypassed some Iraqi units who were poised to fight but failed to counter-attack. The battlefield, eerily quiet and shrouded in acrid smoke from the Kuwaiti oil wells set on fire by the Iraqis on 22 February, was littered with burnt-out wrecks of Iraqi trucks and tanks, victims of the Coalition air force.

At the opposite end of the Allied line, the French *Division Daguet* and its attached US 82nd Airborne Division (the Screaming Eagles), given the task of sweeping around the Saddam Line and securing the offensive's left flank, penetrated rapidly into Iraq, brusquely subduing the Iraqi 45th Infantry Division with artillery and HOT anti-tank missiles from French-built Gazelle helicopters. The 101st Airborne Division, immediately to the east, after a hold-up due to poor weather, mounted one of the biggest airmobile operations in history with some 300 Chinook helicopters ferrying troops to establish an advance position, FOB Cobra, 70 miles inside Iraqi territory.

Iraqi resistance to the Coalition incursions was everywhere so minimal that by late morning Schwarzkopf decided to deal the enemy a further reeling blow, bringing the second phase of the offensive forward to the afternoon of G-Day instead of the morning of G+1. The US 24th Mechanized Infantry Division – Schwarzkopf's old division – along with the 3rd Armoured Cavalry began rolling forward at midday, its mission to cross nearly 250 miles of Iraqi rock and sand and establish itself near the town of Basra, where it would cut off Iraqi forces and engage the Republican Guards. As the 24th roared across the desert it passed weary US Long Range Surveillance Detachments, who had been in Iraq for weeks sending back HUMINT (human intelligence). Also at midday, VII Corps – with 1,300 tanks the biggest armoured corps in history – led by the 'Big Red One', the US 1st Infantry Division (Mechanized), began its breach of the Iraqi line, with the divisions of the Corps following through over the next 24 hours. The British 1st Armoured Division went through the breach in the morning of G+1, the 'anvil' on which the rest of the Corps would hammer the Republican Guards.

To the right of VII Corps, east of Wadi al-Batin, Arab forces from Egypt, Syria, Saudi Arabia and Kuwait began their advance in the afternoon of G-Day, proceeding more circumspectly than their neighbours, the US Marines, in part because they faced one of the most fortified sections of the Saddam Line. The Egyptians found themselves in front of walls of burning oil, but managed the breach in less than five hours after pushing sand into the trenches with their tanks and bulldozers.

By evening all Coalition forces had advanced well beyond their schedule, progress only improved by the Coalition's continuing deception operation, with thousands of Marines – apparently set for a seaborne invasion – waiting off Kuwait's shore, and a highly visible demonstration by the famous 1st Armoured Cavalry Division (the Air Cav) in the Wadi al-Batin. Casualties had been minimal. Among the worst losses of the day were those suffered by the British in a 'friendly fire' incident, when an American A-10 'Tankbuster' mistakenly eliminated a British Warrior Armoured Vehicle; nine soldiers died.

As dawn broke on 25 February, G+1, the scale of the Iraqi rout and disorientation became more apparent. The fast-moving *Division Daguet* had hardly encountered a living soul and continued its spectacular dash throughout the day, reaching As-Salman airfield, 70 miles inside Iraq, by evening, where it had to be ordered to pause. Eastward down the line the 24th Infantry Division (the Victory Division) rolled ever onwards, also without opposition, while the British 1st Armoured Division engaged and defeated the Iraqi 12th Armoured Division before becoming delayed by the throngs of Iraqi soldiers eager to surrender. Elsewhere over the battlefield it was the same story of Iraqis throwing down their weapons. The crush of POWs, indeed, posed more of a problem than the Iraqis who tried to fight; 25,000 prisoners were captured during the day. Only in a handful of places did the Iraqis put up serious resistance. An armoured division counter-attacked the US 2nd Marine Division near Al-Jaber but was heavily repulsed. Iraqi armour which tried to block the path of the 2nd Marine Division and the Tiger Brigade also fared badly. Perhaps the fiercest encounter of the day was at the Burgan oil field near Kuwait International Airport, where the 1st Marine Division met with well-entrenched Iraqi units. These were flushed out by a massive 'time on time' artillery bombardment and then decimated by USMC tanks and Cobra attack helicopters. The Iraqis lost 50 tanks for no USMC loss.

If the Coalition needed any proof that things were going well, it came on the morning of the next day, Tuesday 26 February (G+2), when Baghdad Radio announced that Iraq was prepared to withdraw from Kuwait. Washington's response was brusque: 'The war goes on.' In Kuwait City itself, panic-stricken Iraqis began to commandeer vehicles and flee northwards on the road to the Mutla Gap causing, as one commentator quipped, 'the mother of all traffic jams'. A dozen Coalition F-15s bombed the front of a 1,000-vehicle Iraqi convoy, and then bombed its rear. Coalition aircraft then swarmed down on the luckless trapped Iraqis in a turkey-shoot reminiscent of the destruction of the Wehrmacht as it tried to escape through the Falaise Gap in 1944.

The reason for the Iraqi haste in quitting Kuwait City was that the Coalition's southern groupings were now only miles from the suburbs, although the US 1st Marine Division had run into a sizeable formation of Iraqi armour determined to make a fight for the International Airport. The battle would last throughout the day and into the next, the sky so dark with smoke from oil well fires that flashlights had to be used to read charts. The Tiger Brigade and 2nd Marine Division also met opposition as they curled north around Kuwait City to prevent any retreat.

Meanwhile, far to the west, with the *Division Daguet* holding the left flank secure against Iraqi reinforcements, the XVIII Airborne Corps had consolidated its hold on the Euphrates valley, with the 24th Infantry Division reaching Highway 8 and then surging eastwards down it towards Basra, its helicopter attack regiment in the van. The 24th had the smell of success in its nostrils and was now riding towards the Republican Guard. A brigade of 57 Iraqi T-72 tanks unlucky enough to cross the 24th's path was decimated, the T-72s no match for the 24th's M1A1s and Apache attack helicopters.

Likewise closing on the Republican Guards was VII Corps, with the 2nd Armoured Cavalry making contact with the Guard late in the evening. After completing its rout of the 12th Iraqi Armoured Division, the British 1st Armoured Division had overrun the 17th and 52nd Armoured Divisions, eliminating 300 enemy tanks and armoured vehicles in the process. At midnight the British division reached its main objective, codenamed Waterloo, at the south end of Phase Line Smash. Caught between an anvil and a descending hammer, the Republican Guard realized too late that the target of XVIII Airborne and VII Corps was not Kuwait but the Guard itself.

Over the next 32 hours, by 8 a.m. Thursday 28 February (G+4), the Iraqi Army disintegrated. They surrendered in their thousands, waving anything white they could find. The Iraqi force at Kuwait International Airport was finally overcome, with the triumphant Marines opening their lines to give the honour of liberating Kuwait City to the Kuwaiti 35th Mechanized Brigade, who entered the city at 9 a.m. on 27 February to an ecstatic welcome. Much of the city was anyway already in the control of Kuwaiti resistance fighters.

Along the Iraq–Kuwait border, meanwhile, XVIII Airborne and VII Corps engaged the Republican Guard in what would be the classic tank battle of the campaign, lasting into the morning of G+4. Although some of the Iraqi units in the Basra Pocket put up a brave fight, especially those from the Guard's best-equipped divisions (Tawakalna, Medina and Hammurabi), it was always a one-sided contest. The Iraqis had no air cover and very poor communications, while the attack–attack tactic of the US forces never allowed them time to consolidate. The Coalition was fighting a multi-dimensional modern war while the Iraqis wanted a static war of First World War vintage. The Republican Guard left the field with its pretensions to military elitism in tatters. In truth the Guard was never the force Saddam claimed it to be, or the Coalition feared it to be. Its experience fighting the Iranians had left it not so much combat-ready as combat-fatigued. Moreover, the Guard – its primary function being the protection of Saddam's Ba'athist dictatorship – selected most of its officers for political reliability, not military ability. What was arguably the best Guard unit, *Amn al-Khas* (special security), was judged too important by Saddam to fight in the war, and was kept in Baghdad. Other Iraqi units, made up overwhelmingly of conscripts, had second-rate equipment and little desire to die for Saddam's lost cause. Nor were there as many Iraqi soldiers in the KTO as the Coalition had estimated (500,000); in all probability they numbered fewer than 300,000 – 200,000 fewer than the Coalition.

With the Iraqi Army almost completely encircled, Schwarzkopf would have liked to have continued the war to ensure its destruction. As it was, 700 Iraqi tanks escaped the net. The Coalition's Arab members had no wish to see the complete disintegration of Iraq – which would have unleashed a wave of protest in their countries, where support for Saddam was sizeable – and at 9 p.m. (EST), in a televised address, President Bush announced a ceasefire from midnight – 8 a.m. on 28 February in the Gulf. By the close of the ground war the Iraqis had suffered around 8,000 casualties; another 86,000 Iraqis had surrendered to the Coalition. The Iraqi Army had not only been driven from Kuwait, it had been routed. Coalition casualties during the ground war were minimal: 150 KIA, a quarter of these victims in 'friendly fire' incidents. The Mother of All Battles had taken exactly 100 hours.

TOMORROW'S
TREASURE

East *of the* Sun 1

Linda Lee Chaikin

WATERBROOK
PRESS

TOMORROW'S TREASURE
PUBLISHED BY WATERBROOK PRESS
2375 Telstar Drive, Suite 160
Colorado Springs, Colorado 80920
A division of Random House, Inc.

All Scripture quotations are taken from the *King James Version.*

The characters and events in this book are fictional, and any resemblance to actual persons or events is coincidental.

ISBN 1-57856-513-8

Library of Congress Cataloging-in-Publication Data

Chaikin, L. L., 1943–
    Tomorrow's treasure / Linda Chaikin.
       p. cm.
    ISBN 1-57856-513-8
    1. Mothers and daughters—Fiction. 2. Social classes—Fiction.
3. Jewelry theft—Fiction. I. Title.
    PS3553.H2427 T66 2003
    813'.54—dc21
                            23434   2002013845

Printed in the United States of America
2003—First Edition

10 9 8 7 6 5 4 3 2 1

PART ONE

The righteous man wisely considereth
the house of the wicked.

PROVERBS 21:12

CHAPTER ONE

Summer 1879, Capetown, South Africa

The four white gems of the Southern Cross had just risen from behind Table Top Mountain toward the deep expanse of sky over Capetown Bay. Though the scene usually set her heart humming, Katherine van Buren barely noticed the beauty tonight. Nor could she focus on remembered summer nights on the velvety lawn…for anxiety tightened its grip upon her.

At the baby's soft whimper Katie turned from the cloistered window of her upstairs bedroom in Cape House and went to the bassinet, gently lifting her three-week-old infant. She smiled down at her little girl, whom she had named Eve—now *Evy*—and sat holding her in the rocking chair.

"Poor baby, what shall become of us? But do not worry. Anthony will take us far from here. Yes, he will. Don't cry, my Evy darlin'."

Katie began to gently hum Brahms's "Lullaby." "Your eyes will be amber like mine. Your hair will be tawny gold. But your mouth will be like your father's…a beautiful, sensuous mouth." She hummed the lullaby again as she rocked.

The bedroom door opened. Katie looked up and gazed into the face of her guardian, Sir Julien Bley.

He stood tall and darkly forbidding. His complexion was scorched brown by years of trekking the land of South Africa. His one good light-blue eye burned. His jaw was strong, his sideburns tinged with white.

He came in boldly and shut the door too quietly. Apprehension darted up Katie's spine as she grew aware of the tension in the air—much as it was before a sizzling thunderstorm on the African veldt.

She licked her suddenly dry lips and counted the thuds of her heart in her eardrums.

"So, girl." Julien's voice was gruff, yet low-keyed, which only added to the devastation of his next words. "You insist on keeping the suckling infant though you are unwed."

Katie raised her chin, refusing to let him see she was intimidated. She made a small rocking motion with her infant.

"We must make plans, Katie. I have allowed you to keep her longer than is wise. You must be strong and give her up. It is best for her, for you. Your father, if he were alive, would agree with me. He trusted me to care for you, my girl."

She swallowed, and her arms tightened around her infant. She felt her cheeks turn scarlet at the memory of her godly father, Carl van Buren—memories she had continued to cherish since her arrival here twelve years ago to become Sir Julien's ward. What would her father think of her now, in her situation? Would he be ashamed of her? Embarrassed by her?

No matter what, he would love her. Though she'd been only six when he had died, she'd known his love for her was deep. And though most of her life before her father's death was but a hazy memory after so many years under her guardian's rule, she still remembered him and the religious ways of her Afrikaner people, the Dutch. How shattered she had been, as a small child, upon learning of her father's accidental death in the mine. The site at Kimberly was the first big diamond find he and Julien had made, and they had formed a partnership that went beyond business to a pact of friendship. After the explosion, her mortally injured father had pled with Julien to take his little Katie as his ward.

She stiffened now in her chair as Sir Julien walked up and spoke down at her. "Look at me, girl. Have you nothing to say for yourself? Must I force the infant's removal? Can you not see it is best?"

Her anger began to boil. There had never been so much as a word of condemnation for his sons and nephews who fathered the children he so lightly sent away to distant places, never to be seen again. *Not this time.* She thought and clenched her teeth. *Not with my sweet Evy.* She drew her infant against her heart.

"Well, girl?"

At his gruff demand, she nodded. "Yes, I have something to say, sir! But 'tis more important to me that you hear what Anthony has to say."

His tufted brow inched lower over his deep-set, pale eye. "You persist in laying the fatherhood of this child at his doorstep then?"

"He is the father, and no other, I vow 'tis true."

"You cannot keep the child, Katie."

Her chin lifted. "Anthony wishes to marry me, and I him. If he had not gone to London—"

"So you persist in deceiving yourself? You gaze too much in the mirror at your pert face and not enough at your books of learning." He took a turn up and down the floor. "The blame for your misbegotten baby lies in your willfulness."

She was not willful— She *loved* Anthony, had believed his promises—

"As for Anthony, I have spoken to him."

Her hopes brightened. She looked up at him, her knees too weak to stand and face him with any dignity. Evy was beginning to make little crying sounds, and Katie tried to soothe her.

"Did I not tell you this baby is your blood relation?" She did her best to force a merry note to her voice. Surely Anthony would own his own daughter to his uncle? "She will grow up to make you proud."

"Trying to wheedle me now, are you? It will do no good, my girl. I am doing this for your own fair future. As for my nephew... His marriage into aristocracy is important to the plans of South Africa, and to me. Such tales as laying this child upon my nephew would add to my burden and accomplish little good."

She moaned. Then the unthinkable could be true—that Anthony's marriage was already arranged to—what was her name? Her feverish brain would not let her think.

"Do you think it gives me happiness to see you mourning like this? Do you think I take fiendish pleasure in sending the child away? Nay! But it is your future too that is at stake. You are like my own daughter. Any marriage I make for you among the diamond families of Kimberly will not tolerate an illegitimate child by Anthony Brewster."

"Tales?" She took little note of the rest of what he had said. She gazed up at him, her sweet baby cradled close, and while his brows were tufted and cross, there gleamed a small flicker of pity in his return gaze.

"Anthony has denied everything. That does not surprise me. He is grieved you would try to lay this errant birth upon him, yet he has asked I deal with you gently."

"Of course he would deny it to your face. He fears you! But if you will accept Evy, Anthony will confess how much he loves me, how he wishes the three of us to be together always. Oh, Uncle Julien, can you not see how desperately I want to keep my daughter?"

"You have always been a willful girl bent upon trouble, my dear Katie, yet I have loved you. Part of this tragedy is my fault, I see that now. I should have arranged for you to be married sooner. You became a woman too quickly, and your will and good sense have not kept pace, I fear."

She managed to stand, despite the trembling that seemed to have taken over her limbs. "He is Evy's father, I tell you. Evy is a Brewster. Anthony told me he loved me, that he wished to marry me—"

Her voice cracked, and she sank back to the chair, bending her head toward her baby to avoid Julien's gaze. *He doesn't believe me... He has no feelings for Evy... She's just another baby—a girl at that—when he wants males to carry on his dynasty.*

A sob came from her tight throat.

"Do not be foolish, Katie girl." He spoke with gruff tenderness. "Even if I knew for a fact Anthony sired this infant, there can be no marriage between you and him. Nay, never." He walked to the window and looked out. "The Montieth family in London is important to South Africa, to forming a new state. Maybe Cecil Rhodes will call it Rhodesia."

Katie did not know what he meant, nor did she care at the moment. "South Africa? It is my *child* I care about."

Julien turned and looked at the tiny bundle in the pink cover. Then his square jaw set, the muscles twitching. "It's not a matter of kith 'n kin that's on my mind right now. It's that his Lordship Montieth and his daughter, Lady Camilla, will arrive from London, perhaps very soon. Anthony *must* marry Camilla. I cannot chance having this errant child waiting in the wings."

Katie looked up, brushing the tear streaks from her cheeks. Who were Lord Montieth and Lady Camilla? And what had they to do with her heartache?

Julien's face was wiped smooth of any emotion, and his brittle expression refused her any sympathy.

"Anthony will become engaged to Lady Camilla when she arrives here at Cape House. You are going to Europe for a year, and the baby will be adopted out to a loving family. I shall make sure of that much for you."

Katie's shoulders straightened, then sagged.

"In a fortnight"—Sir Julien's level voice brooked no resistance— "Anthony will place a diamond ring on Lady Camilla's finger."

This pronouncement had the effect of thunder clapping violently over the roof of Cape House. Katie's dry lips parted. She could merely stare at her guardian.

He frowned. "The marriage has been planned since Lady Camilla was twelve and Anthony thirteen. They knew one another while he took his schooling in London. Many a holiday he has spent at Montieth Hall. That he told you none of this does not surprise me." He paced. "But you should have known, Katie, that marriages must be arranged for the betterment of all—yours as well."

Unable to hold back her surging rage, she screamed, "*No!* No! Anthony loves *me!* I will not listen to these lies!"

The startled baby wailed, and Katie embraced her, tears rushing to her eyes. "Hush, hush, sweeting, you'll have your papa, you'll see."

"Stop that, Katie! I must do what is best for everyone concerned."

At her mutinous stare, Sir Julien continued gravely. "With your future at stake we cannot allow a child born out of wedlock to cast shadows on all our paths. You must give the child up. A journey to Europe will give you the maturity to see what is best. At the appropriate time, your marriage will be arranged. Your inheritance in diamonds will insure that some decent son of a government official will look the other way when gossip of a child makes its way into English social circles."

Katie wept into the baby's soft, pink cover. Her stomach ached and her pulse throbbed in her temples. She inhaled Evy's sweet fragrance. *I'll never give you up.*

Sir Julien turned away, shoulders oddly stooped, and walked toward the door and opened it. "I'm sorry, Katie girl, this pains me too. But I have no choice."

As the door opened, Katie saw Inga waiting in the hall. The sturdy Dutch woman held her hands hidden beneath her apron. Her faded gold-gray hair was braided and, as it had been since Katie was a child, coiled around her head like a wreath. Her once-round face and apple cheeks were now sagging and soft, and her small mouth drooped sadly.

"Inga, come in here. Do what you can to comfort Katie."

The old nanny entered the bedroom, bobbed a clearly uncertain curtsy in Sir Julien's direction, and then hurried toward Katie to take the baby from her arms. "There, there, Miss Katie, do not cry so, or you'll be upsetting the baby's milk. Shall I be seeing to her needs now, miss?"

The nurse's low voice—the same voice that had soothed so many of Katie's childhood fears—now filled her with fear. She held onto her baby tightly. What if Inga took Evy away? What if, once Katie relinquished her tiny daughter, Evy would be whisked away to some ship sailing for England or Scotland?

No, she would not let her go.

"I won't give up my baby!" She met Sir Julien's stony gaze. "Do you hear me? I won't! I won't! And no one can make me!"

An austere Sir Julien Bley left the room.

Katie jumped to her feet, still clutching Evy. "I want to see Anthony! Where is he? I want to talk to him! How dare he lie about Evy?"

Inga moved to lay a calming hand on Katie's arm. "Master Anthony is not here, miss. He left last night with them diamond buyers from London and he didn't return. Some say he's on his way to Angola. Something about emeralds."

The last of her hope ebbing away, Katie looked down at her baby girl. "Oh, my precious little one. What shall I do? Whatever shall I do?"

One Month Later

Katie's once-lovely cheeks were hollow and thin. Dark smudges beneath her eyes made them seem a lighter amber. She had made her decision the day after Evy was stolen from her bassinet and taken away from Cape House. *I loathe Sir Julien. And Anthony…*

She had thought she loved Anthony. Now she felt nothing but revulsion and shame. How could she have allowed herself to make such a mistake with her virtue? She had played the fool, and now what would happen to her baby?

"How dare he steal my daughter and lock me in my rooms?" She mumbled the question aloud. "Am I a prisoner? Yes! That is what I am!" For all her initial banging on her locked door, after two weeks she was still confined to her several rooms in Cape House. She ate little and hardly slept. She would have tried to escape when Inga came to care for her needs, but Sir Julien remained in the house as though he knew her thoughts. Inga worried about her, fussed and wiped sympathetic tears from her sagging cheeks, made her hot milk with honey, tried to cajole her into drinking it, but Katie did not respond.

Sir Julien, too, came to see her, frowning, worried creases around his grave eyes…but still he refused to relent.

"It is too late, Katie girl. She is safe with a loving couple. They are devotees of Christ and will treat your daughter as well as you yourself could have. Stop your grieving, and get on with a bright future."

An impotent rage swept her, making her fingers curl into a fist at her sides. "How *dare* you say that to me? What do you know about how a mother's heart aches for her infant? What right had you to steal this little soul from me? She was mine, I tell you, *mine!*" She burst into tears and threw herself in the big overstuffed chair, pressing her head against her arm.

"You leave for Europe in a week." Sir Julien's stiff words drifted through her sorrow. "Once aboard ship you will come to your senses. This was not the only child you will have. You will have others—and a husband and name to go with them."

He left her then, and as the door closed Katie heard the bolt slide into place with solid finality.

She ran to the door and pounded until her hands were sore. "Anthony, I loathe the very memory of your kisses, your wicked lies, the velvety grass that was our bed!"

As the days passed Katie soothed her torn heart with midnight plans and schemes of her own making. "I will escape," she argued to the four walls. "They won't stop me. I won't let them."

She had decided this morning—today was to be the day. She *would* gain her freedom. One way or another. She turned quickly as she heard the outer bolt on her door slide back. That would be Inga bringing afternoon tea.

The elderly Dutch woman entered cautiously, as though she did not know if a woman gone mad might attack her. She supported the tea tray on her hip as she closed the door. Katie noticed two flushed spots on the woman's cheeks. Her small eyes were as bright as polished coins. Sudden hope sparked in Katie's breast and she took steps toward her old nanny.

"What is it?"

Inga glanced back at the door as if it might suddenly develop ears.

"I shouldn't tell you this, miss, but if you knew the sweet baby was safe you'd rest much easier now, wouldn't you?" Her eyes searched Katie's as though looking to reinforce her decision. "Sure now, you would indeed."

Katie latched hold of the woman's arm. "Oh yes, Inga, I would," she whispered. "What do you know?"

Inga's eyes glittered and darted toward the closed door. Katie's old nurse did not like Sir Julien. He was involved in British policy to bring all of South Africa under the Union Jack. Inga had lost her husband years ago in the first skirmishes between the Dutch Afrikaners—the "people of Africa"—and the British. Since then, the Dutch-settled area of South Africa, the Transvaal, had been annexed to the growing realm of the British Empire.

But that did not put an end to the Dutch resistance to British rule.

Inga's low whisper pulled Katie back to the matters at hand. "Do you remember the missionaries who came here to see Sir Julien a year ago?"

"Vaguely." Katie frowned. "What about them?"

"Dr. Clyde Varley, his name is. An' the missus is a young mite. Junia Varley is her name. Junia's sister is married to the vicar of Grimston Way in England. Dr. Varley and Missus Junia have your little one at the mission station near Isandlwana."

Katie stood still, her fingers tightening. "Who told you this?"

"The Zulu woman. The one the missionaries turned into a Christian."

"Jendaya?" A hopeful excitement began to stir. Katie had seen Jendaya many times around the grounds of Cape House. The girl had been driven out of the Zulu *kraal* of beehive huts near Isandlwana, and she lived in danger of being put to death for her decision to be baptized in the Buffalo River near the mission.

Jendaya now spent her time between the Isandlwana mission and the African huts on Sir Julien's estate. Katie had seen the young woman in the stables with Dumaka and had at first mistaken them for lovers, but Jendaya had explained that he was her brother. Though Dumaka was not a Christian, he too had been driven from Zululand for not publicly disowning his sister. Jendaya was still trying to get Dumaka to visit the mission station and talk to the "wise daktari" about the God of gods, but Dumaka resisted. He was angry with his sister for causing him shame—and he was resentful of the "white skins" for interfering with his people. Though he lived and worked at Cape House, his gaze was not warm toward Sir Julien Bley or anyone in Capetown, be they British or Boer—especially the Boer, who were the Dutch.

Katie forced herself to release Inga's arm. "Send for Jendaya! Have her come below my window. I must talk to her."

Inga shook her braided head. "She is gone again, miss. She only came to the back kitchen door asking for me to say your little one was safe with the daktari's wife."

The sound of carriage wheels distracted Katie. She hurried to the window, drew the portieres aside, and looked down into the courtyard. The coach was a hired taxi, and a tall man in black hat and cape was paying the driver. The driver rushed to unload the gentleman's baggage, and the house butler was walking to meet the arriving stranger. Katie was startled when the man looked up toward the Great House.

"What's he doing here?" She turned to Inga. "Sir Julien all but tossed him out a year ago."

Inga joined her at the window. Her mouth pursed. Her glance at Katie seemed hesitant, cautious. "Why, that is Sir Julien's stepbrother, Henry Chantry. He had his eyes on you last time he was here."

How well Katie remembered. Henry was well known for his roving eyes, and she doubted he had changed since she had seen him last before he'd sailed home to Grimston Way, England.

"He's surely come back for diamonds." Katie watched him follow the butler up the walkway to the front veranda. From the looks of his luggage he expected to stay a time. What would Julien say?

Sir Julien and his aunt, Lady Brewster, the Capetown matriarch of the extended family, had long favored Henry, wild as he was. She had even arranged for Henry's blood brother, Lyle Chantry, to marry her niece, the lovely diamond heiress Honoria. But Lady Brewster was a strait-laced woman and so had no sympathy for Henry's lascivious lifestyle. She had stood firmly beside Sir Julien's decision to withhold an inheritance until Henry proved himself worthy of managing such a fortune.

So why had Henry Chantry sailed back here all the way from England after being rejected by the Bleys and Brewsters?

Katie turned her head and looked at Inga. "I wonder if Lady Brewster or Sir Julien expected him."

"Don't think so, Miss Katie. Leastwise there's been no hint of it in the doings about Cape House. And no word of getting his old room ready."

Katie wondered if Henry had known Lady Brewster was vacationing at her Dutch-gabled house at Pietermaritzburg some miles away in Natal, and that Sir Julien was planning a trek out to the Kimberly mines soon.

She turned back to the window. Her fingers ran along the smooth rich texture of the portieres as her eyes narrowed. Cousin Henry Chantry just might be the answer to her present dilemma. The sight of the knave of hearts, baggage in hand, brought Katie a new expectation. Schemes took shape in her mind. Perhaps he could help her escape to the mission station to find her baby, and even arrange passage on a ship to London, and America. Perhaps all was not doomed after all!

As she turned from the window she caught a glance of her image in the gilded mirror. She stopped short, surprised by her own expression. The little upturn of her lips looked sly. For a brief moment her conscience smote her—an uncommon experience since her father's death in the explosion. How disappointed Carl van Buren would be in his daughter if he knew how she had grown up!

Her tawny, wavy hair fell loosely across her shoulders, and her blue velvet empire gown showed a desirable woman. She clenched her teeth. *Too late...too late to undo the past. I am unwed with no prospects of marrying the father of my child. I need money for myself and Evy. No*—she met the amber gaze reflected in the glass—*there is no turning back for you, Katie van Buren. You have set your sails, and now the wild winds must bear you along.*

Ideas churned in her mind, like little weeds growing taller and stronger, and she paced.

How would she get money enough to escape, and a great deal more? It would do no good to flee if she ended up on the streets of New York with a babe in arms, no place to go, and nothing to make her new life respectable. That was no way to start if she was to realize her dream of one day establishing Evy in high society.

I am still young. There can be another love in New York with a respectable name who will marry me and adopt Evy as his daughter. Yes. That was how it would be. After all, she had a right—she was Carl van Buren's daughter. He had been partners with Julien Bley. Why shouldn't she have what had rightfully belonged to her father? What Julien was now keeping!

She must have the Black Diamond, the stone Sir Julien was always enticing buyers from London with by waving it under their noses. Once she had Evy and the Black Diamond, she would be free to do anything she wished.

Her mind made up, she felt nervous perspiration running down her ribs. The Black Diamond. How could she get it?

Henry Chantry was the man to approach about that. He insisted *his* father had found it, and that the diamond was by rights Chantry property, that Sir Julien had used deceit to secure it for himself.

Katie grimaced. She must be desperate indeed to turn to Cousin Henry.

A noise caught Katie's attention, and she spun to see that Inga was about to leave. "Leave the door unbolted. Don't you see? I *must* sneak downstairs and speak alone with Cousin Henry."

"If you get caught, Miss Katie, you know what Sir Julien will do to me for not bolting the door."

"I won't get caught. Please, Inga, I'm desperate."

Inga fiddled with her apron. "Just this once, miss, but do be heedful. Do, please."

"He won't catch me. I promise to be careful."

Katie waited until the woman's steps faded away down the hall, then inched the door open.

It was quiet. She crept to the stairway in time to see Cousin Henry entering the downstairs hall. He was looking toward Sir Julien's office with a dark countenance that matched his swarthy appearance.

Henry Chantry looked as dangerous as any blackguard pirate. He was tall, with black hair and mustache, and Katie suspected he carried a pistol somewhere beneath his white linen jacket. The last she had heard he had been in uncharted territory in Mashonaland on an expedition to locate a mysterious gold deposit that he avowed his grandfather had learned about from some tribal chieftain. No one believed Henry about the gold, although he claimed to have his grandfather's map. Henry's wife had died several years ago on an expedition, and the Brewster family held him responsible. Katie doubted Sir Julien would receive Henry at all kindly.

She stooped behind the banister, not wishing to be seen. She must approach Cousin Henry with caution—Sir Julien was downstairs in his office. What would he do when he heard of Henry's arrival? Perhaps she could learn something to aid her own quest if she could listen in on their conversation. Putting her scruples aside, she hid until Henry walked toward Julien's office, then prepared to sneak down the stairs to listen at the door.

Henry Chantry left the veranda with its bright sunlight and was now standing in the entrance hall looking toward the room he remembered to be Julien's office. His restless gaze flitted over the mansionlike amenities of Cape House, which was just as he remembered. He'd left for England two years ago, after his wife's death of African fever. They had been camped out on the Shangani River on their way back to Bulawayo to bring her to a doctor at the mission station when she had succumbed to the summons of death. Her aunt, Lady Brewster, had never forgiven him for bringing Caroline on the trek.

Henry forced his features into the semblance of a smile when he saw his stepbrother, Sir Julien Bley, standing in the hall beside the door to his office. Julien must have heard the carriage arrive out front.

Henry felt the icy stare of Julien's single eye; it seemed to bore through him with malevolent intent. So, matters had not changed.

"What are you doing here?" Sir Julien demanded, his voice low and chilled.

Henry felt the muscles in his jaw tense. The anger he had been living with ever since Julien had ordered him to leave Cape House blazed, feeling like hot coals in his chest.

"Did I not tell you two years ago"—Julien spoke as though through gritted teeth—"not to come back until you have turned your last allowance into a profitable business?"

Henry recalled that last meeting. He had relived the argument a thousand times over while in England. Each time he replayed the humiliating memory, he promised himself he would one day make Julien pay.

Henry felt his shoulders beginning to sag in the face of his stepbrother, who stood straight-backed, his head high, a diamond stickpin flashing loudly on his black lapel. The day of revenge had not yet arrived. Though Henry had worked hard in London, it seemed that money in his palm turned to straw, while in Julien's it multiplied into diamonds…heaps of them, all flashing brilliantly.

Yet was he not a son of the family as well? Didn't he have as much right to share in the family diamond mines as Julien?

"Well?" Sir Julien's tone was thick with disdain. "Have you come crawling back to me again? Cannot stand on your own two feet, eh? Well, you'll get nothing from me. Do you hear? Nothing. If you want anything to fill your empty pockets, my boy, you can go work in the mines along with the Africans!"

Sir Julien turned on his polished heel and strode into his office, shutting the door.

Henry stood there, tasting bitter gall. His heart slammed in his chest. Tiny beads of sweat formed on his upper lip. It was enough that he had to deal with his own constant string of failures, but when Julien's success was thrown in his face like this, it fed the resentment that ate at his heart like a canker.

I'll get my rightful share of the diamonds—or kill him in the trying. He walked with slow, steady steps toward the office door. His hand was sweaty as he grasped the doorknob and turned it. If it was locked—

It wasn't. He opened it and stepped in, shutting it quietly behind him.

Sir Julien sat behind his polished desk, a small, golden lamp glowing on the surface. The Black Diamond sat glittering under the light like midnight fire. The very sight of it—and the thought of its value on the world market—made Henry's breathing tense.

The corners of Sir Julien's mouth turned up, but his eye held no humor. "So you persist."

Curse the man, he sounded downright bored. Henry schooled his voice to be even, calm. "You will hear me out, Julien. I demand to be treated with respect."

Sir Julien's mouth widened into a smile that Henry loathed, then inclined his dark head with what was clearly mock gravity.

"Very well, I am listening."

Henry walked to the center of the room and stood. The diamond flashed. It was all he could do to keep from gazing at it.

"It was my father who found that." He nodded toward the diamond. "Both Lyle and I want what is rightfully ours—as his sons."

"Everyone suddenly claims to have found the Black Diamond, but I have an eyewitness who has sworn by the laws of England that it was I who discovered it, along with the Kimberly mine."

It seemed to Henry that the black patch on Julien's blind eye began to expand into a gaping pit into which Henry would soon be engulfed.

"A *Chantry* found the Black Diamond!"

"As you found a gold mine?" came Julien's impatient retort.

"I did find a gold mine." Henry braced himself with both hands on the wide desk as he leaned toward Julien. "One day I shall be rich. But I need that diamond to resume my expedition into Mashonaland."

"Don't be a fool, Henry. You've had these expeditions before. The last time it was emeralds. Until"—his voice grew even colder—"you filled your pockets with wind and had to bury your dreams beside Caroline's grave!"

He straightened as though he'd been slapped across the face. "Curse you, Julien. Leave my poor wife out of this!"

"It was you who dragged her into it, hauling her with you across wild, savage land—all while expecting your child! That they are both dead now lies at *your* doorstep—just as surely as though you had killed them."

Henry could bear it no longer. He would shut Julien up if it was the last thing he did! He made a lunge for Julien's throat, but stopped cold when Julien lifted a large caliber pistol from his lap. He aimed it at Henry's chest, his eye flickering in the lamplight—and Henry had the oddest impression that that one eye was a reflection of the Black Diamond.

"You will get nothing from me, Henry. And nothing from Lady Brewster. She blames you for Caroline's death. You robbed her of her only granddaughter—and her unborn great-grandchild lies buried in Mashonaland with her. Do you think either of us would give you a single shilling?" Julien stood. "Now get out of my office…and out of my life."

Dazed from bitter humiliation and weight of his guilt over his late wife, Henry just stood there. He felt as though he were in a trance, and the only thing that got through was the rage toward Julien.

His stepbrother walked around the desk and moved to open the door. He stepped back and gestured, still holding the pistol. "Get out."

Henry turned and walked with leaden steps toward the door, then paused to meet Julien's icy gaze. Neither spoke. Henry straightened his shoulders and walked out, his heels clicking on the polished marble hall.

The housekeeper loitered nearby, glancing from the office door to Henry before she hurried toward the front door and opened it. Her gray eyes darted here and there as she managed a curtsy. "A good day to you, Mister Chantry, sir."

Henry walked out of Cape House onto the veranda. He stood there for a moment, staring at nothing. Now what? What to do next?

He pressed his lips together. If it had not been for that pistol…

Katie had listened at the door of Julien's office through the entire exchange. When the housekeeper noticed her listening, Katie warned her to silence.

Katie hurried out of sight when footsteps approached the door. When Henry exited the office, the housekeeper showed him to the door, then looked only too glad to get away and be about her duties.

The house was still now, with a sense of impending doom. Katie remained hidden behind the bottom of the staircase facing her guardian's office. She was about to come around and go up to her room to think over what she had heard when the office door opened and Julien stood in the doorway. She dared not move...could not breathe. If he saw her, he would twist the truth from her, making her admit what she had overheard.

Julien's dark face was tense. He held something in his hand. At first she thought it was a gun, then she realized it was the Black Diamond.

Katie's heart pounded in her chest. Julien occasionally took the magnificent stone out of its hiding place and set it on his desk to admire it. Afterward he would put it away and go about his work as though he were fulfilled. No one knew where he kept it. He once taunted members of his family with his secret. "Do you think I would trust any of you to know where I keep it, eh? You, Anthony my boy? Or you, Katie?"

She held her breath, waiting for him to return to his office and close the door so she could go up to her room, but Sir Julien did not return to his office. He walked to the front door and stepped out onto the veranda. There was no time to risk going up the stairway. The library was just across the hall, and she sped through the doorway, slipping inside. A window faced the front veranda, and she hurried there to look out. Why had Julien stepped outside? Was he wary that Cousin Henry might come back to the house? Did he know Henry had a pistol, perhaps even under his coat, but had not risked reaching for it?

Katie felt weakened and sick. So much hatred and mistrust. Her hands were cold and tense as she quieted her skirts and peered out through the curtains.

Oddly, she could hear Sir Julien's low voice arguing with someone on the veranda, but she could not see who it was. It had to be Henry again. What if they killed each other? She was about to rush up the stairs to her bedroom when she heard the front door slam shut. Footsteps followed. She waited for them to disappear, but they drew closer. She caught her breath as she realized someone was coming. She did not want Julien to spot her now. He would see through her dismay and guess she had overheard the quarrel in his office. As the library door opened, Katie ducked behind the large leather chair and side table.

Muffled footsteps sounded across the burgundy carpet. She heard someone moving about the room doing something. She ventured a peek from behind the back of the chair and saw Julien's back to her. He stood facing the wall of leather-bound books. Katie realized he was not looking at the library books, but at a table in the corner near the fireplace. A carved teak lion, some elephant tusks, and a wooden box sat on top of the table.

She watched Julien turn his head and glance toward the closed library door. He approached a magnificently carved secretary and opened the two cabinet doors. Then came footsteps in the outer hall, and Julien hurried toward the library door. Katie saw lion etchings on the wooden secretary and two lionhead knobs. Julien bolted the library door and returned to the secretary, taking something from his jacket pocket and looking at it for a moment—

The Black Diamond! Katie's breath caught in her throat as Julien turned his attention to the two lionhead knobs. Once again he turned his back toward her, and she could not see what he was doing. She heard a click and then something like a spring releasing. She had the impression that he was placing something inside a compartment, then he pressed on something as the compartment clicked shut. He closed the secretary cabinet and walked to the library door, opened it and glanced out before he left the room. As his footsteps faded, Katie remained stooped behind the leather chair, too stunned to move.

The diamond was hidden in the secretary.

She moistened her dry lips and sought to calm her galloping heart. She could have sworn Julien had not used any key. Just a secret compartment in a hundred-year-old secretary, most likely used for maps and valuable papers. Why would Sir Julien hide the priceless diamond in a compartment in the desk instead of one of the safes in Cape House where the jewels and priceless items were kept? Perhaps he thought they were too far from his office.

Katie could scarcely take it in. She had actually learned where the Black Diamond was hidden! Her hands shook, but she did not move from her hiding place for an inestimable time. When all was silent, she crept out and went to the desk. She stood staring at it. It was enough to know the secret of the stone's hiding place…at least for now. She crept to the door, opened it a crack, and, seeing no one, slipped out and went to the stairway.

Safely back in her room, she collapsed in a tapestry chair, hugging herself until her nerves calmed and her shaking ceased.

She was still seated there, resting her head on the back of the chair, when Inga tapped on the door and opened it slightly. Seeing Katie, she opened it wide and came in with the afternoon tea tray.

"You're looking ill, Miss Katie. Are you needing a doctor?"

Katie shook her head and watched Inga pour her tea, add sugar and milk, and bring it to her on a gold-rimmed china saucer.

"Here, miss, drink it hotlike. It'll make your insides settle a bit."

Katie took it with a grateful sigh. "Inga?"

The old Dutch woman looked at her, a slight frown on her brow. "Yes, Miss Katie?"

"Did you hear anything in the kitchen about Cousin Henry?"

Inga's pug nose twitched. "Laddie says to his mum, the cookie, that when Master Chantry went to the stables he was mad enough to do Sir Julien harm."

Katie shuddered. "Did Laddie learn anything about where my cousin was going? Did he say he was leaving Capetown or anything of the sort?"

"Master Chantry didn't say a word, miss. Just swung himself onto the horse and galloped away like a hellion. But," she added in a low voice, "if you're wondering where the Master is staying, it's no hard thing to learn. There's all of a half dozen inns and hotels in town that's operating now. Would you be wanting me to send Laddie to find the Master's whereabouts?"

Katie leaned forward, setting her cup and saucer on the little table. "Can he go without Sir Julien knowing?"

"Oh, surely, miss." She grinned. "You know Laddie. He can do most anything and not get himself caught."

"Well, yes, I do not doubt that. Then I wish to write a letter to my cousin and have your nephew deliver it tonight."

Inga nodded gravely. "I'll see it taken care of, Miss Katie. I'll be bringing tea to the others, then I'll come back for your letter."

When Inga left, Katie drank her hot tea and poured a second cup, adding even more sugar and milk. She carried the cup and saucer to her desk, sat down, and drained the cup. When her nerves began to settle, she removed a piece of linen stationery and dipped the pen in the inkwell. She wrote hurriedly, folded the sheet, and sealed it in the envelope. On the outside she scrawled *Master Henry Chantry.* Then she went back to her chair and waited for Inga.

An hour later, the nanny came back into the room. Katie handed her the envelope. "Do not let Laddie tell anyone what he is about."

Inga nodded. "No one, Miss Katie. You rest easy. Laddie will find the Master."

CHAPTER TWO

Katie awoke with a start. She must have dozed off. She was still sitting in the chair, the empty teacup and saucer on her lap. She realized what had awakened her. Sir Julien's impatient voice rang through the open bedroom window.

Had Cousin Henry dared to return?

She set the cup on the tea tray and went to the window, looking down to the front lawn.

A tall young African in knee pants and a long yellow cotton shirt was leading a horse toward Sir Julien, who stood tapping his foot. Dressed for riding, he yelled something in Zulu to Dumaka, who was head groom. Dumaka trotted alongside the gelding, bringing the handsome golden horse to Sir Julien.

Julien mounted, took hold of the reins, and sent the horse galloping toward the gate.

Where was he going? It didn't matter. All that mattered was that with him gone, the task in the library would now be much easier to accomplish.

A soft tap sounded on Katie's door. She hurried to it. A moment later it opened, and Inga's light blue eyes shone.

"Laddie found Master Henry. He's in a room at the wharf. He sent a message to you, Miss Katie." After glancing both ways, she removed an envelope from behind her apron.

Katie read the brief wording from Cousin Henry: *I will meet you in the stables a few minutes after midnight. H. C.*

"Good news, miss? You're smiling pertlike."

Katie clutched the letter to her chest. "Yes! Leave the back kitchen door unlocked tonight. I will come down fifteen minutes before the stroke of twelve."

"Then the master will bring you to Isandlwana?"

"I shall do everything in my power to see that he does. This is my chance to get away, to have my daughter…and a new start in America."

Inga nodded. "With a guardian like Master Julien, it is best to leave if you can, miss. He's ridden to the harbor to meet someone from London. He didn't say who it was, but I don't suspect he'll be back soon. Luck, Miss Katie, is on your side, so it seems. Jendaya, too, has come back to her hut. She didn't leave as I had thought, but was selling vegetables at the open market."

Katie clasped her hands together. "Speak to her about having a four-horse carriage ready for me tonight. If Cousin Henry agrees, Jendaya can bring me as far as Natal. Afterward I can ride horseback with Henry toward Isandlwana." The ride would be rough and not without risk, but Katie would not turn back in fear, no matter how many rumors spread of the Zulus preparing for the first "washing of their spears."

Katie spent the rest of the afternoon on edge. She packed some of her clothing and personal items, then watched the clock on her table for the crucial hour to strike. After midnight the entire household would be asleep. Matters were turning out very well, what with Henry all but agreeing to help her and Sir Julien's being away from the house.

Perhaps almost too well.

Just whom might Julien be meeting on a ship from London? What if he had only pretended to leave for the harbor? He could return to the estate after nightfall, conceal his horse in the thicket, and enter without being seen—perhaps to wait in the darkened library for her and Henry.

"I'm being too suspicious," she murmured to the walls, "but it does appear that the Black Diamond, and escape to Isandlwana, is being handed to me on a silver platter."

Even so, this was the best opportunity to escape and to get Evy back. She narrowed her lashes, remembering the feel of Anthony's arms around her, but thinking of him now brought only a flood of bitterness. *I have borne all the shame, the suffering, the loss, while he tours about London in a fancy coach, sporting Lady Camilla at dinner balls and the theater. Oh, what a fool I was to give myself to him! To listen to his smooth sentimental talk, his declarations of love and protection.*

Well, danger from the Zulus or not, she was going through with her plans to journey toward the Varleys' mission station. There was also risk in Sir Julien's guardianship, considering his loathsome schemes to marry her off to a man of his own choosing. And if she stayed at Cape House, she would lose Evy forever.

I will not lose her! Not if I can prevent it.

As the clock struck eleven, she was dressed and waiting. She was not likely to hear Cousin Henry arrive. She doubted he knew that Julien was away, so he would avoid alerting him. Inga had told Katie earlier that evening that she had spoken to Jendaya, and the Zulu woman would have the carriage waiting behind the cluster of trees by the back road near the African huts. There was a narrow dirt road there that led from the farmland to the township. They could leave without going through the front grounds of Cape House.

Perhaps Cousin Henry was arriving by that road even now!

Once they reached the mission station near Isandlwana, Katie was sure Dr. Varley's wife would relinquish Evy. How could they with any Christian conscience refuse her if she insisted? She was sure they would not. Then, by the time they notified Sir Julien, she and Evy, and perhaps Cousin Henry, would be at Cape Elizabeth, boarding a ship bound for London.

She sat near the door in the darkness, her one bag waiting beside her. *America, yes—it will be a safe place to begin a new life.*

She stood and began to pace the soft carpet. Her feet, encased in stylish flat-heeled morocco slippers, made no sound. She looked at the clock again. At last the hands reached eighteen minutes before midnight, and her heart began to leap. Though it was a warm night, she slipped into her dark, hooded cloak, caught up her bag, and slipped from her room. The upper hall was empty and silent.

Inga had left a small lantern burning near the table by the top of the stairway, and Katie crept down the steps, clutching the banister, her gaze riveted toward Sir Julien's office. No yellow glow came from beneath the oak door.

Below the stairs, hovering like a ghost, Inga waited, a small candle in her hand. Her fair face was taut and looked even more wan than usual.

"The kitchen door is unlocked, just as you said." Her whisper seemed to echo in the silence.

Katie nodded, then threw an arm around the older woman's shoulders. "Thank you, Inga, for everything. What would I have done without you these lonely years?"

Inga showed no particular emotion, but her mouth grew tight. "You be careful now. You watch that Master Henry. You might need him now, but he's a cagey one."

"Yes, yes, good-bye, Inga. You had best go to your room now and lock your door. Do not come out again, no matter what you hear."

Inga handed her the candleholder and slipped away. In another moment, the shadows had swallowed her from Katie's view. Katie glanced back up the stairs. All was well. She stood for a last moment listening. She heard nothing except the drumbeat of her own heart. She made her way along the hall, hesitated by the library, then went toward the kitchen. She would first explain about the Black Diamond to Cousin Henry. When it was taken, they must both be involved.

The kitchen was a huge room, usually warm and bright with a cheerful atmosphere, but in the sporadic moonlight it seemed more like a black cave. She edged her way along the counter and past the immense stove, past the sideboards, the tables, the pantry—

Her breath caught in her throat. What was that over there—that shadow that seemed to emerge from the darkness? Her trembling hand gripped the candleholder. A draft came from somewhere and drew the little flame aside, where it hovered, quavering.

Whoever was in the darkness must have already seen her candle. Too late to hide.

"Who is there?"

A shrill, feline hiss cut through the silence. Katie jumped, and the candle separated from the holder and thudded to the floor, bringing total darkness as the fleeing cat shot past Katie. Her heart fluttered, and she lunged for the back door. As she felt for the doorknob, pulled the door open, and bolted outside, she expected to feel someone's hands grabbing hold of her from behind. She darted to the porch, where damp mops, brooms, and trash barrels seemed determined to hinder her. She rushed down the porch steps and across the yard, toward the distant stables.

She looked back once, afraid she would see lights coming on in some of the lower rooms—but the windows remained dark. The tree branches around her sighed in the night wind. Above, the moon was like a silver disk darting between the clouds coming in from the bay. The beauty calmed her. She must have imagined that shadow, and her own prowling about had spooked poor Tabby, who slept on a padded footstool in the corner of the kitchen.

Katie released a tense breath, turned away from the house, and ran on to the stables to find Cousin Henry.

The stables appeared as low, rambling silhouettes against the backdrop of distant trees. The corral was visible in the moonlight, and a tall, shadowy figure moved away from a shade tree and came toward her. She paused and waited as a horrid thought struck her: What if it was Sir Julien, after all?

She gripped the handle of her bag until the leather strap began to press into her palm.

Cousin Henry came into view, a sardonic smile on his swarthy face, the wind ruffling his dark jacket. He could have passed for a riverboat gambler—not exactly the most trustworthy of folks. Yet she had little choice now except to turn to him.

"You called for me, my dear?"

Katie grabbed his sleeve and pulled him aside to the shadow of the stables. "We must not be seen in the moonlight."

His brows shot up when he saw her clothing bag. "Well, well."

Katie's cheeks heated at his smooth mockery. "So you've finally come to your senses and decided I am worth two of that insipid nephew of mine."

"Henry, you've got to help me. We must act quickly, and I haven't all night to explain. But I will ask that you keep your ill-bred remarks to yourself." She met his gaze. "It is not you I am interested in, but your assistance."

"Sounds typical of you, Katie love. If you were wise you would sound a trifle more...sweet and submissive? Well, go on, we are risking our necks out here if Julien finds us."

"He has gone to the harbor, but we must still be very careful."

"What did you mean by *assistance?*"

She read the hint of suspicion in his tone. Born and raised in England, Henry sounded more British than the rest of the family, who spoke with the Afrikaner accent. Henry's father, Squire George Chantry, owned the grand estate of Rookswood in the village of Grimston Way. Henry's older brother, Lyle, had married one of Lady Brewster's two daughters, Honoria—sister to Caroline, Henry's poor wife.

Katie clamped her jaw to keep her teeth from chattering and lifted her chin, hoping she looked brave when she felt otherwise.

"I have a bargain to present to you."

His dark brows arched at that. "What kind of bargain?"

She looked at him squarely; she needed to at least appear confident. "I overheard your discussion with your stepbrother. You need financial backing for your expedition. A gold discovery, isn't it?"

"You were eavesdropping?"

"Oh, Henry, there is no time for that. Do you want to hear my plan or not?"

"First things first. Why is it you are not turning to your beloved Anthony for help? When I left here two years ago you insisted you were madly in love with the innocuous fellow."

"And you, Cousin Henry, were about to be married."

"After you turned me down."

"That doesn't matter now. Are you interested in listening or not?"

"About my nephew Anthony—"

She tried to hide her consternation. "Never mind him. I don't know where he is, nor do I care! He lied to me. I loathe him." She clenched her hands to still the trembling that threatened to overcome her.

Henry's eyes narrowed as he studied her. Clearly, he was alert and not easily deterred. She should have known he would demand complicated explanations as to why her relationship with his wife's nephew had turned sour.

She stiffened when she felt his fingers on her face. He cupped her chin and turned her toward the moonlight, his gaze searching hers until he must have guessed what she was hiding, for the corner of his mouth tipped.

"So that's how it is, is it?"

She jerked her chin away and stepped back. "Please, don't. Sir Julien has humiliated me enough."

"So, you discovered too late that the cherished Anthony is a louse. I doubt he has given you a second thought since going to London. You should have listened to me. What has he done, abandoned you while he makes arrangements to marry Lord Montieth's charming heiress?"

"Oh, keep quiet!" She felt his words like a blow, and tears rushed to her eyes. She wished to throw his words back into his face, but common sense restrained her. She could not afford to anger him, not when she needed him so desperately.

"Your emotions tell me this is no ordinary jilt. What is it?"

She avoided his eyes and bit her lip, then turned her back. The words lodged in her throat like thorns. How humiliating to have to confess to a man like Henry Chantry that she had been a fool.

"I have a baby." How painful so few words could be!

He remained silent, and she thought he must be stunned.

She whirled to face him. "I *must* escape. I want to leave Capetown forever, to go to America with my baby—to get away from Sir Julien's power over me. He took my baby away." Her voice cracked as pain chipped at her heart. "I've found out she's at the mission station near Isandlwana—Jendaya told me."

"The Zulu woman?"

"Yes. I must go to Isandlwana, find my daughter, and board a ship at Port Elizabeth bound for England. From there, if my plan works, I'll sail for New York."

He looked at her. She began to fear he would utterly refuse her, but then he spoke at last, as brutally honest as she.

"And you want me to rescue Anthony's illegitimate child?"

"She is *my* daughter. I— I've no one else to turn to for help."

"You were a fool to trust him, Katie."

"Yes, I know that now. Will you help me?"

"It will take money to accomplish all this," he said flatly, "and I don't have it. Julien turned me down this afternoon, though I'm an heir to the diamond enterprise the same as he. He controls everything, thanks to old Ebenezer."

Ebenezer Bley. Katie knew he was the first in the extended family to come to Capetown. He'd been at Kimberly when the first diamond was found there, as well as on the river when the first gold was discovered. His wily ability to manipulate was well known. Hadn't he wheedled his way into the circle of just a few men who controlled these finds, thereby becoming wealthy and politically powerful both in Capetown and in London? Ebenezer died a very old man and left his son Julien the controlling interest over the family fortune. He must have felt that Julien would make the best financial patriarch.

Circumstances had proven Ebenezer right, Katie thought bitterly. Sir Julien even administered her portion of her father's fortune to control her future for the benefit of the diamond business as though she, a van Buren, were a relation.

"You understand what you're up against." Henry's question pulled her back to matters at hand. "How do you expect to pay for the ocean passage?"

"By taking some of what is being held back from me and from my daughter. What is partly yours as well. It— It would not be the same as stealing."

"Has Julien ever suggested giving you some diamonds from the inheritance your father left you?"

"He will give me little unless I marry according to his wishes. He took my baby and gave her to the mission and has plans to send me to Europe for a year. As if that would heal my heart! He intends to arrange a marriage for me that suits *his* plans for the Kimberly mines. That is all he devotes himself to—the diamond mines." Her voice quavered, and she cast another glance over her shoulder toward the house, where all was in shadow. The sound of the wind in the treetops and the creaking of the stables sent ripples of fear along her skin. What if Julien was watching, what if he knew? She remembered the pistol he kept. What if he was trying to trap her and Cousin Henry? He had used such a loud voice out on the front lawn—could it have been to draw her attention? To make her think he was leaving?

No, that couldn't be. Sir Julien would never expect her to take the Black Diamond.

"Then are you are thinking of taking some diamonds from Cape House?"

This time it was she who arched her brows. "As though you have not thought that very thing."

"I admit it. But if I help you, what do I get out of this?"

So like Cousin Henry to ask that, yet how could she blame him? She lifted her chin and confronted his hard gaze. She pretended brashness, using a masquerade of boldness to shield her precariousness. "You will get the same as what I intend to have—something of great value, Cousin Henry—the Black Diamond."

His breath stopped short. "The Black Diamond!" he repeated in a soft murmur. "Are you out of your mind? Julien keeps it well hidden—he worships that stone. It would be next to impossible to get your hands on it."

"You think so? It is because he worships it that he keeps his little idol where he can admire it anytime he desires without having to be seen going back and forth, to and from the safe. I know where he hides it."

"Ah!" He seemed taken aback, and she could well believe he wondered how she had managed to discover such a thing. "The Black Diamond. If I could just get my hands on it—"

"You say it belongs to the Chantrys?"

"It does," he stated firmly. "My father was there when it was found. Though Julien denies this, there is even some evidence that my father is the one who dislodged it from the strata."

"*My* father, Carl van Buren, helped to find that mine, yet Julien keeps the mine for himself."

"I can hardly believe you know where it is, Katie. You must be dreaming."

"Dreaming of escape and freedom, yes"—she took hold of his arm—"and desperate enough to take what is mine. I know where the diamond is. We can get it and be on our way to Isandlwana at once. I— I will share with you whatever price the diamond brings on the London market, fifty-fifty."

"It will need to be sold on the smuggling market. London, maybe. Russia, France—the Vatican…"

"But we need money now to get us to England!"

He regarded her, the flicker of condescension clear in his eyes. "If we are going to steal the Black Diamond, my dear, then we might as well help ourselves to anything else we need. In moderation, of course." He laughed and took hold of her arms, pulling her toward him. "We belong together, Katie love. What scoundrels we both are."

She wrenched free. "Speak for yourself, Cousin. I am not a thief."

"No? Dear Julien will come to quite a different conclusion, even though he's the real thief. Not that it matters to me. Evidently it doesn't to you, either."

It did matter. She could imagine her father frowning in sadness if he could see her now. She could remember him reading the Commandments to her when she was a little girl. "Thou shalt not steal… Thou shalt not—"

But all that was behind her now. She had grown up isolated from the religious instruction that had meant so much to her father and the van Buren family of Afrikaners. She would do whatever she must to be free. And to have her daughter restored to her. Surely her father would understand that?

She fixed her gaze on Henry. "Well? Do we have a bargain?"

In the moonlight she saw his mouth turn into a slender smile beneath his mustache. "We have a bargain, Katie. Now suppose you tell me where the Black Diamond is hidden."

For just a moment she could not escape the sensation that she was a fool to trust him—then, feeling his fingers enclose her arm and a tide of warm strength surge through her, she pushed the notion aside. She must take this chance.

"I will take you there. We must do this—together. It's in the library. Come."

"You are certain Julien's gone to Kimberly?"

She was as certain as she could be, and yet…there *was* that uneasy sensation that she was being watched. "I saw him ride away earlier this afternoon, but when it comes to your stepbrother, who can be sure of anything?"

"Here, leave your bag in that brush until we come back for the horses."

Henry was still holding Katie's arm as they came silently up the back porch steps. The door remained ajar from when she had fled. She reached for the knob.

The kitchen was in darkness as they entered, except for the stream of moonlight coming through the high window above the pantry cabinet. Katie stooped and picked up the candle she had dropped earlier. She went to the oven to relight the wick on coals banked in the oven for the morning cook.

Henry knew the house layout perhaps as well as she. He had come here from England several times with his father and Lyle. When his father had married Julien's widowed mother, there had been a time when Henry and Lyle had lived in Cape House. That, of course, was long before trouble developed between Henry and Julien. Lyle had been the silent one, the one who had made friends with Julien and married into the Brewsters.

When Katie turned around with the candle flaring, Cousin Henry was gone. She gasped, looking around. Had he abandoned her? No, she would have heard him if he'd opened the back door and gone out. She went into the hall. No sight of him. He must be in the library, waiting.

She trod the hall floor carefully, trying not to awaken anyone on the ground floor. The live-in Anglo servants all had their rooms near the kitchen and pantry, as did Anthony when he came to visit. Of course, Anthony had not dared show his face for some time. When she had written him about expecting the baby, he had not even replied.

When she came to the library, the heavy door stood open a few inches. She pushed it back and held the candle high. Henry was busy surveying the room of books, maps, and the hunting trophies Julien had collected from his trips into Angola.

She guessed he was checking his intuition as to where the Black Diamond might be hidden.

Katie pushed the door closed behind her. The candle flame reflected a bleak light in the mirror above the fireplace mantle, reminding her of a ghost.

She understood the danger with which she was flirting. Each step brought her closer to an action that she would never be able to reverse. *There is still time to turn back,* a small voice seemed to say.

No, not after getting cousin Henry involved. There is no other way out of my dilemma. I'm going through with it.

Henry came to take her arm. "Where?" His voice was barely audible.

Her hand shook as she led him to the old heirloom secretary. She hesitated—either she trusted Henry or she did not. There was no middle road. If he failed her as had Anthony, she would be twice a fool.

"Hurry!"

At his urgent whisper, she handed him the candle and turned to the secretary. Carefully she pulled aside the two cabinet doors, revealing the lion carvings and the two lion knobs.

"So that's it!" He sounded furious with himself. "A hidden compartment in this old heirloom."

Katie frowned. What had Sir Julien done when he'd had his back toward her? How had the secret door sprung open?

Outside the windows the wind rustled the leaves. The floors and walls creaked as the wood settled for the night. With her right hand she pushed against one lion, and used her left to maneuver the other, nothing happened. She tried again, her urgency increasing with the passing moments.

Her breath came rapidly. Standing beside her, she sensed Henry's impatience.

"Do you know what you're doing?"

"I'm trying!"

"Shh—quiet." His fingers clasped her shoulder as he glanced toward the door.

Katie tensed. Had she heard something? Maybe she had just imagined the sound that day of a spring giving way in a drawer? Now, in the candlelight, she could see there was no keyhole. Julien must have pushed on something.

"There must be a secret lever or something—somewhere." She looked helplessly at Henry.

"I'll try it." He pushed her aside, then set the candle on top of the secretary and began pushing on the lion knobs, then turning, shoving, twisting again.

From somewhere there came a heavier creak. Katie caught her breath and looked at Henry.

He was now so engrossed in trying to figure out the lion knobs and how they worked that he paid no mind. Her heart pounded with heavy beats that took her breath away. She continued to look toward the library door. If Julien had come home... But they would have heard his horse approaching the stables.

As Henry struggled to solve the puzzle, she inched her way toward the door. Was that creak from the wind, or a light footfall? Her mouth was dry. Her palms were slick with sweat, and her shaking fingers worked their way up the bodice of her dress to her throat. If Sir Julien found them here, he would use his pistol on Henry, she was sure of it.

Maybe on her too.

Oh, what have I done? What have I done? She hurried toward Henry, clawing at his arm. "I think I hear someone—"

"Ah!"

The exclamation caught her attention. She heard a faint click, and saw a section of the carved paneling open a crack. Henry pulled it farther out, then picked up the candle and held it close to a small, velvet-lined cavern.

Katie forgot all her fears as the Black Diamond winked at them.

They both reached for it, but Henry grasped first, turning it over in his hand before the candle.

Katie looked up at him. His eyes sparkled with an ugly humor that repelled her. "I've defeated Julien! It's mine!" Greed larded his rough whisper.

She snatched the diamond away from him. "It is *ours.*"

"Look." He took some soft leather pouches out of the drawer, opened a drawstring, and poured some of the whites onto his palm. The diamonds glittered in the candlelight. He grinned, then put them back in the pouch and pulled the drawstring, stuffing three pouches in his trouser pockets.

"Give me that, we don't have time." He snatched the Black Diamond from her, rolled it in the velvet lining from the drawer, and shoved it in his inside jacket pocket. He pushed on the carved paneling and then closed the two cabinet doors.

"To the stables."

Henry surged ahead of her toward the library door. Katie rushed after him, her stomach clenching with fear and guilt. The candle went out, and she swallowed back her fear. Henry opened the library door a crack, looked out, then moved toward the back of the house.

The moon must have clouded over, for the room was in darkness—

just like Katie's aching soul. She was close at his heels when his steps halted at what must have been the kitchen. Her heart, too, nearly stopped.

She turned to look behind just as Henry lunged toward the kitchen door. A gust of wind sent Katie's skirts around her ankles. He reached back, latched hold of her arm, and pulled her toward the porch and down the steps. Crossing the backyard they started running.

When they reached the stables all seemed quiet. Laddie was nowhere to be seen, nor was Dumaka. Of course, they had not expected her to take anything from the house, so why would they be there? They would all certainly face Sir Julien tomorrow to be pounded by questions.

"Where is the Zulu?" Henry demanded impatiently. "She should have been here by now. It's after midnight."

"She's waiting farther down the road, behind the trees."

As he entered the stable for his golden gelding, Katie looked in the brush near the corral for her bag. Carrying it back, she paused, hearing the nervous neighing of the horses in their stalls for the night. Odd that they should be so nervous—probably not used to Henry's horse.

She waited. What was keeping him? She walked to the wide stable doorway and stared into the chasm of darkness, but could not see him. He must be farther toward the back.

She inched forward and whispered. "Henry? Where are you?"

The only sound meeting her was the nervous movements of the horses. She forced herself to enter, surrounded by deep shadows and the pungent odor of hay mingled with manure.

His horse, where was it? And where was the mare Inga had said would be saddled for her?

She turned full circle, glancing desperately about her. Then she heard a creaking sound—a door opening at the far end of the stable. The back door! She saw the wind moving it to and fro on its hinges. This discovery was followed by the one sound she feared: hooves, galloping away.

She ran through the stable and out the back door into the night.

"Henry!" she hissed. In the moonlight she glimpsed him, hunched low in the saddle, rounding a tree-lined bend, where he disappeared in the direction of the African huts.

Her heart sank like a stone. "No! *No!*" Her hands formed fists, and she doubled over. He had taken everything and left her here. *Betrayed!*

Bitter rage filled her mind. She pressed the back of her hand hard against her teeth until it bruised. Tears streamed unheeded down her cheeks. *Henry…Henry, come back! I hate you…hate you…*

She stumbled down the dirt road that led toward the African huts, running, sometimes staggering and stumbling, until she neared the trees. Here, she paused a moment to catch her breath.

A shrill bird's cry startled her. It was followed by a humming sound, loud, then louder still. Katie looked toward the trees. Jendaya had the four-horse carriage waiting in the myrtle trees and was drawing her attention, Zulu fashion, by the humming sound that made Katie shiver.

Jendaya held the reins with one sturdy hand and reached across the seat with the other to pull Katie aboard as she came hurrying up. She clamored onto the seat, gasping for breath.

"Hurry, Jendaya!"

The Zulu woman slapped the reins and the horses bounded forward onto the dirt road.

Katie clutched the sides of the seat as they weaved and bounced ahead. The horses galloped past the African huts. Katie feared the carriage might topple over on its side, but Jendaya handled the horses skillfully.

The warm wind swept Katie's face and sent strands of her tawny hair whipping. Soon, Cape House was left behind in the raw, dusty night.

Any hopes that Henry might be waiting for her along the road, or at the beginning of the township, proved vain. He, too, must be racing through the night astride his horse, the Black Diamond safely stashed in his jacket pocket. He must be throwing back his head and laughing with abandon at her folly for trusting him. She had delivered three pouches of cut diamonds, as well as the prized Kimberly Black Diamond, right into his hands, and he had simply ridden off.

Jendaya drove the carriage from the township and was on the road toward British-controlled Natal as the moon approached the hills that appeared like crouching lions on the horizon. They would reach the mission station near Rorke's Drift bordering Zululand by early morning.

Katie moaned. Her head throbbed, and desolation filled her mind.

Jendaya lifted a long, sleek dark arm with tight, beaded bracelets and made a sweeping motion inland toward the hills. "When the sun rises we will be near the Rock of the Crouching Lion. We will see the daktari and the mission station."

Above, the sky mellowed and cleared as the night wore on, revealing numberless brilliant stars. Thorn trees swept past, horse hooves pounded their drumbeat upon the path, and the South African yellow moon crouched over the hills of Isandlwana. Though exhausted, Katie could not rest. Her heart, sore and distraught, would not let her.

There was little hope of taking Evy away and escaping to America now, unless by some unforeseen chance the missionary Dr. Varley and his wife agreed to help her. Or unless Cousin Henry changed his mind about his treachery and came to Isandlwana? *Too good to be true,* she scolded her hopes. When Sir Julien returned and learned that his diamonds were missing, he would certainly search for Katie. If she failed to escape, how could she ever explain—or convince him that Henry had taken everything and fled?

No, she had no choice but to go on. If only she knew where she was going on to.

CHAPTER THREE

Henry Chantry groaned as he crawled from a layer of hay. He sat up slowly and peered around in the darkness. The stables, that's where he was.

He pushed himself to his feet and staggered a little, then caught his balance on a wooden post. How did he get here like this? He squinted, looking for his horse, for Katie.

Both were gone.

He touched the lump at the back of his head and his eyes narrowed with sudden, burning anger. The last thing he could remember was unhitching his horse, hearing a soft footstep—

So that was it! That treacherous, conniving female had struck him in the dark, then escaped on *his* horse!

Henry groaned as he felt inside his jacket pocket for the Black Diamond. His mouth turned. Gone… Of course it would be. What a fool to have trusted her pretty face.

"The Black Diamond—that rare Black Diamond." His hoarse whisper caught in his dry throat.

When his foot touched something among the scattered straw, he stooped down, wincing as the blood surged to his skull. He snatched up a heavy wooden mallet, glaring at it in the dimness. She might have cracked his skull open! He flung it aside, then started at an outside sound. He looked toward the stable doors. Someone was coming with a lantern—

He felt his trouser pockets for the three pouches of whites, amazed they were still there. The snit must have been in a hurry. He took out the pouches and stooped toward a corner, covering them over with hay. He straightened up as Julien Bley's voice split the night.

"I suspected you would return to do your thieving business. You thought you could get by with it, did you? Then you're a bigger fool than I thought, Henry!"

Someone else was with him. Anthony Brewster held a sjambok, a flexible, rounded whip a little over three feet long, usually made of rhino hide, and first used by the Dutch settlers to drive their oxen.

Was this why Katie involved me? She needed a handy culprit while she escaped? She was far more devious than he had thought.

"Where is the Black Diamond?"

Henry met Julien's angry glare. "I don't have it." He turned to Anthony. "When did you arrive?"

"That's none of your concern!" Julien snapped the words out. "Take that jacket off, then empty your pockets. Anthony, search him, and check for his pistol."

"Don't be a fool, Julien." Henry leaned against the wall, crossing his arms. "Someone clobbered me from behind. While we talk and delay, the real thief is getting away."

Anthony, a broad-shouldered young man with a strong jaw and platinum hair, came toward Henry, frowning. Henry made no resistance as Anthony searched him. He knew there was naught to find but his pistol, which Anthony threw across the stable into the hay. Henry watched Anthony, who seemed to have other concerns on his mind.

"Where is Katie?"

Henry met Anthony's clear suspicion. "Why ask me? You spent enough time with her this past winter."

At least the knave had the grace to redden. "I've not seen Katie for—for months. I've been at Lady Brewster's in Pietermaritzburg with my fiancée until this evening. Julien had just discovered the theft of the Black Diamond when Camilla and I arrived." He turned his troubled gaze to Julien. "Isn't that so, Uncle?"

"Never mind that now, my boy. Search him again. He must have it. Inga says she saw him prowling about the library earlier."

"And knocked myself on the back of the head with that mallet too, I suppose?" Henry didn't even try to conceal his disdain. "Don't be ridiculous, Julien. I don't have the Black Diamond and don't know where it is. And don't forget, I'm an heir of Sir Ebenezer too. I'm just as concerned over its loss as you."

"You'll not convince me of that. And if this were not a family matter I'd contact the authorities at once."

"Would you? I wonder. You and I both know about the diamond smuggling going on recently."

"So what are you getting at?"

"I think you know a little too much about it."

The speculative gleam came cold and hard. "It's your word against mine. But I don't need the authorities to make you talk." Anger burned in Julien's eyes. "Hand me that whip, Anthony."

Henry straightened. "Try that approach, and I will live to kill you, Julien."

"Careful, Uncle Julien," Anthony said. "We must keep these squabbles to ourselves. We'll get to the truth." He turned to Henry. "You still have not told me where Katie is."

Henry smirked. "Dear little Katie has run away with the prize."

"The Black Diamond—? That's nonsense," Anthony snorted.

"Is it? She's determined to get her baby back—*your* baby, Anthony, and she needs the Black Diamond to do it."

A muscle twitched near the corner of Anthony's mouth. His cool gaze shifted away from Henry to Julien.

A footfall sounded behind them. They turned toward the stable entrance, where Henry saw a young woman standing. Her blond hair was elegantly attired and glittering, and there were large diamonds around her throat and at her ears. The tender gray eyes looked with surprise at Anthony, who still held the sjambok. Then she winced, her hand going to her throat. Her gaze swerved to meet Anthony's.

"Oh—"

Anthony looked evenly at Henry, and he got the message: *Say anything, and you will live to regret it.*

Henry smirked. A mere slip of his tongue and Anthony's prospects for marriage to Lord Montieth's daughter would be dust. He smiled and relaxed for the first time. "Maybe we need not be so quick about all this, Julien." He saw from Julien's start that he clearly understood the veiled threat: *Persist, and I just may open Pandora's box.* Lord Montieth was in the British Parliament under Queen Victoria, who, like Julien, wished to bring South Africa into the British Empire. He would certainly abhor any hint of scandal.

Julien's mouth tightened. "Anthony, take Camilla to the house." His words were as stiff as his carriage.

Camilla's questioning gaze swerved to Anthony. He went to take her arm, patting her hand. "There is nothing to be concerned about, my dear Camilla. Uncle Henry has had a minor accident, but he wasn't seriously hurt. His horse threw him and ran off. I'm sure one of the stable boys will find it roaming round the estate by morning."

Henry felt the woman's gaze. A hint of curiosity showed in her face. "A golden gelding?"

"As a matter of fact, yes. You've seen it?"

She cast a glance toward Anthony. "I might have been mistaken about the color," she said in an apologetic tone. "I thought I saw a golden horse trotting loose when I walked up from the house just now. It seemed a little nervous." She twisted her lacy handkerchief. "It may still be there."

"I'll have a look—" Henry started for the doors.

"No need," Julien cut in. "Anthony can do it. Where did you see it, Miss Camilla?"

"By the outer rim of the corral, near the trees."

Henry looked at Anthony, then at the boy's wife-to-be. Was it his imagination, or did Camilla look strangely uneasy?

The woman's mood could be caused by her recent arrival in untamed South Africa. She did not look the sort to adjust well. Although pretty, she was thin and pale.

Then a thought stopped him. If his horse was wandering about, then Katie had not taken it. Had she walked all the way to the carriage waiting near the African huts? Had she intended to run his horse off to keep him from following after her?

"Go back to the house and wait for me, Camilla dear," Anthony was saying. "I will join you there in a few minutes."

Henry looked after them as they left the stables. Their footsteps faded into the windy night.

"What did you do with the Black Diamond?" Julien snapped.

"Don't be a fool. The longer you hold me here, the easier it will be for her to escape. She's already an hour or more ahead of me."

"You are still intent on blaming Katie for this theft?"

"Who else could have done it? You won't find her asleep in her room. Doesn't that tell you something? She told me she was determined to leave."

A moment later Anthony returned to the stable leading the nervous gelding by the reins.

"A bit shy, but otherwise unhurt."

Henry took the reins and led his horse to a stall.

"Then Katie might have been thrown," Sir Julien said. "We'd better get some of the Bantu together and search the area."

Anthony shook his head. "I looked in the trees around the corral."

"You won't find her." Henry looked from one to the other. "She sent a message to my hotel asking me to come here tonight. She had some kind of plan and mentioned taking a carriage. She wanted to escape to America."

"If you are lying—"

Henry cut Anthony off. "Why should I?"

"I can think of a few reasons."

Henry met the younger man's glare. "She had a most compelling reason to run away, thanks to *you*, my lad."

"Enough!" Julien fixed them both with an angry stare. "Henry, where is this message you say she sent you?"

"Naturally, I wouldn't keep it on me. I left it at my hotel."

"Naturally!" Anthony derided.

Henry ignored him, focusing on Julien. "When I arrived from my hotel, she said she was going to get the Black Diamond. She offered to sponsor my expedition to locate my father's gold mine if I would help her find her child and get ship passage. But when I was getting my horse ready, she struck me from behind with that mallet."

"You expect me to believe that?" Julien strode toward him and snatched the mallet up from the barn floor. "If she needed your help so much, then why would she strike you unconscious?" His black eye patch stared back at Henry like a bottomless pit.

Henry frowned. *Why indeed?* "I'm beginning to think the only reason she sent for me was so that I would be left here unconscious...to later waste time answering questions while she escaped in the carriage to the mission station with that Zulu woman."

"You let her leave for the mission station? At a time such as this, without even warning her? Have you gone mad?"

Henry had almost had his fill of this foolishness. "Warning her of what?"

"The Zulus, you fool!" Julien hissed the words. "If you had kept abreast of what London and Governor Frere have been up to these past months instead of chasing after bogus gold deposits, you might have stopped her."

Henry felt his muscles tense. "You'd better explain."

"The Zulus have been given a thirty day ultimatum to comply with British demands to leave the area or face Lord Chelmsford's troops in Zululand. Chelmsford rode toward Isandlwana a week ago."

"The general can expect to meet up with some twenty thousand Impi Zulus!"

Anthony's words struck Henry hard. "I had no idea!" He turned to Sir Julien. "The mission station is located near Rorke's Drift."

"If Cetshwayo's warriors are on the move, no one will be safe anywhere near Zulu territory, and Rorke's Landing sits on the Zulu borders." Julien's tone was dark.

"Uncle Julien"—Anthony looked pale—"we have got to find Katie tonight."

"Send for the Bantu servants, Anthony. I want every available man on the estate armed and on horseback."

"Yes, Uncle Julien."

"Send for Dumaka. He may be useful as a guide."

There wasn't a Zulu alive that Henry trusted, whether they claimed to be Christian or not. So far as he knew, Jendaya could be planning a trick, delivering a white woman as a hostage for the Zulu chieftain.

Julien started for the door. "I'd better send a rider to tell Sir Bartle at Government House. He may be able to send someone to Rorke's Drift."

"There's no reason for all of us to be idle while you gather up an armed force," Henry insisted. "I am well acquainted with the region. I'll ride ahead to Rorke's Drift—and I'll need to be adequately armed."

Julien's one eye glittered. For a moment Henry believed he would not permit him to leave.

"Stop by the house as you ride out." Julien gave a stiff nod. "Take a Martini-Henry rifle and whatever ammunition you need." He turned and stalked out of the stables.

Henry looked after him a moment, a little surprised by his cooperation. Julien must have serious concern for his ward after all.

Henry located his pistol, then retrieved the three pouches of diamonds and hid them deep inside his saddlebag. He mounted his horse and rode to the house for the rifle.

A short time later he was riding toward the Buffalo River at Rorke's Drift on the border between British-controlled Natal and the stony hills of Zululand. There, if he was successful in his quest, he would find not only Katie but also the Black Diamond.

CHAPTER FOUR

And he kneeled down, and cried with a loud
voice, Lord, lay not this sin to their charge.

ACTS 7:60

Rorke's Drift, Twelve Miles South of Isandlwana
House of Mercy Medical Mission

The whitewashed walls of the House of Mercy mission station burned
in the dawn sunlight with the brilliance of bleached bone. The dwelling,
surrounded by wide, shaded verandas roofed with thatch, stood a little
apart from the church and its attendant buildings below the distant
rocky hills that marked the boundary of Zululand.

Dr. Clyde Varley was an early riser. He was fully aware that the
troops under Lord Chelmsford, some seven thousand strong, had already
ridden from Rorke's Drift and were well into Zulu territory. By now
Chelmsford would have divided his men into three groups, the smallest
camped at Isandlwana while the other two were out looking for the great
army of the Zulu chieftain, known to be up to thirty thousand strong.

Dr. Varley was worried. He was not pleased with this British mission into Zululand. The chieftain had ordered all missionaries out of his
land, and the House of Mercy at Rorke's Drift was on the very border
between Zululand and Natal. Varley did not think much of the British
general, for it was clear Chelmsford did not appreciate the strength of

the Zulu warriors. He trusted in his weapons and his experience in battle with other lesser tribes.

But the Zulus were fierce warriors. They had no friends among the other African tribes—too many of them had felt the deadly blade of the assegai, the broad, short, stabbing sword of the Zulu.

Dr. Varley was frowning to himself when a young man he liked, Captain Durbin, came walking toward him at the mission gate.

"Good morning, Doctor," the smiling young captain called.

"Good morning, Captain."

Captain Durbin walked beside a squarely built bear of a man, Hans Kruger, a Boer commander from the Dutch-controlled Transvaal. The Boer was wearing the customary Dutch leather jerkins and hat, in contrast to the British redcoated uniforms.

"Good mornin', Parson," the Boer called.

"You're leaving Rorke's Drift?" Dr. Varley knew they were; he had seen them readying the transport line during the night.

Captain Durbin nodded. "I received word last night from General Chelmsford. I and my men are to bolster the forces at Isandlwana. We wanted to alert you before we left. We know from scouts that the Zulus number about twenty thousand. We don't expect that great a thrust, but it might be wise to send Mrs. Varley and the baby into Natal with the other civilians under your charge."

"You think Cetshwayo will attack this far from Isandlwana?" Dr. Varley couldn't imagine it. Usually seven thousand troops were quite enough—especially when facing fighters with spears.

"I doubt if any of them will get past our troops, but with the woman here I felt I should mention the possibility."

The Boer made a throaty sound of disagreement and fingered his sjambok. "Yah, we have had battles with the Zulu afore now, Captain Durbin." He shook his golden head. "The Zulu must not be underestimated. They are fierce warriors. Cetshwayo's elite Impis are wanting a battle. They cannot marry until they initiate their assegais in enemy blood. Cetshwayo has kept them from war since he took over after his father, but they're wanting it, I can tell you so."

"Maybe. But you Boers tend to exaggerate when it comes to the Zulus." Captain Durbin's smile was indulgent. "If they do attack Chelmsford at Isandlwana, the general will defeat them without difficulty. What are spears against rifles and cannon? I fear it will all be over before I get there."

"You underestimate," the Boer said again. "Your general does not take wise precautions. Trenches should be built at Isandlwana, rocks gathered for defense lines, the wagons drawn in to form a wagon laager." He shook his big head again. "You do not worry enough, Captain."

Captain Durbin's impatient shrug was quick and abrupt. "We cannot waste the time, Hans. After this there will be no more skirmishes with Cetshwayo. He will go scurrying back to his kraal at Ulundi. At any rate, Dr. Varley, I'm under orders to leave soldiers here to man the guns and guard Rorke's Drift. But you might consider sending Mrs. Varley to Natal."

"Yes, Captain. The Scriptures say, "'With good advice make war.' And God be with you."

The three men shook hands, then Dr. Varley watched the soldiers mount their horses and ride toward the column. He continued to watch them until they had been ferried across Buffalo River into Zululand, then he sighed. *Dear Father in heaven, I am worried. War…and death! Souls will be entering eternity totally unprepared for Your holy presence. So few know the beloved Savior.*

Junia Varley cradled baby Evy in her arms and tried to hush her crying. *Father God, how You have blessed me! I feel like Sarah holding Isaac. With Sarah I can say, "Who would have said…that Sarah should have given children suck!" Yet you have given me this precious daughter to raise to know You.*

Perhaps, when Evy grew a little older, Junia would ask Clyde to let her go home to Grimston Way in England for a visit with her sister, Grace, who was married to Vicar Edmund Havering.

Junia secretly dreamed of the quiet rose gardens and village streets of England with its cool misty fog. The stony hills of Zululand, the thorn trees, and the wildlife were all a part of God's wonderful creation, but the heat, dust, and dangers from the different African tribes were a worrisome burden to live with, especially now with a baby.

She heard the sound of horses and carried Evy to the door in time to see the soldiers being ferried across the river to the hinterland. Thank God some soldiers were still left at Rorke's Drift. She walked out into the early morning to join her husband, who turned and smiled down at her and the baby, putting his arm around Junia's shoulders.

"There may be trouble ahead, Junia. The Boer might be right after all. Perhaps I should send you and the baby to Pietermaritzburg until this war with the Zulus is settled."

"They would never cross the river to the mission station, would they?" She did her best to sound calm and confident.

"I do not think so, my dear, but we'll take no chances. I'll arrange a wagon and ox today."

"I'm certain tomorrow will be soon enough, Clyde. Look, someone is coming in a carriage. Why, it's Jendaya…and an English woman. I wonder who that could be?"

"I don't know, but this is the wrong time for visitors to see the mission."

"Maybe they've come to warn us?"

Clyde shook his head. "Seems they would have sent a few men with rifles for that. Let's go greet them."

"She's a lovely young girl. Do you suppose she's one of the soldiers' wives?"

"If she is, I shall need to give her worrisome news. Captain Durbin's troops have ridden to Isandlwana to reinforce the base camp there."

They waited until the carriage drew to a halt, then Clyde lifted a hand in greeting. "Hello, Jendaya, you've brought us a guest?"

Jendaya did not get down immediately, but the young English woman did, as though she were exhausted from the ride. Junia watched her, taking in the dazed expression as the woman stood staring, first at the baby, then at Junia. She smiled again and patted the baby. After a moment of silence, Junia walked toward the woman.

"Welcome to Mercy House. I'm Junia Varley, and this is my husband Dr. Clyde Varley. We're the missionaries here, but I'm sure you've been told that already. Won't you come in and refresh yourself? I shall make tea. And you must be famished too."

The woman walked toward her with slow steps. She swayed a little on her feet, and Junia was relieved when Clyde stepped forward, taking hold of her. "My dear woman, are you ill?"

When she said nothing, he looked up at Jendaya for explanation.

"Bring her into the hut, Clyde," Junia said hurriedly. "She may have sunstroke. Jendaya can explain everything once we get the girl settled."

Odd, Junia thought, leading the way to the mission hut, *how she keeps staring at Evy.*

After they had gotten the young woman indoors on a cot, Junia sent Jendaya to start the water boiling on the outside earthen oven to make tea. Junia went for a jug of water so she could wash the woman's face and hands and feet. She looked so exhausted and frightened and she still had said nothing.

When Junia came back into the hut she stopped. The woman had gotten up from the cot and was kneeling beside Evy's little crib, rocking it gently and humming Brahms's "Lullaby."

Junia felt awash with pity. Was the woman—mentally ill? Had the heat gotten to her that badly on the trip from Natal? Maybe Clyde had learned what this visit was about from Jendaya. She glanced toward the carriage. What was taking Clyde so long? Junia saw Clyde talking with Jendaya some distance from the hut, near where the baking oven was located. She could see Jendaya stooping down while watching the water and talking to him. Clyde was standing, tall and lean and very British looking, a safari hat on his head, his arms folded, paying close attention to the woman. Junia knew her husband well enough after all these years to realize when something troubled him. He was not pleased with whatever Jendaya was telling him.

She turned back to the young woman and smiled at her, wondering what her name was. She must be a soldier's wife in fear for her husband who had decided to chance everything to come here. Some wives were like that when they knew their husbands were being sent into the hinterland during conflicts with the tribes, especially the Zulus. Yet she had not asked about her husband. Perhaps she had seen that most of the soldiers had already left Rorke's Drift and crossed the river. Junia went to kneel down beside the woman and the baby.

"Her name is Evy," Junia said gently, quietly, because the baby was asleep now. "Isn't she a precious one? She's only two months old. She's adopted—or soon will be. We must go to Capetown for that. Then she'll be our very own Evy Varley."

The woman had ceased her singing, but she was still rocking the cradle, staring down at the sleeping infant.

Junia tried again: "What is your name?"

The woman's hand stilled on the cradle. "Katie. Katie van Buren." She looked across the cradle at Junia, and Junia saw a look of tragedy in her eyes that brought a silence between them. The girl seemed to be watching her expectantly, as though she thought Junia would know who she was.

Junia smiled. "Van Buren? That is Dutch. Then you must be a Boer? Did you come from the Transvaal or the Orange Free State?" Although the Transvaal and Natal were no longer under Boer rule, the Transvaal had recently been annexed days after the new British governor and high commissioner, Sir Bartle Frere, had arrived from Bombay, India.

"Do you have family in the Transvaal?" Junia tried to restrain her curiosity.

At this Katie seemed frightened. "I… I don't know anymore." Katie's hand went to her forehead and she rested it there, closing her eyes. "I don't know about anything anymore. I'm so weary, everything is so hopeless…" Despair pinched her voice.

Junia frowned. Katie was indeed ill. "Come, my dear, you must rest for now. We can talk later, after you've eaten something and finished your tea. And a good sleep will do wonders to put worries into perspective."

"May I hold the baby while I rest?"

Junia saw the wistful look on the woman's soiled, sweat-stained face.

"Evy is fast asleep, but yes." Junia could feel the young woman's need to touch something fresh and beautiful. "You lie down, I'll wash you with cool water, and then I'll bring Evy to your arms."

Katie smiled, her lips quavering, and a tear ran down her cheek leaving a line through the dust. "Thank you." She spoke so meekly, so quietly that Junia could hardly hear her.

Worry nudged Junia as she removed the woman's shoes and socks and loosened her bodice. She washed her face and arms, then her feet.

"You're very kind," Katie murmured, watching her.

"It is the least I can do, Katie. A little tea, some food, and when you wish to talk I can listen to your worries. You are welcome at the House of Mercy."

"And you'll let me hold…hold the baby."

"Yes, you can hold Evy." Had Katie lost her own child? Was that the reason for her behavior? Junia felt growing sympathy for her.

Lord, please help this sad young woman. Meet her need, and heal the ache within her. And if I can help in any way, Lord, please show me.

Junia stood looking down at Katie van Buren holding the sleeping baby in her arms. The woman was smiling, her eyes closed. Junia started when Katie spoke in those quiet tones.

"Thank you, Junia. They were right. You are a worthy woman."

Junia frowned. What on earth? She shook her head, then left the hut and stepped outdoors. The afternoon sun was golden; a few fleecy clouds chased each other across the sky toward the distant hills. Jendaya had disappeared, and Clyde was standing alone some distance away by the river, hands in his pockets, staring off.

Something was wrong. She could sense it.

She came up quietly and tucked her arm through his. "So what is this mystery? You look worried, Husband."

He sighed deeply, then looked down at her, a frown between his brows. His deep-set eyes were kind and sympathetic.

"Junia, my dear, you mean Katie has not told you yet?"

"Told me what?" Tension rose within her as she searched his sober face.

"Then she has not." He rubbed his chin, watching her, his love—and his unhappiness—clear in his eyes. "I must say I am surprised by her actions and her silence. Jendaya says that Katie was very upset until she arrived here and saw you holding the baby. Then something came over her, and her emotions seemed to recede into a surprising calm."

"I don't understand." She searched his face for answers, growing more tense as she read his concern. "What's this all about?"

Clyde patted her hand between his, then clasped it tightly. "Katie van Buren is Sir Julien Bley's ward. She is Evy's mother. She's come to take Evy with her to America."

A sword might just as well have pierced her heart. Junia sucked in her breath and gripped his hand tightly, as though she would sink to the ground. He watched her, a worried crease between his brows.

"I see." She looked back toward the hut. "Yes, I see now. That explains her behavior." Her heart thumped, causing an ache in her chest. *Take Evy to America?*

"I do not see how we can turn her away. If she asks us for our help, we must try."

Junia's throat constricted. *Am I so soon to lose this brief time of fulfillment?* Her first cry to God was one of bitter disappointment. *Why? Oh, Father, why? It is unfair!*

"Junia?" he said in a ragged whisper, reaching a tender finger to brush against her cheek. "If she wants her baby..."

She tore her gaze from the hut and looked at her husband. His sympathy was so real, so visible, that his love for her warmed her heart and comforted her.

"Our faith is being tried." After an awkward moment he shook his head. "We can only trust His wisdom, His mercy in bringing Katie here to us. There must be a reason. If God gave us Evy for only a little while, then…though it hurts to release her—"

She had no answers, only questions that throbbed like festering wounds in her soul. Although she struggled for composure, all too soon the inevitable tears flooded her eyes. "Oh, *Clyde!*" She stepped toward him, and his arms wrapped about her and he buried his face against her hair.

"Darling Junia!"

She wept, trying to keep the sounds as quiet as possible, letting her sorrow flow, until her throat hurt. As all her happy dreams of having her own daughter ebbed away, she finally thought there were no more tears to flow. She looked up at her dear husband. "The LORD gave, and the LORD hath taken away; blessed be the name of the LORD."

"Now I know why God gave you to me, Junia." Clyde's voice was hoarse, and his eyes now filled with tears. "There are few as brave and trusting as you. Few with such a lovely spirit of submission to the Lord." He reached over and brushed the windblown dark hair from her face.

She tried to smile. "I love you for saying that, but I feel neither brave nor trusting." She only knew that she must choose to act upon what she knew of God's character. His good plans for them. Comforting words from Isaiah, chapter forty-three, breezed softly across her soul: "When thou passest through the waters, I will be with thee; and through the rivers, they shall not overflow thee: when thou walkest through the fire, thou shalt not be burned; neither shall the flame kindle upon thee. For I am the LORD thy God."

Her sigh seemed to come from the depths of her soul. "I suppose there are reasons… I *know* there are reasons, though I cannot understand them."

"The wounds are too raw, Junia, do not try to ignore the hurt. Wait. Time will prove our Savior can be trusted with pain. Perhaps there are reasons why God has brought us all here now. He knows the future, while we stumble along trying to understand."

She was quiet, just holding him. The wind came up and blew dust and brush along the rocky slope by the river. Though words failed them, their quiet embrace spoke volumes.

"Do you want me to talk to Katie?" he asked after a long while.

"Not yet, Clyde. She is asleep. But perhaps this afternoon, or even tomorrow morning. I wonder if Sir Julien will come here?"

"I'm sure he will. We need to pray about all this before he arrives. We need God's intervention."

Junia looked again toward the hut. Oh yes, they needed that. And His mercy. For without that, Junia feared she would not be able to endure what was coming.

Katie opened her eyes. Her mind and heart churned, and she looked around her. It must be early afternoon. Evy was still asleep in her arms. She held her little girl, running her palm along the baby's back. From outside she heard voices. Someone, most likely Dr. Varley, was reading from the Bible. She could hear his calm, kind voice carried on the wind.

"'The voice said, Cry. And he said, What shall I cry? All flesh is grass, and all the goodliness thereof is as the flower of the field:

'The grass withereth, the flower fadeth: because the spirit of the LORD bloweth upon it: surely the people is grass.

'The grass withereth, the flower fadeth: but the word of our God shall stand for ever.'

"This is a reading from Isaiah forty, verses six through eight."

Katie closed her eyes and felt her tears run down her cheeks and onto a pillow.

There followed a hymn. Katie had never heard it before; it was unlike any she remembered singing as a little girl. Whether because of the words Dr. Varley had read from Scripture, or because of the sweet voices of the missionary doctor and his wife as they sang, Katie felt a strange yearning and tugging at her heart. And for the first time in years, she found her soul crying out.

Help me, God! Help my baby, help these good people—help me do what's right. What do You want of me, Jesus?

The missionaries' voices filled the warm air and drifted in to Katie on the cot, the hymn like balm on chafing wounds.

"Savior, like a shepherd lead us, much we need Thy tender care; in Thy pleasant pastures feed us, for our use Thy folds prepare; we are Thine, do Thou befriend us, be the Guardian of our way; keep Thy flock, from sin defend us, seek us when we go astray."

From somewhere closer at hand another voice joined in, hesitant at first…a deeper voice struggling with the English language, yet resolutely humming the music. It was Jendaya, singing from where she sat on the hut floor: "Thou has promised to receive us, poor and sinful though we be; Thou hast mercy to relieve us, grace to cleanse, and power to free; early let us seek Thy favor; early let us do Thy will; blessed Lord and only Savior, with Thy love our bosoms fill;

"Blessed Jesus, blessed Jesus, Thou hast bought us, Thine we are; blessed Jesus, blessed Jesus, Thou hast loved us, love us still."

The baby stirred.

Katie looked at the sweet, innocent face. *Yes, early let us seek Thy favor; early let us do Thy will.*

She touched the perfectly formed little head, the intricately shaped ear. "May you grow up to do God's will, sweeting," she murmured, "may you learn early to do what is good and pure—"

She stopped abruptly, raising her head from the pillow to look at Jendaya. The Zulu woman had sprung to her strong legs like a lion and stood frozen, looking toward the hut door. She had heard something that brought her terror. Something in the far distance. Something far different than the music of the hymn.

This music did not bring peace.

Katie sat up, fear gnawing at her. She heard it now too. Humming. Humming from thousands of voices, like some great beehive on the move.

Katie struggled to get up, holding Evy to her breast. "Jendaya—? What—?"

"Night of the full moon. I forgot the full moon!"

"What?" Katie's teeth chattered.

Evy began to whimper as though hungry, and Katie tried to quiet her. "What do you mean, Jendaya?"

"Hide!"

"What?"

"Hide! *Hide!*"

"Jendaya!" From outside the distant hum grew still louder, and it seemed the ground shook from the pounding feet of a great and terrible army beating across the plain. Then there came a blood-chilling rattle, a sound Katie knew well. The Zulu Impi—the twenty-thousand strong army of bachelor warriors—were taking their short, wide-bladed spears and beating them against their shields.

Preparing for an attack.

The sounds grew deafening: the humming, the jogging feet, the rattle of blades—

"Oh, God in heaven!" Katie wailed. She ran to the hut door and stumbled out to where Dr. and Mrs. Varley stood shading their eyes with their hands, looking across the South African plain.

Katie looked too, and the sight nauseated her. A sea of black came rolling across the plain toward Rorke's Drift. The great Zulu Impi were trotting forward—thousands upon thousands of black and white cowhide shields. The warriors would charge forward like the buffalo to encircle their victims. They came with their assegais flashing in the sunlight, blinding her. The slow trot was more frightening than if they had been racing. They rattled their blades, humming steadily, coming in a human tidal wave.

The British soldiers were manning their guns, others were on horseback.

Katie screamed, and Junia came running toward her, her features pale but her expression unafraid. "The baby, Jendaya," she ordered quickly, "perhaps you can save her. If God makes a way, bring her to Pietermaritzburg to Lady Brewster. Tell her to send Evy to my sister and her husband in England. Understand? Vicar Edmund Havering! Go now! Take her!" Katie let the woman take Evy from her arms and hand her over to Jendaya.

The Zulu woman hesitated, looking from Junia to Katie, as though trying to think of a way to save them as well.

"If God wills, we will live." Junia pushed Jendaya toward the back of the hut. "Now hide the baby's white skin. Hurry, *hurry.*"

Jendaya took the baby and pushed her down between her breasts, then wrapped herself in the Zulu cloth. She looked at Junia. "Thank you for Jesus, Daktari." With that, she turned and was gone.

Junia threw her arms around Katie, then pulled her down to the hut floor where they knelt. "Pray. Pray to Jesus, our Savior."

Jendaya knew what to do. In the diabolical mayhem, she crawled beneath the black and white cowhide shield of a dead Impi and lay there, hidden, the tiny baby still concealed inside her bosom and covered by her wrap. As death stalked all around her, Jendaya spoke to the God of all gods in the name of His Son Jesus. She spoke for the poor white skins, who had brought knowledge of the Great One to Africa. She asked for safety for the babe and knew that amid the noise its crying was not heard.

The sound of humming stopped. Katie's heart pounded as a terror-filled silence encircled them, and then the clacking of assegais against Zulu shields started up, along with a death drum of pounding feet. Faster, faster came the crashing crescendo. Closer, closer…as many thousands of feet swarmed across Rorke's Drift.

Outdoors, the soldiers fired the guns. The Impi advanced.

Dr. Varley rushed into the hut and knelt beside his wife and Katie, encircling them both with his arms. His surprisingly calm prayer came in a steady voice and filled Katie's ears with amazing words of God's grace, power, and purpose. "God is our refuge and strength, a very present help in trouble. Therefore will not we fear, though the earth be removed, and—"

Katie squeezed her eyes shut and clung to Junia and Dr. Varley. She felt the firm, steady, comforting pressure of their fingers on her cold sweating palms.

"Jesus, forgive my sins," Katie kept repeating. "Forgive me, forgive me. Take care of Evy—"

"Into thy hands I commend my spirit." Junia's whispered prayer was calm, steady. "If you will, please save our baby—"

Katie could no longer hear Junia. The Zulu were all around now. She could smell smoke and hear the fire crackling…hear the dying shouts of the last brave soldiers making a stand outside the hut. The whinny of horses died away. And then…

The Zulus were in the hut.

Tall, chocolate brown Zulu Impi, with bright, fire-hot eyes. Their assegais were no longer silver, but crimson. The young warriors needed a battle before they were allowed to marry. At last, they had their first washing of the spears.

Katie heard Dr. Varley's last shout. Amazingly it was, "Jesus Lord, forgive them—!"

Katie slumped over at the first *whack!*

Strange that she felt such peace, like loving arms embracing her, strange that she was no longer afraid…no longer…

All was quiet in the darkness when Jendaya lifted the shield and crawled away over the bloodied ground toward the river. The mission station was a smoking ruin. Bodies were everywhere. The Impi had performed their ritual of cutting open the bellies of their defeated enemy, and as she crawled toward the riverbank she slipped on human remains. She crawled onward, down the embankment, down toward the Buffalo River, toward clean water. She moved through the water, swimming with floating debris, keeping the baby's head above water.

The stars glimmered in the sky now. Jendaya could see what the daktari had once told her was the Southern Cross. It looked down upon Rorke's Drift, upon Isandlwana, and she thought it looked down at her and the baby with a pure white glow that led the way through the deep, dark night to safety.

The sun rose over the distant hills of Zululand, its dawning rays turning the Rock of the Crouching Lion golden. Henry Chantry sat astride a brown horse looking off toward Rorke's Drift at the smoking ruins. He felt the grim line of his lips, and his fingers tightened on the trigger of his rifle. He was sure no one remained alive. He knew about the Impi rituals. Zulus would make sure everyone was dead before returning inland.

He had not arrived in time to save Katie. If only his gelding had not gone lame... If he had not had to stop at Ladysmith to get another horse...

His heart knew an unexpected pang as he thought of Katie van Buren. There were times in the past when he could have loved her as tenderly as any man could love a woman.

Never again, Katie love. May you rest in peace.

He rode the horse back along the Buffalo River toward Natal, where the stream was wide and low and tumbling over rocks. He saw something near the rocks on the other side of the bank and lifted his rifle.

"I see you, Master Henry. It is Jendaya! I have Miss Katie's child!"

Jendaya stood from behind the rock, holding the baby in front of her so that Henry could see she told the truth.

"I see you as well, Jendaya."

She carried the child close against her while wading across the water, coming toward his horse. She stopped and looked up at him, unsmiling, her great dark eyes shiny pools of sorrow. "They are all dead, Master Chantry. I could not save Miss Katie or Daktari and his wife. Impis surrounded Rorke's Drift, thousands of them."

Henry gave a slight nod. "You did well to save the child."

"I cannot keep child. I go to Ulundi."

Ulundi was the great beehive kraal of King Cetshwayo, where he ruled.

Again, Henry nodded. He accepted her decision, though he didn't fully understand it. To return might mean her death. "Why go there?"

"Because Dumaka will go there. I saw him. He was with the Impi."

Dumaka. Her brother. Then he had run away from Sir Julien's estate. Had he done so knowing of this attack on the British? "You know they may kill you."

"Yes." Her face was firm. "I go to turn him to the bright way."

She came up to the side of the saddle and handed him the infant. Henry took the baby as best he could and held it close to his thigh. The baby was crying, both fists and feet moving. *Your little girl is as spirited as you were, Katie. Let us hope she has the same strong will.*

Jendaya handed him a leather glove connected to a canteen.

"Cow's milk. That is how Daktari's wife feed the baby. I have words from Miss Junia. She says bring the baby to Natal. To Lady Brewster at Pietermaritzburg. Lady Brewster is to send the baby to England. To Vicar Edmund Havering."

Henry's brows lowered...and in that moment he decided. He would do it. He would do it for Katie. He would hire a nanny to make the voyage with him to care for the baby. Lady Brewster could help him locate one. Pietermaritzburg was not too far away. If he started out at once he could be there by noon.

Without a word more, Jendaya walked away, in the direction of Zululand, her head high, her shoulders straight. She was humming— but the sound was not like the humming of the Zulu Impi. Jendaya was humming a hymn that Henry had heard before in the vicarage of Grimston Way, as a boy: "Savior like a shepherd lead us, much we need Thy tender care..."

He frowned again, then looked down at the baby. With a final glance after Jendaya, he studied the track of land ahead of him—the track that led back toward Natal.

Katie was dead. The Black Diamond was missing. He still had no idea who had stolen it from him. Katie? Anthony? Julien himself? Maybe even Dumaka before he had run away to come here to join the Impi? If that was so, the Kimberly Black Diamond would be brought to King Cetshwayo!

Henry turned in the saddle and studied the smoking ruins of the mission station. But if Katie had taken the jewel from him in the stables, it was likely buried beneath all that smoking ruin, ashes, and body parts. His mouth thinned. Not even he would sort through gutted soldiers and women to find a diamond. Let it remain buried at the destroyed mission hut. Perhaps that was a fitting tribute.

He looked down at the baby. "I still have three pouches of whites and the map to the gold deposit in Mashonaland, little one. Maybe someday I'll leave it all to you. In memory of pretty Katie. But for now, you and I are going home to England."

Part Two

He that troubleth his own house
shall inherit the wind.

Proverbs 11:29

Chapter Five

Grimston Way, England
Fall 1890

The earthy blush of the autumn afternoon unexpectedly darkened under a sky heavy with the threat of impending rain. Evy Varley was out gathering lush red and gold leaves for Aunt Grace to use for the fall decorations in the rectory chapel when she realized she had been out too long. It was getting toward five o'clock. She had better find Derwent Brown, the curate's twelve-year-old son, and return to the vicarage before they both got a soaking.

Aunt Grace would be worried about her. Recently her aunt, who had raised her from infancy, seemed more anxious and protective than usual, insisting Evy come straight home from school. She knew Aunt Grace hadn't expected her to enter Grimston Wood today to gather leaves in her pinafore.

With a sigh, Evy started back in the direction of the dirt road. The air she breathed was moist and pungent with the odor of earth, roots, and leaves. Here and there, spicy evergreen scents reminded her of Christmas celebrations in the vicarage.

As she hurried through the woods, lightning suddenly struck above the tall fir trees, and Evy felt a shock of alarm jolt through her. Illuminated in the flash of light was a darkened figure, shrouded amid the trunks. Her skin prickled, for her sensibilities told her whoever it was might have been watching her since she had left the dirt road and entered Grimston Wood.

Thunder rumbled, echoing around Rookswood's gothic towers, with their hideous stone gargoyles. Was this cloaked stranger a visitor who had come to see the squire, Sir Lyle Chantry?

Apprehension tingling through her, Evy stood staring toward the trees. She did not run, as that would only bring her deeper into Grimston Wood. If only she had stayed closer to the road where Derwent was getting wood for the rectory stove! Derwent was the assistant to Evy's Uncle Edmund, the vicar. She had been friends with Derwent for as far back as she could remember, and she wished he would suddenly appear with his bag of wood on his back.

The wind picked up and sang in low, mournful tones through the tops of the fir trees. The first large drops of rain plopped against Evy's bare head, where her tawny hair was braided, pinned, and looped. Her dismay led her to release her pinafore, and the bright leaves she had been gathering fell into a pile at her feet. A mocking wind swept down, threatening to scatter them, seeming to laugh at her fears.

The figure stepped from behind the trees and moved toward her. Her heart leaped. She was sure he meant her harm.

"Don't be afraid, I only want to speak to you."

"Wh-who are you, sir?"

He did not answer, but came closer. She took a step backward, then spun to flee. She heard his footsteps behind, muffled on the thick bed of decaying leaves. She began to run, but a hand reached out and caught her, turning her around to face him. She nearly screamed until she noticed he was looking intently at her face, studying her.

Maybe he didn't mean to harm her after all. "I— I must go now. I'm late. My aunt will be worried."

"Your aunt? Is her name Grace Havering?"

Evy nodded, thinking he was not ugly like the gargoyles guarding the gates of Rookswood estate. He was handsome, with light blue eyes and golden hair. His skin was browned by the sun, and his voice sounded strangely different. Accented, somehow. His clothes spoke of wealth, there was something like a diamond pin in his lapel, and a ring on his tanned hand sparkled with white stones.

"Do you like living with the vicar and his wife?"

She nodded. He looked rather sad, she thought. She felt self-conscious at the way he studied her hair and face…the way he frowned at her scuffed shoes and mended school clothes.

"I must go, sir. It gets dark early in the autumn. I promised Mrs. Croft I'd help with the bread."

"Mrs. Croft?"

"She's the cook and housekeeper. She works at the vicarage."

He nodded, and a little smile lifted his lips. "Do you like helping bake bread?"

"Sometimes—if it's sweet bread. Then I can lick the bowl and spoon."

He laughed, and Evy smiled. There was something strong about him and he seemed to like her, even if he did not appear to like her clothes and shoes.

"I will let you go in a minute, then I will walk you back to the road. Tell me, Evy, do you ever visit Rookswood?"

"Rookswood? Oh no, sir." How did he know her name?

"Would you like to?"

She started. Why would he ask such a question?

"Right now—with you?"

"No, not with me. With the squire's children, Arcilla and Rogan."

Such a thing was impossible! And yet…something about this man convinced Evy he could manage the impossible. She shook her head. "Miss Arcilla does not approve of me, and Squire's two sons, Master Parnell and Master Rogan, think girls are a nuisance. They call me the rectory girl."

His mouth curved again. "I see."

She thought he did. "I'd rather visit there with you," she said impulsively, surprising even herself.

"Would you?" There was a look on his face that she took for sadness. "That might be nice. But you see, I am going away today."

"To London?"

"No, not to London." He looked up toward a riding trail, and Evy looked there too as she heard the beat of hooves.

"I must go."

Disappointment flooded her, though she could not imagine why. "Good-bye... Will I see you again?"

"Good-bye, Evy."

He walked away into the darkened trees as the hoofbeats drew nearer. Soon he had disappeared altogether, and Evy stood looking after him.

In the distance she saw a horse coming closer on the riding trail. Its rider was low in the saddle, and the sound of hooves reverberated among the thick trees. The rider must have noticed her from the corner of his eye as he swept past, for he slowed down a short distance later. The majestic black horse, rippling with muscle, reared up on its hind legs. The rider, seemingly unaffected by such a display, managed the reins and turned the animal around. He rode back to where Evy stood, then calmed the horse by patting its sweating neck and talking to it as though it understood everything he said.

Evy recognized the rider as the squire's younger son, Rogan Chantry. Though she had never spoken with him, she had often seen him riding around the village, his Austrian trainer at his side. She also saw him attending Sunday morning services at the vicarage church with the rest of the squire's family and with a new aunt who had recently come to Rookswood from South Africa.

Rogan looked to be around Derwent's age, but he seemed more mature than the curate's son. Evy thought this was due to Rogan's exposure to a wide range of experiences that Derwent, coming from a poor family, did not have. Rogan had the best tutors. His private tutor at Rookswood came with recommendations fit for royalty. Of course, Rogan had little interaction with the village boys, though he did have friends—the sons and daughters of lords and earls, who came from London to visit him.

Evy stood in the knee-high vines and grasses growing beside the riding trail, eying the splendid horse, remembering how Derwent said Rogan Chantry's first love was racing and jumping.

"Are you all right?"

She swallowed at his low question. "Y-yes."

He wore a dark blue riding jacket and breeches of expensive design. He was quite a handsome boy, with glossy black hair below a cocky cap, and his eyes were a rich chocolate brown with eyelashes as long as a girl's. Those eyes seemed as electric as the coming storm, full of boundless, challenging energy. He was conceited and arrogant too—or so Evy had been warned by Mrs. Croft.

"You might have caused me to crash into those bushes." he stated, his words and tone proving Mrs. Croft right. "I could have been thrown or worse—my horse injured. Never walk on a riding trail, little girl!"

What a lordly young buck! Stung, Evy momentarily ignored the manners so meticulously taught her by her aunt and uncle. "I was not even close to the trail, but *you* were riding too fast!"

He chose to ignore her jibe. "Are you with that silly red-haired boy you play with?" He glanced around, as though searching the wood.

"Derwent is not silly."

"Yes, he is. As silly as a Billy goat nibbling happy weed. You had better leave my woods. There is a thrashing storm overhead about to break."

"You do not own Grimston Wood. So I shall come here as often as I like."

Rogan gave her a rather surprised second glance. "The Chantrys own most everything around here...including the woods."

She should be afraid of him. Certainly she should think twice about challenging him. And yet...all Evy felt at the moment was exhilaration. She might not be a squire's daughter, but she had as much right to be in these woods as anyone of noble birth. "You do *not* own everything. You do not own the rectory, nor my cat, nor me."

"I'm sure I do not want your old cat."

"It is not old."

"I'm sure you are not worth much either."

She jutted her chin out at that. "Oh yes I am. My parents were very important."

He considered that boastful challenge for a moment. "Pray tell, then, who were they?"

"Dr. and Mrs. Clyde Varley from South Africa."

"Were they in diamonds?"

"No…"

A smile touched his mouth. "Then I daresay they were not important."

She stamped her foot. "Yes, they were! They were *martyrs*. Killed in the Zulu War of 1879."

He flicked the riding reins across his palm. "I shall find out about that. I have ways to discover things of importance. Where did they die?"

That stopped her for a moment. "I— I do not know."

"No matter. I'll learn all there is to know about your parents and see if you are only boasting."

"In the meantime I shall walk here anytime I please."

A smile suddenly altered the young man's expression, and Evy stared. So this was why Alice Tisdale, the daughter of the village doctor, tittered about *swooning* over Rogan Chantry.

"Walk here anytime you please, and be ready to meet a bear—a big black one."

"Bears? Here?" She scoffed but couldn't help a glance behind her. The action was not lost on Rogan.

"Why do you think I was riding so fast? It must have weighed five hundred pounds and had big white teeth. If I were you, I'd think twice before I came here alone."

Just then, a voice shouted plaintively from the trees closer to the road: "Miss Evy? Are you there?"

"I'm over here, Derwent."

He came through the trees and stopped when he saw Rogan astride the handsome black horse. Derwent's eyes widened, and he had the awestruck expression of one who had come in contact with royalty. He touched three fingers to his forelock.

"Afternoon, Master Rogan. Fancy meeting you here, sir."

Evy could have cuffed Derwent for fawning over the knave before them.

Derwent ambled toward them, a bag of kindling on his back. He was tall for his age, and looked gaunt in his patched breeches. His crop of russet hair was untidy from the wind, and in the nippy air, his rather long nose, salted with freckles, had taken on a rosy color. He was ogling Rogan's majestic horse and paying scant attention to where he stepped. His thick boot must have caught under a root, for he took a tumble, the bag of wood weighing him down in the moldy damp leaves.

Rogan laughed, and Evy shot him a glare before rushing to lift the bag from her friend. "Are you hurt, Derwent?"

"Ooh…I skinned my palms."

"Poor Derwent." She dragged the wood free, casting a glance at Rogan. The knave was simply sitting atop his beast, watching. Heaven knew it would tax him unduly to come help her!

Evy knelt beside Derwent. "You are always stumbling," she said sadly. "Mrs. Croft says you may need spectacles. Can you stand?"

"His feet are too big is all," Rogan observed with amusement. "Why do you baby him? I do not like girls who bleat like sheep."

Evy shot Rogan another glare. "I do not care *what* manner of girls you like, Master Rogan. If you were a gallant boy, you would have climbed down from your fine horse to help me get that heavy wood off him."

Derwent gaped at her as though she had sassed the king. Rogan, too, seemed at a loss. Then his lips thinned and he tapped his heels into the horse's side. It sprang forward and raced in the direction of the road.

"Ought you to have spoken like that to him, d'ye think, Miss Evy? The Chantrys are important folk in Grimston Way."

"A Chantry or not, he is arrogant and conceited. He's been nourished with exceptional manners, you can count on it, so he ought to use them on everyone, not just the sons and daughters of the aristocracy. I'm as good as any of them!"

At this passionate outburst, Derwent gawked at her. "Sure you are. But, well, Master Rogan's a son of the squire, whereas you and me—"

She jumped to her feet. "He treats us like *servants.* I'm not a servant's child. His father did not know the great missionary David Livingstone like my father did. You know how they were both great doctors. Missionaries," she repeated with emphasis.

Derwent ran his long, restless fingers through his russet hair. "I daresay you may be right, Miss Evy. Dr. Livingstone was a great explorer. I would like to go to Africa and explore the dark regions. I might likely find diamonds too."

"Are you able to walk?" She squinted upward, but the trees were thick, and the dark sky was blotted out. "It's soon to pour."

Derwent took a few steps and tested his ankles. "Good as can be. We best dash for it. Say—what happened to those leaves for Mrs. Havering?"

For some reason, Evy did not tell him about the stranger she had met. "The wind blew them all away."

She hurried through Grimston Wood, and Derwent struggled to keep up, loaded as he was with his bag of kindling.

Evy called over her shoulder: "As for being an explorer…Curate Brown will be unhappy if he thinks you're not going to follow his steps in life."

"Aye."

"You are to be a curate just like he. Sons always follow in their father's steps." She paused to let him rest a moment and catch his breath. "Your future waits here in Grimston Way."

"Aye, and yours, too, I'm thinking."

Evy thought of the gentleman who had spoken to her. Who could he have been? Had he been staying at Rookswood?

More lightning streaked across the darkening sky, prodding them onward.

Thick fir trees hugged the side of the road as they emerged from the woods. She could look up the road and glimpse the big stone gates leading onto Rookswood, so named because of the many black rooks that nested in the nearby wood and made such a fuss in the spring with their cawing.

Rookswood, prominent on the hill overlooking the village of Grimston Way, was even more mysterious and interesting to her now that the stranger had spoken to her and asked her if she wished to visit. Somehow the mere question gave her the exciting sensation of being connected to that huge gray-stone mansion and its forbidden halls. At least, she secretly liked to imagine such things, even though she was not likely ever to be invited there.

Cold splashes of rain from the roiling dark sky splashed on Evy's face, shaking her from her daydreaming. She turned away from the mansion and started down the road toward the rectory.

Derwent switched the heavy load to his other shoulder and followed behind. "Your folks were saints all right, Miss Evy, and important ones too, dying the way they did in Zululand years ago, but most folks in Grimston Way agree that no one is as important as Squire and his family."

It was rather a blow for her to hear that it was not her martyred parents who filled the good villagers with admiration, but the local squire, Sir Lyle. Well, she knew far better. No matter how she might hold the squire in respect as master of the village, the ofttimes arrogant Chantrys could not compare with Dr. Clyde and Junia Varley.

"I do not believe you, Derwent Brown! Why, my parents' photograph hangs in the rectory hall. Aunt Grace says I look just like my mum." She threw him a glance. "I do not see Squire's photograph there."

"She said that? I don't see it, myself. If you don't mind my saying so, your hair is—er, prettier. Goldenlike. Your mum's is black, like your aunt's."

Evy stopped on the road and turned to face him.

"So? My hair will turn darker when I get older. What are you trying to say, Derwent Brown?"

His eyes widened. "Say? Why, nothing Miss Evy. Nothing at all. Just that I think you're prettier—but I wasn't suggesting—" He stopped, red filling his freckled cheeks.

The rain splashed cold and startling against her face. The gusts of wind whipped at her hooded cape as a nameless fear suddenly whipped at her heart. Evy turned and ran down the road toward the village green.

Fancy his saying she did not look like her mum's photograph. Her father had light hair didn't he? Of course he did. The photograph showed that he did. And she'd wager his eyes were like hers too, amber with flecks of jade green. Derwent could be so exasperating at times.

Perhaps Rogan Chantry was right after all. Derwent *was* silly.

At that, her conscience smote her. She must not be so hard on Derwent. He was a kind boy, and she knew he would never deliberately say anything about her or her parents to make her unhappy.

By the time she started across the green Evy was thoroughly soaked. Aunt Grace was going to be upset with her again. "You are so willful at times, Evy," she said time and again. "You must learn to be more like Junia."

Evy saw the old sexton persevering across the rectory yard toward the cemetery. The village gravedigger was carrying a large piece of canvas.

He must be on his way to cover the trench he was digging earlier this morning. If he could keep the rain out, he would be able to finish tomorrow. Uncle Edmund said the sexton was the most superstitious person in Grimston Way, even more so than Old Lady Armitage, who hung garlic on her kitchen door to keep the vampires away on Allhallows Eve. According to the good sexton, if the rain interfered with digging a grave, it meant the Grim Reaper on his horse had been delayed.

Evy waved at the old man, smiling. "No Grim Reaper is going to overtake me," she sang out and took off running toward the church and the rectory house.

The soggy lawn sank beneath her shoes as Evy dashed through the wicker gate and up the walkway, through Aunt Grace's heavily pruned rose bushes. Little remained of the summer flower garden except a few worn-out daisies. The seedpods that her aunt had out on a drying screen for the next spring's planting were getting a drenching. Evy put them under the porch before entering the front door, remembering to wipe her shoes on the mat.

Inside the rectory hall she removed her shoes, then stood quite still, looking up at the photographs that hung over the landing at the top of the first flight of stairs.

Evy went to stand and look as she had done unnumbered times in the past. There they were, Dr. Clyde Varley and his wife, Junia, servants of God to the savages in Zululand. A handsome couple. He had grave but kind eyes. "They are amber colored with flecks of jade green," she assured herself in a whisper. "The color just does not show up in the photograph."

And there was her beloved mother, Junia, with her bright, sweet smile and her dark hair pulled back in a knot.

Evy pulled her own wet hair back from her face and tried to wind it into a knot, but it was so thick, heavy, and wavy, that it ended up spilling from her grasp. She gave up and let it fall about her shoulders. "I look just like you, Mum. I know I do."

She reached a hand to touch her mother's portrait, closing her eyes, imagining as she so often did that she could feel her mother's loving embrace across time, across the miles. *Mother is a heroine.* After all, they died as Christian martyrs, in much the same way other Christian leaders laid down their lives throughout the centuries. Evy was learning about many of those heroes in her Sunday studies at the rectory. "But I wish I had your heart for God too. Your gentle spirit. Aunt Grace says I have a willful spirit. But where did I get it? Not from you. From father?"

Evy could hear Mrs. Croft's twanging voice singing in the kitchen. She turned from the photographs and ran down the stairs and to the back of the rectory, where the fragrant smells of hot bread wafted to entice her.

Aunt Grace was out calling on the parishioners with Uncle Edmund, and they must have been delayed by the rain. She would ask Mrs. Croft about it. Evy had learned early that if one wanted to know anything about what was going on in the village, the person to ask was the sexton's wife, Mrs. Croft. She had a full basket of relatives, so it seemed, and they all apparently worked in Rookswood as parlor maids, downstairs maids, grooms in the stables, cooks and washers in the kitchen, or gardeners. Whatever gossip was astir, be it upstairs or down, it was sure to drift down the hill from Rookswood to the big rectory kitchen to Mrs. Croft.

Aunt Grace would scold them for gossiping if she happened to walk in and catch Mrs. Croft talking to one of her kin. Vicar Edmund, too, would point out the inherent evils of the tongue when unyielded to the lordship of Christ. Nevertheless, gossip flourished "like dandelions in the lawn," Uncle Edmund often stated with a resigned sigh. "Proof the devil walks to and fro seeking someone to devour."

Evy carried her wet shoes and stockings, along with her cloak, placed them by the glowing hearth, then went straight to the oversized kitchen. Her gaze traveled the huge stove, long sideboards, and floor-to-ceiling cupboards stashed with dry foodstuffs, dishes, and great beat-up pots and blackened kettles.

Mrs. Croft had been employed by the rectory to help with cleaning and cooking for as long as Evy could remember, and she was as much a member of Evy's family as her aunt and uncle. In some ways Evy felt even closer to Mrs. Croft, since she could tell her almost anything that troubled her, be it unsavory or fair, and Mrs. Croft would speak her mind plainly. Whereas Evy loved and respected her aunt and uncle and was on her best behavior around them, she could take off her shoes and tuck her feet up under her when sitting in the big kitchen chair in the company of Mrs. Croft.

Mrs. Croft was singing in her off-tune voice when Evy came rushing in, her wet hair loose and wild around her shoulders and back. She breathed in the heady smells of hot, steaming cinnamon scones. "Mmm…I'm starving."

"Humph. You keep eating scones before supper, child, and you'll soon turn into one."

Evy took a mouthful. "Mrs. Croft? Derwent says the Chantrys are more important than my parents."

"Does he now? Still trying to become friends with the squire's young son, is he? Dreams of Kimberly diamond mines and gold fields in the wilds of Africa, that's why. But the good curate won't be letting him go on any such adventure, you'll see. 'Tis best. Derwent will make you a good husband, child."

Evy wrinkled her nose. "That cannot be true about my parents. Not if my father knew David Livingstone! The stories about Mr. Livingstone were in all the newspapers. They don't write about Squire."

She chuckled. "You be right there. Leastwise in the society page."

"Then Derwent is wrong."

"Nay, he be right, I am afraid. Folks in Grimston Way don't be caring much about Master Livingstone, but they do be worrying their heads about the doings of Squire."

"But *why?*"

Mrs. Croft's beady eyes twinkled. "Because Squire be the biggest landowner in Grimston Way, that's why. Most folks in the village works for him. That makes Squire Chantry mighty important in the minds of hard working folk. Not *all*-important, mind you. God be all-important and all-powerful. But folks get their wages, you see, from Squire. Them Chantrys own just about everything, including diamond mines in South Africa."

"Then I wonder why the Chantrys come to Sunday service." Evy sniffed her indignation. "Surely they're too important."

Mrs. Croft laughed, clearly tickled, but when Aunt Grace suddenly came through the kitchen door Mrs. Croft coughed to clear her throat. Evy turned for the door.

"Evy, dear"—Aunt Grace Havering's tone was disapproving—"I am ashamed you would say such a flippant thing about anyone."

Evy winced and automatically pulled her shoulders back, hands tucked behind her. She became aware of her disheveled hair, her wet clothes and bare feet. She curled her toes inward and bit her lip.

Aunt Grace took in her condition and sighed. "Darling, you're soaked. And after you were ill all last week. You can be so careless in your behavior sometimes. You worry me."

Evy looked down at her toes. "Sorry, Aunt. The storm sort of crept up on me and Derwent, and before we knew it—it was pouring."

Just then Evy's cat meowed from under the hardbacked chair. She went to it and rubbed the sides of its golden face, then got up and poured it a saucer of milk.

Aunt Grace went to check on the scones, making sure there were enough to send over to Old Lady Armitage. "She has the grippe, poor old dear," she told Mrs. Croft. "Can you add some cold chicken, Mrs. Croft?"

"Surely, Missus Grace. There's plenty. I'll deliver it on the way home."

Evy watched her aunt as the cat drank its milk. Aunt Grace was a great lady. She was ten years younger than her husband, the vicar, and her hair was a shiny blue-black. Evy held fond memories of being rocked to sleep surrounded by the fragrance of the lavender lotion on her aunt's hair. She wore it in a sedate bun at the back of her neck, much as Evy's mother, Junia, wore hers in the photograph. Aunt Grace's eyes were also brown and often appeared to be sad—

"Were you in the woods with Derwent after school, Evy?"

Evy hesitated at her aunt's unexpected question. Should she tell her about the stranger in Grimston Wood? Her aunt was not the sort of person to approve of meeting and exchanging words with strangers, especially a man in the woods. Even if Evy said she had not wanted to speak to the man, she doubted if Aunt Grace would approve.

"Yes, Derwent was gathering wood for the stove, like Mrs. Croft asked. He should have brought it by now." She glanced toward the back porch, where the wood was stashed in a bin out of the weather. "I thought I'd surprise you with autumn leaves for the chapel," Evy went on. "I knew you would be going there tonight to decorate for Sunday worship."

"That was thoughtful, dear. I did want some leaves. You had better get out of those wet clothes right away. You have a propensity for chest colds, as I do."

"Yes, Aunt." Evy left the kitchen, smuggling the half-eaten scone under her pinafore.

The rectory hall was dim at this hour, and Aunt Grace was going about with a candle, lighting the lanterns. She always did this to make things cheery for when Uncle Edmund came home for supper.

Evy paused on the steep stairway and looked back down. She vacillated. Should she mention the exciting stranger and the interesting things he had said to her? Maybe Aunt knew who he was.

Her aunt became aware that she was standing there and looked at her, waiting. She smiled. "Yes, Evy?"

"I was wondering…do many visitors come to Grimston Way to visit Rookswood?"

Aunt Grace tilted her head. "Yes, why do you ask, dear? Did you see anyone arriving today?"

"No, I just wondered. I suppose they might go walking in Grimston Wood if they did, but hardly on a day when it was about to rain."

Aunt Grace was still. Then she came to the bottom stair. Her face above the glowing flame was unsmiling; her brown eyes shimmered like fathomless pools.

"Did you see a stranger in the woods today from Rookswood?"

Evy swallowed. "No—that is, I do not know where he was from. He did know something about Rookswood, though. He asked if I would like to go there and be with Miss Arcilla."

The candle slipped from Grace's hand and crashed to the floor at her feet. It burned brightly for a moment before going out. The wind lashed the front windows with heavy rain, and the leaded panes rattled.

Quickly, Aunt Grace stooped to the spilled wax and tried to scoop it onto the candleholder. "Oh dear, I've made a terrible mess."

Evy knelt beside her to help, but Aunt Grace had already gotten the candle back onto the holder. "I'll need to scrape the rest up later. Evy, who was this stranger, and what else did he tell you?"

Evy stared into her aunt's face. She looked frightened…but why? Her aunt's fear made Evy's own uncertainties leap out of bounds, so that her voice sounded tight and nervous even to her own ears.

"He hardly said anything. Just asked if I—if I was happy. And if I wished to be friends with the squire's children."

"And what did you tell him?"

"I said I was very happy. That Miss Arcilla did not approve of me."

Aunt Grace did not reply—she only looked down at the candle as though she had never seen it before. Suddenly she stood. "I'd better relight this in the kitchen," she said tonelessly and turned away.

"Aunt? I wonder who he was?"

"I do not know." She spoke quietly, her back toward Evy. "Just a stranger, I suppose. I would not give it a second thought if I were you, dear."

Evy watched her until she disappeared into the kitchen. She stood, taking it all in, then turned and went up the stairs to her room.

In the following days the incident seemed to have been forgotten, though Aunt Grace was more thoughtful than usual and kept a most watchful eye on her niece. Evy began to think she may have imagined the meeting in Grimston Wood. Hadn't Aunt Grace always told her when she was small how fanciful she was? Certainly the thunder and lightning and the darkened atmosphere of Grimston Wood could affect her imagination.

Just a few days later Evy had an opportunity to ask her uncle about her parents. It was a Saturday afternoon, and though the sky was clear and the wind chilly, she was happy to be seated beside the vicar in the horse-drawn jingle as he went calling on one of his parishioners for afternoon tea. Evy held the cloth-covered reed basket of pastries that would be given as a gift.

Evy liked Uncle Edmund's quiet, unassuming ways. She liked how his brown eyes were thoughtful, yet merry. He had a shiny scalp fringed with a mane of gray, and he was full at the waist, blaming it on his love of creamed gravies and flaky cobbler crust. He was the only father she had ever known, and she loved him dearly, despite her daydreams of her missionary parents facing down the Zulus.

"Uncle, Mrs. Croft says you went all the way to Capetown, South Africa, to bring me to Grimston Way after my parents were killed. Is that how I got here?"

He flicked the worn leather reins, and the dappled mare quickened her trot along the wooded road. Squirrels scampered up the tree trunks, chattering as they approached.

"You need to be cautious about listening too much to Mrs. Croft.

She's a splendid woman in many ways, and a great cook"—his eyes twinkled—"but she has a carnal propensity to say things best left unspoken."

"You mean about your trip to Capetown?"

"Oh, I would not say that, Evy." He looked down at her as she looped her arm through his. "Actually, I did not voyage to Capetown at all. You see, the mission board in London contacted your aunt and me about Dr. and Mrs. Varley's death. We had no child, so we were delighted to have you come live with us." He bestowed a kindly smile on her.

She beamed. "Then it was the mission board who brought me here to England?"

"Well, no, as a matter of fact, someone else brought you to Grimston Way. He was a friend of…your mother's…of sorts."

Evy looked at him.

"He brought you here to safety, but he is dead now. An unfortunate death at that."

There was something in his tone that she did not understand. "Who was he, Uncle Edmund?"

"I…er, never met him personally. He came from South Africa. I believe he was an explorer searching for gold. But never mind him. Your aunt and I chose you to be our own. You've made our lives very happy, little lamb."

The words warmed Evy inside. "Was I at the mission with my parents when the Zulus attacked?"

"Yes, you were there." Uncle Edmund sounded so sad, Evy was almost sorry she'd asked. "You would have been killed too, but someone rescued you and kept you safe until you were brought on a ship to London."

"I wonder who he was?"

He clucked at the mare. After a moment, he looked down at her. "Sometimes it is best not to ask too many questions, my dear Evy."

That alerted her. "Why, Uncle?"

"Oh, because some things in the past are best left forgotten. Your life is here in Grimston Way now. This is as God intended. You have nothing in South Africa. A fine marriage will be made for you here, and here you will be happy, God willing. My fondest hope is that you and Derwent will grow up to care for each other. You will make a fine vicar's wife, Evy. You know everyone in the village, and you know all the ways of the rectory. It is so sensible, so right." He reached over and put a protective arm around her.

So sensible, so right. But she couldn't quite still the inner question that echoed within her: Wouldn't marrying Derwent, whom she'd known forever, also be a bit…boring?

As the days passed, the story of her parents and how she had been brought to live at the rectory would not relinquish its hold on her imagination—nor did the meeting with the stranger in Grimston Wood. Both events developed into a rather heroic tale, which she began to embellish until the players had become heroes and heroines of the highest order. As for herself, well, Evy imagined she was somehow most special. She would sit and dream of escaping tribal Zulus brandishing long spears, of being chased through the trees toward a great lion with a flowing mane. She had come to Africa to do good and had been misunderstood, and was now fleeing for her life. All was hopeless, but as she fled a stranger would suddenly appear and ask her if she needed refuge in his mansion. Then the stranger turned into Rogan Chantry, who swept her up on his sleek horse…just in time.

Neither Aunt Grace nor Uncle Edmund spoke to her of the matter in the woods, and Evy believed they wanted her to forget that it had ever occurred. She did not think, however, that they had forgotten. She even heard that Uncle Edmund had called at Rookswood to see the squire and ask if he had recently entertained a visitor from South Africa.

Evy frowned. Why would her uncle and aunt think anyone from that wild, dark continent so far from Grimston Way would be watching her picking autumn leaves in the woods?

CHAPTER SIX

Mrs. Croft was nearly purring with excitement when Evy went into the kitchen on Sunday morning. Aunt Grace had departed earlier in order to choose the hymns, so Evy breakfasted in the kitchen without her before walking to the church.

This morning Mrs. Croft's niece Lizzie, an upstairs parlor maid at Rookswood, had come to see her aunt earlier than usual. Evy guessed this meant that the latest news from Rookswood was of an especially tangy flavor. Lizzie's cheeks had pinked with the rouge of excitement as she hovered near the big stove, chattering like a magpie, while Mrs. Croft whipped the bowl of eggs more energetically than usual into a foaming yellow froth.

"So I says, it's more'n her poor health that's the cause of her leaving South Africa without Master Anthony," Lizzie said in a hushed tone. "Lady Camilla Brewster's important, you know? So she wouldn't just up and leave her husband in Capetown, now would she? I mean, no matter how many giant spiders there is, an' heat, an' them naked heathen. So what if the weather be hard on her, I say. She put up with it all those years—since 1879, so it's said. Now, suddenlike, them savages makes her nervous so she can't sleep. It's all a bit too much for the poor woman's delicate constitution. So the Lady leaves Sir Julien Bley's big house and comes home to sweet England. Anyhow"—she reached across the stovetop for a cooling slice of bacon—"that's the tale." She bit into the bacon, her eyes shining like polished blue stones.

"Seems a bit long for the poor lady to learn the weather was draining her health," Mrs. Croft said thoughtfully, pouring beaten egg onto the sizzling fry pan. "If she went out to marry Master Anthony in '79, that was—" She stopped and pursed her lips, thinking.

"Twelve years ago." Evy offered this information cheerfully. She left the table where she'd been listening and came up to the stove beside Lizzie. Evy reached for a second helping of crispy bacon. She looked into Mrs. Croft's sharp, hazel eyes. "My age," Evy concluded and lifted her brows as she enjoyed the bacon.

"Ouch!" Mrs. Croft jerked her hand away from the splattering grease in the fry pan.

"Who are you talking about?" Evy looked from one woman to the other.

"The newcomer to Rookswood." Mrs. Croft frowned at the eggs, which were turning a lovely brown around the edges.

"A newcomer?" Evy became more alert. Her mind went back to the stranger in the woods.

"Lady Camilla Brewster. Lord Montieth wanted her to return to the Montieth estate in London, but she decided to live at Rookswood."

Evy had never heard of Lady Camilla. "Is she a relation to the Chantrys?"

Mrs. Croft poured Evy a cup of tea. "Anthony is a nephew to Squire."

"Not a blood nephew, though," Lizzie corrected as though teaching a pupil.

"Some of the Brewsters married some of the Bleys. And some of the Bleys married some of the Chantrys."

Lizzie grinned, satisfied whenever Mrs. Croft proved herself capable of explaining a muddled detail. "See?" She nodded to Evy. "It be simple, when you know it."

"Still seems a bit odd to me why Lady Camilla wants to come here instead of going to her family home in London," Mrs. Croft remarked.

"Seems so to me, too. It's whispered her marriage to Mister Anthony were never a happy one, and it's worse now." Lizzie lowered her voice. "Has something to do with a terrible scandal. Stolen family diamonds and a baby born on the wrong side of the blanket."

"So that's the way of it," Mrs. Croft said.

Evy drank her sweet tea. No wonder Lady Camilla was unhappy, if she was married to a scamp who fathered a wrong-side-of-the-blanket baby.

"Mister Anthony must have stolen the family diamond too." Mrs. Croft nodded, sure she was right. "He sounds like a scamp all right."

"That be the strange part." Lizzie joined Evy at the kitchen table. "Nobody knows what happened to the diamonds."

Evy spoke up. "Well, what happened to the baby?"

Lizzie stared at her. "Oh, it's got to be with the mum, what else? Mister Anthony probably paid the woman off and sent her away. That's what they usually do, I've heard. But it makes you wonder why Lady Camilla came here, don't it?"

"You mean she thinks the baby is in Grimston Way?" Evy stared at the older woman. How could such a thing happen?

"I'll wager we'll be learning something more before Lady Camilla leaves Rookswood," Lizzie said firmly. "Oh, I know the ways of these things. I seen it happen oh so many times when I worked them five years in London. Thought it'd be kinder here at home in Grimston Way, but them Bleys, Brewsters, and Chantrys—"

"'Tis the diamond that makes me curious." Mrs. Croft dried her worn hands on her faded apron. "If I'm remembering how it was years ago, it seems to me there was something sinister about that rogue, Henry Chantry."

"Aye, he came from South Africa, all right," Lizzie said thoughtfully.

"There was gossip about a Black Diamond," Mrs. Croft mused.

"That were before I worked at Rookswood. I was a girl here in the village back then. I remember him, faintly. A handsome man, he was. Young Rogan looks more like his Uncle Henry than he looks like his father, Squire Lyle."

Captivated, Evy looked from one woman to the other. A missing Black Diamond? Now *this* was exciting!

Lizzie stood and stretched. "Nobody talks about them days at Rookswood anymore. But I do see Master Rogan sneaking about Master Henry's old rooms sometimes."

"A real feisty boy, that one," Mrs. Croft warned, and Evy thought she glanced her way. Did Derwent tell Mrs. Croft how she'd met him in Grimston Woods?

Mrs. Croft just went on. "Curious, all of it. Curious and a bit scary, too, because Master Henry Chantry were a young man when he died the way he did."

Evy looked up from her plate quickly. "How did he die?"

Mrs. Croft and Lizzie exchanged glances.

Evy watched them. "Did he have an accident?"

"Nobody knows for sure." Mrs. Croft sounded grave indeed. "Some say suicide."

There was quite a scene when Lady Camilla Brewster and the three handsome Chantry offspring arrived that morning to attend the chapel service where Uncle Edmund, his small spectacles low on his short nose, would be reading his sermon. Evy wondered why neither the squire nor Lady Honoria was with them.

Lady Camilla must have been quite attractive when younger, for even now there was a certain prettiness about her, but it seemed any contentment with life had long ago been washed from her heart-shaped face. She entered, with Miss Arcilla, Rogan, and Parnell trailing behind. Many heads turned in their direction. The boys swaggered down the aisle to take their grand family pew at the front of the chapel, situated beneath a stained glass window of the Good Shepherd. Uncle Edmund once said the window was given to St. Graves by the squire's great-great grandfather, Earl Simon Chantry.

At fifteen, Parnell looked bored with Uncle Edmund's sermon as though he already knew more than the vicar.

Rogan, now thirteen, had managed to smuggle a book under his fancy jacket and sat reading it, his expression sober. Evy had once learned from Derwent, who had seen the book, that it contained maps of unexplored Mashonaland, South Africa, with tales about gold deposits. Evy cast Rogan a furtive glance. She always sat in the pew beside Aunt Grace, and he would know that, having seen her here often enough. She thought that the ice may have thawed between them by now, since two days had passed since their meeting at the horse trail. Yet, though she glanced his way several times, he seemed not to notice her. Was he ignoring her?

Evy saw Alice Tisdale, her strawberry-blond curls dancing about her face, and some of the other girls in the village glancing toward Rogan and Parnell. From the silly look on Alice's face, she might have swooned if either of the boys looked her way and smiled. The girls all dreamed of Cinderella romances.

Evy gave a soft snort. Silly twits. Fairy tales never came true.

She wished heartily that Rogan would cast her a glance just so he could see that she was one girl who was not watching him. She lifted her chin a little higher.

Arcilla fussed with her lace-trimmed frock. At twelve, she already had a propensity toward what Mrs. Croft called a "boy-happy" attitude. Not that any of the boys in the village would ever be suitable for Miss Arcilla Chantry. Like her brothers, Arcilla's marriage would be arranged for her. Most likely the three Chantry children would one day marry those from titled families in London—or else wealthy cousins from South Africa. After all, one had to keep the diamond dynasty in the clan.

Arcilla looked about, and Evy was sure she wanted to see what the other village girls were wearing. Just then her blue eyes fell on Evy.

She thinks she's a peacock, and I'm just a little brown wren. Naturally, girls from the families of farmers, merchants, gardeners, and servants, as well as the vicar's niece, would not be wearing frocks that could compare in the slightest with Arcilla's fine wardrobe. Oddly enough, Evy had the impression that this comforted Arcilla.

Poor Uncle Edmund! Was anyone listening to his sermon? Ashamed, she sat straighter in the hard-backed pew and concentrated on his message.

After the service Evy spoke with several of her friends from the village. "Did you see what Arcilla was wearing? Oh, to own a frock like it."

"She always dresses as if she's going to Whitehall instead of church. Mum says she only does it to be noticed."

"What do you think she'll wear next Sunday?"

"Silk." Emily, the blacksmith's daughter, sighed. "Pink. I always dream of owning a pink silk frock."

"Silk is impossible to wash." Evy crossed her arms. "I do not want silk." But even as she spoke, she felt a tiny nudge deep within. Was that completely true?

"Arcilla will wear velvet. Soft blue velvet." Meg, the daughter of the head groom at Rookswood stables, all but crooned the pronouncement. She ran her palm along her rough cotton pinafore as though she could feel the lush velvet on her callused fingers.

"You cannot wash velvet either." Evy said it in an effort to comfort her friend. "Cotton is…more sensible. We must be sensible, you know."

"Well, whatever it is she wears next week, it will make her look beautiful." Meg's sigh was deep.

"Every boy will stare at her as goggled-eyed as an old frog in Grimston's pond." Emily grimaced. "Like our silly brothers do."

"Milt has a terrible crush on her," Meg said with sadness.

"So does my brother Tom. As if Arcilla would *ever* look at him in his overalls. The Chantrys will have picked an earl for her to marry."

"I would not *have* an earl." Evy lifted her chin a fraction as she spoke.

"My brother insists she *did* look at him," Meg said.

"The boys' staring at Arcilla is no more silly than every girl in the village gaping at the squire's two sons." Evy shook her head. "Did you see Alice staring? I nearly laughed at her."

"As if Rogan would pay her any attention."

"Well, I could have told you Arcilla would come wearing the latest London fashion," Emily told them. "Mum says a new seamstress from

London arrived at Rookswood in the Chantry coach. Miss Hildegard, her name is. She is there to make Arcilla, Lady Honoria, and Lady Camilla new winter wardrobes. Mum was cleaning the sewing room when Miss Hildegard arrived. She had all manner of cloth—velvet, taffeta, and silk from India."

Meg and Evy moaned.

All this was fresh on Evy's mind when she returned to the rectory. The next day she was with Mrs. Croft in the kitchen learning how to cook and bake, and how to preserve jams and watermelon rinds in cinnamon. Cooking was part of Evy's schooling so that one day, when she became a vicar's wife, she would be able to bring food to the sick and infirm among the parishioners.

It was fully expected that Derwent would become curate after his father, and one day a vicar. In another few years he would be going away to divinity school in London. Marriage to Derwent would let Evy continue on at the rectory in a comfortable lifestyle. The idea was sensible and practical.

Evy grimaced. If only she felt some excitement when she thought about Derwent! He was like a comfortable shoe. Pushing the disloyal thought aside, she told Mrs. Croft how Rogan and Parnell ignored her and the other girls.

"As though we are a necessary evil to be tolerated."

"You wait a few years." A slight smile tipped Mrs. Croft's lips. "Sudden like, they'll be whistling a different tune. If they be anything like Squire or them before him, they'll be hanging about the girls of Grimston Way like ants around a honey pot. Every decent girl who wants herself a good husband had better watch her reputation. Squire thinks his boys can do no wrong. So if there's mischief to happen, who do you think will be blamed? It won't be Master Parnell or young Rogan—or that sister of his neither, for that matter," she said, showing Evy how to mash the berries for pound cake. "That young Master Rogan has wanderlust, he does, and he is too comely for his own good."

Evy licked the berry juice from her finger, and Mrs. Croft gently slapped at her hand. "Bad manners, missy."

"What does *comely* mean?"

"In the young master's case, pleasing to a girl's eye. Mark my words, little one. That means be cautious of him. He holds promise of becoming a rascally rogue, if you go wanting my opinion."

Evy smiled. Mrs. Croft would give her opinion whether anyone asked for it or not.

"He fits 'is name, I daresay."

Rogan…rogue. Yes, the words even sounded something alike, Evy decided.

Mrs. Croft nodded her gray head. "Aye, but he'll still rise above Parnell, I'm thinking. There's talk about, saying it'll be Rogan who inherits Squire's title, not Master Parnell. Lizzie's heard tales about young Parnell wanting more diamond shares in the Kimberly mines in place of the title and Rookswood lands. Don't know how this will affect Master Rogan, though."

Evy supposed she meant that Rogan, too, wanted to go to South Africa when he grew up, and would not look favorably on remaining in Grimston Way to rule Rookswood lands. However, since most of the villagers living in Grimston Way could trace their lineage back to the time of the Crusades, it seemed that if anyone even so much as wished to journey afar, they were accused of suffering from the reckless disease of wanderlust. Derwent also talked of adventure in faraway places, yet he was even more likely than Rogan to be denied his dreams.

Evy stared down at the bowl in her hands and sighed. Was there no one who could live life the way he—or she—wished?

October blew in on a chilly wind, bearing change in more than just the seasons. The village doctor, Dr. Tisdale, came through Rookswood's gate in his coach and called on Vicar Edmund. The vicar was needed up at Rookswood right away, he said. The long-ailing Lady Honoria, the squire's wife, had passed away in her sleep the night before.

A few days later the sky was roiling with clouds, and the fall wind shook away the few remaining leaves on the chestnut trees. Almost the entire village of Grimston Way lined the road from Rookswood to St. Graves chapel as the Chantry coaches made the slow procession down to the cemetery.

Because the vicar was Evy's uncle, she was permitted to attend. The Chantry family was all in black, including Miss Arcilla. She wore a veiled hat, as did Lady Camilla, who held the young girl's hand. Miss Hortense, the governess, was there too, wiping her eyes on a handkerchief and no doubt recalling being governess to Honoria when she was but a little girl in Capetown.

Parnell Chantry was very somber, as was Rogan, but neither shed tears the way Arcilla did. For the first time ever, Evy's heart went out to the girl. *So she's human after all.*

Evy watched Rogan put his arm around his sister's shoulder when she began to cry, and a warmth filled her. How splendid of him to care for his sister that way. He seemed protective of Arcilla, much more so than Parnell, though one would have expected the older brother to take the lead. Evy recalled what Mrs. Croft said about how the squire's title would be given to Rogan. That was odd, but then, so were many of the details about the Chantrys.

Evy was heartened when the service was all over and they could join the unhappy procession back to the rectory. When Aunt Grace went ahead to check on the tables of food waiting inside the rectory hall, Evy edged up alongside the vicar in his black robe.

"Uncle Edmund," she whispered, "did she go to heaven?"

"My dear child!"

"But Uncle, it's important where Lady Honoria went to."

He smiled and his eyes danced as he reached over to place his loving arm around her shoulders. "You make me a happy man, Evy. Yes, it is all-important where Lady Honoria went. And I feel confident, after having spoken with her many times on the subject of Christ our Savior, that Honoria Chantry is safe in the arms of Jesus."

Evy's relief escaped on a sigh. "Good. Now I can enjoy all the food everyone brought to the rectory."

The vicar threw back his head and enjoyed his laughter, then stopped quickly and cleared his throat when Miss Hortense, the retired governess, shot him a shocked glance over her pince-nez.

There was much food waiting in the hall provided by Rookswood servants, who had been sent down earlier that morning to get everything ready.

Evy marveled when she saw roast ducklings and partridges, a ham, and a big leg of lamb. There were breads, butter, pies, persimmons, and pears. But Sir Lyle, looking most unhappy, stayed only long enough to accept condolences from some of the villagers. Lady Camilla went back to Rookswood with Arcilla and the Chantry sons. Evy felt compassion for them. She had contemplated telling Rogan of her sympathy, but the opportunity had not come. Once again, he had not even glanced her way.

The death of a family member was such a lonely time, but Honoria was not lonely now. She was basking in the joyful presence of God.

Sir Lyle shook hands with the vicar and thanked him for his comforting words of sympathy, then he, too, departed.

The parishioners stayed, and after a while the mood cheered a little. Everyone ate so much that Mrs. Croft teased that no one should be able to eat again for another week, so she ought to take a week off from cooking and go home to clear out her old summer's garden and get it ready for the coming winter.

There was plenty of food left over. The wives all lined up to receive portions, commensurate to the size of their families, to take home. Meg's family got the most, while old Miss Armitage, who was all alone, received the least. She was quite dour about it and did not mince her words to Aunt Grace.

"Hark! An old lady who cannot be waiting on herself at every turn ought to receive a wee bit more. I'll be turning ninety in December."

Evy watched Aunt Grace add their own take-home portion to Miss Armitage's basket, assuring the old lady she was absolutely correct.

Evy sighed and nudged Derwent. "There goes my last hope for a piece of apple tart."

He carried Miss Armitage's basket outside, then drove her to her bungalow before the rains came.

That night Evy prayed especially long for Rogan, Arcilla, and Parnell, who now, like herself, had no mum. She wondered about Lady Camilla Brewster.

The fall rains lingered for several days, making everything chilly, damp, and morosely gray.

A week later Evy was sitting with her fellow students in the rectory hall, which was being used for a schoolroom. Along with her were Meg and her brother Milt, Emily and her brother Tom, Derwent Brown, and Alice Tisdale, the doctor's only child. As Evy sat before her open workbook, Curate Brown spoke.

"It seems Miss Evy is dreaming of faraway places. Do pay attention and begin your Bible lesson."

"Yes, Mr. Brown." Evy felt her face turn hot and she read the parable of the rich fool in the gospel of Luke.

"What happened to the rich fool?" Curate Brown studied the small class when Evy had finished reading.

Milt held up his hand. "He built himself bigger barns to hold it all. No sooner did he have himself a pile, then he up and croaked. He left it all in the barn and never saw it again."

"Just like Lady Chantry," Tom whispered, grinning at Evy. "You know where she went? Deep down below!" He used a deep, baritone voice to say this. He winked, and everyone chuckled except Evy.

"You should not talk so flippantly, Tom," Evy said. "You are gleeful about Lady Honoria's passing because she had so much and you have so little. But you should feel sorry for Arcilla, Parnell, and Rogan Chantry. How would you like to lose your mum?"

"Little Miss Vicar," Tom teased.

"She feels more sorry for Rogan, don't you, Evy?" Alice Tisdale's strawberry-blond hair was wrapped around her head in a braid. Her skin was sallow, and her small mouth puckered. Tom once said she looked as though she had been weaned on a sour pickle.

Evy blushed at Alice's taunt, and the other girl looked positively gleeful that she'd made Evy uncomfortable.

Derwent came to Evy's rescue. "Lady Honoria was a kind and Christian woman. She always came to Sunday services when she was feeling well. It seems her faith in Jesus was more than doing church rituals"—he fixed Alice with a hard stare—"which is more than I can say for others."

When Alice turned away, her cheeks a bright pink, Evy gave Derwent a grateful smile. Rogan wasn't the only one who could be protective. Perhaps life with Derwent would not be so boring, after all.

Three weeks after Honoria Chantry's funeral, Evy watched as Aunt Grace sat in the small rectory office, poring over a pile of papers. Were they debts? Evy wasn't sure, but she had noticed of late that Aunt Grace was mulling over many concerns, far more than the servants' gossip. Maybe Uncle Edmund's health had something to do with her aunt's worries. He had a heart condition that Dr. Tisdale was treating and, after the funeral, had taken to bed with angina. He was still in a weakened condition, so it had been left to the curate, Mr. Brown, to give the Sunday sermons in the chapel.

Toward the end of November, Sir Lyle left Grimston Way for Dover to board a ship for faraway Capetown. Rumor had it that he was to see his stepbrother, Sir Julien Bley. Would he also see Anthony Brewster? Maybe he was trying to bring him and Lady Camilla back together again.

Later Alice Tisdale claimed that Arcilla had needed a long bed rest. "Arcilla's even more unhappy now that her Papa has left. She doesn't improve."

"How do you know?" Evy asked as they walked to the classroom where Curate Brown waited.

A look of smug pride came to Alice's face. "Lady Camilla asked my father if he would send me up to Rookswood to be a companion to

Arcilla. Of course, since I'm the daughter of the village doctor, I'm considered quite suitable. I went last week to read to Arcilla. The house is so grand. Her room is pink and white, and she has dozens of slippers and frocks." Alice's mouth turned up at the corners. "I even saw Rogan and Parnell. They both spoke to me. 'Good morning, Miss Alice,' Parnell said."

"Indeed? Did you faint dead away?"

Alice's smile vanished. Her eyes turned hard. "You're jealous, Evy. And you the vicar's niece, too. You should be better than the rest of us. That's what my mama says."

Your mama says too much about everyone, Evy wanted to tell her, but of course she did not. Alice would run home and tell Mrs. Tisdale, who would then come calling on Aunt Grace.

Besides, Alice was right. Evy *should* be nicer than Alice because her parents had been missionaries and because her uncle was the vicar. She tried to control her tongue thereafter, but trying hard in her own strength did not always work.

When she got home that day, Evy found Aunt Grace in the vicar's office and told her about Arcilla Chantry growing worse.

Aunt Grace leaned back against the desk. "I daresay it has not been easy on her, poor child. Losing her mother, and now Sir Lyle has left for Cape."

"Mrs. Croft says it seems like a curse is on Rookswood. Another death in the family would convince her it was so."

"Nonsense."

"Aunt, who is Master Henry?"

Aunt Grace looked at her sharply. "Why do you ask?"

"Some people say he killed himself."

Aunt Grace yanked off her apron and threw it down on the chair. "I'm going to have a talk with Mrs. Croft."

"It— It really was not Mrs. Croft, but Lizzie."

"Ah, yes, the all-knowing eyes and ears at Rookswood." Aunt Grace sighed, seeming to forfeit any hope of stopping the gossip, and sank tiredly into the chair. "There is no big secret, Evy. Master Henry

Chantry was the squire's brother. He came to Rookswood from Capetown after the Zulu War. He fought in the battles. I think he was quite heroic, but I never met him. He was here in Grimston Way only about a year before he…he met with an accident. Now, enough chatter. I'm taking the jingle out to see Miss Armitage. Want to come with me? Better bring your hooded cloak, dear."

"Yes. Is… Was Master Henry Rogan's blood uncle?"

"Yes. He was somewhat of an explorer in South Africa. He was fairly wealthy, and he never did remarry after his wife Caroline died on one of his expeditions. He favored Rogan and left him everything he owned."

Evy thought of the diamonds, the Black Diamond. Was that how Master Henry made his money? She did not dare mention that to her aunt.

"That means Rogan is going to be a very wealthy man one day, doesn't it?"

Aunt Grace nodded. "Since he will receive a great inheritance from his father as well, yes." She looked over at her husband's desk, where she'd been going over some papers. The mention of money seemed to deepen the worry lines around her eyes. "Ah, well."

Toward the holidays an event took place that changed Evy's life. It was December, and some of the ladies were helping plan for the Christmas festivities at the rectory. Aunt Grace was teaching Evy to weave pine boughs for the garland that would decorate the chapel, and Mrs. Croft was telling the sexton in a low voice to put more pine boughs in the cemetery on the grave of Lady Honoria—"and some on the gate for the late great gentleman, Master Henry Chantry."

At the mention of Master Henry, Evy looked up, breathing in the pungent fragrance of pine. She had not forgotten what Mrs. Croft said about a curse on Rookswood, or that it somehow centered around Master Henry's death. The idea of a curse was just superstition; Evy knew it was foolish, but Mrs. Croft wanting her husband to add extra pine to the gate in memory of Henry Chantry's death convinced her that Mrs. Croft did not think so.

"Better to appease Master Henry," Evy heard Mrs. Croft whisper to her husband.

The tall, thin sexton nodded and ambled away from the rectory yard in the direction of the church cemetery.

Evy stood, about to follow him, intending to ask about Master Henry. But just then the Chantry coach rolled up, as sleek, black, and shiny as anything Evy had ever seen. Mr. Bixby, the footman, always shined it with a cloth, and the yard boy polished the wheels.

Everyone ceased what they were doing, as though royalty had just arrived from London. All eyes were on Mr. Bixby as he climbed down from the driver's seat, his shoulders straight and head high, then opened the coach door.

Though everyone knew Lady Camilla sat inside, they stared at the coach door, breath held, waiting.

Lady Camilla stepped down from the carriage, holding Mr. Bixby's arm. She was gowned in many yards of black satin, and her skin look like purest ivory.

She is prettier than I thought. Evy admired the woman's golden hair, which was so artfully arranged. Her large eyes were the color of slate, and Evy started when they looked directly at her.

Her heart jumped. *Why is she staring at me like that?*

"Good afternoon, Vicar. Mrs. Havering." Lady Camilla's smile was gentle. "I should like to speak with you in the rectory, if you have a few minutes to spare?"

Naturally everyone had minutes to spare for Lady Camilla Montieth Brewster, but Evy thought it rather gracious of her to ask rather than expect everyone to stop what they were doing.

"By all means, Lady Camilla, how good to see you." Uncle Edmund's smile was genuine.

"We were just about to have afternoon tea," Aunt Grace told her with an equally charming smile, and Evy had the clear impression that her aunt liked Lady Camilla.

"Mrs. Croft and Evy have baked fresh scones. I do believe they made your favorite, lemon curd."

Camilla looked over at Evy, and Evy smiled. When Lady Camilla looked quickly away, Evy felt her smile slip. *Is there something about my appearance that bothers her?*

She noticed there was no one else inside the carriage. Rogan must have stayed at Rookswood with Parnell. Parnell had been allowed to return to a prestigious school he attended in London after his mother's death, and was now home for the Christmas holidays. Rogan was to join him at school after the New Year. It would seem a little more deserted once they were gone to London. Evy often saw Rogan riding by on his horse. He would glance her way, pretending not to see her, but she knew he did. Once he had slowed down, but then had ridden on toward the woods, his dog close behind.

Something important must have brought Lady Camilla to see the vicar. Evy decided to help Mrs. Croft bring the tea tray and platter of warm scones into the rectory parlor. Afterward she lingered, hoping to hear what was said.

"I daresay, Vicar, I am at wits' end with worry," Lady Camilla was saying in her quiet voice. "I simply must try everything if Arcilla is to be cheered up. My husband's uncle, the squire, left me in charge of Rookswood and the children while he is away in Capetown. You did receive my message about Miss Evy?"

Evy's gaze swerved to Lady Camilla.

Uncle Edmund placed one hand at his heart. "I can assure you that my niece is a very sensible girl and will cause you no undue difficulty."

"Evy is at the top of the curate's class," Aunt Grace added. "Mrs. Tisdale, the good doctor's wife, also assures me Evy has a great love of and gift for music. It is our ambition to send her to Parkridge Music Academy when she is older."

What was this about? Evy's heart beat faster with anticipation.

"Yes, your niece seems a lovely girl," Lady Camilla was saying as though Evy were not standing right there. "She is quite sensible, indeed, Vicar, I'm well aware of that. I have noticed her in Sunday service. Very well behaved; she is not a little runabout. I have heard no ill talk of her in the village."

Had Lady Camilla been inquiring about her?

"Naturally, everything will depend on what Arcilla thinks. It was a great disappointment to me when she became displeased with Miss Alice. You do know how children fuss and quarrel so. Arcilla sent Alice home last week in tears. Alice has since apologized to Arcilla, but Arcilla has refused to let her visit." She looked at Evy for the first time, and it seemed Lady Camilla's eyes were bright and inquisitive. "Arcilla is willing to have Miss Evy come in Alice's place. Arcilla is very careful about her acquaintances, as you know."

"I daresay," Aunt Grace replied as expected of her.

"If they do get along as I am hoping, I, too, shall be very pleased."

Evy's heart quavered. Rookswood. She was going up to Rookswood, just as the stranger in Grimston Wood had said she might!

Aunt Grace did not look as pleased as Evy would have expected. Her hands were interlocked on her lap and her knuckles were white.

When Lady Camilla departed, Aunt Grace laid a hand on Evy's shoulder. "Dear, I need to discuss this with your uncle in private. Can you help Derwent with the Christmas boughs?"

"Yes, of course."

But as Evy left the parlor, she caught her aunt's quiet question to her husband.

"Oh, Edmund. Do you think this is wise?"

Evy hesitated.

"Perhaps it will be good for the child." Uncle Edmund sounded concerned as well.

"I wonder…"

Knowing she shouldn't dally any longer, Evy hurried out of the room. The next day the decision was announced at breakfast. Uncle Edmund looked at Evy over his lowered spectacles and told her she would become a companion to the ailing Miss Arcilla. Three afternoons a week, beginning on Saturday, she would walk up the hill to Rookswood to visit.

Evy was thrilled. At last, she would go inside Rookswood!

Later that night, Evy slipped from her bed and went to the window. She could just make out part of Rookswood mansion and saw lights glowing in the rooms like golden jewels. *Like diamonds...* She leaned her forehead against the cool glass. *I am going up to the house of diamonds.*

CHAPTER SEVEN

The old sexton, Hiram Croft, was digging a grave when Evy entered through the cemetery gate the next morning.

"Good morning, Mr. Croft."

He was older than Mrs. Croft, very tall, with hunched shoulders and a lined face. It was not polite to say, but Mr. Croft reminded her of one of the rooks that made such a racket in the trees. The birds were noisy now and jumping from branch to branch.

He leaned on his shovel at the bottom of the trench he was digging.

"Mornin', Miss Evy. What brings you here?"

"The ghost of Master Henry Chantry," she said with a teasing smile. "I thought you could tell me all about it."

He grinned. "I remember Master Henry, I do. He used to ride by on a big gold gelding. Was the second golden horse he owned. Lost the first one in Zulu country, he said. He'd ride himself all over the village seeing how folks was. The women all swooned for him. Handsome rascal—some of his blood be in young Rogan Chantry, I'm thinking. More'n likely Henry had himself less concern for how folks was doing and more interest in dallying with the ladies than much else. Master Henry were a busy man when it come to that."

He began digging again. Evy stood on the edge of the trench looking down. "How did he die?"

"Now, missy, don't you go asking me that sort of thing. You ask the good vicar."

"I have. Uncle Edmund says gossip is a sin."

"Aye, so it is. A wise man, the vicar."

She held her hands behind her back. "It doesn't seem to me that my asking how Master Henry died is gossip."

"Well, that do seem a bit true, but when questions are whispered about how a man killed himself…well, then, things change quicklike."

"So it is true? The dark secret is that Master Henry did actually kill himself?"

He cocked one eye up at her. "Shot himself in the noggin, it's said." He tapped the side of right temple. "Right inside Rookswood. Third floor. And on Michaelmas, too. I daresay that will be a mark against him."

The morning seemed darker and somehow threatening. She realized she was holding her breath. Then—"But why would Master Henry shoot himself up there?"

"Why not? Better'n the first floor."

"I don't mean *that*. I mean, it seems a bit odd that a man as important and rich as Henry Chantry would kill himself. From what I've heard he was an adventurer, a bold man, unafraid of most things."

He leaned on his shovel again. "Aye, he was that. Odd, maybe so. I've seen me a whole lot odder things in my time."

"Like what?" She sat down on the edge of the trench, letting her high-button shoes dangle over the side. She wished she had a pair of pretty grown-up slippers like Arcilla wore.

"Well…one foggy Allhallows Eve, I come out here to hang the lighted lantern on the gate over there—so folks could come like they always do and leave things for the ghosts—and lo and behold, I saw the ghost of ol' Henry wandering around here just as plain as though he were alive and kicking. Makes me wonder if Henry killed himself, or if it was more violent than even that."

Evy swallowed, and a chilling breeze made her skin crawl. "You do not mean"—the word lodged in her throat—"he was…*murdered?*"

He looked up at the rooks with a faraway gleam in his eyes. "So some say."

"But who would *do* such a wicked thing?"

"That were long ago, missy. Who's to say? Only Henry's ghost can tell us."

"Oh, Mr. Croft, there aren't any ghosts. Uncle Edmund says ghosts are moldy suspicion from the Dark Ages. Miss Armitage is the oldest person in Grimston Way—nearly ninety—and Derwent vows he saw garlic hanging at her kitchen door. When he asked her why she hung it there, she said to keep vampires away. That's quite silly you know. When a man dies without believing in Jesus, he goes to a place to wait until God judges him. But those who believe go at once to heaven. So if all are accounted for, how can there be ghosts?"

"True enough." He removed his cap and scratched his gray locks, then shoved the cap back on. "I still think there be ghosts."

She smiled. "That is because you *want* to believe it."

He set his jaw. "Seen Master Henry plain as day. He be restless. So he wanders, seeking justice against the kin who killed him."

Evy stared at the man. "You don't think so! His own kin?"

"Aye. Who else coulda done him in?"

"Maybe a thief crawled in his window."

"Ha! You take another look at them tall windows. Why, you'd need to be a rook to fly to one of 'em."

"The bottom windows?"

"Locked, more'n likely."

"But who would that kin person be? And why?" Then it occurred to her. Of course! "The Black Diamond?"

Mr. Croft's eyes fairly sparkled. "Ah…so you know about it too, eh? Could be that diamond. Again, maybe not. Who's to say? Vicar be a good man, but even *he* don't know everything. Spirits wander."

"Human spirits can't wander after death, Mr. Croft. Maybe it was fog you saw instead. You merely thought you saw some unearthly thing wisping about."

"It were foggy that night, all right. So thick and white that swirls wrapped 'round me like snakes." He took a shovelful of dirt and tossed it, then looked up at her.

"There you have it, Mr. Croft. That's what you saw, plain old fog.

You know how thick it can become in autumn. So thick you can hardly see ahead of you."

At the amusement in his eyes, Evy wondered if all this was just one of his jokes.

"Think so, eh?" He shrugged. "Well, you go ahead and think that. Ye'll sleep better, Miss Evy. And Vicar won't be after me for filling your ears with nonsense. But I knows what I saw. And it were a ghost."

"I know a better ghost story, Hiram, but better not tell her more."

Evy nearly jumped out of her skin as the deep voice from behind her went on.

"The rectory girl is probably like Arcilla. My sister squeals and dives under the bed at such tales, and *she* probably does too, especially on foggy nights."

She turned her head to find Rogan Chantry standing by the oak tree, his dog on a leash beside him. Rogan wore a fancy black coat and trousers with gold buttons. His hair was dark and glossy below his cap, and one wave fell across his forehead. He walked up to Evy, and they looked at each other. He took in her scuffed, high-button leather shoes and the plain gray cotton skirt and pinafore she wore. As he studied her, she realized her pinafore was splashed with berry jam from the kitchen. She had not cared about that until this moment. She blushed. His eyes came to hers, and the corners of his mouth turned up as though she amused him.

Evy suspected he was as difficult to get on with as Arcilla. Not only did his father dote on him, but so did the old governess, Miss Hortense. Evy brushed her pinafore, but it did no good. She gave a furtive glance at his shoes. They were shiny—most likely bought in London. His trousers and jacket were of expensive wool, as was his cap. He probably received just about everything his heart could wish for. The leash on his red Irish setter was a shiny silver. The dog, too, seemed to dote on Rogan. It sat humbly at his feet, gazing up with adoring brown eyes.

Evy resisted feeling small and unimportant. Instead, she lifted her chin and folded her arms. "I do not squeal." She swung her high-button shoes. "Nor am I silly."

His smile held a sparkle of mischief. "You would squeal if I took you to my uncle Henry's crypt on Rookswood." Rogan's tone was full of challenge. "My sister is too afraid to go. *All* girls are afraid of everything, is that not so, Buster?" He patted the big dog's shiny head, and the beast whined as if to agree. Rogan's eyes danced as he looked down at Evy. "You see?"

Hiram Croft chuckled, and Evy's fingers itched to cuff that smug grin from Rogan's face. "I would *not* be afraid."

Clearly Rogan did not believe her, but he smiled. "Fine, then, I will take you there. When you come to Rookswood to see Arcilla. If you squeal, I win. Then you will have to do some task to please me."

"What if *I* win?"

The smug smile deepened. "You will not."

Her foot swung faster. "Maybe I will. Then you must do a task for *me*. I will think of one."

"No."

Evy stared at him. "That is not fair."

He shrugged, dismissing the subject, and turned to Mr. Croft.

Evy fumed.

"Now, Hiram, I do not see how you could see my uncle Henry's ghost here in the cemetery when he is not buried here."

"Eh, what? Er, you got me there, young Master Rogan." He chuckled again.

"Unless... Yes, that must be it—if he was riding his gold horse through the cemetery that night when you saw him. My father says his brother Henry was a wanderer."

"Aye, that must be it, all right. Master Henry were on that horse of his."

Evy folded her arms. "Now you are exaggerating, as Uncle Edmund says you do, Mr. Croft. I do not think you saw Master Henry at all, and I am *not* afraid of his crypt." She clambered to her feet, brushing the grass from her skirt.

Rogan shrugged, still smiling. "Never mind his showing up here. My uncle's ghost haunts the third floor of Rookswood Manor all year long. That is where he died. So he is not likely to be here in the cemetery anyway."

Mr. Croft grinned. "I won't be arguing with ye."

Rogan looked at Evy as if to make sure she did not challenge him either. She did not. Instead, to give vent to her miffed feelings, she said, "I will wager those are not real gold buttons." She was staring at his jacket.

"What makes you think they are not?"

"Because Lady Camilla is too wise to let you wear solid gold buttons when you are outdoors riding or walking Buster. You would lose one, and then what?"

Rogan smiled indulgently.

"I think Miss Evy has you there, Master Rogan. If ye did lose one and it were gold, then we'd all be out treasure hunting."

"Finders are keepers," Evy said with a grin. "Because I would find it before anyone."

"No, you would not."

He was positively insufferable! "Why wouldn't I?"

"Because it would be a small chance indeed for anyone to find it, even me."

And of course if *he* could not find it, no one could. How like a Chantry to think that of himself.

"Unless it caught the sun's rays." Rogan snapped his fingers, and Buster lay down. Rogan snapped them again, and the dog stood. "I have taught him a lot of tricks." He folded his arms across his chest and looked down at Mr. Croft. "I am going to find my own gold mine in South Africa. Just like my uncle Julien found a diamond mine in Kimberly. I could find a new diamond mine, but I want to do something different. So I will find gold. Lots. So much gold that I will have solid gold buttons on my jacket. And when I do, I will give you a small bagful, Croft."

"What about me?"

He pursed his lips and studied Evy. "We will see."

She had had enough. "I am not dumb. I would know what to do

with it. As for gold buttons— I daresay, it is a waste to have them. Do you not think so, Mr. Croft?"

Though Mr. Croft chuckled, he would not answer.

Well, she was not afraid to speak her mind. She met Rogan's gaze. "You would only be showing off wearing solid gold buttons."

"Evy!"

She turned to see Mrs. Croft, who was clearly dismayed to think Evy would speak with such flippancy to a Chantry. Mrs. Croft carried a basket over her arm, and Evy knew it contained gingerbread cakes because she had helped Mrs. Croft in the kitchen earlier that morning.

Evy looked down at the ground. "I was just watching Mr. Croft dig."

"You must be remembering your manners." Mrs. Croft smiled an apology at Rogan.

For as long as she remembered, Evy had been taught, whenever she might run into Sir Lyle, to drop a little curtsy and say, "Good morning, Squire Chantry. God bless you on this day and all your house." But this was not Sir Lyle. It was his insufferable son, Rogan, and he nettled her.

"Do not carry on so, Mrs. Croft. Do I look upset? It is nothing."

Evy looked at Rogan, surprised at how weary he sounded.

Mrs. Croft beamed at him. "So generous of you, Master Rogan. Don't you want to thank the squire's son, Evy?"

Evy did *not* want to thank the squire's son. She felt her face turning red. Just then Buster barked loudly and rolled over. Rogan picked up a stone and tossed it. "Go get it, Buster." He unleashed him, and the dog raced to retrieve the stone.

Evy stared at the boy in front of her. How convenient Buster's fetching trick was, coming as it did just in time to save her from embarrassment. Could Rogan actually have tried to help her out of an awkward moment?

Mrs. Croft was smiling at Rogan. "Would you like a cake?" She opened the basket and lowered it between him and Evy. Rogan inclined his head slightly, took the cake, then without another glance Evy's way, he walked off in the direction of the cemetery from whence he had first emerged so unexpectedly.

Evy felt a pang of regret as he left. Perhaps she should have been nicer to him. After all, he had recently lost his mother. He had not behaved sadly though, not like Arcilla, who had been confined to bed over the loss.

Mrs. Croft carried on about Mr. Croft eating his lunch. There was cheese and bread, she told him, and a jar of tea. He climbed up out of the trench and sat on a stump to eat, and Mrs. Croft steered Evy away toward the rectory. "You mustn't keep the vicar and his wife waiting for their lunch. Oh! Your skirt has grass stains, and your hands are smudged. Now Missus Grace will surely be upset. Run and decent yourself, Evy, while I get back to ladle the soup."

When Evy was seated at the polished round dining table, Uncle Edmund gave thanks for the food. Aunt Grace passed the bread plate while Mrs. Croft brought in the soup. Evy guessed from his contented face that Uncle Edmund was in a mellow mood, and even Aunt Grace seemed less worried than she had when Lady Camilla had first come calling. It seemed a safe time to ask questions.

"Where is Kimberly, Uncle Edmund? Isn't that where diamonds were first found in South Africa? It was not on the map I saw in your study."

"You and your curiosity, my girl. Yes, Kimberly is in South Africa, but that map is a very old one. It was not called Kimberly back then. The first diamond was not found there until 1867. At that time it was called the diamond diggings at Colesberg Kopje. It was renamed Kimberly after the colonial secretary who accepted the area into Her Majesty's dominions. After the big diamond was found on the river's bank, Kimberly grew by leaps and bounds. Miners came from all over the world to search for diamonds."

"Did my parents ever visit Kimberly?"

She noticed that her aunt watched her carefully. Did her continued interest disturb Aunt Grace...and if so, why?

"Junia never mentioned going there. Why do you ask, Evy?"

She laughed. "Would it not be a wonder if they had found a diamond of their own? I would be their heir, and we would never need to worry about paying bills again."

Aunt Grace spilled water from the glass she held, and Uncle Edmund reached quickly with his napkin and blotted his wife's sleeve.

"Oh dear," Aunt Grace breathed.

"No harm done, my dear," came Uncle Edmund's soothing tone.

Evy pressed on. "The squire's son isn't so interested in diamonds. He hopes to look for gold in South Africa when he grows up."

Uncle Edmund raised his brows. "You have been talking with Master Rogan, have you?"

"Only a little. It was quite by accident. He came to the cemetery with his dog and overheard Mr. Croft telling me about Master Henry Chantry. Mr. Croft thinks he may have been murdered."

Aunt Grace stiffened, a look of consternation on her face. Evy's uncle was more calm. His tufted white brows shot even higher. "Does he, now! And I suppose he told you Master Henry was murdered for diamonds?"

"He was not certain, just thought he was probably murdered. He did not say why, or who may have done it."

"Well, *that's* a blessing," he said wryly, exchanging looks with Grace. "There is absolutely no proof Henry was murdered."

"Then he killed himself?"

"Evy!" Aunt Grace's sharp tone startled her. "Spreading tales is an evil in which you must not indulge."

"But I did not spread them, Aunt."

"Listening can be just as bad. Words can hurt. Loose tongues can destroy people."

"Yes, and I would never mention this to Meg, Emily, or Alice. They would tell their brothers and it would soon be all over the village."

"I fear it already is." Uncle Edmund sighed. "That tale about Master Henry has been loitering in Grimston Way for many years now. I'm afraid there is not much we can do about it. The Chantrys are deemed mysterious at times by people, and all sorts of tales can spring up about them and grow like weeds."

"He said that Master Henry's ghost walks in the cemetery on Allhallows."

"Very unwise of him. Nonsense."

"That is what I told him, but then Rogan came along and said that his uncle wasn't even buried in the cemetery, so how could he haunt it? Then he told us his uncle Henry was buried in the family crypt at Rookswood." She considered telling them how Rogan offered the challenge to bring her there to see the crypt, but held back. Aunt Grace especially would tell her she could not go, and then she could not prove Rogan wrong about squealing like Arcilla.

"Master Rogan said that Henry's ghost haunts the third floor of Rookswood."

Grace tossed her napkin down on the table, frowning. "Edmund, you simply *must* do something about allowing this sort of chatter. It's unhealthy."

He reached over and laid his hand over hers. "I might as well try and bottle the north wind as end loose talk in the village. Do not fret so," came his soothing tone. "She will hear these tales regardless of our attempt to stop them." He looked across the table at Evy. "I trust you will be wise enough to sort the wheat from the chaff when it comes to truth and foolish chatter."

He trusted her, and Evy felt warm seep through her at the thought. But her aunt's reaction troubled her as much as her uncle's pleased her. Evy disliked worrying Aunt Grace. Lately, she fretted at the drop of a hat. What was worrying her so?

"I suppose you are right," Aunt Grace said uneasily, "but…"

"Aunt, I did not believe what they said about ghosts. How could I? It is silly. I merely thought it was strange about Master Henry. Do you remember him, Uncle?"

"Not well. He spent a good portion of his time in Capetown, as I recall. As to whether he shot himself, I cannot say. There was much confusion at the time." He glanced at Grace, as though to assure her all was well before he went on. "Henry had unwisely permitted himself to become entangled in some diamond scandal or other."

Evy saw her aunt's mouth tighten, and she hastened in another direction. "Master Rogan insists that when he grows up he is going to find a gold mine."

"He does, does he? Ambitious, like all the Chantrys." Uncle Edmund smiled. He took out his vest watch and glanced at the time. "I will be calling on Withers today, my dear," he said to Aunt Grace. "Would you care to come along?"

"I would, except the wind is so chilly. Looks like rain again too. I had better stay and work on Evy's dress. Saturday draws near, when she will visit Rookswood."

He pushed his chair back and stood. Aunt Grace went for his hat and gloves.

Evy came up, placing her arms around her uncle's pudgy middle. "Is it wrong to be ambitious the way Master Rogan is?"

He looked down at her with the kindly smile she loved and patted her back. "Not unless you allow your ambition to rule your heart. God must always have all your heart."

Evy wondered if Rogan would allow his ambition to rule him. "Is there lots of gold in South Africa?"

"I daresay there is a great deal. If you can find it."

"I suppose if you *could* find it, you would be very rich."

"Very rich indeed. And very prone toward trouble. Too much love for gold and diamonds usually brings out the worst in people. Some hoard diamonds and gold because it brings them power. Others put great trust in riches and never learn that possessions cannot give meaning to life. Only a relationship with Christ brings true security and satisfaction."

"Like the rich fool."

His smile deepened. "Like the rich fool, indeed. And we are wise to use Christ's parables to keep us from greed."

"I wonder if Master Henry was murdered for his diamonds and gold?"

"Evy!"

She turned to find Aunt Grace entering the room with Uncle

Edmund's hat and gloves. "You are becoming altogether too involved in this sort of chatter."

Quick remorse swept her. She did not want to distress her aunt. "Yes, I am sorry." With that, she hurried to gather the soup bowls into the kitchen.

When she entered the kitchen, she thought Mrs. Croft might have overheard, or rather had *listened*, for the woman stood by the door, her fingers clutching and unclutching her apron. Evy found her response curious. Why should Mrs. Croft be fidgety?

As Evy stacked the dishes, she began thinking of Saturday and her visit to Arcilla at Rookswood. Her excitement stirred to new life. She hoped it would be a clear and sunny afternoon. It would be such a shame to get her new dress rained on. Sure enough, before the dishes were even dried and put away, it begin to rain. Evy remembered the sexton and wondered if he had finished digging the trench before it became a slippery bed of mud. Mrs. Croft must have been worrying about her husband too, for she went to the window several times and scowled.

Thinking of a grave brought her mind right back to Master Henry. If he had not shot himself, then someone had to have murdered him. But why would anyone wish to murder Master Henry...if not for the Black Diamond?

CHAPTER EIGHT

The wind moaned throughout the rainy afternoon and evening. Though Aunt Grace had sent Evy up to her bedroom over two hours ago, she could not sleep, and so knelt to pray on the newly laundered rag rug beside her bed. She could hear her aunt downstairs in the rectory hall and knew how worried she was. When Uncle Edmund had not returned by supper time, Mrs. Croft told a few of the village men. They had ridden out toward Mr. Wither's farm to see if the vicar's jingle was caught in a bog. They had been gone longer than Aunt Grace thought necessary, and her concern had now turned to gravity.

Evy was still dressed, except for her stockinged feet. Her hands were cold, her stomach had butterflies, and her heart thumped with irregular little beats. She looked up from her prayer book toward the small window, shielded by eyelet curtains. The rain pelted against the leaded pane. A sweeping flash of lightning over Grimston Woods was followed by deep thunder.

"Like the death angel passing over Egypt," she murmured. Above the needling rain, there followed the sound of thudding horse hoofs in the rectory yard below. The jingle and Uncle Edmund!

She scrambled to her feet and rushed to the window, pushing aside the curtain. Even on sunny days the leaded panes kept the rooms dim, and now, with the darkness and rain, it was nearly impossible to see anything. She wiped the moisture from the pane and tried to peer into the darkness below, but she could not see who was hurrying across the muddy yard toward the door. Even up here in her small room she heard the loud rapping. Her heart sank like a stone. It could not be Uncle Edmund.

It was after eight o'clock, and Evy could not imagine a parishioner calling upon Aunt Grace now for any reason except unhappy news. With growing apprehension, Evy let the curtain fall into place and turned to look toward the open bedroom door.

She hurried into the narrow hall and leaned over the rail.

Aunt Grace stood below, Mrs. Croft beside her. Coming in through the front were the curate, Mr. Brown, and Derwent. Curate Brown had taken hold of Aunt Grace's shoulders, and his wet face was set with sadness. Evy saw Aunt Grace stiffen, then her head dropped and her body shook.

"Something has happened to Uncle?" Evy couldn't hold back the cry. She held tightly to the rail, and Derwent looked up at her. His wet face looked drawn and white, and his russet hair was plastered to his cheeks. He tugged at his father's arm and pointed toward Evy, and Mr. Brown looked up. The curate's expression confirmed her fears. He said something to Mrs. Croft, who left the others and moved up the stairs toward Evy.

Evy could not move. Her tearful eyes searched Mrs. Croft's pitying gaze.

"Oh, Evy, my poor lamb," she said gently. "I'm afraid the good vicar has met with a terrible accident. It was the rain and wind, no less. His horse must have bolted from the lightning. Dear Vicar has been taken to heaven."

Evy felt the room start to spin, and the last thing she heard was Mrs. Croft's alarmed cry as she plunged into darkness.

The rains continued on and off, and the perpetual dampness penetrated the old stone rectory. How strange that Lady Honoria would die in October and Uncle Edmund would die just a few weeks later.

Evy stared out the window at the rain. Maybe there really was some sort of curse connected with Master Henry and Rookswood. She could almost believe it if she did not know for sure that Christ was in control of life and death.

The names of the rectors for the past century were inscribed on a tarnished bronze plaque on the stone wall in the front hall, and now Uncle Edmund's name was to be there as well, freshly inscribed by the village engraver.

The Saturday appointment that Evy was to have had with Arcilla at Rookswood was postponed until after Christmas. Evy was confined to the rectory in the traditional state of mourning alongside Aunt Grace.

Though the kindly parishioners rallied to their needs and took turns bringing food, it was evident that in due time Aunt Grace would need to seek employment for the many years that loomed ahead. After all, she was still a relatively young woman.

"Times are changing, Evy," Aunt Grace told her two weeks later. "It's highly probable that you, too, will grow up with the need to seek employment. If that happens you will be aided by a good education. Even if you marry Derwent Brown, life is uncertain. We can depend upon the Lord to care for us, though He surely expects us to use our talents wisely. Consider how He gave the ant the instinct to prepare for winter. If we do nothing, and merely say we are depending upon our heavenly Father to provide, we are close to presumption."

Evy could see how grave and serious her aunt had become, and this affected her as well. After tasting pain and loss, Evy had made a terrible discovery: Life was dangerous.

The parishioners were helping with the many duties that were temporarily in the hands of the curate. No one had much doubt Mr. Brown would become the new vicar of St. Graves. He was well thought of by both the villagers and the bishop, and he was making quiet plans to move into the rectory house with Derwent, doing his best to do so without offense to the vicar's sorrowing widow.

Evy had no idea how this delicate situation would be worked out. It was obvious that once a new vicar was appointed, she and Aunt Grace would have to leave the rectory and find another place to live. The uncertainty was taking its toll on Aunt Grace, coming so soon after Uncle Edmund's death, and Evy felt great sympathy and concern. Life had suddenly become more difficult. The hard places had not been filed smooth. Tears were a portion of her cup. She wished she were older so that she could help bring in financial support. There was also some talk that Dr. Tisdale might arrange for Aunt Grace to live in a cottage on his farm for a monthly pittance, but Evy hoped that would not happen. Alice Tisdale was patronizing enough. She was going about whispering to the other girls that her father would be taking on the care of the vicar's widow and niece, even going so far as to imply that they would be receiving charity. Alice had sounded positively smug when she revealed she might need to go through her frocks to donate garments to Evy so she could continue to attend school. "Perfectly good frocks, too—ones that I want to keep. But Mum says I must be charitable to the poor and deprived."

It took all of Evy's control to not walk up and confront Alice with her silly lies. It wasn't so dreadful for her to say these things to Meg and Emily because they knew what poverty was and they knew better. But Alice was also spreading the tale among the boys. It was horribly embarrassing! Evy shuddered to think just how condescending Alice's manner would become if she and Aunt Grace *did* end up living in the old cottage on the Tisdale farm. *Oh, spare me! I will wear a potato sack before I ever wear a discarded frock from Alice Tisdale!*

Despite all this, as the days inched by, Evy was able to continue her piano lessons twice a week under Mrs. Tisdale, who had studied music when she was young, and whose contribution to the community was noted by the villagers.

"I'm in complete agreement with Mrs. Tisdale. Music is nourishing to the spirit," Aunt Grace said. "I see no reason why your uncle's death should deprive you of your piano lessons. Especially when you enjoy them so much."

There were four students: Evy, Meg, Emily, and of course, Alice. Although the other students paid, Evy was now allowed to attend at no charge since she had been the niece of the dear departed vicar.

Evy knew that Alice did not particularly like her. Alice blamed Evy for losing the chance to go up to Rookswood several afternoons each week to be companion to Arcilla. After all, Alice never ceased to remind Evy, *she* was the doctor's daughter. Though Evy thought her pallid and sullen, she considered herself quite pretty. Besides which, it was no secret that Alice dared to imagine herself romantically involved with Rogan Chantry. Emily and Meg would giggle about the girl's vanity.

"As if he'd ever look at her. He'll have someone special, like Lady Bancroft's daughter, Patricia. Have you seen Miss Patricia?" Meg asked Evy in a whisper.

Evy admitted she had not, nor did she wish to see another pretty girl romping about in fancy clothes and carrying on something awful in front of Rogan.

"She's very rich. She would be, of course; her parents are of the nobility, living in London. They even met Her Majesty at court. Patricia is thirteen now and wears gowns made in Paris. Her hair is auburn and she has what Tom calls forget-me-not blue eyes."

"Rogan is only a boy." Evy gave a sniff. "He is too young to marry."

"They make plans early for marriage among the nobility." Meg nodded, eyes wide and sober. "They even have someone chosen for Arcilla already."

"Oh, do not say so," Evy groaned.

"Indeed, so. Patricia's brother, Charles Bancroft."

"Pity the young man," Emily said.

"How do you know all this? About the Bancroft children I mean?" Evy had heard nothing of the sort from Mrs. Croft.

Meg shrugged. "Because Mum now works in the kitchen at Rookswood."

That appeared to explain everything from Meg's viewpoint.

Emily sighed. "If only I knew I was going to get a handsome husband, I'd be happy."

"Handsome! I should be happy if I get a husband at all," Meg said. "At least you're the blacksmith's daughter. Pa is a groom at the Rookswood stables."

"You'll marry Tom, Emily's brother." Evy patted her friend's hand.

"And you'll marry Derwent," Meg told Evy. "You're lucky. He's so handsome."

Evy's brows lifted. Derwent? Handsome?

Alice had finished her piano lesson and walked up. "You three are always whispering," she said crossly. "It's quite rude you know."

"So it is," Evy agreed, and stood, shaking out her skirts. It was time to start back to the rectory.

"We were talking about the squire's son." Meg's malicious tone made it clear she did not like Alice's superior ways of lecturing them. "Rogan's going to marry Miss Patricia Bancroft. *She's* rich and beautiful."

Alice's lips tightened. "Gossip…probably only from the kitchen of Rookswood. He'll marry whom he wishes to marry. He's very independent." She smoothed her strawberry blond hair with the palm of her hand. She looked at her fingernails with a secretive smile. "He talks to *me* all the time."

"Ta, *ta,*" Meg said, mimicking her lofty voice.

Alice fixed Evy with a cool stare. "It is quite unkind of you to have taken my place as Miss Arcilla's best friend."

"I have not been up to Rookswood yet. Really, Alice, you're being very unfair. Arcilla makes her own decisions as to whom she befriends. I had nothing at all to do with her choice."

Alice shrugged. "The doctor's daughter and the vicar's niece could be on the same social stratum, I suppose. But—"

"Always putting on airs." Emily shook her head. "You're really no better than the rest of us, Alice."

"That's not what my mum tells me. But never mind, both of you. Because now that the vicar has—well, now that he's not here any longer, Mum says Lady Camilla will ask me to return because I play the piano so well."

It was true that Alice was very good at the piano, and Evy longed to become as proficient. Alice was blessed to have Mrs. Tisdale for her mother, but Evy knew better about Alice being asked to return to Rookswood.

Emily looked at Evy and rolled her eyes, and Evy stifled a giggle. It vanished quickly enough, though, when Evy thought again about what she and Aunt Grace were to do.

Whatever was to be decided about the future, there was no question that they would need to find a new home soon.

Uncle Edmund had left Grace a small benefice, but Evy had learned the money would run out in the years ahead. The bishop in London had taken a sympathetic interest in their plight and written a letter to Grace, in which he told her that he would try to arrange something suitable for their sustenance. Grace wrote back that she preferred to find work in a household, perhaps in London.

Taking work in London loomed large in her aunt's thinking these days, when, on the wintry heels of change, the expected announcement arrived that the bishop had indeed awarded the St. Graves Parish to its curate, Mr. Brown. He had been faithful to Uncle Edmund, and, as Aunt Grace told her, it was fitting that he should become the new vicar.

"Your uncle would be pleased if he knew the position went to Mr. Brown. It will be good for Derwent, too, and ultimately for your future as well, Evy."

Evy understood what she meant. She was to marry Derwent.

Mr. Brown immediately offered to let them continue to live at the rectory for as long as they wished, but both he and Grace recognized the arrangement would not be wise. Her aunt declined. As she told Evy, Mr. Brown had lost his wife many years ago, after Derwent's birth, and it did not bode well for a widowed woman to be living in the same house with a widower.

"Besides, if we are to make a match between you and Derwent, we cannot have the two of you growing up in such close confines. You would soon begin looking upon one another as brother and sister."

Evy felt that way now. She had known Derwent all her life. The older she grew, the more difficult it became to imagine herself married to him. Her aunt assured her she would feel differently once she reached her teen years.

"Everything changes when you begin growing up. You will think Derwent handsome and wise."

Evy studied the quiet boy when they gathered for Sunday services the next day and wondered if such a miracle could happen. He was far from handsome, not that his appearance was of primary concern. A heart for God could supplant a handsome body. She thought this because her uncle had told her so. Evy hoped she would be wise enough one day to know this for herself.

Unfortunately, Derwent was not especially bright either, and that worried Evy. Although he was the son of the curate and so was expected to be interested in matters pertaining to the parish church, Derwent took more interest in hunting possum and rabbits and dreamed about searching for diamonds and gold in South Africa. He was quite good-natured, rather gullible about most things, and continued to look on Rogan Chantry with hero worship even though Rogan was a bit younger than he.

Perhaps Derwent would change?

Evy counted the years until she would turn fourteen, clearly expecting that she would wake up on that morning and find herself a new person, and Derwent—the fairy tale prince.

"I shall be taking the train into London to look for work."

Aunt Grace's words snatched Evy from her thoughts.

"Mrs. Croft has volunteered to look after you for the time I am away. I promise to return before Christmas."

Evy pondered this. "What kind of work will you seek?"

"Well, I was a governess before I married Edmund, so I can fall back on that. The difficulty will be in finding a family willing to take us both. We will make this a matter of prayer, Evy." Grace put her arms around her. "You are all I have left. It would not be good for either of us to be separated at this time."

Evy agreed and choked back her tears. What if she needed to live in an orphanage for the next five years? She asked the question that was uppermost in her mind, the one that was usually glossed over with indifference. "Aunt Grace, would not my father have had relatives? The Varleys, I mean? Someone we could turn to for help?"

Evy felt the familiar barrier slip between them. She guessed her aunt's response from the veiled look that came over her tired face.

"No, dear. I believe he had an older brother somewhere in the Cape, but we've never heard from him. He was quite a bit older than your father, so he may have departed this world by now. I believe he was a heavy drinker and a gambler."

Evy felt a rush of disappointment. "Oh...I see."

"Do not worry so. I shall find work. God is our Shepherd. He will provide. If not in London, then elsewhere. Your uncle had many friends and associates in the church. Perhaps the bishop will recommend me to some genteel family."

But Evy's troubled thoughts remained. "And my mother's family and yours?"

A cloud seemed to pass over her aunt's countenance, as though her memories were sad ones. "Our father died when Junia and I were children. I was thirteen and she was seven. There was no one else. Our mother—your grandmother, Victoria—died soon after Junia was born. Father never mentioned her family. When I was nineteen I worked as a nanny for the bishop's daughter in London while also caring for Junia. The bishop introduced me to Edmund, who was a young curate. Edmund and I married, and the bishop arranged for him to come to St. Graves. In due season he became its rector. That was many years ago." Her heavy sigh seemed to fill the room.

It was no use. Evy had heard most of this before. It was like knocking at the door of an empty house. Her aunt was never unkind about Evy's questions, but she was ever and always reluctant to talk freely. Perhaps Evy merely imagined that there was more to understand.

Before Aunt Grace left on the train for London, Evy overheard her talking with Vicar Brown. "We had such fine plans for her. Edmund wanted so much for her to attend music school in London. As you know, she loves the piano, and we both recognized her talent. To have become a music teacher would have suited her well. Now I wonder if I shall be able to manage it."

"These things can only be left to the Lord, Mrs. Havering. Surely God knew all this when He permitted the beloved vicar to meet with his tragic accident. In God's wisdom, what we now view as dark tragedies may be necessary for the final glorious design."

Evy eased the kitchen door shut, and behind her she heard Mrs. Croft sniff. Evy turned around to see the woman wiping her eyes with the edge of her apron. Her heart warmed toward Mrs. Croft. *She does actually care about us.* Rather awed at the thought, Evy walked up and put her arms around the woman's waist, and Mrs. Croft awkwardly patted her back. "There, there," she murmured, "there, there, Evy dear. It's all going to be all right. I daresay the future be brighter than any of us think now."

Evy and Mrs. Croft saw Aunt Grace off at the train depot.

Her aunt kissed Evy's cheek. "Good-bye, dear. Take good care of her, Mrs. Croft."

"Oh, I will indeed, Missus Grace," she said, holding the reins to the jingle tightly.

"And remember, Evy, study hard in Mr. Brown's classroom while I'm gone. It is even more urgent now to make good use of the three *R*s."

Evy blinked back tears. "I will, Aunt. Oh, good-bye, good-bye, and may God give you a wonderful post as governess."

She sat beside Mrs. Croft on the seat in the jingle watching her aunt wave as she boarded the train. A few minutes later the big steam engine pulled out of the way station, and the whistle pierced the cold morning air. Evy covered her ears. They watched the train leaving Grimston Way until it rounded the bend and was blocked from view by a stand of weathered oak trees.

The whistle continued to blow, growing fainter. Evy watched the boiler smoke on the horizon as stillness settled about her.

Finally Mrs. Croft flipped the reins, and the horse turned and started back toward the village rectory.

CHAPTER NINE

During the next few weeks life proceeded as normally as could be expected in such circumstances. Mr. Brown and some of the ladies in the village decorated the hall and church for the Christmas celebration, though the mood was anything but cheery. On the great table beside the host of inscribed names belonging to rectors of St. Graves Parish stood a Christmas bush in a pot. The decorated bush was an old tradition begun by the Cornish, and many in this area of England adopted the festive decoration instead of using Christmas trees. The bush had been sent down from the Chantry family with a hand-decorated card signed by the entire family, from Lady Camilla's elegant script to Arcilla's lopsided handwriting. At the top of the card were the words *Merry Christmas.*

A few days before Aunt Grace's return Evy went with Derwent to the woods near the rectory to hunt for mistletoe and holly. She had spotted a large cluster of mistletoe in an oak tree, and Derwent shimmied up the trunk and onto a branch to reach it. When her basket was past half full he climbed down to rest, and they sat for a few minutes on a fallen log beside the dirt road. They agreed that after resting they would search for holly branches with red berries, then return to the rectory.

Derwent ran his fingers through his russet hair and looked at her. Red suddenly tinged his cheeks.

"Seems to me, if you go away to London to live, Miss Evy, I won't be seeing you anymore. Does it seem so to you, too?"

It did, but Evy tried not to think about it. Still, she couldn't keep her mind from traveling that path. What if she had to move to London? She would be taken away from her friends and from all she was comfortable with! Uncertainty was a constant companion as she wondered what would happen if she *did* move away. Would she and Derwent continue as friends, perhaps through letters? What a poor substitute for being with her lifelong friend!

She pushed aside these gloomy thoughts. "Oh, surely we will see one another. After all, you will be coming to London to attend divinity school in a few short years. And Aunt and I have so many friends in Grimston Way we could never simply turn our backs and disappear into the London throngs."

"Then you will come back and visit the rectory sometimes?"

Evy smoothed a tendril of her hair back into place, wondering why his question brought her a feeling of uneasiness. Perhaps because she noticed the hope in his eyes—a hope that appeared to question her more deeply than she was ready to answer.

"Quite often, I daresay. Aunt will see to that."

He cleared his throat. "I find myself hoping—"

A sudden thundering of hooves drew Evy's attention to the road, where she saw Rogan riding his horse. As usual he looked the squire's son, dressed handsomely in shiny polished boots, a neat hat sitting to one side of his head in a rather cocky manner. He looked surprised to see them sitting together on the log, and he rode up and took in the scene, noting the mistletoe in the basket at her feet. He studied Derwent, then looked at her, as though he had come to some conclusion.

"Is not that mistletoe?"

Evy stood quickly at Rogan's question and picked up her basket. "Yes. For the rectory hall."

"Mistletoe for the rectory hall?" He looked amused and then laughed. "I never thought of the rectory as a place for kissing."

"It's— It's not." Curse his mocking tone and the heat in her face! "It is simply—a decoration."

He held out his hand toward her. "I should like a piece of it, thank you."

Fighting the urge to throw the basket at him, Evy broke off a small twig with three leaves and handed it to him, eyes averted.

"Are you not going to ask me what I shall do with it?" Rogan's dark eyes were dancing.

"It's naught of my business."

Rogan looked at Derwent. "What do *you* do with this?" He waved the twig about, deliberately holding it over Evy's head.

Derwent turned pink, frowned, and shrugged. "Nothing."

"Nothing! I am disappointed in you."

Derwent looked at Evy. "What were you going to do with it, Evy?"

"Evy?" Rogan's tone showed his surprise. "Not *Miss* Evy, but just— Evy. Looks like I have interrupted a little rendezvous by the roadside, after all."

Derwent did not seem to know what to say. He stood and shoved his hands into his pockets, his gaze fixed on Rogan's purebred. Rogan leaned forward and patted the horse's muscled neck. Upon spying their picnic basket, he grinned.

"A little picnic. How charming. Shall I join you for lunch?" He swung down and appeared not to notice Evy's silence.

"Aye, help yourself, Master Rogan." Derwent went for the basket, all too willing to share. When Rogan smiled at Evy, she had the distinct impression he knew she did not want him to stay.

He sat down on the log beside Derwent, who opened the basket.

"Are you not you going to sit between us—Evy?" Rogan moved aside, providing a space.

Evy ignored him and pretended she had not noticed his using her first name. Why did he have to come along and spoil a perfectly lovely afternoon?

She walked over and stood across from them.

"Ah, my favorite!" Rogan seemed to be enjoying himself as he dug out a ham sandwich.

"Do you not get ham sandwiches up at Rookswood?" Evy crossed her arms and slanted him a glare. "I should think you could have any-thing your heart wished for."

"Of course"—he waved his hand as he talked around the sand-wich—"but I do not get to eat my lunch in Grimston Woods." He smiled. "I like picnics. Perhaps I shall have my own one day. I know of a special place on a hill. It's perfect."

"In Grimston Woods?" Derwent glanced about them.

"No. On Rookswood land. There is a grand view from the hill."

Derwent held out a second sandwich and an apple for Evy to choose. She knew he was hungry, so since Rogan was eating *her* sand-wich, she took the apple and bit into it. She nodded to Derwent. "You eat the sandwich."

"What fun," Rogan said, leaning back. "Maybe I shall decide to have a picnic of my own. Let me see… Whom shall I invite?" He looked at Evy, studying her.

"All your friends?"

At Derwent's suggestion, Rogan nodded. "Of course. That defi-nitely means you… What was your name?"

"Derwent."

He sounded so anxious to please the great Rogan that Evy wanted to stamp her foot.

"So it was. How stupid of me to forget my friends' names. Derwent Brown." He looked at Evy, his zesty dark eyes amused. "And Evy Varley. Let us think—where shall we have this picnic?" He hung his velvet hat on a twig above him and leaned back, watching Evy steadily as he ate.

"The hill you mentioned?"

"Maybe the crypt." Rogan ignored Derwent's idea. "Did I not say I would bring you there?" The look he leveled at Evy was replete with challenge. "Perhaps I will take you there after we eat."

What was he up to? He had never showed interest in either her or Derwent before now. A dart of apprehension shot through her secret plea-sure over the way he was noticing her. "It looks like rain this afternoon." She spoke quickly, hoping to cover how unsure she was of Rogan—and herself. "We had better return to the rectory soon, Derwent."

"Your aunt went to London, did she not?"

She met Rogan's questioning gaze head-on. "Yes. She will be back before Christmas."

"The crypt?" Derwent looked like a puppy promised a treat.

Rogan read the other boy's interest, and the smile that crossed his features was definitely smug. Clearly, he was enjoying how Evy's own friend was foiling her attempts to leave.

"Yes. My uncle's crypt. Henry Chantry is entombed there. I know all about the village gossip. They say he was *murdered*."

Derwent stopped eating his sandwich and swallowed hard. "Murdered? I never heard about that."

"You would not," Rogan said meaningfully, "but the rector's niece has, have you not— *Evy?*"

"There is always talk." Rogan was beginning to irritate her in earnest.

He stood suddenly, wiping his hand on a napkin, still looking at her and Derwent. He caught up his hat and put it on. "We will go there now. I always have my way. Up, Derwent. Do not linger." He looked up at the sky and smiled. "Though rain it may, I would say we have at least two hours. That is still enough time."

Derwent was rushing, stuffing the picnic remains into the basket, anxious for the adventure with the future *Sir* Rogan. Evy, on the other hand, was far from pleased at the glint of mischief in Rogan's steady gaze. "I do not think—"

But Rogan had commandeered the moment, and Derwent was all too willing to follow him in whatever he wanted to do.

"Derwent, you can walk." Rogan nodded at the boy. "It is not that far. Evy and I will wait for you at Rookswood by the gate."

"Walk?" Derwent blinked.

Rogan's smile was tolerant. "You would not want to put the load of three on my excellent horse! It will be better if only Evy rides with me." He looked at her, his smile deepening. "You are not afraid to ride with me, are you?"

"Absolutely not," she said, though too forcefully. "Should I be?"

"Absolutely not," he repeated with that upturned smile of his.

Funny how she got the opposite impression from his words. "I will walk with Derwent."

Rogan's gaze narrowed, but before he could argue, Evy snatched her basket of mistletoe from below the tree and started up the dirt road toward Rookswood.

Just what was Rogan up to? Perhaps she ought to turn right around now and go back to the rectory. Yes, that was a good idea. If Rogan let Derwent ride with him on the horse, she would turn back to the rectory as soon as they were over the hill and out of sight.

But Rogan did not ride ahead, nor did he ask Derwent to ride with him. He brought the horse behind them allowing Evy and Derwent to lead the way.

Evy leaned close to Derwent. "Now, why is he doing this?"

"He is nice and friendly."

"I am not so sure."

Derwent's eyes shone, so impressed was he. "This will be quite merry, Evy. I always wanted to see a crypt, especially the Chantrys'."

"Whatever *for*, Derwent? Rogan Chantry will never make friends with you the way you hope." She tried to make the whispered observation as kind as she could, but Derwent was unaffected.

"Oh, I know that, but I'd sure like to hear about how his uncle found gold and diamonds in South Africa. Hunted rhinos, too. Heard there's a big rhino head and a Boer whip in his uncle's rooms."

Evy grimaced. "What uncle was that?"

"Oh…I don't know which one…the one that died here when we were just babies. He came from South Africa."

"Rogan Chantry is so arrogant he will never tell you about the family gold and diamonds."

But Derwent would not be turned aside. "Come on, Miss Evy, he was polite enough to invite us. Besides, I want to see the gargoyles again."

"You know you are afraid of them." She glanced over her shoulder. Rogan was a little way behind them, his posture in the saddle erect but relaxed. He certainly looked at home astride his horse.

The huge gate leading to Rookswood stood open between two ancient stone arches, which allowed them to look through what appeared an exceedingly long avenue that bent around some dark, wet fir trees.

"Sometimes I climb that tree behind us and crane my neck just so," Derwent confided in a low voice. "Then I can just glimpse the mansion. It's all gray, with three stories to it."

Evy looked toward the chestnut tree he was pointing out. "Uncle Edmund always said the mansion has leaded windowpanes, thick walls, gables, and all sorts of interesting porticoes and pillars. And he said there's a great iron-studded door built in the days of the Norman knights. There is a splendid polished suit of armor near the staircase, too, and even Norman swords on one wall." Evy couldn't help a little surge of pride at her knowledge.

Derwent's pale eyes bulged. "Knight's armor? Oh, to see *that.*"

Evy too wished to see it, though she'd never admit it to Derwent. Or to Rogan. Better to change the subject so she didn't stir Derwent's hopes. "Christmas is the time to be invited to the mansion. Those who went caroling there last Christmas with Uncle Edmund got to see grand decorations. There were lots of candles adorning the baronial hall, and the carolers got cups of mulberry punch and sweet cakes. Mrs. Croft's family all came home with bags of tasty tidbits to eat."

Derwent gulped. "I remember. We were sick. Worst luck. How come Mrs. Croft's relatives get to partake and we don't?"

"Because they clean the rooms—so many you can't count them, so Mrs. Croft says. Everyone who works there got a gift, too."

Derwent looked as though he might have traded his position as son of the vicar to be the son of the chief stableman. Evy tried to imagine how each of the squire's children had their own big room with servants looking after them. There was a governess, an intelligent woman indeed, but she was soon to retire. So Mrs. Croft said that Squire was looking for just the right woman to be the new governess to his lovely Miss Arcilla. The old governess had served the previous generation of Chantrys and was to be given a small cottage on the estate where she would live out her final days with a comfortable pension. As for Rogan and Parnell, they had a male tutor, a young man who had studied in Paris and could speak several languages. He was preparing the two boys to be sent away to an exclusive school in London.

Evy looked up at the familiar gargoyles guarding the gate with their stone pitchforks. The rainwater still dripped from their mouths, and they looked like slobbering fiends. Uncle Edmund had told her they were medieval. Evy shuddered as she stared up at their leering faces. They seemed to challenge her, as though they knew something about her that she did not. Remembering the stranger in the dark woods, she trembled as the chill wind blew against her frock.

"Reminds me of the walls of Jericho," she told Derwent.

"Them gargoyles…"

She grimaced. "If I owned Rookswood, I would have angels instead."

"But it would be a pity to destroy them. They are ancient."

"You just say that because anything bearing the Chantry name leaves you awestruck," she half scolded. "I don't think you really like gargoyles."

Derwent's sheepish smile told Evy she was right. She knew he was afraid of the dark and prone to believe in the foolish tales of ghosts.

"Are you not afraid of the gargoyles, too?" Derwent's wide-eyed gaze searched her face.

She looked at the statues again. "They are ugly and—evil looking."

Rogan came up to them, leading his horse by the reins. "Those beastly things are all over Rookswood."

Evy studied him out of the corner of her eye. "When will you be joining Parnell in school in London?"

"Soon. Except I will not go to Oxford. I want to attend a special geological school."

That piqued Derwent's interest. "So you can better find gold and diamonds in South Africa, I suppose."

"Yes. What of you?" Rogan eyed the other boy. "I suppose you will go to divinity school?"

Derwent shoved his hands in his pockets. "It's expected."

"Can you shoot straight?"

Evy frowned. Why was Rogan drilling Derwent like this?

Derwent shook his head. "No, but I'd sure like to—"

"Can you ride well?"

"No, never been on a horse."

"That is what I thought."

At Rogan's bored dismissal, Evy spoke up. "Some *ordinary* people do not have the opportunity to do such things."

Rogan's mouth curved. "Such things as the Chantrys do, you mean?" He gave his horse to a boy who ran up to lead it away, then turned toward them. Evy didn't quite trust his smile. After all, he'd never shown such interest in her before, and she did not know how to respond. Perhaps it would be wiser if she did not.

Apparently Rogan realized she was not going to answer. "Follow me."

Derwent was quick on Rogan's heels, but Evy held back. "How far is it?"

"Not far." Rogan paused and looked back at her, that same irritating, amused glint in his eyes. He stopped when she merely stood there. He folded his arms across his chest. "So all your brave talk at the cemetery with old Hiram was boast. You *are* just like Arcilla and all her girlfriends." He seemed bored by the thought.

Evy's eyes narrowed and she set her mouth and followed. With another infuriating smile, Rogan led the way into what looked to her like a huge garden.

"Aye"—Derwent let the word out on a breath of awe—"it's beastly big, I daresay."

"Big enough," Rogan said.

"Too big." Evy knew she was being contrary, but she didn't care. "There's little reason for anyone to have such a big garden."

"Unless you are a Chantry."

Evy could have boxed Derwent's ears for his defense of Rogan.

"Squire can have anything he wants—and so can his family."

"I usually get what I want," Rogan agreed cheerfully.

"Must be like getting Christmas pudding every day," Derwent said with a sigh in his voice.

"And roast goose, too."

"I would not want Christmas pudding every day." Evy set her jaw. "It would soon become tiring. Then Christmas would seem like any ordinary day."

"But on Christmas we get a lot of other special things," Rogan parried. "So Christmas is never boring." He smiled at her. "You will have to spend Christmas at Rookswood sometime."

Evy said nothing to that. She watched Derwent following Rogan as though he were a prince. Rogan seemed to accept the other boy's sudden devotion as merely proper. That only reinforced Evy's determination to resist Rogan's arrogance—although, if she was honest with herself, she had to admit she could easily have gone to the other extreme and thought him special, too. In fact, he was quite out of the ordinary. She liked his dark, shiny hair much better than Derwent's russet hair. And those unusual dark eyes seemed to sparkle with a challenge of warmth. His smile was charming, yet it was mischievous at times, making him mysterious and a little dangerous—all of which was most intriguing.

Evy always knew what to expect from Derwent, so someone a little unpredictable seemed...appealing. *But I'm not silly like Alice or the rest of them. I shall never swoon for Rogan Chantry!*

The huge lawn was bounded by tall hedges enclosing wide flower beds. Trees behind the hedges made it completely private. Rogan whistled.

They walked through the garden for perhaps five minutes until passing through an arbor between two sections of a neatly trimmed hedge. They entered a courtyard enclosed on three sides with a high stone wall and three small gates. All three appeared to be locked, and Evy's imagination could only wonder at what might lie beyond them. At the end of the courtyard she saw what reminded her of an elevated stage with a roof. There were low, wide flat steps that went up. Below were tables and chairs, but they were old and it looked as if they had not been used for years.

"What is that?" Derwent pointed.

"Oh, we do not use this court any longer. In my great-grandfather's day it was for summer fetes, which I think quite boring. There would be an orchestra, and the girls would sit and listen to the music. The boys were supposed to come and keep them company. The best part was the feasting. That is the only part I would enjoy. Unless the girls were very nice to look at, of course. There aren't pretty girls in Grimston Way." But he looked over at Evy with a little smile.

"There is Evy."

Evy blushed at Derwent's innocent assertion. She turned away, steeling herself for Rogan's disagreement.

Oddly enough, it never came.

"They would roast an entire pig and ox on spits in that pit beyond the gate." Rogan pointed to the western gate. "There were big barrels of ale and wine, too. It became a very noisy celebration after the young girls went home…where they belonged."

Evy cast him a glance and saw his calculated smile. *He is trying to goad me.*

"Revelry, that is what it was." Evy nodded. "And debauchery, no less. Like typical lords, barons—and squires ruling over the fiefdom."

She expected him to get angry, but he looked pleased. "Not lords, barons, and squires, but earls and dukes. Now, admit it. You would be as impressed as my sister if a duke took your hand and walked you among the trees—perhaps with a bit of mistletoe."

"I would not. And if the duke tried to kiss me, I would slap him."

He tilted his head and regarded her, but he looked doubtful—and that worried her.

Evy turned away and shaded her eyes, turning her attention on the stage while Rogan gave a small push to Derwent's shoulder and gestured to the northern gate near the stage.

"That way to the mausoleum."

They walked away, leaving Evy standing there. Evidently Rogan was showing her that he did not care whether she followed or not. As she set down her basket she understood his message: She could go just so far in assuming a manner of equality. Any further and she would meet with his disapproval. She pressed her lips together. If he had imposed such boundaries at his young age, what would he be like at eighteen?

Not that she would ever find out. Nor did she want to!

Well, it was now up to her to either fall in line with his game or turn around and go back to the rectory. She stood there a moment watching Rogan open the gate and pass through without a glance over his shoulder. Derwent was at his heels, following, the happy puppy.

Why do I want to see a musty old mausoleum, anyway? She would not be Rogan Chantry's adoring subject. She was well aware that Alice would have followed him, and so might all the other girls, but—

Evy set her chin, whirled about, and ran back toward Rookswood gate. She would show Rogan he could not control her as he did everyone else. She would show him that Evy Varley was not like all the other girls in Grimston Way.

It took her ten minutes to find the front gate, for she had made a wrong turn and then had to retrace her steps. Rookswood was like a village all its own, she thought, looking around through the line of tall trees shadowing the flagstone walkway that circled around to the front of the estate. And now that Rogan was not there, she could allow her awe to come forth. She had never even glimpsed the mansion yet. It must be a good distance from the front grounds.

She did not see the boy who had been at the gate, so he must have taken Rogan's horse to the stables.

At last she found the gate, and with a lift to her chin, she left Rookswood—telling herself she was not the least bit sorry she had walked away.

It didn't take long for regret to sidle up alongside Evy. Her steps on the dirt road slowed as she made her way toward the rectory. How could she have let herself miss out on such a great adventure? No doubt Rogan would never ask her to accompany him on another one. *You have too much pride, Evy Varley.*

It was not until she went through the vicarage gate into the church-yard that she realized she had left her basket of mistletoe sitting in the Rookswood courtyard outside the mausoleum. *I hope Derwent notices and brings it back with him.*

But Derwent did not return with the basket—in fact, when Evy and Mrs. Croft went to the rectory to fix supper for Vicar Brown, Derwent had not shown up at all.

"A bit odd, seeing as how it's his favorite meal of mutton pie and cider," Mrs. Croft said to her.

Now I'll need to confess about going to Rookswood. Evy bit her lip and glanced from Vicar Brown, who was scowling at the dining room table, to Mrs. Croft, who was clearly worried.

"Odd, I say, Vicar. Derwent is not one to be missing his meals. He asked me just this morning what was for supper tonight, and when I told him, he was very pleased. And you know how he loves his cider."

"Yes, yes, very unusual. I wonder where that boy of mine could be?" The vicar's eyes glossed over the empty seat at the table and alighted on Evy, who sat with her hands folded in her lap, wishing she could vanish into thin air. His eyes fixed on her, and he smiled indulgently.

"Now, now, little Evy, maybe you have seen Derwent today?"

"Of course you did, Evy." Mrs. Croft smiled. "They went together to the woods to pick mistletoe and holly, Vicar." She frowned and looked at Evy. "Can't say I've seen where you put it though. Did you and Derwent not get it?"

"Um…"

Vicar Brown waited, his brows rising a notch, and Mrs. Croft continued to hold her hands under her apron as though it were a warming muff. When Evy fell silent, Vicar Brown's white brows climbed even higher.

"Yes, Evy?"

Bother. There was no way out of it. *Drat Derwent anyway!* "Yes. We went to the woods. We gathered the greenery. I…left it behind and… and"—she bit her lip and her eyes went down to her empty plate— "Derwent went back to find it."

"Ah, well, then, that explains it." Vicar Brown's brow unfurrowed. "He will soon be here, Mrs. Croft. Go ahead and serve supper before it gets cold."

"Aye, and I'll warm him a plateful when he returns."

Each bit of food Evy took seemed to turn to sawdust in her throat. She'd lied—and to the vicar!

After Vicar Brown went to his study, Evy slid from her chair. She had to find Derwent!

"Not feeling well, Evy?" Mrs. Croft eyed her when she cleared the table and saw her food hardly touched.

"No, Mrs. Croft. I shall go to my room if it is all right with you."

"Yes, you run along now. No doubt it's from traipsing about the woods in all this damp weather. I'll be up later with warm milk."

Mrs. Croft turned to leave the dining room, and Evy was edging toward the hall to find her cloak when there was a loud rap on the front door. Evy's heart jumped to her throat. Mrs. Croft went to answer it.

Evy heard voices, and when she entered the hall she recognized some of the fancy dressed footmen in hats and cloaks from Rookswood. They held bright lanterns.

A tall, slim young man with fair hair and skin stepped forward to speak to Vicar Brown, who had come out to see who was at the door.

"Good evening, Vicar."

"Hello, Charles, what brings you here tonight? Come in, come in, have some cider."

Evy hung back. She recognized the young man from Rookswood as Mr. Charles Whipple, the tutor who had come from London especially to teach Rogan.

"I cannot stay, sir. It is about your son, Derwent. He is quite beside himself about seeing Henry Chantry's ghost. We, er, have him outside now… We've taken the liberty of giving him something to quiet him down a little."

"Good grief! Derwent thinks he saw a ghost? What perfect nonsense. I shall indeed deal with him about this, you can be certain."

Evy winced.

"It might be best if you went gently on the boy, Vicar Brown. He is most upset."

"Such poppycock. A ghost! I shall have none of that devilish nonsense in my son. Where is he?"

"In the coach with Master Rogan. The squire's son happened to hear him calling for help at Rookswood and rescued him."

"Rookswood? You mean"—the vicar paled—"Derwent was up at the estate?"

"Yes, he was exploring the cemetery and wound up in the family mausoleum. The wind blew the door shut. He panicked in the darkness and could not get it open again. Master Rogan found him an hour ago. He's been looking after the boy ever since. They are together now." The tutor stepped aside from the open doorway and looked down toward the Chantry coach, parked in front of the rectory. The flames in the lanterns beside the coach doors were flickering.

Evy's cheeks burned and her hands were cold and clammy. Why that scamp, Rogan Chantry! He locked Derwent in the mausoleum, with all those old family coffins. What a dreadful boy he was! She had half a mind to tell on him.

She watched the coachman open the door, and Rogan stepped out, decked in his fancy coat with gold buttons and matching blue hat with a feather in it. He helped Derwent down, and holding to his arm walked him with what had to be feigned gentleness and concern up the path to the front door.

Derwent looked sick, his wide eyes going from his father to Mrs. Croft. His red hair was damp and drooping. Rogan looked calm and grave. He released Derwent, who wobbled toward Mrs. Croft.

"My, word! Why—he *has* seen himself a ghost."

"Nonsense!" Mr. Brown's tone was as stiff as his back. "I shall speak with you later, Derwent. Go to your room at once."

"Yes, Father." He looked anxious to get away. Mrs. Croft went with him, and Evy was willing to bet the woman could hardly wait to hear what the boy would tell her. She could imagine the wild tale that would grow in Grimston Way through the years. In another generation the old ghost story of Master Henry Chantry would increase by leaps and bounds.

Rogan removed his hat and bowed to acknowledge Evy, but not before she saw the slight smile he wore. "Miss Evy."

"Master Rogan, how can I thank you for helping my son?" At the vicar's expression of warm gratitude, Rogan inclined his head. "It was all my pleasure, Vicar." He glanced toward Evy. "Fortunately, Derwent was not caught inside very long." Rogan stepped over the threshold into the hall—clearly he was not anxious to leave. Left with little choice, Mr. Whipple came inside and removed his hat.

"Please, come in." The vicar gestured toward the drawing room. "Would you care for cider or tea, gentlemen?"

"Thank you, Vicar."

Evy stared hard at Rogan. *He can be as fancy in his manners as one would like, but it is a sham.* And yet for all her irritation, she could not deny the spark of excitement at Rogan's presence there.

When the vicar led the way, and Tutor Whipple followed, Rogan held back and turned to Evy. He started to speak but saw that the door was open and that the two serving men were standing with Mr. Bixby, the footman, by the coach. Rogan reached up and closed the door. He leaned against it and grinned, arms folded.

"I think you are horrid!" Evy stamped a foot.

"Can I help it if your beau is a bit of a coward, besides a bore?"

"Derwent is *not* my beau."

"He was only in there ten minutes, and he nearly spooked himself into a tizzy."

It was true that Derwent could work himself up into an excited state, but—ten minutes? She eyed Rogan. "Have you no heart?"

"Depends." He smiled.

"You know very well how superstitious the villagers are."

"He should know better. Is he not the vicar's son?"

"He is gullible."

"Granted." He looked to the ceiling, as though it were infinitely more interesting than their current topic of conversation. "I should think you would have more sense than to fall for a youngster like him."

"I have not fallen for him. He is a friend. A very dear one. As for being but a youngster—as you put it—he is a year older than you."

"One would hardly realize that." He studied her for a moment. "So you ran away from me."

A strange spark of excitement danced across her arms at the warm challenge in his tone. She tried to sound as bored as he did when discussing Derwent.

"I have no interest in being locked inside your family mausoleum."

The corners of his mouth turned upward. "I was not going to lock *you* inside. I was angry when you ran away, so I locked Derwent in to show you what a clod he is."

"So you *did* lock him in."

He placed hand on heart and bowed. "I confess to my warped sense of humor, Miss Varley."

"I shall tell the vicar—and your tutor."

His gaze narrowed. "I would not do that if I were you. They will never believe you."

"They will."

"My word against yours? Never. In their eyes I can do no wrong." He smiled. "So you'd best be wary."

Evy wanted to throw something at him. "So you admit you can get by with anything just because you are Sir Lyle's son."

He leaned there, watching her, but she thought his amusement grew somewhat subdued. "I would be lying if I said no."

"You are forgetting"—she glanced again toward the drawing room—"that it is my word *and* Derwent's."

That smile again. "No. I have convinced Derwent that the wind blew the door shut and jammed it. It took me ten agonizing minutes to get it open."

Evy felt her mouth drop open. What a fib! "He believes that?"

"I told him so." He smiled.

"You are worse than I thought. He believes you only because he is overawed by you. He thinks that giving him a few minutes of your time is a courtesy."

"There. You see? He does not think I am so beastly as you say."

"Because he trusted you."

"And you do not."

"I would never trust you now."

"Never is a long time."

"Not long enough."

"Oh very well, so I admit I took advantage of him a bit." He shoved away from the door, brushing the lapel of his coat as though to erase the incident. "He is rather dumb, you know."

"And to think he *likes* you."

For the first time her words appeared to have stung his conscience, if only briefly. "Very well. I shall be a good boy just for you and apologize."

Her brows lifted. "To me?"

"You are offended, are you not?"

"Yes, for Derwent's sake."

"What a waste!"

Evy stiffened. "You need not apologize to me, but to Derwent. And then confess the truth to the vicar and those at Rookswood you got all riled up over this, including your tutor."

Rogan touched hand to his forehead and groaned. "Heaven forbid. Anything but confession to the vicar."

"He is a nice man. He will likely accept your conduct as a mistaken jest and let it all pass with a subdued smile. That is the only thing we poor villagers can do to the Chantrys."

He tipped his head to one side, and his smile turned wry. "I cannot oblige you. You demand too much. I will not don sackcloth and ashes for anyone." With that, he straightened. "And if I were you, miss, I'd not be foolish enough to accuse me. As I said, I will deny it with great vigor. My word will always prevail over yours or Derwent's."

She felt even more frustration with herself than she did with Rogan. How could she have allowed herself to think for even a moment that he would comply with her wishes? "So you expect this to remain a little secret between us, is that it?"

"Yes, if you wish to put it that way."

For a moment he looked very young as he stood there, a flicker of uncertainty in those hooded eyes, his arms folded, a dark curl falling to his forehead.

"I make no promise to keep your secret." At her stiff words, he eyed her, saying nothing.

She knew she ought to turn and walk away, but she did not. They stood there, looking at each other.

Rogan broke the silence at last. "I think you will, actually. You could have told the vicar everything before now. Why didn't you?"

She had no answer. Footsteps sounded, rescuing her. Immediately Rogan became the perfectly mannered young gentleman. He pushed the lock of hair from his forehead and, hat in hand, put on a smooth expression. By the time his tutor appeared to see what was keeping him in the hall, he was definitely the future Sir Rogan.

He was deceptive and polished, and Derwent, in comparison, was an innocent child. Evy shuddered to think what this scoundrel was going to be like as an adult!

"Coming, Master Rogan?" Tutor Whipple asked.

"I have changed my mind about the cider. I think I shall go back to the coach. I sense that Derwent's ordeal has affected me more than I first realized."

Rogan opened the heavy door. He wore a slight smile as he looked at Evy, and then with a final bow of his head, he went out onto the porch.

"Good night." She forced the words through stiff lips.

"Au revoir," came his low murmur.

Somehow Evy thought he had actually enjoyed the standoff between them. He found it entertaining that she refused to crumple at his feet.

And yet he had warned her too. It was her word against his. When it came to public opinion, she would never win against him. And when he decided he wanted something, he would persist until he got it.

Though she could not explain why, that thought sent a shiver down her spine.

CHAPTER TEN

When Aunt Grace returned to Grimston Way, she did not immediately discuss with Evy what had transpired in London. Several days passed by before she came to Evy's room and suggested they take a walk together into the village.

It was a chilly but otherwise pleasant afternoon, with the sun shining in a grayish-blue sky and the branches empty of the warm golds and reds of autumn. December holly smiled its wintry bloom with flame-colored berries amid waxy green leaves.

Donned in matching hooded capes, they might have been mother and daughter out on an afternoon stroll. Evy glanced at her aunt. She was still an attractive lady, and young enough to remarry. If only Vicar Brown were not so old and gray. But it seemed there were no acceptable widowers or bachelors in Grimston Way. Farmer Gilford had no wife, but his rheumatism was such that his knees were knobby, and he walked bowlegged.

"Will we be moving away to London?"

Her aunt shook her head. "Not yet. We will need more patience."

Then that was the reason she had not discussed the matter sooner. "You did not get the post you wished?"

"I went to several interviews, one arranged by the bishop, which appeared at first to be quite hopeful. Alas," she smiled, spreading her palms, "it did not turn out as hoped. Ah, well. We will trust and wait."

Evy watched her, concerned, and noticed her aunt hesitate.

"I was not what they were looking for in a governess," her aunt explained. "Lady Mildren wanted someone older."

"Was it also because you asked that I stay in the house with you?"

"Oh, that," Aunt Grace said too quickly and placed her hand on Evy's arm. "Perhaps it had a small effect on the outcome. Things will work out in due time. We will rest our need with God. He knows our situation. He has good plans. Bishop will also continue to do what he can to find me a post. In the meantime, I shall try my hand at sewing. Lady Camilla has been talking to Miss Hildegard, the seamstress at Rookswood. Miss Hildegard has kindly suggested she could use a little help now and then." She smiled. "So you see, we will not starve in the streets."

Aunt Grace spoke lightly enough, yet Evy could see she was burdened. How like her to try to put a good face on her disappointment. Evy admired her so, and her own conscience was smitten over her deceptive behavior where the vicar and Derwent were concerned.

"Aunt, I feel ashamed about…withholding the truth from Vicar Brown." She paused on the road, and they faced each other. The breeze tossed their capes. A few clouds blew in and scuttled across the wintry sky.

"It concerns Derwent and the episode at Rookswood mausoleum." Evy forced the truth out. "I suppose by now the vicar told you what happened?" Of course, Evy knew that he had—as far as he knew the truth. She had heard them talking.

"Yes. It is all over the village."

Evy saw an odd look on Aunt Grace's features. Had her aunt already suspected her dishonesty?

"Would you like to tell me about it?"

Evy would not, but knew she must if ever she would be free of the burden. She told Aunt Grace what happened when she and Derwent went in search of mistletoe, fully expecting to see her growing look of disapproval. She was heartened when her aunt revealed no shock. If Evy were telling her tale to Alice Tisdale, she would have behaved as though it were a scandal in need of a town meeting.

"Thank you for telling me."

"I should loathe it if my silence about this caused any excessive difficulties for the vicar."

"I will see to the matter. Derwent has already told his father everything, including how you were with him when the squire's son took both of you to Rookswood."

"But Vicar never spoke to me about it."

She smiled briefly and they walked on. "No. He was waiting for you to tell the truth. He was assured you would once I returned home."

"Oh dear… I suppose I shall need to go to him, too."

"Yes. And he will surely accept your apology."

Evy nodded. This was so humiliating. *And it is all Rogan's fault.* No… She could not blame him for her own response. It would have been much easier to have simply told the truth to begin with.

"Derwent believes the door to the mausoleum was jammed. The squire's son convinced him the wind must have blown it shut."

Her aunt kept walking. "And you do not think it was the wind?"

Evy drew in a breath. "No."

"You were not there, Evy. It is your word against Master Rogan's. We must understand that the Chantrys have special privileges accorded to their position."

"Yes. I understand that." And one of those privileges was that their word was considered law. *More's the pity.*

"I am not suggesting such privileges are right, but it has been that way for centuries, and I suspect it will remain so for centuries more."

Evy had no doubt.

"I think," her aunt said, "that we may need to dismiss this behavior as a boyish prank and let the matter die down of its own accord. Master Rogan did return to let Derwent out. If he were a really cruel boy, he might have left him trapped there all night."

Evy shuddered. "I suppose. He did say it was only around ten minutes, but he also said he did it deliberately."

"Did he? Curious… I wonder why. He did not need to tell you."

"No. I think he had not intended to. I have tried to tell Derwent that Rogan locked him inside, but he's not willing to accept that the squire's son would do such a thing."

Evy knew why, too. Rogan had been friendly to Derwent after the crypt incident. That was unusual because she knew that he thought Derwent *unstimulating*. Rogan normally would not choose him as a companion. Both Rogan and Parnell had many friends their own age in the nobility, who shared the same mind-set, abilities, and background. They were accustomed to involving themselves in all manner of exciting activities with well-educated people. Yet Derwent just a few days ago told her with a ringing voice that Master Rogan had brought him to the Rookswood stables and allowed him to choose a horse. And Rogan had brought him to his father's armory closet and had shown him how to handle a rifle so they could go on a rabbit hunt.

"I even saw the suit of armor!"

Evy could still see the way Derwent's eyes had shone.

"I think it wise that you not try to convince Derwent otherwise, Evy. He will need to make up his own mind about Master Rogan. And if you speak against him, Derwent may think you are merely envious that you were not asked to go riding with them. They seem to be getting on as well as anyone in Rogan's position can with peasantry, and that is what we villagers are considered. Not merely by the Chantrys, mind you. These distinctions reign throughout English nobility, as they do also in France and many European countries."

"In France the peasants overthrew the nobility."

"Ah, the Reign of Terror. Thankfully the peasant class of England holds no such vicious vendetta against the royal family. We are not as hotly volatile as the French peasants were."

Evy agreed. "*We* are cool and calm."

Aunt Grace laughed. "We hope. Then again, we are not treated as badly as were the peasant class in France at that time."

Evy felt a great respect and affection in her heart for the beloved Queen Victoria. She imagined herself, sword in hand, defending Her Majesty from a horde of angry British peasants storming St. James Palace.

That image was replaced by another, but this one was real. How surprised she had been when Rogan came riding up to the rectory to see Derwent two days after the mausoleum incident. Evy had been picking Michaelmas daisies with Mrs. Croft and pretended not to see him. Rogan had climbed down from his horse and talked with Derwent, who was weeding the garden. Then Rogan gave something to Derwent. Derwent brought it over to her.

"Fancy you forgot this," Derwent said with a grin.

It was the basket of mistletoe. Evy glanced from the now wilted greens across the yard to Rogan, but he behaved as though she were not there. He was either too friendly or not friendly at all. Of course, she *had* criticized him the night he had brought Derwent back to the rectory. Now he most likely was reminding her of her rightful place.

"Wager you don't know what Master Rogan just offered me." Derwent looked positively giddy.

"Another look inside the mausoleum?"

"Evy!" scolded Mrs. Croft.

Derwent grinned. "No, goose. A horse from Squire's stables."

"A…horse?"

"For riding. And hunting! Wager you'd never thought to see Derwent Brown going hunting with the future squire."

"No, I never did."

"You'd best cease using the word *wager*, Derwent. Your father is set against gambling," Mrs. Croft warned. "And you be careful how you handle them rifles, young man, lest you go shootin' your foot—or Master Rogan's."

Apparently the adventure turned out well. They had returned safely, and Rogan had made certain Derwent was home in time for supper. Certainly he was on his best behavior. Had her rebuke stung his conscience after all?

Derwent brought home a dead rabbit for the sexton to make a favorite stew, which he remembered from childhood (and which Mrs. Croft loathed and would not cook). Derwent confessed he was not sure whether he had shot the rabbit or Master Rogan had. At any rate the sexton, grinning, had been very pleased.

Recently Derwent was walking around with his head higher and his shoulders straighter than ever before, proud that he should have made friends with Rogan Chantry, who, he said, "rides better and shoots straighter than anyone else in Grimston Way."

"Derwent's unexpected friendship with the squire's son seems to be doing him much good," Aunt Grace agreed as they continued their walk. "He is gaining more confidence."

"Maybe, but Rogan orders Derwent about mercilessly."

Her aunt angled her a glance. "Derwent does not appear to mind. He has been a lonely boy most of his life. Not even the other village boys liked him."

"That is true." Now, of course, the other boys were treating Derwent differently. They gathered around to ask about his latest adventure with the squire's son, and could he use his *influence* with Master Rogan to allow them also to accompany Derwent on the next hunting adventure? Since the friendship had begun, it was as though Rogan had raised his scepter and knighted Derwent Brown.

Of course, Rogan's friendliness would not last. Rogan was to be sent away to school in London in February, and that would be the end of it. She hoped Derwent would not be too disappointed when the princely horse turned into a pumpkin at precisely the hour Rogan left Grimston Way.

So the incident at the Chantry mausoleum was to be dismissed as a boyish prank. She believed her aunt said this because she understood that Evy's persistence would hurt her more than it would teach Rogan a lesson. It was just as Rogan had warned her that evening in the front hall: No one in the village in his right mind would win anything by butting heads with the Chantry family.

Her aunt was right. Better to leave things as they were. Evy could just imagine Alice whispering, "Fancy that Evy just trying to get the squire's son into trouble. She's tattling about him because he won't pay her the slightest bit of attention is what I say. My *mum* says…"

Yes, she could imagine what her *mum* would say. Mrs. Tisdale, too, had influence in the village. Recently she had been trying to win Lady

Camilla Brewster with flattery. So that was that. Evy would not go up against Rogan Chantry.

He has won, but I will be even more cautious of him now. She remembered what Mrs. Croft had once warned her. Evy could not forget the words: "Every decent girl in Grimston Way had better watch out. Squire's two sons can do no wrong, so says Sir Lyle. So if there's any mischief to happen, who do you think will be blamed, eh?"

Yes, she would beware indeed.

CHAPTER ELEVEN

Christmas Day arrived chilly and damp, but the sky was clear of mist. The eve before, villagers from all over Grimston Way had continued their tradition of visiting the parish to enjoy platters filled with ginger cookies, mince pies, and a special cider that Mrs. Croft made each year. This time they also came to call on the new vicar and his son and to pay their respects to dear Edmund's widow and niece.

Evy found it a little odd to hear Christmas wishes and condolences in the same breath, but then, nothing seemed normal these past months. Her heart ached for Uncle Edmund, and she knew Aunt Grace grieved as well. Despite the loss, though, her aunt was determined not to spoil the holy day with her own sorrows.

"At Christmas we should not think only of ourselves, but we should also remember our Savior's birth and how it means good news of great joy for all people."

On Christmas Day, Aunt Grace gave Evy a light blue, barred muslin dress trimmed with eyelet lace, assuredly her prettiest and most adult frock ever—although her aunt admitted that the style was a bit behind the present fashion. There was even a pair of heeled slippers, and Evy admitted she looked quite grown-up. She threw her arms around her aunt. "Why, this is not the same dress you have been working on in the evenings!"

"So I fooled you. Well, good, that was my intention. And here is the one I was working on. Now you have two."

Evy, with the help of Mrs. Croft, had made her aunt a lace bookmark and a small reading pillow with tassels. The pillow had a small pocket in which to tuck away her book and reading spectacles.

There was a mince pie sent over from Mrs. Matheson and Tom, who had tried to be nice to Evy. Emily had wrapped up one of her favorite books of poems and gave it to Evy. Everyone was thoughtful and kind. But perhaps the biggest surprise of all came when the Chantry carriage pulled up in front of the rectory and Mr. Bixby got out, sporting a new shiny hat and looking quite proud of it. He came to their door, arms laden with gifts.

Evy and Aunt Grace each received a new hooded cloak and mittens from Lady Camilla. There was a box of bonbons from Switzerland, fruit-shaped marzipan from London, and tins of various cakes and puddings. And Derwent, to his delighted shock and everyone's surprise, had been sent hunting apparatus from Rogan Chantry.

It would be Evy's last Christmas dinner in the rectory, and they had bought a fat hen from Farmer Gilford so that there could be a feast, with Vicar Brown and Derwent as their guests.

"He shall come down like rain upon mown grass," Aunt Grace read from the Psalms before their meal.

The day became a very special Christmas, one Evy knew she would always look back on with fondness and sorrow mingled. They had known the sharpness of God's pruning, but God's kindness could also be depended upon to send soft, healing showers in this new season of their lives. Tomorrow they would set out once more on a different road, but Evy knew wherever that journey might lead, God would be faithful. Amid their loss had come blessing too.

A few days after the New Year of 1891 began, Evy came home one afternoon from her music lesson at Mrs. Tisdale's and noticed something different about Aunt Grace. Her aunt stood before the window, her small pince-nez clipped to the bridge of her nose, contemplating a letter with some uncertainty—yet also with obvious excitement. A fire glowed in the fireplace where water sizzled on the hob. Evy set her bag and cape down on the wooden bench and went to prepare some tea.

Finally she could stand it no longer. "Aunt Grace, what has happened?"

Her aunt looked up, startled. "Hmm? Oh yes. Yes, everything is going quite well, dear. How was your lesson?"

"It was wonderful. Mrs. Tisdale says I'm nearly as good as her Alice. Meg and Emily are all thumbs, she says. She becomes quite irritated with them because they have calluses on their hands and their fingernails are soiled."

"I hope she did not say such things to their faces."

"No." Evy looked at her own fingernails and was pleased they were clean and filed neatly. But Meg and Emily could not help it. They worked so hard helping their poor families...

"Is that a letter from the London bishop, Aunt Grace?"

"No. It is from Rookswood."

Rookswood!

"Something unexpected has happened." Her aunt's eyes glowed. "Lady Camilla writes me that Arcilla needs a governess. Miss Hortense has retired to the servant's cottage, which is no surprise. Her retirement has been expected for some time."

Evy swallowed. Could that possibly mean...?

Aunt Grace's eyes twinkled. "Lady Camilla wishes to procure me for that position."

Evy caught her breath and stared at her aunt. "Are you going to accept?"

"I will be meeting with Lady Camilla on Wednesday afternoon." Aunt Grace touched her hair. "I will need to wash and arrange it nicely," she murmured to herself. "And I shall wear my gray organdy dress. If all goes as expected, Evy, we shall be moving up to Rookswood. We shall have two adjoining rooms on the third floor, vacated by Miss Hortense. I know that will please you."

Evy clapped her palms together, laughing. "Oh, how exciting! Living inside that splendid house. What would Uncle think if he knew?"

Aunt Grace's face lost some of its glow, and her eyes became grave. "I wonder."

Evy could have bitten back her words. Even so, what choice did Aunt Grace have but to go? Evy clasped her hands together. Her aunt, the new governess at Rookswood! It appeared to be the perfect solution to their present need and would even allow them to remain in the village of Grimston Way, among friends. Their prayers were answered.

And yet… Evy watched her aunt's face and was nearly certain that despite her own enthusiasm for the coveted position, Aunt Grace seemed troubled. It could not be over becoming a governess, since she already desired to do so in London. Nor could it be the wage, since it was known that Sir Lyle paid well. So what was it about going to Rookswood that caused Aunt Grace anxiety?

Evy soothed herself by believing that perhaps it was just the difficulty of being governess to spoiled Arcilla. It was well known that Miss Hortense had struggled for years, first with Parnell and Rogan, and then with Arcilla who was far worse than her brothers.

Aunt Grace handed Evy Lady Camilla's letter to read for herself. The silver lettering on the rich stationery bore the insignia of the Chantry family, and Evy fingered the linen texture of the paper with a degree of awe.

It was known among the village, wrote Lady Camilla, that Mrs. Havering was properly educated for the task of becoming Miss Arcilla's new governess. Grace was a woman of upstanding character and devotional discipline, having produced such a well-behaved young girl as Evy Varley. Therefore she appeared to be the "godsend" Lady Camilla had been praying for to teach Arcilla, who was not handling the loss of her mother well. Added to that grief was the absence of her father, Sir Lyle, still away in South Africa. Then there was the retirement of Miss Hortense, who had been like a grandmother to Arcilla. Lady Camilla remained in charge, and she was confident that offering Mrs. Havering the post, which would include room and board for herself and Evy, plus a decent wage, would please Sir Lyle.

The letter continued: *As we discussed before the vicar's untimely death, it comes to my attention that the calming influence of your niece as a companion for Arcilla will also benefit Evy herself, as she can attend the schoolroom here at Rookswood. The piano lessons would continue under the doctor's wife, Mrs. Tisdale, who has already agreed to hold the music lessons here, bringing her own daughter, Alice. And Evy would further benefit by joining Arcilla in riding lessons and other nurturing events, all of which would stand Evy in good stead in society.*

Arcilla would have another loss to face too. Rogan would be leaving soon to attend a private boys' academy in London for the next few years, and then he would go on to graduate university. Arcilla was especially close to Rogan, and so her brother's departure would certainly sadden her. Since he would be leaving in late February, it was imperative to have Mrs. Havering and Evy at Rookswood beginning the first week in February. That would leave the month of January for Mrs. Havering to conclude her affairs at the rectory.

Lady Camilla went on to write that she was quite sure that Vicar Brown would do all he could to aid them in moving to Rookswood. Camilla would also send two of her servants to help bring their belongings to the suite of rooms they would share on the third floor.

Lastly, Mrs. Havering's influence was deemed to be beneficial as she would be bringing with her the experience of having been a beloved and respected vicar's wife. The teachings of the church were to be used generously during the school day, for Miss Arcilla "is such a willful girl."

Evy frowned. Maybe her new life at Rookswood would not be as thrilling as she thought. She would need to get along with Arcilla regularly! To be her companion for a few hours a week was one thing, but living at Rookswood was likely to be another matter entirely. And while moving to the estate house would certainly provide adventure, Evy couldn't help but feel anxious about interacting with the other Chantrys either. Parnell remained a mystery. Perhaps she need not worry about him, who, being the eldest, would look on anyone younger with disdain—especially a girl from the rectory. Rogan, on the other hand…

Evy grimaced, then comforted herself with the thought that even he would soon be gone. And who was to say that she would even see him before he departed for London? He had, after all, been ignoring her ever since the incident over Derwent at the family mausoleum.

Perhaps that was best, since their previous two meetings had convinced her to tread with great caution where he was concerned. She was a little afraid of his dominant disposition, not knowing what to expect from him or how far his intentions would take him. Although locking Derwent in the mausoleum had been a prank, what else could he get by with if he chose to? She was sure Rogan's arrogance convinced him that he deserved to be obeyed just because he was a Chantry, and that she and everyone else should treat him with complete deference.

And that was one thing Evy knew she simply would not do.

Evy would always remember the day when Mr. Bixby arrived at the rectory in the shiny Chantry coach to bring her and Aunt Grace to Rookswood. As they departed that February for the last time, even the weather mirrored her emotions: temperamental, as though it could not decide whether to turn sunny or cloudy.

She and Aunt Grace had packed the last of their belongings the evening before. Their trunks and a few special pieces of furniture, going back to the youthful beginnings of her aunt's marriage to Uncle Edmund, had already been sent over to Rookswood two days before in a wagonette. So today she and Aunt Grace carried only a small portmanteau.

Vicar Brown, Derwent, and Mrs. Croft stood out in front of the rectory garden gate to see them off. Mrs. Croft tearfully reminded Evy that it wasn't as if they'd never see each other again, "The walk down from Rookswood to the rectory, and coming to my cottage for tea, isn't far at all." Evy agreed, trying to dispel the nagging sadness that all goodbyes tend to bring when what was shall never be again.

The coach wound its way up the road bordering Grimston Woods, and the estate gate came into view. Evy heard the eerie squabbling of the rooks seeking a perch in the gray branches.

Evy sat across from her aunt, who wore her best gray linen dress with matching hat and gloves. Evy, too, was appropriately clothed in her new dress with its frills. It made her feel quite adult and special. All her other dresses were so plain, or, as her aunt said, *sensible.* How Evy had grown to dislike *sensible.* Such dresses lasted too long—until Evy outgrew them—and most were out of fashion, too. Then the frock was taken apart, and the best cloth was recut into a blouse or petticoat. The dresses were all in the darker shades: blues, browns, and even one black dress, which she did not like.

Arcilla's dresses were always bright colors with lots of ruffles, bows, gold and silver threading, some with pearl buttons and trimmed in velvet. They weren't sensible at all. But then, Arcilla was not the one who had to worry about washing them. Some people could afford not to be sensible.

The Chantry horses trotted through the tall, arched gateway beneath overhanging oak branches. Harley, the old gatekeeper, stood near the small rose-covered cottage he occupied and lifted his cap before shutting the gate after them. He was Mrs. Croft's cousin and had been gatekeeper for as long as Evy could remember.

Once inside, the road changed from dirt to small cobbles. Evy looked upon mounds of green turf that gently rolled toward a horizon of trees on the perimeter of more private woods. Was that where Rogan had taken Derwent to hunt? The land went even farther back beyond the woods to farmland cultivated by workers employed by the squire.

The shrubbery along the lawns was meticulously manicured, the handiwork of Mr. Tibbs, Rookswood's main gardener. Not far from the entry gate was a narrower lane that she remembered well. It was the route along which Rogan had taken her and Derwent to the huge garden near the Chantry family mausoleum.

They drove the long S-shaped carriageway to the mansion, rimmed on one side with white birch and on the other with elm. When the horses at last came to the end of the S, Mr. Bixby stopped. Evy stared at the biggest house she had ever seen. And the most forbidding.

Why, it's more like a castle than a house!

A Chantry footman came to open the coach door, and Aunt Grace stepped down to the carriage block. Evy followed, unable to pull her gaze from the crenelated towers and turrets. She had learned from Uncle Edmund during her history lessons that they were from the twelfth century, as was the thick, high wall surrounding the main grounds.

What excitement she'd brought with her mingled with dread as gargoyles with bulging eyes and evil scowls glared at her. Evy imagined soldiers dumping boiling pitch down the castle's machicolations while fiery arrows flew from the tower heights to invading enemies scaling makeshift ladders against the walls. In one lesson at the rectory the curate had told of an early Chantry family fleeing into the woods and hiding for weeks while the enemy took over the castle. Someone in the family had been beheaded, but she could not remember who. Evy shuddered.

There was more than one door to Rookswood, and they were all studded with massive iron nails. Many windows included leaded panes, and Aunt Grace pointed out the intricate Gothic tracery on the stone mullions and arched transoms, looking so delicate in contrast to the grotesque faces of the stained gargoyle rainspouts.

No wonder Rogan behaved as he did. It was quite a change to leave Rookswood with its renowned family history and ride down to the humble village with its farm bungalows.

"What a...wondrous castle," murmured Evy as she followed Aunt Grace from the coach up stone steps that rose to a walled courtyard.

"Yes, indeed. Did you know that the first Lord Chantry went with King Richard to the Holy Land to fight the Saracen?"

"Yes, Vicar Brown taught us last year that Lord Chantry was killed in Jerusalem."

"I believe the present squire keeps the sword in the armory room. Perhaps one day when we study history we shall have a tour of the weaponry."

Mrs. Wetherly, the Chantrys' housekeeper, wearing a black bombazine dress and stiff white apron and cap, greeted them in the upper courtyard. Evy recalled that she was a nice, no-nonsense woman who attended Sunday services. Evy wondered what *she* thought of the nosy Lizzie, as well as the host of Mrs. Croft's relatives.

"Welcome to Rookswood, Mrs. Havering," she said. "Lady Camilla will be meeting with you after luncheon in the library. She didn't sleep well last night and hasn't risen yet. I daresay her health troubles her… Do come this way, and I'll show you and Evy right up to your rooms."

"Thank you," said Aunt Grace. "Evy?"

But a fluttering caught her eye, and she looked up to see Arcilla peering down at her from one of the windows. With gold hair plaited and wearing a maroon satin dress, she might have passed for a medieval princess trapped in a castle. Then the girl stuck out her tongue and wrinkled her nose.

Princess, indeed. More like the toad!

Evy finally followed her aunt and Mrs. Wetherly inside, where she came to a stunned halt in the huge baronial hall, adorned with a magnificent chandelier in its vaulted ceiling. She figured the hall to run at least fifty feet with windows on either side. Sunlight did not penetrate the leaded panes well, though, which made for lurking shadows in the far corners and increased Evy's sense of doom.

Drawing a steadying breath, Evy gazed about her. Crusader weapons lined the wall, and she tried not to see the empty eye sockets of the giant suit of armor at the base of the staircase.

Mrs. Wetherly chattered about balls and other musical entertainments that were held here in the great hall and remarked on how beautiful it was when decorated with Christmas candles and holly berries. "Not that there's likely to be any entertainment soon," she said, "not with Lady Honoria's death. And too, the master's been away, and his niece by marriage, Lady Camilla, isn't well enough at present. When Miss Arcilla grows a little older I'm certain we'll have many balls."

Evy lingered, trying to calm her palpitating heart. She ran her palm along the polished wood banister, feeling the hideous bulging eyes of the same style gargoyles carved so intricately there. Uncle Edmund had told her the carvings were done by superstitious people living in other generations who feared devils and thought to frighten them away by surrounding themselves with monsters equally as frightening. The more religious, he said, filled their abodes with carved relics and religious symbols.

She continued up the stairs, feeling the soles of her shoes sink into the thick garnet carpet. The color reminded her of the diamond-encircled ring she had seen on Lady Camilla's hand. She looked up to the gallery where the housekeeper and Aunt Grace now paused. Flickering candlelight glimmered and tossed shadows all around her. Evy took a deep breath and stopped. Foreboding drifted downward in the silent atmosphere and seemed to rest upon her shoulders.

"Evy?" came Aunt Grace's voice, seemingly from far away.

Evy shook her head, hoping to dispel her alarm, and quickened her steps to join them in the gallery. At least a half-dozen family portraits lined the wall. Evy tried to pick out which austere face would most likely be the *murdered* Henry Chantry. It was difficult. They all wore a faintly disdainful expression, even the women, but she finally settled on a piratical looking man with dark hair, mustache, arched brows, and a smirk loitering about his lips—*a rather cruel mouth,* she thought. *Rogan has some of his blood all right, except he's more charming and handsomer.* That had to be Master Henry.

She shivered, now with a strange excitement. Then motion in the opposite end of the long gallery caught her eye. She turned her head. No one was there. But she *had* seen something… She was sure of it. She stared. It was probably Rogan, trying to frighten her—

Just then, a man stepped through the archway and regarded her evenly. At first she thought it was the man she had met in Grimston Woods, but this was a stranger. He remained in the shadows, yet she could see that he had a black eye patch and wore a short-clipped beard. Certainly he was not a servant. His bearing was too proud for that, and his wardrobe was of the same expensive quality as Rogan's.

Aunt Grace and Mrs. Wetherly had left the gallery, and Evy could hear their fading voices. But she felt transfixed. His face was lean and hard and very brown…just like the stranger's in the woods. The man walked forward and stopped a short distance away. His good eye remained fixed upon her. A strange expression flickered across his face as he took in Evy's eyes and hair.

She could stand it no longer. Evy fled up the next flight of stairs after Aunt Grace and Mrs. Wetherly.

The man must be a guest, some important person in the nobility from London. Why had he stared at her like that? Almost as if he knew her!

Evy tried to concentrate on the housekeeper's words. Mrs. Wetherly explained that the nursery wing and big schoolroom were located on the third floor. Here, also, would be their rooms, not two rooms as first thought, but *three*. They had belonged to the retiring governess, Miss Hortense, who had first come to Rookswood with Lady Honoria after she married Sir Lyle in Cape Town. Miss Hortense had stayed with Honoria to nurse their children, Parnell, Rogan, and Arcilla. Honoria's death, Mrs. Wetherly said, had nearly undone the poor governess. "She loved Lady Honoria like her own daughter."

Mrs. Wetherly left them at their rooms, saying that she would have tea sent up at a half past the hour.

Their quarters proved quite pleasant and dispelled some of Evy's discomfort. A small parlor with a hearth and two adjoining bedrooms welcomed them. Behind a blue curtain was a private powder closet, holding a hipbath, a vanity cupboard, and a white dressing table with a large mirror. In the parlor were two chairs and a settee upholstered in cream brocade with pink roses, several good quality mahogany tables, shaded lanterns, and the secretary desk with matching chair that was sent over from the rectory.

Evy's own room was quite small but cozy. She liked the floor-to-midwall window that looked down on a courtyard. She was up high enough to have quite a nice view, though the woods on the other side of the wall looked ominous.

The four-poster bed was smaller than the one in her aunt's room, and though it did not have filmy curtains that could be drawn closed, she approved of the blue quilted coverlet and thick frilled pillows. There was a white dressing table with a fringed ottoman, also in blue, a hard-backed chair, and a small desk with an oil lamp and writing materials. The floor was not carpeted, but there were several area rugs to warm bare feet.

Only one painting adorned the walls: a young girl in a long blue dress, her golden hair undone, running through a meadow. Evy thought it enchanting at first glance, but the longer she looked the more uncertain she became. A dark forest waited on the other side of the meadow, and Evy could not be sure if the girl ran to escape something or to meet someone she cared about. Perhaps if Evy studied the woods more closely she would see someone standing in the shadows waiting for her.

Evy turned quickly away, trying to smile at her fancies.

Some minutes later, when her things were put away, she joined her aunt in the sitting room again. Aunt Grace smiled at her. "Well here we are, Evy. Our new home. In everything give thanks, and so we shall."

Aunt Grace took Evy's hands in her own. "Father God, we thank You for our new home. Encourage us to learn and accept Your purposes for us while we live here. Help us not to be too shy in showing others how much we trust You with the sudden changes in our lives. And remind us to be content with such things as we have, knowing You have promised in Your Word to never leave us or forsake us. We ask in our Savior's dear name, amen."

A few minutes later there was a tap on the door, and the maid, Lizzie, Mrs. Croft's niece, brought in the tea tray. There were cakes and frosted ginger biscuits sent up from the kitchen as a welcome gift by the cook, Beatrice.

"Welcome to Rookswood, Mrs. Havering, Miss Evy."

"Thank you, Lizzie. Do give our thanks to Beatrice in the kitchen."

"Yes, Mrs. Havering." The girl hesitated, as though she wanted to talk.

Aunt Grace remained noncommittal and expressionless, and Evy knew that she was showing the young woman she would not be engaging in servant gossip. Lizzie seemed to understand and quickly departed.

Later that afternoon Aunt Grace would meet with her charge, Miss Arcilla Chantry. Right at the moment, their unknown future seemed to Evy less than comforting indeed.

Chapter Twelve

Evy's meeting with Arcilla was not going well.

The girl was sitting on the window seat that looked out over the tops of the tall beech trees. She stood, as social graces required, when Mrs. Wetherly introduced her to Aunt Grace, though of course Arcilla was well aware of who she was. Arcilla had been attending the church for years. Evy thought the girl looked pale and docile—though she knew Arcilla was certainly not the latter.

Most likely Arcilla's momentary good behavior could be attributed to ill health over her mother's death or perhaps to her brothers' orders that she mind her manners. There was little doubt that Arcilla set great store by Parnell and Rogan, that she cared for their opinions as much as she did Lady Camilla's.

"Hello, Mrs. Havering." The stilted words were spoken as though she had been forced to practice their simplicity. "I am glad you have come to Rookswood." After a pause her eyes flickered, and it seemed her thoughts fought their way to the forefront to master her demeanor. "Not that *anyone* can ever fill the shoes of Miss Hortense. She was our nurse and governess all our lives—me, Rogan, and Parnell."

Her challenge was clear. If Aunt Grace expected to take Miss Hortense's place easily, there would be resistance.

Mrs. Wetherly made a throaty sound of disapproval, but Aunt Grace remained poised and confident. "I am sure you are right, Arcilla, and I certainly have no intention of taking her place in your heart. I am here to teach you on certain subjects until your father sends you to a private school in London."

"I shall *not* go to London. I shall go to *France,* Mrs. Havering."

"Miss Arcilla, you forget your manners!" Mrs. Wetherly's tone was firm. "Your father has not decided where you should be sent to school, and since that is at least three years away—"

"It is Aunt Camilla who will decide, and she has already promised that I can go to France!"

"Mrs. Havering, I must apologize for—"

Aunt Grace gestured airily with her hand. "No harm is done, Mrs. Wetherly." She turned and smiled at the girl, whose cheeks now showed two bright spots of temperamental pink. "I am sure Miss Arcilla and I shall come to peaceable terms."

The housekeeper was clearly flustered. Evy pressed her lips together. Arcilla was apparently quite used to getting the best of the poor woman. Mrs. Wetherly said, "Are you going to show Mrs. Havering and her niece, Evy, around the nursery wing?"

"No. I wish to be excused. I am not feeling well again." Without waiting for permission from either Mrs. Wetherly or Aunt Grace, Arcilla rose and started to leave. On her way to the door her gaze momentarily fixed on Evy, and she stopped in her tracks. A little smirk touched her rosebud mouth as she brushed past and went out, not even troubling to close the door. Her voice was heard in the hall: "Aunt Camilla! Aunt Camilla!"

Most likely she was running to Lady Camilla with an outburst of dislike for her new governess and the demand that Miss Hortense come back.

Mrs. Wetherly plucked at her crisp white apron. "That girl can be positively horrid at times. She's grown worse since her mother passed away. And Sir Lyle leaving for Capetown so soon afterward worsened matters. She needs a strong hand, and I'm afraid she's not getting it. Lady Camilla means well, but Arcilla is such a strong-willed girl that she dances circles around her aunt."

"I understand, Mrs. Wetherly. These matters cannot be rushed. I have hopes that in time she and I shall cooperate."

"Well, I certainly do hope so," the housekeeper said doubtfully. "The only one she tends to listen to is her brother. The world rises and sets upon him by her estimation."

"Master Parnell?"

"Oh no. Master Rogan."

Aunt Grace's brows arched.

Mrs. Wetherly shook her head. "Now that he's leaving next week, there won't be any of us who can calm her down." She wrung her hands.

It was telling that Rogan could calm his sister's emotions, or would even try. Evy would not have thought it in keeping with his self-indulgent behavior.

"Then I shall have a talk with Master Rogan later, Mrs. Wetherly," Aunt Grace said. "Perhaps he and I can work out something between us about Arcilla before he leaves for London."

"Oh, I am sure he would be cooperative."

Evy held back a snort at that. It wouldn't do well to offend Mrs. Wetherly, who clearly thought well of Rogan. The woman proceeded to show Aunt Grace about the large schoolroom. Evy glanced around, growing more dubious about their new home as the minutes passed. *It will not be easy here.* A sudden longing to be back at the rectory, far away from Arcilla, swept over her.

The room was bright and sunny with many windows and had the smell of books, paper, ink, and blackboard chalk. There were three desks with inkwells, two of which had been pushed aside. They must have once belonged to Parnell and Rogan.

Evy pondered which one she would use. Going to school each day with Arcilla sounded most unpleasant. She did not need to wonder which unused desk had belonged to whom. Both Parnell and Rogan had carved their bold initials into the wood, along with the date when they had left the charge of their tutor. Rogan's was just the month before, when Mr. Whipple had departed from Rookswood. Evidently carving dates was a family tradition, because there were other initials there too, from earlier generations of Chantry children. Evy found it curiously interesting to see the initials *H. C.,* etched by Henry Chantry, the man who had died violently here at Rookswood.

There were numbers of books stashed neatly in the walled bookcase, and a large world globe stood on a table. A world map was pinned to a wall, along with a smaller one of Africa. Someone had placed colored pins with tiny flags at Capetown and Kimberly. There was a blackboard behind the teacher's large desk, and Evy knew her aunt would make good use of it.

Some old toys were grouped on one side of the hardwood floor, apparently from when the Chantry children had been small. Evy looked at the red painted rocking horse and worn teddy bears that must have belonged to Arcilla, and checkers and a card game. The toy wooden soldiers and wooden swords must have belonged to the boys. She could imagine the many bouts and tussles that the two brothers must have gotten into when playing knights, while Arcilla played princess.

The door opened, and Lizzie came in apologizing for the interruption. "Lady Camilla wishes to see Mrs. Havering about the schedule she had in mind for Arcilla."

Mrs. Wetherly soon left to carry on her own work, and Aunt Grace asked Evy to go to their rooms. "Our trunks should be there by now. You can begin putting your things away."

Evy entered the sitting room and saw that the two trunks had been brought up by one of the footmen. There were no locks on the trunk lids, and one of them lay wide open. Lizzie Croft must have thought she was to help unpack. Evy saw that it was her own trunk that stood open, her things rifled through. Who would dare!

She closed the door and went to her trunk, looking down. She stooped to her knees to gather a dress and petticoat, when from the corner of her eye she saw someone standing. She turned her head quickly. Arcilla was framed in the doorway of Evy's bedroom, arms folded, a bored look on her pretty face.

"I do not like your dresses."

Hot words rushed to her lips, but she swallowed them back and managed a stiff reply. "Since you won't be wearing them, you needn't concern yourself."

"They are very dull. More suited for Meg."

Meg's mum worked in the Rookswood kitchen, and her pa worked in the stables. Evy struggled to hold her temper.

"Not everyone can have their own dressmaker." Evy directed a pointed look at Arcilla's satiny frock with its full sleeves, narrow cuffs, and popular braid hem. "But you are a bit young to dress so grown-up."

"I am *not!*" Arcilla fell onto the divan and drew her legs up beneath the knife-pleated underskirt. "I am quite grown-up for my age. I cannot wait to go to France to school. I shall have a dancing master and new gowns."

Evy gathered her frocks together. "It was very rude of you to go through my trunk. You had no right."

Arcilla shrugged. "You have nothing of interest to me."

"Then perhaps you ought to go to your own room."

Arcilla stared at her, mouth open, then laughed. "This whole *house* is mine."

"Not these three rooms. My aunt is awarded them for her work here, which will be quite hard, now that she is *your* governess."

Arcilla's eyes flashed, and for a moment Evy thought the girl would pounce on her like an angry cat, but though her hands formed fists and her mouth tightened, Arcilla controlled herself. Suddenly she grimaced what Evy could only surmise was meant as a smile or a truce. She scanned her curiously.

"You are not like Alice, are you?"

"I am Evy Varley."

"I shall overlook your bad manners." Arcilla sniffed. "I would have expected something much better from the niece of the vicar."

"And I would have expected much better from the daughter of the squire. Excuse me—I must hang my frocks in my wardrobe." Evy gathered them up and went into her room. She began hanging them up in the small wardrobe, fully expecting Arcilla to flounce away, but the irritating girl came into the bedroom and gathered herself onto the middle of the bed, watching Evy, amusement sparkling in her eyes. Evy would have liked to order her out of her room, but she could not do so without Arcilla making a fuss about it to Lady Camilla. And Evy did not want to make trouble for Aunt Grace.

Doing her best to ignore her intruder, Evy came to the bottom of her trunk, to a few games and some books that she loved to read. Arcilla looked at them and wrinkled her nose. "How can you waste time reading?"

"It's not a waste of time. Books teach and broaden your understanding of the world and other people. This one is Jane Austen's *Pride and Prejudice;* it teaches so much about the life of the upper class and their snobbery."

"It looks thick and full of words."

Evy laughed. "It is."

"You should come to my room. I have so many things to occupy my time, and so many dresses that Aunt Camilla orders Mrs. Wetherly to give my old ones away to the poor each Christmas."

"Then you have lots of reasons to thank God."

Arcilla sighed, and her smile turned sour. "That's just what Rogan said you would be like."

So Rogan had told Arcilla about her? How...interesting. "What did he say?"

Arcilla shrugged and wrapped a curl around her finger. "Oh, that you were disapproving and bossy. Always looking down your religious nose at everyone else."

Evy stared, surprised that he would have said such a thing. What shocked her even more was how the words stung. Had he actually put it that way? "I do not think I am any of those things."

"Rogan's right. He is always right. I am disappointed you came." She leaned back against the pillows. "I hoped you might be fun. Flirt with the boys and things like that. We might have fun together if you were different. But you are boring. An old stick-in-the-mud. But maybe not as trying as Alice Tisdale. That old stuffy sock! She actually thinks she will end up marrying Rogan, imagine!" She giggled. "He cannot bear the sight of her. Says she practically throws herself at him."

"He seems to have little good to say about anyone except himself."

"Well, he did not have anything good to say about *you* or that foolish boy, Derwent Brown."

"Perhaps your brother has nothing good to say because he feels guilty for locking the vicar's son in the crypt."

Arcilla shrugged, smoothing her puffed sleeves. "If he got himself locked in, it was his own fault. I hear Derwent is quite gullible."

"It was *not* his fault. He was deliberately locked in."

"Rogan is always right."

"No, he is not."

"He *is!* I am going to tell my aunt what you said about Rogan." She climbed from the bed and marched from the room.

So much for not making trouble. Heavy of heart and spirit, Evy finished her unpacking.

The incident did not die there. Evy mentioned the unhappy encounter to Aunt Grace, who in turn spoke of it to Lady Camilla. Soon afterward Arcilla was called downstairs to the library to meet with her aunt, who apparently told her that she did not have rights to the three rooms belonging to the new governess and her niece, and that Arcilla must not forget her upbringing. She must knock before entering, and preferably she was not to go there at all without being invited. There was no reason that Arcilla should feel upset, since she had access by right to the entire mansion belonging to the family.

Evy saw Arcilla again around four o'clock, when Aunt Grace called her into the schoolroom to inform her when classes would begin. "Tomorrow morning at eight o'clock."

Aunt Grace went to get her teaching desk ready, and Arcilla said to Evy in a low voice, "You can *have* those old rooms. What do I care? The whole mansion still belongs to *me*."

"No, it does not."

"It does!"

"It belongs to your father. Your brothers will inherit before you do. I have heard that Rogan will most likely inherit Rookswood."

"*Master* Rogan to you."

"No doubt *you* will be married off to someone and sent far away."

Arcilla glared. "I will not go to that horrid South Africa. I shall stay in England and marry Charles."

Evy had no idea who Charles was, but she almost felt sorry for Arcilla. The idea that she might be sent to the Cape had brought her genuine consternation.

"Africa is a boring place full of naked savages," Arcilla said. "Rogan showed me pictures of them. They have nothing on but a loincloth and run around with spears."

"I am sure you will marry whoever your father decides is appropriate."

"Evy."

She jumped at Aunt Grace's stern voice.

"We will not discuss personal matters concerning Miss Arcilla and her father."

"Yes, Aunt."

Arcilla shot her a look of triumph.

Later, Aunt Grace went out of her way to warn her against contesting Arcilla. "You must not expect Miss Arcilla or her brothers, when they are home, to treat you as your village friends do in the rectory. I am employed by their father, Sir Lyle. We must not forget we are considered help."

"I know that, but she is so *proud.*"

"You must concentrate on your own manners and pride, dear. You are not responsible for Miss Arcilla's behavior, but your own."

"Am I considered hired help, too?"

Her aunt hesitated, and Evy detected a moment of silence that might have been construed as sadness. "No, not yet."

Not yet.

"You are my niece. Nevertheless, you must be respectful to everyone at Rookswood and do as you are told."

❧ ❧ ❧

The days passed, and Evy settled into her new routine, as did Arcilla. Arcilla's manner had changed a little for the better. Much to Evy's surprise, Aunt Grace said she had spoken to Rogan, who in turn had a talk with his sister.

Evy did not see Rogan until the day before he left for school in London. It was during teatime when Lizzie brought up a tray for Arcilla. The girl asked Evy to stay and join her after Aunt Grace was called to visit Lady Camilla about Arcilla's recreation in the afternoons.

The tray was set nicely with jam tarts and milky tea. "You pour," Arcilla told Evy.

She did so, noticing the lovely chinaware cups with their delicate pink blossoms. "They come from far away in China"—Arcilla lifted a cup to her lips—"and do not take that blueberry tart; its my favorite."

"You are the hostess. You are supposed to allow your guest to choose first."

Arcilla laughed and took the blueberry. "You should know me better by now." She bit into it and rolled her eyes. Evy couldn't hold back a smile at the girl's enjoyment of her prize.

The door opened, and Rogan walked in. He leaned back against the door and watched them for a moment. For some reason Evy believed he was amused to see her here at Rookswood. She assumed it was because he was thinking of her as an employee, which in his way of seeing things would make him feel superior.

"Oh, Rogan"—Arcilla's lip drooped—"I am so sad you are leaving tomorrow. It will be so boring around here."

He walked up and lifted the plate of tarts, deciding which one he wanted. "You will have Miss Evy to keep you company." He chose one, then sat down near the window seat, stretching his legs in front of him.

"Evy is too religious to be fun." Arcilla wrinkled her pert nose. "Now if it was only Patricia—"

"If it was Patricia, you both would get into trouble and send poor Aunt to bed with a headache. You can learn from Miss Evy."

Arcilla laughed. Evy thought that if *she* had said that to Arcilla, the girl would have puffed up with offense.

Evy ate her apple tart and sipped her sweet tea in silence, aware of Rogan's presence, while Arcilla chatted constantly with her brother. He listened, making comments now and then, and all but ignored Evy. He was dressed in rich clothes as usual, with an almost bluish-white shirt that buttoned in the back according to the newest style. His ebony hair was wavy, and though Evy pretended to ignore him also, she was as stimulated by his personality as his sister was. His dark eyes glittered as though he held some secret.

"What do you think of the old vicar's niece living here at Rookswood?" Mischief peeked from Arcilla's gaze as she glanced from Rogan to Evy. Evy remained silent, looking steadily at her own teacup.

"You are the one who requested she come visit you in the afternoons," Rogan told his sister. "What do you think of her?"

Evy bit her lip. Was she but a commodity at scrutiny for the buyer?

"I have not made up my mind, and now I have dear Evy every day in school," Arcilla said with a mock sigh.

"You wanted her to come, and you know it, so stop being silly."

Arcilla looked first at her brother and then at Evy. "I suppose having her for company is better than being alone until I'm sent to school in France."

"If you do not do your studies, no school will want you." He looked at Evy. "I will wager Miss Evy knows her lessons every morning. She will soon show you up, Arcilla."

Arcilla flounced in her chair. "I'm sure I don't care at all. I do not intend to do anything when I grow up except dance at balls and have fun in London."

"Sounds positively wasteful," Rogan said.

Arcilla laughed. "*You* danced with Patricia at Christmas."

"Because I had no choice."

"Parnell's sweet on her too. You had better make Patricia happy, or Parnell will marry her instead. Then you will not get Heathfriar.

You know you want Heathfriar very badly because of Lord William's thoroughbreds."

Evy tried not to let her avid curiosity show. She turned to Arcilla, determined to change the subject. "Once lessons are done in the mornings, your afternoons are free, at least. I have things I must do for the rest of the day too."

"Like helping out at the rectory," Rogan said with a smile. "I suppose you and Derwent have a good time together."

"Derwent." Arcilla made a wearied face. "He is such an uninteresting boy."

"He is a *fine* boy." Evy couldn't quite keep the heat from her tone— or her cheeks. "*He* honors his father."

"Why should he not? His father is the vicar. He has no choice." Arcilla yawned.

"He has a free will, the same as you and the others."

"Always protecting little Derwent." Rogan tossed the last bit of his tart into his mouth.

"When she marries him, she will have to do the same," Arcilla teased. "And all their children will have curly red hair and freckles and become vicars."

"At least Derwent reads the Bible." Evy glared at Rogan.

"There you have it!" He sat forward with a grin. "The vicar's niece cannot *wait* to marry Derwent Brown."

"Oh, spare me," Arcilla cried. "A fate worse than death, if you ask me."

"You need not worry." Evy set her cup down. She stood with as much dignity as she could summon. "I must go now. I need to clean my room."

Arcilla giggled as though she had said the funniest thing in the world. "Oh, Evy, you are so perfectly the studious little girl from the rectory! 'I need to clean my room.'" She laughed again.

Rogan stood. "You cannot leave yet."

"My afternoons are my own." Evy faced him.

"Not for long. I heard Aunt Camilla is going to ask Mrs. Havering to let you take riding lessons with Arcilla in the afternoons."

Evy could not restrain her surprise. Was he just taunting her? She knew that Lady Camilla had mentioned riding lessons, but there had been no promise. The thought of learning to ride filled her with excitement. Rogan seemed to watch her reaction.

"Oh, Evy, do sit *down*." Arcilla waved her hand at Evy's chair. "We promise not to tease you anymore. Will you ride at Milton's Academy, Rogan?"

"Not as often as I would like. On weekends Parnell and I will be going to Heathfriar. I can ride there."

Arcilla turned to Evy. "Heathfriar is Patricia's family estate. You will meet Patricia one day when she comes here to Rookswood. She will marry Rogan. I like Heathfriar better than Rookswood because it's close to London. So many exciting things to do. You are so lucky, Rogan," she sighed wistfully. "Patricia wrote that Lord William will let her attend the theater on her next birthday. I wish Father would let me attend the theater."

"Patricia is older than you. She's my age."

He sounded so grown-up, Evy thought.

"Will you be going to the theater with her and Charles?" Arcilla watched Rogan, eyes wide.

Charles… He must be Patricia's brother.

Rogan shrugged and stood. "That is ages away." He folded his arms and paced the room, looking very wise and handsome. He snapped his fingers. "I have an idea. I know what to do this afternoon. Hurry up with tea, Arcilla. Tomorrow I leave, and I promised Miss Evy I would show her old Henry's ghost. You will come with her." He looked down at Evy, that challenging smile tipping his lips again. "That is, if you have not changed your mind about being afraid. You are so much braver than Derwent, aren't you?"

Arcilla drew back. "No! I hate those rooms. It is damp in there. No one's been there for years and years. It is dark inside too."

"We will light the lamps, naturally. Use your head, Arcilla. I have done it before when I was searching. Don't be such a coward."

Evy frowned. *When he was searching? Searching for what?*

Arcilla pouted. "Do you think we should?"

But Rogan waved her hesitation aside. "Of course." He looked at Evy. "You ran away from the crypt. You were shaking in your shoes that day."

Evy stiffened. "I was *not*. Nor am I afraid of the silly notion of ghosts. It's just—well, I do not think Lady Camilla would approve of me exploring the mansion."

"Oh, that," he said as though it were a minor annoyance. "Do not let that worry you. No matter what Arcilla says, Rookswood will be mine someday, not Parnell's. I do as I wish around here. Everyone knows that. And it is now my wish to show you Henry's ghost. That is, if you really are brave enough."

"I do not like Uncle Henry's rooms." Arcilla emphasized the repetition with a stamp of her tiny foot.

Rogan barely looked at her. "We need to go there. We have a crime to solve."

"How do we do that?"

"We solve his murder, of course," Rogan told his sister impatiently.

"Everyone says he killed himself over diamonds."

Arcilla's whispered comment sparked Rogan's interest. "Who said so?"

"Father, for one."

"Did he?" He seemed thoughtful.

"And Aunt Camilla for another."

Rogan grew pensive, as though Camilla's notions interested him a great deal. Evy wondered why; was it because she had come from Sir Julien Bley's estate in Capetown?

"There is no ridding Grimston Way of the gossip about Uncle Henry," Rogan stated. "Even old Hiram Croft thinks he was murdered."

"Then I do not want to go to his musty old rooms."

Rogan shook his head at his sister's fear. "Here is what we will do. I am the detective, and you and Miss Evy are my helpers."

"*I* want to be the detective."

Evy cast a glance to the ceiling at Arcilla's quick assertion.

"I am the detective," Rogan commanded. "I am older, therefore wiser."

That seemed to satisfy Arcilla, so he turned to Evy. He looked from her to Arcilla. "Are you afraid too?"

Evy refused to be compared to Arcilla! She would show them both she was far braver than either of them. "Of course not."

Rogan grinned, casting a glance at his sister. "Are you as brave as the vicar's niece?"

That brought a frown to Arcilla's face; she obviously did not want Evy to outshine her. She pouted for a moment, then she stood. "I will go if Evy does."

Rogan gave a quick nod. "Hurry. Bring a cape. I have only an hour before my riding lesson."

Evy wanted to refuse. Why on earth was she allowing him to manipulate her? And yet…she found herself growing more and more curious.

She and Arcilla went out the door and followed him down the corridor. It was anyone's guess where he was bringing them! And what if they were caught? The mansion was huge and dark, and she hoped she did not end up losing her way. Aunt Grace would be disappointed and displeased if Evy ended up embarrassing her so soon after she had taken up her position as governess.

Evy pushed these thoughts away as she followed behind Arcilla, who stayed close to Rogan. They came to a dim stairway at the back of the house. It was quiet here, as though it was not often used, even by the servants. At the top of the stairway a rope was drawn from the banister to the wall, closing off the rooms that were uppermost in the house. Rogan went up as though he had come this way often. Evy frowned. What was he searching for in his uncle's suite of rooms?

Her heart thumping, she climbed the stairs after him, one hand on the banister. She tried not to look at the carved gargoyles staring back at them, teeth bared. Arcilla paused, and grabbed Evy's arm. For once, Evy didn't mind the girl's presence. They went up together.

Rogan waited at the top landing. He wore a faint smile, and Evy had the clear impression he was trying not to laugh.

"Come," he said. "You both look as if you swallowed green frogs."

Green frogs, indeed!

Evy stepped forward. She would show Rogan Chantry just how wrong he was.

Chapter Thirteen

Evy waited, her heart in her throat, as Rogan tried the knob to Master Henry's room. When he found it locked, she was surprised at her own disappointment.

If the door to Master Henry's rooms was locked, they must turn back—

But Rogan merely smiled at them and took a key from his pocket. He unlocked the door with a flair.

The door creaked open, and he entered first. Evy was determined to be brave, but it wasn't easy entering the dim room and feeling Arcilla's fingers digging into her arm. For all Arcilla's boasting and professed dislike, she was clearly grateful for Evy's company.

The silent house seemed to close in about Evy. As she entered the room it was as though an eerie coldness touched her. The warm schoolroom was now a whole world away. In a sudden panic, she froze in the middle of the stuffy room. Rogan closed the door and lit a candle. His brown eyes were bright as he held the candle and looked at them over the flickering flame.

"This was Henry's Diamond Room," he said in a low voice. "He used to keep diamonds here from Kimberly to sell in London and Paris. He was also involved in smuggling. There was one particular diamond that he would not sell for any price."

"The Black Diamond?" Evy said it quickly, to show him she knew more than he thought she did.

The surprise on his face brought a smile to her own.

"How do you know that?"

"From Lizzie," she whispered ruefully.

His mouth turned. "You are right, Evy. It was called the Black Diamond of Kimberly, very unusual and as big as an egg."

"Ooh, is it still here?" Arcilla looked around.

"Uncle Julien came here and searched once or twice after Henry's death. So did Anthony."

Evy came alert. "Anthony? Is he another of your uncles from South Africa?"

He shook his head. "No. He's a Brewster—a stepnephew of Julien's, but because Julien had no sons, he decided to adopt Anthony when he married Lady Camilla. The Black Diamond was worth many hundreds of thousands of pounds."

Evy pursed her lips. "What could have happened to it?"

"That question remains unanswered. It is either hidden here somewhere, or—"

"It was stolen?" Evy whispered.

Rogan's eyes glittered. "Most likely at the same time Uncle Henry was murdered."

"Ooh." Arcilla's whisper echoed in the still room.

"Henry's ghost creeps about this room in search of his murderer." Rogan's voice deepened, and when the candle flame nearly went out, Arcilla broke for the door, but Rogan grabbed her arm. "Shh!"

Evy's teeth threatened to chatter, and she gritted them into submission. She looked about the room at a big desk and chair, a library shelf with books from ceiling to floor, and a glass case lined with black velvet.

"That was where he used to keep some diamond jewelry from Kimberly."

It never dawned on Evy to question what Rogan said, or to wonder how he knew this. She supposed his information had come in much the same way that he had gotten hold of the key. He knew many of the secrets of Rookswood and was bent on discovering the rest of what might be hidden.

"Of course there's no evidence Uncle Henry was murdered," he admitted, "or that someone came to Rookswood and stole the Kimberly Black Diamond, but whoever did it would be smart enough to make sure of that."

Evy agreed. Murder and diamonds… It was exciting and terrifying all at once, and she was in the very midst of the scene of the crime!

"D-did you ever see Uncle Henry's ghost?" Arcilla whispered to her brother.

"I once saw what I thought was a ghost," he said calmly.

"You do not think so now?" Evy peered at him in the darkness.

His dark eyes squinted at her. "I'll tell you this much. See that closet over there? That's where I hid when his ghost came creeping out from that door across the room. That was Henry's private room where he would sleep sometimes when he worked up here late. That's the room where he was murdered, but the constable and the family say he killed himself with his own pistol."

Arcilla tugged at her brother's arm. "I don't like it in here, Rogan. Let us go back to the schoolroom and finish the tea and tarts."

"Not until I look in the other room."

"What is it you are searching for? The Black Diamond?" Evy took a step toward Rogan. "You do think it's still hidden here somewhere?"

"I am searching for more than the diamond, but that remains my secret. I won't tell anyone."

Evy knew she shouldn't be here, but she couldn't leave. She was determined to win Rogan's admiration, to make him see she wasn't afraid. So she lingered, even when Arcilla tugged at her sleeve to leave.

"How many people in your family could have taken the Kimberly Diamond?" Evy whispered. "You mentioned Sir Julien Bley and Anthony Brewster—was there anyone else?"

"A passel of them. There are the great-greats. All Chantrys."

"Not all, there's Mama's family, the Brewsters. Lady Brewster, our great-aunt."

"I forgot about her. I think she is still alive. She must be as old as Miss Armitage by now. Henry was married to one of Lady Brewster's nieces, I think."

"Caroline," Arcilla explained. "Mother told me about her. She was a sister." Arcilla looked at Evy, and her blue eyes gleamed. "Lady Brewster's family helped find the first diamond in Kimberly."

"They did not!" Rogan frowned at his sister, as though she were foolish. "Uncle Julien Bley did. And his partner—a Boer."

"What is a Boer?" Arcilla wrinkled her nose.

"Ancestors of the Dutch, who went to South Africa in the 1600s from Holland. Julien is here now visiting Rookswood. He came from Germany on business and will soon be on his way back to South Africa. He didn't know my father had already sailed for Port Elizabeth weeks ago, or that Mother—" He stopped and looked at Arcilla.

Evy knew he had been about to mention Lady Honoria's death.

"Anyway, forget the Boer. Now, Sir Julien is partners with De Beer of South Africa."

"De Beer?" Evy frowned. There were too many names to figure them all out.

"You don't know who De Beer is?" Clearly Rogan found the idea incredible.

Evy realized the man must be someone very important and that if she were to be wise, she must know about De Beer.

"He owns almost all the diamonds in South Africa," Rogan explained. "He has a near monopoly."

"But he doesn't own the Kimberly Black Diamond," Arcilla protested.

"No one owns it now—except the person who stole it from Uncle Henry."

"It's the biggest diamond they ever found," Arcilla said smugly to Evy. "They will find it again, and we will be very, very rich."

"We already are." Rogan shrugged. "I suppose we could have anything in the world that we took a fancy to having." He looked at Evy. "Even people."

Evy's chin came up at that. "You cannot buy and own people."

"Sir Julien Bley bought his wife. He wanted her, so he bought her."

"That's horrid."

Rogan smiled. "Not to Sir Julien. Aunt Catherine Bley was very beautiful. She died as a bride after less than a year of marriage, and he never remarried. That's why he adopted Anthony."

He moved to the second door leading into the bedroom where Henry Chantry had either killed himself or been murdered, keeping the candle flame from flickering out. Evy followed, with Arcilla clutching her arm, the carpet silencing their footsteps.

"How did Master Henry come to have the Black Diamond?" Evy asked.

"There's a big scandal that says he stole it from Cape House—that's Sir Julien's estate."

"I'm afraid," Arcilla whispered.

"Then go back to your room." Rogan sounded as though he was growing impatient.

Arcilla looked at Evy. "Come with me."

She stood her ground. She wanted to see that bedroom.

"I'm going back." With that, Arcilla hurried out of the room, silently closing the door behind her.

Rogan looked at Evy. "Follow me, and because you proved you were brave I will tell you what I'm looking for."

"I already know. Diamonds. Master Henry must have stolen more than the black one."

"There were three bags of whites, too, but that's not what I'm searching for. No. It's a map. Henry's map. He left it to me in his will."

Evy's heart thudded in her chest. A map? "The map is lost too?"

"Or hidden along with the diamonds—that's my thought, and I'm going to find it someday."

"A map to what? A gold mine?"

"Yes, a very old map—hand-drawn by Uncle Henry, who was shown the gold deposit by a Zulu warrior, called an Impi. It shows a gold mine in Mashonaland. But Sir Julien and the rest of the family insist that the notion of gold is a folly. They call it Henry's Folly. But I'm betting on Uncle Henry. He was quite an explorer. He left it to me because he suspected I'd follow his interests. He was right."

She agreed with that.

"When I locate the map, I'll go to South Africa and start my own gold mining business. That's why I've chosen a geological university instead of Oxford like Parnell."

Evy could scarcely catch her breath! Here she was, the niece of the governess, prowling the secret rooms of Master Henry Chantry with the son of the present squire. Somehow everything Rogan did was adventurous and exciting.

No wonder Derwent liked to be around him.

As they slipped into the bedroom, Evy felt as though Rookswood welcomed her into its mysteries. For a short time she had what she had secretly dreamed about: She was important to Rogan and Arcilla. Arcilla needed her. And the more time they spent together as companions, the more Arcilla would depend on her. Rogan seemed to encourage it, as though he thought Arcilla was safe when she was in Evy's company. But Evy knew that while Rogan might accept her at times, as he was now doing by taking her on a tour of forbidden places, he never lost the demeanor that told her she was of a lower station, and that their relationship was a temporary experience. She sensed that as he went away to school and grew older, the relationship would end.

The bedroom was also in shadows. The large bed was made up as though Master Henry were expected at any moment. The room was cold and musty smelling, and the floorboards creaked beneath the carpet as they walked slowly across it toward another desk, smaller than the one in the other room.

"I've looked everywhere." Rogan held the candle high, letting the light play on the walls. "He hid the map in a good place, all right. Otherwise someone would have found it before now. I've tried to think like Henry, but somehow it doesn't work."

"He was much older than you are now. Maybe he knew things about Rookswood you do not."

"A secret hiding place for his map? Yes, I've thought of that. When I go to school in London I'm going to visit the historical libraries to see what I can learn about Rookswood architecture. I do know that Uncle

Henry studied architecture as a young man before he gave it up and went to South Africa."

"I'm sure you will win in the end."

He looked at her, and there was an expression in his gaze that made her breath catch in her throat. Aware of an unsettling tension between them, she hurried to fill the silence. "Because you will not give up searching."

He gave a slow nod. "You are right about that. When I come home from school I will keep on searching until one day I find it. If it's here. I think it is."

Her heart began to beat faster. She gazed at the painting on the wall showing tall Africans in leopard skins, with feathers, bones, and jewels in their headpieces. They carried fierce spears, and their eyes stared back with a regal defiance. Behind them was a lion with yellow eyes, and in the background, a great flat-topped mountain.

Rogan noticed her glance. "That is Table Top Mountain, overlooking Capetown. Those short spears or knives the Zulu are carrying are called assegai."

She shuddered at the sight of the painting. The Africans looked fierce and vengeful. "The Zulus killed my parents at the mission station near Isandlwana."

"Yes. I was looking at your mother's photograph in the rectory last Sunday." He studied her, and Evy felt a quick heat fill her cheeks. She was recalling Derwent's comment that she did not look much like her mother. Did Rogan think the same?

The door to the front hall opened quietly, and there came the dreadful sound of footsteps too heavy to be Arcilla's. Horror washed over Evy. Was she to be found out? Oh, what would Aunt Grace say?

Rogan put a finger to his lips and gestured for her to hide. She dove under the desk.

The moments crept by. Where was Rogan hiding?

She saw a flickering light, but it could not be Rogan's candle, for he had doused it when they'd heard the door open. Slow footsteps moved across the main room, and the stealthy sound of desk drawers opening and shutting followed. Ghosts did not open dresser drawers. Then whoever it was must have noticed the bedroom door ajar, for someone came to the threshold.

Evy held her breath. A man stood in the doorway—the same man she had encountered the morning of her arrival in the upper corridor. He carried a lantern, holding it high, so that the light flickered on his face: squared-jawed, a craggy complexion browned from the sun, thick jaw-length hair the color of ebony, a black eye patch. His good eye was a burning pale blue. He wore a gold satin smoking jacket, and a large diamond ring on his hand flashed in the lantern light. She saw his head lift slightly, like a hunting dog catching the scent of prey.

"All right. Who's in here? Come out at once!"

Evy's shaking hand went over her mouth. She was just about to crawl out and surrender when Rogan came forward.

"Hello, Uncle Julien. You smelled the smoke from my candle?"

"So it's you, Rogan. What brought you here?"

"I leave in the morning for school in London. I like looking at Uncle Henry's maps of South Africa, so I wanted a final look before I went away."

Sir Julien Bley was silent a moment too long, and then he appeared to accept the explanation. "Yes, Camilla tells me you are anxiously looking forward to coming to the Cape after schooling. Well, that pleases me, boy. Especially with Parnell showing so much interest in the diamond business. But I wish you would get this notion out of your head about searching for Henry's Folly. You will do far better in the mines. Prove your worth to me, boy, and I'll leave you a double share in my will."

"I will remember that, Uncle Julien."

He sounded so congenial, but Evy suspected he was pretending.

"Well, Rogan, show me the maps that so intrigue you. I can tell at first glimpse if they're up to date and accurate."

Sir Julien looked around the bedroom, then back down at Rogan. "Are they in here?" The tone of his question implied he knew they were not, which left the obvious question of what Rogan was doing in the bedroom if he were looking at maps. Evy tensed.

But here again, Rogan proved himself quite foxy. "Your stepbrother Henry had a whole drawer full of maps, sir. He kept them here in this ottoman." He went to a round footstool covered with tapestry and lifted the lid. He stooped down and took out a stack of maps, pencils, and several volumes of books.

Sir Julien came to join him. "Well, well. So you *did* find maps. Brilliant, my boy. Ah yes, indeed. I definitely want you in Capetown in a few years."

"I like this one best." Rogan spoke quietly, spreading it out for his uncle to see. "It's of Zululand. Like that painting on the wall over the bed."

Sir Julien followed his glance to the painting that had given Evy shivers.

"That was the Zulu king Cetshwayo," Sir Julien said, unpleasantness in his voice. "His twenty thousand Impi attacked and slaughtered our British troops in the Battle of Isandlwana in 1879. A loss we'll never forget." His jaw tightened. "Reinforcements came in later, and the Zulus were soundly thrashed. We've no trouble with them now—not much, anyway. Let me see that map, my boy."

Rogan stood and handed it to him.

"Ah." Sir Julien nodded, apparently satisfied. "It is Zululand all right. So, you were telling me the truth."

Rogan's eyes widened, making him the picture of innocence. "Why shouldn't I?"

"No reason. Well, good enough. Hand me those maps. I shall have a look through them myself tonight in my room. I, too, am leaving in the morning."

Whether reluctantly or not, Rogan gathered them up and turned them over to his father's stepbrother. He closed the ottoman lid and went toward the door. "I have a riding lesson in fifteen minutes. Do you want me to lock up?"

"Yes. Lock it up."

Evy watched them leave the bedroom and heard Sir Julien ask, "How did you get a key to this room?"

Rogan answered something in a muffled voice. Sir Julien laughed as if Rogan amused him with his antics. The door closed behind them and a grating sound was heard in the lock. Evy's hands were folded and tightly intertwined. She must not be discovered. It would mean trouble for Aunt Grace. Relief washed over her that Rogan had kept her presence a secret. But now...

Her eyes widened. She was locked inside! When, and how, would she get out?

Surely Rogan or even Arcilla would come back and open the door. But Arcilla did not have the key and would be afraid to venture here alone anyway. Evy hoped she would not say anything to Aunt Grace.

Oh, Rogan, now what?

He had to go riding, or the instructor would let it be known to Lady Camilla and Sir Julien that he had not shown up. Then Sir Julien would want to know why he had not kept the appointment. Evy crawled out from under the desk and went into the next room.

She would need to wait until Rogan could come back up here and unlock the door. She hoped he would come before the afternoon shadows began to darken the rooms even more.

She walked toward the door to the hall and tried the doorknob, but it was secure. She made her way to the window and looked out. Unless she had a rope she could never escape through the window. Nor could she imagine herself shimmying down a rope even if she had one. She grew dizzy just staring down into the empty courtyard. If someone had murdered Master Henry, that person would have entered through the hall door.

No, there was nothing she could do but wait. With a heavy sigh, she sat down near the door, her eyes on the big clock. The pendulum was not swinging. Perhaps it had not been wound since Master Henry's dreadful death.

It seemed hours before she heard quiet footsteps outside in the hall. She stood and faced the door. A key turned in the lock, and the door opened slowly. Rogan stood there, looking grave. He studied her face.

"I was afraid you would start screaming in panic."

"I told you. I do not scream."

"You were brave," he admitted, unsmiling.

His words did more to lighten her mood than anything else.

"Come along, hurry. I'll need to lock it again. And whatever you do, don't tell Sir Julien you were in here with me."

"I won't. But he took your maps."

"I didn't want those anyway." He smiled. "I kept them in the ottoman for just such an emergency. I'm more clever than anyone thinks."

She was not surprised. "You don't suspect Sir Julien?" she whispered as they went quietly down the corridor to the steps.

"Of what, murdering Henry?"

Evy clamped her fingers over her mouth. Even to say those dread words sent a shudder through her spine.

"No, Sir Julien doesn't need the Black Diamond, although he wanted it badly. He has diamond mines in Kimberly. He's richer than the Chantrys. He's as hard as a diamond, but some say he has a tender streak too. You would hardly know it by looking at him. Not that I completely trust him. He is greedy."

They came down the steps and across the hall to the schoolroom. He opened the door and looked inside. Arcilla jumped up from the window seat and looked at them, questioning.

"It is all right," Rogan said. "I've got to go back to the stables. Mr. Kline is waiting for me. I told him I had to do something important. Good-bye," he told Evy, smiling, amused again. "I will leave for London early. You have lived up to your boast." He ran down the hall and disappeared around the corner. She heard his footsteps clattering down the main stairway toward the front door.

At least he had admitted she was brave.

When she was alone that night in her bed, remembering, she felt uncertain, even fearful. There was something dark about those rooms… about the maps, the diamonds, and what she'd heard about Master Henry.

But none of it seemed quite so menacing as Sir Julien Bley.

Chapter Fourteen

The days seemed to rush by because so much was new and exciting. Then, one quiet Tuesday afternoon, Lizzie appeared in the corridor outside the schoolroom, waving wild hands to catch Evy's attention.

Evy glanced at her aunt, who was busy with Arcilla on a history lesson. She stepped from the room into the corridor and pulled the door almost closed.

"What is it, Lizzie?"

She'd never seen Mrs. Croft's niece quite so excited. "Lady Camilla is sending for you. She wants you to take tea with her in the parlor." Her bright eyes searched Evy's face as though she might find the meaning of this unexpected invitation written there.

Evy couldn't blame her. She was surprised as well. "Are you certain?"

"*Sure* of it. Something is up, Miss. Lady Camilla's been behaving strange these days. I seen her watching you, nervouslike. She wrote a letter too—to Australia, no less. Then she says to me, funnylike, 'But he ain't there yet.' Only she didn't say *ain't.*"

Evy glanced at the schoolroom door. Did Aunt Grace know about this invitation to tea? If she did, she had not told Evy earlier. She smoothed her cotton dress and looked down at her shoes. Maybe she should change into her new frock, the one she wore on their arrival to Rookswood.

It was quite a compliment to be invited to tea. Evy recalled the way Lady Camilla had looked at her when they first met at the rectory before

Uncle Edmund's death. "Are you certain you're not making a mistake? Maybe Lady Camilla meant both my aunt and me."

"No, she said it to Mrs. Wetherly. I heard 'em talking. 'Bring her now,' her ladyship says. A bit unusual, don't you think, Miss?"

Quite unusual indeed. Lizzie's eyes fairly snapped with curiosity. "And just you alone to tea, without Mrs. Havering nor Miss Arcilla. I said to myself, now what's *this* all about? Lady Camilla has herself something on her mind; wonder what it could be?"

Evy couldn't imagine, unless… Perhaps Lady Camilla Brewster had some interest in her parents? They were martyrs, after all. They had lived in South Africa. It was probably nothing more mysterious than that. Lady Camilla might even have met them at one time and could share some interesting experience.

"And that letter to Australia, I tried seeing who it was addressed to."

Evy tried to conjure up an expression of disapproval. "It isn't wise to be snooping, Lizzie. Whoever Lady Camilla writes to is none of our affair."

The stair creaked. Evy jumped and turned to find Mrs. Wetherly, the housekeeper, stopped on the stairway, brows arched and lips pursed when she saw Lizzie.

"You are supposed to be helping Beatrice in the kitchen, Lizzie."

"Aye, Mrs. Wetherly, I was just going there." The maid cast Evy a secretive glance and rushed down the stairs toward the kitchen.

Mrs. Wetherly sighed. "That girl is a trial to my patience. If it were not for my friendship with Mrs. Croft, I'd have sought permission from Sir Lyle to be rid of her long before now."

"Lizzie's curious about things." Evy did her best to give the woman a patient smile. "She's harmless, though."

"I certainly hope so. She talks so much about everything." Mrs. Wetherly studied Evy for a moment. "I expect Lizzie has already brought you Lady Camilla's request?"

"To have tea in the parlor, yes. Is it— Is it proper?"

"When Lady Brewster requests something, it is proper even if out of the ordinary. You come along with me. You look perfectly acceptable and quite pretty."

"I had better tell my aunt first."

"I will come back and explain."

Evy followed Mrs. Wetherly down the wide staircase into the great hall and then toward another intricately engraved door. She knocked quietly, then opened it.

"Miss Evy is here, Lady Camilla."

"Show her in please, Mrs. Wetherly."

Evy smoothed her hair into place and entered the parlor, taking in the heavy dark wood furnishings done in burgundy and gold. Lady Camilla stood before an upholstered velvet wing-backed chair; she looked utterly elegant and rather royal. Her long, flowing dress of wispy green material flattered her pale skin and golden hair, but seemed more appropriate for relaxing in the privacy of her room than for tea. Evy had heard Lady Camilla was still "rather ill" and wondered if her having asked Evy to tea might have surprised the household.

Oh, to be so lovely...

Lady Camilla smiled wanly. "Come in, Evy. Do sit down."

She moved across the thick carpet and took the chair across from Lady Camilla. A low rosewood tea table was set between them. Mrs. Wetherly brought in the silver tea service and went out, closing the heavy door behind her. Evy smiled to herself. So much for Lizzie coming with some vain excuse to loiter about the door. No one could hear through that heavy wood. It looked to be fourteenth century, when it would have protected a Chantry baron who might fear an ax attack from a warring knight!

"Why don't you pour for us, dear?"

Evy did so, suddenly grateful Aunt Grace had taught her the manners and style of fashion: Always remember to lift the little finger. Point up and not down. Never *grip* the handle as if it were a weapon.

Lady Camilla Brewster watched her, and Evy had the impression the woman was pleased. Evy handed her the tea plate, breathing in the sweet fragrance of the delicately arranged sweet jam cakes. Camilla chose the only one without gooey filling. Evy supposed that said something about her. Evy chose a raspberry, and then wondered how she would eat it without getting any on her chin, which would never do.

Camilla studied her, seeming to take in every aspect of Evy's features. Why had she asked her here? Evy offered a tentative smile.

"I am pleased you are not shy, Evy. Being raised in the vicarage as you were might have turned you into what we call a shrinking violet. Yet you seem confident and interested in adventure."

"Yes, I guess I am, Lady Brewster."

"Why don't you go ahead and enjoy that jam cake and not worry about the raspberry filling?" she said with a sudden smile. "If it splashes, we will keep it our little secret."

Evy laughed. "You knew just what I was worried about." She liked Lady Camilla after all. "I am pleased you would ask me to have tea."

"I have been wanting to speak with you for some time. Just the two of us, ever since I arrived at Rookswood from Capetown. The death of your uncle, the vicar, delayed matters. His death was unfortunate for you, wasn't it? I noticed at the vicarage that you appeared to love him a great deal, and your aunt, too."

An odd observation. Was it not normal to love the only family one had?

"They raised me. I consider them my parents."

"Yes. Assuredly. You would be so inclined. Yet they were not your parents by blood."

Now why was she saying this? "Aunt Grace is my blood aunt. She was the older sister of my mother, Junia Varley."

"Was she?"

Evy looked up from her tea. There was something a little strange in the way she said those words.

"Aunt Grace and my mother? Oh yes, they were sisters by blood."

The corners of Lady Camilla's mouth pinched together, making her look older than her actual years. She could not be over thirty-five, perhaps even younger.

"I wanted to talk to you before Sir Julien returns from London."

Evy watched her, speechless, trying to gain her footing. So that was why she had not seen Sir Julien at Rookswood for the last few days since Rogan left for school in London. Not that she knew much of what was happening in the house. She was mostly confined to the third floor and to their suite of rooms, though she could use the backstairs to go outdoors from the servants' entrance.

"Lady Camilla, I don't mean to be impolite, but why would you have a particular interest in talking to me?"

Camilla's eyes deepened to a violet hue. She leaned forward, her delicate hands clasping together so tightly that the fine hands turned white.

"You really do not suspect, do you?"

Evy tipped her head at the woman's amazed tone. Suspect what?

"They really have managed to keep everything from you. I should have known. When Sir Julien makes up his mind about something, there are few inside the family who would dare oppose him."

The energy with which she spoke appeared to have drained her emotionally, for she leaned back again, or rather slumped. Her heart-shaped face was drawn and weary. "Then, for your sake, my dear, I shall be…delicate about this."

Evy's fingers were trembling now, and her cup rattled on the gold-rimmed saucer. "What do you mean, Lady Brewster? Did you know my parents?"

"Oh yes indeed—I knew them. I knew your father *very* well. Or perhaps I should say, I thought I knew him. As for your mother, I saw her several times. You look very much like her—very little like your father. You have her traits, too, her confidence, her spirit—"

Suddenly Camilla went rigid against the back of the chair, and her face drained of whatever color it had possessed. Her action so startled Evy that she too froze. A door clicked shut, and Evy spun to find Sir Julien Bley standing beside the door to a room she had not noticed.

Evy's fingers tightened on the cup. He appeared just as forbidding as he had in Henry Chantry's rooms. This time he looked angry and intimidating. Perhaps the black patch that covered his eye gave him such a sinister air. But as he stared coldly from that one pale eye at Lady Camilla, Evy decided that the dangerous air was more than mere impression. It was quite certainly reality when his will was thwarted.

And though Evy could not understand why, it was clear that Camilla Brewster was doing just that.

"Sir Julien." Lady Camilla's breathy, thin tone set Evy's nerves even more on edge. Was the woman afraid of Sir Julien? Lady Camilla leaned forward in the wide chair, both hands clutching the armrests tightly. "I thought—"

"I know what you thought, Camilla. I have not yet left for London, as you can see. However, I have decided to take you with me when I do. You can wait in the hotel while I have my meeting with the colonial office. You will be going back to Cape House on a ship departing on Thursday. With Anthony ill and anxiously awaiting your cherished presence, I fear we cannot disappoint him."

Camilla dampened her lips and looked ill.

Evy's heart was pounding so hard that she couldn't breathe. The moment was horrid. She wanted to run out of the room, but her need to understand outweighed her fear.

She set her teacup on the table and stood to her feet, her knees shaking. Sir Julien's good eye swerved and pinned her to the spot.

"So you are Evy."

She tilted her chin and met his hard gaze. *There is no cause to be so afraid. Why should I be?* "That is my name, sir. I was just having tea with Lady Brewster."

His mouth quirked. "So I notice."

"She was about to tell me what she knew about my parents in South Africa."

Any faint amusement vanished. "I assure you, my ailing daughter-in-law can tell you nothing about Dr. and Mrs. Varley. Nothing that in the least will help you get on with your growing up. However, your Aunt Grace tells me you wish to attend music school in London when you are older."

"Yes. With all my heart." Now why was he asking her this? It seemed rather odd.

"You think you are good with music, do you?"

"Yes!"

The quirk showed again. "You have spunk anyway."

"But Parkridge Music Academy is out of the question since my uncle died."

Sir Julien did not respond. Evy shifted under that intense gaze and stole a glance at Lady Camilla. She was still slumped in the chair, defeat on her delicate features. Evy's heart went out to her in sympathy. Sir Julien could be a bully if people let him.

"If you will excuse me… My English class is about to commence." Evy turned to Lady Camilla, who was gazing at Julien. "Lady Brewster, thank you for the tea. Perhaps we can resume our conversation later—"

"I am certain Lady Brewster will be much too occupied packing her trunk for the voyage."

Evy inclined her head to Sir Julien. What could she say? What *dare* she say to such an authoritative man? She turned away and moved toward the door, but he came up, surprising her.

"One moment."

She looked at him, her hand hovering over the doorknob. He was unsmiling, yet Evy thought his rugged, dark features had softened ever so slightly. He reached out and cupped her chin, and she didn't let herself flinch as he lifted her face toward the light coming in from the window. His sharp eye examined her features, and there was no apology in his gaze or in the firm grip of his lean hand. He looked at her eyes, her hair, the line of her jaw and her throat.

Evy could not move.

After a moment his hand fell away and she heard a slight sigh escape his lips. "Yes."

There was nothing in that simple word or his weary tone that she could understand. Evy stepped back. How could he humiliate her this way, studying her like some colt being considered for purchase? And how could he be so mean to Lady Camilla?

"Why did you do that, sir? What did you expect to see?"

"What did I expect to see?"

The sound of rushing footsteps echoed in the outer hall, and the door opened. Aunt Grace stood there, out of breath. Seeing Sir Julien, she stopped abruptly. They looked at one another in silence, then Aunt Grace looked over at Lady Camilla. Finally her gaze shifted to Evy.

"You should not have left the schoolroom without permission."

"It is my fault." Evy turned with a start to look at Lady Camilla. Her voice was soft and childlike. "I wanted her to have tea with me."

"You need concern yourself no further, Mrs. Havering," Sir Julien asserted. "Lady Brewster and I are leaving for London as soon as she is packed. We will be on our way home to Capetown."

Aunt Grace had regained her studious composure. She nodded and looked at Evy. "Miss Arcilla is waiting for you in the schoolroom."

Evy's hands were clenched at her sides. "But—"

"Evy?"

She knew that quiet, determined tone well. There was no use in arguing. "Yes, Aunt." She glanced toward Lady Camilla. For a moment Evy thought she saw an apology in the woman's eyes before she looked away.

"Good-bye, Lady Brewster." Evy turned and saw Sir Julien's heedful gaze. She walked past her aunt into the great hall. She had started for the stairway when she noticed Lizzie dusting a spotless polished table. Mrs. Wetherly was nowhere in sight. Evy ignored Lizzie and rushed up the stairs to the third floor schoolroom.

Arcilla, waiting at the window, rushed at her as she entered. She must have wondered at Aunt Grace's hasty departure from the classroom. She looked as curious as Lizzie had.

"What happened? When Mrs. Wetherly told your aunt you were having tea with Camilla, she dropped everything and rushed downstairs as though the house were on fire. What did Camilla tell you?"

"Sir Julien arrived and interrupted everything. Why is Lady Camilla so afraid of him?"

"Isn't everyone?" She shuddered. "And that eye patch is hideous! And the way he stares at you with that one pale eye—it makes me feel like a butterfly pinned to the wall."

"But why is Lady Camilla so intimidated? She is married to his nephew, the man he adopted as a son. I would think they should all get along quite well."

"You heard Rogan before he left for London. Uncle Julien manages the entire family dynasty. Almost like a king with his realm of subjects. Never mind him... What did Camilla want with *you?* And why was your aunt so upset that you were alone with her?"

That was exactly what Evy wanted to know, but to share her bewilderment with Arcilla now would likely add fire to the matter. No, she must talk to Aunt Grace alone first.

When Aunt Grace came into the schoolroom and went around to her desk, Evy nearly went limp with relief. Arcilla watched Evy's aunt closely as well, and Evy was sure the girl was stymied when Aunt Grace sat down with a calm repose in her hard-backed chair. She lifted the spectacles from the silver chain that hung about her neck and placed them on the bridge of her nose. And then, as though nothing unusual had occurred, she reopened her big textbook.

"Open your workbooks to page ten, please. We shall be a little late with closing our lessons today."

Arcilla groaned. Evy avoided her aunt's eyes. If only she could so easily avoid the questions filling her mind, as though they were burned there with a branding iron.

After school was over, Aunt Grace came to speak with Evy.

"Let's walk in the garden. Better bring our wraps, there's a chill wind blowing."

They went down by the backstairs and out into the garden. The wind rushed through the treetops and sent the clouds scuttling across the sky. Rain threatened them as they strolled through one of the narrow rocky paths deeper into the huge garden. The green willows spread their lacy branches and drooped toward the clipped grassland, reaching out like the long arms of an octopus.

"You must have wondered why I was worried when you were having tea with Lady Camilla."

"What am I to think? It was all so strange and mysterious. And Sir

Julien—the way he looked at me. I felt like a specimen on display. Why is he insisting Lady Camilla leave with him this afternoon? I thought she was going to stay and live at Rookswood."

"So did I. She must have changed her mind. Her husband, I hear, is ill and needs her to return to Capetown. That must be another reason Sir Julien is concerned."

"He treats her like a prisoner."

Aunt Grace walked along, a small frown pinching her brow, her meditative gaze on the rocky path at her feet. Unlike Lady Camilla, Aunt Grace wore sturdy booted shoes.

"You might as well know the unpleasant truth, Evy."

Her heart pounded. Was she at last to understand all the mysteries plaguing her?

"Camilla Brewster is not well. I've learned that she is mentally ill. In the beginning she seemed quite normal, but after suffering through a stillbirth, she has not been able to recover emotionally. Afterward she desperately wanted a child, but the attending physician spoke privately to Anthony and Sir Julien about not taking the risk—a risk even to herself. Since then she has run away from Cape House several times since her marriage to Anthony Brewster."

Evy did not speak for a moment. Lady Camilla unstable? But she had appeared quite sane. She finally managed a question. "A risk to herself?"

"Yes. And there was the possibility of mental deficiencies in the children, as well. Anthony thought it best not to attempt having children again, which brought tension between them because Camilla would not accept such a thing. She was eventually placed under medical supervision at Cape House. And to make matters worse, while Sir Julien was away in Germany, she arrived here in England, looking forward to being with Honoria, only to receive the sorry news of her death. So it's really no wonder Julien thinks it best to take her back when he returns home to South Africa."

Evy paused by the holly bushes, still thick with red berries. She frowned as she pulled some off and tossed them. "I feel sorry for her.

And why was she especially interested in me, Aunt? I could see that she was. I'm sure she was about to reveal something personal when Sir Julien came in and stopped her. His very presence intimidated her."

Grace sighed. "I suppose it has to do with a story I've heard—about a scandal in the family at Cape House. After you hear it you will also understand why it would not have been wise for me to discuss it with you sooner. It must be kept in strictest confidence, as such stories, regardless of their lack of veracity, can ruin reputations as well as important relationships.

"The tale has to do with Camilla's husband, Anthony Brewster. There was talk of a baby. Sir Julien fears she has worked herself into a stressful emotional state after convincing herself that Anthony is the father and—that you could be the child."

Evy stopped cold, staring at her aunt. She tried to speak twice, but nothing came out. Then, "Me!"

Aunt Grace's features softened. "I know how you must feel. It is all wicked gossip and not worthy to be repeated. But you were so upset about Camilla's actions that I needed to explain what I felt was driving her."

"I had already heard about a baby, but—"

"From whom?"

At her aunt's sharp gaze, Evy turned back to the holly bush. "Oh, just Lizzie. She picked up bits of gossip here and there. When she told Mrs. Croft about it, I happened to be there. But why would Lady Camilla think *I* am the child? My parents were missionaries; she must know that."

"Who can explain the irrational notions in the mind and heart of a woman who lost her only child and desperately wants a substitute? Especially when she is convinced that her husband fathered another woman's child, and she cannot risk having one of her own. I believe the scandal includes a tale of diamonds that were stolen from Cape House years ago. She also believes Anthony had something to do with that. As you can see, it is enough to disturb any woman who fears such things about her own husband."

Evy plucked at the holly bush, not caring that she was being rough. "Poor Lady Camilla. I feel so sorry for her. I wonder if that's why Sir Julien looked at me like that?"

Aunt Grace started. "What do you mean?"

"The way he stared at me, searching my face, my eyes. I thought it very rude of him. He thinks he can do most anything." A little like Rogan.

"Yes, Julien can be rude, and yet there are characteristics about him that are also gentlemanly and generous. I am sure he meant you no harm."

"But why stare at me like that? What was he looking for?"

Grace walked on then, forcing Evy to leave the holly bushes and follow.

"Probably because he knew Clyde Varley and my sister, Junia. They occasionally went to Capetown to get supplies for the mission station at Rorke's Drift and would stop by and see Sir Julien at Cape House."

More surprising information. Was there no end to the things she did not know about her own family? "Sir Julien does not seem a Christian gentleman to me."

"I do not know about that. His interest in Clyde centered on a new British colony. Julien came here hoping to get a charter from the Queen to proceed. Originally, he felt that allowing missionaries to journey with the farmers would give the enterprise more respectability and acceptance."

"He intended to ask my parents to join the colony, is that it?"

"Yes. Junia once wrote to me about it."

"I wish you had kept her letters. It would make me feel closer to her and Father if I had them."

When Aunt Grace hesitated to respond, Evy glanced up at her. Was she hiding something? Quick denial and criticism swept Evy. How could she doubt her dear aunt? She must not be suspicious of Aunt Grace now, not after all she had been through, all the while saving some of her meager earnings in the hope of putting Evy through school.

Evy fixed her gaze on the hard ground. "So he stared at me because

I reminded him of my parents?" Could that be the real reason, or was there something else?

"That could certainly explain it. But it would be better to forget him, and Lady Camilla, too. In a way, I'm glad she is leaving."

Evy glanced at her. "Now there will not be anyone to oversee Rookswood."

"On the contrary, Sir Julien told me that before Sir Lyle returns, his maiden sister, Elosia Chantry, will be coming from London. Sir Julien arranged it. She is very fond of Arcilla and Rogan. So let's forget the unpleasant past and walk into the future with confidence and peace. Shall we?" She smiled, but there was a tension around her mouth and eyes that worried Evy.

She tried to smile to ease her aunt's concerns. "I want that too, but I'd still like to know everything I can about my parents. And I still keep wondering about that stranger in Grimston Wood months ago. Who could he have been?"

"Before your Uncle Edmund died, he had a talk with Sir Lyle. It seems that Lady Camilla had arrived from Capetown in the company of her cousin John from Natal. He journeyed on to the Australian gold fields. It may have been John you met."

"Australia?" She remembered what Lizzie had told her about a letter Camilla had written to Australia. "Yes, that's possible. If she confided in him, he might have thought I was related." So that was why he had suggested she should visit Rookswood. And yet…

"But Evy, I must warn you again. There is no end to the pain that reckless gossip can inflict. It is wise not to mention any of this. Lady Camilla's delusions must be kept secret."

Evy envisioned Lizzie repeating the tale, with her own enhancements.

"It is likely you will one day marry Derwent and live in Grimston Way. For your sake, your children's, and their children's, let's not make more of this than absolutely necessary."

Aunt Grace was right. Evy did not care to have any dark mysteries shrouding her parents' past, or her own!

They walked back to the house together and up to their rooms.

Later that afternoon, through a small window in the hall, Evy watched Sir Julien Bley and Lady Camilla Brewster being assisted into the coach by Mr. Bixby.

Was Lady Camilla actually ill? Or was it just a way for Sir Julien to control her? What could be the real reason Sir Julien did not want Lady Camilla to remain at Rookswood? Could there be more truth to Lady Brewster's claims about a secret child than even Aunt Grace knew?

As though she were once again in the tearoom, Evy could almost feel Sir Julien's chill, searching stare…feel the firm grip of those lean, hard fingers grasping her chin, forcing her to look up at him.

Just what had he expected to see—or hoped he would not?

Chapter Fifteen

When Rogan came home from school that summer, he did not mention Master Henry's precious map to Evy again. She began to wonder if it really existed. Had it just been a tale to entertain her and Arcilla, while he hoped to make them afraid of a ghost?

She was relieved no one in the house had suspected them of snooping in Henry's rooms. But one good thing came from it: The incident had triggered the start of Evy's friendship with Arcilla. In the months following that day Arcilla regained her weight, and there was now color in her cheeks. On her fourteenth birthday she carried a gilded mirror with her, which she took out during teatime to study her reflection, quite pleased with what she saw.

"One more year and I shall go to school in France. I can hardly wait. And you?" She turned to Evy. "Will you attend the music school?"

Evy looked away. She knew she did not have adequate resources for such a thing, no matter how much she wanted it. Uncle Edmund's death seemed to have closed so many desirable opportunities. "We must trust the Lord with our disappointments."

Arcilla smiled. "Spoken like a true daughter of the vicarage."

In spite of disappointments and uncertainties, Evy enjoyed living at Rookswood. On Sundays she and Aunt Grace would visit with Vicar Brown and Derwent, usually joining them for Sunday dinner. In the evenings Evy played the piano for them in the rectory parlor, then she and Derwent would walk in the garden and talk about his future. Soon now, he would be attending divinity school in London.

Aunt Grace naturally believed Evy's music would be a help to her as a vicar's wife. It would work well in the church services, and she could always bring a little extra money into the family by becoming a music teacher like Mrs. Tisdale, but Evy prayed for more than that. She wanted to become proficient, to study with the masters.

But how to manage those expensive years of study?

Evy's favorite times of the year were summer and Christmas holidays, for that was when Rogan and Parnell came home. Not that they noticed her, of course. On his first visit home from school Rogan had ignored her. It had hurt, but she told herself it was to be expected. He was there only two weeks before leaving again. She found out later from Arcilla that he had taken his horse to Heathfriar estate, the Bancrofts' home. It seemed that Lord Bancroft's daughter, Miss Patricia, was an avid horsewoman.

No wonder she appealed to Rogan.

Even so, everyday events were pleasant enough, and as time rolled by, Evy all but forgot the strange tales of Henry Chantry's murder, the Kimberly Black Diamond, and the gossip surrounding Lady Camilla and her husband Anthony Brewster. Even Lizzie seemed to have forgotten and turned her attention on Arcilla's comings and goings, as the girl was growing up fast.

Lady Elosia Chantry, Sir Lyle's eldest sister, had arrived the year before to take over the household, and Sir Lyle, whose voyage home to London had been long delayed, finally returned to Rookswood nearly two years after his wife's death.

"Papa, you are home at last!" Arcilla ran to throw her arms around his slim waist. "Do not ever leave again without me."

A wan smile momentarily softened his lean, craggy face. "It is good to be home, Daughter. How beautiful you have become. Where is Rogan?"

Arcilla affected a pretty pout and stepped aside as Rogan met him. "Hello, Father."

"There you are. Ah, a happy birthday, son." The squire threw an arm around Rogan's shoulders, and a happy smile lit his face as he looked his younger son over.

Evy, watching from the gallery, her elbows resting on the rail, thought it was clear which of his children he doted on.

"You are quite the young man at sixteen. Even taller than Parnell."

Rogan laughed, but drew away and pushed Parnell forward to his father. Parnell grasped his father's arms, meeting him at eye level.

It was a curious thing, Evy thought. Rogan so darkly handsome, so bold and adventurous, looked more like his Uncle Henry than he did his lean, ruddy father. It was Parnell who reflected his father's physical image, with chestnut hair and a slighter frame.

"Did you bring me any diamonds, Father?" Parnell asked.

Rogan shook his head wryly. "You sound like Arcilla at five, asking for candy."

"Candy diamonds." Arcilla giggled. "Oh, how tickling."

"Lyle, is that you?"

Lady Elosia came from the other end of the great hall, and Evy watched her brisk walk as she moved toward her brother, her hand outstretched. It was as though he were a guest instead of the squire. Lady Elosia was taller than her brother and, with her large-boned frame and silvery-blue hair, looked little like him.

"It is past time you returned," she scolded. "Dear Arcilla has been *demented* since you left. More's the pity, indeed, coming so soon after Honoria's death. Really, Lyle, you should not have left Rookswood when you did."

The squire dismissed Parnell as though he had not heard his question about diamonds and brushed his wide mouth against his maiden sister's white, powdered cheek.

"Hello, Elosia. I am afraid the call of the Kimberly mines could not wait." His tired voice contained an injured edge to it. "Missing Julien's arrival here at Rookswood as I did, I had to remain at Cape House until he arrived with Camilla. Bixby tells me she wanted to stay here."

"Trust a coachman to see through things. Truly, Camilla had no choice. Julien practically escorted her from Rookswood with a gun at her back. I daresay, I have never liked that stepbrother of ours."

"Jesting about guns after what happened to Henry is not wise, Elosia."

"No, naturally not." For the first time she appeared a little put out. "Well, at least you are home."

"I am very grateful for your being here, Sister."

"You always were doe-eyed and helpless without Honoria," Lady Elosia said in an adoring, albeit scolding voice, and she smiled and kissed both his cheeks. "Come along, dear boy, you must be famished. I say, Lyle! You've lost weight. I must do something about that!"

Rogan looked up at Evy with a half-amused smile.

Sir Lyle glanced in the direction of the great library. "Did my books arrive from the publisher in New York?"

"You mean all those geology books?" Lady Elosia wrinkled her nose the way Arcilla often did. "Sorrowfully, yes. I had Bentley stack them in your office. But look here, Lyle, I simply won't allow you to close yourself up with your books and meditations and ignore your need to find a new life. You cannot mourn dear Honoria forever, you know. By the way, that reminds me—we are invited to Heathfriar next week. Miss Patricia is having her birthday ball."

"Oh how grand!" Arcilla clapped her hands, tagging behind her father. "I shall see Charles Bancroft."

Lyle scowled down at her. "Forget Charles, Daughter. When you reach sixteen your uncle Julien wishes you to meet Peter Bartley. A marvelous man. I went there to meet him."

"Peter Bartley? But Papa, I love *Charles*." Arcilla whirled toward Rogan, grabbing hold of him. "Tell him, Rogan, *tell* him. Tell Papa how you and I are such good friends with Charles and Patricia."

"You have already told him."

"Who is Peter Bartley?" Lady Elosia frowned at Lyle. "We must be careful about Arcilla's future marriage. I will not have her unhappy."

"Now, Elosia, the situation is still several years off. I simply do not want Arcilla getting too involved with Lord William's son."

"Yes, who is Peter Bartley?" Arcilla fussed with the frills on her stylish leg-of-mutton sleeves.

"I know who Bartley is," Parnell spoke up, lightly yanking Arcilla's golden tresses. "He is a very important fellow, isn't he, Father? You see? I have been studying my politics just the way you expected." He tossed a competitive look toward Rogan. "Peter Bartley may head up Uncle Julien's new colony deeper into South Africa."

Sir Lyle turned toward him, brows lifted. "You are right, Parnell. That is why Julien wishes Arcilla to meet him when she grows up a little more."

"I am already grown-up." Her head tilted to the side, and a pretty smile showed a dimple. "But I simply will not go to that savage place, will I, Aunt Elosia?" She went and put her arms around her, looking at her father with what Evy was certain was an unexpected challenge, softened with a teasing tone, as if trying to woo him.

Elosia was quick to agree. "Of course you will not. My land, Lyle! Would you send your own daughter to live among heathen just to please Julien?"

"Uncle Julien controls the diamonds." Rogan's wry observation drew a nod from his father.

"Unfortunately," Sir Lyle said with a sigh.

Rogan tilted his head, regarding his father. "Where is this colony to be?"

"Mashonaland."

Evy noticed the smile fade from Rogan's face.

"Isn't that where Uncle Henry had his last expeditions?" Parnell glanced toward Rogan.

"He insists his interest has nothing to do with the map Henry left Rogan in his will," Lyle said, a little too sharply, Evy thought.

Parnell turned a wicked grin on his younger brother. "Better watch out, Rogan, or Julien will be staking his claim ahead of you."

"That supposed map of Henry's was never located," Lyle countered.

"I agree with Father. It probably does not even exist, Rogan." Parnell sounded almost gleeful. "You're wasting your time searching for it."

Arcilla jumped into the fray. "You are just jealous because Uncle Henry left it to Rogan instead of you, Parnell. Pay no mind, Rogan." She went to loop her arm through his, then reached up and smoothed his dark hair. "When you find Henry's Folly, then it will be Parnell who will look foolish. And you won't get one single gold coin, Parnell."

Parnell chuckled. "*I* won't need it—I will have the diamonds. Remember, Father, Rogan and I have already had our meeting with you and settled our inheritance. I get extra shares in the diamond mines of Kimberly, and Rogan can have Rookswood as he wants."

"And the title." Evy marveled at Rogan's calm tone. He seemed utterly undisturbed by all that had just gone on. "In fact, you can begin calling me *Sir* Rogan now." His face broke into a grin.

"You can have the old title and land. It means little to me. All I want are diamonds! South Africa! And unlike you, Arcilla, I *do* want Uncle Julien to arrange my marriage—to Darinda Bley."

"Who carries a tidy inheritance of her own," Rogan said.

"Listen to you two carry on about titles and inheritance as though I were already gone," Lyle said wryly.

"What do I get for my inheritance?" Arcilla complained.

"Rogan and Parnell will always look after you, Daughter, and of course you will have your shares in the mines."

"And Peter Bartley," Rogan tossed in, glancing his sister's way.

Lady Elosia put her arms around Arcilla. "I'm leaving everything that is mine to you, Precious."

Apparently Rogan had had enough, for he parted company with them as Lady Elosia led the way into the dining room, Arcilla on her arm.

When Rogan came bounding up the stairs, Evy started to return to the third floor.

"Running away again!

She didn't even spare him a glance. "I have my studies to attend to."

"It did not seem to worry you during my father's homecoming."

"I was not eavesdropping—not really." She hated the way heat rose in her cheeks when he teased her. "Aunt Grace thought your aunt might call us to meet the squire. I was simply prepared to go down if beckoned."

"As though my father does not know who you and the vicar's widow are." He smiled. "What do you think of my family?" His eyes glittered, but Evy thought there was a tinge of hurt in the humor.

"At least you *have* a family." She had not meant to sound wistful, but the note, though restrained, was clearly in her voice.

"I've been wondering what you thought of Camilla Brewster?"

Aware that he watched her alertly, she wondered if perhaps he understood more of the scandal originating in Capetown than just the part about the stolen diamonds.

"I felt sorry for her." She met Rogan's steady gaze. "Your aunt was right about the way your uncle treated Lady Camilla. He commanded her as though she were a prisoner instead of his daughter-in-law."

"Maybe being married to his adopted son is one and the same thing."

"At least you do not approve of Sir Julien's control over the members of your family."

"I hear Camilla talked to you before Julien burst into the parlor with his sjambok," he said. "What did she tell you?"

"Very little." Evy almost smiled at his description of the scene. Sir Julien might as well have brandished a Boer whip. She wasn't sure what he knew, and for some reason was loath to reveal too much.

Rogan leaned against the gallery rail, but his gaze never left her, and she felt her cheeks growing warm again under that scrutiny.

"Did she mention the mystery baby?"

So Rogan also knew about that as well. The heat surged from her cheeks into her whole face. It was absurd how she could feel so vulnerable about her past when there could be no truth to Lady Camilla's irrational beliefs. Nor was there any reason to try to hide the tale.

"She did not mention the gossipy tale to me, but my aunt knew about it and explained Lady Brewster's…illness." She hesitated, then gave in to her curiosity. "When did you hear about the child?"

"Just recently. When I came from Heathfriar to welcome my father home. I must say I was surprised to learn about it."

Then he had heard about it yesterday. "It is quite foolish, of course." She spoke with more firmness than necessary. "I know who my parents are. Dr. Clyde and Junia Varley. I was born at Rorke's Drift at the mission station two months before the Zulu War."

His regard of her turned pensive. "Rather a murky issue, though, don't you think? The rectory girl becoming my cousin."

"I cannot see myself as your cousin—or being connected to anyone in this family, for that matter."

"Then again, Anthony Brewster is not related to the Chantrys by blood, only by marriage. But I wonder how things would change should the impossible happen and you discover you are part of this mixed-up, daft dynasty."

"I do not know what you mean." But she did. She merely refused to think about it.

"I *mean*," he belabored the point, "you would be a diamond heiress, much like Arcilla. Julien would be your grandfather by marriage, which would mean he would be meditating on whom to marry you to. After all, he'd have to be sure to enhance his fortune and power."

Evy felt her mouth gape open, and she stared at Rogan. Not for *anything* did she want to be connected to this family dynasty. If she were somehow related to Rogan…

She pushed away the emotions struggling to overwhelm her and tipped her chin. "Sounds a bit frightening to me."

"Frightening?" That caught his interest. "How so?"

"For one thing, I would not want Sir Julien arranging my future. But this discussion is silly because the tale of a mystery child is mere chatter."

"Maybe not. I can see I will have to look into all this."

"Please do not."

His smirk was back. "Why? Are you afraid to learn the truth?"

"Of course not." Really, he was insufferable! "I already *know* the truth. It is gossip I wish to shun. Soon Lizzie or one of the other servants will start spreading tales and turning me into an heiress." She turned away. "Now if you'll be so kind as to excuse me, I must go."

He laughed, and the sound was deep and rich. "Wait. Are you not going to wish me a happy birthday?"

She hesitated. He was sixteen now, more handsome than ever, with a devilish grin and devastating gaze…and every inch a scamp. She pressed her lips together. "Happy birthday."

He mocked a frown. "Is that all?" She started when he reached out to take her hand. His eyes glittered. "All the girls like to kiss me on my birthday."

She could understand that. "Alice Tisdale was no doubt first in line."

"I only like the prettiest ones to catch me."

From the fire blazing in her face, she was sure her cheeks must be scarlet.

"Well?" His brows arched, and his smile deepened.

Did he actually think she would kiss him? She assumed her sternest expression, but could not restrain a small, teasing smile. "There is no accounting for boys with unwise tastes, or for silly girls determined to make fools of themselves."

He laughed. "Leave it to the rectory girl to put me in my place. So you won't kiss me on my birthday?"

"Indeed, no. Aunt Grace says a girl must never permit liberties until she is engaged and the wedding date firmly established. And then only a kiss on the cheek."

His grip on her hand tightened. "It is like that, is it? But you are not actually *that* old-fashioned are you? Where is your adventurous spirit? Why not do something just for fun? It's rather early for till death do us part."

Her heart thumped at the feel of his warm hand around hers, and she tried to wriggle her hand free. The action only amused him.

"Rogan?" It was Sir Lyle, calling from below the gallery. "We are waiting for you at the table."

He let a slow smile work its way across his features and tugged her hand. "At least come down for birthday cake."

"You forget yourself. What do you think Lady Elosia would do if the niece of the hired governess walked into the dining room and sat down at your birthday dinner?"

"She would do nothing because I have just invited you as my guest. I told you before, Rookswood will be mine someday. I will do as I wish here. Everyone knows that."

"I don't doubt it," she said with a rueful smile. "Thank you for the invitation, but I really must go." Easing her hand from his at last, she backed away.

Was that regret in his eyes? She could not be sure.

"If I cannot change your mind, then…au revoir."

He bounded down the stairs to join his father, and Evy watched them retire into the dining room. When they had vanished from view, she made her way upstairs to the third floor. But her wicked mind would not let her be. All she could think of was what would have happened if she had accepted Rogan's outrageous invitation.

She drew in a steadying breath as she sank into a chair. It was hard to know who was more dangerous—Sir Julien with his schemes, or Rogan with his utter determination to have his way with everyone and everything.

In the two years since Evy and Aunt Grace had come to Rookswood, Arcilla had accepted Evy. Still, the girl was not above being catty or demanding her way at times. She had her own set of friends from London's aristocracy who came to visit on holidays and in the summer, and Evy did not belong. When they came to stay, she would occupy herself with practicing her beloved music.

And yet, though Evy was excluded from the circle of Arcilla's friends, she was closer to Arcilla than she would have thought possible. The fact that Evy's temperament was so different from Arcilla's permitted their unusual but complementary friendship to proceed without threat of competition.

"We're nothing alike," Arcilla told her one day, "and maybe that's the reason I like your company, while I cannot endure that imperious snob, Alice Tisdale."

Evy did not tell Arcilla that she, too, was often an *imperious snob*.

Lady Elosia had been thoughtful enough to have a piano brought up to one of the empty rooms on the third floor, and Evy would go there and indulge herself. One such time when London friends were staying the weekend with Arcilla, she came to the door of the music room and stood, hands on hips.

"Will you *stop* that moldy music? You are disturbing my friends."

She nodded to Miss Patricia Bancroft, who eyed Evy with disdain. When they went out, Evy heard Patricia say to Arcilla, "Is *that* the girl Rogan was talking about to Charles?"

"I suppose it was. What did Rogan say?"

"He said…"

Evy grimaced when their voices faded. Down the corridor Arcilla closed her bedroom door, and Evy let her hands crash on the keys. The noisy bedlam filled the room.

So what did he say about me? Was it too much to contemplate that he might have complemented her? *Keep dreaming, Evy Varley.*

That same afternoon Evy noticed for the first time a handsome violin in the corner of the large room. Investigating she saw initials engraved on the leather carrying case: *R. J. C.*

It could not be Rogan's could it? There must be some mistake. Could there be another R. J. C.? Hardly. But the thought of the restless, arrogant Rogan playing violin made her laugh. What an impossible notion.

Arcilla's fifteenth birthday finally arrived, but it did not find her going to France as she had anticipated. Instead, she was sent to a private school in London, which did not seem to cause the degree of disappointment it might have due to her interest in one of Patricia Bancroft's brothers.

Arcilla often talked about Charles, but then she talked about so many boys that Evy merely smiled at her.

"Honestly, Arcilla. You've been in love so often you'll never know when you really *are* in love."

"Oh, you're such a disapproving girl. Really, Evy, I'm serious. By now you should have at least *one* boy you're interested in. Instead all you do is practice your music and read your Bible."

"That is not true. I do lots of other things. But I don't see why I should follow in your steps. They'll most likely lead you into big trouble one of these days."

Arcilla laughed at her. "Well, you do have Derwent Brown."

Evy gave a haughty sniff. "I don't know what you intend to imply by that."

Arcilla's grin was utterly wicked. "I daresay you *do*. You are going to marry him one day. You'll go live at the rectory and grow roses and hold the spring and summer fete. Whereas I"—and she smiled to herself at this and opened her arms wide—"will be able to enjoy the whole wide world. Isn't it positively *grand?*"

"Oh, indeed. Positively." Evy gave her friend a small smile. "But I warn you, Arcilla, you may learn that the whole wide world is not such a lovely place after all. As for Derwent, you appear to know more than I do about our future. Nothing is certain in this life. Only God knows whom I will marry, and that is the best choice I could have."

"Oh, Evy, you are *so* naive, yet I can't help liking you for it. Well, never mind that, what do you think of my new ball gown? Isn't it a dream? I'll wear it at Heathfriar."

While Arcilla had been to several balls by now, Evy had not been to even one. She refused to let Arcilla know she was wistful, or that she secretly dreamed of waltzing with Rogan and not with Derwent. Arcilla would enjoy making fun of her, and if she discovered her daydream about Rogan she might even be mean enough to tell him.

"The ball at Heathfriar—where dear Charles shall sweep me off my feet." Arcilla held her ball gown against her with one hand and placed the other at her heart. She waltzed about the room, eyes closed in dreamy reverie until she bumped into the bed and fell. Evy laughed. Today Arcilla was in love with Charles, and tomorrow—well, who knew? Certainly not Arcilla.

The gown was indeed beautiful, a minty green with a golden underlining so that it shimmered in the light. Arcilla would look lovely in it, and of course she knew she would. She was mature in body, and boys were starting to buzz around her like bees.

"What about Peter Bartley of South Africa?" Evy leaned back. "Your father and Sir Julien have plans."

Arcilla made a face. "I will *never* travel to South Africa to marry a government official. Aunt Elosia agrees with me."

A surprise, indeed, Evy thought, then chastised herself for the uncharitable thought. For all of Arcilla's posturing, it had to be a difficult thing to have one's future decided without regard to what one truly wanted.

For the hundredth time, Evy thanked God that she belonged to a simple and loving family. At least she would never have to worry about being handed off in marriage as a financial or business asset!

A few months later, Evy had her fifteenth birthday, and Aunt Grace handed her an envelope.

"For your birthday."

Evy unsealed the flap, removed a gilt-edged letter, and read.

This is to inform you that Miss Evy Varley has been accepted into her first year of studies at the prestigious and hallowed halls of Parkridge Music Academy.

Shock and then delight shivered through Evy. She jumped up and threw her arms around Aunt Grace. "Aunt! Oh, *thank* you, thank you! But how? How could you manage with our finances as they are?"

Aunt Grace smiled, looking as pleased and excited as Evy. "Oh, I have my little secrets. I wanted to surprise you."

"You have. And I'm thrilled. But your savings—"

"This did not come from my savings."

"Then where—?"

Her aunt merely patted her hand. "Now now, you must not meddle. A birthday gift is meant to be accepted, not questioned. The second year of your studies is another matter, however. We will proceed one year at a time, trusting the Lord."

Evy laughed and embraced her again. "I owe you so much, Aunt Grace."

"It is enough I have your affection." Her aunt's voice trembled, and Evy blinked back tears.

"You will always have that, dear Aunt." She kissed the older woman's cheek, then frowned when she noticed darkening circles beneath her aunt's eyes. She must be tired, Evy thought, but paid no more attention at the moment. Her happiness bubbled.

"I must go and tell Arcilla."

"Tell me what?" Arcilla came into the room, hands behind her.

Evy whirled, smiling. "That I trusted the Lord with my disappointment about going to Parkridge, and guess *what?*"

Arcilla laughed. "He answered your prayer after all!"

"Yes! I'm leaving for London in two weeks."

"I know. Mrs. Havering told me. And now…" She drew her hands from behind her and held out a gaily wrapped package. Arcilla's eyes sparkled as she looked over at Aunt Grace, who smiled.

"We've shared the secret of your going to London, and I bought you something."

Evy's heart overflowed. "Oh, Arcilla, did you really?"

"Of course I did, silly goose. Open it."

Evy tore open the paper and ribbons. "Oooh…" She feasted her eyes on a stylish dress, one as elegant as anything Arcilla owned for evening wear.

"The jade color goes with my eyes." There was no doubting the pleasure in Arcilla's features, as she said this, then went on to exclaim over the lower half of the skirt, which was also embroidered. "It is wonderful."

The neckline was lower, as was appropriate for evening wear, with a delicately embroidered bodice. The sleeves were puffed to the elbow with silk ruching at the bust. The overskirt was pleated, which, Arcilla explained, was quite popular. The gold-fringed hemline on the ornate skirt came to the floor.

Again, Evy let a sigh of pure delight escape her as she touched the glimmering silk.

"And—this." Arcilla stepped back into the corridor, then returned with a hatbox and several smaller boxes. Her mischievous smile drew an answering grin from Evy. "These are from my dear, *dear* brother."

Rogan!

Evy felt her cheeks warming, and lowered her head to avoid Arcilla's sharp gaze. She took the packages and tore off the wrappings, then removed a positively darling green hat with bows, ribbons, and silk flowers that matched the dress.

"The hat is for day wear," Arcilla said.

"It's beautiful." Evy held the charming adornment in her hands as a riot of emotions surged through her. *Don't be absurd!* a sensible voice within her scolded. *He didn't buy this special for you. Good heavens, he probably sent a servant to purchase it. You can't possibly think Rogan would care enough to—*

She removed the fashionable silk flowers with tiny gemstones that were to be worn in an upswept hairdo for evening. Next followed gloves that reached to the elbow, and a lacy fan to complete her evening outfit.

Evy could not find her voice.

"He's busy in London, so he did not come home this weekend."

Evy met Arcilla's smiling look. So she was right. He hadn't bought it—

"But when he saw the dress I'd bought you, he went out and returned with the other accessories. 'For the rectory girl,' he told me, though I confess his tone was a bit goading. No matter. His taste is surprisingly exquisite." She nudged Evy. "Try them *on*. Let's see."

"Yes"—Aunt Grace came from behind her—"try them on, dear." She reached to unloose Evy's garments, then helped her slip into the new dress and set the jaunty hat on her head, brushing back her thick, tawny curls.

"You look lovely, dear." Aunt Grace's voice caught with tender pleasure.

Evy rushed to the mirror and could scarcely believe her eyes. Could that vision in the glass really be her?

"Such conceit." Arcilla *tsked,* an utterly shameless grin on her face.

"I—hardly recognize myself."

"You look quite grown-up," Arcilla agreed, as though she were a few years Evy's senior instead of a few months.

Evy turned back to the mirror, noting how the color of the gown made her amber eyes sparkle with jade flecks. Those eyes widened a fraction as she realized how the dress enhanced her figure.

She fondled the ribbons on her hat, more pleased than she dared admit to know Rogan had actually taken time to shop in London to buy her birthday gifts.

Her gaze slid from the hat to her aunt's reflection, and Evy stiffened. Aunt Grace's eyes shone with pride, but there was something more there.

Concern. Clearly, her aunt was worried.

And Evy had the uncomfortable feeling that it was because Aunt Grace had known what—and who—had been occupying her thoughts.

CHAPTER SIXTEEN

Evy and Alice Tisdale shared a room with two other girls at Parkridge Music Academy in London. Turning fifteen and going to music school had not changed Alice one whit. She was still as haughty as ever. She seemed to live in a dream world, and hinted time and again that she would marry Rogan. Evy discounted that idea, though she never said so to Alice. But it was well known that Rogan and Patricia were often placed together at social functions.

Thus it was a quite a surprise when Alice announced one Thursday afternoon that Rogan had arranged for her to spend a weekend at Heathfriar. Arcilla would be there, as would Rogan and Parnell, and there was to be some sort of lawn party.

"Naturally the Chantrys shall be taking me to Heathfriar with them tomorrow afternoon. We shall return here to the school on Sunday evening." Alice looked across the room at Evy, who was doing her homework. "It is such a shame *you* will be left here all alone, Evy."

Evy refused to rise to the bait. Alice had been insufferable ever since she learned about the pretty hat Rogan had bought Evy for her birthday.

Alice, however, wasn't to be put off. "Isn't it all a bit barmy? I mean, here you are, so much *closer* to Arcilla than I, but you have not even been invited. Then again, maybe not so strange, since it wasn't Arcilla who invited me, but Sir Rogan."

"Are you not rushing things, Alice? He is not Sir Rogan yet. Squire is still in good health, the last I heard."

Alice pursed her small mouth and remained silent, pretending to read.

Evy was not disappointed about not being invited to Heathfriar. She'd had no expectations of becoming part of the aristocratic circle of young friends surrounding Arcilla and her two brothers. Nor did Alice actually belong. It was Mrs. Tisdale who constantly pushed her daughter forward and manipulated events to have her included.

As for Evy, she was under no illusions. She was the governess's niece. The fact she was able to attend a school like Parkridge, where most of the students were wealthy, had been primarily due to her aunt's ability to save. That, however, in no way elevated her in society.

She *was* surprised, though, that Alice would be invited to such an event, knowing how Arcilla felt about the girl. It was even more puzzling to think of Rogan arranging for Alice to come to Heathfriar for any reason. From what Arcilla had told her about Rogan's activities in London, Evy could not imagine him the least bit interested in Alice. He attended riding clubs and was rumored to be seeing several girls besides Patricia. Did she know this? Probably not.

Evy shook her head. Perhaps she was just not familiar enough with Rogan to know for certain. After all, she had not actually spoken with him since his birthday nearly two years ago—and the incident in the gallery had been a singular event. When he did come home to Rookswood, it was only briefly, and then he and Parnell would leave to spend time with their like-minded friends. If it had not been for the sweet little birthday hat, Evy would have suspected he barely remembered her. And even the hat might have been an impulsive gesture because Arcilla showed him the dress she'd bought her.

Ah well…

Evy stole another glance at Alice, who had her smug nose glued to her reading assignment. *Could I be wrong about Rogan Chantry and Alice?* Alice was pretty, in her own anemic way, and Dr. Tisdale was esteemed in Grimston Way, though he was unknown in London's higher circles. That being the case, it did seem strange for Alice to get an invitation to Heathfriar. If Alice were to be believed, then Evy knew even less about Rogan than she had thought.

Stop it! Evy pinched herself. *Stop thinking about Rogan Chantry.* After all, Derwent was corresponding with her. He was well into his training and would come home this summer to become his father's assistant until September, when he would return for his final year.

Evy let a small sigh escape. If only she knew how she felt about Derwent. She had known him for so long that she was perfectly comfortable around him, and she believed he felt the same. Still, at times she thought of him more as a cousin than a beau.

Perhaps the most disturbing change in Evy's life came when Aunt Grace wrote her that her health was troubling her. Now that Arcilla no longer needed a governess, Lady Elosia had arranged with the bishop to have Grace help the new young curate teach school at the rectory. Grace wrote Evy that she was enjoying the work.

I teach three days a week. I am enjoying it and did not realize how much I had missed the vicarage. Walking up the path lined with the roses Edmund and I planted years ago when we first arrived is like coming home again. Next month is the spring fete, and Vicar Brown asked me to be in charge of assigning booths to our dear parishioners to sell their goods. Oh, did I tell you in my last letter? Lady Elosia is allowing me to stay in the governess cottage vacated since Miss Hortense passed away last month. The cottage perfectly meets my needs, and there is plenty of room for your arrival in the summer.

Evy frowned. Was her aunt's writing a little shaky? Aunt Grace was under Dr. Tisdale's care for "weak lungs," but she had insisted to Evy she would grow stronger by summer.

Evy was thankful that Lady Elosia, filling the role of squire for her preoccupied brother Lyle, had been such a help to dear Aunt Grace. Evy suspected most of the Chantrys' kindness toward her aunt was because of Uncle Edmund's position as vicar for so many years in Grimston Way, rather than the few years she had been Arcilla's governess.

Evy returned home to Grimston Way that summer, anxious to see for herself how Aunt Grace was progressing. Though thinner, she appeared well enough when she met Evy at the junction in the one-horse jingle. Or was her aunt merely adept at concealing her problems? Now that Evy was older, she could look back over those early years at the vicarage, and even at Rookswood when Aunt Grace had been Arcilla's governess, and recognize that her aunt had never been one to share her innermost feelings. No, not even when she lost her husband.

Life in the simple cottage on Rookswood estate was cozy and comfortable. Evy loved taking walks in the huge garden, and not entirely because she might *accidentally* meet Rogan. But he, as it turned out, came and went with little notice of her, spending most of his time in London or at Heathfriar.

Evy missed being privy to what was going on with Arcilla and her brothers. Arcilla had many exciting new friends and no longer needed her company as she had when they were younger. Even so, when things went wrong in her life or she had some tantalizing secret she felt she couldn't entrust to her rival girlfriends, she would have a horse saddled and ride down from the manor house to see Evy, bringing another mare with her so they could go riding together as they had done in the past.

"What kind of friends are they if they cannot keep your confidences?" Evy asked her as they rode along the simple wooded trail at a slow pace. It was a warm June day, and the cloudless sky and green trees made for a perfect outing.

"Some of them I would *never* trust with any of my secrets." Arcilla shifted in the saddle to look at Evy. "Whenever they get angry or jealous, they threaten to tell everyone."

"Then they are not friends."

Arcilla's laughter rang out. "That's why I like you. Dear, faithful Evy Varley. I know I can tell you *anything,* and you won't tell anyone, or think worse of me."

"Perhaps because I already know the worst." Evy winked at her.

Arcilla's response was a smirk with a definite secretive edge to it. "Oh no, you don't… And I'm not going to tell you, either."

"I'm quite sure I don't need to hear about it."

It was around this time that Parnell and Rogan both came home from London. Oddly enough, they were going to be at Rookswood the rest of the summer because Parnell, who had graduated Oxford, would be going to Capetown to take a position in the diamond business under Sir Julien.

"When will Parnell leave?"

"August, I think. So Papa and Aunt Elosia wanted them both home together this summer. I don't mind staying at Rookswood this year. We will all be together for a change. Then, too, the summer entertainments will be grand this year, thanks to Aunt Elosia. Papa takes no interest in such things. When my mum was alive, she would always have dinner balls. That is, until she became so ill…" She fell silent, but it was only a moment until she brightened. "And of course Charles will come, and Patricia." She cast an amused glance toward Evy at the mention of the Bancroft girl.

Evy looked off toward the trees. Arcilla was far too quick to discern emotions in other girls.

"Have you heard more about Peter Bartley from South Africa?"

Arcilla grimaced, making her lovely face quite unattractive. "He writes me. His letters are filled with political information. Dreadfully boring. Something about trouble with the Dutch. *Boers,* I think he called them."

"What does Charles Bancroft think of your family's wish to match you up with Mr. Bartley?"

Arcilla bit her lip. "I have not told him yet."

Evy arched a brow at that. "Is that fair to Charles?"

"Do you want me to lose him?"

"No. But you will if Sir Julien and your father agree about your marriage to Mr. Bartley."

"I'm counting on Aunt Elosia. She wants me to stay in England, and she is close to the Bancrofts."

Evy sometimes saw the guests arrive on Friday afternoon to stay the weekend—they were wealthy, well bred, and of high social rank. Usually their sons and daughters would come with them and have their own parties with Arcilla, Rogan, and Parnell. At changing seasons there were foxhunts and pheasant shoots. Sir Lyle had pheasants bred on the estate solely for that purpose. Then, in the evenings, the dancing and dining would begin. The sounds of music coming from the baronial hall would drift down to the cottage. Sometimes, when Evy was in a fanciful, romantic mood, she would feed her dreams by going out to Aunt Grace's small rose garden and sitting on the swing where she could listen to the waltzes. She'd pretend she was there, like Miss Patricia. Naturally her dreams would have her in the loveliest ball gown, and suddenly Rogan would notice her!

"Where have you been all these years?" he would say as he asked her to waltz with him. "Look at you—all grown-up and so very pretty."

Evy laughed at her own folly, yet she would dance in the shadows of the rose garden pretending Rogan was with her. In her dreams, even Derwent understood. "I see you are not the one for me, Evy. I let you go in peace."

"Silly goose," she reprimanded herself. "I am as bad as Alice Tisdale!"

A few times during the summer Evy did see Rogan, but always from a distance when he was out riding with his friends. Those few times they did ride near the cottage, she went on pruning the roses and acted as though she did not notice them. Rogan, typically, would be smiling and laughing at something Miss Patricia said. Evy admired the other girl's blue riding habit, no doubt especially made for her. It went so well with her auburn hair. She was an exceptionally pretty girl. No wonder Rogan was attracted to her. Patricia fairly outdid herself to keep his attention, and she appeared very good at it.

One weekend not long after one of Evy's rides with Arcilla, Lady Elosia and Sir Lyle were entertaining guests from London. Evy was with Derwent in the rectory garden, and Aunt Grace was helping Vicar Brown, as she did every year, to arrange for the late summer fete. As usual, the parishioners would sell everything from elderberry jam and sweet cinnamon pickles to dried herbs in little bouquets. The money from the sale would go to restore the rectory fruit orchard, where disease had damaged the apple and plum trees.

Aunt Grace, as she had done for so many years when Uncle Edmund was alive, was assigning locations for the ladies to put up their booths on the large rectory lawn. Vicar Brown, Derwent, Mr. Croft, and even Bixby the coachman from Rookswood were building a few covered cubicles for the older ladies.

Derwent was home from divinity school and helping run the rectory and aid his father, who was none too strong. Vicar Brown had suffered a mild stroke in the winter. Though Derwent was expected to become curate when he graduated, nothing was settled yet. Some in the village said that he did not have the true calling of a vicar, and these whispers had made their way to him and made him despondent.

"If my father must step down earlier than planned, it will change everything," he told Evy, nailing a piece of canvas onto a booth. Evy would be selling Aunt Grace's tarts. "I suppose I could become a private tutor and live in London, but it would not give the living that the rectory does." At this, he glanced at Evy meaningfully.

Evy understood what Derwent was hinting at. If ever they were to marry, he would need a post at the rectory. If they both taught, then they could afford a place to live in London. But Evy had no strong passions toward Derwent, and the thought of marriage to him seemed little more than duty. And yet, what could be more normal than for a vicar's son and a former vicar's niece to carry on the work at the rectory in Grimston Way for another generation?

"You both know the rectory so well," Aunt Grace often said when they were alone in the cottage.

"I would not worry about a position, Derwent." Evy winced as he struck his thumb with the hammer. He yowled and dropped the tool, which Evy picked up. "Come down. Let me see."

"I was never good at this." Derwent climbed down the stepladder.

"You will lose your thumbnail," Evy told him. "Here, I'll finish."

"No, Evy, you might fall. Besides, girls don't climb ladders and bang nails."

She grinned. "I do." To prove it, she climbed up and proceeded to nail the canvas closed.

"Anyway, Derwent," she said over her banging, "if your father's health forces him to retire earlier than planned, there will of necessity be a new vicar appointed from London."

"True enough."

"Eventually, though, you will get a post here, perhaps as curate. There are a great many duties that fall to the curate, and you will be able to prove your spirituality."

"I suppose." He ran his uninjured hand through his russet hair. "I sometimes wish… Well, I'd best not say."

"What do you wish?" She hammered another nail.

"You won't laugh at me if I tell you?"

She gave him a scolding glance. "I think you know me better than that."

"I sometimes find myself wishing I was going to Capetown, like Rogan and Parnell." His eyes shone with a longing Evy had not seen before. "I would like to work in the diamond business. I suppose you think I sound ungrateful. The church has been good to me, allowing me the grant to go to school as they did. I wouldn't be able to attend if they hadn't. I owe my best years to the church."

Evy listened, aware how much Derwent still admired Rogan. She could not deny that Rogan's plans in South Africa seemed much more adventurous than being vicar. The lure of diamonds and faraway places had set Derwent to dreaming.

"The work in the church is far more important eternally," she encouraged. "Nourishing God's flock is a great honor."

"Oh, I know that. That's what troubles me. I don't feel worthy. And let's face it, I'm not the spiritual teacher your uncle Edmund was, or even my father. Though his mind seems to be going on him. His memory is, anyway. I'm helping with his sermons. I mean in no way to make light of it, but perhaps some of the talk going on about me is more true than not. Not every son is called to follow in his father's steps. The Lord does not always gift father and son the same way. If He did, there would be something to say for godliness and spiritual gifts being passed on through heredity and environment rather than sovereign will and grace. I don't see the Scripture teaching that."

She turned her head and smiled down at him. "The fact that you say these things tells me you *know* the Scripture well enough to be vicar someday."

A crooked smile lifted his mouth. "That will need to be a long time from now, Evy. I mean it." He frowned at his sore thumb, then shook his head.

Evy turned back to her nails. "A long time... Well, that is not really surprising. It's hardly wise for the bishop to appoint a young man like yourself to fill the vicar's position so soon. You must be tested by time."

"Aye—I mean *yes*," he hastened. "A *seasoned* man is how they say it. A man who's walked with the Lord for many years." Again he shook his head. "But gaining a living will be hard."

"I doubt if sailing to the Cape to search for diamonds will give you anything more in your bank account. You may end up with a whole lot less."

"That is true, of course. They say Kimberly is a wild and woolly place."

"That's why my parents went there so many years ago to present a witness for God."

"And they died for it."

She hammered a nail, not responding to this somber reminder.

"Evy, I just hope— Oh, why hello, Rogan!"

Oh no! Evy froze, then looked down over her shoulder. Rogan sat astride his horse, an alert, surprised flicker in his gaze. He studied her with sufficient intensity to freeze the smile on her lips into self-consciousness.

At first she thought he was dismayed to find her atop a ladder—not exactly a ladylike activity. But something in that dark gaze told her that what had startled Rogan had little to do with ladders and nails...and a great deal more to do with Evy herself.

She shivered, though the day was still quite warm. Rogan looked quite grown-up. His wavy ebony hair still had a tendency to fall across his forehead. His slashing dark brows, bold eyes, and strong jawline gave him a handsome, roguish appearance. How different he was from Derwent.

Evy became aware she was staring, and scolded herself for that fact just as Rogan seemed to recover from whatever surprise she had given him.

"You have grown." The comment was deep and rich, and his gaze held hers.

She loathed herself for blushing.

"Miss Evy, Derwent"—Rogan looked at Derwent as though suddenly becoming aware of him—"this is Miss Patricia Bancroft." Though he nodded to the young woman at his side, his gaze came back to rest on Evy.

Her gaze swerved from Rogan to confront the girl sitting proudly on the horse beside Rogan's magnificent mount. She seemed expert at handling her horse, another reason for Rogan's interest. The cold appraisal Patricia gave Evy made her cling more tightly to the ladder. Clearly, it had not been Patricia's idea to turn aside from the road to say hello. She looked disapproving and even hostile. Did she resent that Rogan would show friendliness toward her and Derwent—or had she noticed the look he'd given her?

Evy glanced away. What was she supposed to say?

"Time goes by so quickly." The words sounded foolish, even to her own ears.

Rogan's smile deepened, and his gaze told her he was aware of her discomfiture. "So it does. We were out riding before lunch and saw you both from the road. Is Derwent teaching you carpentry, or does he prefer the shade?"

She ignored his amusement, but Derwent held up his injured thumb. "Alas, I'm a poor teacher indeed."

Rogan laughed.

Derwent, apparently unmindful of the undercurrent between Rogan and Evy, sighed. "I was telling Evy how I might enjoy choosing to go to Capetown and work in the diamond business. I admire you and your brother."

"And give up the opportunity for a quiet and peaceful life here at the rectory?" Rogan's measuring glance seemed to question whether Derwent might also be relinquishing his plans for Evy.

"Well, there is that, of course." Derwent glanced about the vicarage grounds, as though contemplating all of Grimston Way.

"It would surprise me if Miss Evy would approve of your giving up rectory life for the uncertainty and dangers of African diamonds."

Evy felt herself stiffen. Rogan talked as though she were not present.

"I'm sure," she said, hoping to sound casual, "that my wishes will not be the sole criterion for deciding Derwent's future."

Rogan's brows lifted. "I would expect your wishes to count a great deal in Derwent's thoughts about anything, but most especially the future."

She ignored his assertion, grateful that Derwent looked as if he hadn't understood Rogan's implication. She started down the unsteady ladder, clutching the hammer in one hand. Rogan gestured for Derwent to help her.

Derwent jumped up to hold the ladder, and Evy felt the heat in her cheeks. What was it about Rogan that flustered her so?

"Thank you," she said, not looking at any of them. She set the hammer down and wiped her hands on a cloth, choosing her next words carefully. "It shouldn't be all that surprising for me to have interests in South Africa as well. Most everyone knows how my parents worked there and were killed in the Zulu War." She looked up and met Rogan's challenging stare.

"You are not afraid to go to the Cape?"

"No, though I've no reason to think I shall ever do so."

"I suppose not. I was thinking of Arcilla. You have two more years at Parkridge Music Academy?"

"Three years."

"That's right…you are younger than she."

"Only by three months."

At her hasty correction, Rogan regarded her. "Then you are enjoying your schooling?"

His seeming interest warmed her, and she smiled. "Very much so." She had not yet thanked him for the pretty hat, but she dared not do so now. Patricia was already fuming. The girl was flipping her small horsewhip, chewing on her rosebud lips while Rogan spoke with Evy.

Patricia looked over her shoulder toward the road, as if expecting company. "It is getting late, Rogan." She sounded a bit cross, and Evy had to fight a smirk. "We are to meet Parnell and Christine for luncheon. Remember?"

He did not appear worried about luncheon, nor even the obvious tone of her voice, but obliged her by turning his horse.

Derwent's gaze rested on the horses. "Handsome animals. How is your riding proceeding, Rogan?"

"I shall know next month."

"Next month?"

He smiled. "I shall ride in the Dublin horse show."

Evy had heard much about the show and realized he must be very good indeed if he was in that competition.

Rogan gestured to the booth. "Yours?" he asked Evy, studying her features again.

"My aunt's." She shifted, longing for the cool of evening—and freedom from that dark gaze, "The annual summer fete you know. The proceeds will go to buy new fruit trees for the rectory," she managed, brushing her heavy hair away from her shoulder. Anything to cool her face a bit. If only he would stop staring at her so!

"Interesting and commendable. We will make sure to visit Mrs. Havering's booth, won't we, Patricia?"

"Oh, by *all* means." Patricia made no effort to hide her irritation.

"It is well that Vicar Brown gets some new fruit trees." Evy felt the situation deteriorating quickly and dragging her down with it.

Again, Rogan smiled. He watched her as though trying to figure her out, and Evy felt a tinge of trepidation dance across her skin. How could one look both alarm and please her so? It was the kind of look she had secretly dreamed Rogan would give her, yet it made her feel guilty and afraid.

Breaking his gaze from her, Rogan touched the tip of his smart-looking hat, nodding first to Derwent, then to her. "I will try to visit the fete. When is it?"

Evy tried to swallow, though her throat felt suddenly bone dry. "Saturday, but I doubt if it will interest you."

His look told her he knew she was trying to discourage him. "Oh, I am quite interested already. Au revoir." With that, he maneuvered his horse and rode after Miss Patricia, who had galloped ahead.

Evy sank to the footstool, her legs suddenly unwilling to support her.

"A talented young man." Derwent looked after Rogan.

Evy felt an unreasonable surge of irritation. Did Derwent understand nothing? Didn't it even bother him to have Rogan looking at her the way he had? It certainly had bothered *her*...far more than it should have.

But Derwent seemed oblivious to anything amiss. "Rogan is quite different from his brother. Some think he will gain notoriety in the Dublin horse show. It takes discipline to reach that level. He also graduates next year from the geological school, and is in the top of his class. Parnell was not so inclined and spent a good deal of time in London away from his studies, with friends. Parnell is leaving for the Cape in September, did you know?"

She did, and she knew Rogan was likely to sail there after his graduation. What she didn't know was whether she was glad about that...or utterly devastated.

CHAPTER SEVENTEEN

It rained on the day of the fete, which prompted a rush to reorganize inside the rectory hall. Of course it was impossible to move so many booths indoors, so there was a scramble to locate enough tables for the ladies to display their baked goods and preserves in the rectory hall.

"To think we spent all that time on them booths," Mrs. Croft complained to Evy. "It won't be nearly as attractive now. Let's hope the villagers turn out."

It was a tradition for the squire's family to support the fete, so about an hour into the event Lady Elosia arrived in the family coach with Arcilla and Parnell. Evy looked around for Rogan, but did not see him. Patricia Bancroft, she thought. If she could keep him away, she would.

Apparently, though, Patricia hadn't succeeded, for Rogan came a short time later. Patricia was not with him.

Evy admitted her surprise that Rogan had actually shown as he said he would. Maybe the Bancrofts had returned to London, and he had nothing to entertain him. Evy watched Rogan and Parnell from where she stood behind a long serving table covered with a white lace cloth embroidered with spring tulips.

Dr. Tisdale's wife was at the next table dipping a ladle into a huge bowl of punch, while Alice cavorted about as though she were a guest. Evy could not remember a time when Alice actually assisted her mother at any of the events. But then, Mrs. Tisdale thought her daughter too important for such menial work as the other rectory girls endured. Mrs. Tisdale looked none the worse for manning the table alone. She was doing a brisk business selling her punch, and she smiled as the coins continued to plunk into the container.

Alice stopped by to see what Evy was selling. "Our punch bowl is Viennese crystal." She flipped her hair back. "Mum bought it in Vienna when we went there on tour two years ago." The pitying glance she directed at her set Evy's nerves on edge. "You should have *seen* the music theater! *Too* awfully grand! I simply *must* go again."

Evy held her tongue, but her thoughts would not be silent. *Alice will be in for a bumpy landing once she comes down from her high horse. How can she possibly expect to marry Rogan when Patricia Bancroft has already been approved by the Chantry and Bancroft families?*

Evy turned her attention from Alice to Parnell Chantry. He looked a great deal older since having finished at the university. He divided his time now between Rookswood and the London branch office, where he was learning about the family's South African diamond business.

Both brothers looked dashing in their rich attire as they stood beside Lady Elosia and Arcilla. They were soon performing the social duties of the squire's family, bowing to the ladies and complimenting them on their goods.

A woman holding a tray approached Evy's table. Evy held the tongs to a fat apple tart, watching Rogan as Alice approached him.

Rogan clearly was the more friendly of the squire's sons, with an easy smile and an appealing way about him that made him more likable in the village. It also made him more dangerous. The village girls were already hopelessly beguiled by him, a fact that both amused and irritated Evy as she looked on. Alice was fanning herself with a new white Vienna lace fan though it was not a bit warm. In fact, Evy had contemplated putting on her wrap. Alice's giggle carried on the breeze, and Evy glanced at her just in time to see her toss her strawberry blond curls and mince about in her blue dress.

Evy huffed when Rogan smiled at the ridiculous girl and carried on a polite conversation. But just as Evy was about to look away, Rogan glanced in the direction of her table. He caught her gaze, and his smile broadened.

"Oh! I am so sorry, Miss Armitage!" Evy's cheeks blazed as she looked down at the dear old lady's tray. She had just released the apple tart over her cup instead of her napkin! The cup instantly overflowed, and punch ran across the tray.

"My *dear* girl," Miss Armitage said, alarmed.

Evy grabbed a cloth and hurried around the table to where the elderly woman stood, clearly offended.

"Oh, my dear Miss Armitage, I do hope the Holland lace is not stained." She tried to blot a spill that had run from the tray to the woman's bagging sleeve.

"*Tsk, tsk,* Evy. You simply *must* pay closer attention to what you are doing."

"Yes, Miss Armitage. I am so very sorry."

"You've said that already." The woman turned her silver head with its outdated 1860 hairdo and looked across the hall toward Rogan and Parnell. The two young men wore tolerant smiles as they talked with Meg and Emily, who had joined Alice. The three girls chattered like excited sparrows.

"So that's it." Miss Armitage's features pinched even more than usual. "I might have known it."

Evy pretended to not understand. "Beg pardon, Miss Armitage?"

"You know very well what I mean, I daresay. I would think a sensible young lady such as yourself, Evy Varley, would know better than to get absorbed in the likes of those two scamps. And you, with your upbringing in the rectory, should know better than to be daydreaming about them." She straightened her spectacles and looked around. "Where is that aunt of yours?"

"She's a bit ill, I'm afraid. We thought it best that she avoid the rain." Evy wished she could sink through the floor and hide from those shrewd gray eyes that fixed upon her. "Shall I— Shall I get you another tray of punch and a tart, Miss Armitage?"

"You do not expect me to eat *this* mess, do you?"

"No, of course not. Here, I'll take that tray away."

"I should hope so."

A short time later, Evy returned with a tray of fresh punch and another of Aunt Grace's apple tarts. But before she could escape, Miss Armitage grasped her sleeve.

"You watch those two scoundrels." The old woman's voice was low and full of dire meaning. "They will dance circles around a good girl like you every time. You are no match for them. They've been well trained in the house of Master Henry, and now that their father, the squire, is widowed—he could very well have his eye on your aunt."

Evy must have looked blank, because Miss Armitage made a sound of impatient dismissal. "Untrustworthy scamps, those boys. Word has it from my sister in London. She knows. Oh yes, indeed. Those two have already caused talk in London. Matilda read about it in the society page."

With that, Miss Armitage walked away toward Vicar Brown, no doubt to fill his ears with whatever she had read in the London papers. Evy watched her leave, then glanced at Rogan and Parnell. What on earth had the papers said about them?

She shook her head. Never mind. Whatever it was, it had to be just gossip.

She took a deep breath and sighed to herself. *Lord, do not let me become a gossipy hen when I grow old.*

At least Miss Armitage was gone. Evy moved back behind the table, glancing around her. Had anyone noticed the embarrassing incident? Fortunately, everyone seemed too occupied with conversations to pay attention to her disaster. She looked toward Arcilla, who was as lovely as ever, her hair plaited with silver threads and her summery frock of daffodil yellow satin flowing about her. She had matured into a beautiful young woman.

Evy's own dress was quite ordinary by comparison. Cotton, pale blue, with simple white cuffs and a high collar with a bit of lace. The long skirts were quite dignified and proper, and while the dress was no match for Arcilla's and Alice's, she would need to be blind to see herself every day in the mirror and not be aware that she, too, had blossomed into a beauty.

Arcilla was nearing seventeen now and was anxious to complete her last year at the finishing school in London. After that she would have her coming-out in London society when a marriage would be arranged, either to Charles Bancroft, if Arcilla and Lady Elosia had their way, or to Peter Bartley of South Africa, if Sir Julien Bley ruled his family realm. Evy, if she believed in wagering, would bet that Sir Julien would win.

Evy glanced about, seeking Derwent. She finally spotted him with Tom and Milt. All three were agog, watching Arcilla, who smiled and charmed them, making each one feel special. One thing about Arcilla: She never blushed. *If all the boys stared at me that way, I'd turn pink as a new rose!* Evy sighed at her lack of poise. Arcilla knew her effect on the young men and played it to full advantage.

Evy grimaced. Could Derwent and the others not see through the girl's insincerity? Even so, Evy could not help being fond of Arcilla. She was what she was, and it was simple as that.

"My Alice is having such a wonderful time." Mrs. Tisdale's voice drew Evy's attention. The woman was talking with the solicitor's wife. "I daresay she is very near the marrying age now. The doctor"—she always spoke of her husband in third person, as though he were nobility—"is seriously rethinking her future. Naturally, Alice wishes to graduate from music school in London, but we are thinking an engagement might be wiser. We have *just* the proper young man in mind."

Was it Evy's imagination, or did Mrs. Tisdale glance sideways at her?

"Derwent and Rogan are *quite* friendly with Alice," the woman went on. "They rode over yesterday to visit and stayed for tea and cakes."

So that was where Derwent spent yesterday afternoon. Evy had wondered when he did not show up to help with the final preparations on the booth. It should not surprise her that he had opted to take an afternoon ride with Rogan, who must have lent him a horse. But she'd never dreamed they had ridden over to the Tisdales'. Derwent said nothing of where he had been when he came by later, and she had not thought it her business to ask him.

So he'd had tea and cakes with Alice. Well, that was fine. It didn't bother her. Not nearly as much as the fact that Rogan had done so as well!

"Alice is a very nice girl," the solicitor's wife agreed.

"And very dutiful to her religious faith," Mrs. Tisdale said.

Evy knew differently. The entire time she'd roomed with Alice, the girl had never read from her small Bible and tried to avoid chapel.

A sudden frown pulled Evy's brows low. Why was Mrs. Tisdale suddenly talking about religion…and Derwent? Could she have Derwent in mind for Alice?

Evy looked across the hall at Alice, adorned in an extravagant apple green dress with matching slippers, her braided hair coiled about her head. That dress must have cost Dr. Tisdale a pretty pound. It was Mrs. Tisdale's idea, of course. Evy watched Alice carry a large basket of summer daisies, handing them out to the ladies and girls in celebration of the summer fete. She was doing so with a certain fanfare that drew attention to herself as she walked about the hall, making certain Rogan noticed her. Or was it Derwent she sought to attract?

She handed a double daisy tied with a pink ribbon to Arcilla, then stopped in front of Rogan and Derwent to talk. She was playing the coquette and looking quite silly, but what irritated Evy the most was that Rogan was smiling. Alice was looking up at him and turning from side to side while she held her basket behind her back, her apple green skirts rustling.

If Alice were outside in the garden, and if it were nighttime, she'd probably let Rogan kiss her! Then Evy caught herself and bit her lip. *How catty I'm being.*

She jumped when a voice beside her drawled lazily, "Hello, hello, hello."

Parnell Chantry had come up without her noticing and stood there, a small plate in hand. He dropped a goodly handful of coins in the offering container. "Did you make those tarts?"

Unlike Rogan's dark hair, Parnell's was chestnut and curly, and his eyes were hazel-brown. He was an inch shorter than Rogan, and was slim and agile. A small, dark mole on his chin gave him a rather a knavish appearance. Evy couldn't recall seeing Parnell smile, but, like all the Chantrys, he was comely.

Evy used the tongs to move the tarts around so they would show better. "My aunt baked them. I'm afraid all I did was dust them with sugar. Which one would you like?"

"The one with the most apples. Yes—that one. Delightful."

He held out his plate, and she placed it with careful precision, taking no chances of repeating her accident with Miss Armitage. Imagine the horror of doing such a thing to Parnell Chantry! She glanced at the lace on his velvet cuff. Clearly he enjoyed dressing with more French flair than Rogan. She watched him taste the tart with his fork.

"Absolutely smashing." He looked across the hall toward his brother and took another bite as Rogan looked past Alice and his gaze came to rest on them. Evy had the oddest impression that the two brothers were challenging one another.

Parnell turned back to her. "Your aunt is ill?"

"Yes, for some time now. We hoped the summer weather would benefit her, but it has not."

He nodded. "I'm glad we had her as Arcilla's governess for as long as we did. My sister is most fond of her."

Evy was not aware that this was so, but perhaps he was trying to be kind. "Thank you. My aunt is quite patient."

Again, he nodded.

There was a moment of awkward silence, as though he tried to think of something to say to her. She already knew she was not as easy to talk with as other girls, who giggled and said silly things. But Evy would eat a mouthful of dirt before she would dither and show off in such a coquettish way.

Parnell shifted, suddenly looking as though his shirt collar was too tight. Undoubtedly he was aware of the wide disparity between their social positions. Evy took pity on the poor man.

"You are through at the university now." She smiled at him. "I suppose you will be sailing to South Africa. Are you looking forward to it?"

He brushed the spotless cuff of his jacket. "Yes, it should prove deeply interesting."

"Will you be leaving soon?"

"It will be a few months more. There is so much to learn at the London office."

She nodded. "I can well understand that. What does your family do at the London office?"

"For one thing we hire master diamond cutters. It is painstaking work, but lucrative. Businesses the world over come to buy from us. I'm pleased to say I will not be involved in that part of the business. I haven't the steady nerves for it. Our father expects me to be involved in running the mines. I'll learn all that from my uncle, Sir Julien. My family is partners with another side of our extended family in South Africa as well. You may have heard of the them...the Bleys and Brewsters?"

"Yes, indeed. Sir Julien Bley is an important name in diamonds, or so I've been told."

"Very important. You have heard of De Beer Consolidated in South Africa?"

Evy considered this. "Well, yes, I suppose I have. He is the diamond mogul, isn't he?"

Parnell seemed pleased at her knowledge. "To be modest, yes. De Beer owns one of the four main diamond companies in Kimberly. Sir Julien is managing director of De Beer under the great Cecil Rhodes. Uncle Julien is one of the largest shareholders. And Mr. Rhodes and Sir Julien intend to make De Beer the owner of the other three companies one day."

She supposed that if one's values and worth were determined by their ownership of diamonds, then Sir Julien would be a very great man indeed. "Do the other three diamond companies agree that Mr. De Beer should own a monopoly on South African diamonds?"

Parnell's expression told her he was being tolerant of what he considered her ignorance. "One does not *ask* permission for such ventures. One prods and pushes until walls fall down."

Evy looked down at the tarts on the table. "Sounds very...cold-blooded."

"At times, yes." She noted he offered no apology. "So you see, Rogan and I have grave responsibilities ahead of us in South Africa."

Her heart constricted at Parnell's words. "Then the squire will send both you and your brother to the Cape?"

"Uncle Julien has requested him to do so. Father is in close correspondence with his stepbrother."

From what Evy had seen, Sir Lyle was apt to do whatever Julien told him. Which did not bode well for Arcilla and Charles.

"I believe Rogan is nearly finished with his geology studies at the university," she commented. "He once mentioned searching for gold in South Africa."

"My brother has ideas...some strange and wild ones. I think he will set them aside when he arrives at the Cape."

"Am I interrupting something important?"

Evy turned with a start, and her gaze collided with Rogan's. He had come up without their realizing it. How much had he overheard? She would have preferred not to be found discussing him with his brother.

"Hello, Miss Evy." He smiled, a sultry contrast to his light-haired brother. He offered the small bow expected of young gentlemen of aristocratic birth, but he seemed disingenuous. What was he up to?

Evy felt a shiver of caution and set her guard against him. Rogan appeared to notice the change in her demeanor, as his smile deepened and seemed to challenge her. Could it be that in distancing herself from him, she actually interested him all the more? The answer was clear: Rogan's conceit would make him determined to break down anyone's resistance.

Evy bit back her annoyance. Apparently, by just being herself, she presented a different challenge than the other young ladies around them. And, much to her dismay, this had sparked interest in both brothers.

So this was what a hart felt when encircled by two hunters.

Old Miss Armitage's dire warnings echoed in Evy's mind, and she glanced in the woman's direction. Sure enough, Miss Armitage was watching them, shrewd interest gleaming in those pale eyes.

Rogan took another look at his brother, and his jaw tensed. Thankfully, Parnell did not appear to notice his brother's displeasure. Evy did not want a scene right there in the rectory hall.

She almost clapped with relief when she saw Lady Elosia coming toward them.

"Ah, there you are, Parnell, Rogan. Have you made the rounds? We cannot stay long, you know. Sir Lyle has received correspondence from Sir Julien, and he wishes to meet with you both in the library at four o'clock. Ah, Evy, and how is Grace? Any better?"

"I'm afraid not, Lady Elosia, but thank you for your concern. Dr. Tisdale will see her before supper."

"Ah, yes, the dear woman. I'm glad she did not venture out in the rain. Such dreadful weather for June. Well, if there is anything we can do up at Rookswood, my dear, you send word up right away. Your aunt is such a hard worker. It is no wonder she's having difficulty recovering from last winter's chest cold. You tell her to drink herb tea."

Evy thanked her, and Parnell bowed and took his leave. Evy waited for Rogan to follow suit, but he lingered.

"Mrs. Havering is ill again?"

She explained that Aunt Grace had been fighting a lung ailment since last fall.

Rogan's frown seemed sincere. "Maybe she ought to visit a physician in London. There are specialists in bronchitis."

"I mentioned it to her, but I think you know something about my aunt. She would feel it a waste of time and expense to travel there and stay in a hotel."

She was surprised by his genuine sympathy, but strangely, instead of bolstering her spirits it undid her defenses against him. And that was far more disturbing than she liked. She changed the subject, not wanting to let her rioting emotions show. She did not want his sympathy, not when it made her feel so vulnerable toward him.

"I believe Lady Elosia mentioned you are expected at Rookswood." She sounded more disapproving than she felt.

His brows arched. "How like a teacher you sound." He gestured at the tarts. "I shall try one for this evening. You can wrap it up? Anyway, I rode my horse down, so I don't need to return in the coach. And my father's always late. She said four, so that means more like half past five."

She wrapped the tart while he put money into the container, and she noticed he put in more than Parnell. She handed the tart to him. "I must not keep you." She took special care to avoid that dark gaze.

"You make me feel so appreciated."

She would not be swayed by his teasing. "I am sure you are."

A faint, sardonic smile showed. "But not by you."

"I do not know why you say so."

"It is obvious. You disapprove of me."

She busied herself rearranging the remaining tarts. "That should not trouble you. My opinion is not important."

"Then you do still disapprove of me?"

"I did not say so."

"Your eyes say so quite clearly."

"Then you must not try to read them."

A quick heat filled her cheeks at her effrontery, but Rogan merely smiled. "They are interesting...and *very* readable."

"You are mistaken—"

"Unusual color, I think...like amber. Or is it tawny? Almost the color of a lion I saw in a painting from South Africa." He leaned toward her for a closer look, and Evy stepped back.

Oh, this cursed warmth in her cheeks! She searched for a way to distract him from his study of her eyes. "Truly, what does my opinion matter? You do not remind me of someone who worries about what people may think of you."

"Depends on the person, of course." His smile was almost her undoing. "Maybe I would appreciate your good opinion."

The idea was so absurd to her that she laughed, easing the moment and breaking his spell. Since there were no other customers, she sat down on the stool and glanced about the hall, as though uninterested in him. But she was almost painfully aware of him leaning there, amused, watching her.

"Still looking for Derwent?" The smooth question was replete with meaning.

Her gaze came to his, and his dark brow lifted. He glanced about the hall. "I think he is with the Tisdale girl. Interesting thought. Derwent and Alice." His eyes came back to her. "They make a charming couple, don't you agree?"

She knew what he was trying to do, and she would not rise to the bait. "I have not thought about it one way or the other."

"Maybe you should."

She paused at that, and his smile returned.

"I mean that Derwent is obviously such a very good friend of yours. You should be interested in his...affairs."

"I consider him a good friend, yes."

"Only a friend?"

She ignored the question, and he went on. "Ah, well, you need not explain. You have so much in common, you and Derwent. Everyone says so."

She tried not to let her irritation at this show. "Do they?"

"Don't you think so? You both were raised in the rectory. That should give you much to talk about."

"Yes, I suppose that is true."

He pursed his lips. "Derwent may one day wish to reconsider taking his father's position when the vicar retires. Especially if he had another offer, and of course, if the vicar approved the change in his career."

What was Rogan getting at? "Derwent wasn't serious when he mentioned South Africa, you know." She folded her hands in her lap, hoping to still their trembling. Rogan in such close proximity was far too disturbing for her peace of mind. "Derwent is almost obligated to enter the church. Vicar Brown would be heartbroken if his son became an adventurer instead of a parson."

Rogan inclined his dark head. "True enough, I am sure. And there is nothing like being plagued with guilt for disappointing the expectations of family. Yet Derwent freely admits he does not feel worthy of that position."

Evy's uneasiness grew, and she also wondered if Rogan might actually know something of the same burden...if he bore the weight of disappointing Sir Lyle. However, even his notion to mine for gold in South

Africa, which was a departure from the family interest in diamonds, had not been met with displeasure.

"Derwent will become curate." She nodded to emphasize her certainty. "I don't believe he would shirk his responsibility."

"You think he is really that dedicated, do you?" There flickered an inquisitiveness in his dark eyes. "How highly you've elevated him above the rest of us adventurous scoundrels."

She managed a smile. "I am impressed by the humble manner in which he deals with the difficult expectations placed upon him."

"You mean, compared to us Chantrys, who are arrogant and utterly lacking in humility. Well then, being a rectory girl, you should be qualified to teach me how to be humble."

Such a suggestion sent her heart skipping, but Evy managed to keep her voice light and steady. "I am sure there is little I could teach you, Master Rogan, that you would accept."

A warm smile lit his features. "Then we must find out."

Evy wished the ground would open up and swallow her. Either that, or swallow him! Rogan's veiled suggestion that he was interested in her was utterly ridiculous, she knew that. There could never be anything to his intent beyond a light and frivolous flirtation. So why did the idea set her poor head spinning so?

"And since you are so impressed by Derwent"—he inclined his head—"is it possible that I know him better than you do?"

Now that was absurd indeed! "I hardly think so."

"We shall see."

Evy felt her gaze narrow. "What do you mean?"

He lifted a hand, every inch the royal dismissing a lesser being. "Perhaps he has confided in me." His eyes glinted, and Evy was sure he was laughing at her. "After all, having taken advantage of our docile and trusting Derwent when we were boys, I may feel compelled to offer him advice and, shall we say…opportunity?"

Oh no! Poor Derwent! He had always looked on Rogan with such admiration. If Rogan should somehow convince him to give up the rectory life to follow him out to South Africa—

"If you should make the mistake of luring him to South Africa, you shall be doing him, and others, an injustice."

A veil seemed to fall over Rogan's expression. "I'm disappointed you would see it that way. May I assume that when you mention an injustice done to *others,* you speak of yourself?"

"I speak first of Vicar Brown."

"And yourself second?"

Evy had had enough. She slid from the stool and planted her hands on her hips. "There has been no promise made between myself and Derwent, if that is what you are hinting at. My concern has nothing to do with *my* unwillingness to pursue a future in South Africa. It has everything to do with what is best for *Derwent.*"

His mouth thinned, and she saw clear disdain in his dark eyes. "Is it necessary, then, to protect him as though he were a child, with no wisdom or determination of his own?"

Words failed her at the cold accusation. Was that what she was doing? She remained silent, considering.

After a moment, he changed the subject. "You are returning to the music school soon?"

She pulled herself from her pondering and nodded. "Yes...in a few weeks."

"Maybe I will see you in London."

"I do not see how or why you should bother."

A sardonic hint of smile touched his mouth at her candor. She hoped he did not believe she wanted to elicit some reason why he wanted to see her. She had not meant it that way, but he was quite capable, in his conceit, of thinking so.

"Ah well, I must be going or I'll be late for my father's meeting in the library. That would never do. Every letter from Sir Julien is a grand occasion. My uncle always has his way—even from across the Atlantic."

"Perhaps the letter has to do with your brother's voyage to South Africa," she said, trying not to sound too interested.

"Yes. And mine, no doubt. The family in Capetown have a sudden and particular interest in us, which is curious"—a slight frown settled on his brow—"and a little worrisome."

What could he mean by that? What *particular interest?* But Rogan did not elaborate, and she would not be so forward as to ask. Instead, she headed the conversation another direction. "Do you remember the time we were nearly caught by Sir Julien in Master Henry's rooms?"

She would have thought the memory would bring him a smile, but instead a certain thoughtful concern showed in his gaze, as though his mind traveled far away, perhaps to Sir Julien himself in Capetown.

"Yes, I remember. But he only caught *me* there. He has since made light of it, but somehow I do not think he really accepted my explanation."

"Did he ever learn that I was with you?"

Rogan shrugged. "I never told him. I would have expected him to question you if he knew. Then, again, Sir Julien is rather odd. Sometimes I think he did know. By the way, have you heard from Lady Camilla since she was here?"

"No. For her sake I hope she has come to know I am not her husband's mystery child."

Rogan didn't respond. He simply studied her features.

She met his gaze, wondering at the shift in his mood, and he smiled a little.

"Well, Miss Evy, it's been...interesting. We will talk again. Au revoir." He turned and walked away.

She watched him leave through the front hall door. Why had he brought up Lady Camilla? And why did she get the distinct impression that Rogan did not quite trust his Uncle Julien?

As she turned back to the table of tarts, she could not help but shiver. Rogan...Sir Julien...Master Henry... Try as she might, she couldn't escape thinking about them. Nor could she dislodge the uneasy feeling that their family secrets were more than a touch sinister.

She could only be grateful they had nothing to do with her.

CHAPTER EIGHTEEN

Evy's uncertainty over Aunt Grace took a swift upsurge during the next several weeks. It was late August, and Dr. Tisdale informed Evy that her aunt was suffering from a serious attack of bronchitis that might linger into the winter months ahead.

"She is quite frail and will need care."

She stood beside him in the doorway to her aunt's small room, watching Aunt Grace sleep. Her sallow cheeks were pronounced, as were the purplish shadows beneath her eyes.

"Keep the room warm and dry." The doctor nodded to Evy, and left—taking with him Evy's hopes of returning to London and music school.

She found solace in long walks in the woods, where she thought and prayed. She knew there were scant resources for her schooling, and her aunt's health required that she remain with her.

Evy wished she could go to the stables to borrow the horse she learned to ride when she first came to Rookswood, but with Arcilla away for a short stay at Heathfriar to visit Patricia and be near Charles, she was reluctant to impose upon the squire's kindness.

She went out in the late afternoons, when the sun dipped low and cast a shimmer on the yellow-red leaves of August. The starkness of color, combined with the moan of the wind through the treetops in the otherwise pervading silence, touched her spirit with a melancholy she could not understand. Walking seemed her only solace.

Once on the little-used trail that led into the woods, she could walk undisturbed until she came to a small hill. Here, she could see Rookswood, especially the west side of the great house.

How she had enjoyed her early years, both in the rectory and at Rookswood. Everything was changing now that they were nearly grown and out of school. What would the future hold? If Sir Julien arranged for Arcilla to marry Peter Bartley against her will, that would of necessity end Evy's friendship with her. Arcilla would be busy with her new life in Capetown, distance and change would leave no opportunity for a continued relationship with her old governess's niece. Their lives would be so different.

And what of Evy's plans? Everything was so uncertain. She only had three months of paid classes left. Once Evy returned for the Christmas holidays, they would have to pay for any further schooling. But even more important, her ailing aunt needed her here.

No, Evy had little choice. She would have to find work teaching piano to children in the parish. There would always be new Megs and Emilys who would come along. Already the two girls were engaged to marry next year, and they would soon be having babies. Evy smiled to herself, for she could almost hear Uncle Edmund's voice on the wind in the autumn leaves, quoting one of the Bible verses he had asked her to memorize: "For I have learned, in whatsoever state I am, therewith to be content."

As she stood on the windy hillock looking off at Rookswood, the dry colorful leaves on the trees rattled in the breeze, accompanied by another sound…hoofbeats?

She spun just in time to see Rogan maneuver his horse from among the trees onto an open area, holding the mount steady.

"I thought I'd find you here."

Although his presence disturbed the tranquility of her emotions, she felt a rush of exhilaration. Rogan always brought her a challenge.

He looked down at her. "I saw you walking up the trail. You come here often. You must enjoy the view."

She drew her shawl tighter as the wind swirled her cotton skirts at her ankles.

"Rather a bleak day for a comfortable walk." He lifted his face to the wind. "There wasn't much of a summer, was there?"

Somehow she read more into his words, hearing the truth that the carefree days of youth were fast coming to a close. There would be inevitable partings, some of them permanent.

"I like to walk in the cool brisk wind," she said just to be contrary and to avoid emotions that weakened her resolve not to respond to his almost magnetic appeal.

"Well, there's no accounting for people's tastes. I am surprised Derwent is not with you, though. An aptly secluded spot for a late afternoon rendezvous." He glanced toward the dim woods as he slid from the saddle. "Or did he see me and decide to hide?"

How could she be so attracted to one so very irritating? "Once again, you are wrong. And I think you know it. I did not come here to rendezvous with Derwent or anyone else. Besides, Derwent is no doubt busily attending to the vicar's needs, just as I must do shortly with my aunt."

"What is wrong with the vicar?" He walked up to stand near her on an edge overlooking the grassy meadow.

"Age, I fear… How do you know I come here often?"

His smile was quick and warm. "I cannot tell you all my secrets."

Had he seen her in the afternoons from a window in the west wing? Interesting that he had never troubled to join her until today.

"I remember you often enjoyed riding with my sister. Why do you avoid the stables now?"

"It would be rather bold of me, I daresay, since your sister remains at Heathfriar."

"Ah, you are timid about riding alone, then. That can be remedied. I don't leave for London until next week."

His nearness was entirely too distracting, and she forced herself to look away, struggling to appear indifferent. "I am so busy now."

"Why not go riding with me?"

"You misunderstood me about being timid. How I feel about my access to the Chantry stables has nothing to do with the fear of riding alone. I have always enjoyed being alone, to some degree. I meant that it would be bold of me to make use of the Chantry stables on my own. It was different when I was Arcilla's companion. The only reason I even learned to ride was because Lady Elosia wanted a companion for Arcilla during her lessons."

It was no secret that Arcilla actually felt reluctant about riding. She did so merely because it enabled her to be out and away from family eyes. Evy was the only one who knew that Arcilla had used those occasions to chatter with village boys.

"Granted, that is the reason you learned to ride"—Rogan inclined his dark head—"but now it is I who need a riding companion. So you can accompany me while I am here."

She gave a short laugh. "I hardly think you have difficulty finding a suitable companion."

"That is where you are wrong." His smile sent a shiver of awareness dancing up her spine. "I gather you think because I am a Chantry I can have everything I want?"

"Most everything."

"Ah, wrong again. It is not so. I am particular, you see. And I wish for your company. Who better could I have than the girl from the rectory, chosen by my aunt for our sweet Arcilla's betterment?" He reached out to pat his horse's neck. "I am sure my aunt would also agree that your company would benefit me."

Evy could find no suitable retort. What was he trying to do? Wrapping her shawl tightly around her, she warned her emotions to be still and moved away from him. "It is later than I thought. I must be going now."

He ignored her statement. "Arcilla never really enjoyed riding, but I noticed that you did. I doubt if she ever would have mastered it if not for your lead. Though she was nervous about it, she felt motivated not to be outdone."

Evy hesitated, turning back to him. "I'm surprised you recognized that."

"It goes along with her tendency to be in the spotlight." He laughed. "I know my dear sister very well indeed. Now it is balls and outings. Of course, Charles is ready to flatter and charm her. I think he has already fallen for her."

"Arcilla is a beautiful woman. Naturally men will notice."

"Yes. And she does many foolish things. I suspect she gets the tendency from not having a mother to teach her. Lady Elosia, bless her heart, is, well—Lady Elosia."

Evy smiled, rather surprised to hear him speak this way. He had never given any evidence that he thought Arcilla was unwise where men were concerned.

He met her smile with one of his own. "Feel free to use the stables whenever the fancy takes you."

The clearly sincere offer warmed her in ways she knew it should not. "Thank you, but presently walking suits me just fine. It offers me time to think."

"And you can't think while riding?" His smile told her he didn't believe her. "I thought you handled your mount in a very relaxed manner. You could learn to be an excellent rider. A shame I will not be here long enough to give you some advanced lessons."

At his meaningful smile, Evy looked away.

Run! her mind screamed. *Stay!* her heart pled.

She cleared her throat. "You are leaving for the university?"

"Next week." His tone turned cajoling. "Yet there is time for a few lessons."

He was nothing if not persistent. "The sun will set in an hour. I must get back."

"We have time. You needn't be concerned. I will see you back to the cottage."

"I— I really must get back. You see, I never stay here long. It is mostly the walk I enjoy."

"You rise early. Meet me at the stables at eight. You can ride with me just as you rode with Arcilla."

It was all she could do to meet that steady gaze. Her heart beat rapidly, and she scolded it, furious with both Rogan and herself.

This is nothing more to him than a mild flirtation, an amusing entertainment. A culmination of their childhood relationship before he went away. It would go nowhere, nor was it supposed to. But for all that she knew that was true, Evy felt as though a dangerous and life-changing trap was closing about her. She must not get involved with Rogan. Not even lightly.

"I have so much work to do tomorrow—"

"It cannot be all that urgent. I shall have you back before ten o'clock."

"It is urgent."

A dark brow shot up, and he offered the cryptic smile she was beginning to know so well. He did not believe her. He leaned his arm against the saddle, studying her. She could only guess what was in his mind.

She glanced away from him. "I told Derwent I would choose the hymns for Sunday. I usually go there by half past eight."

"How long can it possibly take to choose a few hymns? No more than twenty minutes, is my guess, not to make light of hymns, you understand. Actually, I am very fond of church music. I have even studied its history."

She turned and looked at him. He watched her evenly, as though measuring her response. Was he trying a different bait?

"You…studied church music?"

"There! You see?" He looked utterly wounded. "*Everything* I do is suspect!"

She couldn't help but laugh. "Not quite *everything*. But you do not remind me of someone interested in music or history."

"Suspicion, suspicion. My interest in church music should convince you not to avoid me."

Her brows arched this time. "Avoid you?"

"Like a frightened little bird, ready to peep and fly away the moment I come into view…especially when you are alone." His voice dropped to a soft murmur. "What could you be afraid of, I wonder?"

Her heart felt as though a hand had seized it, squeezing it with fierce determination. She spun away from him, striding down the path in the direction of the cottage and Aunt Grace, back to safety and security.

He was far too close to the heart of her true feelings. How had he known? It did not matter, but it was risky that he knew. What else could he guess from reading her eyes?

"Then I will see you at the rectory in the morning." His laughing voice chased her down the hill. "I will help you choose the hymns, and we will have our little ride afterward."

"You would not enjoy choosing the hymns," she called over her shoulder.

He caught up with her at that, leading his horse. A smile touched his mouth again. "You think I am really that crass?"

She jerked to a halt, facing him. "That's not what I meant."

He leaned close to her, and the warmth of his breath on her face nearly stopped her heart. "Then I shall surprise you, Miss Evy. Did you know I am quite adept at playing the violin?"

Her mouth fell open. The violin she'd seen in the piano room. So it had been his. She narrowed her gaze. Or had it?

"You?" She allowed a slight laugh. "I can't imagine such a thing."

Was there regret in his smile as he shook his head at her. "Oh, my dear Miss Evy, you've been quite wrong about me."

She crossed her arms. "You never played the violin before going to school in London."

"That is where you are wrong again. My mother hired a maestro to teach me for years until she died. After that I rebelled and wanted nothing to do with it. But when I went to London I realized I could not shake off a love for good music."

Could she believe him? He sounded so sincere…but then, he was a master at that.

"So I've been practicing again. Why should that shock you?"

She felt the telltale heat enter her cheeks, and turned to his horse to stroke its smooth nose. "Because I can hardly see you playing beautiful music."

"Then I must play for you sometime. How about Paganini's Violin Concerto no. 2 in B Minor?"

She stared at him. "You're not serious. It is a glorious piece! You're jesting, surely."

Clearly he found great satisfaction in her astonishment.

Piqued, Evy tossed her head. "Nothing you *say* you can do surprises me, but if you can *really* play Paganini—well, I shall certainly eat my words."

His eyes glinted at that, and Evy felt a sudden dread. "Then we will one day put an end to your misconceptions, Miss Varley, and I shall play for you. On one condition—that you also play for me. I should like to hear Beethoven's Piano Concerto no. 4."

She winced at that. "You ask a great deal of me."

She couldn't tell if the glint in his gaze was mockery or admiration. "I am sure you can prevail. Do we have an agreement?"

She hesitated. "Yes…but I would feel more confident if knew I was returning to school for more training."

"If?" He looked genuinely surprised. "I thought you loved piano."

"I— I do. But things are not well for us at this time. Not with my aunt the way she is."

At his thoughtful look she changed the subject. "If you give me enough time to practice, I will agree."

"Then it's done. This is wonderful. I have discovered something that proves you wrong about me."

She almost laughed at the delight in his voice. "I really must be going now."

"I will walk you back to the cottage."

"There is no need. I do this most every afternoon."

His smile opposed her. "I insist. I have detained you longer than usual, and the sun is setting. You need not be afraid of me."

"I am not!"

His sideways glance was skeptical. "Then why do you not wish me to walk you back to the cottage?"

It was clear he was going to have his way. It ought to have nettled her, but secretly, it did not. She could not fight him on this, so she would simply give in to the pleasure of his company. For the moment, anyway.

"I simply thought you were out for a ride and would wish to carry on with it." She knew the protest held little force.

He placed hand at heart, affecting a somber stance. "I shall be completely forthright, Miss Evy. I have been aware of your habits recently and suspected you would come here, so I followed. I fully expected to see our dear Derwent, but lo, such a happy turn of fortune—I discovered you alone. You see, I wanted to talk with you. After all, being such a close neighbor and knowing you for so many years, I think it is time we became more…personally involved. Do you not agree?"

That half lazy smile pulled at her, and she forced herself to look away toward the path. "We are not actually neighbors. It cannot be lost on you that I live with my aunt in one of the Chantry cottages on Chantry property."

"Now, now, there's no need for that kind of talk. Anyway, we've shared a few secrets in our time, which goes a bit of a way in making a bond between us. Don't you think so?"

"The secrets, I admit, were very intriguing. But I am not aware of the bond you hint of."

He smiled. "Then I need to cultivate it to bring your thinking around to mine. Let us see"—he pursed his lips—"perhaps in London, when you get there. In the past there was a time or two when I thought to contact you, but one thing or another came up. This year, I will simply make things happen. I am rather a prodder, you know. I want things to happen, and I usually help them along. And we now have an agreement."

Would he really arrange to see her in London when she returned to Parkridge Music Academy? She hoped not. She hoped so. Oh, she didn't know *what* she hoped. Their agreement to play for each other clearly made a way for them to meet, which otherwise might never come to fruition. But in London—away from the vicarage?

"One day," he continued, "I will show you Uncle Henry's map. If

I did not want to develop this…*friendship* with you, would I make such a promise?"

She had no sensible answer and was fairly certain that was just what he wanted.

"Then you actually found Master Henry's map?"

"I told you I would, remember? When I make up my mind to accomplish something, I do not give up until I have victory. Yes, I found it. And I have plans for when I arrive at the Cape. You see? I've even let you in on my secret. No one in the family realizes I have the map. Naturally, no one ever believed it was real, except perhaps Julien," he said thoughtfully. "I think that's his reason for backing a new colony in Mashonaland. He would love to get his hands on the gold deposit that Henry made such an issue about."

"You will tell Sir Lyle, of course. And your brother, when you arrive at the Cape?"

He lost his teasing grace at that. "Parnell? I doubt I will. First I need to locate the area where Henry claimed there was gold."

"The map does not show it?"

"Most of that area of Africa is unexplored by Europeans. Livingstone may have gone that way, but Henry had difficulty drawing the map as precisely as he must have wanted. Someday, of course, they will all need to know I found the map, but not until I own one of the greatest gold deposits in the area. What I'm hoping for is that Julien's colony is nearby. If it proves to be, then I will have a base to work from."

"The colony is deep in Mashonaland?"

"They are beginning to call the town Rhodesia—after Cecil Rhodes, who sponsored the colony—but it's known now as Salisbury. Julien is hoping the colonial office will send Peter Bartley there to represent the Crown."

She looked at him. "Arcilla would be most unhappy if she were forced to marry him and go to such a savage place."

"Yes," he frowned, "Aunt Elosia will have a fainting spell."

"Surely your father would not wish his daughter to go to such a place?"

"Sometimes I do not think he knows what is happening. Or cares."

Before she could think better of it, she put a hand on his arm. "Oh, please, you don't mean that."

Something flicked in his dark features as he looked down at her hand, and when he lifted his eyes to hers, she found her mouth going suddenly dry at the intensity of his gaze. She had the odd sensation of drowning…and pulled her hand away.

He hesitated, then fell into step beside her again. "I do, actually. Since my mother died, Father is not the man he once was. At first we thought it was Arcilla who would not recover. It turns out she is doing very well, but my father seems to have lost all real interests. He stays in the library most of the time and studies his books."

"I am sorry."

"Anyway, I will go to Salisbury."

What once seemed Rogan's boyish dreams Evy now saw were an ambitious man's determination to prevail. She knew he was quite capable, for Arcilla had boasted of her brother's grades in the university. A professor of geology had great hopes for his success, Arcilla had said.

Rogan could be quite serious when he wished to be, but she knew little of that side of his character. She was still learning just who Rogan Chantry really was. Indeed, he had surprised her today. She suspected there would be more surprises in the future. His declared interest in music both startled and pleased her greatly.

And yet, despite all this Evy still did not wholly trust him, not when it came to her heart. She must not become foolishly enamored with him, for she was sure that would lead to unhappy consequences.

Too late, too late, a voice within her chided. She ignored it. "I am sure you will succeed, or die reaching for your goal. Where did you find the map?"

"In Uncle Henry's rooms. Just as I had thought. The Black Diamond may be there too. I'd hoped it would be with the map, but it was not. But I did find a few very interesting letters."

He gave her a curious glance, and Evy sensed a cause for concern. "Letters?"

"Old letters, written in 1879. From Cape House."

"Oh? Are you going to tell me their secrets?"

His smile was as guarded as his words. "Not yet. I have my purposes first."

She waited, but he said no more, and silence reigned until the cottage came into view. Aunt Grace had already lit a lantern, and a golden glow was showing through the front windows, welcoming her inside.

Rogan opened the small wicket gate, where the bushy white roses grew in sprawling mounds. He bowed her past with exaggerated decorum, as though he knew she did not trust him to be a gentleman. She passed through, and he followed her. It was a short distance to the cottage door, and relief swept her when he did not attempt to see her there, or—even worse—force her to show hospitality to the squire's son and invite him in for tea.

"Au revoir, my dear Miss Varley."

She smiled at his typical parting. Never good-bye, but always "until later." He was letting it be known that he intended to see her again.

When she reached the porch, she glanced back. He was mounting his horse for the ride across the estate grounds to Rookswood. He caught her glance and touched his cap in a little salute, turned the horse, and rode away.

Her eyes half closed, and she tried to discern the emotions rioting within her. Pleasure and excitement that he had contrived the meeting on the hillock, and that he'd arranged for a meeting in London. And something else.

Apprehension.

She was no fool. She was on dangerous ground, and she knew it.

Inside the cottage, she stopped to peer into the small mirror hanging before the table with its bowl of autumn mums. She took careful consideration of her appearance.

Her thick hair, amber eyes, and blossoming figure were surely the reasons Rogan's head had turned in her direction. All wrong reasons, of course, but there it was.

She turned from the glass. Yes, she would need to be cautious indeed. It would have been far safer for her to remain a little brown wren when the fox was near the coop. She lacked father, uncle, or brother to safeguard her from interested hunters.

Well, I have my Christian upbringing to give me wisdom. I shall tread slowly and wisely in temptation's garden.

Hadn't Evy seen how beauty had spoiled Arcilla? And how it made Rogan sometimes too confident and bold? At a snap of their fingers, they could have just about anyone they wanted.

Well, she was not so foolish as to think Rogan truly wanted her. No, she would not be caught in his trap. She would let him spend time with her, but nothing more.

Certainly there could be no harm in that.

CHAPTER NINETEEN

The next morning dawned with a cool, crisp early autumn breeze that tousled Evy's hair as she walked down the narrow dirt road past Grimston Wood to the rectory. Derwent was already up and waiting for her.

"How is the vicar this morning?" she asked as he walked with her into the chapel.

"I found him in his study when I got up. He was seated at his desk, his Bible open to the Psalms. I think he fell asleep there last night. I daresay he looked very unrested." He scowled, running his fingers through his red hair. "I should have gotten up to check on him last night. I saw him to bed, but I'm a sound sleeper; he must have gotten up and gone down to his desk to read."

Evy sympathized. Hadn't she spent days and nights worrying about Aunt Grace during her illness? "You must not feel guilty because he slept at his desk, Derwent. The vicar is not a child that you must make all his decisions and feel guilty when he chooses one with which you disagree. I remember how Uncle Edmund sometimes rose at four in the morning to read the Bible in his office alone with God before duties pressed upon him."

"Yes, but, my father is growing so forgetful. I worry he will hurt himself someday. The stairs to his loft are steep, as you very well know from having used them."

She nodded. Toward the end of her uncle's life, Aunt Grace had expressed similar worries about Uncle Edmund climbing and descending those very steps. Yet neither her uncle nor Derwent's father ever wanted to give up the loft as a cloister.

Her gaze rested on Derwent's strained features. "I can see your present concerns lie far away from divinity school in London."

He made no reply, but he didn't need to. He bowed to her at the front steps of the chapel and walked back to the rectory. She went into the small church office used by the vicar and turned her attention to choosing the hymns for Sunday's worship service. She had several hymnals open on the desk when she heard footsteps behind her. She looked over her shoulder toward the office door, then stood as Rogan entered. She had not believed he would come.

"Hard at work, I see." He came up to the desk, noting the hymnbooks spread before her. He was dressed for riding. "You look surprised. I told you I would come."

Evy held a hymnal against her. "I suppose I thought you would change your mind."

"Why so? When I commit to something meaningful, I pursue it." Apparently he saw the small flash of alarm in her eyes, for he gestured to the hymnbooks: "I confided in you yesterday and shared my interest in music, remember?"

She looked down at one of the open hymnbooks. "Yes, I daresay, I still find the idea rather startling."

He offered an easy smile as he picked up a hymnbook and leafed through it. "Yes, it would be…if you think me a scoundrel. Well, I suppose it was not so very long ago that my family's ancestors *were* scoundrels. Barbarians who would just as easily throw their enemies to the bears as bother with them. But to get back to the present, Evy—I may call you by your Christian name? Thank you," he said before she answered. "By the way, what is Evy the familiar form of? Eve, is it not?"

"Yes, so Aunt Grace tells me."

"I rather like that…Eve." He walked to the shelf of theology books and glanced over them, still holding the hymnbook.

She drew a steadying breath. "Eve sounded a little stilted for a baby, so my mother began calling me Evy."

"A month at the mission station was not very long to have you."

"A month?" She frowned. "It was longer than that. More like a year. Why do you say a month?"

He rested his shoulder against the bookcase and studied her. "All right, a year. Let's not discuss that now—you keep looking at the door—are you expecting someone? Derwent perhaps?"

"No, he has work to do this morning. Is there anything I can help you with?" She made her tone quite businesslike.

"Yes, remember how you told me you were going to select the hymns? Well, there is quite a history behind church music. Were you aware that eighteenth-century hymnbooks were usually only collections of texts which did not include musical notes?"

That did interest her, which she fully believed he had expected. "No, I was not aware of that."

"Or that the first American hymnal to place music together with text didn't appear until 1831? In fact, there weren't many hymnbooks at all, even here in England. The usual way of singing was called lining out. The leader would say one line, and the congregation repeated it. Hymnbooks were rare and too expensive." He turned the book over in his hands, as though savoring the feel of it. "What's more, most parishioners could not read, so they did not sing one verse immediately after another as we do now."

She studied him as he put the book down and picked up another, noting the open page she had chosen.

"Charles Wesley… It might surprise you to know how many hymns he wrote in his lifetime."

She folded her arms. What a fount of information Rogan had become. If only she could believe it was out of true interest in the subject rather than out of a desire to entice her. "I suppose you know?"

"Of course. I told you of my renewed interest in music, did I not?"

Her bewilderment must have shown on her face, for he broke into a teasing grin.

"Really, Evy, you must learn to trust me. As for Wesley, he wrote

8,989 hymns! And even more poems than William Wordsworth. Charles completed a poem about every other day. Prolific, wasn't he?"

"I must say, I am quite surprised when I thought—"

"When you thought I'd no appreciation for the finer things of life, which in your opinion would be music and religion."

She walked to the desk and straightened the hymnbooks, dismayed to see how her fingers trembled.

"So hard-working and dedicated. I think a change of routine, a bit of relaxation, would not harm you. Why not dine with me tonight at Rookswood?"

Her brows lifted, and she struggled to keep her pleasure from showing. "I hardly think Sir Lyle and Lady Elosia would approve."

"By now it should be clear that I keep the company I choose."

"Still, it seems hardly suitable…"

"Let me be the judge of what is suitable. Tomorrow night?"

"I can hardly accept such an invitation."

He came up beside the desk, standing next to her, speaking in a low tone of what sounded for all the world like entreaty. "Come riding with me, at least."

She wanted to. Oh, how she wanted to. "Thank you, but I cannot. Not today."

"Why are you afraid of me?"

"I am not!" But as she spoke, she made the error of looking up, and her protest fell as his gaze held hers. She wasn't certain how long they stood thus, but when she grew aware of the warmth in her cheeks, she looked down at a book again. She picked up her pen and drew a piece of stationery toward her. "Whatever gave you the notion I was afraid of you?"

"It's obvious. No use denying it."

"That is quite absurd."

"It is quite accurate." There was laughter in his voice. "You look as though you're being stalked by the big bad wolf."

Which may not be far from the truth.

"You must not be afraid of me, you know. " His smooth voice did odd things to her heart. "There is no reason for it, really. In fact, I am fond of you."

She caught her breath, but refused to look at him. "Indeed?"

"Yes. And we have known each other for so long that I take a particular interest in you."

"I did not know I was of concern to anyone at Rookswood."

"Then I must try harder to convince you."

She straightened and met his eyes. "Why should I suddenly be convinced of something that has never been so?"

"Your question shows how little we understand one another. Surely a matter deserving of remedy. In fact, I admire you and your dedication to things Christian, such as your attendance at music school."

"I am pleased you approve, though I have my own reasons for doing so."

"Which is as it should be. You see, that is one of the things that interests me about you. Most young ladies seem so shallow in their attempts to impress me."

True…and a goodly number of young ladies at that.

"I was serious yesterday when I said that we should go riding together. There are areas where you could improve in riding, and I would enjoy helping you."

She picked up her pen and shuffled the books on the desk. "I am certain anyone who will be riding in the Dublin show, such as yourself, would be well qualified as a teacher, but as I have said—"

"There is so very much work to do for our dear and humble Derwent." His smile was close to being derisive. "Then I dare not keep you any longer. I must say our little confab has been informative, however. I think I understand you a little better now. I will see you again—soon."

When he had gone, she found it difficult to stop thinking about him. She recalled his interest in the violin—or so he had claimed—and his knowledge of Christian worship hymns. He had seemed genuine there. Was she being unfair with Rogan?

When she returned to the cottage she was surprised to find Aunt Grace sitting at the kitchen table waiting for her. She held a sheet of Rookswood stationery in her hand and looked up as Evy came in through the kitchen door. Pale and thin, nevertheless her aunt was cheerful.

"There you are, Evy. I've a message from Rookswood. From Lady Elosia. She wishes to see you for tea this afternoon."

"Lady Elosia invited me to tea?"

"Yes, a lovely invitation, I daresay. It will do you good. I fear I've demanded too much of your time. A young girl such as yourself needs some diversions."

Evy looked at the sheet of Rookswood stationery. Aunt Grace's words sounded vaguely familiar. Had Rogan suggested to Lady Elosia that she invite her? "Rather odd she would suddenly find time and desire to invite me to tea."

"Perhaps not so odd. I understand she has heard from Arcilla in London. Arcilla would surely have asked about you and perhaps even sent you a letter."

"I doubt if Arcilla has time in her thoughts or schedule to be wondering about me. But I shall enjoy tea at Rookswood."

As Evy entered Rookswood Manor that afternoon it was like old times. Gazing about the halls stirred to life memories of living upstairs, of days spent with Arcilla, of Rogan...

The leaded windows still lent their aura of shadow and secrets to the dim corners of the baronial hall, and the solid, ironwork grandeur carried her imagination to another century of Chantry dominance over the village serfs.

Her steps echoed in the stone chamber beneath the vaulted ceiling. Above the stairs in the upper gallery, paintings of ancestral Chantrys gazed down upon her with robust disfavor and amused superiority.

The housekeeper, Mrs. Wetherly, had since retired, so this was Evy's first meeting with the new butler, Mr. Ames. The man's thin, angular face remained unaltered as he led her across the hall to her audience with Lady Elosia.

"This way, miss," he stated in a lofty voice, and led her from the hall toward what Evy knew to be Sir Lyle's large library. The butler discreetly tapped on the solid oak door, opened it, and stepped in with a slight bow.

"Miss Varley is here, sir."

Sir? Evy started as Rogan's voice drifted to her: "Show her in, Ames."

Evy entered the library, rich with polished dark mahogany, wine-colored carpet, and walls of leather-bound books. The door clicked shut behind her.

Rogan stood near the fireplace, looking satisfied with himself. He stood with hands behind his back, feet apart, and wore a faint smile as he glanced over her Sunday afternoon dress.

"How good of you to come."

Could he mean it? Since when did Chantrys welcome someone of lesser social stature to Rookswood, as though that person's presence favored them? She glanced around the room for Lady Elosia. She was not there.

The log in the fire crackled invitingly and emanated a woodsy aroma. Rogan walked toward her, gesturing for her to take a comfortable chair near the marble fireplace, and he did the same.

"Where is Lady Elosia?" The warmth from the fire was pleasant after the chilling walk up from the cottage. She had brought no wrap and shivered slightly.

"She developed an unexpected headache and retired to her room for the afternoon." He wore a grave face, but his dark eyes danced. "Most unfortunate."

She resisted the exhilarating excitement that wanted to weave its tempting spell around her. She stood. "I am sorry to hear that. Then I shall go and come again when she calls for me." She started toward the door.

"Wait—Evy, please."

She paused in the center of the room, though it was against her better judgment.

He walked up behind her. "I have offended you. Why?"

She turned slowly to face him. "You must ask? Because you arranged this, not your aunt."

His mouth curved. "Is that so terrible?"

"Need I remind you of your social status, and of mine?"

"No. I told you I was fond of you, did I not?"

"Surely you are aware, a man of your background, that neither your aunt nor your father would approve of your being *fond* of me, as you like to put it. Nothing can come of this so-called fondness, and you know that better than anyone. Your attentions are—are quite unsuitable and—" She bit her lip, angry with herself more than with him.

"I am going away in a week. I wanted to see you alone."

"So you arranged a ruse."

"I arranged to see you, yes. But it is not a ruse. I asked you to ride with me this morning at the rectory, but you refused. I at least thought I could help you to select the worship hymns, but you refused that, too."

"I'll wager Lady Elosia knows nothing about this so-called afternoon tea."

"I wouldn't wager, if I were you. Your uncle, were he alive, would not approve such an activity." His smile was warm, teasing.

"Nor would he approve of your deceit."

"Oh, come. Your reaction is a bit overdone, is it not? You behave as though I have committed some great wickedness by inviting you here. Did I not invite you earlier to dine with me at Rookswood? Then why so shocked over a bit of tea?"

"You did not invite me to tea. Lady Elosia did. At least it was her name on the stationery."

He smiled wryly. "If I had signed *Rogan Chantry*, you would not have come. You made that clear at the rectory."

"You deceived my aunt. She believed the invitation was from Lady Elosia." She turned and walked to the door, but he was there ahead of her.

She had thought he would be frustrated by now, but he was still smiling. "You are a most maddening young woman. I know a dozen brats in London who would be flattered by my attention, yet you shield yourself like a prickly pear."

"Brats!"

"I can tell, however, that you are not as cool toward me as you like to pretend. Your eyes deny your indifference."

She was furious. He was right, and she felt unmasked. But he seemed to think she evaded him because she enjoyed being chased.

He leaned his shoulder against the door, looking down upon her, and did not step aside. "I think I shall keep you here."

She looked at him evenly, wavering in her resolve.

"My aunt did send that invitation to Mrs. Havering. I know that surprises you, but it is true. And she did come down with an attack and take to her bed. I merely took advantage of an opportunity. Fault me for that, if you wish. I confess, instead of sending word to cancel tea as she suggested, I decided it might be helpful to see you before I depart, as there is a matter that I wish to discuss with you." He reached inside his coat and pulled out an envelope, handing it to her. The envelope bore a London postmark, and she recognized Arcilla's handwriting.

He watched her for a moment, as though trying to discern whether she would cooperate. He must have decided she would, for he straightened from the door and walked toward the center of the room.

Evy turned and watched him. There had been a palpable shift in Rogan's mood. He seemed pensive, as though involved in some internal debate. A minute must have passed before she spoke. "What do you wish to discuss?"

He looked at her, and the gleam in his eyes was grave, even a little intimidating. For once, there was no suggestion of a smile on his face. "Your father."

"I do not understand."

"You will." She wondered if he was truly as calm as his tone implied. "As you suggested, Miss Varley, it is time to set aside any fondness." His gaze narrowed a little as he held an arm toward the door. "It is necessary for you to accompany me to the top floor, to Henry's old rooms. I cannot hint of a ghost as I did when a boy, but I can unlock the mystery of the Kimberly Black Diamond. And that of your parents."

Evy's breath caught, and her heart constricted. Her parents? There was no mystery surrounding her parents…was there?

"Shall we go?"

For once, Evy didn't argue. She simply nodded and followed Rogan from the room, nearly overcome with an odd sense of dread, as though her life was about to change. And she wasn't at all sure she was going to like the results.

Chapter Twenty

The stairway to the third floor was dark as Rogan allowed Evy to lead the way. They passed the familiar rooms she and Aunt Grace had occupied, went by the schoolroom and across the narrow, dimly lit hall to another smaller stairwell that was uncarpeted and bleak. It looked even dimmer toward the top landing. Evy paused, hand on the rail, looking up.

"Childhood fears of ghosts?"

Evy ignored Rogan's question and pushed aside the cowardly impulse to run. With resolute steps, she moved upward.

The rooms once belonging to Henry Chantry were much as she remembered. Little if anything had been done to them in the years since Rogan had brought her and Arcilla here. A musty odor of old furniture and draperies hung in the air. Rogan went to the window and threw it open. A chill, damp wind stirred the curtains as he turned to face her, arms folded, gaze firm, and a trace of a smile on his lips.

He took a key, opened an old metal box with engravings of lions and elephants on it, and took out a lump of what looked to Evy like rough rock.

"That is not gold, is it?"

He took her wrist and placed the lump on her palm. She rubbed her thumb over the rough surface, thinking only that it was unimpressive.

"There is a crystalline structure running through the rock. See it?"

It looked dull and was marbled with flaws and fissures.

"That's quartz you're looking at. It's held together by a substance that fills every crack and fault line." His eyes met hers. "Gold."

Evy looked at the thin layers of bright metal that twinkled in the light from the window. "Master Henry found this?"

"He and the Hottentot must have taken it from the ridge. It is gold, all right. If this ore is typical of the vein, it is an unusually rich find."

Considering Rogan's geological studies, she would take his word for it.

"Henry learned about this deposit as a young man in the mining camps around Kimberly. An old Afrikaner of Dutch ancestry from the Transvaal had a Hottentot slave who led them to the ridge of gold somewhere in what is known as Mashonaland. The Afrikaner and Hottentot were attacked by tribesmen and killed. Henry writes that he barely escaped with his life thanks to a fast horse and his skill with a rifle and pistol. During the next year he tried to retrace his steps back into the area to relocate the gold deposit, but was unsuccessful. His efforts gave rise to the suggestion that he was a deluded adventurer. That's when the mocking notion of Henry's Folly began. Soon afterward the Zulu War broke out, and his return to the region was impossible. So he drew a map from memory, detailing the trek with the Hottentot. I found his map, which he left me in his will, here with the quartz."

Evy looked from the rock to Rogan. "But if this proves there was gold, why did Henry come back here to Rookswood after the Zulu War? Why not return to Mashonaland and search?"

"That"—he took the rock and put it back in the box—"is the mystery I have sought to understand for several years. It never made sense that he returned to England. How could he be content knowing, yet not acting? He wanted another expedition. I know that for a fact. He wrote about it. Well, I now have an answer."

He locked the box and looked at her, his gaze steady and even. "Evidently Henry had to leave Capetown and promise never to return. If he came back, Julien would turn the matter of the theft of the Black Diamond over to the law. Henry was in quite a dilemma. His individual shares in the diamond mines were all in South Africa, as was the gold deposit. And yet he dared not go on another expedition without Sir Julien's permission."

"The law? Then it was Henry who stole the diamond?"

"Not according to Lady Brewster, his older aunt by marriage. I found a letter she'd written to Henry. It was with the map. She apologized for accusing him of stealing the Black Diamond and for rashly joining with Sir Julien to send him away."

Rogan paused, as though hesitant to go on, to unveil what came next. But why should he be? Surely there was nothing in this story that mattered to her?

She moved to sit in a nearby chair, disregarding the dust. "Then, if Lady Brewster claimed that Master Henry did not steal the Black Diamond, did Sir Julien ever locate it?"

"No, not that I am aware. No one yet knows what happened to the diamond once it was stolen from Julien's library at Cape House. Heyden insists it was brought here to Rookswood, that Henry was the thief."

"Heyden?"

"Heyden van Buren. The van Burens are Boers, of Dutch ancestry. At one time Carl van Buren was Julien's partner. They were both young men then. They located their first diamonds together in the river diggings in West Griqualand, close to the river Vaal. Van Buren was killed in the same mine explosion that cost Julien his eye. Later, Julien bought out Carl's younger brother for a handsome sum, and the man reverted to farming in the Transvaal. Heyden van Buren is his son."

She noted an edge to Rogan's voice. "You sound as though you do not trust this Heyden."

"Perhaps I do not. He is here in England now, traveling with representatives from the Boer Republic under their leader, Paul Kruger. The Boers are protesting British incursion into the Transvaal. There are rumblings of war. Heyden van Buren, from what I have seen of him, is a Boer zealot."

"Surely none of this concerns my parents?" Yet even as she spoke, uncertainty nudged her. Evy searched Rogan's face for clues. "What can you possibly know of my father or mother?"

"I knew next to nothing about what Mrs. Junia Varley was like until I read Lady Brewster's letter. A very telling letter that mentions Junia.

I wrestled with whether to share the information with you, since it is unpleasant. I decided I must since it involves the theft of the Black Diamond, and, unfortunately—your mother's involvement."

She stared at him mutely. "Oh, but surely there is some mistake! It just cannot be."

"I am sorry. The letter to Henry mentions that your mother was in Cape House the night the Black Diamond was stolen."

She watched him, trying to take this information in. "How could that be? How could she have been at Sir Julien's estate when she was with my father at the compound at Rorke's Drift?"

"Your mother knew not only Henry, but Sir Julien. Lady Brewster's letter makes that clear."

"Impossible, I tell you."

"Lady Brewster had no reason to lie. She wrote years ago, after Uncle Henry returned here to Rookswood. The letter was private. Neither Lady Brewster nor Henry expected anyone other than themselves to know its contents."

Evy jumped to her feet. "Preposterous! What would my mother be doing at Sir Julien's house on that night or any other? There is some mistake, there has to be."

"There is no mistake. Sit down, Evy." He came around from behind his uncle's desk. "There was no romantic affair, if that thought is upsetting you. That would indeed be a tragedy, would it not? If we were blood cousins. No, this ugly matter involves not the fire of passion, but cold, hard greed."

She caught her breath. "Then of what do you accuse my mother?"

He shook his head, the shadow of his usual smile on his lips. "I do not accuse her of anything. Someone else has accused her. Lady Brewster's apology to Henry in her letter pointed out the fact that it was your mother who stole the Black Diamond and ran away from Cape House."

Evy gasped and stood so abruptly that she swayed a little. Rogan reached to catch her, but she wrenched away.

"You *dare* suggest that my mother stole your family diamond? She was dedicated to teaching Christianity. If she had been greedy for gain, she would not have become a missionary with small hope of having anything more in this world than a medical hut. She certainly would not have been risking her life in Zululand, where she gave her life in martyrdom."

"I understand the complications, even the contradictions, but Lady Brewster wrote Henry that the family nanny finally confessed that she had helped your mother escape by arranging with an African worker to have a buggy ready near the stables."

"There is no proof to any of this. There can't be."

"It's all in the letter. Your mother stole the Kimberly Diamond, then ran away from the Capetown estate, taking the diamond and the buggy."

"I want that letter." Her voice shook, but she didn't care.

He frowned. "No. Not yet."

She stamped her foot. "You are lying."

His dark eyes flickered, and she shivered at goading him so. But it had to be a lie. It had to be.

"For what reason would I lie, Evy?"

"Only you would know. You brought me here to flaunt this in my face. Why that should be, I do not know."

"I brought you here to show you…this." He took the letter from his pocket and held it in front of her. "No one else knows about it, just as they did not know of the map. Sir Julien has accepted what he believes is the inevitable loss of the diamond. Henry was the only other person who knew about your mother, and he's dead, as is Lady Brewster who wrote this incriminating letter. There is talk, of course. But without this letter dated many years ago, it is only a tale. As far as everyone else is concerned, the guilt lies with my uncle. I could destroy this letter and there would be nothing in writing to incriminate the memory and reputation of your mother."

She searched his face. Why had he said this to her? What was on his mind?

"I was going to show this letter to your Aunt Grace and draw the truth from her. Your mother was her sister. She could have written Grace, who may be keeping matters quiet."

This was too much! "So now you are insinuating that Aunt Grace knows where the diamond is hidden!"

His frown was quick, impatient. "I did not say that. However, she may know something, and I need any information she has."

Evy hesitated. "Yet you did not go to her. Why?"

"When I learned of her frail health, I decided against speaking to her. If she knows anything about the diamond, it is for you to find out—at the appropriate time, when you believe it is safe to question her. This"—he held the letter up—"will remain in my control. One day I may surrender it to you to do with as you wish. But not until I have all the information I can get on the Black Diamond."

Evy stared at him, and one simple fact filled her mind: She simply must get the letter.

Before he could guess what she was about, she snatched it from his hand and darted to the door, flinging it open and dashing into the hall. Rogan reached her before she hit the dark stairwell. His strong fingers closed about her wrist, and he retrieved the letter from her trapped fingers.

She spun to face him and was met by his smile. "Your determination is commendable, my dear Evy, but I'm afraid I must disappoint you."

She hissed her frustration and lunged to grab the letter back.

Her fingers tweaked it from his grip, surprising both Rogan and herself. A burst of energy shot through her as she sped down the steps. She traversed the corridor, running hard past the schoolroom, past the rooms she and Aunt Grace had once occupied, and toward the flight of stairs to the main house.

She heard him behind her, yet she kept her pace down the stairs, the hall, and then the second flight of stairs.

Evy glanced over her shoulder and saw him. She would never make it back to the cottage. It seemed as though he was letting her stay ahead, knowing he could overtake her when he pleased, perhaps outside—

unless she surprised him again. Was there time enough to take his horse? She had noticed it tied near the tree.

Did she dare? The feel of the letter in her hands brought her the answer: yes. She had no other choice.

She ran past the gallery of Chantry faces, down toward the final flight of stairs into the baronial hall. Rogan took a shortcut over the banister and ran ahead, reaching the front door, smug and smiling. Evy paused. He blocked her exit, and yet…off to one side was the library. *The library! With the fire still crackling in the fireplace! Yes! Yes, of course—*

She reached for the library door, looking up to see his smile vanish. Could he stop her? She must not let him.

Evy burst into the library. *Yes!* The fire still burned. Gasping to catch her breath, she held the letter in her hand…and time seemed to move in slow motion. She all but stumbled toward the fireplace, ready to hurl the horrid letter to the consuming flames, when there came a movement from a high-backed chair facing the hearth. A man stood and turned to face her.

He looked as surprised as she felt. She had not seen him before. His hair was fair, his eyes a wintry blue, his build rather slender.

Rogan burst into the room and also stopped in his tracks when he saw the man standing there. Evy was caught between the two of them, the letter clutched in her trembling hand.

"Heyden!" The surprise in Rogan's voice wore a thin veneer of…what? Dislike?

"Hello, Rogan. Am I—er—interrupting anything?"

A tense silence fell between Evy and Rogan. His dark gaze glittered, and she could almost believe he had enjoyed the pursuit down three flights of stairs, while she was gasping and holding a cramp in her side. Rogan smiled, casting a quick, calculating glance from her to the flames. Then he sprinted suddenly in her direction.

Evy made a dash for the fireplace.

Rogan intercepted her, catching her wrist and whirling her straight into his strong arms, holding her fast. He plucked the letter from her fingers and stashed it inside his jacket. He was smiling again, his dark eyes dancing.

"You are a tougher competitor than I would have thought, my dear. But alas—though I promised I may surrender to your whims one day, that day has yet to arrive." And then, as though they were the only two in the room, he drew her closer. Before she could protest, his warm lips covered hers in a kiss that sent her senses reeling and a shiver scurrying down her spine.

When he finally released her, there was a faint look of surprise on his face.

Evy didn't think. Couldn't think. She simply reacted. She drew back and slapped him. The resounding smack split the silence of the room. Rogan did not even flinch.

She dragged breath into her lungs, painfully aware that her breathing trouble had nothing whatsoever to do with the chase she'd just been in. No, it was the capture that had stolen the air from her lungs.

Heyden looked on in silence, and, choking back a sob, Evy ran from the library and out into the hall.

The butler was waiting by the front door, wearing the same dignified expression as before, quite as though he had neither seen nor heard anything amiss. But Evy knew he must have seen part of the chase with Rogan.

The butler opened the heavy door and bowed as she swept past and out onto the front steps of Rookswood.

"A good day to you, Miss," he said with the same lofty voice.

Down the steps she went into the cold afternoon, the sky a blue-gray with oncoming clouds as the promise of an early autumn sent leaves scuttling along the stone courtyard about her feet. Though exhausted, she hurried on, sniffing back angry tears, forcing her head high as she made her way home.

How dare he kiss her? How dare he make her feel…things she simply *shouldn't* be feeling!

"He's a cad," she hissed to the darkening sky. "A frustrating, impossible cad!"

CHAPTER TWENTY-ONE

Evy did not return to the cottage immediately lest Aunt Grace question her about the teatime she was to have taken with Lady Elosia. Instead, she hurried along one of the garden paths, hoping against hope to rid herself of emotional upset and calm her facial expression.

And to give herself time to forget the feel of Rogan's lips on hers...the way his arms had both imprisoned and sheltered her...

"Stop it!" She clenched her teeth. "Stop thinking about the cad!"

She had wanted the truth about her past, and yet it loomed as a dark, ugly cloud. How could either of her parents possibly be involved in stealing? Especially the theft of something as valuable as the Black Diamond?

No! It was utterly preposterous. She refused to accept any such notion.

She rushed on, the wind cooling her feverish skin. Wasn't the horrid innuendo about her mother terrible enough? How could Rogan have compounded this awful day by taking hold of her that way...by lowering his dark head until all she saw were his eyes and the light burning in their depths?

"Oh, stop it!" Evy pressed her hands to her burning cheeks. How could he have kissed her? And in front of Heyden van Buren! Yet it had not troubled Rogan at all. He had seemed to enjoy the spectacle! Well, of course. Why wouldn't he? The cad had probably planned all along to take advantage of her. What a fool she'd been to trust him, to follow him to Master Henry's rooms.

"Cad!" she hissed to the blowing wind. Yet…she could not stop thinking of him.

She kicked at a rock in the path. *I should be indignant and dislike him heartily.* Unable to deny the truth, she looked to the sky and wailed, "But I don't!"

Her shoes crunched the leaves on the path. She came to a bench on the green beneath an overspreading oak tree. She brushed the leaves from the bench and sank down, limp.

"Oh, Rogan…what have you done?"

She closed her eyes. Could there be any thread of truth in Lady Brewster's letter? Could Evy's mother have been involved in stealing the diamond?

For all her staunch denials, fear nibbled at her. Fear that what appeared impossible might somehow be true… Oh, the idea was humiliating! And made even more so because she'd heard it from Rogan.

She sat mulling over the dark disclosure, over the picture of her mother changing from Christian martyr to thief. The cracked image left her shaking. First Lady Camilla's wild claim, and now Lady Brewster's letter.

Evy straightened. She must talk this over with Aunt Grace.

But even as she was ready to stand, her traitorous mind recalled occasions when Aunt Grace had behaved oddly. Rogan's tale could certainly explain why Aunt Grace had always avoided discussing details about Evy's parents. And there was her strange reaction when Evy mentioned Master Henry's death to Uncle Edmund several years ago.

Could it be…? Was her aunt wary of some sort of scandal coming to light? When the old sexton, Mr. Croft, had mentioned the possibility that Henry did not commit suicide but was murdered, Aunt Grace had been particularly upset. Evy had thought it was just the topic that upset her, but now… Could there be more to it? She frowned. If Aunt Grace discussed the notion of murder openly, wouldn't that eventually introduce the topic of the stolen diamond and her sister Junia?

As though she could not help herself, Evy remembered the strange anxiety Aunt Grace had shown when asked to become governess and live at Rookswood. Perhaps she had known Sir Julien was visiting at Rookswood and feared he might tell Evy that he blamed her mother for the diamond theft.

Feeling as though the weight of a thousand wagons rested on her shoulders, Evy stood and trudged back to the cottage and up the front steps.

"Evy, you are back so soon?" Aunt Grace regarded her, wide-eyed.

"Yes. Lady Elosia developed a headache and took to bed." Evy struggled to keep her voice from betraying her emotional exhaustion. "I shall put the tea on for us."

She poured boiling water into the teapot, then covered it with the faded cozy. A counter divided the small kitchen and sitting room. Chairs encircled the small fireplace. Though far from luxurious, the cottage was comfortable and, until the last few weeks of her aunt's illness, cheerful. Now the chilly wind blew about the chimney and windows, and the once sunny summer atmosphere took on a lonely isolation.

Evy stole several sharp glances at her aunt. How to bring up the stark subject gnawing at Evy's soul without making her aunt ill?

I will ask about the Black Diamond without mentioning Lady Brewster's letter... I could bring up Lady Camilla again...

Evy brought the tea tray with sweet biscuits made by Mrs. Croft to the low wooden table and sat down opposite her aunt.

Aunt Grace was propped up with pillows on two overstuffed chairs pushed together, improvising a daybed. Outside the window the bare branches on the old apple tree moved in the wind.

"Looks as though rain is on the way again." Grace lifted her teacup to her lips.

One look at her aunt was all it took for Evy to swim in dismay. Aunt Grace was watching her, her large brown eyes troubled and wide with alarm. Evy's heart knew a pang of guilt when she noted the gray in the woman's once brown hair. Aunt Grace had lost so much weight that the skin on her face was taut, showing the fine sculpture of her bones. The bluish splotches under her eyes persisted despite the energy tonic Dr. Tisdale prescribed.

Evy swallowed hard. Aunt Grace had raised her, loved her, and with Uncle Edmund had provided for her earthly needs. Even this cottage was an entitlement granted her because of her aunt's faithful service to Grimston Way. To badger her now with questions of the past seemed…cruel.

How can I break her heart by letting her know that I've heard the very worst, what she desired to keep from me, about my mother?

Evy bit back sudden tears. What if burdening Aunt Grace with questions now about a stolen diamond and possible murder shortened her life? She had been so upset over Lady Camilla's suspicions, what would she do about Lady Brewster's letter to Henry Chantry?

No. I cannot do this to her. Not now… She swallowed her disappointment and desperation. *Dear God, help me to be wise, to wait upon You.*

"You worry too much, Evy."

At her aunt's unexpected comment, Evy started.

"You heard Dr. Tisdale. My chances for recovery are excellent. Mrs. Croft has offered to come and help me while you are away at school in London."

Evy sighed. It was well enough that her aunt took her subdued mood for worry about her health. "School? Dear Aunt, we both know that it is out of the question now. It seems selfish of me even to contemplate using the little you have saved for another year at Parkridge. I would much rather take you to London to see a specialist. Dr. Tisdale is a fine man, but I am sure there are better doctors. And Dr. Tisdale, too, expects to be paid. I've been thinking. I could take a leave of absence from my studies and return in, say, another year or so to graduate. Perhaps I can take your place teaching school with the curate. Derwent may be able to arrange for it. He could convince Vicar Brown to authorize my acceptance, I'm sure."

Aunt Grace set her cup down. "I'll not hear of it, Evy dear. Your learning is more important than ever. Should something happen to me, which is entirely in God's timing, then I want to depart with the peace of knowing your education will provide for your upkeep. If not, I shall feel a failure in spite of my service at the vicarage with Edmund."

Aunt Grace went on: If Evy graduated music school she would be qualified to teach in London. But once a student left the path of learning to start earning a living, it could become difficult to return to that narrow path.

"Once in a race, it is wise to keep going."

Aunt Grace would know better than anyone about that. And then Evy paused; for once Aunt Grace did not suggest that marriage to Derwent would bring the secure life that she had always planned for Evy to have.

"Not that I am suggesting marriage to Derwent is the wrong choice for your future," Grace said as though she had read Evy's mind. "I am certain he will be a good and kind husband for you. Even so, it is wise to have something to fall back upon when I am gone. Just in case."

Evy shuddered. She could not imagine the quiet, isolated cottage without Aunt Grace, or even living in the rectory. Peering into the future to plan her life was like trying to see through the fog on the London wharf. Only God could see ahead. She did know that peace always came to her when she thought of His wise and caring nature.

Evy's decision came swiftly. She went around the table and knelt beside the daybed. "Aunt, I— I do not mind staying here in Grimston Way. I've had one wonderful year at Parkridge, and I have learned so much. Even now I'm able to teach children and receive a wage for it. True, it will not be much, but I am sure I can get two, possibly even three students whose parents will pay for piano lessons. Madame Ardelle at the London school believes I have talent as a children's instructor. I think she would be willing to write me a letter of recommendation."

Grace squeezed her hand. "Yes, I am sure you are qualified now. I was talking to Mrs. Tisdale only yesterday. She tells me she will soon need to give up her piano lessons and mentioned the possibility of you taking over for her."

"There! You see?" Evy really did try to sound enthusiastic. "God will provide for His children."

"Yes, even so, it isn't necessary yet that you not go back to London."

"But—the money. How will we manage?"

"I have the money."

Evy stared at this calm pronouncement. "Where did it come from?"

"Now, dear, did I not tell you before that I must be allowed my little secrets? It is enough that the money is available. No, you will finish your schooling, and who knows? Derwent may receive a living at a vicarage in another section of England with better possibilities than Grimston Way. Should he end up in London, you could get a position teaching in a music school. So you see? There's not a thing to worry about, Evy."

Evy could have told her there was plenty to concern them, but not wishing to put further stress upon her aunt's thin shoulders, she said nothing and simply returned her bright smile. She would keep her fears about her mother and the future locked inside her heart.

"If you say so, Aunt. I have much to be thankful for, I know. My future, it seems, is in God's hand."

"Most certainly. Like the pillar of cloud leading the children of Israel, there is One directing our path through the wilderness."

Despite her aunt's assurances that all was well, Evy still struggled with uneasiness. Concern—unnamed, unknown—loitered in the background like some ominous phantom of darkness ready to spring upon her. She took solace in the words of the psalmist: "My times are in thy hand."

During the following days, before returning to London, Evy tended to Aunt Grace's vegetable garden and fruit trees. In early September Mrs. Croft came, and they enjoyed time together with Aunt Grace, preserving the bounty.

Evy prayed often that whatever their allotted time together might hold, the favorable hand of their heavenly Father would overshadow and protect her and her aunt. Much to her dismay, she did not see Rogan again before he left for his final year at the university. She suspected that Heyden van Buren had also left with him for London.

It is just as well, she told herself time and again. She still fumed when she thought of the way Rogan had taken such liberties with her. He would not have dared if he had not been a Chantry.

As the days slipped by and she prepared her winter wardrobe to return to London, she wondered if the divine promise of God's protective oversight might not be gracious preparation for what awaited. For disappointment came only a few days before Evy and Derwent were to board the train together for London and their respective schools.

It was around five o'clock in the afternoon, and Aunt Grace was taking a nap, something she needed far more frequently of late. Evy was alone in the kitchen, kneading dough for the following day's bread, when Derwent showed up on the bungalow porch. He always tapped and looked in through the window on the door. She saw him outside, his hands pushed into the big pockets of his faded coat. She raised floury hands and gestured he should come inside.

He opened the door, and a gust of wind followed him.

"Brrr, it's getting colder by the day. Autumn's coming sooner this year."

The sun was dipping low in the pearl-gray sky, and she motioned toward the lanterns. "Would you light those for me, Derwent, please?"

"Sure enough." He looked over at the counter by the big black stove. "What are you stirring up?"

"Bread dough for tomorrow. I'm all done." She went to wash her hands, then removed the apron that had been Aunt Grace's. "I will put the teakettle on."

"Um...I really cannot stay that long, Evy. Thanks, anyway."

She was rather surprised. He usually had tea, then cleaned out any sweet biscuits left from the morning. "Is anything wrong?" She looked at him in the lantern light.

He shifted. "I would not say it that way, but, well, I would rather just get on with the news that brought me here."

"Well, all right." She sat down on the kitchen stool. "What is it?"

He cleared his throat. "I will get right to it. I won't be returning for my final year at divinity school."

Evy stared at him, not sure she'd heard right. Her first thought was that Rogan must have had something to do with this. He had already planted a song of high adventure in Derwent's mind. *South Africa again,* she thought shortly. *Gold fields and diamond mines!*

"So you are going to Capetown."

"No… That's not how it is, Evy. It is my father. I've been noticing it all summer, and maybe you have too, but it is getting unmanageable. He is just growing old, I expect. He forgets things. That's all right, if it does not hurt anyone, but that's the pain of it, you see. Last night he decided to make himself a mug of tea before bed. Next thing I knew, I woke up smelling smoke."

"Oh no! Derwent!" She reached out to take his hands.

"That's what I told myself. 'Oh no!' I went rushing down to the kitchen not knowing what to expect and found the water in the kettle had boiled away. The kettle was black and smoking up the kitchen. I took care of things, then checked on him. Do you know he was fast asleep! If I hadn't been home and smelled smoke, the rectory could have caught fire. And that isn't the first time… Two weeks ago he left some candles burning off the holder. Mrs. Croft found them." He squeezed her hands. "He is getting worse, you see. You know what that means."

"Is there any damage to the kitchen?"

"Oh, some smoky darkened areas by the stove. Mrs. Croft says she won't attempt cleaning up unless I help, so naturally I will. Wouldn't think of leaving the mess all for her, especially the ceiling. We'll do it tonight."

She almost smiled when he released her hands to reach for the plate of sweet biscuits. He frowned as he chewed. "My father's losing his clarity, that's plain to see. It is getting worse by the week. Seems to be coming on awful fast. He can no longer prepare his sermons. No one knows that yet. I've been helping him all summer. He has merely been reading them from the pulpit. So you see"—his tone was heavy, resigned—"I wouldn't feel good about myself if I just up and left him for school. You understand, don't you, Evy? You feel that way about Miss Grace sometimes. But she's not half as bad off as my father." He searched her eyes, as though seeking some kind of confirmation from her. "If it were just his leg or a knee, I could handle that. I could just get the sexton to come and help him with personal matters while I was away at school. But his mind…well, it is different. Sometimes he gets frustrated and cross about it. And he says I imagine it all."

Her heart nearly broke for him. "Derwent, I am so sorry. Of course I understand your dilemma. I wish there were something I could do to help."

"There's nothing anyone can do. He is my father, and I will look after him. But it does throw a corker into matters, doesn't it? I will need to delay graduation, and if I must do that, then I'll need to delay— well, a lot of other things." He took her hands again. "You know what I mean, Evy?"

"Yes, of course I do." And she did. But what she didn't fully understand was the rush of relief the news brought her. "That is very understandable. You must not worry about any of that now. You have enough on your shoulders."

"It is not that I was worried, or that I'm thinking things are too burdensome. It is just that setting future things by the stovepipe is inevitable right now. I worry something dreadful could happen. If I went away now, the rectory could burn down, or he could take a fall and break a hip."

"That would be dreadful indeed."

"So, at least until the bishop appoints someone to take over the rectory, I cannot return to school."

As he spoke she had the oddest impression that he was just a trifle relieved over the postponement.

Derwent gave a deep sigh. "When a new rector comes, then I can carry on at divinity school."

Evy nodded, but Aunt Grace's warning drifted through her mind, about the difficulty of getting back on the path to learning once one stepped off the narrow way.

Derwent stood, then hesitated, as though he wanted to say something more and could not find the words. He shuffled his feet and put the collar up on his coat. "Well…you will be leaving soon for music school, I daresay."

"Yes, in three days now."

"I will write you about how things are going here."

"Yes. And I will write you."

He maneuvered his way to the door. "Try not to worry about Miss Grace. I will look in on her every day, and so will Mrs. Croft."

She nodded. "That will be a great blessing for me." He was such a kind man. Why couldn't her heart react to him as it did to Rogan? "Thank you, Derwent."

He hesitated once more, then opened the door and stepped out to the porch. "G'night, Evy. See you tomorrow."

"Yes, good night. And I will be praying for you and the vicar."

He smiled. "I knew you would. You are good at that sort of thing. Better than I. It was your upbringing."

He shut the door, and she heard his feet leaving the porch. From the kitchen window she saw the chilling purple twilight settling into darkness.

Soon it was time to pack her trunk, and then Mrs. Croft drove her and Aunt Grace to the train depot in the one-horse jingle. Evy boarded the train and waved good-bye as the train chugged out of the station on its two-hour journey to London.

Now she would play the piano every day. How she had missed it. Of course, she'd played at the rectory when she had time to walk there, but now music would fill her life, her soul. What joy! Oh, to fill her mind and heart with glorious music and forget everything unpleasant that had plagued her these summer months.

Everything…and everyone.

As Grimston Way and Rookswood estate faded into the distance, Evy wondered if even her love of music would be able to free her mind of the dark clouds of suspicion surrounding the Kimberly Black

Diamond and Henry's mysterious death. Or if it could keep her from dwelling on the unthinkable—that somehow her mother had been involved in theft and deception.

Would Rogan let the ugly past alone? Could she? She did not know. She could only pray for God's wisdom and guidance.

CHAPTER TWENTY-TWO

On the first day of the new school year Evy and the other students were assembled in the great hall, where Madame Ardelle, who reigned over Parkridge Music Academy as though she were its queen, addressed them. She was clad fully in black, except for a bit of white lace here and there. Though formidable and demanding, she was otherwise a pleasant woman, who commanded the respect of her students, most of whom were pleased to be in this serious learning environment.

Madame emphasized how fortunate the students were to be here and that they must now live up to the reputation of the school. This seemed to worry her a good deal of the time, for Master Eldridge would teach the final year at Parkridge. She seemed to have no greater chagrin than that her music students would not measure up to his expectations. She constantly reminded them that Master Eldridge had played piano throughout Europe and was considered one of the great musicians in England.

"I think Madame is in love with Master Eldridge," Victoria, one of the girls in Evy's room said.

Another of the girls, Frances, dismissed this notion. "She's too old."

"Who said old people do not fall in love?"

"It seems quite obvious that romance and marriage are for the young."

"What nonsense!" Victoria grimaced. "Who wrote the great romantic plays, pray tell? Men with gray hair."

Frances considered, then shrugged. "Maybe you are right. I never thought of that."

Alice Tisdale was not in Evy's room this year. In fact, Evy had looked for her at all the large gatherings but had not found her. That seemed a bit odd. Was all well with Alice? She had seemed rather wan and quiet all last summer, as though something had been troubling her. In Evy's next letter to Aunt Grace, she asked about the Tisdale family and whether Alice had been seen in church.

The weeks went by slowly because Evy was concerned about her aunt. Also, she could not quite stop thinking about Rogan—and the memory of that moment in his arms would return at some of the most inconvenient times, such as during practice, when her fingers would miss a key and she would instantly glance up to see Madame Ardelle's sharp black eyes.

In the second year there was a good deal more freedom for the students. Sometimes in the afternoons and often on Saturdays the students would hire carriages and go to Regents Park, or take boat rides on the Thames and afterward have tea in Piccadilly. Evy enjoyed choosing a bakery treat and taking it out to one of the sidewalk tables, joined by her two roommates, Frances and Victoria.

Life was molded around a pleasant routine. Besides her music, there were language classes, dancing, and twice-a-week classes on deportment and conversation. Evy took them all, as though she knew her days for such opportunities were short. But piano was a grueling five hours a day, overseen by the watchful madame. Sundays, of course, were worship days. A good many of the students did not attend, but Evy would find her way to St. Paul's each Sunday morning where she hung on words the minister gave from the pulpit of the great cathedral.

When Frances told her about Grand Tabernacle, she began attending and was awed and inspired by the preaching of the great Reverend Charles Spurgeon. After hearing him she began taking a greater interest in the Scriptures. Evy had been raised to believe in Jesus and His redemptive work, but through Spurgeon's eloquent exposition, Christ became more precious and personal to Evy's heart. She read the Bible before bedtime now, whereas before it was mostly a book for Sunday at the rectory. Her prayer life also became less dependent on the *Book of*

Common Prayer, and hymns took on new meaning. She read about Wesley, Isaac Watts, and Newton, and gained a new appreciation for Bach and Handel as she recognized that their inspiration came from their Christian faith.

The month of November rolled around, and letters arrived from Aunt Grace explaining that Alice would not be returning to music school.

She may take her final two years in France, with this year as a sabbatical. She has been such a help at the rectory, taking over many of the duties you performed so well. I must say I'm surprised. Alice never appeared committed to the Lord until this year. Derwent is depending on her help a little too much, I fear. At any rate, we are all so grateful Alice can help since neither I nor Mrs. Tisdale is quite able to do all that we once enjoyed.

Derwent and Alice?

Derwent also wrote telling Evy of his father's regression and of how difficult things were for him. *I do my best, but I have always said that I am not as gifted as my father. Miss Alice thinks I should speak of my concerns to Sir Lyle and Lady Elosia.*

Evy looked up from the letter. What was Alice doing advising Derwent like this? He seemed quite satisfied to allow it. What was going on back in Grimston Way?

She read on...

We all know what a great influence Sir Lyle and Lady Elosia have over the rectory and what goes on here. Did I write you about the good man and his wife who may take my father's place as vicar when the hour comes? I daresay, everyone likes him. He was here for a week last month to meet the villagers. The bishop is likely to appoint him. He and his wife will be coming in the spring, around Easter, to hold services and get to know the parishioners better. There is some assurance that I may become the new curate...

Evy heard from Arcilla now and then. Her Montague finishing school was nearby, so she sent Evy secret messages through one of the staff girls so they could meet at Regents Park. A message came on Friday afternoon, delivered by one of the maids who worked at the prestigious school: *Meet me at Regents Park at noon on Saturday. There is news to tell you.*

More than likely there was also someone Arcilla wished to meet.

Despite curtailed freedoms, the young woman had managed to rendez-vous with several men from the university, all while claiming that her heart belonged steadfastly to Charles Bancroft.

Evy went to the park and waited for Arcilla by the fountain. It was a sunny Saturday, and a good many Londoners were enjoying the day in spite of the chilly November weather. The lawn was well kept and filled with a scattering of colorful autumn leaves. An array of birds and pigeons were about the square and near the fountain. Evy wondered what kind of news Arcilla wished to tell her. Perhaps it was merely about her holiday plans. Arcilla usually anticipated gala affairs months in advance so she could have her father arrange for additions to her wardrobe. She told Evy that she did not wish to go home to Rookswood this year for Christmas, but preferred Heathfriar.

"Rookswood is too far," she had said. "Guests must stay the week-end or at least the night, and this limits many from attending. It's Rogan who prefers Rookswood; he likes the country setting."

"Well, with his dedication to riding, he would."

She remembered Arcilla's mock horror. "Riding! The very thought spoils everything."

Evy smiled at her extravagant friend. "You'd prefer dancing with a dozen attentive young men vying for your smile."

Arcilla laughed, then sighed in mock ruefulness. "Ah, how well you know me, Evy."

Evy was pulled from her musings by the sound of Arcilla's voice call-ing: "Evy, over here!"

She turned from the fountain and saw the parked carriage near the curbside. Arcilla was leaning out the cab window, beckoning her to come.

Now what? Arcilla usually walked down from Montague. Evy hur-ried across the grass toward the cab.

"Quickly, inside!" Arcilla scooted over, and Evy climbed in, the cabby closing the door.

"The gem show," Arcilla called to the cabby.

Evy looked at her as the carriage pulled away from the curb. "Gem show?"

"I'll explain in a few minutes. First, I've other news."

Arcilla was a beautiful sight in her stylish frock, hat, and fur-collared coat. She appeared quite the sophisticated young woman on the doorstep of marriage. And yet there was an unusual tension in her voice, and she was absent the hand gestures that she normally used for emphasis. She learned early on that she looked charming with a hand going to her heart as she expressed her sincerity, or up to a stylish hat when flirting, or reaching forth in a gesture of pathos when she wanted one's help.

The fact that she'd abandoned her favorite mannerisms told Evy that she was genuinely upset.

"*Everything* has gone wrong!"

"Surely not everything." Evy tried to smile at Arcilla's wail. "A few more months at Montague and you will graduate. That is something for you to be pleased about. No more schools, no more guardians—that should make you deliriously happy."

"I am serious, Evy. I've heard distressing news from Rogan. He came over to the school last night to see me. We talked in the parlor."

Evy's interest picked up.

"He showed me a letter he received from Parnell, who is in Capetown. Two pages, mind you. That should tell you how seriously Parnell takes his mission."

Evy raised her brows. "What mission?"

Arcilla's large eyes shone with misery. "Sir Julien is going to convince my father that I should marry Peter Bartley! So dear traitorous brother Parnell wrote Rogan telling him all the reasons why he must convince me, and why I should go through with it! Parnell has met with Mr. Bartley. In fact, Rogan has warned me that the man is here in London. Rogan said he arrived from the Cape a week ago. I'm expected to be introduced to him before we leave London for Christmas holidays."

Evy could see the worry in the other girl's eyes and dropped her teasing. "Parnell wants you to marry Peter Bartley? But why? I thought he and Rogan were both friends with Charles. They've certainly spent enough time together at Heathfriar these past few years."

"Well, Rogan is Charles's friend. It is Sir Julien who wants my father to arrange marriage with Mr. Bartley. Parnell wrote Rogan explaining what was being planned." Arcilla's mouth set in the stubborn line Evy knew all too well. "I won't do it, I tell you. I positively *don't* want to marry any man but Charles."

Evy was not surprised by Arcilla's unhappy news. She remembered hearing Sir Lyle discussing Peter Bartley and how Julien believed Bartley was the right man for her. But what did shock her was the role her brothers were playing. Parnell had to know his sister would resist.

"Why would Parnell want you to marry Mr. Bartley?"

"Oh, you know Parnell. He is for anything Uncle Julien is touting." She rested her chin in her hands, clearly despondent. "That's what he told Rogan in the letter too. It turns out that Mr. Bartley is related in some way to the Bleys, so I suppose he's in diamonds. Uncle Julien wrote Father that the marriage will bring a certain diamond mine under family control. So it is very important to him—and to the Chantrys. It is all quite involved, you see."

Evy could not help but notice that this fact—that it was considered important to the family diamond interests—seemed to appeal to Arcilla's pride. Evy knew she had always adored being the center of anything important. Well, if such a thing could sway her, then did she really love Charles?

"Does Rogan agree that it is wise for you to marry Peter?"

"Rogan told me he favors Charles. They're such good friends. Of course, Patricia is Charles's sister, and that has something to do with it, I suppose, since Rogan will marry Patricia. He has not proposed to her yet, but the family expects him to, perhaps before he leaves for Capetown next year. Parnell is also being groomed to marry into Uncle Julien's family. Even though the girl—I forget her name—is too young now. She is fourteen, I think."

She turned to Evy with wide, helpless eyes. "Oh, Evy, it is so dreadful. How lucky you are to be so inconsequential. No one wants to marry you—except Derwent."

"Thank you, Arcilla."

Arcilla batted at her arm. "Oh, you know what I mean. You are quite pretty, really. Except you are too prim. That frightens men away."

It did not seem to frighten her scoundrel brother, Evy wanted to tell her. She wondered what Arcilla would say if she knew of the advances Rogan had been making toward her. But Evy preferred that no one else know about it.

"Rogan is not convinced about Mr. Bartley," Arcilla was saying. "Parnell knows that Rogan favors Charles. That's why Parnell wrote him. You should see the letter. It was absurd. Rogan said it looked like a lawyer's treatise."

"I do not see how you can thwart your family's purposes, Arcilla."

"Not *everyone* in the family agrees, I tell you. Rogan is not convinced. He has yet to meet Mr. Bartley."

"What did Rogan advise you to do? He would side with your family's wishes, would he not?" After all, there would be family wishes and plans for *his* marriage as well.

"He will meet with Mr. Bartley and make his own judgment, then speak with Father about it over Christmas holidays when we all return to Rookswood."

"He would want a match that would be most sensible for you."

"I suppose Parnell does too, but he seems greatly swayed by Sir Julien since he went to Capetown. Thank goodness for Aunt Elosia. At least she thinks a match with the Bancroft family would be favorable."

"Then perhaps you have no cause to worry unduly."

"I wish it were that simple. Mr. Bartley will also be coming to Rookswood to meet with my father during the holidays. Now I'll have to go home for the season instead of being with Charles at Heathfriar, as we planned. But I *won't* marry Mr. Bartley."

Evy leaned back against the cushion. "You must not do anything rash."

"You are the only true friend I have. You must help me. If you don't, I won't have anyone to turn to."

"You have Rogan."

"Yes, but he would not stand for my running off with Charles."

Evy stiffened. Run off? Would Arcilla really do something so foolish? "I do not see what I can do to help you." What would Charles do if Arcilla suggested running away and getting married? Such a thing would bring sure scandal, and Charles would lose the favor of his family. Evy could not see Charles Bancroft giving up his right to inherit Heathfriar.

"There is something you can do for me." Arcilla was pleading now. "I'm to meet some friends at the museum at one o'clock for the diamond show. I want you to come with me."

"Me? But why?"

Arcilla looked away, and little alarms began to sound in Evy's mind. What was the girl up to now?

"Oh, just because I feel so unsocial. I need you there for support."

Evy laughed. "Since when do you need me to give you courage in a social gathering? Besides, I doubt my presence will be appreciated by your friends."

"Well, *I* shall appreciate it. Oh, Evy, do not protest. It will all be rather boring, actually. Diamonds from all over the world…but one can't *wear* them, can one? All one can do is *look*. And the event is really a show honoring diamond cutters. I need your company."

This was certainly not typical of Arcilla. Evy did not know what to think of her motive.

"Now, do not get that huffy look and say no before I explain. Because I need you to help me."

"To do what?"

"I'm meeting someone—alone." Arcilla waved off Evy's protest. "Oh, do not look at me that way. It is perfectly harmless."

Evy was not convinced. "If your brother does not wish you to go off alone, do not expect me to shield your recklessness. I've no desire to come up against his displeasure." Indeed, she'd faced enough of that in her race down the three flights of stairs at Rookswood.

"It is important, I tell you!" Arcilla's lip shot out in a pout. "Are you my friend or not?"

"It seems I am a friend when you need me to get you out of trouble."

Arcilla laughed. "Do not be silly, Evy. Of course we are friends. We have been together since childhood. Oh, very well. I will tell you. I'm meeting Charles. There…now you know. Is that so dreadful?"

"No, of course not. Then why must you slip away like this? Do you not see him most weekends at Heathfriar? And he *is* Rogan's friend."

"That's just the problem. They are close friends. Oh, do you not see my difficulty?"

"You are not being totally honest with me, Arcilla, and I shan't cooperate with your schemes unless you are truthful. I've my own reputation to safeguard, you know."

"But I *am* being truthful. Charles knows about Mr. Bartley, and we must meet alone and discuss the future."

"He learned so quickly?"

"Rogan met with him yesterday. Charles saw Parnell's letter. Rogan explained the difficulty facing my father should he oppose a marriage Sir Julien thinks is important to all of us. You look curious and confused, I know. I do not understand everything either. Rogan never explains all to me. He says I wouldn't understand. It does concern the Chantry interest in the diamond mines owned by Sir Julien. That should help you understand the horrid situation I've been forced into. I'm a pawn in the plans of relatives in Capetown as well as here in England. Rogan told Charles not to see me during Mr. Bartley's stay in London. Don't you see? It is so unfair to me and Charles."

"I'm sorry you're in this situation. But if you are not supposed to see Charles, then a secret meeting will only make matters worse."

"How will Rogan find out? You won't tell him, and neither will I."

"I'd rather not become involved in this."

"Of course not. But I must see Charles once more! Please, Evy!"

Evy was sympathetic, but she could just imagine her own difficulty if things went awry and Rogan discovered she had abetted his sister in something so reckless.

"Just this once." Arcilla placed a hand on Evy's arm. "I won't ask your help for a clandestine meeting with Charles again. I promise."

As if Arcilla could resist further opportunity to see the man she claimed to be in love with. And what of Charles? Did he not realize the situation he was placing Arcilla in by agreeing to meet with her in secret?

"If Charles is such a good friend of your brother, why is he willing to deceive him?"

"Oh, Evy, you are such a *novice* about love." She clasped her hands together, intertwining her fingers. "Charles and I are *deeply* in love. We should rather *die* than be forever torn apart."

"That sounds much like Romeo and Juliet. But I think you have felt the same way about several other men in your life."

Arcilla actually looked a bit wounded at that. "You laugh, but that is merely because you are so dour you do not know what love is."

Evy stiffened. "I know enough to realize that deceiving family and friends for a secret meeting is not likely to come to a good end."

"No lectures." Arcilla held up her hands. "I have endured enough of them!"

"Then I will go now and trouble you no longer."

"Oh, Evy, you are impossible. No, please, do not go. Say you will help me—just this once."

A heavy sigh escaped her. Did Arcilla have any idea how troublesome this could become? Did she even care? "How long will you be gone?"

"Not long. Thirty minutes, maybe less. All you need do is occupy Heyden van Buren with conversation until I return. Ask him all about the gem show. That will keep him talking. He is as boring as Rogan on the subject of diamond cutting. I will be as quick as I can. I promise."

Heyden. Evy fought the heat that threatened to surge into her cheeks. She hadn't seen the man since he'd witnessed that dreadful scene in the Rookswood library. "What is Mr. Heyden doing at the diamond show?"

Arcilla's pretty brow furrowed. "You look rather affected by him. Do you know him?"

"I met him in the library at Rookswood last August."

Arcilla gave her a quick scrutiny. "He will never marry you, so do not hope for such a thing."

Evy could not stop the bark of laughter that escaped her. "Whatever gave you such a silly notion?"

Arcilla arched her brows. "Oh, come. I know that wistful look."

"You know nothing of the sort."

"His family was one of the early *voortrekkers*."

"Boers, mostly farmers." Evy had studied up on the Hollanders, who had first gone to South Africa in the 1600s, while the Puritans had gone to America.

"Yes, well anyway…" Arcilla lifted her hand, showing she had little interest in history. She had hardly passed the subject when Aunt Grace taught it at Rookswood. "Rogan thinks that Heyden van Buren's family agree with the cantankerous Boers when it comes to who rules South Africa. Heyden's family is not well off, though he has a good education."

"I assure you, I have no romantic interest whatsoever in the man." Evy kept her tone calm and cool.

Arcilla's trilling laughter filled the cab. "That is why I like you, Evy. You are not afraid to say what you think. Too many others fear I will exclude them from my balls and dinner parties if they speak their true minds." She turned in the seat to face Evy, her hand extended like a waif pleading for crumbs. "Then you'll come with me to the museum?"

Evy nodded. She had her own reason for attending now. If Heyden van Buren would be there, then a few questions about the theft of the Black Diamond were appropriate. Rogan had said that Heyden had some suspicions of his own about who had taken it from Cape House.

"As long as you promise me you will not use this occasion to run away with Charles Bancroft, I'll go with you."

"You have my promise."

Evy gave Arcilla a quick look. The girl's meek response did not bode well…but never mind. Surely she would not be such a ninny as to run off with Charles. And even if she would, surely Charles had more sense.

At least, Evy fervently hoped so.

CHAPTER TWENTY-THREE

The carriage drew up alongside the museum, and they were assisted out.
Evy saw Heyden van Buren standing on the wide steps. He came forward, smiling, and removed his hat, his eyes fixed on Arcilla. She
exploited the moment, despite the negative things she had said about
him in the cab.

"You are late, Miss Arcilla. I was beginning to worry. I should have
met you at Montague and escorted you."

Her tinkling laughter showed delight, as though pleased he had
worried.

"You are looking beautiful," he told her. "You shall put the diamonds to shame."

Again, she laughed and favored him with a sweet smile. "How kind
you are with your compliments, Mr. van Buren. You make a humble
young lady such as myself blush."

Evy was astounded she kept a straight face, and remained in the
background unnoticed until his wintry blue eyes recognized her. There
came a visible start of surprise as he must have recalled the scene in the
library, then a small glimmer of approval as his eyes dropped over her.
Evy resisted his flattery.

"Miss Varley, isn't it? This is a surprise. I think my friend Rogan
Chantry failed to properly introduce us at our last encounter." He smiled
and bent over her hand, his fair hair catching the sunlight. "Permit me to

introduce myself. I am Heyden van Buren, and as you would know by now, my family is acquainted with Sir Julien Bley of South Africa."

"Yes. I have been informed. Will you be staying long in England?"

At the glint of curiosity in his eyes, Evy felt a twinge of apprehension. Was he putting events together? Was he linking her with her mother, and did he believe her mother had been at Cape House and run away with the Kimberly Black Diamond? The idea was so egregious that she felt her cheeks tint. If only she could disprove it and salvage her mother's reputation.

"A few more weeks," Heyden was saying. "Then it's home again to South Africa."

He was older than she had first thought, perhaps ten years Rogan's senior, which would make him around twenty-eight. He was browned from the South African summers, and the lines at the corners of his eyes were not the work of aging but of the sunshine. His accent was rather strange too, bringing to mind the man Evy had met in the woods so long ago. She preferred the richer tones of Rogan's precise British.

Inside the museum, guards were everywhere. One quiet, vaulted chamber of marble and glass was roped off, and diamonds of all shapes and sizes—some in the rough—were displayed on a background of black velvet under shimmering light. Special guests were invited to a catered luncheon to hear lectures by some of the most revered diamond cutters from around the world. In spite of her first inclination to refuse Arcilla's request to accompany her, she was now pleased she had come, not merely to ask questions of Heyden should the opportunity arise, but to see the glorious display of the world's diamonds.

Heyden seemed to appreciate her avid interest and informed her which diamonds had been sent from Capetown for the show. He pointed out a blue diamond, which was catalogued, "The Blue Rand, Kimberly, 1876."

"Sir Julien Bley's." There was tension in Heyden's pronouncement.

"I understand your Uncle Carl van Buren and Julien Bley were at one time partners in a diamond mine." She did her best to sound casual.

His brow twitched. "Yes, I was a small boy then. You probably know of the mining accident and how Sir Julien bought the van Burens out. We are not on the best of terms now… You have heard?"

"That you are an Afrikaner, yes."

"In British Capetown, Miss Varley, there is a great dislike for the Boers, to use a British term. Most of my people are loyal to Paul Kruger and the Transvaal Republic. That's where I grew up with my grandmother. Though it's presently under Dutch rule, that may all change soon. Since gold has been found in the Transvaal, the British officials in Capetown, including Sir Julien, are trying to influence London to seize the area. They will not be satisfied until war is provoked with the hope that British sovereignty will be established throughout all South Africa."

Evy was aware of the recent newspaper accounts of disagreements between the British government and the Dutch farmers, but she had not formed an opinion on the matter. Perhaps that might change later, but with other, more personal concerns on her mind, trouble with the Boers seemed far away and of little consequence.

"Sir Julien Bley rightfully questions my allegiance to British rule in South Africa. I've never made any bones about my political convictions. But I do not fret… There are other ways to win my rightful seat at his banqueting table."

He studied her so thoughtfully that she grew uncomfortable. His look was much the same as Sir Julien's when he'd scanned her so intently in the parlor with Lady Camilla.

She gave a small shrug. "Sir Julien still has a great interest in what became of the Black Diamond."

"Then Rogan told you of the scandal surrounding your mother?" Evy started, and his mouth turned down. "That is most unfortunate. I feel she was unfairly blamed."

His words caught her off guard, and she gave him a smile of relief. "Somehow I thought you believed in her guilt and offered Rogan your convictions."

"I shall tell you a secret, Miss Varley. One of the reasons I came to England was to arrange a meeting with you about your mother. I have information that you will find very interesting. We cannot talk here,

however. I had hoped to speak with you at Rookswood, but Rogan"—
he smirked—"actually threatened me, the young cub. If I set foot again
on the estate, I'm quite sure he will have me thrown off."

She looked at him, trying to fathom this new development. Why
would Rogan not wish her to meet with Heyden about her mother?
"You feel my mother was innocent?"

"I do. If she took the diamond on the night of the storm when she
fled in the buggy, then what happened to it? I've questioned the old
Zulu woman."

"The one they say helped my mother escape in the buggy?"

"Yes, Jendaya. I've made a trip into Zululand since the war. I am the
only one who has managed to speak to her. She said there was no diamond because your mother was convinced that Henry Chantry betrayed her and ran off with it. Jendaya entrusted you to Henry who took
you to Natal. From there, arrangements were made to bring you to
Grimston Way."

Master Henry had betrayed her mother! Rogan had not mentioned
this...so he must not be aware of it. "Then it really *was* Master Henry
who stole the Black Diamond."

"I am convinced of it."

That could only mean Lady Brewster had been wrong when she
wrote him absolving him of guilt. But how to prove it? And how to convince Rogan?

Lady Brewster's letter would not help—in fact it would likely discourage Heyden. She did not think even he knew its contents. Rogan
had been quite closed about the matter.

"You do not know how your words lighten my burden, Mr. van
Buren."

"Heyden, please."

"I thought I was the only one who believed in my mother's innocence. I think the charge is incredible. She was a Christian missionary."

His golden brow went up. "A missionary?"

"Yes, of course, at Rorke's Drift. Why she would even be at Cape
House makes little sense to me. I told Rogan so, but he insisted my

mother was there that night. But I cannot imagine she would know Master Henry. So this supposed betrayal makes no sense. Unless— Yes, it is quite possible that my mother was at Cape House that night for some Christian purpose. A duty to perform, no doubt. I intend to find out someday."

She looked at Heyden and was startled at his intense regard. "I see… I believe you are in…some confusion about your mother, Miss Varley. We do need to talk. But now is not the right moment. When can we meet again? Alone?"

"I can meet you at Regents Park the first Saturday in December."

"Yes, very fine."

That Heyden understood her dilemma was tremendously reassuring. At last she had an ally.

"Tell me if I am out of line, Miss Varley, but witnessing that startling scene in the Rookswood library has troubled me on more than one occasion recently. May I ask what Rogan Chantry may have told you about the theft of Sir Julien's prized diamond?"

"Only what I just mentioned, that Sir Julien no longer believes it was his stepbrother Henry who arranged the theft, but my mother."

He was thoughtful again. "Do you mind telling me what was in the letter that made you want to throw it into the fireplace?"

She wondered how much to tell him, and yet why should she not trust him? He believed her mother innocent, when Rogan did not.

"Then Rogan did not explain?" She was opting for time to think.

"Rogan Chantry is a most secretive young man."

"It was an old letter from Lady Brewster apologizing to Henry Chantry for accusing him of stealing the diamond. She blamed my mother."

"Then…Rogan believes your mother was a missionary."

She blinked. What an odd thing to say. "Yes, of course he does."

In the thoughtful silence that followed, Evy came suddenly alert. *Arcilla…*

She turned from the showcase and glanced about the chamber, her heart plummeting. Arcilla was nowhere to be seen. Evy wasn't even sure which direction she had gone to meet Charles Bancroft.

Several couples entered the chamber, talking and laughing quietly. Evy's gaze rested on them, and suddenly she found herself confronting Rogan and Miss Patricia Bancroft.

Rogan was obviously surprised to see Evy—and when his fervent dark gaze found Heyden, Evy was sure he was displeased.

She assumed those with him were several of his university friends, along with the typically pretty aristocratic young ladies who would be dining with them after the diamond show. Why didn't Arcilla mention that Rogan would be here this afternoon with Patricia?

Evy hated to admit it, but Rogan and Miss Patricia made a handsome couple. Suddenly she felt herself a sparrow among peacocks—she hadn't dressed formally at all. She turned away as though to look down at the blue diamond Heyden had been pointing out to her just moments before.

Evy looked over to the clock. Arcilla said she would take less than thirty minutes. Her time was up. What on earth was delaying *dear* Arcilla? She endured a moment during which she wanted to turn and leave the museum at once and take a cab back to Parkridge Music School. She should have known better than to trust a Chantry! *She has left me here to make excuses during her absence, but this time it won't work.*

Heyden was watching her, and she tried to focus on what he was saying. "I understand you study piano at a notable music school. You must play quite well."

She managed a smile. "There are times when I wonder if I truly play at all. I shall have my concert solo in the first week of December. If I merit even a nod of approval from Madame Ardelle, I shall be delighted. It is very grueling."

"I can well imagine. I admire such determination. I have always wanted to play, but lacked the discipline to do it well. A public performance, is it? Then I should like very much to come and hear you."

Pleasure filled her at the thought. He was a most agreeable man.

The concert, she told him, would be held on a Saturday evening near the end of the term before the school breaks for Christmas and New Year's holidays.

"I shall make a note of the date and be in attendance."

"Am I missing out on something? Sounds like a party?"

Heyden turned to face Rogan. "Hello! Quite a display, is it not?"

He inclined his head, but his gaze was on Evy, not Heyden. "Quite. Only the Black Diamond is missing. I see Sir Julien's Blue is here. Stunning, isn't it?"

At the mention of the Black Diamond, Heyden fell silent. Evy tensed. Rogan must have known speaking of it would make the moment uncomfortable.

Rogan gave Evy a tenuous smile. "What a pleasant surprise. Where is Arcilla?" He glanced about.

"Arcilla?" Evy gripped her hands together. "She could, in fact, be anywhere by now."

Rogan was regarding her carefully. She could tell he suspected she was hiding something. Oh, a plague on Arcilla for putting her in such an awkward position!

If Heyden had not been there, Evy would have mentioned Arcilla's desire to see Charles. But family matters between brother and sister over a future marriage should be kept in a tight circle. Her inability to explain to Rogan left her no choice but to give an illusive answer. "She was right here with us when we came in." Evy cast what she hoped was a casual glance about the chamber. She saw Patricia talking with the friends they had arrived with earlier. She avoided Rogan's gaze and was relieved when Heyden, who saw nothing unusual about Arcilla's behavior, or perhaps did not care, went back to discussing diamonds.

"Sir Julien's Blue is attracting attention from the world markets," he told Rogan, "including the Vatican, but there's doubt Sir Julien will sell. Some suggest he's growing sentimental."

"About the Blue?" Rogan's smile was almost derisive. "It is not sentimentality that holds back the sale, but what Julien considers weak bidding. If the offer were high enough, he would sell in an instant. No, there is no sentiment lurking in my uncle's cool mind, unless it's over the loss of the Kimberly Black."

Evy frowned. Was Rogan baiting Heyden? She wanted to tell him that Heyden did not believe her mother was guilty, but decided against it. Besides, Rogan had not been looking at her when he mentioned the Black, but at Heyden.

Heyden turned a smile Evy's way and reached out to take her hand. "Miss Evy was telling me of her piano concert to be held in December."

Rogan lifted one rakish, dark brow. "How interesting. You invited Heyden to your performance?"

Oh, this was insufferable! "Well, yes…anyone is welcome. It is to be near the end of the term."

"But a solo concert nevertheless." He smiled. "I am sure I will find it of interest as well."

Heyden was looking across the chamber. "I see an old friend from the Angola diamond mines. He called and told me he'd be here. I worked for him some years ago. That was when I foolishly thought Angola diamonds were superior in color and clarity to South African." With that, Heyden walked across the museum chamber past several intimidating looking guards.

A man had entered the chamber and now stood by the door. Evy saw that he was very heavy, and in his fifties with a smallish, egg-shaped head. His warm-weather white Panama suit and wide-brimmed hat were most inappropriate for the setting.

Rogan, too, regarded him with mild interest. As the man and Heyden walked to one of the glassed-in security tables to look at the glittering array of stones, Rogan turned toward Evy.

"Who is he?" she asked. "The heavy man in the Panama suit?"

"One of the Boer officials from the Transvaal Republic. One of Paul Kruger's right-hand men. They came to see Her Majesty's Prime Minister to avert war. And now—where *is* that foolish sister of mine?" His gaze locked with hers. "With Charles?"

He knew. "You are wrong if you think I came here to help arrange her rendezvous."

"Then it is Charles?"

"Yes. I knew nothing of the museum showing until I was already in the cab with her. She asked that I meet her at Regents Park, and once I was in the cab she pleaded for me to come with her. She was upset over the family decision to have her marry Peter Bartley."

"Then she told you? I thought she might. Where does Heyden come into this?"

Evy cocked her head. "Why should you think he does?"

"Because he wanted to see you, and I warned him to stay away. He used Arcilla to bring you here so he could talk to you. What did he tell you?"

Her brows lifted. "*He* happens to believe my mother is innocent. He found out Master Henry betrayed my mother that night and ran off with the Black Diamond. Jendaya, the Zulu woman, told him so. He thinks Lady Brewster was quite wrong to have absolved Master Henry of guilt in the matter, all of which is very reassuring concerning my parents. Why then should I not want to talk with him?"

"Because he is more trouble than you are ready to handle." Rogan's gaze was as hard as his tone. "I'm asking you to stay away from him, Evy. At least until I have more time to look into the matters he's told me about."

"Then…he did tell you my mother was innocent?"

A look she had never seen before crossed his face. "Let us simply say he told me about your mother. The information he wishes to drop at your feet is not what you are expecting." Was he worried? He certainly sounded so. "I don't think you are ready to hear it yet. Stay away from him. The van Burens hate my family for a number of reasons I cannot get into now. Heyden will do anything to ruin us. He cannot be trusted."

She watched him, troubled, uncertain…yet unable to promise what he wished of her.

"Do you know why he is here in London?"

She looked to where Heyden stood talking with the heavyset man. "No, though he said wanted to talk with me."

"That's not all of it. As a Boer, he despises the British. He actually wants war. We consider him a serious troublemaker, trying to urge Paul Kruger to throw down an ultimatum to the British Government to get out of the Transvaal."

"I know little about the conflict," she admitted. Her interest in Heyden van Buren had to do with her parents, and Rogan knew it.

"This is the first time you've talked with him?"

"Yes. I have not seen him before except in the—" She caught herself before mentioning that debacle in the library, but it was too late.

He smiled, his eyes scanning her face briefly. "Ah yes…the library." The words came out in a deep, caressing rumble. "A fond memory indeed."

"I really must be going now." She turned to survey the room. "There is nothing I can do about finding Arcilla. I'm sorry it turned out this way. Sorrier still that she drew me here to enable her to escape more easily."

"Please accept my apology for her. We both know Arcilla well enough to understand her. But as long as she is with Charles, I won't worry unduly. I merely wish she had used her head and refrained while Bartley is visiting. He expected to meet her here tonight, and from the hound dog look on his face, his pride has been injured."

Evy could not help but smile.

"There is no telling when she will return," Rogan said. "I suppose she's gone off in Charles's carriage. Well then, you will need a ride back to Parkridge. I'll call you a cab."

"There is no need. I can arrange it myself, thank you."

His smile was broad. "I would not *think* of allowing you to go off alone. If I concern myself with Arcilla, I also feel some obligation toward you. After all," he said silkily, "you would not have gotten into this if it hadn't been for her conniving. I'll get you a cab."

"I am not helpless, Rogan. I have done my own arranging many times. I shall be quite safe."

He ignored her completely, falling into step with her as she headed for the door. The man was inexorable, and she could only wonder why.

Unless... She restrained a small smile. Perhaps his insistence had something to do with a vague notion that Heyden might feel obligated to bring her back to Parkridge.

True to his word, Rogan hailed a cab, rather imperiously, she thought, and handed her into the seat. "I shall let you know about Arcilla." He lifted her hand to his lips, and the contact sent shivers running through her. "Au revoir."

She sank back against the seat cushion, grateful to be free from the many layers of tension she'd just encountered. As she ran through the conversations in her mind, she felt her resolve grow.

She would talk with Heyden again and hear what he had to say. No matter what Rogan Chantry thought.

CHAPTER TWENTY-FOUR

Evy had trouble concentrating in class the next morning, so deep was her concern about Arcilla. What if she had actually convinced Charles to run off to France and get married?

After classes, Madame Ardelle entered the dormitory room that Evy shared with Frances and Victoria. Her round, olive-toned face was animated, and her brown eyes turned to Evy, who sat curled in chair with her music history book in hand.

"You have a caller, Miss Evy." The woman always used the formal *Miss* before the names of her students, even after three or four years under her tutorship. "Rogan Chantry waits for you with a coach. He is asking permission to escort you out to dinner, but I told him that was highly irregular for a Thursday night. I hope I have not disappointed you too severely. You may speak with him in the parlor if you like, but you must insist he leave for his university by eight o'clock."

Frances and Victoria slipped over to the window and peered down into the carriage yard.

"Oooh...look at that divine coach."

"Never mind the coach. Look at him!"

"Miss Frances, Miss Victoria?" Madame Ardelle looked at them, brows raised, then turned again toward Evy. "It is not befitting to keep a young man of such good breeding waiting."

What Madame Ardelle meant, of course, was that the Chantry name was associated with South African diamonds.

Evy hurried to freshen up and run a brush through her hair while

Frances and Victoria gave her advice on what would make her look her prettiest. She calmly changed into a pretty dress and added the saucy hat Rogan had bought her, setting it carefully on her thick, tawny hair. Again she noted how the ribbons and color emphasized the jade flecks in her eyes. Would he notice?

Evy smiled and left the room. Once away from the girls, she admitted to herself that she was not as indifferent toward her dashing caller as she pretended. She sped to the stairway and looked down into the quiet front hall. She hoped Madame Ardelle had not loitered, and she sighed when the woman was not in sight. Evy came down the stairs, looking toward the door that led into the parlor. It was ajar, and she knew Rogan had entered and was waiting.

She hoped the news on Arcilla would be good. Interesting...that Rogan had wanted to go to dinner.

She entered the parlor, where the gloomy late November weather was chased away by a glowing log burning in the grate. The large parlor was furnished in Madame Ardelle's old-world taste. Heavy wine-colored draperies, Louis XIV furniture, and a matching wine and cream Persian carpet. Through the floor-to-ceiling windows the bare branches of trees were starkly fingered against a pale five o'clock sky. She paused, lifting a hand to touch her smooth hair.

At the same moment, Rogan left the bookcase and came toward her, scanning her with obvious pleasure. He took in the hat. "Very charming. A perfect match of green." His genteel manner was in contrast with the lively gleam in his eyes. He took her hand, that enigmatic smile dancing across his features.

"How good of you to see me on a Thursday evening, Miss Varley. Madame has made it clear you need your sleep, and I am not to keep you up past eight."

From his exaggerated gravity, it was clear he was amused by Madame's strict code of rules for her music students. Yet his actions were smoothly calculated to represent the pinnacle of gentlemanly graces.

"Our first class starts at half past five," she said with a rueful smile.

"So, unlike spoiled fourth-year university students, we must adhere to a strict discipline."

He smiled. "So you still believe I am spoiled and arrogant. I'll have you know I am agonizing over final exams for graduation and going without sleep."

"Should I believe you? I wonder... You look well rested and alert."

"I cannot help what your stimulating presence does to me."

She laughed. He really was a rogue—and far too appealing when he was like this. She breezed past him toward the window, sitting primly on the cushioned window seat, her folded hands on her lap.

He watched her with a ghost of a smile, and she had the sense that he was still trying to understand her. She hid a smile of her own. Good. Let him wonder. He was altogether too accomplished in understanding young women as it was.

"I told you I'd come to let you know about Arcilla."

She inclined her head. "Thank you. I've been concerned for her. However, you could have sent a message and saved yourself a trip from the university."

"Would you have preferred that?"

She lowered her gaze, affecting a demure posture. "I was thinking of your busy schedule."

"I'm rarely too busy to see someone whose company I find so... intriguing. I was hoping you would come to dinner with me. I'd forgotten you were held under lock and key by the stalwart madame."

"I did not receive an invitation to attend dinner with you."

"Ah. A word to the wise, eh? I am expected to arrange things well in advance. You do not like surprises, then."

Did that displease him? She could well imagine that Patricia Bancroft rearranged her schedule to be with him whenever he wished.

"I assure you it is Madame who is inflexible." She quickly changed the subject. "I take it then that Arcilla is back at Montague, safe and sound?"

His wry smile was nonetheless indulgent. Clearly he cared about his sister. "Yes, alas, the emergency is over—for the present. My sister, as you know, is not above creating new storms to bring a bit of unwanted excitement into everyone's lives. Thanks to Charles, everything worked out reasonably well. He is from the old school of thought and prefers the status quo. Meaning he is not interested in galloping off to Paris in the dead of night to marry secretly. He knew what was expected of him and carried it through to the proper end. Instead of fleeing with her like two escaped lovebirds to France, he kept a stiff upper lip and brought her back to the school."

Charles Bancroft most likely had experience in avoiding awkward social positions, and Evy was fairly certain he must know Peter Bartley had arrived. Had Arcilla put up an emotional fuss and begged her beloved to flee with her to Paris? Poor Charles! The temptation to surrender to her pleadings must have been difficult to resist.

Rogan walked up to the window seat and looked down at her.

She refused to let his nearness unnerve her. "What do you think Mr. Bartley might have done if they had come back into the museum together?"

"I'd rather not imagine. But ol' Bartley does seem to be rather a sport. Like someone who would dutifully drink poison for the cause, rather than lose favor."

She laughed.

"In this case, it's Sir Julien whose favor Bartley fears losing. Not that matters are anywhere near being resolved where Arcilla and Charles are concerned. It's a gummy situation. Two men want to marry her, and the family must decide, but not according to which man will make her life most contented. That would be too simple. The choice must be based on social agendas."

And on what will bring more success to the diamond dynasty, she thought, remaining silent. She was a little surprised at Rogan's cynicism for his own social stratum.

He leaned against the wall near her. "I'm relieved the decision is in my father's hands. Naturally, I'll give him my opinion. I've promised Arcilla I would. I like Charles"—from the sincere tone of his voice,

Evy believed this—"though he's a bit of a lockjaw. He can be very pompous sometimes. But I do trust him. We've been friends since we were boys. But Bartley…" His gaze drifted to the far wall. "He is Sir Julien's golden boy. I don't see a bright outcome for Arcilla and Charles. Julien holds the purse strings to the family cache of diamonds—and mines."

"I'm surprised you can view the situation so clearly."

A brow lifted. "You think I am blind to the sins and foibles of the aristocracy? Only one who has never studied the French Revolution could be so. Sir Julien has feet of clay, as do we all, including the poor and downtrodden, by the way. I've never been one to believe in the righteous poor and the evil rich. What is that old saying? 'The Colonel's lady and Rosie o' Grady are sisters under the skin'?"

"I don't doubt that Rosie might pass herself off as the Colonel's lady if given half a chance," she said. "Anyway, I should hate to be forced to marry a man I did not love because his family had a stake in my marriage—and in the cache of diamonds."

"You are not suggesting that the aristocracy are the only ones who hold to the opinions of family and society, are you?"

She met his challenging gaze. "Yes, indeed. It does appear to be so. Arcilla has little to say about her marriage."

"You think she would make a wiser choice if it were left up to her?"

That stopped her. She had to be honest. "Well…in Arcilla's case—"

He smiled. "And in your case?"

"In my case"—she rose from the window seat and turned to look outdoors—"the same criteria do not apply. Your sister and I are worlds apart."

From the corner of her eye, she saw him contemplate the small explosion of wood and flames in the fireplace. "So your world is more generous with its young daughters, you think?"

She hesitated. She could see a trap coming, but she would not retreat. "Yes…I believe so."

His gaze came back to capture hers, and she thought she saw a fire reflected in the depths of his eyes. "Then why, unless something happens to force a change, is your future all but chiseled in stone? Why will you return to Grimston Way, become Mrs. Brown, and carry on in your aunt's footsteps?"

She started to respond, but he cut her off.

"And please do not tell me it is because that is what you wish, for I will not believe it."

Evy walked to the settee and sat down, refusing to let his taunts ruffle her. "I did not realize I was being forced to marry Derwent."

His cryptic smile set her nerves on edge. "Then am I wrong in thinking a match was made between your uncle and Vicar Brown when you and Derwent were still babes in arms?"

She had no answer for that—it was, of course, quite true—and so she simply remained silent. But when the stillness in the room grew oppressive, she gave a sigh. "Perhaps I wish to be a vicar's wife."

One brow arched. "Derwent and you, the perfect vicar's wife... I wonder. Ah, well. Life can be full of little surprises, can it not?" His unexpected smile was disarming. "Despite all the plans of mice and men, and, I might add, despite the promise of diamonds, people are known to do very strange things."

"I indeed hope so. I should be disappointed to think otherwise."

"Love wins out in the end, is that it?"

"I think so, yes."

"A man throws away everything for the woman he loves. Very romantic, but do you really believe that can happen?"

"Not often perhaps. I suppose, like Arcilla, more marriages are made to accommodate wealth and position than love and faith."

"Faith. I wondered if you would bring that into the equation. A vicar's daughter—in your case a niece—must marry her own kind, just as we must marry our own kind. Or as you would say it, someone *socially suitable*."

"One must marry of like faith, yes. Not because one is related to a vicar, but for obedience."

His head tipped at that. "Explain. I am interested."

"I am obliged as a Christian to marry a man of the same genuine commitment to the Christian faith as my own."

"'Be ye not unequally yoked together.' Is that what you mean?"

She stared at him. Was Rogan actually quoting the Bible? "Yes."

"So we are back to Derwent. You would marry him because he is…suitable. Very enlightening."

She did not argue, partly because he was right. But she also was reluctant to give away her doubts about marriage to Derwent. She was not in the least doubtful that it would be a comfortable marriage. But was that enough?

Rogan startled her by pushing away from the wall and going to snatch his coat and hat. Quick disappointment stabbed her that he was so ready to depart. Not, she assured herself, because she wanted his company, but because she had a question.

She leaned forward. "Why do I somehow think—dare I say it?—that you do not like Sir Julien?"

His cool gaze came back at her. "Whatever gave you that idea?"

She shrugged. "When you mention him I've noted…a bit of doubt in your voice."

"I did not realize my feelings showed so easily." He smiled. "I'd better watch myself around him, or he'll disinherit me."

She sat back, hands in her lap again. "Now you are being cynical again."

"Am I?"

"You did not answer my question. Maybe because you do not want to reveal how you think?"

He hesitated, then pursed his lips. "Maybe *dislike* is not the right word to describe how I feel about him. *Distrust* may be closer. I've never fully trusted him, not even when I was a boy. Remember when we were children and I brought you to Henry's rooms?"

"How could I forget? Sir Julien came in, and you told me to hide. It was frightening."

"I saw Julien search Henry's rooms the night before we went there. It was very late, so obviously he did not wish to be seen. I sometimes think he came to Rookswood to search."

To search…for what? She stood and walked toward him. "He was looking for the Black Diamond? Then he does not think Henry was innocent, as Lady Brewster maintained in her letter!"

His gaze held hers, but his thoughts seemed to be elsewhere. "I think it was the map he wanted. I wonder if it wasn't also the letter from Lady Brewster." He focused on her. "What did Heyden tell you about the diamond?"

She hesitated, then decided to tell Rogan exactly what Heyden had said. He needed to know there was at least one person in his family who did not hold her mother to blame.

Rogan listened, growing ever more thoughtful. "I suppose Heyden wanted to learn what it was you hoped to destroy in the fireplace that afternoon the three of us met."

"Why would he not be curious after such a dramatic, shocking scene?"

A small smile tipped his lips. "True, but he was far too curious long before that day. What did you tell him?"

"He already suspected that I wanted to destroy a letter. I told him it was from Lady Brewster."

"You told him what the letter was about?"

"Yes."

A frown drew his brow down. "That was a mistake."

"He believes in my mother's innocence. I saw no reason not to trust him."

"I *gave* you reasons. He wishes to use you for his own political purposes."

"But—"

"Never forget he's a ruddy Boer, disloyal to the British Crown. If a war breaks out in South Africa, which I fully expect, and perhaps sooner than anyone thinks, Heyden will support Dutch rule under Paul

Kruger. I've no intention of cooperating with him about the Black Diamond. Or"—his burning gaze swept her face—"about you."

After a moment of charged silence, he smiled. "Well, I'd best be on my way."

Evy followed him into the hall to lock up for the night.

"I regret you are not having dinner with me."

Swift pleasure warmed her, but she schooled her features, careful not to give him the notion that she, too, was disappointed. "It would have been pleasant."

"Another time perhaps, when you are not so limited by Madame." He took her hand and lifted it to his lips, but rather than kiss the back as she expected, he turned it over and pressed a kiss to her palm. At the warm pressure on her skin, she caught her breath, suppressing a shiver. His smiling eyes told her he was well aware of her reaction. And pleased by it.

"Au revoir," he murmured and went out the door.

Evy watched as he entered the coach and shut the door. A moment later she heard the clop of hooves as the coach pulled away. Her gaze followed the coach down the cobbled drive until it disappeared into the London fog.

She bolted the front door and turned to the staircase. How Rogan disturbed her. She could still feel the touch of his lips on her hand. There was more to Rogan Chantry than the surface revealed. He disapproved of Heyden, but there was much he was not telling her. Somehow she was sure it involved her—and her parents.

But Heyden had a side to him that she found rather comforting; he had been sympathetic about her mother, and he lacked the social status—and the accompanying arrogance—so nettling in Rogan.

Evy went back upstairs to her dormitory room and tried to concentrate on her language studies, but Rogan's words echoed in her mind: *I've no intention of cooperating with him about the Black Diamond. Or about you.* What had he meant? Could he have found out about her upcoming meeting with Heyden?

On Friday a letter arrived from Aunt Grace.

Vicar Brown died peacefully in his sleep of heart failure on November 3, and the new vicar has arrived. It is all quite sad for our sakes because we will miss him, but not sad for Vicar Brown, who has joined your uncle in the presence of Christ.

At the end of the letter, she wrote part of the verse from the first chapter of the epistle to the Philippians: "...to depart, and to be with Christ; which is far better."

Evy wrote her condolences to Derwent. It was far too soon after the loss of his father to inquire about his plans for the future. Though she fully expected that in time he would become the new curate, he would first need to return to divinity school for his final year.

Life was definitely changing by large steps and small. Sometimes it seemed the most significant changes came by way of the most unlikely events. Yet over all things, great and small, the Lord God reigned supreme. Only in moments of human weakness did doubt and fear steal away her confidence and set her heart beating uncertainly.

If only those moments did not center so very often on Rogan Chantry.

CHAPTER TWENTY-FIVE

The end of the school term and the Christmas holidays drew near…as did the night of Evy's concert. The other girls were as excited as though they had been chosen to do the solo performance for an audience of London's avid music lovers.

"I know you'll do well," Frances told her. "I have listened to your practice, and it's flawless."

Evy laughed. "I think you're too generous. I'm far from becoming a concert pianist, and this whole thing has put butterflies in my stomach."

"You will do well," Frances said again, and left Evy to her practice. She was having a new dress made in a London shop for the occasion. Aunt Grace had known of the honor since October and had written Evy insisting a gown be made for the evening of Evy's performance:

Do not concern yourself for the expense, dear. To have been selected from among the students to be the featured pianist is obviously a thrilling event, and I want you to have the best. You have worked hard indeed and deserve a special gown. I only wish my strength were such that I could be there to hear you play. My prayers will be with you, and I'll be waiting anxiously for you to come home for the holidays to tell me all about it.

Evy was thrilled. She had worried about what dress to wear, for she had nothing elegant enough for the occasion. She wasted no time in trying to find the right shop and seamstress. Madame Ardelle recommended a French shop, for she was acquainted with its widowed owner.

"You are making a mistake," Frances said. "Do what Madame says, and you'll be wearing stiff black taffeta on stage. I can hear it now as you bow before the audience and sit down at the piano. Then you'll begin to play the funeral dirge." Frances began humming a doleful march.

"Oh Frances, you are being silly," Evy said, laughing. "Just because Madame wears black doesn't mean her friend cannot work with colors. What color do you think I should choose?"

"Burgundy," Victoria sighed.

"Emerald velvet," Frances countered. "It suits your eyes."

Evy pursed her lips. "Emerald green. Velvet, yes. Luxurious velvet."

And so it was. Accompanied by her roommates, Evy went to the shop in downtown London and chose from the available patterns and materials. When she returned two weeks later to collect the gown, Evy tried it on before the mirror to make certain everything fit. It was all Evy could do not to echo the *oohs* and *ahs* of her two friends. She turned before the mirrors as the seamstress looked on proudly at her handiwork. The skirt was long and flowing; the tightly fitting bodice, according to the latest style, had a lower neckline for evening wear, and the popular sleeveheads were large and puffed. "Do you think it's a bit too daring?" she whispered to Frances and Victoria.

"It fits you so well, Evy. Anything else would make you look stuffy and disapproving. Besides, it is just a *wee* bit off the shoulder."

"And you *did* choose that pattern." Frances eyed her. "So you must have wanted that style."

"Yes, it is so lovely… I saw Patricia Bancroft wearing a style like this at the diamond show at the museum some weeks ago."

"There! You see?" Frances clapped her hands. "You are all set for the musical. Hurry now, let's go back to the school to show the other girls. I cannot wait to see their faces. And wait until we do your hair the night of the concert." She sighed. "'Tis a pity Rogan Chantry won't be there." She cast Evy a sly glance, but Evy avoided her eyes in the mirror.

Now the night of the concert had arrived. Evy had had one disappointment that morning—a letter from Heyden. It had read quite simply:

Dear Miss Varley,

I regret that I cannot keep our appointment at Regents Park for this Saturday. Urgent political concerns demand that I accompany Paul Kruger to the country home of the Officer of Colonial Affairs. I look forward to contacting you as soon as possible.

H. van Buren

But she scarcely gave him a thought now. Dressed in her gown, her hair meticulously upswept in curls and waves, Evy had to admit she felt like Cinderella going to the ball. Victoria had lent Evy her mother's pearls and matching fan comb. And Claudine, who hailed from a wealthy London family, lent her a darling pair of velvet slippers and a feather fan. Victoria, who had as little as Evy, kissed a lace handkerchief and turned it over, a twinkle in her eye. "From great-great grandmother Fanny Wilshire, for blessing."

Fifteen minutes before Evy went on stage, she waited near the entrance to the raised dais in the great hall. She was shocked to see Arcilla, adorned in a lovely outfit of blue satin, come floating into the room.

"Arcilla!" Surprised delight filled Evy at the sight of her friend. "What are you doing here?"

Arcilla's tinkling laughter was warm as she came up to take Evy's arm and turn her about. "*C'êst magnifique.* Evy, I hardly recognize you. What do you mean, what am I doing here? Would I miss your crowning moment?" She grimaced. "Mr. Bartley is here with me. He's my escort tonight. We were to attend a dinner party, but once I knew this was your night to shine, I insisted he bring me to hear you play. Afterward we are all going to our family townhouse on the Strand for a little dinner—and you are coming with us. We must toast you and make a fuss over your success, you know."

We? Evy's heart thumped irregularly. Was Rogan actually there?

The butterflies in her stomach were getting worse. Even her hands felt cold and clammy. Suppose her fingers fumbled over the keys? *Dear Father, please help me to play for Your honor tonight.*

She tried to focus on Arcilla. "Me? Go to the Chantry Townhouse?"

"But of course. We think highly of you, you know." She laughed. "We have a surprise for you there as well, but you won't learn what it is until you get there. We'll take you in the carriage. That way you can meet my Prince Charming, Mr. Bartley." She looked toward the ceiling, as though he were anything *but* Prince Charming.

But Evy's mind was too full to think about Arcilla's problems right now. *"We* have a surprise? Who is *we?"*

"Rogan, of course," she said airily. "Most of this was his idea. He was the one who told me you were playing solo tonight, chosen from among all the students at the school. And this"—she produced an orchid—"is from both of us. Here, let's pin it to your gown, it goes so well."

Rogan *was* here! Evy's agonies increased at the thought. What if she gave less than her best performance?

Madame Ardelle appeared and drew Evy from among her well-wishers. It was time. A few minutes later, Evy stood beside Madame in the dimly lit utilitarian backstage area behind enormous curtains. She must be calm, Madame told her quietly. Yes, she would be confident, and play from her soul. Madame would not have chosen her if she thought otherwise.

With these words in her mind and a prayer on her tongue, Evy waited for the end of her introduction. She found herself leaving parted curtains and walking onto the stage, something she had practiced scores of times. She walked to the grand piano, turned to face the large audience, whose faces she could not see, offered the practiced little curtsy, then sat down on the bench. The keys stared up at her, waiting, as though holding their breath. *Play us well,* they seemed to implore, *with all your heart.*

Evy's fingers took command of the keys, and glorious notes resonated throughout the hall. It was no accident that she had chosen Beethoven's Piano Concerto no. 4. She smiled as she imagined Rogan's reaction. He would have no doubt that she had fulfilled her part of their music bargain made on the windy hill overlooking Rookswood, when he had challenged her to play this very concerto for him.

But she dared not imagine him sitting out there, watching her and listening. Not unless she wanted her nerves to go out of control. Instead, she gave herself up to the piece, and soon she forgot everything but the glorious images in her soul that the music stirred to life.

She went on to play a number of pieces for her finale, including some Chopin nocturnes. When her fingers stilled and the last notes drifted on the still air of the room, there was a moment of hushed silence. She held her breath—and then it came: applause, breaking out in waves of wholehearted approval, but she understood it was for more than her ability. The enthusiasm was for the matchless music itself filling the listeners' souls with wondrous joy, even as it had her own. And if she had been able to elicit this emotion in the audience, she had accomplished her goal.

Evy stood, blinking back tears, thankful to her Creator for endowing her with the abilities she had been able to cultivate and use tonight. This achievement had been years in the making, and many were her enablers, not least Aunt Grace at home in Grimston Way, praying for her as Evy knew she would be. Aunt Grace, ill, yet wholeheartedly involved.

Thank you, Father God.

Evy bowed to the audience.

When she left the dais, Madame was there in the waiting room, her hands clasped and her eyes shining. "Magnificent."

At the woman's simple praise, Evy smiled her delighted gratitude.

"Now you must meet some guests. They are waiting to congratulate you."

It was some time before she met Arcilla and Mr. Bartley. She looked behind them and felt a small stab of disappointment. No Rogan.

"Evy, you were grand!" Arcilla turned to Mr. Bartley. "Was she not, Peter?"

"Indeed, most excellent, Miss Varley. I look forward to hearing you again."

"Thank you," Evy repeated over and over to her well-wishers. But her focus was elsewhere. Where was Rogan?

She turned and almost bumped into him. He was unaccompanied. Evy's heart tripped. Where was the ever-present Patricia? Had she not wished to accompany him? Or had he decided against her company tonight? She felt a little thrill at the possibility.

Rogan's eyes shone, and the unrestrained admiration in his dark gaze brought a warmth to her cheeks. Unlike the others he took her hand and bent over it, kissing it. Once again her heart leapt at his touch.

"You were wonderful."

His low murmur moved over her like a sweet summer rain. "Thank you," she managed, withdrawing her hand, but still feeling his touch. "Did you approve of my first choice?" She barely restrained a grin.

A faint, knowing smile touched the corners of his mouth. "It was superbly done."

Evy had never known such joy as filled her in that moment.

It was some time before she could break away, and when Madame Ardelle gave permission for her dinner out with the Chantrys, she escaped with them to the coach. Arcilla and Mr. Bartley got in first. Arcilla was busy chattering as Rogan handed Evy inside. He then got in beside her, shutting the door. The horses' hooves clattered across the damp cobbles on the way toward the Chantry Townhouse located on the Strand.

Arcilla was still laughing and chattering with Mr. Bartley, looking very unlike the forlorn young lady she had portrayed only a few weeks ago. So much for the deep, undying love she had vowed! Or was this apparent happiness only affectation? It was difficult to tell. Evy would rather believe Arcilla had decided Peter Bartley was not such a dreadful choice after all.

She glanced at Rogan, meaning to look away again, but his gaze would not relinquish hers.

"Unlike some others, I am not surprised at how lovely you look tonight. I have always credited myself for seeing beyond the unadorned rectory girl to the real woman who is Eve Varley."

That gave her pause. "I am and always shall be the rectory girl, Rogan."

His smile wrought havoc on her already heightened nerves. "I hope so. It's the rectory girl I find most appealing. She remains the same, even when adorned in pearls and velvet. Someday it must be diamonds."

She flushed, nearly overcome with a pleasure she did not want. She must not feel this way... It made her foolishly vulnerable. It had been a mistake to come with him tonight, to act as though she belonged to this social echelon. And yet, there was not another place she would rather be than sitting beside him, warmed by his attentive interest and what appeared to be genuine compliments.

And so for a moment, she allowed herself to deny that she was climbing a precipitous cliff. Or that the fall, should it occur, would be a dreadful one.

Aware of a sudden silence in the coach, Evy looked quickly across at Arcilla. It would be dreadful if she could read Evy's thoughts! Arcilla had already seen fit to warn her not to fall for Heyden van Buren. What would she think if she knew her true feelings toward her brother, upon whom Arcilla thought the sun rose and set?

The Chantry Townhouse was exactly what Evy would have expected: It stood in a class all its own surrounded by other two-story houses in the socially elite area of the Strand, known for royalty and titled families.

"Mum used to like coming here," Arcilla reminisced, after exiting the coach. "Do you remember, Rogan?"

Of course he would, and made no unnecessary comments as Arcilla continued in her nostalgia. "There was something about the rose garden that was special. Mum would say, 'You can smell them tonight. The little fairies are out playing on the velvet petals.' No sooner would we all arrive than Mum would take my hand and we'd go off to check on her special scarlet roses. If she thought anything was not just right, she'd call Simms—our old butler, the dear—and she would chide him about the health of her *babies*. Simms used to be so gentle with Mum, as though she were a child herself."

Rogan interrupted, but there was gentleness in his voice, as though he felt sorry for his sister. "Come along, Arcilla. We'd best go inside. Simms won't like it if the supper gets cold. Besides, I suspect after giving so much of herself tonight that Evy must be hungry."

Actually, she hardly had an appetite. She was too excited. As they went up the walk she knew she would always remember this special night when she had played to an approving audience and dined in December moonlight with Rogan Chantry.

The townhouse must indeed have been one of Lady Honoria's favorite places away from Rookswood. Evy could see it in the choice of furniture and paintings. The rooms were narrower, the house taller, and the intricately carved steep wooden staircase had been refinished so that it looked like a polished wooden gem. Three narrow flights of steps wound upward in a half spiral. The gallery railing on the middle floor was also highly polished, and ornate and lovely crystalline chandeliers shone and glittered like carved chunks of ice.

"It is beautiful," she murmured as Rogan took her wrap and handed it to Simms.

Simms and his niece, a young woman with berry cheeks and thick brows, had prepared a cozy room facing the garden for the supper. There was a long table covered with festive linens and full of platters of all sorts of foods and delicacies. Candles gleamed on either end and above another smaller chandelier.

Comfortable chairs were arranged in a semicircle about a round table with a mammoth bowl of Christmas flowers and greens. Evy kept the surprise she felt to herself. She had expected other guests to be here, but the comfortable arrangement was set for a foursome.

She gazed about, aware of the thought that had gone into this. Warmth filled her at the realization of the care and honor that had been afforded her. Was it Rogan or Arcilla who had been the driving force behind it all?

They each were to choose whatever delectables they preferred. Evy felt as though her head were spinning. *Here I am, dining cozily with social aristocrats in a townhouse that once, long ago, entertained King Charles!* Surely this opportunity would not have been possible without Rogan. He must have been the instigator. The thought was exciting and dangerous—but she didn't care. She was here, in her new gown and hairdo, after a successful performance, enjoying the attention of quite possibly the most sought-after young bachelor in London.

Miss Patricia Bancroft was not here, but Evy Varley was.

The dining was quite pleasant and the company exhilarating. Even Arcilla, with whom Evy was so accustomed to chatting, entered whole-heartedly into the relaxed conversation. Mr. Bartley, or Peter, as both Arcilla and Rogan called him, talked extensively about South Africa and Capetown. Evy found it all quite intriguing. Peter told them he had been born in England and taken to Capetown when he was three years old, when his father was appointed a governing official.

"Peter may be appointed to aid the governor-general in dealing with the troublesome Dutch," Arcilla told Evy.

"Boers," Peter corrected her, though Evy noted his tone was most patient. "A proud and uncivilized band of farmers. Do you know much about them, Miss Varley?"

"No, I cannot say I do. I understand they settled there before the English arrived."

"That is true. They call themselves voortrekkers. Their commander is Paul Kruger. A thornier, tougher-minded old Dutchman you'll not likely meet."

Evy thought of Heyden at that, and her eyes met Rogan's. He looked a bit provoked.

"War is inevitable, don't you think, Peter?"

He studied Rogan at that. "If we do not force the Boers to accept British rule, then the Union Jack isn't likely to be flying over any new Rand that may be discovered. Therefore war, in my mind, is a necessity."

"The Rand?" Evy asked.

Rogan turned his head toward her. "Witwatersrand. Where the first big gold rush took place. The name was shortened to The Rand."

Had Rogan mentioned his idea of a second great gold find to his future brother-in-law? She guessed that he had not. Rogan listened more than he spoke, as though willing to learn everything he could from those who had been born and raised in South Africa. It was this ten-dency that made her think he would become an expert in whatever he set out to do. More and more she realized that he was not arrogant, as she had once thought, but confident. His interest in the Cape, in gold especially, had not waned since childhood. Nor had his belief that he would be successful.

"Why do you think there will be a war?" Evy directed her question to both Peter and Rogan.

Arcilla yawned and nibbled at her dessert, a small custard tart with raspberry sauce.

"I can sum it up for you in one meaningful word, Miss Varley," Peter said with a twisted smile. "Kruger. The soldier, the warrior, the stubborn Dutchman who refuses to see the sunrise of the British Empire spreading across Africa."

She shifted in her chair at this passionate outburst.

Rogan had long since finished his supper and was stretched in his chair opposite her, hands behind his dark head. He had removed his dinner jacket and loosened his white frilled shirt around his throat.

"Gold and diamonds," Rogan told her lazily. "You've heard of Cecil Rhodes, have you not?"

She looked at him. *I would have studied up on this before I came if I'd known I'd be drilled on South Africa.* She feared she might look as blank and bored as Arcilla. "I believe your father mentioned a colony…somewhere in Mashonaland."

Rogan nodded. "Rhodes wants to push farther into the region and form a new outpost that he dreams will one day be a small country all its own—Rhodesia. Named for himself, of course. There are likely to be diamonds, gold, and perhaps emeralds in that region. He has gained a charter from the queen allowing him to form a company of settlers to make the trek inland. Peter is likely to be sent to Rhodesia as an official representative of the governor-general in Capetown."

Evy looked at Arcilla to see her reaction. She had come alert and looked with shock, first at Rogan, then at Peter. "Rhodesia? You're being sent there by the governor-general?"

Peter looked a trifle uncomfortable and glanced at Rogan as if to ask why he'd told her so soon. But Rogan sipped from his glass, his expression bland and unreadable.

Had he done this deliberately? She recalled how he had said that he preferred Arcilla to marry Charles. Perhaps she had settled in too comfortably with Peter, and Rogan was trying to alarm her, to make her put up more of a fight for the man she wanted. Did Arcilla wish to travel deeper into Africa as the wife of a commissioner?

But while the news had startled Evy, too, she found the idea of such a journey as exciting as it was dangerous.

"The governor-general of Capetown and your uncle, Sir Julien, will be sending me," Peter said.

"Leave it to Uncle Julien," Rogan commented. "He has his fingers in everything."

"What of the tribes in the area?" Evy looked to Peter. "Do they agree on allowing more white settlers?"

Rogan cocked a brow and looked at Peter. "What say you, Peter?" Amusement tinged his casual words. "Will they welcome Rhodes with open arms, do you think?"

Peter emptied his glass in one gulp and set it down with a click of determination. "They will. All we need is more time to convince them it's in their best interest."

Rogan looked over at Evy, a faint smile playing at his lips.

Arcilla was frowning, most likely imagining herself in a company of new settlers moving off into the unknown wilds of Africa. Evy saw her shudder a little, and at that moment her heart went out to Arcilla. Did Sir Lyle understand what he was doing by allowing Sir Julien to dictate his daughter's marriage?

Rogan stood, startling Evy, and looked at his timepiece. "I think we need a change in mood. One moment." With that, he left the room.

Arcilla lapsed into thoughtful silence, and Evy did her best to carry on the conversation with Mr. Bartley, steering clear of his future in Rhodesia. Was he finding everything in London as he had expected? Was the cold weather difficult on him? How were the seasons in the Cape? Then she heard it.

The vibrant notes of a violin.

Emotions washing over her in waves, Evy sat straighter and turned her head. Rogan had reentered the room. He had his dinner jacket back on, his shirt collar buttoned precisely, and held a magnificent violin. He bowed to Evy.

"I keep my promises, Miss Varley. After your superb performance at Parkridge, tonight seemed the perfect time."

Arcilla's face was wreathed in smiles. She clapped her hands, looking at Evy with a childlike delight. "I *told* you we had a surprise for you."

She stood and offered a sweeping curtsy. "Ladies and gentlemen, may I bring to your august attention the musical expertise of Master Rogan Chantry playing...?" Apparently she had forgotten the official name, for she covered her mouth with a laugh and looked over at her brother for help.

Rogan bowed deeply to Evy. "Paganini's Violin Concerto no. 2 in B Minor."

As he set bow to strings, Evy leaned back in her chair, her eyes drifting closed. The music rose and swelled, filling the room as completely as it filled her heart. Rogan's suave yet dynamic performance of Paganini's concerto left a tingle running down her spine. She opened her eyes and saw his gaze fixed on her, and knew he was playing for her. Her breath caught in her throat at that, and she gave him a smile from the depths of her heart.

After Paganini, he broke into "La Campanella." She would never have guessed Rogan had such drama and beauty of interpretation in him. The rendition called for a quivering command of the strings. She envisioned a lone violin player late at night on the streets of Paris telling a story of love, danger, and loss with just a touch of wry humor. How well that piece fit Rogan's personality.

When he finally lowered his bow, Evy stood with the others, applauding madly.

Rogan's questioning gaze held hers, and she knew what he wanted. She did not hesitate to give it to him. "It was marvelous."

"Encore!" Arcilla's eyes shone as she looked at Evy. *This is my brother,* they seemed to say to her. *He is a Chantry. He is exceptional.* "Encore."

He gave his sister a small bow and played Bach's Violin Concerto no. 1. And as Evy sank back into her chair, she thought she would never know another night such as this.

The evening ended as it had begun, at Parkridge Music Academy. Rogan escorted her to the door and inside to the front hall, while Arcilla waited with Peter in the coach.

She gave him a warm smile. "Good night, Rogan. Thank you for the lovely evening. I enjoyed it very much—especially your violin."

"It is you who are the musical talent. You won accolades tonight, you know. I suppose you'll go on for your final year. What then? Have you any special plans?"

"Everything depends on my aunt's health." And their finances, but naturally she did not tell him that. Aunt Grace wanted to keep her in Parkridge, but the final year would be almost twice as expensive, since Madame Ardelle's graduates would attend classes at Eldridge Music School under the direction of Master Eldridge himself, a very demanding instructor.

Rogan nodded, and Evy thought there was sympathy in his eyes for Aunt Grace's health. But there seemed to be a question as well. "I suppose Derwent has written you of his plans now that the vicar has died."

Derwent! She hadn't thought of him once that night. She looked away, wondering what that meant. "I think it far too soon for him to make any decisions."

"He only has two choices, as I see it. Return to divinity school and hope for a vicarage, or find other employment."

"He might get the curate's job in Grimston Way."

"At St. Graves Parish, you mean?"

"He mentioned it in his last letter."

"I suppose that would please you. You could remain in Grimston Way. That is, unless you're the adventurous sort who wishes to travel and see something of the world."

Was there a question behind this casual statement?

Evy didn't hesitate. "Unlike Arcilla, I think I would very much like to go to South Africa. But...I suppose I shall settle in Grimston Way and carry on as I always have."

"Ah, well, there is still this year of studies to complete, isn't there—for both of us. That reminds me, I have horrendous exams in the morning. I had better get back to the university. If not, I may be out on the streets playing my violin for a tuppence."

She laughed at that. "I hardly think you'll need to worry about such a thing."

He opened the door, his thoughtful gaze lingering on her face. "One never knows. Especially if I end up balking against Julien's will and plans." He smiled. "Good night." The door closed behind him.

Evy stood there, wondering. What did Rogan mean? Contesting Sir Julien Bley's will and plans? Did Rogan have Arcilla's marriage to Peter Bartley in mind, or something else? His own marriage, perhaps? Could there be someone special that Sir Julien wanted Rogan to marry? Maybe a girl in Capetown?

Evy realized she'd been biting her thumbnail and lowered her hand.

Or maybe the confrontation would come over Henry's Mashonaland map? It was no coincidence, was it, that Cecil Rhodes's ambition for a new colony was directed toward Mashonaland?

She pushed all this from her mind, determined instead to remember and relish every moment of the exceptional evening. She wrapped her arms around herself and stood there, basking in the warm afterglow. She could still feel the pressure of Rogan's hand holding hers as he had helped her from the coach.

But it was another moment they'd shared—one long ago in a darkened library before a blazing fire—that was indelibly burned upon her lips. And her heart.

CHAPTER TWENTY-SIX

Evy returned home to Grimston Way for the Christmas holidays. She had expected Derwent to meet her at the train depot but he did not appear. It was Mrs. Croft who was all smiles, driving the jingle. Strange…that Derwent did not come.

"That Derwent be a foolish young man," she snorted, but would say no more when Evy questioned her. She spoke instead of Aunt Grace's deteriorating health. "Though she won't be admitting she's failing to anyone, leastwise to you, Miss Evy."

Evy suspected her aunt wished to keep Christmas a joyful and hopeful season for them both. When she arrived at the cottage, Aunt Grace met her on the porch with a smile.

"Welcome home, Evy dear."

"Aunt Grace." Evy took hold of her shoulders and looked at her thin, pale figure. "You haven't worn yourself out getting everything ready for Christmas, have you? You know I would have enjoyed doing the decorations and baking with you. You must not tire yourself."

"No, no, I am fine now." She laughed. "I've been so looking forward to your coming home since last month. Just a mild winter cold again."

Evy looked about the cottage with warm pleasure, well aware that their home came from the generosity of the Chantrys. "Everything is just as I remembered it. Oh Aunt, it's so good to be home again." She threw her arms around her. "I only wish you could have been there the night of my recital. It was thrilling, stunning, and even Arcilla came— and Rogan."

Aunt Grace's brows shot up. "Indeed? Rogan? My! Well—I shall need to hear every exciting detail. I've got a nice pot of tea on, and Mrs. Croft brought over some peppermint cookies."

Evy smiled her pleasure. They stayed up late talking about everything while slowly decorating the cottage with baskets of fresh pine and berries.

"Where did you get the pine?" Evy did not think her aunt could go foraging in the woods as she used to when stronger.

"Alice brought them over. Very kind of her, I thought."

Evy paused, turned, and looked at her. "Alice? Yes, I'm surprised, too. How is she?" Evy had never quite understood why it was that Dr. and Mrs. Tisdale, who were comfortably affluent, had held back from sending Alice to pursue her music. They could afford to send Alice to France, considered to have the crowning glory of music schools.

"Oh, Alice is well enough."

Evy waited, expecting more explanation, but it did not come. "She is not ill, is she?"

"Oh, my no. She is—just the same girl she always was. More grown-up, of course. She is quite a young woman now, a year older than you."

"Yes, she's Arcilla's age. I suppose I'll see her during the season."

"I'm sure you will." Aunt Grace added a red bow to the pine garland she had strewn atop the fireplace and stood back to judge its effect. "The new vicar and his wife are giving the traditional afternoon Christmas tea on Saturday. You'll like Vicar Osgood and his good wife, Martha. She is just as busy and hard-working as Martha of Bethany. Vicar Osgood served a parish in Runnymeade before being sent here to us after Vicar Brown's departure. You'll like them, dear."

"I'm sure I shall." Evy was still wondering about Alice. What could have happened to her? Aunt Grace did not seem to want to discuss it, and Evy thought it wise to drop the subject for now. She was sure she would learn more in the days to come.

They baked ginger cookies and mince pies and placed them in the little pantry to cool. They would wrap them up and tie them with ribbons and then go calling on the villagers to wish them Merry Christmas on Sunday. She had joined Aunt Grace on this traditional outing since she was a little girl riding along in the jingle, the big basket of goodies on her lap. Oh, the happy days of childhood. And yet how the holidays, so precious in their Christian foundation, could also bring painful memories of lost loved ones and a world no longer sunny with childhood expectations!

Dear Uncle Edmund. Evy could see him busy at his rectory desk preparing his sermons, smiling at her with such patience if she loitered in the doorway of his office hoping for attention. Evy sighed. She missed him terribly at times like this. And it brought a qualm to her heart as she looked at her aunt and saw the visible decline in her health, clear warning that their time together was drawing to a close.

Don't think about it, she told herself. *Enjoy the time God has graciously given you. Who knows what a day may bring forth? But my heavenly Father does, and that's my consolation.*

This year would be a special holiday, one that she would always look back upon with fondness. She would make sure of it and enjoy it to its fullest.

The next day she did not see any of the Chantrys, though Arcilla and Rogan had both returned to Rookswood within a day of Evy's arrival from London. Peter Bartley was to have come back with them to meet Sir Lyle and Lady Elosia. Evy wondered about Heyden van Buren. She was disappointed that he had not gotten back in touch with her yet, but she fully expected him to do so.

The next day the Chantry coachman, Mr. Bixby, delivered the yearly goose for Christmas dinner. And for Aunt Grace there was a sealed envelope containing a generous gift of money from Lady Elosia.

"Bless her! Now we can buy presents." Aunt Grace's features lit up. "It's a sunny day too. Perfect for a bit of shopping in the village. We will have a few days for wrapping as well."

"It should be enjoyable, but are you sure you're feeling strong enough?"

"I'm feeling fine," Aunt Grace said with determination.

"I'll drive the jingle. And maybe we can stop afterward at Miss

Henny's shop for tea and some of those honey cakes I remember from childhood. It seemed back then the cakes were the most wonderful in all England."

Aunt Grace laughed. "I suspect you will still enjoy them, even though they may be a bit lumpy at her age."

The shopping trip was as fun as expected, and they laughed riotously as they tried to buy a gift for one another while the other turned her back and pretended ignorance. Afterward they stopped at Miss Henny's tea shop and enjoyed a pot of the best tea in Grimston Way along with the slightly overdone honey cakes baked by the eighty-year-old proprietress, who was delighted to see them.

"Bless my soul, but you're getting prettier with every year, Evy. And so talented with that music learnin' of yours that Grace tells me you're studying." She shook her gray head. "I just can't understand the likes of the vicar's son."

Before Evy could ask what she meant, the door opened, and Mr. Croft came shuffling in. He looked unchanged since the days of Evy's childhood, when she watched him digging graves. He saw her but did not appear to recognize her. He grinned at Aunt Grace, however, and removed his sock cap. "Afternoon, Mrs. Vicar. A pleasure to see ye out and about on such a sunny day…ah, that be *you*, Miss Evy? Praise the Lord, it is!"

"Hello Mr. Croft," she said with a warm smile. "How are you?"

"Oh, I be fine, yessir, just fine. Ye be coming to the new vicar's Christmas tea, miss?"

"I'm looking forward to it."

"Mrs. Croft be helping out the new vicar's wife that day. She be glad to hear you'll be there, miss."

He went to order his lunch of milky tea and sweet biscuits, and Miss Henny went to wait on him.

Evy studied Aunt Grace as they drank their tea. "Why did Miss Henny say that about Derwent?"

Her aunt contemplated her tea as though it were quite profound. She gave a heavy sigh. "Because Derwent has been seeing a great deal of

Alice. Let's not worry about that now. Derwent will come to his senses. His mind is filled with South Africa, and I feel certain Alice is encouraging him in this."

Evy set her teacup in its saucer, giving a slow nod. "I thought it might come to this. He has always wanted to go there, since we were children."

"Nothing is certain yet."

She thought she should feel something, some disappointment perhaps. But she didn't. It was strange… She felt so little concern about Derwent and Alice, so little disappointment that her old friend hadn't come to see her. But let her wayward mind conjure one image of Rogan Chantry paying close attention to Patricia Bancroft—perhaps kissing her palm as he had Evy's, or—*forbid it!*—kissing her the way he had kissed Evy in the library that day…

She closed her eyes. *I not only feel like I've swallowed a rock but as though I could cry my heart out! Drat Rogan Chantry!*

When they finished their last cup and the teapot was empty, they said good-bye to Miss Henny and went out to where the jingle was parked and waiting with their packages.

As Evy walked to the jingle, she saw Mrs. Tisdale and Alice just getting out of the family carriage. Mrs. Tisdale looked over to see Evy and Aunt Grace, and she smiled and waved. "Oh, hello!"

Evy held the reins while mother and daughter walked up.

"Well, Grace, you are looking much better today. Must be Evy's homecoming. Hello, Evy, how are you?" Mrs. Tisdale went on talking to Aunt Grace, so Evy turned to Alice.

"Alice, hello!"

Evy had not seen Alice for nearly a year. Aunt Grace was right— Alice indeed had changed, at least on the outside. She was nineteen now. Her strawberry blond hair was elaborately styled under a blue hat with a matching satin rose. The colors made her already pale face look waxen. The narrow chin, the tight little mouth, the rather wide forehead with a coquettish curly lock deliberately arranged there seemed testimony to Alice's usual self-satisfaction. Her light eyes reflected whatever color she wore, so that they now appeared gray-blue, fringed with reddish lashes.

"Hello, Evy." She played with her gloves, looking at Evy's bare hands holding the horse's reins. "Congratulations on being chosen to play the solo at the school concert. Mrs. Havering told us about it."

"Thank you. I'll always remember that night."

Alice smiled. "I don't suppose the competition among Madame Ardelle's students was very rigorous this year. So many of *us* that would have competed weren't there."

Evy ignored the clearly self-serving remark. It was, after all, Christmas, and the season of goodwill. "Are you still playing, Alice?"

"Not as seriously as before. I enjoy playing the piano at the rectory each Sunday." She paused, and Evy thought her look held some special meaning. "Unless you wish the position now that you're home again? You always used to do it."

"I'm sure you do wonderfully." Evy hoped she showed no curiosity over Alice being involved at the rectory. She had never appeared to like such involvement before. She had changed all right…because of Derwent? But was her faith genuine? Derwent had best find out.

"Then I shall keep the plans as they are," Alice said. "I'll be playing the carols in the chapel on Christmas Eve as well."

"Perhaps you should ask Rogan to join you on the violin." Alice looked startled, and Evy smiled. "He plays beautifully. So serious, yet he has a certain flair for lightness."

Alice's brows went up. "Rogan?"

Evy felt a small prick of pleasure at Alice's discomfiture. Now Alice was aware how little she knew about Rogan.

Mrs. Tisdale had concluded her chat with Aunt Grace and was bustling herself and Alice off toward the local seamstress shop. "Miss Hildegard has opened her own shop, Evy, did Grace tell you?"

Miss Hildegard had been sent for by Lady Honoria some years ago to make dresses for herself and Arcilla. At that time Miss Hildegard had lived at Rookswood. Since Arcilla had long ago departed for London and had all her clothes made there, the seamstress had opened up a small shop in Grimston Way. Evy wondered if she received much business other than that of Mrs. Tisdale and Alice—and perhaps Lady Elosia.

"We visit her shop often." Mrs. Tisdale's rather proud tone grated on Evy's nerves. "Naturally Alice likes to look well. Especially now." She smiled, and Evy thought, as Mrs. Tisdale glanced sideways at Alice, that the two acted as though they shared some special secret. Alice offered a little smile and touched the rose on her hat. Changed or not, she still had that sidling way about her.

Evy's suspicions grew.

"Well, we're off, girls. We must run. Toodle-oo. Come along, Alice. I'm anxious to see the lace from Brussels."

Evy picked up the reins to drive back to the cottage, smiling at her aunt to show the Tisdale women did not worry her. Aunt Grace, however, was not smiling. She looked ahead, down the narrow village street.

"Mrs. Tisdale still seems the same," Evy commented, but not without affection.

"Yes, indeed. Beatrice has always forged ahead with her plans and needles Dr. Tisdale into using every ounce of his influence in the village to get things done the way she wants them."

Evy glanced at her aunt. It seemed Aunt Grace was more disturbed by the Tisdales than she had been in the past. She must not be feeling well.

"Beatrice has managed to become friendly with Lady Elosia."

She pondered this. "That should please both Mrs. Tisdale and Alice. They were always quite concerned about getting on socially with Rookswood."

"Oh, it isn't social, exactly. That is, Beatrice gets on with Lady Elosia on some matters that concern the village and rectory, but the relationship ends there. Neither Arcilla nor Rogan is likely to include Alice in their inner circle. But Beatrice does influence Lady Elosia on some important decisions connected with the rectory."

Evy waited, but her aunt must have decided she had fallen into gossip, because she stopped and said nothing more for the ride back to the cottage. Evy couldn't help wondering if some of those decisions included Derwent. The gay holiday mood had evaporated. Perhaps her aunt had overdone herself. Evy would insist she rest for the afternoon until she made their supper. *Tonight I shall make sausage and eggs, and use some of the sweet white bread we bought at the bakery.* Derwent would be coming over as he usually did on Friday evenings. This would be her first time to see him since her return from school. She was anxious to discuss matters with him about divinity school—and his deeper friendship with Alice.

That evening after Evy wrapped her Christmas presents and put them in the cupboard out of sight, she set about to fix their supper. It was six o'clock when Aunt Grace came out to join her. She looked much more peaceful.

"Why the third place setting, Evy?"

"Derwent always comes on Friday nights."

"Yes, of course, I should have told you. He's in London."

"London?" Evy turned to her aunt.

"Yes, he said he had some business there."

"When did he go there?"

"Oh…a day or so before your return." She shuffled her dinnerware around.

Evy watched her. "What sort of business could he have?"

Aunt Grace either did not know or did not wish to discuss it. She simply said, "He will be back before Christmas."

Evy dropped the matter and forced a smile, trying to seem cheerful so as not to worry her aunt. "I do not mind the extra sausage and eggs. I can warm them over for breakfast. "

Christmas drew closer, and Evy could see the various coaches arriving for the drive up the winding road to Rookswood to attend the dinner balls. She did not see Arcilla or Rogan, but she heard from Mrs. Croft that Lizzie had told her that Miss Patricia Bancroft had arrived for the weekend. Her brother Charles was noticeably absent.

"I hear Miss Arcilla has herself a new beau," Mrs. Croft said with a curious glint in her eyes. "There was quite a going-on up there, before them guests arrived, there was, says Lizzie. Miss Arcilla is in a weepy state one day, then all stoic, and cheerful as a wee elf the next, but keeping firm company with that Peter Bartley from Capetown."

Evy did not tell Mrs. Croft that she already knew what was happening in Arcilla's life. Sir Lyle must have decided that his daughter would indeed marry Peter. Evidently Mr. Bartley's pending political position in South Africa was deemed more important than any danger of war upon Sir Lyle's only daughter.

Evy shook her head at the idea of spoiled, flighty Arcilla in South Africa! How would she ever endure?

On a crisp, sunny morning near Christmas, Evy walked the trail up to the hillock, where she could enjoy the wide, sweeping view of Rookswood and the surrounding estate grounds. She'd come here nearly every day since her return…though she finally admitted it wasn't for the view.

Sadly, Rogan did not once ride up to the hill as he had that day in what now seemed the distant past. It was foolish to expect him to come, of course, with Patricia staying in the great house.

Evy pressed her lips together. How had she ever permitted her emotions to get out of hand? It was unwise to wish to see him again, to walk here thinking he might show up, but neither could she stay away.

It was his presence in London at the concert that made her think so unwisely about him, and his playing the violin. She had mistaken his interest in her plans for an interest in her. *Foolish, foolish girl,* she chastised herself. *That will never be.* It was clear that when Patricia Bancroft occupied his time, Evy Varley did not enter the picture. She was, and always had been, little more than Arcilla's childhood companion—the rectory girl.

Clearly attending her concert and inviting her to the Chantry Townhouse for supper had been suggested as much for Arcilla's sake as for Rogan's.

Nevertheless she remained on the hill, determined to enjoy the view, looking toward Rookswood. She drank in the sight of the sun shining on its windows, fondly recalling events, then turned away and walked back down the trail.

She came to the bottom of the hill. Before she turned on the path leading toward the cottage, she heard male voices and the *clop* of horses' hooves. Reluctant to meet anyone with her emotions still so raw, she stepped aside where trees grew close together. A few moments later she was surprised to see Rogan and Derwent riding by, side by side.

They rode past her, going away from the cottage, and Derwent was laughing.

Evy waited until they rounded the fork in the road and then resumed her walk home.

The rooks gabbled in the tops of the trees, and a chill wind blew against her. Strange that Derwent had not been by the cottage to see her since he had returned from London yesterday... Or was it? Perhaps stranger still, that he was to be found in Rogan's company.

What, if anything, did it mean? The happy ring of his laughter had conveyed a carefree message she believed was clear.

CHAPTER TWENTY-SEVEN

Christmas tea took place as it always had at the vicarage, with one distinct difference. Derwent did not attend.

"Derwent is working today," Vicar Osgood told Evy when she inquired.

"Working?" Evy was unable to conceal her surprise.

"For Rogan Chantry. He's been spending quite a lot of time at Rookswood with the Chantry horses. We are hoping the position of curate opens soon… I'm certain it will."

His sympathetic look told Evy he understood that marriage could only take place once Derwent received the position. Evy's annoyance with Derwent was growing. How much had he told the new vicar?

It appears as though he is doing a good deal of explaining about his situation to everyone except me.

So Derwent was working at Rookswood estate for Rogan! Then that explained why she saw them riding together yesterday.

Derwent was not the only absentee. Lady Elosia, who made it a point to maintain her influence in the village, did not attend either. Someone mentioned she was "a bit under the weather." In fact, none of the Chantrys were present, nor were the Tisdales. Evy's girlhood friends Meg and Emily, now married, were there. Meg had married Emily's brother, Tom; Emily was married to Meg's brother, Milt. Both women were expecting babies. They were quick to embrace Evy and welcome her home, smiling and congratulating her on success at music school. Evy had always liked the two. They were plain, humble, and genuine. But even they watched her as though they were on the verge of asking her a question about some matter that troubled them. An exchange of glances between the two appeared to discourage either one from doing so.

When the first group left early to take their children home, Evy used their departure as an opportunity to get away. She left Aunt Grace chatting with the new vicar's wife and wandered out the rectory gate, onto the road. It was odd how everyone watched her. Could her worst fears be true? Could gossip have escaped Pandora's box somehow about her mother stealing the Kimberly Diamond? No, that could not have happened. Not many knew about it, not even Lizzie or Mrs. Croft. Rogan, while a scamp in some ways, would not embarrass or hurt her reputation in the village.

But might Heyden have been here asking questions?

Evy walked along the road toward Rookswood. Aunt Grace would come home in the jingle, so there was no need to worry about her. Evy wanted to be alone.

Though it was far from an unpleasant day, she could think of little to cheer her mood. The holiday festivities no longer seemed as bright as when she had arrived three days ago. The excitement of returning to Grimston Way had fizzled. Except for seeing Aunt Grace, little remained of the old life she remembered when Uncle Edmund was the beloved vicar. Even Derwent and her village friends had changed. It was as though she were no longer one of them. Even Aunt Grace seemed different…a little sad, perhaps? Or perturbed? Yes, that was it. Perturbed. It must be on account of her poor health. *Undoubtedly she misses her life as it was in the rectory, too.* What else could it be except disappointment with Derwent?

Evy thought of the Kimberly Diamond again. So far, she had avoided upsetting Aunt Grace by discussing it with her. But if Heyden had been asking around the village and word had gotten back to her aunt as well, perhaps it was time to speak to her about it.

Rogan believed her aunt knew something, though even he had not forced the issue with her. He would graduate soon and be off to South

Africa, so surely he would want to learn everything he could before leaving Grimston Way.

Evy cast a glance at the sky now turning as dark as her mood. Yes, perhaps it was time.

The next day, however, Aunt Grace took to bed with a mild fever.

"You must not worry so, Evy. I overdid it a little at the tea, is all. A rest in bed today and I shall be feeling much better tomorrow. But perhaps you should go ahead with our plans to deliver presents today. That is if you do not mind going without me?"

"No, I wouldn't think of your going. The weather has taken a turn for the worse. It looks like a foggy evening."

"Then do not be late. Mrs. Croft is coming over to make us a good chicken soup."

Evy's mood was far from festive as she loaded the basket with the cakes and candies they had made on her arrival and carried it to the jingle.

She rode into the village alone, forcing a cheery spirit and trying to leave a blessing in the homes where she called. She delivered the preserves and cakes to Old Lady Armitage, who was still spry and alert in her advanced years. The old woman came out her door to the wicket gate and up to the side of the jingle. The wind blew her thin white hair, and she drew her fringed shawl around her bony shoulders. A gleam flickered in the still-shrewd eyes.

"So it's you, is it, Miss Evy? I daresay you've changed a bit since tripping off to London to play that piano. You look a mite too pretty for the young scoundrels of Grimston Way." She studied Evy up and down. "Unless it's that chief scoundrel, Rogan Chantry, you've an eye on."

"Merry Christmas, Miss Armitage." Evy forced a smile and ignored her comments. "Aunt wanted me to bring you some of her summer preserves."

"Bless her soul. True blue, she is. Always was. Can't say the same for the rest of 'em... And now Vicar Brown is gone to his reward too. The new vicar laughs too much. I don't care for it. That silly boy of Vicar Brown's hasn't half the wit of his father, either. Derwent lets himself be pushed around like a wet mop. You'd think he'd stand up on his hind feet and demand to chart his own life, wouldn't you? But oh no, not him. Knuckles under to Lady Elosia like a puppy grabbed by the scruff of its neck. A shame, really... Ah, thank you, dearie." She took the box of preserves and cakes. Evy had put extra inside, along with a new shawl and bonnet she had bought for the woman in the village.

"You're not missing much when it comes to Derwent Brown." Miss Armitage gave a sage nod of her head and a wink. "Let him have that silly Alice if that's the way of it. Well, Merry Christmas, Miss Evy. You keep playing your piano."

It was a few moments before Evy could reply, but she finally gathered her scattered wits. "Yes, Merry Christmas, Miss Armitage."

So that was it! Derwent and Alice! *My suspicions were right.*

Evy drove on, and by the time the jingle was empty, she was in a better mood. In fact, she almost overflowed with relief! She did not love Derwent the way a girl should love a man. She'd known it for some time but never really admitted it, mostly because Aunt Grace had always expected the union. *I was told from a child I should marry Derwent.*

The relief she felt over admitting this, combined with giving and sharing Christian love with others, cheered her heart and utterly lifted her burden. She was humming "silent night, holy night" when she left the village proper and was on the road back to Rookswood estate. She had not gone far when she met Arcilla riding one of the mellow mares from the Chantry stables. She called to Evy and waved for her to pull over. She came riding up, her cheeks tinted pink with cold and her blue eyes bright. The wind tossed her hair beneath the pert riding hat.

"Hello and cheers! I've been looking for you, Evy. Your aunt said you had come into the village."

"What brings you out riding alone?"

"I'm a big girl now," Arcilla jested.

"Yes, but surely any mission important enough to get you on horseback must be worth some kind of escort," Evy said with a laugh.

Arcilla played with her whip. "Exceedingly important, if you want to know."

"A dinner ball?"

Arcilla stared at her, clearly amazed. "How did you know?"

Evy laughed. "I know you. When is this one?"

"Tonight. And you *must* be there."

"Me, tonight? Oh come, Arcilla, you are teasing."

"No, indeed. There is an emergency, and I need you."

"Well, it is so grand to be wanted, even if only when an emergency demands it."

"Oh, you know what I really mean."

"Yes."

Arcilla laughed. "Now don't be so moldy. You need some fun as well, so let us conclude we are helping each other. Do say you'll come. Aunt Elosia approves of you, and so does my father. They wouldn't have had your aunt as my governess years ago if they hadn't."

Evy toyed with the reins. Would Rogan be there? Of course... Patricia Bancroft would no doubt be at his side.

"Aunt Grace is not well and needs me to be home tonight."

"I already spoke to her. She tells me she will have the company of Mrs. Croft. A party will do you good, she says. So there! No more excuses."

Arcilla was never one to mince words when it came to protecting someone else's pride or feelings, and she did not do so now. "It's Rogan's friend, Abbot. He's here at Rookswood. I had planned for Cicely to be Abbot's partner tonight, but she became ill this morning. And you have the perfect gown to wear, too. The one you wore to your concert in London. It looked very pretty on you, I must say."

Evy knew Arcilla would give her no peace if she did not capitulate. "Very well, I will come."

"I *knew* I could depend on you." Arcilla's smile beamed on Evy. "I will send Bixby to bring you up to the house around seven."

❖   ❖   ❖

It was raining when Bixby helped her into the coach and closed the door.

Evy arrived at the front carriageway, and the footman came to open the door. He carried an umbrella for Evy and escorted her up to the open doorway of Rookswood.

The glittering chandeliers, the decorations of pine and berries, red and gold ribbon, all glowed with festive color. Lilting voices reached her ears, and she realized they came from the expanded ballroom off to her left. Evy held her breath as she waited near the wide double doorway that led into the aristocratic foxes' lair.

Arcilla saw her first and rushed toward her, bringing a handsome young man in evening dress with her.

"This is Abbot Miles. Abbot, my very best friend, Evy Varley."

He bowed over her hand and smiled. "Fortune has smiled upon me."

He took her arm, and they stopped at the doorway of the ballroom as their names were announced to the small group, all of whom had turned in their direction. Then Lady Elosia came toward them, a smile on her face, her elegant hand outstretched, the gems glittering on her fingers and wrist.

"Ah, dear Evy, how charming of you to come. And how positively enchanting you have become."

"Thank you indeed, Lady Elosia."

"Come, let me introduce you to the others."

In the next few minutes Evy found herself murmuring all the right responses to all the right greetings from all the right holiday guests— mostly lords and ladies, of course—from London's elite. She felt a little breathless when introduced to an earl and his countess. Then, of course, there was Peter Bartley, looking quite distinguished. Even Arcilla seemed more mature than when Evy had seen her that afternoon. She actually seemed to change in Peter's company, to stand straighter and carry a more somber demeanor. Evy could not help note, however, that the girlish glow that had shone in her eyes when with Charles Bancroft had dulled to a look of resignation.

A stir passed through the gathering as everyone turned to look toward the doorway. The handsome younger son of the squire himself had arrived, Patricia Bancroft on his arm. Rogan's dark gaze slipped over the faces of those present and then focused on Evy. He looked genuinely shocked for a moment before he recovered. His jaw hardened, and Evy frowned. He did not look pleased.

He did not know I would be here.

"Rogan Chantry and Miss Patricia Bancroft," the male reader intoned, and the couple advanced into the ballroom, Patricia's hand resting lightly on Rogan's arm. They made the rounds of the guests, exchanging greetings, until they came to Abbot and Evy. Evy felt her heart skip a beat as her gaze met Rogan's.

Yes, he was displeased. She could see an angry spark in the depths of his eyes, and it brought a heat to her cheeks.

"Why didn't you tell me you had such a beautiful neighbor, Rogan?" Abbot grinned. "Or maybe I should say now I *know* why you didn't tell us all these years."

"Where is Cicely?" Patricia asked the question of Abbot, though her narrowed gaze was fixed on Evy.

"Ill, in her room."

Patricia's cool gaze slipped from Evy, and she looked at Rogan. "There is Peter... Come, Rogan, I think dinner will soon be served."

Evy refused to be intimidated by the cool reception. Had she not told Arcilla it would be this way? But she had not expected Rogan to be in opposition to her presence. Was it because he was with Patricia? Rogan had not actually spoken to her yet and now walked Patricia away toward his sister and Peter Bartley.

They all made their way to the table, and Evy lifted her chin. She would not dart away like a timid mouse. She determined to enjoy the evening no matter how coolly Patricia treated her.

Never had Evy seen such elegance. It almost made her head spin with the wonder of it all. The long dining table was adorned with silver and crystal, all aglitter under the great chandelier. The dining hall must have witnessed many splendid occasions through its years, but never more so than tonight, she thought. Flowers had been brought in from Rookswood greenhouses and were in great ceramic pots on urns and side tables. Candlelight did wonders for the gowns and jewels that adorned the women, as well as the gentlemen adorned in dinner black with startling white frilled shirts. Evy sat toward the end of the long table to the left of Abbot, and though she was aware of the interested glances cast her way from the young men in attendance, she pretended not to notice.

If only she could also have ignored the fact that Rogan was fully attentive to Patricia.

The meal was sumptuous. Evy had never seen such food, including three kinds of roasted meat and a number of side dishes and breads. The conversation as well was stimulating. On her right was an older gentleman, a friend of Sir Lyle's. Evy carried on a fascinating discussion with him through the meal about the prospects of war between England and the Boers of South Africa. He was in favor of ousting the "Boers under that uncivilized Paul Kruger" and planting the Union Jack squarely in the Transvaal, the area controlled by the Dutch.

After an assortment of English and French desserts, teas, and coffees, liquor was served in the next room. Evy declined and accepted lemon water with a sprig of mint.

Later in the evening the dancing began in the ballroom. Sir Lyle and Lady Elosia led the first waltz, followed by Rogan and Patricia, then Arcilla and Mr. Bartley. Afterward, Sir Lyle and Rogan performed their social duty by choosing other partners from among their guests.

Evy's heart fluttered when Rogan stopped in front of her, bowed lightly, and escorted her onto the glossy floor. As she moved into the circle of Rogan's arms, she could sense Patricia's cool indignation. Sir Lyle chose Lady Elizabeth, and the four of them waltzed about the huge ballroom floor. Despite her pleasure at being chosen for such an honor, she couldn't help a touch of nerves.

If I miss a step, I shall wish to sink through the floor. Happily, she did not, and soon she relaxed and let the music overtake her.

It was an astounding moment to be in Rogan's arms, with the grand notes of Johann Strauss's music echoing about them. She was waltzing where great ladies of the blood had done for nearly two hundred years, and the man she was with was heir to its history and future. For a moment she felt like Lady Eve Varley, her beautiful skirts swirling in a show of color and promise. She was aware of Rogan's nearness, of the way he held her, his arm around her waist, the other hand enclosing hers…

For just a moment, her rebellious memory flashed to the moment in the library all those months ago, when his kiss had sent her head spinning and her heart dancing. For a moment, all was magical and all her girlish daydreams were coming true. For a moment…

Her gaze met Rogan's. He stared back evenly.

"You have made me the center of attention," she said breathlessly.

"You already were. The rectory girl is not supposed to be so beautiful, or so poised and polished."

Her heart beat faster at that. *He thinks I'm beautiful!* "Everyone will talk, now that you asked me to share the first waltz. You dance well."

"It is not hard when holding you." Something burned deep in his gaze. Something heated and disturbing. "Yes…I would like the waltz to continue indefinitely."

She let her gaze drop. "You must not say such things."

"I could say a great deal more."

"But it would not be fitting for you to do so…*Master* Rogan."

At her use of his title, they lapsed into silence. Evy focused on enjoying the music. Waltzing beneath the glowing chandelier was like a fantasy. And like any fantasy, it would certainly come to an end.

She might be as beautiful as any woman there, but she was, and always would be, the rectory girl.

She pulled her dismal thoughts another direction. "Arcilla does not look happy tonight, but subdued."

"I'm hoping she will get over losing Charles. She's young."

He spoke as though he himself were old and seasoned in such matters.

"Then you've changed your mind? You think Mr. Bartley will be a proper husband?"

His shoulders lifted. "I doubt either man would be a proper husband, as you mean it. They love their pleasure too much for both marriage and their ambitions. It's not that I have changed my mind about Arcilla's marriage. South Africa does not suit her nature—she is too flighty—but my father has decided the matter, as is his right. She will marry Peter and go to South Africa."

"Soon?"

"Quite soon."

Evy lapsed into silence for a moment, then, "She will be forced into a marriage she does not want, to a man she does not love. How could it be worse?"

"It could be worse, because as we discussed that night in the townhouse, Peter is likely to be sent inland to the Rhodesia colony. Can you see my sister as the governor's wife?"

No, she could not. Arcilla would be most unhappy. She belonged in London among her elite friends. "Then—it could come to that, do you think?"

"I hope not. I've discussed the matter with my father. He has yet to convince Sir Julien, though. Perhaps when Julien meets her at the Cape, he will understand and change his mind about the governor's post, at least. Sending Arcilla with Peter into Mashonaland is like sending a lamb into the wolf pack. She would become ill and depressed."

"You *must* convince them."

One brow arched, and he met her earnest gaze. "I have tried, and will continue. It is kind of you to concern yourself. You have been a good influence on her from the beginning."

She was pleased that he would think so.

"But you mustn't worry too much about Arcilla. You have your own concerns, it appears. I hear you have lost the humble, kindhearted boy your aunt expected you to marry these years."

Derwent.

Rogan's lively dark eyes studied her a moment too long, and then a hint of something like satisfaction showed itself. Whenever Rogan wore that satisfied smile, she worried.

He cocked his head. "Then you have not heard the romantic news?"

"I have my suspicions and"—she inclined her head—"a bit of gossip from Miss Armitage, but I have heard nothing from Derwent, and until I do…" She let her words fade.

His smile loitered. "Why, I am indeed scandalized that Derwent— fine upstanding saint that you say he is—has not come to you to explain the change in his future plans. What could he be afraid of, I wonder?" He scanned her lightly. "Do you have a temper, Miss Varley? They say hell has no fury like a woman scorned."

That got her. "Afraid! Of me! Because of an interest in Alice?"

"Rather shoddy of him not to tell you sooner. Even if his courage is lacking, he might at least have written you while you were in London to prepare you for the surprise. You are surprised by this turn of events, are you not? Come, admit it. Surely your reticence does not come from your feminine pride being stepped on?"

She was tempted instead to stomp on one of his finely clad feet. "If you have news worthy of being believed, and not mere gossip, then please do get on with it."

"My, my, such lofty indignation. The news that has the village buzzing of course is marriage, what else? Between Derwent and Alice Tisdale."

Then Old Lady Armitage had known what she was talking about after all. Evy might have expected this outcome about Derwent, but hearing it now so bluntly put was startling. For a moment she was tongue-tied under Rogan's alert gaze.

"Did Derwent tell you he wanted to marry Alice?"

"Yes, when we were out exercising the horses recently."

He watched her, but she scarcely noticed. She was turning the news over in her mind. If Derwent had confided in Rogan, it must be true.

His arm tightened around her. "I am waiting for you to faint in utter despondency over your loss. Do I take it then that you are not disappointed?"

She pulled away a little, finally finding her voice. "Disappointed? Perhaps I was expecting it. But until Derwent himself tells me, I think it best not to rush to conclusions."

"Mrs. Tisdale has been calling on Aunt Elosia for the last few weeks. There was a lengthy discussion between them just a few days ago. It appears there will be an arrangement made between Dr. Tisdale and Lady Elosia to have Derwent and Alice marry in the new year."

Apparently Mrs. Tisdale had decided Derwent would be a good catch for Alice. But why? What had changed Mrs. Tisdale's mind so that she would seek out Derwent?

She realized Rogan still watched her with keen eyes and forced a smile to her lips. "If what you say is true, then I hope they shall be very happy."

She thought that beneath his grave mood there was satisfaction.

"They are well suited then, you think?"

"I would not know." Her words sounded stiff even to her own ears, and she tried to ease the tension in her voice. "That is for Derwent to decide...and Alice." No wonder Alice had looked smug and secretive when she had seen Evy the other day in the village.

"It is just as well then, that you are not too disappointed. Derwent will soon be going to South Africa with his new bride. Thanks to my father, Derwent has a job that pleases him—and the Tisdales. Derwent will be working for the family. He will also get some training in geology. I understand his pay will be generous. And that, along with his prospect of owning shares in any new gold discovery, has made everyone happy."

She stopped dancing. "So *that's* it!" She struggled to keep her tone hushed. "You were partly behind all this. What did you do, bribe him to abandon divinity school, marry Alice, and go to South Africa?"

He gave her a look of utter innocence. "What suspicions you nurture. I am shocked you would think this of me. My thoughts toward Derwent are supportive and kind..." His gaze captured hers. "As they are toward you. Besides, we know, do we not, that he's long spun dreams from cobwebs about South Africa."

In fairness to Rogan, yes, she did know this about Derwent. Nevertheless—

"Come, Evy, you are not in love with Derwent."

The music ceased, and she stood on the ballroom floor, still held captive in his arms, staring at him. She had no trouble reading the challenge in his eyes, yet she refused to give in. How could she, when doing so could only mean disaster for her?

"How would you know *what* I feel?" No sooner had she said this, than she wished ardently she hadn't.

His arm around her waist tightened a little. "Because you are not as indifferent toward me as you pretend."

"Indeed?"

"Nor am I indifferent toward you." There was a husky quality to his voice that sent shivers tingling across her nerves. "You must know that."

Of course she knew it. She'd known it for years. But she also knew any relationship between them had only one end. And it was not a good one.

"Don't you see, Evy? I am not willing to lose you so quickly. You are too young to be snatched away from me."

She swallowed as a trembling seemed to take hold of her. He sounded so determined. *Lord, how am I to resist him when all I want to do is give in?*

"I do not want to come back from South Africa in a few years and find you the wife of Derwent Brown. Or of anyone else, for that matter."

She closed her eyes. And when he did come back, what then? His family had their expectations, and they would hardly be willing to permit the marriage of Master Rogan to Evy Varley—not, she reminded herself, that Rogan had ever mentioned marriage.

"You should be pleased you are not like Arcilla," he said, "being forced to marry without love. Derwent is a fine fellow, but losing him to Alice is not the end of the world."

She raised her chin. "How do *you* know what is best for me?"

"You forget, my dear Miss Varley, that I, too, have known you since childhood. If Derwent wishes to go, you should reconsider your feelings toward him."

"What do you mean by that?" And yet, she knew quite well what he meant.

"Is it not obvious? He either allowed others to make up his mind for him, which does not bode well for his courage, or he freely made up his own mind. Which is it?"

"The latter, I suspect, with a bit of bait dangled before his eyes."

He shrugged and a brow lifted. "The glare of gold blinded his vision, you mean? I won't deny life is full of testings and temptations. One must still show what one is made of by one's decisions. I say Derwent wants to marry Alice and go to South Africa. In which case, free him to go."

That was too much. She stared at him, letting her irritation show. "I have no intention of holding him here!"

He flashed a smile. "Good. His only mistake, as I see it, is his timidity in coming to you and admitting it face to face. I shall have a little talk with him."

She stiffened. "Please do not."

"If he feels he cannot face you, then he can write you a letter."

She narrowed her eyes, but Rogan seemed to ignore her. After a moment, she tilted her head. "Very well, you may be right about all this. Even so, there must be some other reason for his not telling me of his change of plans sooner. We've been friends since childhood."

He gave a nod. "Though I don't know this for a fact, I suspect his reluctance stemmed from his concern over the convictions he believed he must live up to in becoming a vicar. That they worried him, I think, is not a surprise to you."

She did not reply, but he must have seen from her expression that he was right. He gave another nod. "Perhaps Derwent simply cannot face disappointing you, and others."

He was probably right, but she did not want to hear it now. She turned. "I am going back to the cottage."

He refused to release her hand. "Wait. Leave now, like this, and we will both be the talk of the village gossip tomorrow. We are being observed by everyone in the ballroom. Besides, the coach is not ready, and it's pouring rain."

She glanced about the room—he was right. They were indeed being observed.

"Shall we dance this waltz also?" Not waiting for a reply, he led her in step with the music.

She eased back into his arms, letting him direct her, letting his arms support her. *Only for a moment,* she told herself.

His low voice whispered in her ear. "Forget Derwent. He was never truly right for you."

"You are so certain…"

His embrace tightened again, and he leaned close so that his warm breath caressed her face. "Oh yes. Quite certain."

CHAPTER TWENTY-EIGHT

It was only two days before Christmas, but Evy could not bring herself to ask the sexton, Hiram Croft, to come and kill the white Christmas goose already delivered from Rookswood.

"You've a tender heart, that's what," Mrs. Croft said.

"She is so white-breasted, so sleek of neck," Evy said. "It seems a pity to destroy her—especially when neither Aunt Grace nor I have caught the festive mood for a big Christmas feast."

"She is right."

They turned to find Aunt Grace joining them to look over the wire fence at the goose walking under the willow tree.

Mrs. Croft rubbed her chin. "I saw a hen already prepared at Tom's butcher shop."

Evy looked at her aunt, who smiled. "Very well. A hen it is. We ought to have a small celebration at least, in honor of the Savior's birth."

Evy agreed, though she could find little to be joyful about this year. She had not yet mentioned the news about Derwent and Alice to her aunt. It was true that she was not in love with Derwent; but she was fond of him…had been connected to him since childhood.

"You best get indoors where it's warm, Miss Grace; this be bad weather for chest colds."

When Aunt Grace went to take her afternoon nap, Evy was alone with Mrs. Croft in the kitchen, and the silence between them lengthened. Mrs. Croft was helping Evy bake the week's bread supply, a task she had done on her own when Evy was in London.

"I do not know what Aunt Grace and I would do without you, Mrs. Croft. You and Mr. Croft, both. He chopped wood for us on Saturday. And you've been such a help and consolation to us."

Mrs. Croft smiled, and pleasure shone in her eyes. "You're both as much family to me as my own kin, Miss Evy."

At Mrs. Croft's subtle glance, Evy wondered if she knew about the upcoming marriage. There was little she did not know of the goings-on in the village. How could anything of this magnitude escape her?

"You are very glum," Mrs. Croft acknowledged. "Ever since you went to that ball up at the big house. Did it not go well for you, child? You looked so pretty that night. I'd have thought you would be asked to waltz most of them dances."

"Oh, it was a lovely ball. That's not what is troubling me."

"That Master Rogan again, I suppose." Her lips were pinched. "A sly one, he. Has his eye on you plenty, I'm thinking, and with no good purpose in mind. He can do little else 'cept marry that Miss Patricia even if he wanted someone else."

Evy realized with a sinking heart that if she did not explain soon, Rogan would be blamed for trifling with her. Well, no time like the present. "I think you already know about Derwent and Alice Tisdale, Mrs. Croft."

Mrs. Croft frowned. "Aye, I do. The story's been buzzing about since you went off to school in London. It's why Mrs. Tisdale kept Alice home, I'm thinking. To make their sneaky plan for catching poor Derwent. I'll tell you something else too. Miss Grace knows all about it."

"I thought she might."

"She was hoping—probably still is—that Derwent would come to his senses. He'd never be allowed to get by with this foolishness if Vicar Brown was alive. You were away at school when Mrs. Tisdale came to see your aunt. She came all huffy like. Insisted Derwent had fallen in love with Alice and was reluctant to break the news to you. In love, my *foot.*" She sniffed her disapproval and held up her floured hands. "It's the job working for the diamond family that Derwent wants. I say the

Tisdales helped arrange it with the squire, knowing it would lure Derwent away from his schoolin' and marriage to you. Squire gave Derwent the job offer because Lady Elosia agreed he ought to marry Alice. Promised him shares in a mine. And that offer went hand in hand with marrying Alice. Well, it figures, I daresay. Derwent never was much bent on following the vicar's footsteps."

She slapped and kneaded the lump of bread dough with robust force. "Miss Grace went on hoping and praying Derwent would see the light. But the glitter of gold and diamonds has him packing his bag. That's what Mrs. Tisdale is excited about too."

"About the diamond mines?"

"I daresay. After all, her Alice will be married to Derwent when Rogan Chantry strikes gold—if he can make good on his Uncle Henry's map. That's how they're thinking, anyway. Her and the good doctor both. And Alice thinks Derwent could end up with a great reward from Rogan if he shares the burden of the work."

Evy could see the way Alice was thinking, that Derwent might even end up partners with a Chantry. That would never happen, of course. Neither Rogan nor the family, including Sir Julien Bley, would allow anyone to become a partner.

"Diamonds, and now gold." Mrs. Croft said it as if discussing measles and the plague. "That's what's been rattling 'round in Derwent's head. Believes all of Master Rogan's talk. There isn't anything he wouldn't do for Rogan Chantry."

As Evy had known since childhood. Just as she'd always known she saw Derwent more as a brother than a beau. It had just seemed the easiest path to agree to what everyone expected: that they would one day marry. She'd spent so many years walking that path without ever really wanting to do so. Not to say that her pride was not stung by his turning her down for Alice and employment with Rogan at Kimberly. Without the prospect of marriage to Derwent, her future was decidedly unsettled. But perhaps it had always been so.

"Maybe you ought to be counting your blessings. You found out early enough what Derwent was like," Mrs. Croft said.

"What do you mean, what he is like? It's true I have always known about Derwent's dreams of going to South Africa."

"Well, that's so, it's plain as the nose on your face if you ask me. But what I mean is, he could be bought, couldn't he? And he was quick to betray you to get what he wanted."

At this echo of Rogan's words at the ball, Evy frowned. "I do not know if I see it as betrayal."

"What else? Nice young man, indeed! He's not strong enough for you, that's what I say. And you're worth two of Alice."

Evy smiled. "You are loyal to me, that's all. Alice is all right."

"I don't understand you, Miss Evy. I'd be hopping mad if she stole my beau from beneath my nose like that."

"Maybe I'm not really in love with Derwent, Mrs. Croft."

She looked at Evy, brows raised. "You was planning to marry him for years."

Evy had no response for that. But she knew, deep inside, that while she'd been planning it, she hadn't been looking forward to it.

Aunt Grace said very little about Derwent after Evy told her she knew of his decision. "You'll graduate from Parkridge next year," she assured her. "You will be able to get a decent position teaching music."

Evy understood, and even agreed. If there was no one else to marry, she would at least be able to support herself doing something she loved.

Christmas dawned damp and foggy. Evy dressed in a frilled white blouse and ankle-length skirt of blue, then brought the present she would give Aunt Grace from its hiding place in the cupboard by the window. It was a cluster of red, blue, and green glass hummingbirds formed into a wind chime. Aunt Grace loved wind chimes, and Evy had found this one in a shop in London. It had taken most of her meager savings, which she had earned while sometimes helping out in the kitchen at school, but every coin she had spent would be worth the sparkle in her aunt's eyes when she hung it from the window and the first spring breeze sent it tinkling.

Aunt Grace must have heard her getting dressed, for when Evy came into the kitchen she was waiting. Evy took a deep breath of the aroma of fresh-brewed tea. Aunt Grace was sitting at the table with her worn Bible open.

"Merry Christmas," Evy called with deliberate cheerfulness. She bent and kissed her aunt's cheek.

"Merry Christmas, dear. Shall we have breakfast first, or open our presents?"

"Oh, you should not have troubled yourself," Evy said, but was pleased to see the scrambled eggs and ham slices on cornbread staying warm on the back of the stove. Aunt Grace must be feeling stronger.

"Believe me, it's like old times," Aunt Grace said. "I enjoyed being able to cook for a change. Mrs. Croft has already been here—look."

Evy followed her smiling gaze to the decorated pine bush, where two small packages sat next to their own presents. Evy saw that her present to the Crofts, along with Aunt Grace's for them, was gone. She hoped Mrs. Croft liked the new shawl she had bought for her. She knew Aunt Grace had made Mrs. Croft a new woolen nightgown and cap.

"Since breakfast is staying warm, let's be like children and open our gifts first!"

Aunt Grace laughed. They handed each other a gift, then tore them open with exclamations of joy. Aunt Grace had bought her a new blue-gray hooded woolen cloak, and Evy was delighted. She realized what it must have cost and how little money they had between them, yet somehow, strangely enough, Aunt Grace always seemed to have whatever money was needed—both for schooling and for school clothes. Whenever she asked about it Aunt Grace would always say cheerfully, "Oh I have my little secrets, dear."

"Aunt Grace, you shouldn't have—"

"You'll need it. You still have a year and half of schooling, do not forget. The other was getting frayed."

"It is the perfect color. I adore it, thank you."

Aunt Grace made much of the glass birds, and Evy could see by her happy expression that she truly liked the gift. "Ah, a sweet sign of spring and better days ahead," Aunt Grace predicted.

They made the most of their Christmas and then prepared their dinner, ready to receive several village friends who were coming to offer well wishes. Emily came by with her husband, Milt, followed an hour later by Meg and Tom. Once again Mr. Bixby showed up from Rookswood with several gaily beribboned gifts. Arcilla had sent Evy new gloves and a small beaded handbag. A second gift was wrapped in shiny red paper with a golden ribbon. Evy stared, speechless, when she removed a pair of golden earrings with emeralds. They could not be real…could they?

But they were. The gift card was signed simply: *Merry Christmas, Rogan.*

She gazed at the gift, knowing she could not possibly keep them, yet also knowing she would never be able to afford anything like them on her own. She took them out and ran to the small mirror by the hat tree and tried them on, pushing her tawny hair aside and turning her head in both directions so the flash of gold and green would dazzle her.

"Oh…they're stunning." She sighed.

Aunt Grace watched her, a slight frown on her brow. "From Master Rogan?"

"Yes."

"I thought they might be."

She did not say why she had thought so, and Evy avoided her gaze in the mirror. She waited, expecting her aunt to tell her she could not keep them, but Aunt Grace was silent and went to the stove to bring their breakfast to the table.

"They are expensive and beautiful."

Evy studied them again in the mirror. "Yes, I cannot think why he would give me such a gift."

Aunt Grace looked over at her. "Perhaps he is trying to cheer you after the disappointment with Derwent."

Evy looked at her reflection. The emeralds brought out the flecks of green in her amber eyes. "I hardly think so, Aunt. When he told me about the upcoming marriage, he seemed rather glib about it, as though he liked the idea of Derwent going to South Africa."

"That is what I mean."

Evy turned and looked at her aunt. "I beg your pardon?"

"It has not escaped me that Master Rogan has noticed you on more than one occasion. I've known from way back, even when I was governess at Rookswood, that he always took a special interest in you."

"Oh, I hardly think so—"

"Yes, he has. No use denying it, dear. Mrs. Croft has noticed it too. The question is, what does he have in mind?"

Evy flushed and reached up to pull off the earrings. "Nothing. He has nothing in mind. He will marry Miss Bancroft and go away to Capetown."

"Naturally the squire and Lady Elosia expect him to do so. You saw what they expected of Arcilla. I suspect she will be married off to Mr. Bartley very soon now. The family has their expectations and they will not be easily thwarted. Especially Rogan's uncle, Sir Julien Bley."

Evy placed the earrings back into the small red velvet box and closed the lid. "Yes, I know. If you are trying to warn me not to fall for Rogan Chantry, you need not worry. I am well aware of his reputation…and that no Chantry will ever marry beneath his social level."

"I do not worry, dear. I know you have twice as much sense as the silly young ladies who make fools of themselves chasing after him. You have too much dignity for that. I suspect that is one of the things about you that captures his attention so."

"Why have you not told me to send the earrings back?"

"Because you do not need me to lecture you. You will do what is best."

"Suppose I wish to keep them?"

Aunt Grace poured tea. "Then you will do so. You are nearly grown up now."

"They are worth a lot of money. If worse came to worst I could sell them. A little nest egg, so to speak."

"Yes." She looked up from the teacups. "Do you want honey in your tea?"

She trusts my judgment. Evy smiled, knowing she would not disappoint her aunt. She would make the appropriate decision.

But oh! How she wanted to keep the earrings!

With the New Year upon them, it was soon time to return to London. A day before Evy was to board the train she received a letter from Derwent. Mrs. Croft delivered it.

"Aye, Derwent is knowing what I think of him," Mrs. Croft said shortly. "I told him before he left Grimston Way."

Evy took the envelope and held it for a moment. Then she looked at Mrs. Croft. "You must not be too hard on him, Mrs. Croft. I told you, I'm not in love with Derwent. I suspect he did not want to hurt me and couldn't endure a face-to-face meeting. Down deep in his heart he probably believes he did betray me. His father, too, and Aunt Grace. Expectations were so high it never gave either of us much choice. I'll need to let him know I hold nothing against him. I only wish Alice and him well. Has he left the village?"

"He has, indeed. Squire sent him off to do some work in London at the family company there. Seems Master Rogan will be giving him some training now that Rogan's graduated from that university. In about a year's time they'll both be going to the Cape…after Alice ups and marries him, that is."

Evy opened the envelope.

"Well, you've guessed how it is. He writes 'cause he can't look himself in the mirror. He don't have the courage to look you eye to eye either and admit he betrayed you," Mrs. Croft stated.

Evy shook her head. "I do not think he betrayed me, Mrs. Croft.

This may sound strange, but Derwent and I never talked of marriage outright, or even said we loved each other."

"Well, it were certainly planned by the good vicar your Uncle Edmund before he were killed the way he was that stormy night. I daresay he would be upset with Derwent for turning his back on you and running away to the diamond mines. Adventure, that's what he wants, and that silly little Alice. Mark my words, she'll regret it once she gets over to that land of savage Hottentots. An' I'll wager Derwent will want to kick himself once he's been married to her a time. He'll be thinking back to the vicarage and the old ways and what he gave up for big dreams." She gave a sharp, quick nod. "He'll be regretting his quick decisions, all right. I've been around too long not to know that's how life goes. You reap what you sow, that's how it is…"

Evy was barely listening. She read to herself as she sat on the kitchen stool.

I have Squire to thank for this grand opportunity. We talked at some length in the library at Rookswood. It is no secret to you how I have wanted to go to the Cape to make my life and fortune. I never was cut from the cleric's cloth the way my good father was, or your Uncle Edmund. When my father was so ill and I filled in for him behind the pulpit, even writing most of his sermons, it gave me the opportunity to learn that I was not called to the vicarage, and do not at this time have a strong desire to return to divinity school. You are such a fine, upstanding girl that I guessed long ago I was never good enough for you, Miss Evy. Even Lady Elosia said you would never be pleased with me because I was not like your uncle. Alice thought so, too. Lady Elosia thought marrying Alice and beginning a different life in the Cape would be the wisest thing I could do for you, and for me…

I hope you will forgive me if I led you to believe falsely of my intentions toward you. It was always more what your aunt and uncle, and my father, wanted than what either of us wanted. I love you as a sister and think highly of you and always will.

As ever, faithfully your friend,
Derwent T. Brown

Evy blinked back tears. She folded the letter and replaced it inside its envelope.

"That rascally scoundrel, Derwent!" Mrs. Croft scowled, evidently taking Evy's tears to mean heartbreak.

"My tears are for fond childhood memories, Mrs. Croft, not over losing Derwent. You see, he is right," she said firmly. "And I think we all did him an injustice in not listening to him these years. He was not *called* to be a vicar. I'm seeing now that his gifts and abilities lie elsewhere than behind a pulpit."

"Humph. I'm not convinced any." She shook a finger. "Bad company corrupts good behavior, is what I say. It's that Master Rogan who planted all those restless seeds in Derwent's mind from the times they was boys."

Lady Elosia said you would never be pleased with me because I was not like your uncle... Marrying Alice and beginning a different life in the Cape would be the wisest thing I could do for you, and for me...

Evy stared at the letter. Strange...about Lady Elosia.

The January morning was cold and frosty as Evy boarded the train for London. The evening before, when Evy questioned whether or not they could afford her return to music school, Aunt Grace assured her all was well.

"We will manage the expenses somehow. It's even more important now that you continue your music studies."

Once back at Parkridge, school life and her love of music overshadowed past disappointments. She wrote a brief letter to Derwent in care of the Chantry Diamond Company assuring him that his decision to marry Alice Tisdale and go to South Africa in no way caused her either unhappiness or disappointment toward him. She wished him and Alice much joy and prayed God's blessings on their union. She also wrote Rogan:

Dear Rogan,

I thank you for the exquisite pair of earrings, but I cannot accept a gift so expensive. It would not be suitable. They are now safely stored at the cottage with my aunt, Mrs. Havering. If you would have Arcilla stop by and claim them, or do so yourself on one of your visits home (perhaps for Arcilla's wedding?), I would be appreciative.

   Miss Evy Varley, Parkridge Music School, London

In the months that concluded Evy's third year of studies, she did not hear back from Rogan, nor did she hear again from Derwent. As for Rogan, it was unclear when he would sail to the Cape. The last she had heard, he remained in London becoming familiar with the inner workings of the family company under the headship of Sir Julien.

Since Arcilla had already graduated from Montague, she remained at Rookswood, as did Peter Bartley. Aunt Grace wrote her that the engagement had been announced and that the marriage would take place in April. Within a week they would then sail for the Cape.

During this period Evy heard from Arcilla twice. She had sent a letter bemoaning the fact that she must go to South Africa, and deplored the notion that Peter might get a government post inland at the colony to be called Rhodesia.

I feel as though I am being sentenced to prison.

Evy felt compassion for her plight, but what was there to do? At least Peter Bartley had seemed a patient man who would deal kindly with Arcilla's whims.

Another letter came at the end of March.

I am getting married at the rectory on the 15th. Everyone will gather at Rookswood afterward, including Rogan. He has finally accepted Peter as a future brother-in-law. They are getting on quite well now. I would invite you to the ceremony, but you would need to miss some of your exams, and that doesn't seem wise considering you lost Derwent to Alice. You may need to work as a music teacher in the future, so you had better study hard.

   That reminds me—Alice is such a copycat! A week after my marriage, she will marry Derwent in the rectory. Amusing, don't you think?

We sail for Capetown immediately after our marriage, and Derwent and Alice will sail in May. I don't know if I shall see you again before I sail to my doom… If not, I wish you well on your music and future teaching. I will write you from Capetown.

Arcilla

In April, Evy read of Arcilla's marriage in the society page of the London paper. "Diamond Heiress Marries South African Government Official," the caption read.

There was a stunning photograph of the wedding. Arcilla looked like a princess in white, and Peter Bartley was quite distinguished. But it was Rogan who stood out, and in the background stood Miss Patricia Bancroft as bridesmaid. She held the bride's bouquet. Would she be next to marry?

Aunt Grace did not write about Derwent's marriage, which followed a week later, but she mentioned that Arcilla and her husband had indeed set sail for the Cape, and that Derwent and Alice, now Mrs. Brown, would sail on the first of May.

Evy turned her full attention to her graduation next year from Parkridge. She wondered and prayed about her own future, what she would do, and what God might have in store for her.

And yet, despite her best efforts, she could not shake the awareness that Rogan Chantry had not yet become engaged to Patricia Bancroft.

Chapter Twenty-Nine

Near the end of the school year came the emergency that Evy had been expecting. The letter was from Vicar Osgood: *Your beloved aunt is quite ill. Dr. Tisdale has concurred with me that it would be wise if you came home as soon as possible.*

Evy wasted no time packing her portmanteau and boarding the train for Grimston Way. She had sent a wire to Dr. Tisdale asking that he inform Mrs. Croft of her arrival.

Mrs. Croft was waiting in the jingle when she arrived. She appeared haggard and discouraged.

"It's that nasty business with the lungs, dearie. Doctor says she has pneumonia."

Evy's heart grew even heavier when she saw Aunt Grace, who was feverish and delirious.

"She has congestion and inflammation of the lungs." Dr. Tisdale's grave tone and countenance told Evy more than she wanted to know. "This is serious business, my dear. I would not have asked you to come home if it were just another of her colds."

Evy nodded and knelt beside the bed, taking Aunt Grace's hand in both her own. She searched her feverish face anxiously. "I'm here, Aunt Grace."

Aunt Grace's eyes fluttered open, and she tried to focus on Evy's face. She managed a faint smile, to reassure her, Evy was certain, that she would be all right. How like her aunt. Unselfish to the end. A woman who had stood by her sister—and her sister's child—through thick and thin. A woman who had wanted children of her own, had been denied them by God's providence, and had opened her arms to embrace Evy as her very own. She had worked to help support Evy, had been a faithful vicar's wife, had been stout-hearted to the end.

"Many daughters have done virtuously, but thou excellest them all," Evy whispered in her aunt's ear, quoting from the last chapter of Proverbs. Although Aunt Grace was too ill to answer, Evy sensed that she had heard.

The next days were some of Evy's unhappiest. To see Aunt Grace lying there, propped up with pillows, her skin hot and dry, her eyes glazed... It was almost more than Evy could bear. It came to her then...the sad truth that her aunt's chances of recovery were as feeble as her body. Evy prayed, as did all their friends in the rectory. Mrs. Croft stayed with her, helping to care for her aunt's needs and lending loving strength to Evy as well, making sure she had her soup and enough rest.

"It was bound to come to it, child," she said more than once. "Miss Grace's been on borrowed time from the Lord some years now. She knew it too, but she tried to keep joyful for your sake. If it weren't now that the Lord was going to bring her home, it would be next winter, or the winter after that. She's been sick like this before, but never this bad."

Aunt Grace's eyes opened. "Is...that you, Evy?"

She came quickly to the side of the bed. "Yes, Aunt, I'm here."

Mrs. Croft murmured she would put tea on and left them alone, closing the door behind her.

"Evy, I am going home to be with our heavenly Father...and dear Edmund..."

Sorrow choked Evy's throat. "Oh, Aunt, try to get well. You must! What will I do without you? I have no one else...no one." Tears trickled down her face as she clutched Aunt Grace's hand. She suddenly felt alone, abandoned, an orphan once more. She was losing everything she cared about. First her Uncle Edmund, then loyal Derwent, and even Arcilla was gone...silly, spoiled Arcilla, yet her dearest friend. And now Aunt Grace. What would she do alone?

"You must be strong..." Her aunt's voice was firm for all that it was weak and thready. "God is a very present help in trouble. You can trust Him to provide, dearest… His plans are well laid…all for your good."

"Don't talk, Aunt, you must save your breath and rest. You'll get better. This will pass."

She shook her head, and Evy could see what the action cost her. "Not this time…I know. There is something I must tell you…about your mother."

Evy stiffened and met her aunt's fevered gaze. Aunt Grace reached a hand toward her as if to touch the side of her face. "Rogan came to me…months ago… He asked, and I told him the truth. I could do naught else. I sinned in not telling you, but I did not want you unhappy… You were so proud to be the daughter of missionaries—martyrs—that I kept it from you…"

Evy swallowed, her throat suddenly dry and raw. She leaned closer, catching every syllable. "What…truth?"

"Clyde and Junia… They were going to adopt you…"

Evy clutched her aunt's hand. "Adopt?"

"Your mother was a van Buren…Katie…Sir Julien's ward…"

Evy felt unable to catch a breath. Her heart pounded in her chest as she struggled to absorb those words. Her mother…not the wonderful missionary she'd always believed? But a van Buren? How could this be?

"My mother is…Katie van Buren?" Saying it out loud didn't help. She couldn't believe it.

But Aunt Grace's weak nod told her it was so. "She ran away. From Sir Julien…because he took you from her. She tried to find you…to get you back. But she was killed. At the mission station. With Junia."

Evy swallowed again as understanding began to dawn. "Then it was Katie—my mother who took the prized Black Diamond? When she ran away?"

Aunt Grace closed her eyes, as though the effort to speak had drained all her energy. She moistened her cracked feverish lips. "That, I do not know…only that Katie was your mother… I know not who your father was."

Evy laid the side of her face against her aunt's hand and let the sobs come. "It matters not," she said over and over again. "*You* are my mother, dear heart. The only mother I've ever known. Do not fret."

Aunt Grace looked at her with pleading eyes and managed another weak smile. "You mean that?"

Evy buried her face against her aunt's thin chest. "Oh yes! I love you, Mum."

Aunt Grace smiled and reached a trembling hand to Evy's tumbling hair. She caressed it gently, and Evy recognized the action for what it was. A farewell.

Aunt Grace died in the night during the prayer vigil led in her room by Vicar Osgood. Prayers and scriptures were read, while candles flickered and cast trembling shadows on the cream walls beside the bed. Evy was silent, remembering all that they had been through together, well aware that she now trudged the future's path alone.

Grace Havering was buried in the churchyard at the rectory on a summer day in late June, next to the grave site of Vicar Edmund Havering. No gray day, this. The sky was a cloudless blue, and the birds sang merrily.

Only Evy's heart still felt the grief of winter. What would she do now? This was why she had gone to music school, of course…to work as a music teacher and support herself through the years. Her aunt had sacrificed financially to make sure of her education. But would she be able to finish her final year?

To represent Rookswood, and in fond memory of Vicar Edmund's wife, Lady Elosia came to the funeral. To Evy's surprise, Rogan stood with her in solemn black. Mrs. Croft and the sexton were there too, and Meg and Emily and their families. Even Dr. and Mrs. Tisdale came.

But Evy was aware of little else except her sense of sadness tempered by the Christian hope of being united once more with loved ones who had gone before. The words of Christ echoed in her mind, bringing consolation: "I am the resurrection, and the life: he that believeth in me, though he were dead, yet shall he live."

❧ ❧ ❧

Mrs. Croft returned with Evy to the cottage to spend the night. "You ought not to be alone," she said.

Evy was grateful for her company. The cottage was empty and too quiet. She went to her bed and tried to rest, for she was exhausted. At last she slept and awoke to drink the strange tasting tea that Mrs. Croft gave her.

"A sedative from Dr. Tisdale," she explained.

Evy did not awaken until midmorning the next day. The song of birds filled the room with hope. Life went on. Summer went on. Her heavenly Father was sovereign and reigning on His throne, her future in His hand.

The future, however, did not share its secrets with her. It only stared at her blankly. *I am the daughter of Katie van Buren.* The thought rattled around in her mind until it was joined by another. *Then...I must be related in some way to Heyden van Buren!* She shook her head. *And my father? Will I ever know who he is?*

Then, as though stepping from the mist of her memory, she saw again the stranger in Grimston Woods...remembered the look of sadness in his eyes as he had scrutinized her. What had he seen that made him so sad? Could he actually have been some distant cousin of Lady Camilla's, as Evy had been told? John...that was his name, wasn't it? Had he really gone to Australia?

And on the heels of that thought came another. Lady Camilla had been sure that her husband, Anthony Brewster, had fathered a child in secret. Evy's heart pounded at the question that nagged at her: Was it possible there was truth to this, after all...and that Evy was that child?

Her blood thundered in her ears. She sat up in bed and stared at the fluttering curtain. She pressed her trembling hand against her forehead, and her eyes closed as she tried to make sense of all the ideas tumbling about in her mind. Of course it could be true! Anything could be true now that she knew her mother was Katie van Buren, Sir Julien's ward. Sir Julien Bley! No wonder he had searched her face the way he did that day in the tearoom with Lady Camilla. Was it he, then, who had covered all this up? And Heyden van Buren—he had wanted to tell her something about her mother, but had suddenly vanished from her life. Why? Sir Julien again?

Evy tried to quiet her emotions. She must be calm and not jump to conclusions, though the truth appeared to be staring her in the face. She must give her heart time to adjust.

She forced her thoughts away from her parents. It was still too new and painful to ponder for long. The truth would be there tomorrow. There was time to let things settle, to let the shock ease a bit. Instead, she looked to the future. She supposed she would return to school in September, but that would depend on finances. She had known little about them; Aunt Grace had managed the purse strings. Evy knew she would have to look into what she had to depend on. Her aunt always kept their money in a small metal box hidden away in a trunk that held her and Uncle Edmund's mementos. Evy slipped from bed, dressed, and went to find the trunk. She removed the metal box and opened it to count the contents.

There was ten pounds in it. She was shocked. She would have expected at least a hundred. And making matters worse, now that Aunt Grace was gone, her retirement wage for faithful service to the vicarage would not continue. Even the cottage had been theirs to use only because Lady Elosia had awarded it to Aunt Grace because of Uncle Edmund. Evy had benefited, but now that would all change. She did not think those at Rookswood would immediately ask her to go, but she would need to leave sometime, and probably soon.

Ten pounds. Evy sat down hard on the ottoman. How had her aunt possibly believed she could attend her final year at Parkridge if that was all she had?

I will not be able to go back. That's clear. I must make careful use of this money. It will be some time before I can make any on my own.

Yes, she would need to find work by September, either here in Grimston Way or in London. This revelation coming on top of her sorrow made the burden far heavier to bear. For a moment she was tempted to give way to self-pitying tears. *No.* She clamped her jaw. There was no other recourse than to find work. She would be unwise to spend what she had knowing there would be no more until she earned it.

Still, she consoled herself, she had nearly three years of training, enough to possibly get a position as music teacher—if not at a prestigious girl's school, then certainly she could find young private students in London.

Evy took her Bible and found solace in reading the Psalms and Isaiah. She prayed for guidance and strength, to be wise and trusting. Over and over, verses that told her to fear not seemed to jump out at her. "Fear thou not; for I am with thee: be not dismayed; for I am thy God.... Fear not: for I have redeemed thee, I have called thee by thy name."

Later that afternoon Mrs. Croft came to Evy, clearly reluctant to impart her message. Lips pinched, she finally said, "Master Rogan wants to see you. Shall I tell him you aren't up to seeing visitors just now?"

Evy's heart skipped a beat. Did she dare see Rogan now, with her emotions in such a riot? But she could not bear to have him come and be turned away.

"No, I want to see him. I'll be there in a few minutes."

Mrs. Croft looked none too pleased. Evy knew she blamed Rogan for taking Derwent away from her, but at least the woman didn't say anything. She just nodded and left the room.

Evy brushed out her hair and smoothed the skirts of her black taffeta funeral dress. She glanced at herself in the mirror, frowning at the wan and distressed image that met her. She pinched her cheeks, trying to bring some color into them, and smoothed her thick, unruly hair. She scowled at her image. She looked young and frightened.

Determined not to appear so to Rogan, she bound her long hair up into a semblance of dignified order and, drawing a deep breath, went out to meet her caller.

Rogan paced about the small room and turned when he heard her enter. He came toward her, took a careful look, and a frown formed. He took both her hands into his and looked into her eyes. "No need to tell you how sorry I am at your loss."

She knew she should withdraw her hands, but she did not. "Thank you. I saw you and Lady Elosia at the funeral. Thank you for coming."

"But of course I would come. I would have called on you sooner, but I knew you needed time to be alone. Are you up to talking for a few minutes? I would not disturb you now, except I have little choice. My plans to leave for Capetown were already made before this happened, and my ship leaves next week."

"Oh"—her dismay was swift and fierce—"then you are leaving so soon?"

His jaw tightened. "Yes, I must. Why not come to Rookswood to dinner? It will do you good to leave the cottage for awhile."

"I couldn't…"

He inclined his head. "I understand. Then we will talk here or go for a walk. It is a pleasant enough afternoon. You could use some fresh air, I think."

He probably wanted to talk with her alone, without Mrs. Croft loitering in the kitchen with one ear peeled in their direction.

"I really do need to talk to you, Evy."

Evy. The warm way he said her name sent her heart scurrying. She knew she should not… Walking unescorted with a man when one was single and alone in the world was more than enough cause for gossip.

But he was leaving next week. "All right, a walk. Excuse me a moment first. I want to get something from my room."

"I'll wait for you outside."

Evy went to retrieve the earrings Rogan had given her for Christmas. He had never come to claim them. She slipped them inside her handbag, then took a black scarf that had belonged to Aunt Grace and put it around her hair.

Rogan waited near the gate, opening it for her as she joined him. She allowed him to lead the way. He was right: Being outdoors, feeling the afternoon sun on her skin, breathing fresh air, and hearing birds and humming bees filled her heart like a refreshing breeze. All was not lost. Her wonderful heavenly Father still ruled.

They walked for a while in silence.

"That black scarf is rather disconcerting."

Slowly, she removed it and let the breeze play in her hair. "It is not proper to go out so soon after a funeral without black."

"The villagers all know you. There isn't one of them in their right mind who would think ill of you if they saw you, which they will not. We are alone. As I already suggested, I would have waited to see you except there is so little time. I leave for London in the morning, and I do not know when I will be back to England. A year, maybe two."

Evy remained silent, but her heart cried out against this news. Two years! He was leaving for two years. She would not have him...or Arcilla...or Derwent...

He turned toward the grassy area facing the pond. There were benches here, and the ducks, geese, and peacocks were enjoying the grass and the water. Evy sighed. "Aunt Grace told me about my mother before she died."

His head turned sharply toward her. "Did she tell you I had spoken with her a few months ago?"

She nodded.

"What did she tell you about...your mother?"

"The truth. That her name was Katie van Buren, and she was your Uncle Julien's ward. That Dr. Clyde and Junia Varley adopted me...or had planned to do so. And"—her throat constricted, but she forced the words out—"that Katie very likely stole the Black Diamond."

She blinked away the tears that burned at her eyes. "Lady Brewster's letter was accurate after all. But when she spoke of my mother, she meant Katie van Buren, whereas I was thinking of Junia Varley. That's why her being a"—she could not say it, could not call her mother a thief—"made so little sense to me."

Rogan was silent for a moment. Then he nodded. "I was under the impression Lady Brewster was speaking of Junia, as well." He regarded her. "But there may be more to all this than what we now know, Evy. While I'm in Capetown I shall find out the entire story from Sir Julien."

She turned to face him. He would do that…for her?

"I was not going to say anything yet. I still need to do some research." His gaze grew warm, and she wondered whether it was sympathy that she saw there…or something more. "But you have had enough depressing news, and I'd like to leave you with something on a more hopeful note." He took her elbow and walked her across the grass toward the pond.

"There is something about this tale of your mother betraying my Uncle Henry that has troubled me since Grace told me who your real mother was. And that is the death of Henry."

"Yes, Henry… What about his death?"

"*Think,* Evy. If neither Katie nor Henry had the diamond, then why would someone follow him here to England—someone who murdered him? It suggests to me that someone followed him here for another reason. The map, most likely. I always thought that. And if he *was* murdered, that implies that he knew something that placed him in danger."

She began to understand, and her heart quickened. "He may have found out who had the Black Diamond?"

"Quite possibly."

"Perhaps the man who murdered him?"

His nod was quick. "Yes. Henry may have confronted whoever it was and threatened to unmask him."

"But that would imply the person was living in Rookswood!"

"Not necessarily. Someone may have followed him to Rookswood. I think," he said firmly, "that Heyden knows more than he is telling me."

"I am quite likely a relative of his, you know." Evy still could not believe that. "He had planned to meet me in London long ago and tell me more about my mother."

"Yes, I know. He came to me and told me. I asked him not to say anything to you about Katie. I wanted more information first, and I did not want you hurt. I had no idea your aunt would confess before her death. But now that she has told you—yes, Heyden is your cousin. He has returned to South Africa—with a few thousand pounds in his bank account."

"Oh, Rogan! You gave him money to go away?" She stared at him, not sure if she should be angry or pleased.

"It is over and done. What pleases me is that you are not too unhappy to know you are the daughter of Katie van Buren."

She gazed out across the pond. "I don't know how I feel about all this yet. I am still dazed. But Rogan, how would someone from Capetown get inside Rookswood to confront Master Henry without some of you remembering him?"

"There is no secret there. Members of all sides of the family were nearby in London when Henry died. My mother's family, the Brewsters, were here also. For that matter, so were Anthony and Sir Julien. Even Camilla."

"Oh, surely you do not think—?"

He frowned. "I don't know yet what I really think about all this."

"Then…what you're saying is that it could have been any of them?"

"They all had opportunity to silence Henry."

She walked over to the bench and sat down. "Thank you for telling me this. It helps more than you know. Is this the matter you wished to see me about?"

"No." He walked over to the bench and stood looking down at her. "I will come straight to the point. It is not lost on me that you are alone now. I should like to go away to South Africa knowing you are well taken care of."

Her brows lifted, and she could not hold back the rueful words. "Do you wish to arrange a marriage for me with the village shoemaker, Rogan? Perhaps you regret the haste with which Derwent was taken from me after all?"

A glint of derisive challenge burned his dark gaze. "You misunderstand me. I think you already know what I meant."

She met his gaze, barely daring to breathe. *Did he mean…?*

"I do not."

"I certainly am not advocating marriage—to anyone, least of all the shoemaker. And you misjudge me about Derwent."

"I am not altogether convinced of that. I believe you were involved. Derwent said so in his letter back in January when I returned to Parkridge. The only thing that is unclear to me is why you would meddle."

"Meddle." A small smile played at his lips. "Such a potent little word, implying malice. I would think my interest in the matter should be simple to understand. I did not fancy the notion of your marrying him while I was away. I already told you that at the ball, back in December."

His bluntness embarrassed yet elated her. "Why should it matter to you?"

His smile was full now, and she saw the imp dancing in his dark eyes. "What a leading question, Miss Varley! Naturally, as I've told you before, I am…fond of you."

"Fond of me?"

He placed hands on his hips. "I have known you most of my life. I find myself concerned for your future. I did not twist Derwent's arm to get him to marry Alice. He did so of his choice and at the prompting of Mrs. Tisdale and Aunt Elosia. It was my father who offered him a good position in Capetown." He gave her a slanted look. "Of course, offering him some shares in the gold I expect to discover did not hurt the prospects either."

She folded her arms and tapped her foot. "Well, you proved yourself quite successful."

"Just between you and me, I am not the least sorry Derwent is gullible and, where you are concerned, foolish."

The way he looked at her, as though she *belonged* to him, did odd things to her heart. She folded her hands in her lap, forcing herself to breathe slowly. *Do not be foolish,* she scolded. *His interest in you is as a friend, as one who wants the best for you. That is all.*

He crossed his arms, watching her closely, as though trying to read her reaction to his words. "I have the feeling Derwent and I will be friends for years to come. He trusts me. I will be forced to honor that trust."

She smiled at that. "Sometimes I think you actually are fond of Derwent."

"If I confessed, that would spoil your convictions that I am arrogant and a scoundrel."

"Oh? Is that how you want me to think of you?"

"I think I told you before that I would prefer your good opinion of me."

The breeze blew against her, and she watched it ruffle his shirt. "Your opinion that casts my mother in a new light is definitely in line with your wish."

He bowed lightly. "Thank you. And now I shall get straight to why I wanted you see you. I am aware that your expenses must weigh heavily on your shoulders, particularly at this time."

She thought of the ten pounds in the treasure box. She did not like to discuss such a personal matter with him, but he seemed quite relaxed about it, showing no embarrassment at all.

"That is why," he continued, "since I must go away for some time, I would secure a measure of peace knowing you had sufficient funds to care for yourself. Lest you think the removal of Derwent is to blame for this, I hasten to contradict the idea. I knew for some time about your aunt's dwindling finances. She confided in Mrs. Croft—and we know, do we not, that Mrs. Croft loves to chatter. So it is no wonder it all got back to me. You have ten pounds. Am I right?"

Quick heat filled her cheeks. *Oh, Mrs. Croft!* Though pleased by his concern, she wondered why he felt it. She searched his features, seeking some clue to his motivation...but he was veiled.

"Naturally I would be sorry to see your final year at the music academy foiled. I would be quite amenable to seeing the tuition paid—as I've paid the first three years."

She sucked in her breath, then surged to her feet. *"You?"*

"Why not? It was our little secret, your aunt's and mine. She wanted you to attend so badly that she accepted the gift as a loan. If it makes you feel better, we can consider the final year a loan as well, with the idea you would pay it back at some time in the future."

Evy silenced an intake of breath. Could she possibly be hearing right? "Are you saying you wish to give—lend me more money?"

He inclined his head, looking as though he was fighting a smile. "Yes. Enough to pay for your final tuition, and then to set you up in your own music school. Preferably here in Grimston Way. London is full of scamps. Here Mrs. Croft could keep an eye on you, as would the new vicar and his wife."

She could not take it in. "But—*why?* Why would you wish to do such a thing?"

"I told you I am fond of you...actually, quite fond." He walked toward her. "It was always your aunt's wish that you should support yourself. If you are financially independent, then there will be less reason for the well-meaning but errant ladies of the village to try to marry you off to the farmer's son"—he allowed the smile now—"or the shoemaker. And you will be under far less pressure to agree. You will have time to...make decisions."

"That is exceedingly thoughtful and generous of you."

"I have my own reasons as well. We both enjoy a genuine interest in music. I would like to see you pursue it."

Evy did not know what to say.

"If, in your proper way of thinking, you believe taking money from me is unsuitable, then we could work through a third party. Vicar Osgood, for instance, would do nicely."

"You are serious, then."

"Of course. I hoped I made that clear. Well?" He smiled again. "Is it a bargain?"

"But I... Well, it is very considerate on your part. I must say I am astonished. What can I say? You have already paid my schooling for three years."

"I enjoyed the little secret."

She could well imagine he did. "However, it is quite out of bounds to even consider taking money. And I must pay you back what you've already paid." She closed her eyes. How on earth would she do that? It had to be thousands of pounds... *Oh! What would people think if they knew?*

"Nonsense."

Her eyes opened at his firm assertion. His expression was as unyielding as his tone. "Everyone in the village knows you are virtuous."

How did he do it? How was it he could read her thoughts so easily? Did he know her feelings toward him as well? *Oh, please...no.*

His gaze softened. "A loan is not as improper as you imply. After all, I am the squire's son. One day I will inherit Rookswood and my father's title, and I shall be squire. All that has been settled years ago."

Her eyes widened at this. So Rogan would not inherit the Chantry shares in De Beer Consolidated. "Is that why you have your own interest in locating gold?"

"Partly. I always wanted Rookswood; Parnell always wanted the diamonds. So for once you hear of two brothers who have completely agreed on the inheritance that will be left them. Arcilla, of course, will share in the diamonds, but most of the shares go to Parnell. That is one of the reasons my father and Sir Julien thought it so important for Arcilla to marry into position and wealth through Peter."

"I see..."

"Look, never mind about me. As I said, I am interested in *your* future, Evy. I want to make sure you will be financially secure. Please, will you allow me to help you?"

She looked away from the kindled warmth in the dark eyes, afraid of what was there, knowing that it could never come to fruition. "I— I will need to think about it. Thank you for your offer."

He looked amused at her grave hesitancy. "All right, think about it, pray about it. But you will need to make your decision soon. I leave for London tomorrow early, and for the Cape next Thursday morning." He handed her a calling card. "Here is my town address in London. Contact me before Thursday. In the meantime, I will go ahead and draw up the necessary papers. How do you wish it to be written? Through Vicar Osgood and the rectory, or directly to you?"

He smiled faintly. "That is, of course, should you decide to go along with this."

She plucked at the black scarf in her hands, aware of the wind, aware of him, of his gaze and how near they stood. She looked away toward the pond. "If I decide to accept your kind offer, I should prefer to deal through the vicar."

He smiled. "Very proper. Then the vicar it is. As a matter of fact, I have already talked to him about this. He is in full agreement."

She looked at him and saw his smile. Suddenly she smiled too. "You were quite certain I would accept."

"I was hoping."

"My own music school." The mere thought of it filled her with inexpressible joy. "Oh, Rogan, how could I resist? It is something I've always dreamed of, but never thought possible. I thought marriage to—" Rogan's mouth turned slightly, and she hastened on, "I expected my life to be different."

"I think you will agree that life's plans are not always tied up in neat little packages. Occasionally we find ourselves at unexpected crossroads with more than one opportunity from which to choose. Time itself is often the best indicator of which decision to make, for it can tell so many things that are now hazy. Do you not think so?"

His soft words, his warm gaze wrapped around her, enfolding her. Once again, her heart beat faster. "Yes…only time will tell."

The awareness between them all but crackled in the warm air, and she forced her gaze away from his, reaching into her handbag and drawing out the small red velvet box. She hesitated, then handed it to him. "I see that neither you nor Arcilla came by for this, so I wanted to return it now. Again, it was kind of you to think of me at Christmas, but…"

"I think of you a great deal, Evy. There is a special relationship between us."

She was not so certain about this special relationship and believed he was not either. "But a Chantry heirloom…"

"It is not from the Chantry family jewels. I chose this myself in

London while looking over some of the diamond and emerald collections at the Company. The green and yellow diamonds reminded me of your eyes. Please accept it from me, Evy. It is simply a Christmas present."

She was overcome. "But, Rogan—"

His eyes glittered. "If you will not accept it, I will toss it into the pond."

She gasped. "You would not!"

"I will. I can be rash sometimes."

There was a half smile that denied this challenge, and laughter bubbled up from deep within her. She snatched the red velvet box back from his hand.

"Such a display of emotion on your part, Master Rogan, would not be fitting. But...since I never know how far you will go to surprise me, I will humbly accept this gift and will treasure it always." All jesting gone now, she let her sincerity show in her eyes. "Thank you. I am afraid I did not have a proper gift to give you at Christmas, however—"

"However?" His gaze dropped pointedly to her lips.

Her breath caught in her throat. "*However,* I am sure you understand."

His smile was rueful. "Hmmm. Indeed. Well, with that settled, I am sorry to say I must be on my way. I will walk you back to the gate. Unless you wish to sit a while by the pond and enjoy the sunshine?"

He was leaving... And though he was making a generous financial provision for her security and safety, who knew when she would actually see him again? Or whether she ever would? Anything could happen in two years. Anything. He might find someone he cared for in Capetown. He might forget all about her. She had heard that there were quite a few English girls there with well-to-do families serving Her Majesty's government.

Or Miss Patricia might join him in Capetown, and they might marry...

No, nothing was certain, least of all this shaky relationship that she and Rogan seemed to share. Yes, he said he was *fond* of her—a fact this present generosity seemed to support—but fondness was not undying love.

His brow lifted as he watched her, but his tone was gentle when he spoke. "You are frowning."

She looked away. "Was I?"

"Still disappointed about losing Derwent?"

Oh, Rogan! She looked at the box in her hand and shook her head. Moisture filled her eyes and before she could stop the flow a splotch dropped on the velvet, darkening it.

"Evy." Sympathy deepened his voice.

No... That was the last thing she wanted from him...

She looked up at him, and her heart contracted. Their gazes held, and he reached with gentle hands to take her arms. As the June breeze blew her hair and rustled the skirt of her mourning dress, Rogan's arms encircled her, drew her close. A small sigh escaped her as his lips lowered to hers.

A searing flame scattered the dismal shadows and the blackness of gloom. The moment was wonderful, even if it was only a moment. This was *now.* This she would always remember. The memory of his lips on hers would warm her in the long, lonely nights ahead. Her arms went around him, and he held her tightly, his kiss deepening, lingering.

After what seemed an eternity of wonder, Rogan withdrew. His hands moved to her shoulders.

"I will come back, Evy, and when I do, I expect to find you here waiting for me. Until then, it is never good-bye." He studied her face, as though memorizing it. "It is merely au revoir."

She was unable to speak, though her heart cried out when he released her and turned to walk away toward Rookswood...and Capetown. Her gaze followed Rogan until he was out of view, then she turned, blinking back scalding tears, and looked toward the silvery-blue pond rippling in the warm breeze. A graceful white swan glided peacefully toward the shade of a willow whose long branches swayed over the water. A meadowlark sang in the lilac tree nearby, while out of view in the distance its mate answered sweetly, confidently.

Evy turned and looked back toward Rookswood, where Rogan had disappeared. Out of sight, she thought with a sudden glimmer of hope and confidence, but not forever gone.

"Au revoir, Rogan," she whispered. "I promise I will be waiting for you when you return."

ABOUT THE AUTHOR

Linda Lee Chaikin has written eighteen books for the Christian market. *For Whom the Stars Shine* was a finalist for the prestigious Christy Award, and several of her novels have been awarded the Silver Angel for excellence. Many of Linda's books have been included on the best-seller list.

Behind the Stories, a book about writers of inspirational novels, offers Linda's personal biography. She is a graduate of Multnomah Bible Seminary and taught neighborhood Bible classes for a number of years before turning to writing. She and her husband presently make their home in California.

Dear Reader,

I hope you will look for the second book of the East of the Sun trilogy in 2004, when the story of Evy Varley and Rogan Chantry continues to unwind toward their destiny in Capetown, South Africa.

I would be pleased to hear from you. You can write to me through my publisher:

Linda Lee Chaikin
c/o WaterBrook Press
2375 Telstar Drive, Suite 160
Colorado Springs, CO 80920

Sincerely,

Linda Lee Chaikin

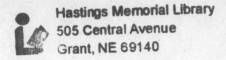